On the Way to Somewhere Else

FARANDOUL MORMON. THE ROLL CALL OF THE SPOUSES.
Robida, Voyages très extraordinaires, *185*.

On the Way to Somewhere Else

European Sojourners in the Mormon West
1834–1930

Edited by
Michael W. Homer

University of Oklahoma Press
Norman

LIBRARY OF CONGRESS CATALOGING-IN-PUBLICATION DATA

On the way to somewhere else : European sojourners in the
Mormon West, 1834–1930 / edited by Michael W. Homer.
p. cm.
ISBN 978-0-8061-4083-4 (paper)
Includes bibliographical references (p. [385]-408) and index.
1. Mormon pioneers—West (U.S.)—History—Anecdotes.
2. Mormons—West (U.S.)—Social life and customs—Anecdotes.
3. Frontier and pioneer life—West (U.S.)—Anecdotes. 4. West (U.S.)—Social life
and customs—Anecdotes. 5. West (U.S.)—Description and travel—Anecdotes.
6. Travelers—West (U.S.)—Anecdotes. 7. Europeans—West (U.S.)—Anecdotes.
8. Travelers' writings, European. I. Homer, Michael W
F596.3-M8 O5 2006
978/.02092309 22 2005033476

The paper in this book meets the guidelines for permanence and durability of the Committee on Production Guidelines for Book Longevity of the Council on Library Resources, Inc. ∞

Copyright © 2006 by Michael W. Homer. Published by the University of Oklahoma Press, Publishing Division of the University. Paperback published 2017. Manufactured in the U.S.A.

All rights reserved. No part of this publication may be reproduced, stored in a retrieval system, or transmitted, in any form or by any means, electronic, mechanical, photocopying, recording, or otherwise—except as permitted under Section 107 or 108 of the United States Copyright Act—without the prior written permission of the University of Oklahoma Press. To request permission to reproduce sections from this book, write to Permissions, University of Oklahoma Press, 2800 Venture Drive, Norman, OK 73069, or email rights@oupress.ou.edu.

Contents

Foreword 9
Acknowledgments 13
Editorial Procedures and Translations 21
Introduction 23

1. "The Mormonites": The First European Observers, 1830–46   29
   Alexander Philipp Maximilian: They Complained Bitterly — Samuele Carlo Mazzuchelli: To See and Speak with a Heresiarch — Albert Karl Koch: A Place I Had Wished to See for a Long Time — Alexander Ziegler: The Completed Temple Was Arranged as a Barracks — Pierre-Jean De Smet: Mr. Young, an Affable and Very Polite Gentleman

2. "Polygamy is a Sword of Damocles":
   Overland Travelers in Utah, 1849–55 47
   Leonetto Cipriani: We Don't Think Polygamy Can Last for Long — Jacob Heinrich Wilhelm Schiel: I Saw Not a Single Beautiful Woman — Jules Rémy: More Power Than Any Potentate in the World

3. "Gathering to Zion": European Converts in Utah . . 85
   Stephen Malan: The Test Was a Severe One — Daniel Bertoch: Oh How Toff He Was — John Ahmanson: Joyfully We Drove in to Zion — Louis Bertrand: Everyone Flew to Arms

4. "But Brigham Young is Still Governor":
   Mormonism's Secular Control, 1859–69 115
   Israel Joseph Benjamin: The Heart of Mormon Country — Enrico Besana: The New Road of Iron Will Destroy this Anomaly — Olympe de Joaral Audouard: An Enormous Caravan, Including Some Ladies

5. "The King of the New Jerusalem":
   Riding the Rails through Utah, 1869–77 147
   Joseph Alexander, Baron von Hübner: Sovereign of the Desert — Rudolph Schleiden: He Disapproved When Any Mormon Drank Wine or Beer — Louis Laurent Simonin: Stenhouse Promised to Introduce His Two Wives — Max Joseph August Heinrich Markus Buchner: Brigham Young Sat on His Sofa Slumped Down — Victor-Henri Rochefort, Marquis de Rochefort-Luçay: Mr. Stenhouse . . . Resolved to "Confine" Us — Francesco Varvaro Pojero: He Would Convert You Immediately — Baron Arnold de Woelmont: One of the Most Astonishing Figures of Our Time

6. "Excursions in My Own Mind":
   European Fantasy Accounts of the Mormon West . . 187
   Paul Duplessis: Abandon All Hope of Leaving — Heinrich Balduin Möllhausen: Polygamy is Common amongst Them — Jules Verne: At a Speed of Twenty Miles an Hour, A Course of Mormon History — Albert Robida: They Were Too Tired of the Solitary Life — Karl Friedrich May: We Will Not Give Up — Emilio Salgari: Strange Rituals and Polygamy — Guillaume Apollinaire: So Much Fertitlity after the Sterility of the Salt Desert — Pierre Benoit: Let Me Remind You . . . I am Infallible

7. "The Country of Apotheoses":
   The First European Visitors to Southern Utah . . . 259
   Th. Gr. [Anonymous]: Mormons are Communists — Albert Tissandier: Wild, Forsaken Places — Carlo Gardini: A Little Worried the Indians Would Scalp Me

8. "The Many Scandinavians Who Live in Utah":
   Northern Literary Lights in the Mormon West . . . 303
   Vilhelm Kristian Sigurd Topsöe: The Era of Mormonism is Irrecoverably Over — Jonas Jonsson Stadling: Mormons Pay for Theatre Tickets with Watermelons — Paul Peter Waldenström: Here Comes Satan! — Paulus Henrik Cavling: You Have Seen God's Face

9. "Bitter, Salt, and Hopeless":
   The Last Struggle for Statehood, 1878–96 319
   Charles-Louis-François André: An Undulating Plain Garnished with *Sauges en Brousailles* — Rudolph Meyer: A Lot Can Be Learned from the Mormons — Giovanni Vigna dal Ferro: Do Not Believe That the Mormons are Savages — Friederick Martin von Bodenstedt: A Variety of Things Are Missing Here — Gabriel-Paul-Othenin de Cléron, Comte d'Haussonville: Polygamy—That's What Always Troubles the Gentiles — Stéphane Jousselin: I Demand to See the Women

10. "Americans Like All the Others":
    Accommodation after Statehood, 1896–1930 343
    Jules Huret: Christians with Mohammedan Instincts — G. A. Zimmer: Such Blind Fanatical Zeal — David Bosio: I Was Lucky Enough to be Able to Gather Many Waldensians — Comtesse Madeleine and Mlle. Jacqueline de Bryas: The Mormons Looked Just Like All Other Human Beings — Zopito Valentini: I Did Raise the Subject of Polygamy

Afterword. "Hunters of the Picturesque": Utah in the Twenty-first Century 377
Bibliography 385
Index 409

Illustrations

The roll call of the spouses	*frontispiece*
Samuele Mazzuchelli	35
Pierre-Jean De Smet	44
Brigham Young	45
Great Salt Lake, Utah	46
Leonetto Cipriani	50
Social Hall, Salt Lake City	79
Daniel Bertoch	92
Saltair resort	95
Louis Bertrand	100
Israel Joseph Benjamin	119
Olympe Audouard	125
"Mormonism in Paris"	127
"L'académie transformée"	128
Salt Lake House	146
Townsend House	153
T. B. H. Stenhouse	166
Salt Lake Theatre	168
Jules Verne	208
Elder Hitch preaches on the train	211
Albert Robida	216
The departure of the sailors for the city of the Mormons	217
The formal reception at Salt Lake City	219
The toast to the amiable divisions of Mandibul	221
Sectional view of a Mormon home	224
"View of the Great Salt Lake, Utah"	267
"The Salt Lake, Utah: Bathhouse and Open Air Cafe"	270
"The House of Nathan Adams"	273
"Main Street in the Village of Kanab (Kane County, Utah)"	274
Walker Opera House, Salt Lake City	295
David Bosio	365
Emmeline B. Wells	370

Foreword

Western history is full of surprises, and Michael W. Homer's *On the Way to Somewhere Else: European Sojourners in the Mormon West* reveals the remarkable treasures awaiting scholars who undertake a serious study of travelers who have written about the Latter-day Saints (or LDS) people. Most collections of European travelers' tales about frontier Mormons are predictable, typically being the benign views of English gentlemen who passed through Utah Territory, often supplemented by the more accurate perceptions of one British swashbuckler, Richard Francis Burton.

Mr. Homer has ignored this tradition and, in the process, breaks new ground. This volume contains his discoveries in an Aladdin's cave of European reports about the early Mormons and the American West. Ranging from the encounters of Prussian, German, Italian, and Belgian travelers with "Mormonite" religious revolutionaries on the Missouri and Mississippi rivers in the 1830s and 1840s to the faith's transformation into a theocratic empire in the Far West and its painful accommodation with American culture and the twentieth century, this volume captures a kaleidoscopic picture of the Mormon West.

The voices heard here include those of an outraged Catholic priest, an intrigued German prince, a liberated Frenchwoman, an insightful Italian count, a devout French convert, and an embittered Danish apostate. Their descriptions of meetings with the denizens of the American frontier—fur traders, Indians, journalists, and soldiers—enhance their always-colorful encounters with the fiercely dedicated devotees of early Mormonism. The travel accounts Mr. Homer has located of real voyagers sometimes outdistance the hilarious and extraordinary fantasies concocted by European writers who never set foot in North America.

In an age when the offended morals of Victorian Americans produced dozens of denunciations of life in Utah, negative views of the young religion dominated most outsiders' writings on the Mormon Kingdom. In contrast, European visitors expressed cosmopolitan perspectives about the Latter-day Saints and their odd marriage customs. (Their encounters with tiresome Puritans in the East may have predisposed such visitors to a favorable impression of a people adventurous enough to embrace polygamy.)

As he bestrode his time and region, Brigham Young dominates many of these accounts. A visit with the "Pope of Mormonism" was a prerequisite of any European's stay in Utah Territory until 1877, and the charming President Young always obliged his visitors with a visit worth reporting. The homespun prophet and philosopher clearly enjoyed his meetings with European intellectuals and nobles, and they rewarded him with almost uniformly favorable reviews.

Given their aristocratic backgrounds, it is hardly surprising that many of these commentators often viewed Brigham Young's autocracy much more favorably than they did the chaos of American democracy—although one Austrian aristocrat (probably a natural son of that architect of oligarchy, Prince Metternich) saw "not a shadow of enthusiasm or pleasure on those gaping faces, or in those bent bodies" among the crowd at an Ogden railroad depot as they rendered obsequious honors to Brigham Young, the "sovereign of the desert"; this European autocrat concluded that the prophet's devotees dreaded far more than loved him.

These continental perspectives cover almost one hundred years and capture the physical development of Utah and the political evolution of Mormonism. These visitors paint a wonderful picture of the growth of Salt Lake and its transformation from a ramshackle collection of mud huts to a mining and railroad emporium. They painted engaging word portraits of characters such as shootist Porter Rockwell, innkeeper James Townsend, and journalist T. B. H. Stenhouse, who gave the American Mecca much of its local color.

These narratives show how the two oddest elements of the city's architecture, the tabernacle and the temple, fascinated and either impressed or appalled European tourists. And they were all taken with the city's spectacular location and fascinated with what Albert Tissandier called "the mysterious Salt Lake."

Many of these travelers' tales will surprise the most knowledgeable scholars of the Mormon West. "With families so rapidly increasing," future prophet John Taylor told Count Cipriani in 1853, "we don't think polygamy can last for long." Louis Bertrand's forgotten memoir contains the earliest known LDS account of the Utah War. Its detailing of Mormon war plans in the spring of 1858 explodes the myth conjured up by Utah apologists decades later that features Brigham Young as an injured and innocent peacemaker. And certainly, few Latter-day revelations are as astounding as the story of a pirate band converted to Mormonism and polygamy, only to run afoul of the Danites.

This collection represents decades of work by a dedicated scholar. Michael W. Homer is a descendant of European converts from the Waldensian valleys of northern Italy who were among the first immigrants to Utah. After growing up in Utah and Oregon, Mr. Homer served a mission for the Church of Jesus Christ of Latter-day Saints from 1972 to 1974 in Italy. He attended Georgetown University, the University of Utah, and the University of Nebraska and is now a trial lawyer specializing in real property and construction litigation. He has used this expertise to write extensively on legal issues in America's western territories and is a recognized expert on new religious movements, Spiritualism, and Arthur Conan Doyle. His book, *Spiritismo*, was published in Italy in 1999. His article "'Similarity of Priesthood in Masonry': The Relationship between Freemasonry and Mormonism," which appeared in *Dialogue: A Journal of Mormon Thought*, is widely hailed as the finest work on Mormonism and Masonry and won awards from the Mormon History Association, the John Whitmer Historical Association, and *Dialogue*. Mr. Homer practices law in Salt Lake City, serves as chairman of Utah's Board of State History, and is my next-door neighbor.

Enjoy the results of decades of work by an excellent scholar.

WILL BAGLEY
Salt Lake City, Utah

Acknowledgments

I first became interested in Europeans who had traveled to Utah when I was concluding my LDS mission in Italy in June 1974. The mission president, Dan C. Jorgensen, graciously agreed to accompany me and my companion, E. Carl Goodman, to the Waldensian valleys where both of our great-grandfathers lived before converting to Mormonism and emigrating to Utah in the 1850s. In the small village of San Germano Chisone we met Mario Beux, a cook at Pension de L'Ours, who knew the owner of the home where my great-grandfather Jacques Bertoch was born. Mario introduced us to Aldo Jahier, and both men accompanied us to the "frazione" of Gondini, where the eighteenth-century Bertoch home still survives. Goodman and I later walked through his ancestral village of Roccapiatta where his great-grandfather, Philippe Cardon, was born.

These experiences captured my imagination, and when I returned to Utah I began searching for accounts written by Bertoch, Cardon, and other Waldensian emigrants. During this process I became acquainted with LDS Church Historian Leonard Arrington, who kindly shared his transcription of Stephen Malan's journal, which is included in this anthology, and his notes on Leonetto Cipriani, an Italian diplomat who visited Utah in 1853. Cipriani was so charismatic I decided to visit his birthplace in Corsica. In Bastia I met Maître Angeline Tomasi, *avocat a la cour*, who is Cipriani's descendant and conservator. Maitre Tomasi graciously allowed me to examine Cipriani's original papers, which are still located in his original travel trunk, and she directed me to Cipriani's crypt in Centuri.

I have returned to Italy to investigate other travelers and to better understand the multi-layered and complex lenses through which they viewed our Utah communities. My visits to the Waldensian valleys have been aided by

Flora Ferrero, Gabriella Ballesio, Stefano Seppè, Giorgio Tourn, and Aldo Jahier. Flora has shown me the "nooks and crannies" of the "valli Valdesi" and has taken me to all of the surviving homes of Mormon converts who left the valleys during the 1850s, including the home of Stephen Malan. She also introduced me to archives located in Torino, Torre Pellice, and Pinerolo.

I have also been given great support by other Italians, including Giovanni Marianetti, Roberto Mongia, Oriana Fallaci, and Massimo Introvigne. Giovanni Marianetti, whom I met in Torino in 1972, introduced me to Italian editions of Albert Robida, Richard Burton, Louis Simonin, Joseph Alexander von Hübner, and Jules Verne. He has also been my "maestro" concerning the Italian Risorgimento. Roberto Mongia, whom I met in Milan in 1973, introduced me to bookstores and libraries in Milano, Torino, Aosta, and Torre Pellice, and shared his perspectives about European history while we were sailing aboard his "piccola barca" on Lago Maggiore. In 1988, while Roberto and I were searching the shelves of Libreria Malavasi in Milano, one of the Malavasi brothers showed us a book that mentioned a young Milanese Dominican priest named Samuele Mazzuchelli and his book, published in 1844, in which he described his encounter with Joseph Smith.[1] I was fascinated by this account and eventually visited the small convent in Sinsinawa, Wisconsin, that Mazzuchelli founded in the 1840s. There I met Sisters Marie Laurence and Nona McGreal, who were extremely gracious and provided me with additional information concerning Mazzuchelli, including some of his unpublished notes and articles he wrote about Mormonism after his encounter with Joseph Smith, plus a "Positio" submitted to the Vatican for his beatification.[2] Sixteen years after being introduced to Mazzuchelli in Milano, I finally located a copy of his memoirs from another Milanese bookseller, Il Polifilo Libri Rari, at the New York Antiquarian Book Fair. I met Oriana Fallaci in New York City, while she was writing a yet-unpublished novel about her family, and later in Florence, where she arranged a private tour of Biblioteca Laurenziana and

---

[1] The book I found at this classic bookshop, located near the Duomo, was written by Italian senator Luca Beltrami, who was Mazzuchelli's nephew. Beltrami recounted Mazzuchelli's encounter with Smith and that the Milanese priest founded a Dominican House and college in Sinsinawa, Wisconsin. See Luca Beltrami, *Padre Samuele Mazzuchelli*. Roberto Mongia located Luca Beltrami's 1928 article, "I Mormoni nelle memorie di un missionario Milanese."

[2] For additional information, see Codazzi, *L'opera del missionario milanese Padre Samuele Mazzuchelli*, as well as Mazzuchelli's critique of *The Book of Mormon* written shortly after his visit to Nauvoo.

lectured me about Dante and Grand Duke Leopold II. We visited San Gimignano, where we discussed medieval towers, and San Miniato, where she talked about Napoléon's Italian ancestral roots. I met Massimo Introvigne in 1987 at the annual meeting of the Mormon History Association. Since that time he has become family. He has introduced me to bookstores in England, France, Hungary, Italy, Brazil, Latvia, and the U.S. He and his wife Silvia have taken me to some excellent restaurants in Torino, Sirmione, Vallegio, Lanzo, Bardonecchia, and Foggia.

I have benefited from my association with other Italian friends, including Aldo Scarpignato, Roman bookseller, who explained the Risorgimento from a Roman perspective and introduced me to hundreds of titles on the Risorgimento; Gino Fletzer, Judge, Court of Cassassion, Rome, Italy, who showed me the many hidden bookstores and libraries in Venice and gave me his opinions concerning the third war of Italian independence; and Alfredo Mantovana, an Italian cabinet minister, who explained the events of 1848 to 1870 from a Roman Catholic perspective.

My rich associations in Great Britain have also been invaluable in researching this book. In 1991 I met Dame Jean Conan Doyle, the daughter of Sir Arthur Conan Doyle. Dame Jean and I had many delightful discussions in her flat in Sloan Square, where she showed me the books her father gave her and related her memories of Salt Lake City in 1923. She also accompanied me to some of the finest military clubs in London. Through Jean Conan Doyle I became acquainted with Doyle scholars. Owen Dudley Edwards, University of Edinburgh, accompanied me to Doyle's boyhood homes in Edinburgh as well as some of his favorite bookstores in that city; Malcolm Payne, of the Conan Doyle Crowborough Establishment, took me on a walking tour of Crowborough in Hampshire and told me about a paper delivered at the Portsmouth Literary Society that was probably the catalyst for Doyle's *A Study in Scarlet*; Georgina Doyle, also of Hampshire, accompanied me to Doyle's "psychic retreat" in New Forest at Bignell Wood and to the Scottish author's final resting place in Minstead, where she shared many family stories about Doyle's travels on behalf of Spiritualism; Richard Lancelyn Green showed me his impressive Doyle archive at his flat in Kennsington and we scoured bookshops in London and Cambridge looking for books by Willie Hornung; David Kirby, Cambridge, England, first told me about what he thought of Arthur Conan Doyle at a roadside pub near his home and introduced me to some of his less-known works; Christopher Roden, Chester, England, shared his considerable knowledge concerning the writer while exploring the city wall surrounding his city; Dixon Smith, of Rupert Books, Cambridge, England, shared many insights on Doyle's religious outlook as we sat in the lobby of Langham Hotel in London and at his office in Cambridge; and Michael Halewood, of Halewood and Sons, a fifth-generation bookshop in Preston, England, who introduced me to his immense stock of Doyle and travel books and sat next to me with paddle in hand at both Sotheby's and Christie's.

I am indebted to many individuals and institutions who have either influenced my studies in general or this book in particular: Will Bagley has become a friend and confidante and has made this book possible through his great generosity, patience, and editorial skills; Richard Bennett, Winnipeg, Manitoba (who has since moved to Brigham Young University in Provo), opened the University of Manitoba archives, which greatly facilitated my study of Doyle; Martha Sonntag Bradley, University of Utah, taught me about the Second Great Awakening, Bernini, Brunelleschi, and Bramante; Mario DePillis, University of Massachusetts, Amherst, shared his vast knowledge of world history as we walked the streets of Torino, Aalborg, Guardia Piemontese, and Palermo; Antoine Faivre, University of Paris–Sorbonne, navigated me around numerous book stores on the Left Bank; Robert A. Gilbert, of Bristol, England, facilitated my visit to the Masonic Library at the Grand Lodge in London and shared information concerning Freemasonry in colonial America; Carmon Hardy, Cal State–Fullerton, taught me the connection between nineteenth-century Mormonism and European thought and with his wife, Camiglia, shared supper in Torino, Paris, and Salt Lake City; Tancred King, Worcester, Massachusetts, took me to a Paris book fair in Montmartre where we discovered a rare French edition of Albert Robida; Jean-François Mayer, University of Fribourg, has accompanied me to bookstores in Switzerland, called my attention to the writings of Guers, Favez, and De Gasparin, summarized Alborg's memoirs, and gave me and my son, Matt, a "Cook's tour" of Fribourg; Peter Meadows, Cambridge University, showed me the famous Waldensian manuscripts that Samuel Morland deposited in Cambridge; J. Gordon Melton, Institute for the Study of American Religion, Santa Barbara, California, tutored me about new religious movements during book hunts in Budapest, Riga, London, Paris, Torino, Milano, and Los Angeles; Pierre Nordon, University of Paris–Sorbonne, among the best biographers of Doyle, discussed his insights concerning "Angels of Darkness" on several occasions as we lunched on the Left Bank; Phil Notarianni, Director of the Utah State Historical Society, shared information about Zopito Valentini and took me on a guided tour of Guardia Piemontese and the beach in Diamante, Calabria; Bernadette Rigal-Cellard, University of Bordeaux, shared her perspective on French travelers while we ate nachos at Cricket's in Waco, Texas; Jesse C. Trentadue, Salt Lake City, introduced me to the writings of George Ruxton while we visited bookstores in New York, London, Paris, and Stillwater, Wisconsin; and Giovanna Spagarino Viglongo, of Torino, shared previously unpublished material written by Emilio Salgari.

Lavina Fielding Anderson, Paul Anton-Nelson, Gabriella Ballesio, Eileen Barker, Maureen Ursenbach Beecher, Curt Bench, Andrea Cassinasco, Peter Delafosse, Larry Draper, Eric Dursteler, Dennis Evans, Robert Frew, Rick Grunder, Richard Neitzel Holtzapel, Lyn Jacobs, Richard Jenson, Walter Jones, Priscilla Juvellis, John Keahey, Manuel Kromer, Richard Loomis, William MacKinnon, Giovanni Maschero, George Miles, Michael Marquardt, David Miller, William Mulder, Joan Nay, Floyd O'Neil, Bill Peifer, Kent Powell, Francesca Rocci, Andrew F. Rolle, Ken Sanders, Jeff Shields, William Slaughter, Frank Suitter, Giovanni Tata, Linda Thatcher, Gregory Thompson, James Toronto, Giorgio Tourn, Salvatore Velluto, Sam Weller, Tony Weller, Susan Whetstone, Marco Zatterin, and PierLuigi Zoccatelli gave me sound advice and assistance.

This book would not have been possible without the translation services of TSC, Paris, France; Eva Lefevre, Hugh MacNaughton, Rose Edwards, Adrianno Comollo, Rick Grunder, Gaston Chappuis, Wouter Hanegraaff, and Roberto Mongia. I also acknowledge the following translators and publishers that have previously published material by the referenced authors and have granted permission to use their translations: the Arthur H. Clark Company and A. Evan Lloyd [Maximillian]; the Priory Press and Sister Maria Michele Armato, O.P., and Sister Mary Jereux Finnegan, O.P. [Mazzuchelli]; Champoeg Press and Ernest Falbo [Cipriani]; Moody Press and Gleason L. Archer [Ahmanson]; University of Oklahoma Press and Thomas N. Bonner [Schiel]; Southern Illinois University Press and Ernst A. Stadler [Koch]; Alfred A. Knopf and Florence and Victor Llona [Benoit]; and the Donald

R. Moorman Collection, Weber State University Archives and Gaston Chappuis [Bertrand]. I would also like to thank Sandy Ricks, Cathy Dixon, Jennifer Bodell, Jennifer Scott, Dana Henson, and Alana Romney, who transcribed much of the material included in this volume.

The following institutions provided materials and assistance that were invaluable in this study: The Church of Jesus Christ of Latter-day Saints, Historical Department and Family History Library, Salt Lake City, Utah; Societá di Studi Valdesi, Torre Pellice, Italy; Centro Culturale Valdese, Torre Pellice, Italy; Editrice Claudiana, Torino; The Sinsinawa Guild, Sinsinawa, Wisconsin; The British Library; The University of Edinburgh Library; The Library of Congress; Biblioteca Nazionale [Torino, Florence, and Rome]; Biblioteca di Storia e Cultura del Piemonte della Provincia di Torino, Torino, Italy; Biblioteca del Museo Nazionale del Risorgimento Italiano, Torino, Italy; The Newberry Library; The Huntington Library; Boston Public Library; New York City Public Library; Chicago Public Library; University of California, Bancroft Library; Biblioteca Querini Stampalia, Venice; Biblioteca Comunale, Milano; San Francisco Public Library; Salt Lake City Public Library; Utah State Historical Society; Nebraska Historical Society; University of Utah, J. Willard Marriott Library; Brigham Young University, Harold B. Lee Library; University of Manitoba Library, Special Collections; Harvard University, Widener Library; Yale University, The Beinecke Rare Book and Manuscript Library, and Mudd Library; The London School of Economics; Cambridge University Library; The University of Paris–Sorbonne; Princeton University, Firestone Library; University of Chicago, Regenstein Library; The Center for Studies on New Religions, Torino; The Institute of the Study of American Religion, Santa Barbara, California; and The Reform Club, London.

Of course I recognize that while these individuals and institutions have given me invaluable advice and assistance, the mistakes and defects in this volume are my own.

Finally, I thank Becky Homer for her understanding and support. My son, Matt, accompanied me to bookstores and libraries in London, Paris, Rome, Milan, Toronto, and New York. His patience was surely tested as we drove around Lake Geneva—in both directions—and as he slept in a hotel bar in Bayeaux, France, during a D-Day commemoration. My twin daughters, Marcia and Marisa, have remained exuberant even as they have become infected with the travel and book-collecting bug. Together we survived the summer of 2003 as we stood in line at the Eiffel Tower and the Louvre while the mercury registered 107° F. Finally, I could not have completed this book without the complete understanding, encouragement, and love of Nancy A. Browning, whom I was so lucky to meet while she was on her way to somewhere else: *Omnia amor vincit, et nos cedamus amori.*

Editorial Procedures and Translations

This collection of travel accounts attempts to represent the original accounts faithfully in a readable format. The translations are not literal but attempt to preserve the style and intent of the original authors in their native languages. I have edited and updated antiquated language that appeared in a few of the nineteenth-century translations to make the text easier for a modern reader to comprehend, but I have not eliminated the racial anachronisms, such as "savages" or "redskins," that say so much about attitudes of the time. I have done my best to provide translations and transcriptions that are as accurate as possible, but this arduous task does not encourage any claim to infallibility.

The material is organized into chapters, authors, and documents. Each document contains an abbreviated heading identifying the source and its location. Full citations for these items are found in the bibliography. Footnotes cite published sources by author, title, and page number. Where available, newspaper citations are to page/column: 2/3. The bibliography contains a complete listing of all the books, fantasy accounts, periodicals, theses and dissertations, and manuscripts cited in the footnotes. I have italicized book titles and put article, thesis, and dissertation titles in quotation marks. Manuscript citations appear in plain text without quotation marks. Materials from the Archives of the Historical Department of the Church of Jesus Christ of Latter-day Saints in Salt Lake City, Utah, are cited as LDS Archives.

Occasionally I have added or deleted paragraph breaks for readability.

I have not always been successful in locating biographical information concerning each author. When I have not, I have attempted to place the entry in historical perspective. In those cases where I have located biographical information in standard references, such as Jenson's LDS *Biographical Encyclopedia;* Thrapp's *Encyclopedia of Frontier Biography;* Garr, Cannon, and Cowan's *Encyclopedia of Latter-day Saint History; Dictionnaire de Biographie Française; Dizionario Biogafico degli Italiani;* Rosi's *Dizionario del Risorgimento Nazionale;* or *Neue Deutsche Biographie,* I have not always provided citations.

Introduction

"We were very curious to see these famed Latter Day Saints, as they modestly call themselves," French feminist Olympe Audouard admitted as she approached her first Mormon settlement in 1868. After a cable from Brigham Young informed her group that a "Mormon family awaits you," she "cried out with joy. At last we were going to contemplate these seventeen-strong families with only one man!"[1] Like Audouard, virtually every traveler who visited Utah during the nineteenth and early twentieth centuries was curious about Mormons. Europeans were particularly focused on the religious claims and practices of the extraordinary new American religion, and they arrived in Utah hoping to see frontier prophets, temples where holy rituals took place, and people who practiced plural marriage as they reenacted the Old Testament in the heart of the Great American Desert.

Salt Lake was not the first city that drew travelers because of its religious origins. For centuries religious and secular sojourners have made pilgrimages to the world's holy places, beginning with Jerusalem, which David made the new capital of his kingdom, even as his son Solomon transferred the ark of the covenant from a portable tabernacle to a permanent temple for Yaweh. Pilgrims visit locations in Jerusalem associated with the birth, death, and resurrection of Jesus Christ. Saint Helena, mother of Emperor Constantine, journeyed to Jerusalem in 325 A.D. and discovered the site of the crucifixion, the Holy Cross, and the Crown of Thorns. She took relics to Rome, where visitors can still see three large pieces of the cross, a nail from the cross, and two thorns from the crown of thorns.[2] Pilgrims thereafter flocked to Rome to visit the "New Jerusalem," Augustine's prophesied "City on a Hill" for God's chosen people. Just as Solomon reinvented

---

[1] Audouard, *A travers l'Amérique: Le Far-West*, 292. [2] Ortolani, *S. Croce in Gerusalemme*, 86–92.

Jerusalem, the Renaissance popes reoriented Rome from its old pagan center in the Forum to the traditional site of St. Peter's crucifixion on Vatican Hill. From 1475 to 1483, they built the Sistine Chapel in the dimensions of King Solomon's temple, and from 1506 to 1615 they rebuilt St. Peter's Basilica. Symbolic of this change was Michelangelo Buonarotti's redesign in 1538 of Campidoglio (Capitol Hill), considered to be the center of the universe, and which was reoriented from the Forum to the Vatican. John Winthrop and other early Protestant immigrants relocated "the city on a hill" to America in 1630 when they covenanted with God that in their new settlement "we must consider that we shall be as a City upon a hill. The eyes of all people are upon us."[3]

Two hundred years later, building on Winthrop's idea of American exceptionalism, Joseph Smith translated and published a book of sacred scripture in 1830 that not only identified America as the chosen land but even reported a previously unrecorded visit of Jesus Christ to the Western Hemisphere. Smith soon relocated ancient sacred geography, including the Garden of Eden and the "center place" where a temple would be built, from the Middle East to the American Midwest, placing God's chosen people and holy lands in Missouri. Unlike Solomon and the Roman pontiffs, Joseph Smith was not a head of state, but he did claim special prerogatives, including an exclusive license to act in God's name, as "king" of the Kingdom of God.[4] He and his successors were Old Testament–style prophets, seers, and revelators who instructed their followers to remain separate and apart from the world, gather to "Zion," practice polygamy, and become ritually endowed and married for eternity in structures patterned after Solomon's temple.

These early heady days of Mormonism occurred just as European travelers began visiting America. During the 1820s and 1830s new turnpikes and canals led the more hardy—or foolhardy—travelers to the American frontier. The travelers highlighted in this volume were the successors of pilgrims and "grand tourists" who had visited the Holy Land, Italy, and eventually the United States.[5] During the nineteenth century, visitors

---

[3] Winthrop, *Life and Letters of John Winthrop*, 1:19.   [4] Hansen, *Quest for Empire*, 155–58.
[5] The "Grand Tour" was discontinued during Napoléon's self-deluded reign, but when the "great shadow" went into exile privileged young men returned to the continent. One of the best summaries of the Grand Tour is Withey, *Grand Tours and Cook's Tours*. See also Hibbert, *The Grand Tour*; Chaney, *The Evolution of the Grand Tour*; and Chard, *Pleasure and Guilt on the Grand Tour*. Baedeker and Murray began publishing their first modern guidebooks for European venues, and similar guides were eventually prepared for travel in the U.S. Withey, *Grand Tours and Cook's Tours*, 71–72; and Sillitoe, *Leading the Blind*, 1–7.

appreciated the pristine scenery of Niagara Falls, the Hudson River, and the Shenandoah Valley. Later travelers extended their tours farther west. While these travelers were duly impressed with the American landscape, they were also anxious to criticize the institutions and behavior of the new country. They shared Europe's skepticism about America—particularly its political system and religious pluralism: "'America' has been an object of foreign suspicion for even longer than it has been a beacon and haven for the world's poor and downtrodden."[6]

Many of the travelers "on the way to somewhere else" who visited the raw Mormon settlements at Kirtland, Jackson County, and Nauvoo—which were located near major transportation routes—shared this skepticism. What could be more relevant in a tour of America that would demonstrate the foibles of the new country than to visit newly founded settlements of an American-born religion?[7] When Brigham Young led his followers in 1847 to the Salt Lake Valley—whose natural geography was similar to the Holy Land, with its salt sea connected to a freshwater lake by the "River Jordan"—he believed that their "New Jerusalem" was a fulfillment of Isaiah's prophecy that in the last days "the mountain of the Lord's house shall be established in the top of the mountains, and shall be exalted above the hills; and all nations shall flow unto it."[8] Like his predecessor, Young built settlements in accordance with the "plat of the City of Zion," which was similar to cities planned under the Northwest Ordinance but which were also reminiscent of the Greco-Roman grid pattern.

Many of the travelers who spent a day or two in Utah continued to be just

---

[6] Judt, "Anti-Americans Abroad," 24. Frances Trollope (1780–1863) was particularly determined to expose American foibles, and "her book was popular in Britain because it documented the stereotypes of cultural inferiority and boorish materialism that the Old World was avid to have confirmed about the New." See Schama, "The Unloved American," 37. Alexis de Tocqueville (1805–59) was less extreme and admitted that American manners were "often vulgar, but they are neither brutal nor mean." See Tocqueville, *Democracy in America*, 248–51. Charles Dickens (1812–70) observed that Americans "are not a humorous people, and their temperament always impressed me as being of a dull and gloomy character," but their tendency "to assert their self-respect and their equality" did not offend him. See Dickens, *American Notes*, 296, 298. Although Dickens did not visit Nauvoo, he boarded the ship *Amazon* in Liverpool in 1863 and spoke to Mormon converts immigrating to New York. See Mulder and Mortensen, eds., *Among the Mormons*, 334–44.

[7] Judt, "Anti-Americans Abroad," 24. Talleyrand's comment that America had "32 religions and only one plate" was consistent with the observations of many French travelers who ridiculed the number of new religions and the simplicity of American cuisine. "It is ironic that Mormonism, as native to the United States as Indian corn," William Mulder notes, "once seemed notoriously un-American." See Mulder, *Homeward to Zion*, 274.

[8] Isaiah 2:2. For an analysis of "spiritual geography," see Francaviglia, *Believing in Place*.

as critical of Americans as they were of Mormons.⁹ Like Italian traveler Francesco Varvaro Pojero, they often read Tocqueville, Trollope, and Dickens to prepare for their voyages to America.¹⁰ Mormons were obvious examples of what the flawed American experiment produced. Neither America nor its religious experiments matched up well to their own notions of European superiority.¹¹ Evidence of nationalistic bias is apparent in many of these accounts—surely some writers felt an obligation to be critical so that it would not appear that they had been appropriated—but it is also true that many Germans and Italians had less national identity than the British and French and that religious and cultural forces may have been just as important. "With few exceptions," Italian traveler Carlo Gardini wrote, "I have always found that French, German and English writers always have little benevolence toward America and often render flawed and partial judgments."¹²

Europeans with no strong religious beliefs, such as Olympe Audouard and Jules Huret, were less offended by Mormonism's "heretical" doctrines and practices, including plural marriage, than god-fearing believers such as Samuele Mazzuchelli and Pierre-Jean De Smet. Similarly, those with autocratic tendencies, such as Leonetto Cipriani and Comte d'Haussonville, were more likely to admire Brigham Young's strong leadership style than those from more democratic backgrounds.

Regardless of nationalistic or religious bias, the observations of travelers are snapshots of a very limited landscape. Jules Rémy visited Salt Lake for one month and Richard F. Burton was in the city for three weeks, but most travelers spent no more than a day or two in Mormon settlements before writing their accounts. "All impressions of hasty travel are chaotic," Daniel J. Boorstin observed, and Utah and the Mormons were particularly vulnerable to caricature.¹³ Travelers who obtained inside information or possessed great

---

⁹ I have borrowed the title of this book from H. V. Morton, who observed that "in spite of its attractions, Milan has always been one of those cities visited *on the way to somewhere else.*" See Morton, *A Traveler in Italy*, 38, italics added. ¹⁰ Torrielli, *Italian Opinion of America*, 20.

¹¹ This anti-American sentiment was not unique. "Most Grand Tourists seem to have traveled and returned home with their religious, political and racial prejudices unchanged and an enhanced notion of their own superiority, categorizing those they met as 'men, women and Italians,'" as one reviewer recently observed. "To them, Italy was not only a foreign country but a land of the past, as it was long to remain in the eyes of North Europeans." See Honour, "Italianizzati," 11.

¹² Gardini, *Gli Stati Uniti-Ricordi*, 1:125.

¹³ Dickens, *American Notes*, vi. Daniel Boorstin has observed that during the mid-nineteenth century it was quite common for literate travelers to "publish generalizations about 'America' or 'Americans' after a few weeks in New York or New Orleans.... It was an age of uncritical generalizations, especially by Englishmen about Americans." See his introduction to Isabella Bird, *A Lady's Life in the Rocky Mountains*, xix.

powers of observation were destined to write better accounts. Observers who were lazy or relied heavily on travel guides, the accounts of other travelers, or even stereotypes were destined to write weaker travelogues.

In addition to traditional travel accounts I have included selections from picaresque fantasies. Some of these stories have remained in print since their initial publication and were read by a much wider audience than most of the real time travel narratives in this volume. George Orwell's observation that autobiography is the "most egregious form of fiction" explains in part why no bright line always separates travel narratives from "historical fiction." A recent example of the controversy a novelist can generate by claiming that all of the events described in a book are based on facts occurred when Dan Brown assured his readers in the preface to the *Da Vinci Code* that "all descriptions of artwork, architecture, documents, and secret rituals in this novel are accurate."[14] Since the first edition of the book was published in 2003 there has been an explosion of religious responses by Catholics and Evangelicals and secular critiques by art historians, architectural historians, and historians of religion.[15]

Brown's book also demonstrates that fictional accounts that focus on religious beliefs usually generate more fire than purely secular stories. It is also true that books by popular fictional authors are sometimes the only source consulted by many readers about obscure religious beliefs and that many authors emphasize what he or she considers to be the most bizarre aspects of the religion. Michael Austin has concluded that for "most of the twentieth century, *A Study in Scarlet* has been one of two classic works of genre fiction (along with Zane Grey's *Riders of the Purple Sage*) responsible for keeping common nineteenth-century stereotypes of Mormonism in continuous circulation among readers and writers of popular fiction."[16] Doyle's story, which was steeped in polygamy, patriarchy, theocracy, and murder in Utah, presents a frozen image of a distorted snapshot of nineteenth-century Mormonism. Even so Doyle claimed, like other fictional authors, that

---

[14] Brown, *The Da Vinci Code*, 1.

[15] Dan Burnstein has published an anthology of responses in his *Secrets of the Code*. James A. Beverley, an evangelical Christian scholar, has summarized and criticized the various responses in his *Counterfeit Code*. For a Catholic viewpoint, see Olson and Miesel, *The DaVinci Hoax*.

[16] Austin, "Troped by the Mormons," 51. Doyle's *A Study in Scarlet*, which introduced Sherlock Holmes to the world, was very important in shaping the European image of Utah and the Mormons. Several years ago an experienced book dealer in Stockholm assured me that the best accounts in Swedish concerning Utah were written by Arthur Conan Doyle, before selling me Swedish translations of Doyle's *A Study in Scarlet* and his travel narrative, *Our Second American Adventure*.

"all I said about the Danite band and the murders is historical, so I cannot withdraw that, tho it is likely that in a work of fiction it is stated more luridly than in a work of history. It is best to let the matter rest."[17]

Like Doyle, most of the authors of the selections in this book concentrated on those aspects of Utah, Mormonism, and the West that were of interest in Europe. Just as accounts of the Grand Tour created and perpetuated a popular and distorted image of Italy, these travelers' tales became the primary sources that shaped European opinions about Utah and the Mormons. They have been consulted as source material by novelists, playwrights, and movie makers and still inspire detective fiction, westerns, comics, movies, plays, and television programs.[18] As much as Utah has changed during the past 150 years, these authors continue to "speak from the dust," sometimes convincingly, to readers in the twenty-first century, some of whom remain "very curious" to visit a Utah that no longer exists and probably never did.[19]

MICHAEL W. HOMER
Salt Lake City, Utah

---

[17] Correspondence from Doyle to G. Hodgson Higgins, 10 May 1923, LDS Archives.

[18] Comics, such as *Tex* in Italy, still highlight Mormonism in its nineteenth-century context. See also *Lanciostory* no. 45 (1980); and *Skorpio* no. 44 (1979).

[19] The phrase "speak from the dust" is from Doyle, *Through the Magic Door*, x.

Chapter 1

"THE MORMONITES"
The First European Observers, 1830–46

After the organization of the Church of Jesus Christ of Latter-day Saints in Manchester, New York, in April 1830, Joseph Smith and his followers joined the westward tide of emigration. The following November, Mormons on a mission to the Indians on the Missouri frontier encountered Sidney Rigdon (1793–1876), a Baptist preacher and disaffected disciple of Alexander Campbell, in Ohio, and the church soon transferred its headquarters to Kirtland near Lake Erie, where it remained for most of the decade.[1] Joseph Smith received more revelations in Ohio than in any other location, and the first Mormon temple was built and dedicated there in 1836. The church simultaneously identified Missouri as Zion, and a rush of converts to the state led to bitter conflict with those who did not agree with Joseph Smith's beliefs and practices, including the later notion that Independence stood near the site of the Garden of Eden.

During the 1830s Mormonism attracted a host of sectarian critics who called church members "Mormonites" and attacked their revelations, doctrines, and economic and social innovations.[2] An Ohio critic reported in 1831 that "[t]hey have all things in common, and dispense with the marriage covenant."[3] Three years later newspaper editor Eber D. Howe, whose family had converted to the new faith, published *Mormonism Unvailed* [*sic*], a stinging personal attack on Joseph Smith. Philastus Hurlbut's interviews with men

---

[1] Marquardt and Walters, *Inventing Mormonism*, 153–72. For a Campbellite perspective on Rigdon's conversion and influence on Smith, see Hayden, *Early History of the Disciples in the Western Reserve*, 209–22.

[2] For the first reviews of *The Book of Mormon* by Alexander Campbell, Jason Whitman, and *The Western Messenger*, see Vogel, ed., *Early Mormon Documents*, 2:217–50; and Mulder and Mortensen, eds., *Among the Mormons*, 71–75, 80–81, 86–88.

[3] *Evangelical Magazine and Gospel Advocate*, 47.

who knew of Smith's career as a necromancer in New York and his charge that Smith had plagiarized *The Book of Mormon* provided generations of critics with a blueprint for attacks on the nascent religion. Almanacs and gazetteers described "Mormonites" throughout the 1830s, sometimes dispassionately but more often negatively.[4]

American and British travelers occasionally criticized the doctrines and character of Mormons they met in New York, Pennsylvania, Ohio, and Missouri. Baptist minister David Marks attended a Mormon meeting in Fayette, New York, in 1830, where he met David Whitmer and "two or three of his sons and others to a number of eight, who said they were witnesses of a certain book just published, called 'The Golden Bible' or 'Book of Mormon.'" Believers in Ohio lent Marks a copy of *The Book of Mormon*, and he read part of it.[5] While preaching in Kirtland in 1831, Nancy Towle encountered prominent Mormons, including William Wines Phelps, Martin Harris, Sidney Rigdon, and Joseph Smith.[6] Alvan Stone, a Baptist ministering in Illinois in 1832, repeated gossip about a "Methodist exhorter" who was converted to Mormonism, became "violently deranged," and "blasted the hopes of Mormonism in this region for a season."[7] Congregational minister Samuel L. Parker found "a small neighborhood of Mormons" in Liberty, Missouri, in 1835. "They had fled from Jackson County, which they call their promised land, and to which they say they shall return," wrote this Oregon-bound missionary. "They are a poor deluded people, and when they speak of their persecutions, they seem not to possess the spirit of our Saviour."[8]

Secular travelers also took notice of the Latter-day Saints. Nathan Hoskins wrote in 1832 that "Mormonites have spread considerably in the

---

[4] A relatively dispassionate account that relied on information provided by Mormons is Hayward's *The Religious Creeds and Statistics of Every Christian Denomination*, 130–42. For a negative treatment relying on Howe and others, see J. Newton Brown's 1838 *Encyclopedia of Religious Knowledge*; J. M. Peck's *A Gazetteer of Illinois*, which noted that there was "a small society of *Mormons* in Green county" in 1836; and Alphonso Wetmore's 1837 *Gazetteer of the State of Missouri*, which devoted four pages to attacks on the Mormons.

[5] Marks, *The Life of David Marks*, 340–42. After his death, Marks' wife published a second edition with an additional paragraph telling how Mormon missionaries urged him to buy a copy of *The Book of Mormon* for $1.25, even though an angel had told them to sell it for $1.75. "They replied, 'The angel said we might sell it for that sum, but did not say we should not sell it for any less.'" When Marks' journal first appeared in serial form in Limerick, Maine, he wrote only that "we went to Fayette & held one meeting" and did not mention his encounter with Mormons. See *The Morning Star*, 28 April 1830, 1.

[6] Towle, *Vicissitudes Illustrated*, 150–59.

[7] Stone, "Extracts from the Memoir of Alvan Stone," 85–97.

[8] Parker, *Journal of an Exploring Tour beyond the Rocky Mountains*, 30.

Ohio" and that "[n]umbers of people from very respectable families embraced [Joseph Smith's] doctrines; spending a considerable portion of their time in reading, prayer and exhortation, and were very zealous."[9] Ornithologist John Townsend, who traveled west with Nathaniel Wyeth's fur-trading expedition, and Josiah Gregg, a renowned Santa Fe trader, commented on Mormons in their travel accounts.[10] Edmund Flagg encountered a Latter-day Saint family in the Midwest on its way to Missouri. Flagg pretended to be a Mormon to gain their confidence about "'the reasons of the faith that was in him' and the ultimate, proximate, and intermediate designs of the party." Despite expressing his disbelief, he admitted that the father was "by no means an ignorant fanatic."[11]

While traveling to Lockport, New York, in 1832 or 1833, British traveler Thomas Hamilton passed "several parties of what were called Mormonites, going to join a settlement established by their founder, in Ohio." He compared Mormonism to the teachings of British Utopian Robert Owen.[12] E. S. Abdy, a Fellow of Jesus College at Cambridge, wrote in 1835 that while he "had no opportunity of visiting any Mormon settlement," he heard descriptions of Joseph Smith and the Mormons in Ohio, as well as accounts of the religion's history and doctrines.[13] D. Griffiths Jr. described *The Book of Mormon* and debated a Mormon elder in Ohio in 1834. Griffiths considered the new religion "[o]ne of the most remarkable instances of credulity and fanaticism existing at the present time in the United States," but he believed "many of the Mormon people are perfectly sincere [as] is pretty evident from the sacrifice in property they make."[14]

When Joseph Smith transferred church headquarters to the east bank of the Mississippi in 1839, the new Mormon capital at Nauvoo, Illinois, grew rapidly and soon became a prominent river town. During the next decade Mormon truth claims and history became the subject of an increasing number of books and newspaper reports, often written by Protestant clergymen or disaffected Mormons. Nauvoo was easily accessible by steamboat for travelers who hoped to see a few Mormons and perhaps speak with the young American prophet. Protestant ministers such as Daniel Kidder and Jonathan

---

[9] Hoskins Jr., *Notes Upon the Western Country*, 40–41.
[10] Townsend, *Narrative of a Journey across the Rocky Mountains*, 29–30; and Gregg, *Commerce of the Prairies*, 93–99.
[11] Flagg, *The Far West*, 1:109–13.
[12] Hamilton, *Men and Manners in America*, 309–12.
[13] Abdy, *Journal of a Residence and Tour in the United States*, 1:324–25, 2:40–42, 54–59.
[14] Griffiths Jr., *Two Years' Residence in the New Settlements of Ohio*, 132–41.

B. Turner and Episcopal priests John A. Clark and Henry Caswall visited Nauvoo and wrote accounts of their encounters with the Mormons.[15]

Continental European travelers were drawn to frontier America in the 1830s and 1840s. Explorers Prince Maximilian and Albert Karl Koch were primarily interested in hunting and natural history, while Roman Catholic missionaries Samuele Mazzuchelli and Pierre-Jean De Smet sought to convert the new world to the true faith. Mazzuchelli, Koch, and German traveler Alexander Ziegler made special trips to Nauvoo to visit the Mormon capital. Like their American and British counterparts, they each were curious about the new religion and recorded their impressions of the Mormons they encountered in Missouri, Nauvoo, and Council Bluffs, Iowa.

Alexander Philipp Maximilian:
They Complained Bitterly

Alexander Philipp Maximilian, prince of Wied-Neuwied (1782–1867), served as a major general in the Prussian army during the Napoleonic wars.[16] During his military service he developed a strong interest in the natural sciences and planned a trip to America. Maximilian visited Brazil in 1815 with a scientific expedition and spent two years in South America studying the flora and fauna of the Brazilian rain forests. His account of his adventures appeared in Germany in 1820 and 1821 and was later translated into French, Dutch, and English.

The prince arrived in North America in 1832 to explore the upper Missouri River, commissioning Swiss artist Karl Bodmer to sketch the American frontier and its aborigine inhabitants. His party wintered at Robert Owen's Utopian colony at New Harmony, Indiana. In spring 1833 he launched his expedition to the western frontier from St. Louis. The party conducted a scientific exploration of the upper Missouri, visiting Fort Cantonment (now Fort Leavenworth), Bellevue (below present-day Omaha), Fort Pierre, Fort Clark (near today's Bismarck, North Dakota), and John Jacob Astor's American Fur Company outposts at Fort Union and Fort McKenzie, where the party spent nearly two months. The expedition collected examples of Indian culture, including weapons and shamanistic artifacts, as well as fossils. Bod-

---

[15] Aitken, *Journey up the Mississippi River ... to Nauvoo, the City of the Latter Day Saints*, 35–36.

[16] For Maximilian's life, see Thwaites, ed., *Travels in the Interior of North America*, 3:9–20.

mer sketched the scenery and the Indians, creating an invaluable record of cultures that would virtually vanish within a few years before the onslaught of smallpox. Maximilian returned in the spring, arriving at Fort Leavenworth in May 1834 and leaving New York in July.

Fur-trader Alexander Culbertson accompanied the fifty-five-year-old Maximilian on part of his trip and described the prince in his journal:

> In this year an interesting character in the person of Prince Maximilian from Koblenz on the Rhine made his first appearance in the upper Missouri. The Prince was at that time nearly seventy years of age, but well preserved, and able to endure considerable fatigue. He was a man of medium-height, rather slender, sans teeth, passionately fond of his pipe, unostentatious, and speaking very broken English. His favorite dress was a white slouch hat, a black velvet coat, rather rusty from long service, and probably the greasiest pair of trousers that ever encased princely legs. The Prince was a bachelor and a man of science, and it was in this latter capacity that he had roamed so far from his ancestral home on the Rhine. He was accompanied by an artist named Boadman [Bodmer] and a servant.[17]

On his party's return in May 1834, Maximilian encountered Mormons aboard a steamboat near Williams Ferry (today's Missouri City) on the Missouri River. Maximilian's two-volume account of his experiences in America was published for the first time in German in 1839–41, in French in 1840–43, and in English in 1843. The chief value of his work was its ethnology, which was "highly interesting as an historical description of natural conditions west of the Mississippi." Reuben Gold Thwaites wrote that a traveler "gliding across the plains and along the windings of the Missouri in a palace-car, may follow the pages of Maximilian and the plates of Bodmer, and thus obtain as clearly as words and pictures can express, an accurate presentation of the trans-Mississippi region in 1833."[18]

MAXIMILIAN, *REISE IN DAS INNERE NORD-AMERIKA IN DEN JAHREN 1832 BIS 1834* [TRAVELS IN THE INTERIOR OF NORTH AMERICA], 119–20.
TRANSLATED BY H. EVANS LLOYD.

Our vessel was crowded with curious persons, and, besides these, an unwelcome intruder had intoxicated the greater part of my people. Among our inquisitive visitors there were several men belonging to a religious sect known here by the name of Mormons. They complained bitterly of the

---

[17] Thwaites, ed., *Travels in the Interior of North America*, 3:17–18. For Culberston, see Wischmann, *Frontier Diplomats*. [18] Thwaites, ed., *Travels in the Interior of North America*, 3:19–20.

unjust treatment which they had lately experienced. They had lived on the other side of the Missouri, and, as they asserted, had been expelled, on account of their doctrines, by the neighboring planters, their dwellings demolished and burnt, their plantations destroyed, and some of them killed, on which they settled on the north bank of the river. I was not able to learn whether all this was true, or why, after an interval of one or two years, they have not obtained redress from the government. So much, however, is certain, that, if these people spoke the truth, it would be a great disgrace to the administration of justice in this country, which calls itself the only free country in the world.

According to their account, an angel appeared in 1821 to the founder of their doctrine, and brought him golden tables of law, on which the contents of a certain chapter of the Bible were engraved, and which is the substance of the doctrine. The inscription was translated, and the angel took the tables away. They spoke also of a prophet Mormon, but I was not able clearly to comprehend the mystical meaning of their words. A sensible old man gave me some notion of their doctrine, to which he seemed to be much devoted. He affirmed that their sect was perfectly harmless, and never molested others, a point respecting which their neighbors might, perhaps, give a different testimony.

SAMUELE CARLO MAZZUCHELLI:
TO SEE AND SPEAK WITH A HERESIARCH

Samuele Mazzuchelli (1806–64) was born in Milan, Italy. When he was six his mother died and he was sent to Catholic boarding school in Lugano, Switzerland. At seventeen he joined the Dominican Order in Faenza, Italy, transferred to Rome, and was ordained a sub-deacon in 1827. That year Frederic Rese visited Rome, on behalf of Bishop Edward Dominic Fenwick of Cincinnati, Ohio, to recruit Catholic clergy to serve as missionaries in the United States. Mazzuchelli responded to Rese's call, and in December 1828 he arrived in Cincinnati as a Dominican novice. He was ordained a priest in September 1830, and Bishop Fenwick assigned him to minister at the fur emporium on Mackinac Island.[19]

During the next five years Mazzuchelli served in Green Bay, Winnebago, Prairie du Chien, and Crawford, Wisconsin. He designed and directed the

---

[19] For more on Mazzuchelli, see McGreal, *Samuele Mazzuchelli*; Alderson and Alderson, *The Man Mazzuchelli, Pioneer Priest*; and Marolla, *Mazzuchelli of Wisconsin*.

SAMUELE MAZZUCHELLI (1806–1864).
Courtesy of The Sinsinawa Guild,
Sinsinawa, Wisconsin.

construction of churches and organized schools for Indians and Catholic parishioners. In 1835 Mazzuchelli was assigned to DuBuque, which soon became part of Wisconsin Territory. He visited Mississippi River settlements from Fort Snelling on the north to St. Louis on the south, including Galena, Iowa City, Muscatine, Benton, and New Diggings in Illinois and Iowa. He eventually established twenty-one frontier churches.

Like many clergymen in the Midwest, Mazzuchelli was curious about the activities of Joseph Smith. He discussed the Mormon prophet with Father Alleman, a Dominican priest who served in Fort Madison, Iowa, which was across the Mississippi River and about ten miles north of Nauvoo. He also read Jonathan B. Turner's *Mormonism in All Ages*.[20] In February 1843 he decided to visit Nauvoo and stayed briefly with Father Alleman before crossing the frozen Mississippi from Fort Madison to Nauvoo on a horse-drawn sleigh. Soon after his visit to Nauvoo Mazzuchelli returned to Italy, where in 1844 he published his memoirs anonymously in Milan and devoted a chapter to his visit to Nauvoo and a general discussion of Mormon history and doc-

---

[20] Ironically Mazzuchelli relied on Presbyterian minister Jonathan Turner, who in addition to being anti-Mormon was extremely anti-Catholic. See Turner, *Mormonism in All Ages*, 8.

trines.[21] But the memoirs failed to reveal that Mazzuchelli had made forty-five pages of careful handwritten notes while reading the third edition of *The Book of Mormon* and that he had also analyzed Parley P. Pratt's *Voice of Warning*, which has been described as "[p]erhaps the most important book outside the 'Standard Works' to be issued in Mormondom."[22]

Mazzuchelli returned to the U.S. in 1845 and organized the Dominican Order of Sisters of the Convent of Sinsinawa. Mazzuchelli remained interested in Mormonism during the last decade of his life as he continued to minister from Fort Benton. He submitted three articles to Bishop John N. Neumann in 1858, in which he analyzed Pratt's *Voice of Warning*, and requested permission to publish them in *The Catholic Standard*. Perhaps the Utah War and Pratt's murder in 1857 rekindled Mazzuchelli's interest in the religion and reminded him of his unpublished studies. Mazzuchelli died in Fort Benton in 1864 after residing in America for more than thirty-five years.

One hundred and sixty-one years after Mazzuchelli arrived in the U.S., the Sisters of the Convent of Sinsinawa prepared a Positio Super Vita, Virtutibus et Fama Sanctitatis, and submitted it to the congregation for the Causes of Saints seeking his canonization.[23] On 6 July 1993 Mazzuchelli took the first step toward sainthood when he was declared venerable by Pope John Paul II.

MAZZUCHELLI, *MEMORIE ISTORICHE ED EDIFICANTI D'UN MISSIONARIO APOSTOLICO* [HISTORICAL AND EDIFYING MEMORIES OF AN APOSTOLIC MISSIONARY], 295–303. TRANSLATED BY SISTER MARIA MICHELE ARMATO, O.P., AND SISTER MARY JEREMY FINNEGAN, O.P.[24]

It was in February 1843 that the Missionary [Mazzuchelli] desired to see and speak with a heresiarch known for several years, in every part of the

---

[21] [Mazzuchelli], *Memorie istoriche ed edificanti*. Following Mazzuchelli's return to the U.S., the same publisher issued his *Casa di Missioni e Collegio Fondati sul Sinsinawa Mound*. Mazzuchelli was mentioned frequently in a Catholic magazine published in Milan. See *L'Amico Cattolico* (October 1843), 312–13; (May 1844), 344–48; (May 1845), 390–92; (December 1845), 447–56; (January 1847), 37–39; (June 1847), 450–64. Mazzuchelli was the first Italian to publish his observations about Mormonism. Events in Utah began to be reported only after Mormon missionaries arrived in Piedmont in 1850.

[22] Whittaker, "Early Mormon Pamphleteering," 58.

[23] *Positio Super Vita, Virtutibus et Fama Sanctitatis*. The *Positio* mentions Mazzuchelli's visit with Joseph Smith and his observations on Mormonism.

[24] This translation originally appeared in *The Memoirs of Reverend Samuel Mazzuchelli, O.P.* The first English translation of Mazzuchelli's *Memoirs* appeared in *The Young Eagle*, a magazine published by Santa Clara College in Sinsinawa, Wisconsin, from February 1898 to December 1901. See Mazzuchelli, "Memoirs of Rev. Samuele Mazzuchelli, O.P."

Republic and even in England.²⁵ With this objective, I left Burlington for a few days and went to Fort Madison where the Reverend J. Alleman was exercising his holy ministry. After descending the frozen Mississippi for ten miles, I arrived at Nauvoo, the famous city of the Mormons. There the well-known Prophet Joseph Smith, founder of the sect, has his home. . . .²⁶

The false prophet and heresiarch, Joseph Smith, founder of the sect of Mormons or "Latter-Day Saints" is a man of thirty nine [37] years, tall and well-proportioned. His expression does not indicate friendliness nor good judgment, his looks show anything but piety, his manners are somewhat rough. Born of poor parents, he did not have the advantages of an ordinary education. He has a wife and children. His influence over the sect is almost unlimited, and he seeks by every means to keep the Mormons in the belief that he is a prophet of the Most High, with whom he says he has frequent conversations and by whose inspiration he directs and governs the new church of the Latter-Day Saints. On the occasion of my visit to him, he solemnly declared that he had many times seen God face to face and had more revelations than the Apostle Saint Paul, to whom, he asserted, he was not inferior in goodness. So flagrant was his imposture and effrontery that, in one sermon, he proclaimed himself great as Moses and as Jesus Christ.²⁷ Even among his followers there was much comment on his immorality. The false prophet owes the propagation of his heresies to the cooperation of several interested associates; among the more notable of these are Sidney Rigdon, Parley P. Pratt, and John Taylor. The religious ignorance of the Protestant people also contributes to this growth. . . .

It may be observed here that any religion, however extravagant and absurd in its teachings, always finds followers among Protestants, whenever its founders know how to quote many passages from the Bible to defend it. The

---

[25] Mazzuchelli wrote his *Memoirs* in the third person, which the translation changes to first person. Twelfth-century Roman Catholic clergy used the term "heresiarch" to refer to preachers—usually not ordained—who advocated purification of the church from clerical corruption and innovations in church practices such as infant baptism and veneration of the crucifix. The Albigensians and Waldensians originated in France, and both groups were eventually excommunicated and persecuted. Contemporary orthodox clergy organized the Franciscans and Dominicans.

[26] W. W. Murphy's biography recorded details not in Mazzuchelli's *Memorie*. "On his arrival at Norvoo [sic] he called on Joseph Smith, the head of the Mormon Church, and at the request of Smith, remained his guest over night and they sat up until three o'clock in the morning, Father Mazzuchelli endeavoring to arrive at the tenants of Mormonism and in discussing other theological questions." See Murphy, "Biography of Father Samuele Mazzuchelli." See writings by Mazzuchelli's great-nephew, Luca Beltrami, *Padre Samuele Mazzuchelli*, 55–57; and "I Mormoni nelle memorie di un missionario Milanese." See also Crépeau, *Un apôtre dominicain aux Etats-Unis*, 201; Alderson and Alderson, *The Man Mazzuchelli*; and Marolla, *Mazzuchelli of Wisconsin*.

[27] I have found no record by Joseph Smith or any of his associates of Mazzuchelli's visit to Nauvoo. Smith's diary confirms that the Mormon prophet was in Nauvoo during February 1843 and that he traveled to Shokokon, a settlement across the Mississippi River from Burlington. Mazzuchelli lived in Shokokon that winter. See Smith, *An American Prophet's Record*, 301–12.

Mormon preachers have so thoroughly studied the Bible that they were able to convince the hearers that their dogmas were a continuation of the prophecies and the Gospel. In this way they converted innumerable people, and not a few Protestant ministers. It seems almost incredible that a people can be so intelligent, so astute in the business of this world, so enterprising, and so fond of reading as the Americans of the United States, and at the same time so ready to believe all the errors invented by artfullness and religious fanaticism. But of what are men not capable outside of the Catholic Church? Will they be able to find the truth without it? Will they be able to hold firmly to any doctrine? Will they find any foundation on which to build? . . .

Returning to the town of Burlington after my visit to the false prophet, I remained there until the first week of Lent, when I left for Galena, 180 miles distant. I made a portion of this journey on the frozen Mississippi, a very easy way to traveling with horse and sleigh; but the cold was more intense than in other years, the temperature being ten degrees below freezing for the greater part of March.

Albert Karl Koch:
A Place I Had Wished to See for a Long Time

Albrecht Karl Koch (1804–67) was born in Roitzsch, in the duchy of Saxony. Little is known about his life before Koch visited the United States as a twenty-two-year old. He lived in Erie, Pennsylvania, and perhaps St. Clair, Michigan, before moving to St. Louis. By 1836 he had become the proprietor of the St. Louis Museum, which housed wax figures of Andrew Jackson, Don Antonio López de Santa Ana, and Seminole chief Osceola and his wife. Other attractions featured panoramic views of ancient cities and battles, illustrations of natural history, paintings of Indians, and stuffed and live birds and animals, including bears and alligators. The museum occasionally served as a theater for ventriloquists, magicians, bird imitators, singers, and actors.[28]

An enthusiastic collector of fossils, Koch traveled the Mississippi River Valley searching for exhibits for his museum, and in 1840 he successfully supervised a four-month excavation of the fossilized remains of a mastodon. He assembled the bones and displayed them in St. Louis before selling the

---

[28] For a brief description of Koch's life, see Ernst A. Stadler's introduction to Koch's *Journey Through a Part of the United States*, xvii–xxxv; and McDermott, "Dr. Koch's Wonderful Fossils," 233–56.

museum and setting out with a traveling exhibit to New Orleans, Philadelphia, and other cities. Koch took the exhibit to London and Ireland for two years beginning in 1841, and while in England he met the Mormon apostle Parley P. Pratt. Koch sold his fossil collection to the British Museum and returned to the United States. On 21 November 1844, while traveling on the Mississippi to Alabama (where he eventually discovered the remains of a sea serpent called zeuglodon), he visited Nauvoo, where he again encountered Pratt. He exhibited his new sea serpent in Germany in 1846 and eventually sold it to the Berlin Royal Anatomical Museum. He returned to Alabama in 1848 and recovered another zeuglodon fossil that he shipped to Germany, where he displayed it a year later. Koch exhibited his sea serpent in New Orleans in 1853 before settling in St. Louis with his family. He conducted geological explorations in Tennessee and developed real estate in Illinois, where he died in 1867 at Golconda. Koch recounted his adventures in North America from 1844 to 1846 in a narrative published in Vienna in 1847, from which these edited excerpts are taken.

KOCH, REISE DURCH EINEN THEIL DER VEREINIGTEN STAATEN [JOURNEY THROUGH A PART OF THE UNITED STATES], 67–68. TRANSLATED BY ERNST A. STADLER.

Thursday, the 21st of November [1844]. This morning I arrived again with the Steamboat *Iowa*, safely at the rapids of the Mississippi, but the boat had such a heavy load that half of it had to be loaded into two large barges. This took four hours' time away, but shortly before that we landed, to my joy, in Nauvoo, the city of Latter Day Saints, a place I had wished to see for a long time. This town, which was built only 5 years ago, lies in Illinois on the right bank [*sic*] of the Mississippi on a plane which rises gently from the river. The river here has flat rocky banks and a good landing place. Some distance from the river is a very fertile land. In the middle of the city, on its highest point, rise the walls of the not-yet-completed temple, which is 170 feet long and 80 feet wide and is of a very original architecture. The walls are strong and massive and decorated by some 30 columns that were worked by skilled sculptors. In this temple is a very interesting place intended for the baptism of those who want to join this sect. It is an oblong fount borne by twelve life-sized oxen. The oxen are real masterpieces of workmanship, and if viewed from a short distance would be taken for live animals. At present they are painted white with oil paint, but they, like the fount they carry, will be gilded. Two of the oxen stand at each end of the container, and two pairs on each side, and between them there is a staircase that leads up to the pool;

from each side, stairs lead down to the water, where the person who is going to be baptized, like the Baptists, will be submerged by the preacher. Not far from the temple is the foundation for an arsenal, for the Mormons are able, should they be in any danger, to field 3000 men, a fact of which they are very proud. An apostle of the Mormons, a certain Mr. Pratt whom I knew from Liverpool, showed me all the interesting sights. After I looked around town for awhile, I went to the bank of the Mississippi to see whether I could discover anything in respect to geology. At first it looked as if I would not find anything, but suddenly I saw an undamaged petrified bone at my feet. At closer inspection I found it to be the thighbone of a Labyrinthodon, or primeval giant frog. Judging by the size of the bone, this frog must have weighed approximately 50 to 80 pounds and have had unusual muscle strength. But curiously this bone was the first petrifaction of an animal belonging to the reptiles that was discovered below the bituminous layer. I say the first fragment because in a short time I found also a part of the tibia and a humerus of the same animal.

Alexander Ziegler:
The Completed Temple Was Arranged as a Barracks

German traveler Alexander Ziegler (1822–87) was born in Ruhla in the Thueringer Woods and studied geography and economics before becoming a prolific writer of travel narratives. He first visited the U.S. in 1846, spent time in Cuba, and returned to New York. On his voyage down the Mississippi he visited the battle-scarred and largely abandoned settlement at Nauvoo. He was an eyewitness to the aftermath of the "Battle of Nauvoo," when some eight hundred Illinois militiamen defeated three hundred defenders on 12 September 1846, killing three members of the Mormon "Spartan Band." The victors occupied and desecrated the temple and evicted most of the city's remaining inhabitants.[29]

Ziegler returned to Germany in 1847 and wrote a two-volume account of his travels that appeared the next year. He described the conditions of German immigrants he met in New England and discussed agricultural and religious conditions in the U.S. He advised Germans to settle in Wisconsin because of its favorable agriculture prospects and suggested that the German government organize a program of immigration to assist the poor. Ziegler published a volume on American democracy in 1848 and in 1856

---

[29] Allen and Leonard, *The Story of the Latter-day Saints*, 234.

wrote a catechism for German travelers and immigrants that addressed commonly asked questions about the U.S.[30] During the 1850s Ziegler continued to travel and write about his adventures, touring Spain, Morocco, Algeria, Tunisia, Egypt, Palestine, Syria, Asia Minor, and Greece, and at the end of the decade Scandinavia, Finland, and the isles of Orkey and Shetland.[31] Ziegler died in Wiesbaden in 1887.[32]

ZIEGLER, *SKIZZEN EINER REISE DURCH NORDAMERIKA UND WESTINDIEN* [SKETCHES OF TRAVEL THROUGH NORTH AMERICA AND THE WEST INDIES], 243–47. TRANSLATED BY WOUTER HANEGRAAFF.

In the late afternoon we sailed past Fort Madison, and some hours later we reached Nauvoo. After we had left the boat here—which moored a bit later farther down at the other shore at Montrose—so that we could visit the city of the "Latter-day Saints" we went, over a softly ascending slope, from the shore to the slightly-distanced, spaciously constructed Mormon city, which consisted of small houses, and were highly surprised to find here the temple not only open, but also a troop of cavalry before it, considerably armed and equipped with three-pounders. The vestibule, as well as the inside of the church, was filled with variously armed folks, looking like highwaymen, and the completed temple was arranged as a barracks. Not a little surprised about this military equipment, we asked for the reason, and learned now that a few days earlier a battle had been waged against the Mormons, that infamous religious sect, which had settled here since several years, and that all had been driven away. These had put up a large army on the other side of the Mississippi, and were for a part still busy with the retreat out of Nauvoo, where the population had amounted to over 17.000 Mormons.[33] Only now did we notice the destruction of the houses in the city, which were sorely ravaged by bullets and were abandoned by their inhabitants. The battle and the attack on the city had been all the more violent, because the Mormons had fought for their city with much courage and great bravery. Many of them had been wounded, and many remained dead on the spot. In accordance with the treaty achieved by the mayor of the city of Quincy, the Mormons had to leave the state of Illinois, but were permitted to sell their land and their buildings through authorized agents. The Jesuits speculated on the Mormon temple, and had already, as we heard, made an offer, which however had not yet been accepted. As we were further informed, the neighbors of

---

[30] Ziegler, *Republicanische Licht und Schattenseiten* and *Der Geleitsmann*.
[31] Ziegler, *Reise in Spanien; Meine Reise im Orient;* and *Meine Reisen im Norden*.
[32] For more on Ziegler, see his entry in *Allgemeine Deutsche Biographie*.
[33] Contemporary population figures for Nauvoo tended to be inflated. Leonard, *Nauvoo, A Place of Peace*, 179, estimated Nauvoo had 11,057 residents in 1845.

the Mormons had become bent on their beautiful and fertile properties, and apparently for this reason had undertaken a military expedition against them. On the other hand, some advanced as the reason for this fight that the Mormons had committed many abuses and vices, by which the security of persons and property, as well as of public morality, had come to be endangered. As a result of the community of property existing among them, their priests had in a scandalous manner lived together with the women in a so-called "spiritual marriage."

The Mormon temple in Nauvoo is built in a very noble style. It has a length of 108 and a breadth of 80 feet, is surrounded by a large, heavy, not yet completed wall, and produces an impressive sight.[34] The front side of the building has a flight of stairs, along which one reaches three large, arched entrance doors. Through these one enters the vestibule, and after that the simple church, separated in three naves and decorated with some tasteful sculpture. Here neither an altar nor a pulpit was to be seen, but only a row of raised seats with separate church chairs. On the right side there was a staircase, by which we first entered the octagonal tower of the building, in which were several halls, and finally on the roof of the temple, from which we enjoyed a wonderful view over the endless prairies and the great Mississippi stream. While climbing down we saw in one of these halls the general staff of the occupation army sitting at a table, smoking and playing [cards].

By the light of the moon, in a boat in the company of some Mormon fugitives, we sailed to the other shore of the Mississippi, where those who were driven away had put up their army. We discovered the mooing flocks of cattle, laden carts, household goods, beds, small white tents and brightly flaming fires, and some women preparing food, while the men had gathered around the fires in gloomy groups. They intended to set out for California.

After we had walked unhindered through the Mormon army, we had to cross the wide mouth of a large, deep creek that discharges into the Mississippi to reach our steamboat. Instead of a bridge we found nothing but a round tree-trunk floating on the water and a broad plank. While I preferred the trunk, my traveling companion, who had an inclination to dizziness, tried to reach the other side by making use of the plank. However, his dangerous crossing was not smiled upon by a lucky star. . . .

Due to the lower rapids of the Mississippi, which begin here and cannot be crossed, the steamboat could not go further. The captain therefore asked us to pass these rapids by land, and then to continue our journey to St. Louis on another steamboat. We made good use of this evening to write our diaries, while the ladies sang and the gentlemen played cards.

---

[34] By contrast Koch estimated the length to be 170 feet.

Pierre-Jean De Smet:
Mr. Young, an Affable and Very Polite Gentleman

One of the most remarkable characters of his age, Pierre-Jean De Smet (1801–73) was born in Termonde, Belgium, and may have logged more miles in the American West than any other traveler in the nineteenth century.[35] As a youth he entered the Preparatory Seminary at Mechlin and first traveled to the United States in 1821, where he entered the Novitiate of the Society of Jesus in Whitemarsh, Maryland. In 1823 he was sent to help found a Jesuit church in Florissant, near St. Louis, Missouri, and was ordained a priest in 1827.

De Smet founded a mission among the Pottawatomie Indians in 1838 near present Council Bluffs, Iowa. He made his first extended venture into the West in 1840, traveling to the Pacific Northwest, where he eventually founded St. Mary's Mission in the Bitterroot Valley and St. Ignatius' Mission among the Kalispel Indians. He visited Fort Benton—the residence of Father Mazzuchelli—as well as New Orleans, Louisville, Cincinnati, Mobile, Chicago, Omaha, Milwaukee, Washington, Baltimore, New York, and Central and South America. De Smet sailed to Europe as many as sixteen times to raise European consciousness of Indians, and he published accounts of his missionary labors in six languages to solicit contributions.

On his way from Oregon to St. Louis in 1846, De Smet visited Council Bluffs, where he shared his knowledge of the Great Basin with Brigham Young, for the Latter-day Saints were closely questioning every western sojourner who passed through their refuge camp at Winter Quarters near today's Omaha. His account demonstrates his sympathy toward the Mormons and the persecution they had encountered in Illinois. The Jesuit priest's subsequent observations were less charitable: he advised sending missionaries to Utah in 1850. This was "so much the more urgent to-day, when the Mormons (a sect of fanatics) and the French socialists under the lead of Cabet are proposing to go and form new States in the midst of the great desert," he wrote. "The Mormons are there already, 50,000 to 60,000 in number.... The poor simple savages will be their dupes, unless we forestall them and implant as much as possible the truths of our holy religion in their hearts."[36]

---

[35] For De Smet, see De Smet, *Life, Letters and Travels*; Margaret, *Father De Smet, Pioneer Priest of the Rockies*; and Carriker, *Father Peter John De Smet, Jesuit in the West*.

[36] De Smet, *Missions de l'Orégon*, 272; and De Smet, *Life, Letters and Travels*, 611.

Pierre-Jean De Smet (1801–73). Used by permission, Utah State Historical Society, all rights reserved.

De Smet joined the Utah Expedition as chaplain in 1858. Having read the accounts of several disenchanted Mormons, particularly John Hyde's *Mormonism: Its Leaders and Designs*, he was predictably more critical of the Mormons, characterizing them as "that terrible sect of modern fanatics, flying from civilization, settled in the midst of an uninhabited wilderness." When the Utah War ended, De Smet was traveling to Utah, on the south fork of the Platte 480 miles west of the Missouri, and he returned to Fort Leavenworth and resigned his commission. De Smet died at St. Louis University in 1873 and is buried at the Jesuit Novitiate at Florissant, Missouri.[37] Despite his battles with the Mormons and the fact he never visited the Salt Lake Valley, he is remembered on "This is the Place Monument" at the mouth of Emigration Canyon in Salt Lake City as one of the great explorers of West.

De Smet, *Missions de l'Orégon et voyages aux Montagnes Rocheuses* [Oregon Missions and Travels over the Rocky Mountains], 272, as quoted in *Life, Letters and Travels of Father Pierre-Jean De Smet*, II: 611.

On the 18th [November 1846] we found ourselves within view of the old Council Bluffs, which was once a great military post. Since my last voyage in 1842, the river has made considerable changes here, and has dug itself a new bed in various places. Council Bluffs, which was then on the edge of the river, is now more than three miles from it. During the day we saw the ruins

---

[37] Hyde, *Mormonism: Its Leaders and Designs*; and De Smet, *Life, Letters and Travels*, 1408–15.

Brigham Young (1801–77).
Used by permission, Utah State Historical Society, all rights reserved.

of several old trading-houses. Not far from there, in a vast and beautiful plain, is a temporary establishment of the Mormons, driven out from their city of Nauvoo on the Mississippi; there are more than 10,000 of them here. I was introduced to their president, Mr. Young, an affable and very polite gentleman. He pressed me very earnestly to remain a few days, an invitation which my limited time did not permit me to accept. The unheard-of-persecutions and atrocious sufferings endured by these unhappy people will furnish a sad page to the history of the great valley of the west.

Cinquante nouvelles lettres du R. P. De Smet
[Fifty New Letters of R. P. De Smet], as quoted in
Life, Letters and Travels of Father Pierre Jean De Smet, I: 56.

In the fall of 1846, as I drew near to the frontier of the State of Missouri, I found the advance guard of the Mormons, numbering about 10,000, camped in the territory of the Omahas, not far from the old Council Bluffs. They had just been driven out for the second time from a state of the Union. They had resolved to winter on the threshold of the great desert, and then to move onward into it to put distance between themselves and their persecutors, without even knowing at that time the goal of their long wanderings, nor the spot where they should once more build for themselves permanent dwellings. They asked me a thousand questions about the regions I had explored and the spot I have just described to you [the basin of the Great Salt Lake]. I pleased them greatly from the account I gave them of it. Was that what determined them? I dare not assert it. They are there.

Great Salt Lake, Utah.
Produced by Currier & Ives, a New York City lithographic company, circa 1870.

Chapter 2

"Polygamy is a Sword of Damocles"
Overland Travelers in Utah, 1849–55

At dusk on 27 June 1844 an angry mob shot and killed Joseph Smith in Carthage, Illinois, sealing the Mormon prophet's mission with his blood. Two years later his foremost successor, Brigham Young, led the Mormons from Nauvoo to Council Bluffs, Iowa, across the Missouri River to Winter Quarters, and finally in 1847 to the Great Basin. Great Salt Lake City became "the halfway house" of the California gold rush and the most important way station on the road west. The discovery of gold at Sutter's Mill in 1848 insured that a host of world travelers would visit Great Salt Lake City on their way to El Dorado.[1] The Mormon hierarchy's determination to continue the practice of polygamy and eventually to do so publicly provided irresistible enticements to European sojourners to visit the "modern Mohammedans," and "cast the die" for a confrontation with the federal government that would rage for the rest of the nineteenth century. Polygamy guaranteed it would be impossible for this new American religion to integrate into the American mainstream, and that it would become the object of ridicule and attack until it was forced to abandon the practice after almost forty years of strife.

Early western travelers encountered Mormons as they journeyed west from Nauvoo. In New Mexico, George F. Ruxton, a British army officer,

---

[1] For a small sample of the hundreds of overland narratives that describe visits to Salt Lake in 1849 and 1850, see Barnes, ed., "The Gold Rush Journal of Thomas Evershed"; Langworthy, *Scenery of the Plains, Mountains and Mines*, 82–114; Stansbury, *Exploration and Survey of the Valley of the Great Salt Lake*, 77–216; and Gunnison, *The Mormons, or, Latter-Day Saints*.

met members of the Mormon Battalion, including a veteran of Wellington's peninsular campaign. Edwin Bryant found Mormons in California who had arrived with Sam Brannan on the ship *Brooklyn*. Although he had heard rumors about the battalion in Missouri that had created fear among the 1846 emigrant parties, he did not see any horns or zealous fanatics but instead noted two young women "neatly dressed, and one of them may be called good-looking." Bryant returned to the East with Gen. Stephen W. Kearny, whose "Life Guards" consisted of Mormon Battalion veterans. Francis Parkman encountered Mormons near Pueblo, Colorado: "As we came up the Mormons left their work, seated themselves on the timber around us, and began earnestly to discuss points of theology, complain of the ill-usage they had received from the 'Gentiles,' and sound a lamentation over the loss of their great temple at Nauvoo."[2]

The Mormons had been settled in Salt Lake Valley for five years when Apostle Orson Pratt publicly announced that the church's hierarchy permitted and even instructed its members to practice polygamy.[3] Four years later the newborn Republican Party condemned bigamy as one the "twin relics of barbarism," and soon two of Utah Territory's federal judges suggested that polygamists could be prosecuted under the "Common Law."[4] President Buchanan sent federal troops to Utah to quell what some had described as a theocratic rebellion, and during the same year Mormons executed the Mountain Meadows massacre. While trouble brewed in Utah, the Saints were being observed by numerous travelers who passed through the territory on their way to California, federal officials and their wives, U.S. Army surveying parties and the artists who accompanied them, and even a few backsliding Mormons who retreated from Salt Lake.[5]

Utah Territory also attracted attention in Great Britain. William Kelly and William Chandless were among the first British adventurers to record

---

[2] Ruxton, *Adventures in Mexico and the Rocky Mountains*, 205; Bryant, *What I Saw in California*, 15, 26, 304; and Parkman, *The California and Oregon Trail*, 332. For these Mormon Battalion encounters, see Bigler and Bagley, eds., *Army of Israel*, 234, 277–79, 301, 305–7, 310–15.

[3] The revelation on "the new and everlasting covenant" of eternal marriage and the plurality of wives had been given to Joseph Smith on 12 July 1843 in Nauvoo. See *D&C*, 132.

[4] Homer, "The Judiciary and the Common Law in Utah Territory," 105–6.

[5] Ferris, *Utah and the Mormons*; Ferris, *The Mormons at Home*; Ingalls, "Report," Senate Exec. Doc. 1 (34:1), Serial 811, 2:152–68; Belisle, *The Prophets; or, Mormonism Unveiled*; Hyde Jr., *Mormonism: Its Leaders and Designs*; Green, *Fifteen Years among the Mormons*; and Franklin, *A Cheap Trip to the Great Salt Lake City*.

their encounters in Utah.[6] In addition, sectarian critics continued to write about Mormonism and its missionary activities.[7] But the biggest publicity came from Charles Mackay's book, *The Mormons*. Mackay wrote several articles for Liverpool's *Morning Chronicle* in August 1850 about Mormon emigrants who were bound for America. His articles were collected in a single volume, without attribution, that was published in 1851. This book was quite popular and was republished, with attribution, in many English editions and appeared in France, Germany, and Sweden, where it helped fuel continental European interest in Utah and the Mormons.[8]

Milanese patriot and political exile Antonio Caccia passed through Utah on his way to the gold fields in 1849, and noted in a novel published in Monaco in 1850 that Mormons had a "theocratic government with a community of goods and a plurality of women."[9] Italian diplomat Leonetto Cipriani stopped in Salt Lake in 1853 while driving cattle to California and recorded his experiences in his memoirs. That same year German geologist Jacob Heinrich Wilhelm Schiel visited Great Salt Lake City as a member of the Gunnison Expedition. Two years later French botanist Jules Rémy, in company with his British naturalist friend Julius Brenchley, stayed in Salt Lake for a month on a side trip from California. The accounts of Caccia, Cipriani, Schiel, and Rémy were eventually published in their own countries, but only Rémy's book had any impact on future travelers, since Cipriani's memoirs were not published until 1934, and Schiel's book was not widely read outside his native Germany. In contrast, Rémy's two-volume account of his experiences in Utah appeared in French and English and influenced many of the travelers in this anthology, becoming one of the primary sources travelers used to plan their visit to Utah and the Mormons.

---

[6] Kelly, *An Excursion to California*, 1:221–51; Chandless, *A Visit to Salt Lake*, 112–287; Snow, "British Travelers View the Saints," 63–81; and Mitchell, "Gentile Impressions of Salt Lake City, Utah, 1849–1870," 334–52.

[7] William John Conybeare criticized Mormon doctrines and proselytizing in the *Edinburgh Review* in 1854, subsequently included in *Essays, Ecclesiastical and Social*, which was translated into Danish, French, and Italian. The Religious Tract Society published at least four tracts on the Mormons: *Mormonism* (1851); *The Doctrines of Mormonism* (1853); *Is Mormonism True or Not?* (1853); and *Reasons I Cannot Become a Mormonite* (1851). The Society also published a book containing seventeen pages on "Mormonites." See *Remarkable Delusions, or Illustrations of Popular Errors* [1851], 171–88.

[8] Mackay, *The Mormons: or Latter-Day Saints*. Wilfried Decoo notes that Amédée Pichot published an abridged French translation of Mackay's book in 1856. See Decoo, "The Image of Mormonism in French Literature," 1:162. Theodor Olshausen published a German translation under his name. See Walker, Whittaker, and Allen, *Mormon History*, 25 n.37.

[9] Caccia, *Europa ed America: Scene della vita dal 1848–1850*, 414–19.

LEONETTO CIPRIANI (1812–88).
Cipriani, Avventure della mia vita.

LEONETTO CIPRIANI:
WE DON'T THINK POLYGAMY CAN LAST FOR LONG

Leonetto Cipriani (1812–88) was born in Centuri, Corsica, but his family roots were in Tuscany.[10] Cipriani's ancestors, like Napoléon Bonaparte's, emigrated to Corsica where the families maintained close relations. After Waterloo, Cipriani and his family went into voluntary exile at Livorno (Leghorn) where he established a successful mercantile business. Cipriani, who was the oldest of eleven children, became actively involved in his father's business and traveled to Algeria, Trinidad, London, Paris, Washington, and New York. When his father died in 1837, he became the guardian of his siblings and the owner of the family business. Like his father, he established connections with lawyers and politicians in Tuscany and maintained close ties with the Bonaparte family.

Cipriani became a colonel in the army of the grand duke of Tuscany in 1848 and served in Lombardy when the duke committed six thousand troops to fight on the side of his brother-in-law, the king of Sardinia, against the Austrians (the grand duke's countrymen) during the First War

---

[10] The Cipriani papers are located in Bastia, Corsica. See Vasoli, *Un Uomo del Risorgimento nella California del "Gold Rush"*; and Vasoli, *L'archivio privato di Leonetto Cipriani*. Some primary documents are also located in the archives of the Provincia di Torino.

of Italian Independence. Cipriani was captured during the conflict and incarcerated in Mantova.[11] After King Carlo Alberto and Lord Palmerton obtained his release, Cipriani returned to Tuscany. Grand Duke Leopold II appointed him as governor of Livorno [Leghorn], but Cipriani escaped when some of the grand duke's soldiers defected to reactionary forces.[12] Also forced into exile, Leopold asked Cipriani to seek the assistance of the king of Sardinia and from Louis Napoléon, who was elected president of the second French republic in December 1848, and through their efforts he was restored as the grand duke of Tuscany. Cipriani fought on behalf of King Carlo Alberto at the decisive Battle of Novara in 1849, a defeat that resulted in the king's abdication.

Cipriani decided to leave Italy in the aftermath of the First War of Italian Independence (Giuseppe Garibaldi left for New York in June 1850), and the new king of Sardinia, Vittorio Emmanuele II, appointed Cipriani as consul in San Francisco. Cipriani left in October 1851 and, like many government officials, he was anxious to both serve his government and make his fortune. During his tenure as consul, Cipriani failed in several real estate ventures, and within a year he resigned his post to join a cattle drive from St. Louis to California, which included an outfit of eleven wagons, an omnibus, a thousand head of cattle, and ten tons of cargo. His account of this venture is the only central overland narrative written by an Italian. Cipriani left the company "with a guide and eight horses, four saddle horses and four pack horses loaded with provisions," and after traveling on "horrible roads," he arrived in Great Salt Lake City on 14 August 1853. "I am writing from Salt Lake. I am on the plains west of the mountains in the Salt Lake valley, where the Mormon sect has established itself," Cipriani wrote to his son Beppe. "I will tell you later who these Mormons are and why they have settled in this isolated place." Cipriani met Brigham Young and John Taylor and recorded his observations for seven days before he continued overland to San Francisco.[13]

Cipriani returned to Europe in 1855 but briefly visited the U.S. three years

---

[11] Mantova was one of four cities located in a strategic zone in Austrian Lombardia-Veneto known as the Quadrilateral. Each city had fortresses (Mantova, Peschiera, Verona, and Legnano) that played decisive roles in Italy's early wars of liberation and were not captured until the Third War of Italian Independence (1866). Metternich's envoy, Alexander Joseph von Hübner, who later visited Utah, was imprisoned by the "provisional government" in Milano in 1848.

[12] Carlo I of the Medici dynasty was the first grand duke of Tuscany. When the Medici line ended in 1737, the Austrian dukes of Lorraine inherited the grand duchy. They remained in power—except for the Napoleonic interlude—until 1860 when Tuscany became part of the Kingdom of Italy.

[13] Cipriani to Beppe Cipriani, 14 August 1853, Cipriani Manuscript collection, Bastia, Corsica.

later to marry an American girl. He became a consultant to Napoléon III and accompanied the French emperor during the Second War of Italian Independence. Following victories at Solferino and San Martino and the partitions of Lombardy, Romagna, and the duchies in Tuscany, King Victor Emmanuel II nominated him as the governor of Romagna. Cipriani accepted but resigned after a short tenure because of concerns that his relationship with Napoléon III made it impossible for him to balance competing political interests. After resigning Cipriani learned that his wife had died in childbirth and he retired from public life. Cipriani spent 1860 to 1864 in the United States. When he returned to Europe he was nominated to the Italian Senate and given an Italian knighthood, which included the title of count. In June 1865 he returned to Centuri, Corsica, where he completed his memoirs, which were not published until 1934 when the Italian consul pressed for their publication.

CIPRIANI, *AVVENTURE DELLA MIA VITA* [MY LIFE ADVENTURES].
TRANSLATED BY ERNEST FALBO,
CALIFORNIA AND OVERLAND DIARIES OF COUNT LEONETTO CIPRIANI, 101–17.

Friday, 12 August 1853.

At noon we were on the summit of the mountains that overlook the lake, and being only twelve miles away, we rested for two hours. At three in the afternoon, we sighted directly ahead the City of the Mormons, and at four we were in the plains where a wide, shaded thoroughfare led in a straight line to Salt Lake City.

Shortly afterwards, we met up with a man on horseback, fashionably dressed and accompanied by two young and fair Amazons who were probably his wives. I asked him how far the city was and where we might find the best inn. He said that we were still three miles away from the city and that if we proceeded straight on, we would come to the square of the Temple where we would find the only inn. Arriving at the square, I asked a passerby the location of the inn. Noting from his strange accent that he was not American, I asked of what country he might be. The old fellow said he was Neopolitan, a music teacher, and that his name was Gennaro Capone.[14]

---

[14] Falbo suggested that Gennaro Capone was actually Domenico Ballo, the musical director of the Social Hall Orchestra. See Falbo, ed., *California and Overland Diaries*, 116–17. Nadia Vasoli argued that Capone, an eccentric Neapolitan street singer, could not be Ballo, whom M. E. Henderson described as a refined Italian who was a graduate of the Milan Conservatory, an able clarinetist, and a teacher at West Point Military Academy before arriving in Utah. See Vasoli, *Un Uomo del Risorgimento*, 199–200. But Falbo is probably correct, since Jules Rémy described Ballo as a Sicilian whose orchestra played very good music, and Ballo's obituary states that he was born in Sicily. See Rémy, *A Journey to Great-Salt-Lake City*, 1:213–14; and *Deseret News*, 12 June 1861. Naples was the capital of the Kingdom of the Two Sicilies, and Cipriani probably employed some hyperbole in his description of Ballo, knowing that his readers in Tuscany and Piedmont would enjoy such stereotypes.

"I am delighted," I said. "Let me shake your hand."

"Are you Italian?" he asked.

"Yes, thank God."

"And of what region?"

"I'm a Florentine," I answered. "Come to see me tomorrow at the inn. I shall give you news of your King 'Bomba' and you can tell me if you are now a Mormon because of him."[15]

"May he find a bitter end! For thirty years I have had to wander the earth because of him! But let me accompany you to the inn. The owner has two fine daughters who sing and play. My two best pupils."

And loosening his tongue, he gave full vent to his Neopolitan garrulousness. He assailed me with questions, hardly giving me time to answer. When he heard of the caravan awaiting me at Pyramid Valley, he exclaimed, "How's that? You are traveling with thirty people? You must be a prince then, eh?" And he lavished me with his "pardon me's" and "excuse me's," doffing his hat and addressing me as "Excellency."

We came to the inn. On the porch was an entire Mormon family, father, two mothers, and eight children. Seeing Don Gennaro, the two mothers and the children ran up to him and welcomed him excitedly and with open arms. I was struck by the curious resemblance of all the children to the Neopolitan music-master. The Mormon father and his eldest son remained out on the porch. They were both smaller than Tom Thumb, pot-bellied and short-necked, their heads disappearing in their shoulders so that they looked like a couple of seals.

After such an effusive welcome from his pupils, Don Gennaro announced me to the whole company as a rich Italian prince, and everyone, the two seals included, received me in a manner of great respect and consideration. They immediately busied themselves in preparing for me the best room, the finest linen and whatever accessories of the toilette that were available, including toothbrushes already used, and made ready the bath in the little room next to my room.

Don Gennaro, who had set everything in motion, acted as proprietor and host and showed me to my room. I expressed the need for a shave and a hair cut before taking my bath. "Let me do it for you. I've been a hairdresser, too," he said. And no sooner had he said it than he took off his coat, washed his hands, shaved my beard, cut my hair, washed it with the rum and a juniper water that Americans use, and would not rest until after my bath, when he had trimmed my toenails as well. Later, I dressed with the help of Gosto, who handed me whatever was cleanest and driest from my modest wardrobe. Then, while waiting for the princely dinner announced by the "Maestro," I lay down on a sofa and fell asleep.

---

[15] King Ferdinand II of the Kingdom of Two Sicilies was nicknamed "King Bomba" because he literally bombed the chief cities of Sicily following their revolt in 1849.

I was aroused by Don Gennaro's sonorous "Your Excellency is served!" I found the dining-room brightly illuminated, and a sumptuous table laid out in the Russian style, and the whole family regally attired and waiting for me. It was such an unexpected surprise for me that for a moment I believed that I was not among the Mormons at all but in a splendid European palace. The dinner was excellent, thanks to Don Gennaro who later confessed to having been a cook once in New Orleans. It was served by the two eldest daughters—beautiful girls—with such grace and ease that I could overlook the lack of servants.

After dinner we passed into the large parlor such as is found in all American homes and hotels, known as the *salotto buono* in Tuscany. There was an Erard piano with its jaws wide open, ready to devour my valuable time and rest. But unhesitatingly, I rose, and said goodnight to everyone and went to bed, foregoing the piano recital which Don Gennaro had undoubtedly arranged in my honor. I left the discomfited Don Gennaro with his mouth open wider than usual.

Saturday, 13 August 1853.

In the morning, solicitude and concern for my well-being and comfort increased to the point of annoyance. While I would have preferred a light breakfast in my room, Gosto informed me that a huge table had been laid out with every imaginable sort of food, and that Don Gennaro had even prepared macaroni. Men of temperance and moderation are subjected to temptations they cannot resist, and so am I. I ate such a huge portion of macaroni that I thought I would explode, and I vastly honored the rest of the meal as well.

Afterwards, I asked to be taken to the first apostle, Taylor, to whom were attributed the many English and Swedish converts and who was the right-hand man of the Prophet Brigham Young.[16] Taylor received me courteously, but I noted that Don Gennaro was not in his good graces, for he at once excused him, saying, "You may go. I'll look after the gentleman."

When we were alone, Taylor asked me, "Who are you? Why have you come to Salt Lake? What do you wish of me?"

"I am Colonel Cipriani, an Italian. I was crossing the plains on my way to California with my covered-wagon train when I left it at South Pass in order to visit your city. I should like to make the acquaintance of your Prophet and to be informed of your interesting settlement at Salt Lake. And if you can believe me, I should like to know about your religion."

"We ask for nothing more than that a European may know us personally,

---

[16] Cipriani overstates the rank of Apostle John Taylor, who was not a member of the First Presidency and was outranked at this time by Orson Pratt and Orson Hyde in the Quorum of Twelve. In addition Taylor was not the "right-hand man" of Brigham Young. That honor belonged to Heber C. Kimball.

but past experience forces us to be hesitant. Many, like you, have come to visit us. We opened our homes, and I could almost say our hearts, to them, and in our presence they seemed pleased with us and with our institutions. Once away, however, they printed every sort of infamy and slander against us."

I quickly reassured him on my account, even showing him letters, which fortunately I had with me, from the Bonaparte family and from other prominent people. Taylor was completely satisfied and arranged an appointment for me with the Prophet for the following morning. In the meantime, he conducted me around the city and indicated its principal monuments. The first was their temporary temple, which was a stone building sixty meters long and thirty meters wide, proportionately high, forming an arch, with large windows on all sides. Inside there was no altar of any kind, but only a pulpit propped up against one of the side walls, and some handsome pews.[17]

The new temple under construction, still only a few meters from the ground, was to be larger than St. Peter's and of granite blocks. We visited then the public library with its large reading room, which was illuminated by light entering from above, and other rooms all around, one of which was used for meetings of the apostles and bishops, and another room holding the public archive. Other places of interest were the School of Drawing (Accademia di disegno); a school of fine arts and crafts boasting a small museum of mechanical models; classrooms for children, located in every quarter of the city; and the small but elegant theatre.[18] It was astonishing to think that all this had been accomplished in just a few years and with merely the tithes contributed voluntarily.

After dinner, feeling obligated to Don Gennaro and the two fair hostesses, I spent the evening in their company. One of the girls played the harp and piano fairly well; the other sang Italian in a manner that would have driven a deaf person to flight. And Don Gennaro, strutting about like a peacock, could not contain his satisfaction. He fell back to crude gesturing and shouting, habits which he had lost in twenty years of living with impassive beings like the Mormons who, like the clergy of all faiths, by assuming an attitude of long-faced renunciation, finally succeed in making it look convincing.

Sunday, 14 August 1853.

After breakfast, Taylor met me at the inn and took me to the Prophet, who welcomed me with courtesy. He was a fine type of ancient patriarch, with his white hair falling to his shoulders in ringlets. He gave me all the

---

[17] Cipriani visited the first tabernacle built on Temple Square, which was a meeting house and not a temple. Constructed in 1851–52, it was an adobe building with a sharply pitched roof covering the partially subterranean interior of the building.

[18] Cipriani apparently visited the Old Council Hall and Social Hall.

information I wanted and promised to send me a letter (which he later did), written in his own hand, concerning the Mormon settlement at Salt Lake, with some indications on their beliefs. All the information which follows was taken from his letter.

As the regular visiting hour was drawing near and the antechamber was already filled with people, I took leave of the Prophet. I went with Taylor to the southern part of Utah county to visit the small cities of Neki and Palmira which were in a plain all marked off like a chessboard, rich in lush vegetation and in all breeds of stock. The cities, however, were only villages, modeled after the capital and similarly centered around church and school.[19]

Monday, 15 August 1853.

I went on an excursion to Utah Lake and its outlet, the River Jordan, which empties into Salt Lake, and crossed the lake by boat as far as the fishermen's wharf at the far end of the thoroughfare facing the Temple.

I had dinner in the evening at the home of the apostle Taylor. He was one of the richest Mormons and had a brick house built in the Near Eastern style, that is, a ground floor built around a courtyard with a water fountain spouting forty feet, and an array of every variety of plant and flower. All around the house there was a covered promenade that gave access to all the rooms, and behind that, another courtyard onto which opened the kitchens, stables, and barns.

I was greeted by a beautiful young Swedish lady of twenty and by a grave, matronly woman whom Taylor introduced respectively as his young bride and his old wife. The latter had borne him two children, one of whom was then in Europe, while the other was serving as a militia captain in the campaign against the Indians. He had not had children from his young wife, but he said he hoped to soon have them.

After dinner I had an interesting conversation with Taylor, and although my questions on such a subject had to be discreet, I did ask him if the Mormons, generally speaking, were satisfied with polygamy.

"For the time being, yes," he answered. "But with families so rapidly increasing, we don't think polygamy can last for long."

"And what is the reason for that?" I asked.

"Because as long as religious authorities can watch over the development of families and direct them morally, the plurality of wives is possible. But when families are left to themselves, without control, arising discord will make it necessary that we ourselves demand the abolition of polygamy. This is the opinion of the Prophet and of the apostles."

"May I ask you a question?"

---

[19] Cipriani is referring to Nephi and Palmyra in Juab and Utah counties. The same day he wrote a letter from Salt Lake to his son Beppe, which is preserved at the Cipriani Archives in Bastia, Corsica.

"Certainly."

"Do children born of different wives live in harmony with one another? And do the wives?"

"Presently, yes," he said, "But the secret of harmony among them is wholly artificial. It is based on continual work."

"What do you mean by that?"

"Every wife," he explained, "has a special duty. The oldest wife manages the household. One works in the kitchen, another in the garden, and so on. Just as they were in the time of Abraham, with the difference being that Abraham, in addition to his wives, had many slaves who were also wives in the physical sense, while we have only wives, some of whom are spiritual wives."

"What are spiritual wives?"

"They're the wives who can no longer bear children and who look after household duties."

"According to your principles, can you marry as many wives as you like?"

"No, not without the Prophet's consent, which is not given except to one who has already given proof of great morality and who has the means, especially, to assure a comfortable living for a large family. Generally, the Mormons have only one wife. Only a few, among them the Prophet, have four, and a hundred or so have two or three wives. Almost all of those with several wives live in the city. For several years now, the Prophet has not granted permission to anyone to have more than one wife. I was the last person to be granted this permission, since I had only two children and my fortune was more than enough to support another wife."

"What is your opinion about the increase in population?" I asked. "Is it greater with polygamy or monogamy?"

"When it is a question of a society wholly dedicated to work, it is undoubtedly greater with monogamy. We have studied the matter carefully and have arrived at the conclusion that where several wives are concerned, even when they are all young, only one is the favorite sexually and it is she who makes possible the large families. Of the other wives, some have a first child, who is also their last. Most women known when they marry that they can never be anything but spiritual wives. I think that virginity and chastity are natural in a woman, unlike in men, when her body is, I repeat, chastised by continuous toil."

"But human passions, jealousy—have they no hold on your wives?"

"They have, but these passions are suppressed by constant work, by their husbands' conduct, and by the religious influence of the Prophet and bishops."

"Have you had cases of wives rebelling against the household? How do you punish or correct them?"

"We've had very few such cases, and rarely at that. We correct them, by admonition and with gentleness, and when that does not suffice, we impose silence, a punishment which we have found to be the most effective with a woman."

"What do you mean by 'imposing' silence?"

"I mean never speaking to her, either at home or outside, and never answering her questions. Few women can withstand such treatment. Some have been driven mad by this, others have committed suicide, but with the majority of them, their morale breaks down and they become like lambs. I repeat, however, these cases of rebellion are rare, and in most families an exemplary harmony reigns."

"Are you satisfied with public morality? Do you have frequent cases of adultery?"

"Only one case in twenty years, and that occurred six years ago."

"How did you punish it?"

"They punished themselves by running off to Mexico."

"But you said that there is a court here under Federal jurisdiction. What are its functions?"

"The same as those in the Union. But since it has been here, it has never had to judge a single civil or criminal case. All civil and criminal cases among the Mormons are discussed in a friendly manner and judged by a third party or by the bishop, and, in the more important cases, by the Prophet. We have never had a single criminal case to try."

"So you have neither lawyers nor prosecutors in your city?"

"Not even one. They would starve to death."

"You are a happy people indeed! May God keep you free of them as of a plague or a hailstorm! You have stated that all the great works that I have been admiring were built by the community. With what means were they built?"

"With voluntary services and tithes."

"Does everyone pay exactly a tenth of all his income?"

"Yes, conscientiously. And some even pay more, and personal services are offered with commendable zeal."

"Do you pay Federal taxes?"

"No, because U.S. territories are exempt from all taxation."

"But don't you have postal service each month with the states on the Atlantic?"

"Yes, but it is a special service of ours, paid for by the community."

"The Prophet, the apostles and the bishops, who are, I believe, both your spiritual and temporal authorities—are they remunerated?"

"Not even a cent. Public revenue is used only for works in the public interest."

"What about the maintenance of roads and irrigation ditches?"

"Streets and roads are kept up by those whose property fronts on them. Only the irrigation systems are financed by the entire community."

"I admire what you say. But tell me, how is it that you have such a poor reputation in the United States and Europe?"

"The reason is a very simple one. Our countrymen on the Atlantic envy our prosperity and the rich and independent way of life that we have made for ourselves. Envy has given rise to all sorts of slander which has been taken up by the publicists and journalists and believed by the general public. Several times we would have fought them with their own weapons, that is, through the press, but we have always given up the idea because it would have meant spending too much to obtain so little. The newspapers that we might have founded or subsidized would have been only an infinitely small minority against so many others in America. We have thought it more in our interest to keep silent in order to be forgotten. But, briefly, it was only a short time ago that Congress declared the Salt Lake valley a territory of the United States. As such, as a territory, we have assigned to us a Federal judge, a new one every year since they never want to stay here. Judges without lawyers and without trials are like fish out of water, and since we distrust them and therefore do not admit them into our homes, they leave in desperation. And what is worse (and I don't think I have told you this), if you were to offer a thousand dollars for it, you would not find a bottle of brandy in the whole city. You would find wine, perhaps, but in only two or three homes."

"Oh, is the use of alcohol and wine prohibited, then?"

"Entirely, and this is one of the causes contributing to the betterment of our society. A few bottles of wine are allowed, for medicinal uses."

"But I saw some fine vineyards. What are they for?"

"We eat the grapes."

"Are beer and cider allowed?"

"Yes, but very little of it is consumed."

"Consequently, you use only tea and coffee. How do you obtain these products, which for you are primary necessities?"

"We have made some attempts in the south, where the climate is almost tropical, and we have already succeeded in producing some coffee and sugar. Nor are we discouraged about growing tea, which is essential for us. As for coffee and sugar, the Mexicans bring it to us in exchange for dried legumes and other products, which makes for a thriving export trade."

The two wives were listening to this conversation without taking part in it, for the good reasons that the old lady did not understand a word of French and the young woman spoke it only a little. Though I had not, throughout the conversation, fixed my eyes on her, I noticed that when Taylor was telling me about the Mormon women and their punishments, I saw the young wife smile faintly. It would have been interesting to have heard her opinion on the question, but approaching her would have been overstepping the limits of curiosity.

After tea, I left. Gosto was at the door of the inn and told me that some beautiful young girls were waiting for me, singing and laughing boisterously and making music, with Don Gennaro as orchestra conductor. But I went straight to my room to write these notes, and the girls down stairs continued to make noise until they learned that there was no longer any hope of meeting me, the "prince."

Tuesday, 16 August 1853.

I made ready for my departure. I bought two good mules and the provisions for the trip. In the evening, Mr. Taylor took me to the theatre.

The Mormons have made of their theatre what it should be everywhere, a school of morality in action. The actors are amateurs, all of them unmarried, belonging to the best families. The plays to be performed are selected from the repertoires of all nations and are translated and revised by a competent committee. The theatre is operated at the expense of the community, the proceeds consisting of ten-cent admission fees. Inside, the theatre is formed like an amphitheatre, and has a seating capacity of fifteen hundred, the women sitting on the right, the men on the left.

The orchestra was large, but left much to be desired in the way of harmony; this was the fault of its director, Don Gennaro, who did not, Taylor said, devote enough time to it. Strangely enough, Don Gennaro was dressed for the role of a missionary and was not recognizable in the play. Such is the power of discipline and the mysterious spiritual force which dominated the lives of the Mormons.

They were performing an episode from the life of Solomon. The actors were excellent, particularly the young woman who played the Mother, and a well-dressed audience filled the theatre. In brief, I spent a stimulating and delightful evening.

Wednesday, 17 August 1853.

I finished preparations, which were not insignificant considering the fifty miles of desert country I would have to cross. During the day, I left my calling card with the Prophet and several of the apostles, and gave a ring with my coat of arms to Don Gennaro. I gave other rings, which I had bought in town, to the fair young ladies of the inn. To the "seal" innkeeper I paid my bill, which was very reasonable, amounting to eighty dollars for the eight days, for the three of us and our eight mules.

Thursday, 18 August 1853.

Though I had asked them not to get up earlier than they did ordinarily, the Mormon family was all up at dawn the next morning to say goodbye to me. I kissed the two wives on their cheeks, the two daughters on their foreheads, shook hands with the two seals, and left.

Jacob Heinrich Wilhelm Schiel: I Saw Not a Single Beautiful Woman

Jacob H. Schiel (1813–98?) was the surgeon and geologist in the John W. Gunnison (1812–53) expedition, which surveyed the proposed central route for the transcontinental railroad in 1853 and 1854.[20] He was born in Stromberg and was educated nearby at the University of Heidelberg, where he became a lecturer in chemistry and geology.[21] Before the end of the 1840s he traveled to America, where he remained for approximately ten years.

Schiel joined Gunnison's company in Westport, Missouri, and in June 1853 the expedition traveled west between the 38th and 39th parallels. Part of the company camped on the Sevier River on 25 October 1853 about sixteen miles from Sevier Lake, where Gunnison and twelve of his men planned to do a reconnaissance. Pahvant Indians attacked the poorly defended camp at dawn. In addition to Gunnison, three soldiers, the company's botanist and artist, as well as one civilian guide, were killed. Gunnison's assistant, Lt. Edward Griffin Beckwith (1818–81), investigated the incident and wrote an account of the massacre that was initially published in the *Deseret News*. After wintering in Great Salt Lake City, Beckwith completed the survey and he issued an expanded report of Gunnison's death and the survey in his Pacific Railroad Report.[22]

Schiel also submitted an official report and kept a personal journal. After he returned to Germany he wrote an account of the expedition, relying in part on Beckwith's account and his personal notes, which was published in Schaffhausen in 1859. The work is a readable narrative of the expedition and includes interesting details concerning the residents of Utah, whom he observed during the winter his company resided in Salt Lake City. It is unclear when Schiel died, but it appears that he could have lived until 1883 or possibly 1898.

---

[20] Gunnison was a member of the Corps of Topographical Engineers who served as an aid to Capt. Howard Stansbury (1806–63) during his survey of the Great Salt Lake in 1849 and 1850. The company spent the winter in Salt Lake City, and Gunnison's one-volume history of the Mormons was published in 1852 after he returned to Washington. The book was one of the first generally sympathetic portraits of the Latter-day Saints.

[21] Thomas Bonner notes that "Schiel possessed no medical degree" but apparently was "quite familiar with diseases and their remedies, as [his] book reveals." In the geological report written by Schiel for the expedition's official report, "his name is followed by M.D." Perhaps Schiel "deceived his superiors" about his training, but more likely, "Americans unfamiliar with the German university system" assumed his doctor's degree in philosophy was a medical degree. See Schiel, *Journey through the Rocky Mountains*, xi.

[22] Wagner and Camp, *The Plains and the Rockies*, entries 263 and 264.

Reise durch die Felsengebirge [Journey Through the Rocky Mountains], 77–82, 91–94. Translated and edited by Thomas N. Bonner.[23]

Salt Lake City lies sixteen miles away from the Salt Lake at the western base of the Wasatch Mountains at 40° 45′ 30″ north latitude and at an elevation calculated at 4,350 feet above sea level from our six-month barometer readings (from November to May). The city is very amply laid out and visible from a great distance when approached from the south. Yet it does not make a very friendly impression, for though the streets are straight and wide, and almost every house has a little piece of enclosed land, everything bears the mark of poverty and makeshift. The streets, to be sure, have sidewalks, that is, by-ways separated by ditches from the street, but they are as impassable in bad weather as the streets themselves. In all parts of the city away from the central district, but especially in the southern part, pedestrians, riders, and drivers all have the same trouble in wading through the soft mud in the bad season.

The ditches mentioned above serve to conduct the fine water of a stream known as City Creek from the nearby mountains through the entire city, an arrangement which offers the inhabitants many conveniences. The houses are constructed chiefly of so-called adobe (air-dried brick), one-story high, and covered with shingles. Log cabins are relatively scarce since wood must be brought a distance of thirty to forty miles from the Wasatch Mountains and consequently must be used sparingly. In the central part of the city there are some two-story houses as well as the new house of Brigham Young, the tithing office, and the statehouse, the latter the only house in Utah built entirely of stone. The tabernacle is also located here, a strange building constructed of adobe like all others in the city with a roof reaching almost to the ground.[24] Since this house is to be used for church services only until the large temple is completed, the saints found it practical to adapt the underground space, normally used as a cellar or basement, for use as a kind of auditorium. The benches are arranged in amphitheatre fashion so that the speaker standing below can be seen and heard from all sides. As the ceiling of this hall is also the roof of the house and has the shape of a tunnel-vault, the height proved to be sufficient, and the two side-walls of the house needed to be no more than four or five feet above the ground.

The church service of the Mormons usually begins with a prayer of the high priest, followed by a song from the congregation which is accompanied by a good six-octave melodion in the absence of an organ. An Englishwoman, whose husband died on the way to California, is the organist and

---

[23] The translation by Thomas N. Bonner was originally published in Schiel, *Journey Through the Rocky Mountains*, 70–72, 77–84, 91–94. I also consulted *The Land Between: Dr. James Schiel's Account of the Gunnison-Beckwith Expedition.*

[24] This is the original "Old" Tabernacle on Temple Square.

plays the instrument passably well. After the song comes a discourse by one of the directors chosen previously. The Mormons assert, of course, that the speaker learns only shortly beforehand that he is to speak, the speeches are made extempore, and anyone can be called upon to speak on a given subject. This is an excellent artifice to strengthen the people in the belief that revelations and divine inspiration occur continuously among the elect. After the service the tithing work is announced; every Mormon returns not only the tenth part of his labor but also the tenth part of his time. The congregation, however, is never given an accounting of the use of the tithe. When I remarked one day to the apostle Taylor, regarded as one of the most learned pillars of the church, that this was against the spirit of American institutions, he tried to explain to me that it was better in the end for the wiser and more learned to care for the affairs of a people than that the people themselves should bicker about everything. He pointed in all seriousness to China as his ideal of a form of government.

It was more irritating than amusing to observe how the poor, spiritually famished, generally very ordinary working people from Wales, Denmark, and Norway—these constitute the main population of the valley—are manipulated, fanaticized, and turned into pliant saints. It is not a new, but certainly an instructive, sight for the philosopher as for the statesman to see right under his eyes how a supposedly revealed religion arises and matures and how the crassest nonsense and most obvious deceit serve in the founding and establishment of a state for the purpose of exploiting the humble. Yet it cannot be said that the leading men of Utah are especially gifted or even talented. By far the greater part of them are indeed extremely ignorant and of limited understanding. Even religious fanaticism, which spreads like a contagion, is not found among them. They possess at most the fanaticism of selfishness, ambition, and leadership, which are common to shallow and deep minds alike, both inside and outside Utah. Even Brigham Young is no more than an unusual person. In a conversation of several hours which I had with him, I found neither knowledge nor unusual understanding on a variety of subjects. Yet he has great administrative talent, which is not exactly uncommon in America, a good measure of shrewdness, and he knows his flock well. A mythical teaching with high-sounding promises of worldly and eternal happiness has always captivated the ignorant, thoughtless man, and what must appear to the educated, thinking man as an unpardonable blasphemy is often welcomed by the great multitude and suited to its dim perceptions and way of thinking. There are many examples among the women of Utah of how the most foolish beliefs and religious fanaticism are able to repress or at least hold back the strong passions of mankind. In general the women in Utah are opposed to the doctrine of the plurality of wives, yet many are entirely resigned to it. I have even heard several of them express the wish that their husbands might take more wives, for "the more wives, the more salvation," as they expressed it. The wife can be saved only through her husband, according to the teaching of the Mormons, and it is therefore the duty of the man to save as many as possible. Psychologically, the most remarkable case of proselytization that I came across among the Mormons was that of an English family in which the wife and her two grown daughters went over to the Mormon religion, while the father remained unconverted but, because of a pliant disposition and the love of peace, came along to Utah. The women are sealed to the men by the prophet, an apostle, bishop, or patriarch—there is an unlimited number of these worthies in Utah—but although the relationship is legally called marriage and is considered such in practice, it is nothing else but concubinage so far as the ease of its dissolution and the position of the wife are concerned. If two men agree that they want to exchange one or another of their wives, they explain to the prophet or one of his representatives that they have had a revelation that they cannot save their wives but believe that the other one can. The other one has likewise had a revelation in which it was made known to him that he is the true savior. The sealing and unsealing has no further propriety than this.

Only the first wife has the position of a housewife in the Mormon household. Only she arranges everything and gives orders to the succeeding wives. While she bears the name of her husband, the other wives are called only by their first names and, at most, "second, third wife, etc. of Brother N." The lady elect always lives in the immediate vicinity of her husband, but the others live crowded together in special rooms or even in neighboring buildings, do the work of servants, and occasionally see their husband. Many of the apostles even have a number of wives in the neighboring communities and visit them only now and then.

The saints boast that their religion is a cheerful one and that a hypocritical gloominess such as found in Europe is impossible among them. The husband, they say, wants to see his children properly happy and prosperous, and this is not the worst side of their dogma. They love music and the dance; their dances, where both old and young dance, are usually introduced by prayer and song. Since spirituous drinks are not on hand, there are no excesses at their festivities, at most only too much dancing. Besides the dances, the theatre, naturally an amateur theatre, is one of the chief pleasures of the saints in the wintertime. I must say to their credit, although I admit the dubious nature of this praise, that their theatrical personnel played as well and sometimes better than what is seen on the stage of the larger cities of the West. The acting of a Mrs. W., even in tragic roles, must be called excellent in view of the conditions. They were not content with shorter plays but played such things as *The Lady of Lyons* by Bulwer, *Othello* by Shakespeare, *The Honeymoon*, and others. A favorite was *Jugomar the Barbarian*, the English version of *Sohn der Wildniss*. The stage was narrow and the equipment very scanty, but a great deal of effort was expended on costumes, which did not always correspond to the time and place of the dramatic action. Thus the pseudo prince in *The Lady of Lyons*, which takes place at the time of the French Revolution, appeared in the childish finery of a medieval dandy. After the play there was usually another song, which was or became a comical song, in which the public in the pit (and the entire spectator space was all in the pit) sang the chorus, especially when the favorite Mormon Song was sung. In order to give the reader some concept of this trans-wasatchian poetry I will add a verse of this song in the original:

A Mormon father likes to see,
His Mormon family agree,
The prattling baby on his knee
Cries: Daddy, I am a Mormon!
Eh! the merry, oh! the merry, Eh! the merry Mormons
I never knew what joy was before I came amongst the Mormons!

The last two verses are repeated by the chorus. I regret that I cannot add the melody of this song for it fits the content completely. The orchestra, which accompanies these songfests and is also active in the tabernacle, possesses a number of string and wind instruments. Although most of these are played incorrectly and often completely independent of one another, this does not stop the saints, completely unspoiled in a musical sense, from calling their music "the sweetest music on earth," an appellation whose harmless pride can well be pardoned. This "sweetest music" is like a large brewery which I was once told about in Salt Lake City. After finding the establishment in company of the topographer of our expedition,[25] following a long search, I found in the corner of a kind of shed a brewing copper, which could hold approximately one hogshead, and a cooler that approached three feet in length and was no wider. The brew which came out of this apparatus was a bitterly sour travesty of the brewer's art. The descriptions of the Mormons concerning their own country are pure hyperbole and can be accorded little belief.

Even the descriptions of climatic conditions in their land are extraordinarily favorable and pleasant. If one would believe them, the climate of Utah is the most beautiful in the world. Sickness never occurs, and the few cases encountered are healed by faith, i.e. through the laying on of hands by the apostles. All of this is naturally the purest humbug. During our stay in Salt Lake City, an epidemic of scarlet-fever and measles raged, from which quite a number of children died. Several of the Mormons were bent upon

---

[25] Expedition topographer Richard H. Kern was killed with Gunnison. J. A. Snyder, the assistant topographer, is probably the individual identified by Schiel.

buying the pharmaceutical materials which I could spare, and one of their apostles, whose wife had become ill, was so far from expecting healing by the laying on of hands that he did me the honor of asking me to visit the sickbed and give the orders. . . .

When one sees what the Mormons have made of their country since taking it over, he cannot withhold praise of their diligence and perseverance, but the great admiration which they have for themselves has not been earned. Compared with what has been accomplished in California in lesser time by the overland emigration, their accomplishment seems very small even when all of the differences are taken into account. The person who does not mistrust the descriptions of the Mormons as exaggerations and deliberate lies must come to the conclusion in reading them that the Jordan Valley is a paradise in which wonder crowds on wonder. In reading of wonderful national workshops where everyone can find employment until he can make himself independent, one has to think of some sheds with several workbenches, circular saws, vises, and lathes standing in them, all in rudimentary condition, with less than a dozen men working at them so far as I could see. The workshops appear to enjoy no great favor even among the saints themselves. It is similarly the case with their educational facilities. They exist only as an idea. The school system in Utah has not gone beyond the elementary level, which is of course understandable and quite common. Even their great cotton manufacture is a chimera. In an attic room of the statehouse the Mormons keep several expensive scientific instruments which they offered to me for my use during the time of our stay in Salt Lake City, since they still had no one among them who knew how to use them. There was an excellent Ross microscope of the newest design, and the astonishment of some of their learned scribes at the real marvels which the little instrument revealed to them, when I showed them several objects, was very great. They had no fewer than six barometers for measuring elevation made by the well-known English inventor, Troughton, but all had gotten air in their vacuums or had been otherwise damaged by careless handling. Not a single one was usable. A chemical apparatus in the form of a large reagent box was also there, likewise a telescope and some smaller measuring instruments. A part of the library, for whose creation Congress had earlier granted five thousand dollars, recently went up in flames. In addition to the great English encyclopedias, the science of jurisprudence had been rather well represented, and it is asserted that the fire was started with the foreknowledge of the Mormon authorities to whom jurisprudence was especially unwelcome.

The description I have given of the land of Utah is not clothed in the rosy colors of the saints, but it is, I believe, a true picture of conditions which have aroused general interest on this side of the ocean and even more on the other side. It gives me special pleasure to be able to give assurance that in the entire Territory I met no more than three Germans who had entered the community of the Latter-day Saints and the faith of one of them, at least, was not built upon rock. The principal of these three worthies was a penniless student, who from necessity had translated the Book of Mormon into German and then followed the missionary, for whom he had done this work, from Hamburg to Utah. He was the city engineer in Provo, the second city in size, and was waiting impatiently for the Holy Ghost to reveal to him the theorem of congruent and analogous triangles, since without this knowledge his vocation was turning very sour.[26] The second countryman was a barber, who hoped to trim the beards of all nations following their conversion, but in the meantime, complaining about the high price of shaving soap, he did some doctoring in the big city. The third was a very ordinary man. In making the acquaintance of the first of these three Germans, a coincidence was revealed which deserves to be told. One of the Mormon apostles (Apostle Taylor) asked me one day if he could introduce to me a young German who lived in Provo and was very anxious to see one of his countrymen.[27] As I was agreeable, he brought the young man to me several days later. It was the translator of the Book of Mormon....

If I have done any injustice to the Latter-day Saints in this foregoing description, I would regret it the more since I must close with a great incivility to the women of Utah. I make this transgression in the interest of consoling those of my countrymen who may look with silent envy and perhaps secret desire upon the prerogatives of the saints. In the entire valley I saw not a single beautiful woman, or even one approaching it, and only one girl who, while quite pretty, was not the type to "shake the saintship of an anchorite"; yet she can await salvation with certainty, for compassion still lives in Utah. May all the daughters of Utah forgive me that I have no better opinion of their charms.

JULES RÉMY:
MORE POWER THAN ANY POTENTATE IN THE WORLD

Although Robert Baird's *The Religions of America*, published in French in 1844, contained one of the earliest references to Mormonism that appeared in France, it was not until the first LDS missionaries arrived in Paris that the

---

[26] George Viett was converted in Paris where he taught German.

[27] John Taylor met George P. Dykes (1808–88), a Mormon missionary who was serving in Prussia, in London in 1851. Taylor agreed to help organize a mission in Prussia and they traveled together to Hamburg, where they solicited George Viett's help. Taylor directed Dykes and Viett to translate the *Book of Mormon* into German. Viett was undoubtedly the primary translator and the convert referred to by Schiel, but he initially received no credit for having done so.

French press began paying attention to the American religion. On 20 April 1850 B. H. Révoil published an article about the new "bizarre sect" in *L'Illustration, Journal Universel*, which relied heavily on articles from the British press.[28] He also referred to Charles Mackay's newly published book, including illustrations that had originally appeared in American publications, such as *Harper's Weekly*. During the next ten years prominent French writers such as Philarète Chasles, Alfred Maury, and Prosper Mérimée also commented on Mormonism.[29]

While visiting San Francisco in July 1855, French botanist Jules Rémy (1826–93) and British naturalist Julius Brenchley decided to travel to Great Salt Lake City. They arrived in September and remained for thirty-one days. After leaving Salt Lake Rémy wrote thirteen letters that appeared in the French-language newspaper *Echo du Pacifique* under the title "A Trip to Salt Lake." These letters were translated and published in the *California Chronicle* between December 1855 and March 1856, and in the *Louisville Courier* between March and May 1856.[30] Of course, no one paid much attention to Rémy's letters, and scholars have hardly noticed them since the publication of Rémy's handsome two-volume narrative in Paris in 1860 and an English translation the following year in London.[31] The French edition was credited to Rémy, while the English edition listed both Rémy and Brenchley as authors. Elisée Reclus, Hippolyte Taine, and a few lesser-known French authors reviewed Rémy's *Voyage au pays des Mormons*.[32] This book became one

---

[28] Baird, *De la religion aux Etats-Unis*, 329–37; and Révoil, "Souvenirs des Etats-Unis," 251–52. The article on Mormonism was one in a series on "bizarre religions" in the U.S. The same newspaper made subsequent references to Mormonism. See *L'Illustration, Journal Universel*, 16:393 (6–13 September 1850), 146. Révoil later translated Maria Ward's exposé as *Les harems du Nouveau Monde*.

[29] Chasles, *Etudes sur la littérature et les moeurs*; Maury, "Sectes religieuses au XIXème siècle," 965–68; and Mérimée, "Les Mormones" in *Mélanges historiques littéraires*. See Decoo, "The Image of Mormonism in French Literature," 1:157–75, 2:265–76. Other French commentators on Mormonism included Desmons, *Essai historique et critique du Mormonisme*; Erdan, *La France mystique*; Carlier, *Le mariage aux Etats-Unis*; Dababie, *Récits et types américains*; and Eyma, *Excentricités américaines*.

[30] Wagner and Camp, *The Plains and the Rockies*, third edition, 476, cited these articles through an 8 March 1856 notice in the *Western Standard*, the Mormon newspaper that George Q. Cannon published in San Francisco from 23 February 1856 to 6 November 1857. Cannon's comments in the *Western Standard* were republished in *Writings from the "Western Standard,"* 21–24, 44–51.

[31] Excerpts from the book have been published in Mulder and Mortensen, *Among the Mormons*, 278–81; and in Rémy and Brenchley, *An Excerpt from A Journey to Great-Salt-Lake City*.

[32] Reclus, "Le Mormonisme et les Etats-Unis," 881–914; and Taine, "Nouveaux essais," 271–79. For an English translation of Taine, see Fife, "Taine's Essay on the Mormons," 40–65. Lesser known authors include Comettant, *Les civilisations inconnues*; and Reybaud, *Etudes sur les réformateurs, ou socialistes modernes*. Louis Bertrand, a Mormon convert, also commented on Rémy.

of the most consulted studies of Mormonism by Europeans who visited Utah or wrote about the Mormons during the next fifty years.

The book included some items that were not in the letters. For example, Rémy republished John Hyde's account of the Mormon temple from *Mormonism: Its Leaders and Designs*.[33] The Mormon hierarchy chose not to comment on the accuracy of description of the Temple ceremony, although Bertrand mentioned it in his memoirs.[34] Rémy also commissioned Théodule Devéria, an Egyptologist at the Museum of the Louvre, to examine the facsimiles published of the "Book of Abraham." These facsimiles were republished in *The Pearl of Great Price* in 1851.[35] Devéria identified the "facsimile from the Book of Abraham" as "a funeral illustration for a corpse named Horus." Devéria's opinion concerning the authenticity of Joseph Smith's translation initiated a fight, which continues to this day.[36] The inclusion of these seemingly bizarre aspects of Mormonism was a transparent attempt by Rémy to appeal to his readership.[37]

---

[33] Hyde gave several reasons for disclosing the temple ceremony despite his oath not to reveal its secrets. Rémy and Brenchley, *A Journey to Great-Salt-Lake City*, 2:75, suggested Hyde would have done well to suppress his reasons.

[34] Bertrand, *Mémoires d'un Mormon*, 209–10, 216–171. Bertrand was a Freemason and interested in Rémy's treatment of both the Endowment and the Book of Abraham. Both Bertrand and nineteenth-century church leaders recognized and accepted the similarities between the Endowment and the rites of Freemasonry. See Homer, "'Similarity of Priesthood in Masonry'," 1–113.

[35] Giovanni Pietro Antonio Lebolo (1781–1830) recovered artifacts in Egypt between 1817 and 1823 while working for a former French consul to Egypt, Bernardino Drovetti. See Ridley, *Napoleon's Proconsul in Egypt: The Life and Times of Bernardino Drovetti*. Lebolo sold artifacts to the Vatican Museum, the Kunsthistoriches Museum in Vienna, and the king of Sardinia in Torino, and retained the rest. Following his death in 1830 eleven mummies were consigned to Trieste merchant Albano Oblasser for the benefit of Lebolo's surviving children. Oblasser shipped at least four of these mummies to New York in 1833, and they eventually came into the possession of Michael Chandler. Chandler sold these mummies to Joseph Smith in 1835. Dan C. Jorgensen completed the first study of the discovery of the mummies and their connection with Lebolo. See Jorgensen, New Facts.

[36] From 1835 to 1842 Joseph Smith translated the papyri found in the mummies he purchased from Chandler. Smith's work appeared as "The Book of Abraham" in the *Times and Seasons* and in the *Millennial Star*. "The Book of Abraham" was republished as part of *The Pearl of Great Price* in Liverpool, England, in 1851. T. B. H. Stenhouse republished Devéria's study of the Book of Abraham facsimiles in his potboiler *The Rocky Mountain Saints* in 1873, which prompted the LDS church to respond to Devéria. In 1879 George Reynolds published a pamphlet in which he argued that Devéria's translation could be incorrect. See Reynolds, *The Book of Abraham*. One year later the LDS church canonized *The Pearl of Great Price*, including "The Book of Abraham," as its fourth book of sacred scripture. Episcopal Bishop Franklin Spencer Spalding wrote a spirited response to Reynolds in 1912, citing eight experts who confirmed Devéria's conclusions. After the Metropolitan Museum of Art presented a portion of the original papyri to the LDS church in 1967, a new battle began about the authenticity of Joseph Smith's translation. See Nibley, *The Message of the Joseph Smith Papyri*; Larson, *By His Own Hand*; Gee, *A Guide to the Joseph Smith Papyri*; Thompson, "Egyptology and the Book of Abraham"; and Ritner, "The 'Breathing Permit of Hor' Thirty-four Years Later."

[37] These same topics continued to captivate the French. See De Charencey, *Le mythe de Votan* (1871); and Anquetil, ed., *La maîtresse légitime* (1923).

Like his book, Rémy's letters contain occasional mistakes about the details of LDS religious belief and practice (Mormons did not upon first seeing Salt Lake "prostrate themselves upon the earth, like the Mohammedans when they discover the edifices of Mecca"), but for his time and culture, the Frenchman presented a remarkably fair and insightful perspective on the millennial colony.

Rémy's book is best known for his observations about Utah and the Mormons, as well as his descriptions of both the journey from Sacramento through Carson Valley and of his return to California through Provo, Nephi, Fillmore, Beaver, Parowan, Cedar City, and Las Vegas, which are full of detail. Perhaps the most intriguing reference in the book is Rémy's report of an experience that occurred in Lehi, Utah, when "we were literally besieged by a crowd of boys, who seemed all the more inclined to sit up the whole night . . . [and] evinced a singular desire to be made acquainted with everything concerning us . . . [and] seemed determined to get at our secrets. All our movements were watched, it was impossible for us to utter a word without being overheard, or without our hearing comments on our own remarks; neither could we move a dozen paces without being followed." Following this experience, Rémy wrote: "I recommend all governments which find the maintenance of a police force too costly, to commit its functions to the impudence of young street scamps; they will be sure to find in them very zealous if not very clearheaded agents."[38] This incident may well be the genesis of the famous Baker Street Irregulars. *A Study in Scarlet*, Arthur Conan Doyle's first Sherlock Holmes story, includes a subplot involving Mormonism in Utah Territory and describes a group of the Irregulars as a "division of the detective police force" who, after reporting to Holmes, "scampered away downstairs like so many rats, and we heard their shrill voices next moment in the street."[39]

When Rémy passed through Las Vegas he wrote another memorable passage. After noting that the name of Las Vegas means "fertile fields" in Spanish, he observed that "it is easy to foresee that it will never become considerable, inasmuch as the soil capable of cultivation is extremely limited, and the surrounding desert extends to a considerable distance. But, such as it is, there can be no doubt of its real utility, and of its having all the

---

[38] Rémy and Brenchley, *A Journey to Great-Salt-Lake City*, 2:318–19.
[39] Doyle, *Angels of Darkness*, 173.

elements requisite for becoming a valuable halting-place, where the mail, and travelers in general, may renew their stock of provisions."[40] Although Rémy would witness the creation of the new Paris by Louis Napoléon and Georges-Eugène Haussmann, he understandably lacked the imagination to visualize the recreation of Las Vegas with Parisian landmarks.

JULES RÉMY, "A TRIP TO SALT LAKE," NO. II,
CALIFORNIA CHRONICLE, 5 JANUARY 1856
[Translated for the *Chronicle* from *L'Echo du Pacifique*].

Fifty-eight days after leaving Sacramento we entered Zion, and took lodgings at the United States Hotel, kept by the Honorable Mr. Kinney, U.S. Judge for the Territory of Utah.[41] This city resembles no other upon the face of the earth. It is rather a vast assemblage of villas than a city. All the streets are 120 feet wide, cross each other at right angles, watered on each side by a brook of fresh water brought from the neighboring mountains, and ornamented by rows of cottonwood trees. Except the palace of the Governor all the houses are of adobes, but all are substantial and elegant. Some of them are very large, but they are generally small. Every house stands back at least twenty feet from the street, and is surrounded by a small garden. Each block has a bishop, whose duty it is to know every thing passing within his jurisdiction, and to examine every week into the moral and material condition of each family, and to report to the Governor. The bishop has elders and deacons to assist him.

On the morning after our arrival we found ourselves without money, and determined to apply to Gov. Brigham Young for aid. He is a man about 50 years of age, of medium height, and of a corpulent figure. "Brother Brigham," as he is styled, has seventeen wives of different ages, at least one of whom is a great beauty, to my certain knowledge, for I accidentally saw her. As to the number of his children, that is unknown. Last spring nine were born to him in one week. All the Mormon world boasts of the attention which this model patriarch pays to his offspring.

As President of the church, Brigham possesses more power than any potentate in the world. He is the absolute ruler of action and thought in

---

[40] Rémy and Brenchley, *A Journey to Great-Salt-Lake City*, 2:412

[41] John Fitch Kinney (1816–1902) had a long and colorful career in Utah. His controversial first term on the territory's bench taught him "that the authority of the Priesthood is and shall be the law of the land." After he returned as chief justice in 1860, "Never again would he step out of line and question the authority of Brigham Young." See Bigler, *Forgotten Kingdom*, 134–35. Kinney's hotel, the Union House, stood on the northeast corner of 100 North and 200 West across from Union Square near today's West High School. See Homer, "The Federal Bench and Priesthood Authority: The Rise and Fall of John Fitch Kinney," 104 n.19.

Mormondom. Before this man we were presented. We found him in his civil office, dictating orders to his Secretaries while preparing a chew of Virginia tobacco. He was sitting in, or rather squatting on, an arm chair. On his head was a large yellow slouched hat. His dress was of a dull green, and very large in size and loose in fit. His socks were white, and his shirt was slightly wilted. When we were introduced he received us coldly, without even giving us a word. He held his head down almost to his knees, and did not dare to look at us. He imagined, as we afterwards learned, that we had come to assassinate him. We went out, and he learned his error.[42]

We afterwards had a second audience, for which occasion he had called together his grand Council. The two Vice Presidents, five or six apostles, two Generals, the historian of the Church, the director of the constitutions, and a young patriarch, son of Hyrum Smith, the martyr, were present. Brigham uncovered his head before us—an act of condescension which it is said he had never shown to any other person. We were afterwards told by persons familiar with him, that he never forgot his conduct when we first appeared before him, and he was always embarrassed in our presence.

No. III (17 January 1856)

In the course of the conversation I asked whether his missionaries were making many proselytes in France. He answered: "The French are not accessible. Too deeply imbued with the philosophy of Voltaire, they care little about religion, and occupy themselves only with science. But they understand nothing of science; when they shall learn something of it, they will see the truth is found in the book of Mormon, and that our doctrine, sooner or later, must reform society." These words, worthy of notice in more than one respect, were spoken without affectation, and with a manner of conviction so profound that they lead us to believe in the good faith of Brigham— though we had entertained a different opinion in regard to the leading ordinary Mormons. This impression in regard to the President was confirmed by subsequent observations that the present prophet was neither the instigator nor the accomplice of the fraud of the great imposter Joseph, but simply the honest dupe. This is equally unfortunate, but it is far less blameable

---

[42] Young provided a very different view of this conversation to George Q. Cannon on 3 January 1856. "The English Lord, as he represented himself, and his french valet, Dr. Rémy turned out as I expected," Young wrote. "They enquired if I could speak french, I told them I could not, they then commenced talking french in my presence to each other, I told them I had no room for private conference with them and walked out of my office as I felt insulted by their conduct, they followed me out and walked along with me till they could get to speak to me privately, and then asked to borrow money of me. They came here as any other loafers would, without money or recommends." He indicated Cannon might "have some knowledge of a certain Mr. Brenchley who lived several years in the Sandwich Islands where he kept native men and women to minister to his wants and pleasures. Well this is the same man, only he has picked up this french Rémy to attend him in his pregrinations [sic] and pander for him." For Young's complete letter, see Ekins, ed., *Defending Zion*, 159–60.

in him. This opinion, entirely disinterested on our part, will lead us to judge of the Saints with pity than severity, and to hope that they may be left to enjoy in peace in the midst of their mountains, the tranquility and solitude which is necessary to them for the development of their principles.

Before taking final leave of the President, we visited the palace which he has built for his harem. It is a model of Mormon architecture. It is 90 feet long by 36 wide, built of various kinds of rock, among which are some pieces of magnificent granite. Thirty sultanas are to be placed in this new structure, which, though it has already cost $30,000, is far from being finished.[43] The private property of Brigham Young is said to amount to $400,000.

The distinguished reception which Brigham Young gave us attracted much attention for us among the Saints. They imagined that we had made our toilsome voyage for the purpose of joining their church, and rumor, with its hundred tongues, published the accession of two important converts. It was asserted positively that we had been baptized one morning at sunrise, by an apostle, at a warm spring near the city. We were treated with great consideration. Many of the Mormons applied the term "brother" to us.

This was exceedingly amusing to us. Some spoke of choosing us for apostles, or at least for bishops; others asserted that we were very rich, and would advance money enough to finish the temple. Every body spoke of giving sureties for us. We were invited to dinner and supper. On one occasion the band of the church came to serenade us, with the *Marseillaise, God Save the Queen, Yankee Doodle, Hail Columbia,* portions of the sacred music of Mehul and Mozart, and bits of the operas of Meyerbeer and Rossini; and the music was indeed better than any we had heard in San Francisco. A ball was given in our honor, where each gentleman danced with two ladies, an innovation which proves that Brigham had good reason to say that Mormonism would reform society. All these honors were done to us, we saw it well, only as bait to entice us into the trap of the Mormon Church.

The same kindness was shown to us by the Gentiles, as the Mormons style all persons not of their own faith. The Gentile house of Livingston, Kincaid & Co., loaned to us, without interest, some money, of which we were very much in need, and for which we still feel very grateful. The entire number of Gentiles at Salt Lake may be 100—a small proportion to 10,000 Mormons in their city, and to the 40,000 or 50,000 in the Territory of Utah. This small number of Gentiles is composed of merchants, physicians, federal officers, and some men without occupations, who live upon the generosity of the Mormons, or by unknown resources. During our stay at Salt Lake we were robbed twice, and on each occasion by Gentiles. This fact is worthy of notice, for the Mormons may often have been charged with

---

[43] Rémy was witnessing the construction of the Lion House, which still stands in Salt Lake.

crimes committed by persons not of their faith, but residing among them. Nevertheless, the Saints confess that there are some among them unworthy of the name of brethren, and who commit those thefts of cattle, of which the im[m]igrants have so often complained. If theft be common among the Mormons, it is not because the crime is not severely punished. We have heard the "President" advise his people to lynch upon the spot any man taken in the act of stealing.

This exemplary severity is far, it will be seen, from the Communism which has been charged upon the Mormons. Their Communities bear not the slightest resemblance to Communistic society. The phalansterian association sometimes apparent among them is due entirely to the necessity of uniting to protect themselves against the Indians.[44] But in every case the rights to individual property are well marked. It would be equally erroneous to consider the frequent barter of coarse articles among them as an evidence of Communism. This exchange is necessary because coin is very scarce among them. The barter is conducted in a very simple manner, and according to a law made each season to determine the value of each article. While traveling in their settlements it was frequently necessary for us to resort to barter, for the purpose of obtaining the articles necessary for our use. For example: we gave a pound of coffee or tea for a pound of butter. There are towns in Utah, of more than a thousand inhabitants, who, altogether, have not two dollars in coin.

No. IV. (23 January 1856)

From time to time Brigham sent word to us with invitation to visit him, and he excused himself for not calling to see us, by saying that the reputation of the Gentile (Judge Kinney) with whom we lodged was so black that he is afraid of soiling his own fame by entering the house. He complained that Kinney, whom he had received in a kindly manner on his (K's) first arrival, and with whom he, Brigham, had compelled his whole seraglio to dance, had abused his (B's) confidence on numerous occasions, and among other cases, had aided the United States troops to carry off some Mormon women. In this affair of the abduction of the women, the officers made themselves so odious that if the men were to return, there would be war at once, and if any other soldiers should go to Salt Lake, they would be put under a rigid and perpetual quarantine at once.[45] The President had another reason for disliking the Judge. The house of the latter had been used for

---

[44] *Phalansterian* is a reference to the movement of socialist François Fourrier, the *phalanstère* being a phalanx of his followers.

[45] Troops bound for California under Col. Edward Steptoe spent a raucous winter in Salt Lake in 1854 and left with as many as one hundred women in 1855. Although Kinney assured Brigham Young he "exceedingly disliked" the troops' conduct, Young distrusted Kinney for conspiring to become governor of Utah, a post Steptoe declined. See Homer, "The Federal Bench and Priesthood Authority," 95.

interviews, which were very suspicious in the eyes of Mormon modesty. Polygamy does not prevent jealously. The Saints are the most jealous people on earth—jealous even as the gods, among whom they intend at some time to take up their abode. It is in part to this sentiment and partly to their belief in the eternity of matter that their law making adultery a capital offence may be ascribed. They believe that in the highest sphere of heaven, where those will be admitted who have been virtuous on earth, the Saints will become genuine gods, and those who were their wives will be so many queens, forming a seraphic escort, after the manner of *Jesus Christ who every morning in heaven, takes a ride on a white horse, surrounded by the queens, who were his wives on earth*.[46] These extravagances are regarded as articles of faith not only by the ignorant Mormons, but they are even published by Orson Pratt, one of the twelve apostles, and without contradiction, the best educated of all the Saints.

Judge Kinney is not loved by the Saints. He irritates them by vain attacks, and furnishes them with an occasion to accuse the Federal Government of corruption. The habit which we have in Europe of seeing in magistrates the personification of honor and integrity makes us feel as though we had fallen from the clouds when in the United States—the country represented to us to have a perfect government—we see the majestic sceptre of justice in the hands of venal and vile men. This fact alone is sufficient to cast a great discredit upon a political organization, very admirable in many respects. With the present system, where the judge is removed every four years, and a successor chosen at the polls, the evil is beyond the reach of a remedy. Now the American magistrate, who has his position for a short term, is compelled, by the money-seeking spirit of his nation, to soil his robe of office with trade if not with venality. Such is the position of the Judges of the United States at Salt Lake City. But that is not all. With the system of change and low salaries, it is often impossible to get competent men for the position of judges. It is in consequence of this defective system that the Hon. Mr. Kinney, Supreme Judge of the Territory of Utah, exercises at the same time the functions of judge, grocer, inn-keeper, and jockey. Another Judge, Kinney's associate, dared to proclaim before us that *his God is money*, and he shamelessly added that we could put that in our journal. A third judge turned Mormon in defiance of his Government, which surely did not appoint him for that.[47] If I have touched upon these subjects, it is because it galled us to have the Saints appeal to example of the Federal Judges to prove that Christian Society is corrupt and needs the regenerating and purifying influences of Mormonism.

---

[46] This is a literal translation from the French, which is in italics in the *Chronicle*.

[47] Rémy named the judges in his book: the notorious William Drummond, who was accompanied to Utah by a prostitute; and George P. Stiles, who was in fact a Mormon before he came to Utah.

No. V. (29 January 1856)

Next to the lawyers, the most notable "Gentiles" at Salt Lake are the American and English doctors, who are reduced by the caprices of the Church to the necessity of eating their own mustard. A Mormon who should have the weakness to go to a doctor, would be considered so weak in the faith that a new baptism would be necessary to work out his unbelief. Brother Brigham threatens all the pusillanimous souls who employ anything but olive oil and herbs of the field, in the cure of their diseases, with the wrath of Heaven. The power of working miraculous cures resides in all believers, but more especially in those who have been ordained to some ecclesiastical office. We were told of thousands of miracles, wrought by prayers and sweet oil, and although I was not fortunate enough to witness a solitary one, I nevertheless believe them on the testimony of truthful and disinterested persons. Faith may have sufficient influence upon the imagination to create prodigies—even among the pagans. While upon the subject of medicine, I may say that President Young told us one day that he had received a great number of letters from doctors in the Eastern States and San Francisco, asking for information as to the prospect of getting a good practice at Salt Lake, and offering to become Mormons. It is scarcely necessary to say that Brigham does not reply to such impertinences.[48]

The purity of the atmosphere in Utah, and the constant serenity of the sky, gave content to our minds, disposed to be on the sharp look out in the midst of society, described by the Gentiles as cut-throats to all visitors of our kind. It was indeed not very agreeable to hear that such and such persons suspected by the Saints had disappeared suddenly without leaving the least trace. For some time we were under the influence of such fears, but in the end we were satisfied that they were all chimeras—an isolated fact being insufficient to satisfy us that the Mormons were given to murderous practices. Calumny when it is used to attack individuals is hateful and dangerous to the assailant, but when used to attack large societies it becomes a two-edged sword, and frequently produces an effect directly contrary to its purpose. Have not the doctrines of Joseph, the prophet, enough weak points to be attacked, without charging unfortunate men with crimes of which they never were guilty—with customs which they have not, and with practices which they do not observe? While I am disposed to use the right of telling the evil which I saw, I am only obeying a sentiment of justice in declaring that the Mormons are not infamous and immoral, as they are frequently represented, and it is even my duty to declare that they have many qualities

---

[48] Rémy was wrong. In 1851 and 1852 Young corresponded with David Adams, a physician residing in Wayne County, Illinois, who asked a number of questions about Salt Lake, the health of the inhabitants, whether there were other physicians, and whether the common law had been adopted. Young not only responded but published both Adams' letter and his response in the *Millennial Star* 14:212–16 (29 May 1852).

and virtues which entitle them to our esteem in more than one respect. We could not fail to admire the order and tranquility, and the industrial and agricultural activity which were everywhere visible.

The whole mass of this people move like an ant-hill, completely justifying the emblem of the bee-hive placed by the President of the Church on the cornice of his palace. Masons build, carpenters cut and saw, gardeners spade and irrigate, blacksmiths hammer, harvesters cut grain, furriers prepare rich furs, children shell maize, butchers drive their herds, wood-cutters come from the hills heavily laden with wood, carders comb wool, laborers dig ditches for irrigation, chemists make saltpetre and powder, gun-smiths make and mend rifles, tailors, shoe-makers, brick-makers, potters, sawyers, and indeed men of every trade work at their respective occupations. There are no lazy or idle persons. Every one, from the simple believer to the bishop and the apostle, works with his hands.

The sight of this people at work is sufficient to enable one to comprehend the progress of this colony, which began in the month of July 1847, and is now in a very advanced and flourishing condition. And this activity, admirable in itself, as well as for its results, is not, as might be supposed, the consequence of an organization of labor, so much dreamed about by some European economist. Each one works for himself, or for his family, under the spur of necessity, and for the general welfare. The poorer persons, and they are generally the newly arrived, work for the rich; or if they cannot get work otherwise, they demand work of the church, which always has work to be done, and which pays with clothing, provisions, and fire-wood. There are no groggeries, no gambling houses, no places of debauch. The only places of assembling are at the temple, the schools, the field of military exercise, and sometimes in the dramatic saloon or "social hall," where they dance and sing, where they have theatrical performances, and lectures on science and history. There are no violations of the public peace in the street; fights are never seen; criminal suits are rare; and the law, according to the assertion of the Judges, is of little use, except as a guide to decide in regard to old debts.

No. VI. (8 February 1856)

Although there are no grog-shops or liquor dealers at Salt Lake, it is not to be presumed that the Saints are all "tee-totallers," or connected in any way with any temperance society. No commandment compels them to reject certain products of nature or art. But Joseph Smith, in a sermon entitled "Words of Wisdom," advises the true believers to abstain from fermented drinks and from tobacco, and recommends this abstinence as a means of perfection. The most zealous church members obey these injunctions ordinarily, but occasionally drink a little. Many of them use beer, for the purpose of making which they cultivate the hop in their valleys. Some drink wine when they can get it. Others content themselves with whisky, which they distill from potatoes. The families generally spend the evenings at home in conversation, singing, preaching, reading the Bible and the sacred books, and the papers published by their own sect. We seldom saw a woman in the street at night, a fact worthy of remark in a country where there are more women than men, and here it seems that polygamy should give better opportunities for seduction. It is a sight at least curious, if not highly interesting—that of a society, so industrious and steady, composed of so many different elements, and of persons from the lowest classes of society.

In making our enumeration, according to the number of their contributions to the church at Salt Lake, we found English, Scotch, Canadians, Americans, Danes, Swedes, Norwegians, Germans, Swiss, Poles, Russians, Italians and Frenchmen. All these people, from under different and hostile creeds, mostly bred in the deepest ignorance, and with the grossest prejudices, some having lived honestly, and others in the most complete abandonment to the coarsest instincts—all these people differing in blood, country, language, customs, laws, and tastes, have been assembled, and are continuing to assemble, to live as brothers in a perfect harmony, in the centre of the North American continent, where they form a new, compact and independent nation, as little subject to the Government of the United States as to the Sultan of Turkey. These things give cause to believe in the possibility of an universal fusion of all nations into one Republic. And such is the hope, and the aim, more or less avowed, of these privileged descendants of Abraham. He would be deceived who should suppose that the Mormons have no political purposes, no aspirations for power. The Saints, counting already upon the active cooperation of the Indian hordes, whose sympathies they have obtained, wait only for the order of the Prophet. Happily for the human kind, and more particularly for the United States, polygamy, to which they have had recourse to multiply the soldiers of God, brings with it the seeds of a probable social dissolution. This danger which I merely mention here, of a Mormon irruption [sic] will appear more clearly from facts to be mentioned elsewhere.

A week had scarcely passed after our arrival, before we perceived that it was difficult for "Gentiles" to learn the domestic habits, and be familiarly admitted into the houses of the Saints. It is true we were received in the houses of several polygamists but our presence caused a restraint which prevented our acquiring many details, which we were burning to know. The information given us by the "Gentiles" was unsatisfactory, and too contradictory to appear credible. Finally, we conceived the plan of inviting a number of the most sincere and zealous Mormons, both educated and uneducated, to visit us in the evenings. The great desire which we showed to be edified upon every subject, led them to think that we were already half

SOCIAL HALL, SALT LAKE CITY.
Special Collections, J. Willard Marriott Library, University of Utah.

converted and deprived them of all distrust. We put no sharpness in our discourse, or dogmatism in our discussions, and they took pleasure in reply to all our questions. In this manner we passed very agreeable and instructive evenings. We never had reason to admire the force of their logic, for it is impossible for anyone of them to follow up an argument judiciously and sensibly, but we collected many facts. A blind faith prevented the most intelligent among them from perceiving the falsehood in their citations, and the arbitrariness of their interpretations of the sacred book. If we confounded them with quotations from the Holy Scriptures, they pretended that all our versions were incorrect, and that the only reliable one is that of Joseph Smith, and that is unfortunately not yet published. Several times they escaped from embarrassing positions by saying that all *would be clear* after we should be baptised; all that was dark and absurd in their doctrines would be clear and satisfactory under the light of faith. All pretended that by the effect of baptism, and entire submission to the dogmas of the church, a sudden and marvellous change had been effected in their minds, the principal result of which was their transformation into beings resembling God in knowledge, so that they could understand by intuition even those problems which our greatest philosophers despair to solve. They said that the great majority of their church members were not able to read or write before their conversion, but that immediately afterwards they learned in a few years more than Gentiles could have learned in the course of years. What astonished us the most was that they knew the Bible by heart, from one end to the other, and could cite the numbers of chapter and verse.

No. VII. (11 February 1856)

Let us cast a glance upon the prospects of Mormonism, considered in connection with the present condition of the children born and bred under the influence [of] polygamy.

Like delicate flowers, of which the tender petals are soiled and discolored by the least breath of impurity, so are children easily corrupted by the pernicious contagion of evil examples. The immediate consequence of the beastly education of the Mormons, is the destruction of the germ of the most beautiful of the virtues. Love, the lever of societies, the most admirable present which the Deity has made to man—this sentiment so precious, so noble, so magnificent; which raises us above the coarse realities of life, and transports us into unknown regions, and gives us a foretaste of the delights reserved for the world of spirits—is this beautiful sentiment found among the young generation which is now growing up in the shade of Mormonism? Alas! It is necessary to acknowledge the fact; depravity, impiety, obscenity of language, and acts against nature, may be made the just reproach of the young saints at the Salt Lake. It would be necessary to go among the savages, degraded and brutalized by intercourse with the dregs of our civilization, to find horrors comparable to those offered us by the heirs of the saints.

The veil, behind which polygamy concealed itself from us, appeared to be partly raised by the influence of this injurious system upon the minds of the young. This influence is so disastrous, that we must abandon the thought of describing its effects. The evil is beyond expression, and as there is no effect without cause, and as an innocent turtle-dove could not generate a hideous harpy, we are forced to see by its fruits, in despite of all exterior appearances, that polygamy is a baneful monstrosity, which would soon degrade men to the level of the most brutal monkeys. Thus notwithstanding a thousand efforts to conceal itself from our examination, the system of a plurality of wives has betrayed itself by its results, and confirmed the opinions which we had in advance formed of it.

These considerations upon the wickedness of the children of the saints, permit us to foresee that if Mormonism shall disappear like an astonishing and anomalous meteor, the principal causes for its annihilation will be found in polygamy, the very expedient to which the Mormons had recourse to build up and perpetuate their sect. It is thus that when man abandons the order of nature to violate the eternal law of the universe, he always finds that his sins contain their own punishment. A people cannot exist without morality, and the habits of the children of the polygamists are the very reverse of moral. Unfortunate Mormons! you roast the frozen body which you have sought to warm into life. You have taken into your bosom the snake which will kill you. Polygamy is a sword of Damocles for you, heavy and threatening over your heads.

The theory of the Saints in relation to legitimate and natural children is most strange. The sympathy of the sexes, and not the ceremony of marriage, is the measure of legitimacy. A child conceived beyond the limits of the matrimonial state, if born of a father and mother who loved each other tenderly at the time of its conception, is a legitimate child. But the child conceived of parents indifferent towards each other, is only bastard, even if the parents were formally united under the laws of the church. These theories do great honor to the high intelligence of him who drew them from chaos.

I have already said that the Saints themselves confess to a certain point, the precocity of evil among their children; but in this precocity, they see only a proof of their future intelligence, or at most a natural consequence of their long travels over immense deserts, and deceive themselves upon the facility of the means proper for the correction of the "little rascals." They say—"Our children are smarter than the children of the Gentiles, that's all; and why should it not be so, since they belong to the race of Ephraim—and besides enlightened at an early hour by the Holy Spirit? They do not always speak decently, but all that will be corrected at school." The Mormons thus abuse themselves by believing that the common schools will suffice to purify the evil nature of their children. Notwithstanding the numerous cares at the establishment of the new Society, there are already thirty schools in Salt Lake City.

The teachers are paid "in trade" by the families, and cost nothing to the government. Here is a notice which I found fixed on the door of an academy: "We, teachers of the school of the city and county of Cedar, to all the brethren, greeting:—Monday, the 19th of November, the anniversary of the day of the massacre of 185,000 Assyrians by the Angel of the Lord, has been fixed for the re-opening of my lectures upon the Divine Sciences, reading and writing: and whereas, we are now in famine in consequence of the seventh year after our arrival, the prices for every pupil, boy or girl, will be as follows: For one month, a bushel of wheat, or corn, or two bushels of potatoes, and considering that it is winter, every pupil must bring a stick of cedar every fortnight. And considering that those who cannot pay in grain, may be able to pay with other articles, we will receive bear-meat, salted lard and cheese, and considering that we have nothing to eat at present, and that I am in want, every pupil must pay me for a fortnight in advance." . . .

No. XI. (6 March 1856)

During our sojourn at Salt Lake, a three-day conference was held, at which we were present. There were two sessions per day, and the meetings were precisely like those held on Sunday.⁴⁹ At every sitting the exercises began with sacred music from Mozart, well executed with voices and instruments. After the music was done, the President arose, and, keeping his hat on, like his apostles about him, he made an extemporaneous prayer in English. At the end of the prayer all the faithful responded "Amen." Then a high priest, or some orator, arose, and keeping his hat on, spoke diffusely on all kinds of incoherent subjects.

These modern Demosthenes were never in want of words. Sometimes they would pour forth their slang in a calm and phlegmatic tone, standing motionless, with their hands in their pockets; and then all at once they would begin to jump about like imps, and go into all possible contortions and throw their arms about like boxers; and frequently in the fire of their inspiration they would knock their hats down over their eyes. Among their oratorical positions, I have noticed some superb attitudes. Nearly all, even to the President himself, whose natural eloquence is nevertheless remarkable and sometimes touching, did not observe the bounds of modesty in their speech, nor did they abstain from indecent pleasantries and buffooneries, which excited bursts of approving laughter. The large Heber C. Kimball, first counsellor of the presidency, and by virtue of that position Vice-Pope of the Mormons, is so comical in his manner, that the hilarity which he causes, is almost enough in itself to repay a journey to Salt Lake. When the want of dignity is considered which these priests exhibit even in their churches, a stranger might suppose that he was present at a meeting of idiots; and with the exception of the two brothers Pratt, who made sensible and eloquent discourses before us, I could easily believe in the insanity of all of these preachers.⁵⁰

A missionary named Ballantyne, lately arrived from Hindostan, made a narrative of his voyages, and related how, in a violent tempest, the ship captain having lost all hope of safety, and wishing to destroy himself, he [the missionary] said to him, [the captain] *"What do you fear, man of little faith? Do you not carry a minister of God?"* And the wind fell, and the waves grew smooth, and the vessel was saved!⁵¹ The President, Brigham, made in his turn a discourse, in which he said, among other things, "There are more devils among the Mormons than in all the rest of the world! The church owes the sum of $70,000 for emigration; you must pay this debt, and if you do not I will sell your property; and if your property should not be enough, I will sell your

---

⁴⁹ Rémy attended sessions of the LDS semiannual conference that was held in October 1855.

⁵⁰ The Pratt brothers are Orson Pratt and Parley P. Pratt. Both were apostles and eloquent speakers.

⁵¹ Born in Scotland, Richard Ballantyne (1817–98) joined the LDS church in 1842 and immigrated to Nauvoo the next year. He was called on a mission to India in 1852, served in Calcutta, and returned to Utah in September 1855. Ballantyne is best remembered for starting the LDS Sunday School movement in his Salt Lake home in 1849.

wives and children. Hasten to get married; let me see no more boys over sixteen years of age, or girls over fourteen years. Tell the Gentiles that I am fully determined to cut off the head of the first one of them who attempts to seduce our daughters or our wives." Another preacher, in the midst of his discourse, made this eloquent apostrophe: "Almighty God, Father of the Saints, precipitate, I conjure you, to the bottom of hell, all the enemies of our holy religion." After the Mormon orators had all finished, the Mormon Pope arose, stretched out his arms, addressed a short prayer to Jehovah, and dismissed the Assembly.

Such is the Mormon worship as it is practised in the grand temple of the new Jerusalem. The facts speak for themselves; I will abstain from comment. . . .[52]

No. XII. (19 March 1856)

The spirit of brotherhood which reigns among all the Mormons, is shown by an inviolable hospitality toward the brethren, and by sentiments of hostility toward the Gentiles. A Mormon is, at all times and in all places, received as a brother, while the Gentiles are kept at a distance, in the name of the church, which forbids all intercourse with them. We have heard Brigham say to his flock, "Have nothing to do with the Gentiles: If you sell to them the fruits of the earth, charge ten times their worth; if you lend them money, let it be at three per cent. interest." These facts suffice to show the hatred and vengeance which the saints desire to exercise toward the Americans, their persecutors. All the Mormons entertain the hope, dear to their hearts, of reconquering, by the force of arms and the help of Jehovah, the lands of which they were despoiled, on the banks of the Missouri. It is with this view that they follow a kind and generous policy towards the Indians. They think rightly that the numerous warlike tribes which inhabit the interior of the American continent, may be of great service to them when the moment has arrived for the great war which they propose to make against the United States. Their calculations on this subject have been already justified by the fact that the Indians, comparing the treatment which they receive from the Americans with that which they receive from the Mormons, show themselves almost always inoffensive toward the latter. Within the feeble range of human foresight, it seems childish to attach the least importance to these ambitious projects. Nevertheless, if we remember that

---

[52] Rémy also commented on the Deseret alphabet, the University of Deseret, and "polygyny (many-wifery)," which he considered "not only a monstrosity but an injustice." He did, however, "boldly declare that we saw nothing indecent in polygyny, as it is practiced among the Mormons," and acknowledged that Mormon children were "beautiful, strong and vigorous." He also described LDS church organization: "Their ecclesiastical hierarchy contains a descending ladder of quorums, the first of which is the quorum of the presidency consisting of the president and his two grand councillors; a patriarch, a historian and a bishop. . . . With such an organization schism becomes almost impossible."

the powerful eagle comes from an inert egg, that more than once a handful of barbarians has been enabled to overthrow great armies, that disastrous effects are sometimes the result of almost imperceptible causes, we may treat with less disdain the plans which, if they do not succeed, will not the less be tried in execution.

Relying on the justice of their cause, and upon the intestine dissensions which threaten to dissever the Union, the Mormons are silently developing their resources, preparing their means of action, and looking for a favorable opportunity to commence operations; and if there is a temerity on their part which may appear blind, we yet cannot say that success is impossible for them. Does not history tell us that fanaticism does wonders, that faith moves mountains, that perseverance conquers the most stubborn obstacles, and that fortune has the greatest favors for the boldest enterprises? Does not the stage of life offer to us every day the most unexpected facts, previously regarded as impossibilities? The Mormons have that confidence of power which is given by religious fanaticism. When we saw the soldiers of the desert gather every week on the grand *planza* [plaza?] of Zion, experienced in all kinds of danger, accustomed to a precarious and almost a savage mode of life, clothed in rags, armed with revolvers, with sharp eyes, active bodies, and strong limbs—when we saw them under the order of a general in tatters execute with precision complicated operations of strategy, we could not refuse to believe that an army of these people would certainly beat twice their number of other troops.[53]

---

[53] Rémy ended this letter with a comment on Mormonism's lay clergy and tithing policies. A final letter dealt with religious beliefs and practices, noting that the "sinful are condemned to be the slaves of the good" and the "wicked will thus be reduced to the rank of negroes, who according to the Mormon code are destined to remain eternally in slavery." He was astonished to hear a high priest "make a long eulogy of Mohammedanism." Rémy could scarcely believe that an educated Protestant could "become the apologist of Mohammedanism in the XIXth century."

Chapter 3

"GATHERING TO ZION"
European Converts in Utah

In October 1849 Brigham Young instructed three of the twelve apostles—John Taylor, Erastus Snow, and Lorenzo Snow—to travel to Europe and organize missions in Scandinavia, France, and Italy.[1] The Mormon hierarchy had monitored the revolutionary activity that had destabilized the continent for almost two years and it was convinced that these events created an opportunity to expand the church from England—where missionaries had labored since 1837—to the European continent.[2] The leadership incorporated the Perpetual Emigrating Fund to assist financially challenged converts to immigrate to the United States. In June 1850 missionaries arrived in Denmark, France, and Italy, and soon others were sent to Switzerland and Prussia.[3]

Mormon evangelists in Denmark, France, Germany, and Italy translated and published *The Book of Mormon* as well as books, periodicals, and pamphlets to support their proselytizing.[4] When local clergy read these sectarian works,

---

[1] For the northern European missions, see Mulder, *Homeward to Zion: The Mormon Migration from Scandinavia*. William Howell was called to open the French mission on 13 August 1848. He arrived in France on 9 July 1849. The first branch was organized in Boulogne-sur-Mer on 6 April 1850, but mission president John Taylor did not arrive until 18 June 1850. See *Millennial Star*, 1 September 1849, 263–64; 1 October 1849, 294–97; 1 January 1850, 11–14; 15 March 1850, 91–92; and 15 May 1850, 157–59. For Italy, see Stokoe, "The Mormon Waldensians"; Homer, "The Italian Mission, 1850–1867"; Homer, "The Church's Image in Italy from the 1840s to 1946: A Bibliographic Essay," 83–114; Homer, "LDS Prospects in Italy," 139–58; and Ferrero, "L'emigrazione valdese nello Utah nella seconda meta' dell'800."

[2] See *Millennial Star*, 15 March 1848, 90; 1 April 1848, 103–4; 15 April 1848, 119–20; 1 June 1848, 169; 15 July 1848, 209–11; 1 October 1849, 297–300; and 1 February 1850, 37–39.

[3] Lorenzo Snow sent T. B. H. Stenhouse to Lausanne to open the Swiss mission in 1850. George P. Dykes worked in a German-speaking area of Denmark in 1851 until he was banished and began preaching in Hamburg. In September 1851 Brigham Young sent Daniel Carn (later Garn) as first president of the German mission; that same year Orson Spencer began proselytizing in Berlin.

[4] See "The Sesquicentennial of Four European Translations of the Book of Mormon."

Mormonism became a new foil for Protestant and Catholic writers. Scores of publications challenging the new religion began to appear. Despite this reaction, thousands of continental Europeans were eventually converted to Mormonism, and many of them immigrated to Utah Territory with the assistance of the Perpetual Emigrating Fund. These travelers were not on the way to somewhere else: they were gathering to Zion. William Mulder calls LDS converts' "break with the Old World . . . a compound fracture: a break with the old church and with the old country."[5] Dean May noted that the converts, unlike other European immigrants to the West who were "moving out of their old life into relative freedom," found themselves in "tightly structured, hierarchical, closely knit villages where pressures to conform were great."[6]

Some, like John Ahmanson, were disappointed with their new lives in Utah and left the territory as bitter critics of Mormonism. Their accounts were loud and derogatory, but they represented a minority among the many immigrant voices. Most remained in the territory and abandoned their national languages and customs to become part of Mormon society.[7] French revolutionary Louis Bertrand is perhaps the most striking example. In France he was a well-known journalist who was embroiled in the aftermath of the revolutions of 1848. Yet, following his baptism, he left his family (who did not convert) and gathered to Zion. He eventually returned to France as mission president and published his memoirs in which he celebrated Mormonism in Paris. Other converts, less prominent and with softer voices, will never be heard, but a few stories, such as those written by Stephen Malan and Daniel Bertoch many years after their arrival in Utah as teenagers, are now published for the first time.

Stephen Malan: The Test Was a Severe One

In June 1850 Apostle Lorenzo Snow, T. B. H. Stenhouse, and Joseph Toronto arrived in the Kingdom of Sardinia and began proselytizing the only indigenous Protestants in Italy. The missionaries believed that the Waldensians,

---

[5] Mulder, "Through Immigrant Eyes," 47; Mulder, "Mormon Angles of Historical Vision," 20.

[6] May, "Mormons," in Eliason, *Mormons and Mormonism*, 55.

[7] Helen Z. Papanikolas noted that "the logic of submerging national origins, languages, and customs to give strength to the new church, reverence for English as the language in which the Book of Mormon had been translated, and the wholehearted acceptance of Utah's Zion as the immigrant's permanent home kept resistance low." Papanikolas, "Ethnicity in Mormonism," quoted in Eliason, *Mormons and Mormonism*, 166–67.

with their long history of dissent, were better candidates for conversion than the Catholics.[8] The Waldensians lived under desperate economic conditions, residing in "[a] few narrow valleys, which are, in some places, only a bowshot in breadth" and "[t]he inhabitants are far too numerous, according to the nature of the soil." Much of their land was not suitable for farming. Snow estimated that "two-thirds, or more, present nothing but precipices, ravines and rocky districts, or such as have a northern aspect."[9]

After Snow and his companions arrived in the valleys, Snow wrote and published a pamphlet, *La voix de Joseph* (*The Voice of Joseph*). It explained the Mormon doctrine of gathering converts to America in anticipation of the millennium and the church program—the Perpetual Emigrating Fund—that provided financial assistance to those who could not afford to emigrate. Snow described Great Salt Lake City as "a beautiful valley beyond the 'pass' of the Great Rocky Mountains . . . where peace and happiness dwell." Concerning life in "Zion" Snow wrote, "Oh, what a life we live! It is the dreams of the poets actually fulfilled in real life. . . . Here, too, we are all rich. . . . There is no real poverty; all men have access to the soil, the pasture, the timber, the water power, and all elements of wealth, without money or price."

The Malan family lived in the small village of Prassuit in the Val Angrogna and was among the first Mormon converts in Italy.[10] Jean Daniel Malan was a well-respected member of the community prior to his baptism by Mormon missionaries. He was a candidate to be a Waldensian elder before he revealed during an interview that he no longer believed in the church. Jabez Woodard, Lorenzo Snow's successor as mission president,

---

[8] When Snow arrived in the valleys in July 1850 he estimated they were home to 21,000 Waldensians and 5,000 Catholics. "They appeared to my mind like the rose in the wilderness, or the bow in the cloud," he told Brigham Young. See Snow, *The Italian Mission*, 10; and his sister's *Biography and Family Record of Lorenzo Snow*. For Toronto, see Toronto, "Giuseppe Efisio Taranto: Odyssey from Sicily to Salt Lake City," in Van Orden, Smith, and Smith Jr., eds., *Pioneers in Every Land*, 125–47.

[9] Snow, *The Italian Mission*, 11, 13. The Waldensians produced grapes, wheat, rye, maize, oats, mulberry barley, potatoes, and fruit trees and raised cows, goats, and sheep. See Monastier, *A History of the Vaudois Church*, 431–32. Protestant missionaries in Italy reported that some Waldensians were attracted by Mormonism's program of subsidized immigration to the U.S. See Homer, "The Italian Mission," 19–21.

[10] At least 171 Waldensians joined the LDS church during the seventeen-year history of the Italian mission. Seventy-three immigrated to Utah in three groups during 1854 and 1855. The Italian mission record indicates that between 1850 and 1866, 184 persons were baptized, 58 immigrated, and 73 were excommunicated. These figures are inconsistent with the rosters of immigrant ships that name at least 73 Waldensians who migrated between 1853 and 1866, possibly because some of the children were not baptized Mormons. See "Emigration Records and Ship Roster" and "Record of Membership of the Italian Mission," LDS Archives.

baptized the entire Malan family in February 1851, including Jean Daniel, his wife Pauline, and their seven children: Marie Catherine, Jean Daniel, Jean Étienne, Jeanne Dina, Madeleine, Pauline Amelia, and Barthélemy. Thereafter the missionaries held Sunday services in the Malan home.[11]

The Malan family left Italy in February 1855 with the second group of Italian converts.[12] They departed from Liverpool aboard the *Juventa*, arrived in the Salt Lake Valley in October 1855, and settled in Ogden. "We found 'Zion' a comparative desert, but with patient industry, perseverance and heaven's blessings, we've noticed it gradually transformed to a beautiful and most desirable land to dwell on," Madeleine Malan recalled. Amidst a general famine brought on by drought, the family survived the first winter on a diet of weeds, bran bread, and fish caught with traps made from willow twigs. During these difficult times Madeleine worked for Joseph Toronto, doing domestic chores at his home in Salt Lake and making hay at his ranch near the Great Salt Lake. Despite these hardships, Jean D. Malan Sr. was called in 1857 to return to Italy as a missionary.

Jean Etienne Malan, now known as Stephen, wrote a holographic autobiography in 1893, almost forty years after arriving in Utah, in which he described his initial disappointment with "Deseret." But one senses in Malan, as well as many other early converts, that they were often more comfortable discussing church doctrines and beliefs than they were speaking about their own history. In 1912 he published a small book, *The Ten Tribes: Discovered and Identified*, that he had researched for thirty years.

STEPHEN MALAN, AUTOBIOGRAPHY AND FAMILY RECORD, LDS ARCHIVES.

I will not omit to mention here that inasmuch as I had been raised in those fair valleys of Piedmont where nature exhibited so many gifts, where one would inhale the sweet fragrance of the thousands of variegated flow-

---

[11] Jabez Woodard, born 7 October 1821 at Aldenham, England, joined the LDS church in 1849. He arrived in Italy in September 1850 and subsequently served as president of the Italian and Swiss missions. Woodard emigrated to Utah in 1854 and died 2 May 1870 in Morgan, Utah.

[12] The first group sailed from Liverpool to New Orleans aboard the *John M. Wood* on 22 March 1854; the second left Liverpool on the *Juventa* on 14 March 1855 bound for Philadelphia; and the third boarded the *John J. Boyd* on 30 December 1855 and sailed for New York. Most of those who did not immigrate, a total of seventy-three people, were excommunicated and presumably remained members of the Waldensian church. The stated reasons for these excommunications were negligence, rebellion, infidelity, evil and immorality, apostasy, absurdities, unbelief, criticism, nonchalance, cowardice, lying, bad conduct, fear of the world, and deceit. See "Record of Membership of the Italian Mission." Mormon missionaries in Italy converted almost 1 percent of the Waldensian population, which caused great concern among the pastors in the valleys.

ers which the ever green meadows produced so exhilarating to the senses, I could not, having witnessed other climes and scenes, form a correct idea of the aspect that an arid western waste would offer to my view. I could not sense the description given while in my native land, of the flowery border of the River Jordan, nor of the virgin prairies of the valleys of Deseret, nor of the dense forest, and shrubs of its mountain dales and limpid water brooks, and salubrity of its climate. Having never seen it, I conjectured something of a similarity to my country's nature's gifts. Hence with this reflection upon my mind after having for weeks traveled over sandy deserts, and the wilderness across the Rocky Mountains, what a contrast would appear to my view when gazing upon Salt Lake, the fine city of the Saints and the luxurious vegetations covering the surrounding country.

I was so eager for this contemplation, and so expectant of the contrast which my anxious gaze would witness, that on the day that we were to cross the last summit of the mountains [at] Emigration Canyon I started at day break [and] left the company without my breakfast, and made rapid strides to reach the long sought land of Zion. Somewhere down the canyon, I met Samuel Burt our captain of guard. He peremptorily ordered me to go back and help to drive the loose stock. I answered him that I had as he knew full well that I had always promptly obeyed his orders; but that in this instance I would refuse, saying that I was so near Zion and anxious to see the Salt Lake that I would not return to camp for all the stock was worth. I thought he was only trying a tease, for after hearing my argument, he started off with a laugh, seemingly as to say, "fool, your eagerness will be checked; when you'll see the sagebrush fields."

I arrived with perspiration and almost breathless; upon a slight elevation at the mouth of the canyon, my eyes surveyed the whole landscape from the spot upon which I stood; nothing but desert was visible; from the East to West mountains, I could not perceive any thing indicative of anticipations. Seeing some teamsters on their way up the canyon I actually inquired of them where was that great valley of Salt Lake and where was the city located; with a burst of laughter they asked me if I was deprived on my eyesight. "I see," said one of them, "that you appear rather fresh," so he pointed westward; "there," said he, "is the city there a little further off is the Jordan River," but I could not see the flowers on its borders. "You see the lake or part of it, now said he, are you satisfied?"

I was satisfied, and so much so that the contemplation not only dimmed my eyes [but] actual tears rolled down my cheeks was it joy to be gazing upon Zion's hills that produced the agitation? No! It was disappointment, that was conceived through my ignorance of the aspect which I was to witness and the abortiveness of my sanguine anticipations.

The test was a severe one but it was momentary. As I walked along the road the fragrance of the sage was beginning to cause a cogitation upon my mind that this indigent plant growing so profusely could be changed into a fruitful orchard, and gardens by man's industry, and that the whole valley could eventually be converted into that condition which I had contemplated. It is now so to a great extent.

While thus cogitating upon these matters my eyes were not at all affected by the latent tears; but they otherwise became clearer of vision, but my stomach was becoming unruly; and commanded my attention. I first entered the eastern part of Zion's city or tail end. I began to admire the width of the street, and the sparse small dwelling houses. When a man seeing me so absorbed, in observation and as he was standing upon his door step, addressed me by saying "hello there, you must be a stranger in these parts, judging from your scrutiny upon the surroundings." I said "yes," and was upon studying in what manner, in my then very imperfect language of English to ask for something to satisfy the cravings of my stomach, but he anticipated my tardy studied sentence and called me in; after a few inquiries about our journey, he invited me to a sumptuous repast the best since I had left home it was considered so after three months journey across the plains; it is sufficient to know that day to this I, whether willingly or forcibly through force of circumstances, [have] adapted myself to the ways and rules which predominated [in] this western climes, and would shed more tears if I had to forsake this vales of the mountains than those I shed for entering them.

DANIEL BERTOCH: OH HOW TOFF HE WAS

Jabez Woodard also baptized Jean Bertoch, a widower, and his five children, Jean, Daniel, Jacques, Antoinette, and Marguerite, in August 1853. The Bertoch family lived on a small farm near the village of San Germano in Val Chisone. One of Jean's brothers-in-law, Jean Pierre Meynier, was the mayor of San Germano. Shortly after Jean and his family joined the Mormons, Meynier was selected as an elder in the Waldensian church. Another brother-in-law, Daniel Vinçon, was a church dissenter who became disillusioned during the "Risveglio" or reawakening of the 1830s.

Following his conversion to Mormonism, Jean Bertoch prepared his family to immigrate to Utah. He paid 200 lire in October 1853 to obtain a military deferment for his eighteen-year-old son Daniel from the Kingdom of Sardinia. Without this deferment, he would have been required to serve in the army for at least two years.[13] In December 1853 Jean sold the family

---

[13] Archivio di Stato di Torino, Registro delle Insinuazioni, 1853, vol. 1046, 425–26.

home and farm for 2,200 lire. It was a bold move since the land, located on the steep mountains above San Germano Chisone, was the place the family raised crops and pastured cows.[14] The next month he sold a separate piece of farm land in Pomaretto, farther up Val Chisone, for 300 lire.[15]

When Woodard asked Bertoch to remain in Italy to preside over a newly organized branch in San Germano, he agreed but insisted that his children be allowed to immigrate to Utah with the first group of Italian converts.[16] He donated the proceeds from his land sales to the church, and in February 1854 his five children left the valleys. In March they boarded the *John M. Wood* in Liverpool and three months later arrived in New Orleans. Marguerite died of cholera a few weeks later on a small island near St. Louis, Missouri, and a few months after that the eldest son, Jean, died near Fort Kearny, Nebraska Territory. Daniel, Antoinette, and James [Jacques] arrived in Great Salt Lake City in October 1854.[17]

It is unlikely that Jean Bertoch ever learned the fate of his children Jean and Marguerite. He was the branch president in San Germano until he immigrated to Utah with the second group of converts in February 1855. This group included Stephen Malan and his family.[18] Like his two children, Jean did not reach Utah. He died in Mormon Grove, Kansas, during the

---

[14] Archivio di Stato di Torino, Registro delle Insinuazioni di Pinerolo, 1854, vol. 1049, 477–78.

[15] Archivio di Stato di Torino, Registro delle Insinuazioni di San Secondo, 1854, vol. 562, 157–59.

[16] An LDS branch was organized in St-Germain on 8 May 1854, and by fall the Council of the Swiss and Italian Missions learned that three branches had been established in Italy. See *Millennial Star*, 3 June 1854, 350; and *Millennial Star*, 11 November 1854, 707.

[17] Even before the first LDS converts left Piedmont, the Waldensians were monitoring the status of the "separatisti," which included not only Mormons but a few Darbyites as well. The report made reference to "Mormoniti" in Pramollo and Angrogna and noted that there had been "Mormonite" activity in Torre Pellice. They also reported on their departure to "California." Even the Waldensian church moderator, Jean-Pierre Revel, discussed the "Mormon problem" with Joseph Malan, the Waldensian deputy in the Parliament. Revel attended the Presbyterian General Assembly at New York in May 1853 and discussed the religious environment in the Kingdom of Sardinia and solicited funds for a Waldensian theological seminary. See Mitchell, *The Waldenses*, 368–69.

[18] On 30 August 1854 Joseph Malan asked Revel if there were Mormons in the valleys who were attempting to "seduce the people." If there were, "it should not be difficult to repeat the same compliment that was given two years previous, to drive them out immediately." See Malan to Revel, 30 August 1854, Lettres du Modérateur, 1850–59, Archivio della Tavola Valdese, Lettera, 6:67. Malan wrote to Revel again to ask whether he should "apply the principle of freedom of conscience" or take a position that did not "completely approve the decision to expel them, a role that I would personally prefer, rather than follow the Prime Minister Camillo Cavour's opinion . . . and adopt coercive measures." See Malan to Revel, 18 September 1854, ibid., 6:134–35n69. I am indebted to Flora Ferrero for sharing these records. Malan knew that under Cavour's formula he balanced freedom of religion with the likelihood of public disorder if non-Catholic missionaries pressed too hard. He probably concluded that the Mormons were harmless, since they were achieving modest results outside the Waldensian Valleys.

DANIEL BERTOCH (1835–1923).
Used by permission, Utah State Historical Society, all rights reserved.

summer of 1855, and he is buried with others who shared a similar fate in a large pasture next to the campground. At the time of his death his three surviving children were living on Antelope Island on the Great Salt Lake, where they worked for Brigham Young and Joseph Toronto.[19]

DANIEL BERTOCH, AUTOBIOGRAPHY, UTAH STATE HISTORICAL SOCIETY.

We arrived in Salt Lake City, October 28, 1854. It having been nine and one half months since we left our native land. Our oldest brother, John, had died on the plains somewhere near Fort Kearney. Our first camp was made back of a dirt wall, just north of John Sharp's dwelling.[20] We first settlers all had confidence in our leaders, and we were satisfied with Salt Lake City.

Joseph Toronto came and took me to his house where I met my brother and sister. In a few days we went to Antelope Island to work for President Young, under the direction of Mr. Toronto. I had to go to the canyon every

---

[19] Homer, "An Immigrant Story," 208–9. Jean's youngest son, Jacques, returned to Europe as a Mormon missionary in 1891. He spent almost nine months in the Waldensian valleys, where he visited his father's home and boarded with his cousins, whom he had not seen for almost forty years. See Bertoch, *Missionary Journal and Letters*.

[20] John Sharp (1820–91) began his career as an eight-year-old Scottish coal miner and rose to become one of the most powerful men in Utah Territory. He converted to Mormonism in 1848, migrated to Utah in 1850, managed the church's quarrying operations, and became the first bishop of the twentieth ward in 1854. He served as a director of the Union Pacific Railroad and superintendent of the Utah Central Railway but was stripped of his church offices when he pleaded guilty to unlawful cohabitation in 1885.

day for wood, which resulted in wet feet. For my shoes were so bad that I was obliged to tie them on with strings.

Late in spring, Toronto and myself started for Salt Lake with a piece of bran bread in our pockets. We were trying to find the head [*sic*] of the Jordan River. We came across a large flat boat filled with water, we stayed to empty it, but before our task was done it began to get dark, so we started for the nearest light. We stayed with Mr. Keits at K's Creek. At breakfast I was seated next to a young lady about eighteen years old, dressed in a clean calico dress. Imagine my humiliation, for I was dressed in dirty greasy canvas, that Toronto brought from New Orleans. Next day we went back to complete our task and a terrible storm came making it impossible.

We were in danger of our lives so Toronto called to us to come into the boat, and we began to pray in English. When we finished he called upon a Danish boy, and he prayed in Danish; then he asked me. I prayed in French for the first time without my prayer book. It wasn't very long before the storm quieted down and we got away safely. After drying our clothes by a fire we began to hunt for a place to stay.

The next day we started in quest of the Jordan River, we found it in late afternoon. We got in our boat and traveled up the river, we camped that night at Bakers. The next day we arrived in Salt Lake and went to Toronto's. I stayed with him long enough to get a pair of shoes then I ran away. I roamed around for a while then I started to work on the temple.

In about 1-½ months the work stopped. John Sharp then started me to work on the canal. From Big Cottonwood to the mouth of City Creek.[21]

We received ½ pounds of shorts, 1-½ pounds of flour and meat the size of a mans two fists to last one of us a week. I worked there until late in the fall, and everything was closed up for the winter. I went to Sharp for my money, he told me there was no money, only what we ate.

I was left penniless and without a place to stay. The Mormon Company arrived the day I left Sharp and told me my father had passed away. My brother and sister were living on the [Antelope] island [on the Great Salt Lake]. I felt pretty blue and alone in the world. Having run away from Toronto I hated to go back, but I did and he took me back on the island in the fall of 1855. On our way we were obliged to roll our trousers up above the knees and wade through grasshoppers to reach land.

Toronto learned that the large boat, we had tried once before to get, was at Saltair, so he and I went to recover it. We started to dig a trench to let the water in so that we could float the boat out to the lake. Soon we were out of provisions and Toronto went to Salt Lake to get some. I waited for a day and a half and he didn't return so I started on foot for the city. I reached Toronto's and found the house locked, so I hunted for something to eat. I

---

[21] This canal, intended to transport granite from the canyon to the temple site, was never completed.

found a squash, ate all I could and then returned to Saltair. I saw nothing of Toronto, so I started for the island. While in the lake a dreadful storm started. I was drifted all over and thought any minute I would be tipped over and drowned. I was very frightened and so I prayed and then trusted the Lord. I was carried safely to the island and stayed at the church that night. The next day I went on to my brother and sister. I remained here until the fall of 1856, and then left Toronto.

I started to work for George D. and Jedediah Grant. The winter of '55 and '56 was a hard one. The spring of 1856 was one of the hardest that the people had to pass through. Many a family had to sit down to the table and ask the blessing on the food and there was nothing but a dish of greens to be seen.

In the fall of 1856 we separated, my brother James [Jacques] stayed with Mr. Toronto, Antoinette married Louis Chapuis and went to Nephi to live.

DANIEL BERTOCH TO JAMES [JACQUES] BERTOCH AND ANN CUTCLIFFE, 14 FEBRUARY 1922, UTAH STATE HISTORICAL SOCIETY.

Brother and Sister I think very often of our early days in Utah especially on the [Church or Antelope] Island when we eat that big Ox . . . [Joseph] Toronto said the Grando Bovo will Die we better kill him and eat him oh how toff he was. I would [have] good teeth yet if it hadn't been for eating of that Ox and—many other things we did eat makes me sick to think about it now. When John Smith the Patriarch told me that the Lord had answered my prayers I begun to think at that time how many prayers I had offered up to the Lord wasn't many I can tell you.

JOHN AHMANSON: JOYFULLY WE DROVE IN TO ZION

John A. Ahmanson (1827–91) a Danish bookbinder, served a mission to Norway before emigrating from Denmark and arrived in Utah in November 1856 with the James G. Willie Handcart Company. Following a bitter winter he returned to the Midwest and eventually settled in Omaha with other former Mormons from Scandinavia.[22]

Two years after leaving Utah, Ahmanson sued Brigham Young in Nebraska, claiming that the LDS church had not returned some of the personal effects he had stored in Nebraska and had failed to compensate him for acting as a captain of a handcart company from May to November 1856. Young's lawyers responded that the LDS church was not responsible for

---

[22] *Omaha Times*, 6 May 1858; *Omaha Nebraskian*, 8 July 1857; and Mulder, *Homeward to Zion*, 184.

SALTAIR RESORT, C. 1908.
Special Collections, J. Willard Marriott Library, University of Utah.

Ahmanson's cached goods and that the Danish convert had never been an employee of the church, but that he had been chosen by other immigrants to be a captain for their own protection.[23] More than a year after Ahmanson filed his petition seeking compensation, a jury heard the evidence but was discharged when it could not reach a verdict. On 1 November 1861, another jury found in favor of Ahmanson and awarded him $1,297.50 in damages. The verdict is not surprising, considering the mood of the nation concerning the Mormons. Congress was debating the first anti-bigamy law at the same time the jury was listening to the evidence, which included disparaging comments about Mormon beliefs and practices. Brigham Young filed an appeal on 1 April 1863 with the Nebraska Territorial Supreme Court, but the court never considered the appeal since the parties settled the dispute for $1,000.[24]

[23] Pleadings filed with the Nebraska Territorial Supreme Court, 21 August 1863.
[24] Martin, "John Ahmanson vs. Brigham Young," 1–20.

Ahmanson wrote his memoirs in Danish and in 1876 published them in Omaha, almost twenty years after leaving Utah. He described his conversion to Mormonism in Aalborg, Denmark, the handcart ordeal, and his departure from Utah after a stay of four months. Most of Ahmanson's book concentrates on Mormon doctrine and history, but he included personal recollections of his experiences in Great Salt Lake City.[25]

JOHN A. AHMANSON, *VOR TIDS MUHAMED* [A MOHAMMED OF OUR TIME], 24–25, 35–37; 32–33, 44–46; 39–44, 52–55.
TRANSLATED BY GLEASON L. ARCHER.

On the eighth of December [1856] after passing over the Big Mountain we looked down for the first time on the valleys where the Lord's people had taken up residence, and where the promises which awaited them were to be fulfilled. Many forgot the tribulations they had endured upon glimpsing this sudden vista, and on the following day, which was a Sunday, we all broke formation, and as we exchanged expressions of eager anticipation we drove down speedily through the twelve miles of the long, snow-free Emigration Canyon to the great Salt Lake Valley, where we caught sight of Salt Lake City, seven miles distant, the capital city of Mormonism and Brigham Young. From that distance the city with its light gray adobe houses looked like a huge encampment, and the Salt Lake Valley, which had a breadth of about thirty miles from east to west, resembled a basin or dried up lake, with its huge mountain masses ranging upward on all sides.

Although the vegetation was now dead, and the eye of the observer met only a desolate treeless valley, surrounded by bare, reddish mountains, yet the impression made by the whole scene was still very pleasing. The climate was still mild and pleasant down there, and the enormous cliffs and mountain masses, which towered skyward on every side, gave way to an impressive, almost romantic, appearance.

In the afternoon our wagon train reached the city. As we came to a halt just in front of the palace of Brigham Young, the bishops and many of the ministers of the nearby Tabernacle came up. The prophet did not honor us with a personal visit; presumably he was ashamed to look upon our miserable and wretched condition, the result of his own shortsighted and ill-conceived plan, but he had bidden his bishops to hold themselves in

---

[25] This translation, with minor modifications, is by Gleason L. Archer and was published as *Secret History: A Translation of Vor Tids Muhamad* by Moody Press in 1984. Ahmanson had little impact on the image of Mormonism in Scandinavia compared to translated works by John W. Gunnison, Maria Ward, William Chandless, William Hepworth Dixon, and W. G. Marshall. See Mulder, *Homeward to Zion*, 68–69. A bookseller in Stockholm once assured me that the "classic" Utah travel account in Swedish was W. G. Marshall's *Genom America*, even though the author was British.

readiness for our arrival, in order to take care of billeting us in their various districts in the city. I myself was soon surrounded with several old acquaintances from Denmark who had been living for some time in Utah. They took me to their own homes with great friendliness—after my traveling companions (most of whom I saw for the last time) had been provided with lodging.

The last emigrant train of this year, namely Martin's Handcart Company, and the Independent Wagon Company to which my wife belonged, arrived at Salt Lake City on the seventeenth of December in a condition (if possible) even worse than our own. The wagon company had lost nearly all its draught animals and consequently had to leave their goods behind and their wagons as well along the way. They left some of them behind in Laramie, but the greater part of them were in Fort Bridger or by the Devil's Gate. It was one of the severest winters ever known. The snow lay a foot deep in the valleys and about two or three feet on the mountains. I had been very anxious about my wife and little son and tried in every way to get myself sent out with a departing relief train to meet them, but in vain. I only succeeded in sending a buffalo hide and a little coffee and sugar with the wagons, which were supposed to bring them to my wife and son. She received the buffalo hide but nothing else. On the seventeenth of December I went personally to meet the wagon company and reached them at the base of Little Mountain. Who could describe my joy at finding both of my dear ones in the best of health? Forgotten were the hardships of the journey and the long separation, and joyfully we drove in to Zion. . . .

In each of the districts of the city there is a meeting house, in which everyone has a right to step forward and give expression to his inner feelings; otherwise it is conducted by the bishop of the district. Bishop Wooley's meeting house was the one most respected in the city, because Brigham and many of the respected Mormon families belong to it, and there we paid our first visit to the meeting houses.[26] Something we got out of the visit was a proof for the claim that Mormonism possesses all of the spiritual gifts like the first Christian church, for there was a lady who stepped up from the audience and began to speak in a strange "tongue." She showed no sign of an unusual spiritual emotion and appeared to be quite calm, but it was impossible to understand a word of what she said. When she fell silent, the bishop stepped up and asked whether there was anyone to interpret the tongue? No, there was no one who had received "the gift of interpretation," and so the bishop said that although he would rather have understood the

---

[26] Ahmanson's bishop was Edwin D. Woolley (1807–1881), who oversaw Salt Lake's Thirteenth Ward, "one of the most prosperous, if not the most prosperous" in the LDS church. See Arrington, *From Quaker to Latter-Day Saint: Bishop Edwin D. Woolley*, 325.

"tongue" that the sister concerned had spoken in, yet he understood enough of it to know that "she had praised God in a foreign tongue!" Yet it is in a strange way that God distributes His gifts among these people, for a gift of speaking in tongues that no one understands should be regarded as a curiosity that our Lord would hardly concern Himself with. On the same evening an old, white-haired brother came forward as well who was full of the Spirit and related great visions and revelations which the Lord had shown him. He had seen "Zion besieged by the armies of the heathen," and he saw how their weapons and cannonballs fell harmlessly to earth. Then finally he had seen "one of Israel's warriors chase a thousand heathens in flight as in ancient times."

The third district in the city was made up of the so-called Danish District. The bishop there was a poor old American named Hill, who was married to two hefty young English women who were natural sisters.[27] His first counselor was an old acquaintance, Jensen—or Pottemager [Potter] Jensen, as he was called—from Horsholm in Denmark. Jensen was an honest man and highly regarded by the Danish population in Salt Lake City. His nature was steady and thoughtful, and his house stood in a pleasant open area where Danish heartiness and hospitality were still kept up, despite the harsh intolerance which invariably derives from Mormonism. Jensen made his living from ceramics and was a good businessman. . . .

The bishops stand immediately under Brigham Young's leadership and are chosen with regard to their unconditional reliability and obedience to him. They receive their instructions from the prophet and send in their reports to him, and like him they combine in themselves an authority both political and ecclesiastical. This is the political setup of the Mormons, but like all other despots the prophet has his secret police, or his private murder gangs completely compliant to his will, who in line with the rest of their sanctity are called "Danites" or "destroying angels"—Porter Rockwell and Bill Hickman have become notorious in the history of the Mormon community as the commanders of these gangs. The sinister feature about this system is that it is permeated by an inescapable spy system, which like a poisonous lizard slithers about and nourishes itself in every family. . . . The Yankees . . . sometimes have busied themselves idolizing Brigham Young because of the great material advances that Utah has made under his leadership. His administrative ability has been emphasized as something unique, which possibly outweighs the civil and spiritual slavery into which he has debased his people. But thousands of other men could

---

[27] This apparently was Isaac Hill (1806–79), a blacksmith and brick maker who converted to Mormonism in 1833 and served as bishop of Salt Lake's Second Ward from 1854 to 1864.

have done the same and accomplished the same results if they had been in Brigham Young's place and possessed his avid desire and impudent unscrupulousness. Brigham reaped the glory, but the poor, simple people who in their poverty and want have not only transformed a desert mountain country into a fertile land, but also a poor ignorant Yankee into a millionaire, are hardly ever thought of....

Even in regard to the faithful, the Church and the Prophet sometimes do not conduct themselves quite honorably in financial matters, as the reader will see from a few examples. In 1852 a lady named Fresne migrated from the island of Jersey to Utah. At her departure she had more money than necessary for the journey, and she offered the Church a loan of $2,500 for six months. The money was accepted with gratitude, and S. W. Richards, the agent of the Church in Liverpool, England, signed a pledge of repayment and a promissory note or bill of exchange drawn on Brigham Young for a specified sum. Upon her arrival in Salt Lake City the old lady presented the bill of exchange in the belief that the money would be repaid her with the willingness as she had lent it to them, but she was bitterly disappointed in this. The bill was neither acknowledged nor repaid, and when she requested an explanation, she was told that she could take a city lot with an old house on it; if she was not satisfied with that, she would get nothing. The lady registered objections, and they just laughed at her....

[When a Brother Wheelock asked about repayment of a loan,] he received the following ruling from the Prophet: "If an elder borrows money from you, and you find that he is in the process of forsaking the faith, then you can put the screws on him. But so long as he is ready to preach the Gospel without purse or script, then it is not up to you how he uses the money he borrows from you. The Lord wants money for them to spend; let it go and don't be concerned how he spends it. If you raise a complaint against this elder, it will be to your own condemnation. The money is not yours, but the Almighty gave it into your hands to see what you would do with it."

In reality Mormon doctrine itself is stripped of all Christian morality; it has only one great commandment: "blind, unconditional obedience" to the prophet and the leaders of the Church....

It was my decision to leave Utah in company with several compatriots and go to California early in the following year, but because of the fearsome threats that were constantly uttered in the Tabernacle and meeting houses against "apostates and heathens" from then on like an echo from mouth to mouth among the people, our decision was altered and we determined to travel back to the eastern States in company with the larger groups that were gathered in Salt Lake City and organized for mutual security.

Louis Bertrand, ca. 1870.
Image from The Improvement Era.

Louis Bertrand: Everyone Flew to Arms

Born at Roguevaire, near Marseille, France, on 8 January 1808, Jean-François Elie Flandin abandoned his religious studies at age sixteen to follow the sea to Brazil, China, and the U.S., where he became a citizen in 1832. Seven years later he returned to France and became interested in wine production. After living in Paris and Bordeaux, he spent four years in Guinea and four months in China. Flandin returned to Paris, where he began his association with Philippe Buchez's "cercle radical," studied Hoëné Wronski's "Messiamism," and became a disciple of Utopian socialist Etienne Cabet, known as "the pope of communism." Flandin was political editor of Cabet's *Le Populaire* and for unknown reasons adopted the nom-de-plume Louis Alphonse Bertrand before joining the Revolutionary Committee of 1848.[28] Cabet fled to America following Louis Napoléon's counterrevolution and established an Icarian community at Nauvoo, Illinois, in March 1849, while Louis Bertrand was imprisoned for three months.[29]

Apostle John Taylor and Curtis Bolton met Bertrand at the offices of *Le Populaire* in the fall of 1850. Taylor baptized Bertrand and five other converts

---

[28] Dominican Friar Preacher Louis Bertrand (1526–81) was born at Valencia, Spain. A popular preacher, he arrived in the New World at Cartagena in 1562. His reportedly converted ten thousand natives, who all "continued steadfast in their faith." He was ordered home seven years later, but his missionary work won him the title of "Apostle of South America." Clement X canonized St. Louis Bertrand in 1671.

[29] This sketch is based on Richard D. McClellan's excellent studies. See his BYU Honor's Thesis, "Louis A. Bertrand: One of the Most Singular and Romantic Figures of the Age"; and "Not Your Average French Communist Mormon: A Short History of Louis A. Bertrand," 3–24.

in the River Seine in December.[30] Bertrand was discharged from *Le Populaire* in November 1851 when Cabet returned to Paris following his unsuccessful communal experiment at Nauvoo. After the Bonapartist coup that killed one hundred revolutionaries and about thirty-five bystanders, Bolton fled Paris on 4 December 1851, having reported the "danger for Bro Bertrand for he was some years ago one of the head men of the revolution party of red republicans."[31]

When Louis Napoléon's war minister ordered John Taylor to leave France in December 1851, Bolton became mission president and Bertrand helped him complete the translation of the *Livre de Mormon*, which was published in January 1852. By the next year both Bolton and Bertrand followed other political refugees to the Isle of Jersey. Bolton soon left for Utah, but Bertrand remained for two years. Besides doing missionary work—he preached to Victor Hugo and his followers—he translated the *Doctrine and Covenants*, Parley P. Pratt's *A Voice of Warning*, Orson Pratt's *The Seer*, and a book of French hymns.[32]

Using the pen name Alexandre Erdan, Alexandre-André Jacob (1826–78) reported a conversation with a Mormon elder (either Bertrand or Bolton) at the time *The Book of Mormon* was published in France.

>   ALEXANDRE ERDAN, *LA FRANCE MYSTIQUE* [MYSTICAL FRANCE],
>   290–91. TRANSLATED BY HUGH MACNAUGHTON.
>
> It was at the time of the printing of the French translation of the Book of Mormons that I had a chance to see some of these Mormon adepts. I especially remember an interesting conversation between one of the heads of the French mission and my good friend, Marc Ducloux, the Huguenot printer [of the French edition of *The Books of Mormon*]. The conversation went a follows:
>
> *Marc Ducloux*: Really, you hope to be able to conquer this society?
>
> *Mormon Missionary*: I tell you that the WORK will dominate the world. There is more than one way to conquer the world, and we do not neglect any of these ways. Social truth belongs to us; it has to triumph.
>
> *Marc Ducloux*: What do you think of the accusation made against you that you condone polygamy? I must tell you that this is one of the things that most antagonizes our French Protestantism toward you.
>
> *Mormon Missionary*: Really! Isn't it correct that there have been and there still are other religions which, following in the foot steps of the Mosaic law, have permitted and still permit polygamy?

---

[30] Bertrand had a wife and two sons at the time of his baptism. None of them joined the LDS church or emigrated to Utah. [31] Bolton, Journal, 2 December 1851, LDS Archives.

[32] Bertrand to Erastus Snow, *St. Louis Luminary* (23 June 1855), 123.

Alexandre Erdan: Allow me one observation, Sir. I think it would be good politics, if one wants to establish a sect, to be severe regarding morality. Men, as hypocritical animals, have a tendency to join those who present severe theories to them, even though they do not put them into practice. It seems to me that Mormonism fails in this respect.

Mormon Missionary: What you say was true in the past for mankind, but it will be false in the future. We are entering a time when society will not allow sects to play with their earthly lives anymore. Society is in control of itself today. Society needs happiness: she will only follow those who will give her happiness.

Marc Ducloux and I stared at each other in astonishment and our eyes seemed to say: this is quite strange, quite outlandish, but really powerful!

It will be soon two years since this conversation took place. Poor Marc Ducloux, a noble suffering nature, has since passed on; as for me, who outlived him, I repeat what our eyes said that day: there is something truly powerful in this sentence: "MANKIND WANTS HAPPINESS: THEY WILL ONLY FOLLOW THOSE WHO WILL GIVE IT TO THEM."

Bertrand sailed from Liverpool aboard the *Chimborazo* in April 1855 and immigrated to Utah with help from the Perpetual Emigrating Fund. Stephen Malan and Jean Bertoch were in Mormon Grove (near Atchison, Kansas) during the same summer as the former French communist.[33] Bertrand settled in Great Salt Lake City as an ardent disciple of *"le pape des Mormons"* and began growing fruit trees. Emulating agronomist Agoston Haraszthy's dream of transplanting French grapes to California, Bertrand hoped to produce wine in Utah Territory, where the "Word of Wisdom" that now forbids Mormons to drink alcohol was not yet widely observed.[34]

Bertrand witnessed the unfolding drama of the Utah War. During 1858 he lived one block west of the new courthouse in Salt Lake's Fifteenth Ward, writing documents he predicted would be "copied & translated by every European daily paper."[35] He reported on the conflict in the French press and met its principal participants, including Albert Sidney Johnston, Alfred Cumming, and Thomas L. Kane, another product of French socialist thought.

---

[33] While Bertrand camped with Stephen Malan's mother in Kansas in July 1855, she "began to pronounce unintelligible sounds in an unknown tongue but naturally and without exaltation.... None of the persons present having understood her, she proceeded to give the interpretation of her prophecy herself in French." This was evidence that the "gift of tongues, of healing, and many others possessed by the early church do exist in our Church." See Bertrand, *Mémoires d'un Mormon*, 1078, as quoted in McClelland, "Louis Alphonse Bertrand," 47.

[34] Haraszthy, *Grape Culture, Wines, and Wine-making*. By the time Bertrand returned to Utah, his friend Haraszthy was operating "Buena Vista," the first commercial winery in California. Buena Vista is still a successful winery in Sonoma, but the Bartholomew Winery owns the original Haraszthy vineyard.

Bertrand had a unique insider's perspective on the Utah War and is the earliest account of the conflict from a Mormon perspective. He presents an entirely different interpretation of events than the one subsequently repeated in faith-promoting annals, which had a misunderstood Brigham Young working arduously to make peace.[36] The reality was quite different: according to Wilford Woodruff, Young feared the U.S. military no more than he would "an Armey of Grasshoppers." If the government tried to reinforce the Army of Utah, he planned to "use up this army first & then we will use up the others before they get to the South Pass." Young would "let the Army alone this winter. They will die many of them and others desert & many be weakened with the scurvey & in the spring we will wipe them out if necessary if they do not go away."[37] Bertrand's history reveals how close this aggressive campaign plan came to becoming a reality.

Bertrand returned to France in 1859 as mission president, reuniting with his wife and two children and visiting his extended family in Marseille. He traveled, continued writing for newspapers, and became active in French Freemasonry.[38] During his mission he wrote and published *Mémoires d'un Mormon*, which was primarily a missionary tract for Mormonism.[39] The book blasted French writers who had criticized the religion, including B. H. Révoil, Agénor de Gasparin, and even Jules Rémy.[40] Concerning Rémy he wrote:

---

[35] Bertrand to Young, [ca. January 1858] and 26 October 1858, Brigham Young Collection, LDS Archives.

[36] Arrington, *Brigham Young: American Moses*, 250–71, presents the traditional Mormon view of the conflict. The best works on the Utah War are Furniss, *The Mormon Conflict, 1850–1859*; and Bigler, *Forgotten Kingdom* and *Fort Limhi*.

[37] Woodruff, *Wilford Woodruff's Journal*, 5:114, 116.

[38] After Bertrand's return to Paris, the French press published occasional articles about Mormonism. See "Temples des Mormons," *Magasin pittoresque* (May 1859), 172–74; "Source Baptismale des Mormons," *Magasin pittoresque* (July 1859), 229–30.

[39] Bertrand, *Mémoires d'un Mormon*. The book was republished in Paris by E. Dentu and was reviewed in the *London Daily Telegraph* (15 May 1862); *The North American Review* (April 1863); Charles Dickens' *All the Year Round* (14 March 1863); and in French newspapers and periodicals. It was eventually reviewed in *The Improvement Era* 11 (December 1907), 80–89.

[40] Révoil wrote one of the first articles about Mormonism in France, "Souvenirs des Etats-Unis. Religions bizarres professées dans l'union américaine.—Les Mormons," *L'Illustration, Journal Universel*, 15:373 (20 April 1850), 251–52. See also ibid., 16: 393 (6–13 September 1850), 146. Révoil translated *Female Life among the Mormons*, attributed to "Maria Ward" but perhaps the work of Sarah Hollister Harris, wife of a former Utah territorial secretary, as *Les harems du Nouveau Monde*. Bertrand admitted that de Gasparin "had much to do with getting me to go and study on the spot the society of these 'religious bandits' in their dreadful lair of the Salt Lake. Thanks to Mr. de Gasparin, I know now, better than ever, what to think of the erroneous assertions he made against the Mormons." Bertrand also criticized reviews of Rémy's book: See the review of Hippolyte Taine, a prominent philosopher, in *Les Débats* (31 January 1861), and Elisée Reclus, in *Revue des deux-mondes* (15 April 1861).

"Three things struck me in this work: the laudable, though often infelicitous efforts of its author to remain impartial; the solemn praise he lavishes everywhere on the Mormons, but above all, the inanity of the arguments he produces to demonstrate the imposture of the founder of this religious organization. For him, Joseph Smith is nothing but a 'sort of rough-cut, gigantic Tartuffe,'[41] more curious than the other, but who, even though he may have done more wrong, is perhaps less worthy of scorn." But Bertrand admitted: "Now, were one simply to prune a few pages, his book could even be made to be a genuine apology. The history of the Mormons written by our tourist is generally accurate, except in a number of apocryphal inventions he was misguided enough to include, on the say-so of our enemies."[42]

Unable to build a church organization in France or even convert his wife and two sons, a disillusioned Bertrand decided to return to Utah in 1863. He settled thirty miles west of Salt Lake City in Tooele Valley, where he continued to write for Parisian newspapers, in particular *La Liberté*, and became involved in several unsuccessful commercial ventures.[43] He remained enthusiastic about his experiments with "a large 'Mormon' collection of hardy French and American grapes" that he believed would "produce fine table grapes, some excellent light wines, and other luscious raisins." Even though "Utah is now the tail of the United States," the French convert firmly believed "it will sooner or later become the head in everything: that is its 'manifest destiny.'" Bertrand was sure "our parent agricultural society will certainly make our mountain home the most flourishing fruit country on this continent."[44]

---

[41] Tartuffe was Molière's character who cloaks his villainous nature with shows of religion.

[42] Bertrand criticized Rémy for concluding, from the translation of the papyri by a young Egyptologist at the Louvre, that *The Book of Abraham* was not a literal translation: "[Devéria] found in [the papyri] only funeral rituals of Osiris. His interpretation, published synoptically with that of Joseph Smith, entirely differs from it. After that invocation of science, Mr. Rémy concludes triumphantly in these words: 'After the revelations I have just made, if the Mormons persist in believing that their prophet did not know how to lie, they will nevertheless concede that the divinatory power of the Urim-Thummim [Urim and Thummim] is not infallible. . .' But now that science has spoken, who can say to us that its verdict is final? Who will prove that the rules laid down by Champollion for deciphering the Egyptian glyphs are immutable? . . . It is premature and exaggerated to see in this secondary and somewhat obscure incident a scientific Waterloo of Mormonism." See Bertrand, *Mémoires d'un Mormon*, 217.

[43] Journal History, 8 June 1864 [*Millennial Star*, 26:414].

[44] Journal History, 16, 17 July 1868; *Deseret Evening News*, 16, 17 July 1868. Luther Hemenway, a grape enthusiast who resided in St. George, agreed with Bertrand that "excellent wine can be made in large quantities at moderate prices. The importance of the subject is not realized by our community." See Journal History, 18 January 1869.

Bertrand had sent silkworm eggs and a French manual to Swiss convert Octave Ursenbach, who used them to begin a silk industry in Salt Lake County. The first mulberry seeds were planted on Brigham Young's farm and in spring 1868 the church president directed the transplanting of about one hundred thousand trees. On his return, Bertrand operated a cocoonery and tried to find a cash market in France for Utah silkworm eggs. His commercial ventures were such notorious failures that he was referred to in the *Salt Lake Herald* as "a questionable expert in the silk line."[45]

Life in Utah must have been frustrating for the wifeless, childless, and aging Bertrand. The *Deseret News* reported in March 1875 that he had lost his mind, and Bertrand died, apparently with his mental state restored, at age 67 on 21 March 1875.[46] His dream of producing Utah wine from transplanted French grapes ended with his death, but his remarkable life and memoirs continue to illustrate the forgotten appeal of nineteenth-century Mormonism to radical intellectuals.

LOUIS BERTRAND, *MÉMOIRES D'UN MORMON* [MEMORIES OF A MORMON],
117–24 TRANSLATED BY GASTON CHAPPUIS;
196, 207, 208–11, 216–17, 224–26
TRANSLATED BY HUGH MACNAUGHTON.

On July 24, 1857, Mormons celebrated the tenth anniversary of their entry in the Valley in one of the most scenic canyons of the Wasatch Mountains. Gathered there were representatives of all the nations of the Old and New worlds. During the proceedings two riders covered with dust brought important news. In thirteen days these two men had crossed the distance of four hundred leagues separating the Missouri from Salt Lake City. Their first news was of the departure of a division of federal troops from Fort Kearney [*sic*] to chasten the Mormons; the other was the suspension of all mail traffic beyond the Rocky Mountains ordered by the cabinet at Washington. The last measure was considered by us a real declaration of war. . . .

In answer to this energetic call everyone flew to arms. The elite of our youth went to the threatened border, and the capital of the Saints, a truly pastoral city, became an armed camp overnight. The Utah militia, comprising all men from eighteen to forty-five years of age, form a special military organization called the Nauvoo Legion numbering approximately sixteen thousand combatants. We already possess the elements of a respectable

---

[45] *Salt Lake Herald*, 25 June 1870. For the silk industry, see Arrington, "The Finest of Fabrics: Mormon Women and the Silk Industry in Early Utah," 376–96.

[46] Journal History, 11, 22 March 1875; *Deseret Evening News*, 22 March 1875.

army. We have some artillery and even a body of topographical engineers.[47] The excellence of our horses and the fine horsemanship of the Mormons constitutes the greatest strength of our militia. A peculiar thing about our military organization is the fact that both officers and men are expected to arm, equip, and even feed themselves at their own expense, so that the upkeep of our militia, in peace as in war, does not cost the Church one penny. . . .

Our best troops had been directed toward Echo Canyon. There, under the direction of Daniel Wells, commanding officer of the Nauvoo Legion, they scattered along the trail, occupying all the strongest positions throughout the winter. Some important defensive preparations were immediately undertaken at various points in order to make the position impregnable. . . .

Day after day the march of the federal troops became more and more laborious. Snow soon added to their difficulty. Since the region occupied by the troops ran three thousand feet higher than the level of Salt Lake, it was much more exposed to cold and blizzards than our valley. Soon they were buried in four feet of snow. Their animals died by the hundreds from starvation. Then came discouragement, insubordination, lack of water and food, sickness and all plagues broke loose at the same time in the army of invasion. By deserting, a sizeable number of the soldiers found a comfortable home for the winter among us. But the chances of desertion were slim as an active watch was maintained by the officers. In all European countries it is the soldiers who guard the officers; the opposite is true in the army of the United States, where non-commissioned officers, and even commissioned officers, keep watch night and day to prevent desertion from the ranks.

This unhappy expedition would have been blotted out of existence had not Colonel Johnston, replacing General Harney in command, directed [Colonel Edmund] Alexander to come back to Fort Bridger. His return was a real disaster because of the intense cold and abundant snow. After untold and useless sufferings, the colonel finally arrived back at his starting point.[48] From then on the campaign was over to all intents and purposes. Without having burned a single cap and leaving our adversaries just enough food to keep them from starving, we rendered them powerless to hurt us. A column of a thousand men selected from neighboring villages had already taken position along the Weber to watch the enemy's movements and prevent any attempt at invasion

---

[47] In January 1858, Adjutant General James Ferguson reported the Nauvoo Legion consisted of 6,004 troops, of whom about 2,000 were prepared for combat. Chief of Ordinance Thomas Ellerbeck reported the poor state of the Legion's armaments and ammunition supplies on 14 January 1858. See Nauvoo Legion Papers, Beinecke Library.

[48] The army actually marched to a camp on Hams Fork and then proceeded for the first time to Fort Bridger, which the Mormons had burned. The army built Camp Scott, its winter quarters, a short distance up Blacks Fork.

from the north. These men were all released. The body of our active army, numbering about six thousand infantrymen and three hundred horsemen, returned to their cantonments along the impregnable Echo defile....

The cabinet at Washington issued secret instructions containing some pitiless orders for the expedition launched against the saints. Here is a summary of them: take Brigham Young, his two counselors, the twelve apostles, and our most eminent men to the first convenient trees and hang them without any process of law, then proceed with a mass extermination of their followers and sack and burn the whole territory, thus extirpating forever the leprosy of Mormonism from the soil of the United States....[49]

Upon his arrival at Fort Bridger, General Johnston proceeded to put his soldiers on half rations. This drastic measure lasted for seven months. Certain American newspapers bitterly upbraided President Buchanan for having rewarded that officer's inaction with a promotion to general. It must be said in his behalf however that whatever his instructions may have been, lacking as he was in means of transportation and closely watched by our forward posts, Johnston truly was not in a position to take any offensive action. As early as the latter part of November, he was already compelled to send Captain Marcy to New Mexico to fetch horses and mules. A few days later Colonel Cooke arrived from Kansas with the second regiment of dragoons, serving as escort to Mr. Albert Cumming, the newly appointed Governor of Utah by the federal Government. This regiment arrived in a pitiable state. It had crossed the Rocky Mountains through the snows and had lost more than a third of its horses and a good portion of its baggage....[50]

January and February 1858 were spent in making our last war preparations. The only task unfulfilled was the organization of an armed body large enough to take the offensive in the spring. Twelve squadrons of mounted riflemen of one hundred each were recruited and equipped in a few days. Each supplied with two horses, a revolver and carbine, and sufficient food for six months, these twelve hundred cavalrymen, the cream at our youth, constituted an imposing elite force.[51] Our campaign plan was as follows;

---

[49] Mormon leaders were firmly convinced the Utah Expedition received such "secret instructions," but the army's subsequent conduct contradicts such charges. As Capt. Stewart Van Vliet explained to them in September 1857, the army's intent was "to form the Territory of Utah into a military department, similar in all respects to the Military Department of New Mexico, the Pacific, and other geographical Military districts into which are country has been subdivided." See Hafen, ed., *The Utah Expedition*, 39.

[50] Johnston reduced his army's rations but maintained high morale among his troops, who suffered few privations.

[51] Bertrand described the Standing Army of Israel, which the territorial legislature created to serve as a full-time professional army. Mormon historians have ignored the existence of this remarkable unit, which was the brainchild of Brigham Young. See Young to Wells, Taylor, and Smith, 17 October 1857, Brigham Young Collection, LDS Archives. The Standing Army remains "one of a kind in American military history." See Bigler, *Forgotten Kingdom*, 183–84.

seize South Pass to intercept any reinforcement of troops and supplies coming from the United States through this channel; assign two squadrons to the task of overtaking the horses and mules Captain Marcy was to bring back from New Mexico; then resume positions along Devil's Gate, that steep mountain chasm straddling the road just ahead of the Sweetwater and offering a series of formidable strategic points. This plan, as simple as it was practical, would no doubt have been crowned with success... [General Johnston] would have found himself in the dire necessity at surrendering without even the satisfaction of having fired a single cap. But fortunately for the honor of American arms, the intervention of the political enemies of President Buchanan radically changed our war plans.

On February 21 [1858], Colonel Kane, using the name of Dr. Osborne, arrived from Washington by way of Panama and San Francisco on a mission to feel out Brigham Young and to prepare a settlement.[52] After having exposed the object of his secret mission to our governor and assured himself of the latter's intentions, he immediately left for Fort Bridger, where he literally fell as a bombshell in the midst of federal officers. Let us leave him to struggle with our uncivil conquerors and let us see what impression his visit left upon the mind of Brigham Young.

A few days after the departure of the Washington envoy, our twelve squadrons of mounted riflemen were discharged to the great discontent of our saber wielders. Measures of a totally different nature were adopted. On March 21, a special conference was convened in the Tabernacle where Brigham Young revealed to us in a remarkably clear discourse his new plan of action.[53] It involved a series of dispositions affecting the whole Territory. All eventualities had been carefully foreseen, all measures dictated in advance. Here is a summary of them: evacuate all our northern settlements as well as the valley of Great Salt Lake, the population to proceed southward in strong columns toward the Mexican province of Sonora. Provo, our largest southern city, became the pivot and central point of our rendezvous. But it was little enough to thus abandon the fruits of twelve years of labor. It was unanimously agreed that houses, palaces, public buildings, small cottages, fruit trees, shade trees, fences, woods, hay stacks, grass and feed of all kinds—in a word, anything that could burn—would be consigned to ashes at the time of departure. The Deseret News, in its official column,

---

[52] Thomas L. Kane, son of a powerful Pennsylvania federal judge, was an old political ally of the Mormons. He carried letters of recommendation from James Buchanan, but Kane had no authority to represent the government or to conduct negotiations.

[53] Young's remarks in Watt, *A Series of Instructions and Remarks by President Brigham Young at a Special Council, Tabernacle, March 21, 1858*, came after the Mormon offensive strategy collapsed upon learning that Shoshone and Bannock bands had attacked the remote LDS settlement at Fort Limhi. See Bigler, *Forgotten Kingdom*, 186–87.

announced the decision: "In a general conference, held in the Tabernacle on the 21st of this month, it has been unanimously agreed to abandon Sebastopol to our enemies if they persist in following the unconstitutional policy of the present administration."

It became morally difficult to make war against a people who announce to the whole world their intention of burning from thirty to forty million dollars worth of property, the fruits of twelve years of work, with such laconic and stoic indifference. To want to subdue such resolute men, capable of conceiving and executing such a plan, is like attempting to put out Vesuvius with a glass of water.

After a short stay in the federal camp, the president's envoy one day told Governor Cumming: "Leave here all this war paraphernalia, these cannons, these carbines, these revolvers, just take a tooth pick with you. I will see that you conquer the impregnable Territory of Utah, Brigham Young, the Twelve Apostles, the two priesthoods, and all the polygamous and non-polygamous Mormons." And they left alone on horseback. When they arrived at our forward posts, a guard of honor of twenty horsemen escorted them to our general Headquarters, established in a grotto, toward the center of our Thermopylae. They reached it by nightfall and were nearly famished. But an excellent dinner awaited them: all the delicacies imaginable, domestic and imported, were served: this meal was all the more welcome since for five months His Excellency had been reduced to skimpy rations.

Following this banquet, a concert of vocal and instrumental music was improvised to celebrate the arrival of our new Governor. Deseret, too, has its poets, among whom we must mention Miss Eliza Snow, the pearl of our local bards; and William G. Mills, who has given us an admirable translation of La Marseillaise and a war song that has become extremely popular in the army.[54] His Excellency was honored with all our artistic productions inspired since we rose up in arms. A curious episode fitly concluded this celebration. At about ten o'clock, numerous fires, simultaneously lighted on the highest peaks of these fairy mountains, suddenly flooded the entire area of our Thermopylae. Thereafter salvoes fired by the troops followed by deafening hurrahs, and band music multiplied by echoes, climaxed this celebration. At a given signal burning coals, reminiscent of erupting volcanoes, were suddenly thrust down from the highest peaks overlooking the defile, thus forming a double cascade of flames, Finally the blaze became general and constituted the climax of these giant fireworks whose reflection upon the abrupt and arid slopes produced an indescribable effect. . . .

---

[54] Eliza Snow was a widow of Joseph Smith and plural wife of Brigham Young. William G. Mills, a member of the Salt Lake's short-lived musical and literary Polysophical Society (which ended when Jedediah Grant denounced it as "a stink in my nostrils") had sailed with Bertrand on the *Chimborazo* and kept the official record of the voyage.

On Sunday April 28, the Prophet solemnly presented the new Governor to the congregation at the Tabernacle. In his first address, Mr. Cumming declared modestly that he was not an orator and that, not being accustomed to public speaking, he would merely limit himself to state that President Buchanan's objective in sending a military expedition to Utah was not intended in any way to molest the Mormons but to establish posts over the Territory to protect its inhabitants against the Indians. This strange declaration provoked a burst of laughter throughout the audience, whereupon the Governor invited those present to freely address their opinions before him. One of our merchants, Mr. G. [Gilbert] Clements, an Irishman, immediately arose and expressed the feeling of the assembly in regards to our difficulties with the Federal Government. His discourse, faithfully rendering the universal opinion of the citizens present, was often interrupted by enthusiastic applause.

Mr. Cumming sought to mitigate these charges, but John Taylor, one of our best orators, refuted the assertions of His Excellency. However, soon overtaken by the general enthusiasm and overcome by his own feelings, he was unable to continue his discourse. Last eyewitness and survivor of the murder of Joseph Smith, himself the victim of atrocious persecutions suffered by the Mormons in Missouri and Illinois, Taylor had been unable to dwell upon those sad memories without deep emotion. The Tabernacle was no longer a calm and peaceful assembly, listening worshipfully to the admonitions of our prophets. The clumsiness of the governor had momentarily transformed it into an uproarious political rally. But Brigham Young arose and went to the pulpit. He pronounced a few sentences and this stormy sea was calmed at once. Whereupon Mr. Cumming had a document read by which he invited all dissatisfied persons to address themselves to him to obtain means of transportation to return to the States. Fifty-three persons, including thirty children, requested his protection and took the road back to the States.[55]

I was very anxious to meet Colonel Kane. I found him deeply grieved at the news of the death of his father, once one of the most enlightened magistrates of Philadelphia. The Colonel was sorely tried by this loss, suddenly added to that of Doctor Kane, his brother, famous for his travels in the arc-

---

[55] Some sources charged that the vaunted "Move South" was carried out at gunpoint and that a "secret guard" kept Governor Cumming isolated from unhappy Mormons. James W. Simonton reported that an emigrant company from Salt Lake sought refuge with the army on 1 June 1858. "They are unanimous in the declaration that the United States troops would never have met with any serious opposition in attempting to enter the Valley, and that if protection should be afforded to them by the troops, fully one-half the entire Mormon community would embrace the opportunity to flee." Simonton contended these apostates felt Cumming had been "utterly deceived" about the number of those who wanted to leave Utah. See Simonton, "Letter from the Army of Utah," *San Francisco Evening Bulletin*, 21 July 1858, 3/2–4.

tic regions.⁵⁶ I was struck by his small stature: it was practically that of Louis Blanc.⁵⁷ A political writer of note, Mr. Kane had begun his diplomatic career at the American Embassy of General [Lewis] Cass in Paris. For a long time, he was correspondent of the newspaper *Le National.* This is enough to show that he is very familiar with the French language. After fifteen minutes of conversation we were already old acquaintances. He showed himself full of goodwill toward the Saints in general. In our private conversation he was quite communicative. His mission to Utah, at the direction of President Buchanan, was not of an official nature. The secret instructions given to the federal troops had truly been of a ruthless nature. But time has not come to say any more on this subject. The following day I had the privilege of lunching with the Colonel and Governor Cumming. I was for both of them the object of an intense curiosity. Born in the State of Georgia and one of the most influential members of the Democratic party, Mr. Cumming promptly won the love of his new constituents because of his integrity and mildness of character. . . .

The first dispatch received by Mr. Buchanan from his envoy prompted him to take a forthright decision. As soon as he learned that the saints really intended to burn everything of value in Mormondom and were actively engaged in evacuating once more the territory of the United States, he refused, as our ex-governor had foreseen, to accept the moral responsibility for this catastrophe which would have been en eternal blemish upon his administration. He finally decided to close the affair just where he should have begun, that is by sending two commissioners, Senator [Lazarus W.] Powell and Major MacCulloch [Benjamin McCulloch], with a long proclamation. He magnanimously offered us full and complete amnesty. This proclamation will remain in history as the strangest mystification any President of the United States, from the days of George Washington, ever foisted upon the American people. It contained but a single truth, which I give here translated literally: "During the journey of the United States troops, an unprotected convoy of wagons was attacked and destroyed by a corps of Mormons with all food and ammunitions burned."⁵⁸

To give more weight to his threat of general emigration, Brigham had

---

⁵⁶ Elisha Kent Kane (1820–57) was a national hero because of his participation in polar expeditions. He was secretly married to Margaret Fox, who, with her sister, is credited with ushering in modern spiritism in 1847 in Hydesville, New York.

⁵⁷ French writer Jean-Joseph-Charles-Louis Blanc (1811–82) was a leading socialist theorist and spokesman for the provisional government of 1848, but his enemies used his short stature to caricature him as "that king of gnomes."

⁵⁸ Buchanan's proclamation read, "While the troops of the United States were on their march, a train of baggage wagons, which happened to be unprotected, was attacked and destroyed by a portion of the Mormon forces, and the provisions and stores with which the train was laden were wantonly burned." See Hafen, ed., *The Utah Expedition,* 334.

given orders to begin its execution. The President's commissioners found the city of Salt Lake almost entirely deserted. Barring four hundred men charged with the task of watering the gardens, all its inhabitants together with those of our northern counties had abandoned everything to gather around the church leaders at Provo. A population of more than eighty thousand souls was gathered there with its flocks, ready to emigrate toward the province of Sonora. Among these choice souls, there were some who had already sacrificed their welfare and possessions four or five times for the sake of their religious convictions. We understand why in this century of selfishness, in which the worship of the golden calf has become universal, such behavior has been labeled fanaticism. But the spectacle of a people ready to leave its new homes, to burn these comfortable dwellings and all its properties to push on four hundred leagues farther into the desert to create a new haven where it will be able to worship God according to the dictates of its own conscience; yea such a spectacle as this in the middle of the nineteenth century merits a pause for reflection.

Fortunately, the more conciliatory dispositions of the Government spared us this sacrifice. On the 11th of June our chief leaders returned to Salt Lake. The following day a meeting was held in Council-House between the federal commissioners, members of our legislature, and the leaders of the Church. The session was a long and a stormy one; the conduct of President Buchanan brought forth unrestrained expressions of censure. Having to withstand the perorations of our Volga boatmen, the envoys from Washington were treading upon hot coals. Agreement could not be reached upon a single point. But at the conclusion of this session, the commissioners solicited a personal interview with Brigham Young. The latter went to the Globe Hotel with his two counselors and peace preliminaries were signed during a secret session that evening. It was agreed that to safeguard the honor of the federal government and to preserve appearances, our troops would evacuate Echo Canyon and the American army would cross the city without stopping and would camp beyond its limits.[59]

The following day the morning session at Council-House was public. . . For an hour and a half [Brigham Young] held his listeners spellbound. In closing he stated: "For twenty years men have put a price on my head, yet it is still solidly fastened to my neck, perhaps more so than that of any other man living. Before I die, I shall see the entire universe vainly beleaguered against Mormonism; it has been revealed to me from above."

---

[59] Sen. Lazarus W. Powell and Maj. Benjamin McCulloch, a hero of the Texas Revolution, carried a presidential pardon for sedition and treason to take effect if the Mormons accepted the territorial officials, as well as a promise not to interfere with their religion. The commissioners refused to negotiate with the Mormons, who grudgingly accepted the terms. See Furniss, *The Mormon Conflict*, 195–96.

A word here about this "first pope of the Mormons." Worthy successor of Joseph though not quite so literate, he exercises a moral dictatorship over his people the likes of which one would vainly seek elsewhere in the world today. If he lives another fifteen years, he will accomplish political miracles unlooked for by European nations. Physically, he is a man of medium height. Though sixty-one years old, he appears to be barely fifty because of his blond hair and his robust but calm appearance. His diet is the same as that of the first Christian hermits. He is a perfect gentleman, very distinguished in manner and conversation. He has all the natural gifts, all the perfections of eloquence; his gesture is graceful, his elocution distinct, his voice is deep and very agreeable. He is expert in the handling of irony, but his charity knows no bounds, his tolerance for political opinions and toward other faiths is beyond belief. No man has ever had more devoted friends here on earth. The authority of Moses was constantly challenged by the descendants of Jacob while he was yet alive. That of Brigham over modern Israel is sovereign and limitless. Much has been said lately of his unbounded ambition, of his political and religious despotism. These declarations are totally lacking in truth. In one of our last semi-annual conferences he has publicly declared that he considered the designation of prophet, seer and revelator as being merely honorary titles. It is absolutely true that though his word is considered as the word of God by all the Saints, he has never uttered any prophecy that has become law to the Church. He frequently states that Mormons have enough revelations to damn themselves, unless they heed them. As for his alleged political ambitions, the future alone will tell. . . .

Chapter 4

"But Brigham Young is Still Governor"
Mormonism's Secular Control, 1859–69

The Utah War ended when Brigham Young recognized the authority of Alfred Cumming, the newly appointed territorial governor, and grudgingly accepted President Buchanan's "free pardon for the seditions and treasons" committed during Utah's "rebellion against the United States."[1] Nevertheless, Cumming correctly observed that "Brigham Young is still governor of the people."[2] Yet even in his new role as *de facto* ruler of Utah, Young could not perpetuate the isolation his people had enjoyed for more than a decade after their arrival. Following 1858 there was a dramatic and steadily growing influx of soldiers, merchants, railroad workers, miners, and visitors into the territory.

The Civil War initially diverted the nation's attention from the Mormons, but in 1862 U.S. Army volunteers from California arrived in the territory to keep a watchful eye on Brigham Young and his followers. The Republican Congress passed wide-ranging legislation that transformed not only Utah but the American West: the Homestead Act redefined land distribution in the territories; the Railroad Act funded the transcontinental railroad that opened the West to the world and sharply increased the number of visitors to Utah; and the Morrill anti-bigamy act fired the first shot in a thirty-year battle to force the Mormon hierarchy to abandon polygamy.

During the next decade a parade of prominent writers visited Utah Territory, and their accounts would have an enduring impact on the territory's

---
[1] Hafen, ed., *The Utah Expedition*, 336.
[2] Stenhouse, *The Rocky Mountain Saints*, 445.

image.[3] In 1859 *Harper's Weekly*, which had a circulation of over 100,000 subscribers, commissioned Horace Greeley, the editor of the *New York Tribune*, to interview Brigham Young and write his impressions of Utah. During his almost three-week stay in Salt Lake, the Mormons convinced Greeley that, although misguided, they were not charlatans, and that they would eventually abandon polygamy and survive as a monogamous religion.[4]

One year later, Capt. Richard Francis Burton, the renowned British explorer, visited the territory for three weeks in August 1860 and published his observations in *The City of the Saints*, the most influential European volume ever written about the Mormons. Burton was the most prominent traveler who was drawn to Utah by the practice of plural marriage. He spoke with sinners, Saints, and Gentiles. Although he expressed admiration for Brigham Young, he admitted that the Mormons had "an inner life into which I cannot flatter myself or deceive the reader with the idea of having penetrated." In the wake of the Utah War, he sensed a "gloom" at Great Salt Lake City. One of Burton's biographers believed "*The City of the Saints* is one of his best works but it is sadly overlooked."[5] Few travelers have matched Burton's intellectual curiosity, natural instincts, and background. *City of the Saints* was translated and published in many European languages and set a high standard for all subsequent travelers who wrote about the Mormon Kingdom. And yet, some reviewers were very critical of Burton's "liberal" views on polygamy.

Samuel Clemens, soon to write under the nom de plume of Mark Twain, passed through Utah in 1861 with his brother Orion,[6] and in 1864 Charles

---

[3] Other Americans who helped create Mormonism's national image during the 1860s include Fitz Hugh Ludlow in 1864; Samuel Bowles in 1865; Alexander Kelly McClure in 1867; and John Todd in 1869. The less-prominent James Knox Polk Miller read Burton and, wanting to "deserve the name of 'traveler'" worked in Salt Lake City during the winter of 1864–65. Neither Mormon services in the tabernacle nor theatrical productions in the Social Hall impressed him, but Orrin Porter Rockwell did, although Miller's claim to have encountered the illiterate gunman reading Burton's description of him is suspect. See Rolle, ed., *The Road to Virginia City*, 33–62. British travelers included William Hepworth Dixon and Sir Charles Wentworth Dilke in 1866; William A. Bell and Frederick Trench Townshend in 1868; and Frederick Whymper in 1869.

[4] Greeley, *An Overland Journey*, 218, 238, 241. Greeley predicted that "there will be a new revelation, ere many years, whereby the saints will be admonished to love and cherish the wives they already have, but not to marry any more beyond the natural assignment of one wife to one husband." Ibid., 241.

[5] Rice, *Captain Sir Richard Francis Burton*, 431.

[6] Although he visited Salt Lake City in 1861, Twain's observations were not published until 1872 in *Roughing It*.

Farrar Browne, whose pen name was Artemus Ward, performed his one-man show "Among the Mormons" at the Salt Lake House.[7] During the summer of 1865 the speaker of the House of Representatives, Schuyler Colfax, visited the territory accompanied by two reporters, Albert Richardson of the *New York Tribune* and Samuel Bowles of the *Springfield* (Mass.) *Republican*, to gauge Mormon attitudes in the wake of the Civil War. According to Richardson, Brigham Young convinced several of his colleagues that polygamy would be allowed to die a natural death. "I do not say that he willfully deceived us," Richardson later admitted, "but he certainly gave us this idea."[8]

Virtually every subsequent visitor to the Mormon West consulted the accounts of these travelers and humorists.[9] In addition, new guides, such as John C. Van Tramp's 1866 *Prairie and Rocky Mountain Adventures*, encouraged travelers to visit the attractions of Salt Lake City. Meanwhile French, Italian, and German travel writers provided a curious audience in continental Europe with exotic descriptions of Utah and the Mormons.[10] Among them was Olympe de Joaral Audouard, who in 1868 was the first European woman to visit Utah who recorded her experiences. This crucial decade witnessed increasingly significant alterations in the territory's population and culture, and at its end the arrival of the railroad opened the floodgates of change.

---

[7] Ward did not visit Utah Territory until 1864, but he began performing his famous show about his "visit" to the Mormons in 1860, while his published version of the same, "A Visit to Brigham Young," appeared in *Artemus Ward: His Book* in 1862. When he finally visited Utah he was quite concerned about "having my swan-like throat cut by the Danites" because of his "wholesale denunciation of a people I had never seen," but he was reassured by T. B. H. Stenhouse. See Hingston, *The Genial Showman*, 282–336.

[8] "A Mormon Trouble Brewing—Seditious Preaching in Salt Lake City," *Rochester Daily Democrat* 33:504 (14 November 1865).

[9] Burton's *City of the Saints* was published in France, Spain, and Italy, while Dixon's works appeared in Germany and France. Mayne Reid's most famous Mormon tale, *Les deux filles du squatter*, appeared in French. Other accounts of Mormonism in English by less-known authors such as Samuel Griswold Goodrich's *Les Etats-Unis d'Amérique*, were occasionally translated and distributed on the continent.

[10] French monk Emmanuel Henri Domenech mentioned Utah and the Mormons in several books; see his *Journal d'un missionnaire au Texas et au Mexique*, which appeared in English as *Missionary Adventures in Texas and Mexico*, 339; and his *Voyage pittoresque dans les grands déserts du Nouveau Monde*, which was published in English as *Seven Years' Residence in the Great Deserts of North America*, 192–99. Italian writer Gustavo Strafforello adapted a German text by Federico di Hellwald in *America Settentrionale secondo le notizie più recenti*. Strafforello included graphics from a French translation of Burton's *City of the Saints* and added a short history of the Mormons, claiming they were the most important social and political sect in the United States since they had created "a state within a state." Ibid., 135.

Israel Joseph Benjamin:
The Heart of Mormon Country

Jewish writer and traveler Israel Joseph Benjamin (1818–1864) was born in Falticeni, Moldavia, in 1818. Beginning in the late 1840s he traveled to the Far East, Middle East, and Russia to discover the lost ten tribes. He visited the U.S in 1859 to investigate the conditions of Jewish communities, and in 1861 he arrived in San Francisco after a brief trek across Panama. Benjamin passed through Salt Lake that summer while returning to the East by overland trail.[11] Within a few years of his return to Europe, Benjamin died in London in 1864.

As Benjamin reported, there were Jews living in Utah Territory at the time of his visit. Solomon N. Carvalho, the artist in John C. Frémont's 1853–54 expedition, was among the first Jews to visit the territory.[12] Julius Gerson Brooks and his wife Fanny arrived in Utah in 1854 and later were the first Jews to settle permanently in the territory. In 1858, Nicholas S. Ransohoff was one of the first non-Mormon merchants to establish a store in Salt Lake City, and an increasing number of Jewish settlers arrived in the aftermath of the Civil War. They played a prominent role in civic and cultural life and were among the first Freemasons and Odd Fellows in Utah Territory.[13]

> Israel Benjamin, *Drei Jahre in Amerika, 1859–1862*
> [Three Years in America], 46–48, 83–84. Translated by TSC.
>
> Early on the afternoon of July 15th I arrived in Salt Lake City, the heart of Mormon country. I sent my calling card to President Brigham Young, the current leader of the sect, and was invited for a visit that same evening. His two-story house is located in a sort of yard surrounded by a wall that is half as high as the house itself. His office and parlor are, of course, found on the ground floor while his private living quarters and harem are on the upper floor. There are other buildings behind the house where a beautiful garden appears to be located. The emblem of the Mormons, a beehive (or Deseret as it is called in the prophecies of the Mormons), is affixed to its roof. A doorman stands guard in front of the house.
>
> I found Brigham Young to be a healthy, robust and slightly portly sixty-year-old man of average height. He has a closely-trimmed red beard with

---

[11] Wagner, Camp, and Becker, *The Plains and the Rockies*, 653–54.

[12] Carvalho, *Incidents of Travel and Adventure in the Far West*.

[13] Watters, *The Pioneer Jews of Utah*, 16–21, 42–43; and Stone, *A Homeland in the West: Utah Jews Remember*, 1–12.

Israel Joseph Benjamin (1818–64) was a Jewish traveler who visited Utah and spoke with Brigham Young in 1861. *Special Collections, J. Willard Marriott Library, University of Utah.*

some gray already mixed in it. American-born, he speaks only English. His facial features reveal a lot of courage and enterprising spirit. His attitude towards strangers is very friendly and courteous, particularly towards Hebrews, who are called Brother Jews by members of the sect. A few Jews have joined his church. According to their assertions, the Mormons are descendants of the ten tribes, particularly the tribe of Ephraim. I indicated to him the falseness of this assertion by making a number of pointed counter-arguments, one in particular being that the sect is composed of people issuing from the greatest variety of countries and nationalities, namely of Englishmen, Americans, Swedes, and Germans. In answer to this, he was only able to refer me to the divine revelations he has received. I spent a full hour with him, our conversation dealing only with religious topics. As he had already become acquainted with my name and the purpose of my trip through the newspapers and saw that it was my sincere intention to devote a section of my travel book about California to a thorough and unbiased description of the history and beliefs of his Church, I could not give myself permission to express myself as freely to this friendly man as I would have liked. Rather, I requested and was willingly given permission to use all historically significant documents about the Mormons.

Afterwards, I spent another hour and a half speaking with a few apostles. Through information provided by members of his church, I discovered that Brigham had hardly received any academic or general schooling in his youth. In fact, I was even assured that for a long time he had been unable to write even a single word, and the Mormons claim that he became very educated by means of special revelations from God. I replied that I could not accept any of this as being true, but was most sincerely willing to admit that a man who can keep together a religious society of 70 to 80,000 people from the greatest variety of nationalities and languages must be most gifted by nature. As just mentioned, his followers believe him to be a prophet. This is, in fact, one of their most important articles of faith and they therefore believe that he does not do anything without receiving a specific revelation.

Of course, I could not very well go and inspect his harem, but in this respect I felt I had been taken back to the Asian continent, for I got to see as little of the ladies of the house in Utah as I had in the Orient. The women very rarely go out. Mr. Young has a total of fifty-two children and thirteen wives. The ten of his children whom I saw ranged from eight to twelve years in age. Absolutely none of them had handsome features, nor were any of them appropriately dressed. Even so, I did see the wives of other Mormons, including some of the Apostles. There was nothing remarkable about their clothing aside from their hats which had very far protruding visors or sides, presumably to protect their faces from inquisitive glances or from the sun. A Mormon who does not hold a church office is not required to have more than one wife. Officials of the church, on the other hand, such as presidents, apostles, bishops, elders, etc., are bound by religious law to have at least two wives. Most women who share one husband do not live very peaceably together. They are treated very well by their husbands. However, as within many Oriental societies, in proven cases of infidelity, they are quietly dispatched from this life. This information is based on a reliable source and, indeed, such cases have already occurred....

The population of Salt Lake City numbers somewhere between 13 and 15,000. Only a few of the residents, mostly Americans, are not members of the sect. Five Israelites reside here, two of whom profess to being members of the sect. The other three are merchants who have thriving businesses. In general, however, there is little business trade in this city, for most residents are farmers.

As we have already mentioned, the city is the capital of the Utah Territory. It has a very beautiful courthouse and the governor's residence. It covers an area two miles long by two miles wide. The houses are very attractive and are mostly surrounded by trees and gardens. It is laid out into 45 streets. There are water channels along both sides that allow dirt to be easily removed. A bishop is in charge of each of the 20 wards into which it is divided. Each ward has a public school. All of the schools are built in the same style. The air here is very healthy. In general, summer is very warm with few rainy days. Winter is very snowy and lasts for about three months. The city has two theaters, one large and the other small. A third, which is becoming quite grandiose and beautiful, is still under construction.[14] There are two weekly newspapers, one political and one ecclesiastical, which could not be published during my stay because of a paper shortage. . . .

The eighty-mile long and forty-mile wide Salt Lake is fifteen miles to the west of the city. At its center, there is a whirlpool. It definitely earns its name, for its water is so salty that no living creature can be found in it and three barrels of its water yield one barrel of salt. There are several islands in the lake which are fertile, have beautiful ornamental gardens and good spring water. Many geese and other fowl can be found on them. The entire region around the lake is infertile due to lack of water. Recently, about 3,000 acres of land have been mechanically irrigated and, as a result, have proven to be very productive.

There are 70 to 80,000 Mormons in the Territory. The area they have settled runs from 330 miles south of Salt Lake City to 100 miles north of it.

Enrico Besana:
The New Road of Iron Will Destroy This Anomaly

Enrico Besana (1813–77) was a political activist, a soldier in the Italian Risorgimento, and a professional traveler. As a medical student in Pavia he joined *Giovane Italia* (Young Italy), a secret organization dedicated to the creation of a united, liberal, and republican Italy. After wounding an Austrian officer during a duel in Milan, he went into exile in Lugano, Switzerland. He returned to Milan to participate in the First War of Italian Independence in 1848, and in 1859 he fought with Garibaldi in Lombardia during the Second War of Italian Independence. In 1860 he was elected to the Italian House of Deputies, and during the Third War of Italian independence in 1866, he fought in southern Italy. Besana completed his first journey around the world in 1868, traveling through the Suez Canal to Ceylon, China, Japan, California, Philadelphia, and back to Italy. He later visited Peru, Hawaii, New Zealand, Australia, and India. During his travels Besana contributed articles to Italian periodicals and newspapers in which he sought to give a more balanced perspective than British and French authors on American nation-building. He believed that American immigrants "are really reborn into a better life."[15]

---

[14] The Social Hall served as Utah's first theater in 1852, but its productions basically ended with the Utah War. In 1859 Philip Margetts organized the Mechanics' Dramatic Association, which performed in Henry Bowring's home. The success of Bowring's Theater helped persuade Brigham Young to spend $100,000 to build the Salt Lake Theatre, which opened in March 1862.

[15] Torrielli, *Italian Opinion on America*, 260.

Besana traveled from San Francisco to Salt Lake City in a six-horse, twelve-passenger stagecoach during his first trip around the world in 1868 and spent several days in Salt Lake City. *La Perserveranza* of Milan published Besana's letters in 1869. Like many travelers, Besana relied on other travel accounts—and replicated their errors—in his description of LDS church history, and his editor used illustrations taken from American and British publications and grafted background information from other sources, including British author William Hepworth Dixon's account of his 1866 visit to Utah in *New America*, into Besana's reports.[16] The editor was particularly struck by Besana's revelation that there were Italian converts in Utah, and Besana and Emilio Treves assured his readers that although he was not "a literary professional, he wrote better than one, and narrated with clarity, seeing not only with his own eyes but observing with the eyes of his mind."[17] When he died in 1877 Besana had visited every country in Europe and Asia and had circumnavigated the globe three times.

ENRICO BESANA, *NOTE DEL VIAGGIO DI UN ITALIANO:*
LE GRANDE PRATERIE AMERICANE E I MORMONI [TRAVEL NOTES BY AN ITALIAN: THE GREAT PLAINS AND THE MORMONS], 60–64.

Salt Lake, the capital city, is beautiful and very clean. There are 22,000 inhabitants and some very remarkable buildings. They claim that the tabernacle can accommodate 15,000 persons. They are constructing a very large organ in it. They want their new temple, which is beginning to rise from its foundations, to be even more luxurious than the temple of Solomon. They are using a very beautiful quality of marble. There is also a very beautiful theater that is open year round in which very zealous Mormons participate in productions, including three of the Prophet's daughters. Brigham Young attends every evening in a balcony next to the stage, accompanied by some of his wives, since polygamy exists here, which was initially limited to Church dignitaries, but which today is open to all. This is the black spot for which this sect is hated and ridiculed by the citizens of the United States. Thus, in the middle of a free people, the most despotic power has been born. In a country where there is not a state church, a church has been established that is beyond the laws of man and one sees born again, in the middle of the nineteenth century, social forms of the pagan world. The

---

[16] A Milanese weekly published a series of articles on "The Railroad of the Pacific" with detailed descriptions of Utah and the Mormons. The series included illustrations of Salt Lake City that had appeared in *Harper's*. See "La Ferrovia del Pacifico," *L'emporio pittoresco* 5:206 (9–15 August 1868), 90–91; 5:207 (15–22 August 1868), 102–3; 5:208 (22–29 August 1868), 118–19; 5:209 (29 August–5 September 1868), 139–42.

[17] Torrielli, *Italian Opinion on America*, 25, quoting *Giornale popolare dei viaggi*, 1:161 (1871).

Mormons openly renounce the most precious gains of science and philosophy: personal liberty, family life, representative government, a free press, an independent judiciary, and equal justice. They repudiate all of these good forms acquired by modern society with such effort, and place themselves blindly under a fanatic who is intelligent but coarse and barbarous. The consequences of this social disorder will not take long to be felt. The liberal education, the reading of secular books, and above all the new generation that is far from the state of moral and physical degradation that characterized their fathers when they arrived from Europe, all of these things will produce their natural effects, and that is not all: liberty and civilization, which will advance even more quickly because of the new road of iron from the shores of the Pacific to the Atlantic, will in the end destroy this anomaly, which during my visit was still experiencing great prosperity.[18]

Olympe de Joaral Audouard:
An Enormous Caravan, Including Some Ladies

The prominent and fiery French feminist, writer, and lecturer Olympe de Joaral Audouard (1830–90) married an unfaithful Marseille notary, but they were separated for many years before their eventual divorce in 1885.[19] With her liberation from matrimony, Audouard began traveling to Egypt, Turkey, and Russia, writing accounts of her adventures.[20] She moved to Paris, where she began writing novels and polemical feminist works that ridiculed men by referring to them as "frogmen," "butterflymen," "mosquitomen," "duckmen," and other lower forms of insects and animals. She also edited two feminist journals, *La revue cosmopolite* and *Le Papillon*, gave lectures, and published books that argued for women's rights.

When the government of Napoléon III opposed her efforts to transform the *Cosmopolite* from a literary to a political journal, she traveled to the

---

[18] In the original version published in *La Perseveranza*, Besana wrote: "That which is certain is that a liberal education given to these youth, and the reading of secular books, will produce their effects, and this phenomenon of mysticism and ecclesiastical tyranny cannot survive beyond the time that liberty and civilization spreads itself from the shores of the Atlantic to the Pacific and passes through these deserts."

[19] Audouard and her husband took advantage of France's first divorce law, passed in 1884. Her comment that she already knew "about Mormonism by experience" indicates infidelity played a role in the divorce.

[20] Audouard was part of a select group of literary women, including Mary Wollstonecraft (1759–1797), Mary Shelley (1797–1851), Frances Trollope (1779–1863), and others, who enjoyed the freedom to leave home and travel, and who possessed the talent to write popular accounts of their travels. Audouard wrote *Les mystères du sérail* in 1863; *Le canal de Suez* in 1864; *Les mystères de l'Egypte dévoilés* in 1865; *L'Orient et ses peuples* in 1867; and *A travers l'Amérique* in 1869.

United States, where she described the differences between "perceptive" American women and "brutish" American men. Few literary women ventured to the Far West before the completion of the transcontinental railroad, and Audouard's book is the first account written by a European woman who visited Utah. Other contemporary female perspectives of the territory were written by those who claimed to be victims of Mormonism's peculiar marriage system, and it was not until after the completion of the railroad that an increasing number of female writers visited Utah.[21]

Despite her militant feminism, the puritanical nature of Mormon polygamy, especially when contrasted to European standards of male marital fidelity, and the strong defense polygamous wives offered for the practice completely won Madam Audouard's sympathies. On her return to France, she published an account of her Western adventures that appeared in at least three editions in 1869, 1871, and 1889. She resumed the lecture circuit, and described Utah and the Mormons in such glowing terms that she was lampooned in the French press. Albert Robida—who may have first heard of Mormonism as a result of publicity for her lectures and who later lampooned the Mormons in several books—drew several cartoons for the 13 March 1869 issue of the Parisian journal *Paris-Caprice* entitled "Mormonisme à Paris." One of them jested that Audouard's lectures "are beginning to produce an unexpected effect . . . half of Paris has already converted to Mormonism!!!!"[22] Audouard eventually became embroiled in new controversies with the de Broglie government because of her feminist conferences. In 1874, in the midst of an upsurge of interest in spiritualism in France, she published *Le monde des esprits ou la vie après la mort*. Prior to her death in 1890 Audouard wrote a memoir and continued to travel and promote feminism.[23]

---

[21] The first women to record their visits to Utah were the wives of federal officials, including Cornelia Ferris, whose husband served as territorial secretary from 1852 to 1853, and Elizabeth Cumming, wife of the territory's second governor. See Ferris, *The Mormons at Home*; and Canning and Beeton, eds., *The Genteel Gentile*. The purported tale of a plural wife, *Female Life Among the Mormons*, appeared anonymously in 1855, but later editions used the pseudonym "Mrs. Maria Ward." Perhaps the work of Sarah Hollister Harris, wife of a former Utah territorial secretary, the book was published in Danish, Swedish, French, German and even Hungarian, and became a model for later accounts written by Fanny Stenhouse in 1872 and Ann-Eliza Webb Young in 1876. Neither Isabella Bird (1831–1904) nor Ida Pfeiffer (1797–1858), two of the most famous female travelers of their age, visited Utah, but Pfeiffer encountered schismatic Mormons in Wisconsin who followed James Strang. Other prominent women travelers included Sarah Jane Lippincott (writing as Grace Greenwood), who visited Utah in the fall of 1871; Mrs. Frank Leslie in 1877; Lady Duffus Hardy in 1881; Emily Faithful in 1884; and Frances Merriman in 1894.

[22] "Le Mormonisme à Paris," *Paris-Caprice* (No. 63 of 13 March 1869).

[23] Audouard wrote *Les nuits russes* in 1876 and *Au pays des boyards* in 1881.

Olympe Audouard (1830–1890).
Audouard is on the far right. *From* L'Eclipse, *5 July 1868.*
Courtesy of L'Association des Amis d'Albert Robida.

OLYMPE DE JOARAL AUDOUARD, *A TRAVERS L'AMÉRIQUE: LE FAR WEST*
[CROSSING AMERICA: THE FAR WEST], 291–313, 332–70.
TRANSLATED BY HUGH MACNAUGHTON.

From Green River on, Mormon workers were building the railway. Their leader, Brigham Young, and his three sons bought up this line on a contract basis.[24] Everywhere in the mountains Mormons can be seen encamped, and I can assure you that they are working briskly. Since the Mormons took over the construction, they are building up to six miles a day.

The great Mormon leader, knowing that Mr. Durand was coming to him with an enormous caravan, including some ladies, had telegraphed orders to each Mormon camp to have a good place to rest made ready for us, and arrange for a good meal.[25]

We were very curious to see these famed Latter-day Saints, as they modestly call themselves. Mr. Durand showed us a cable from Brigham Young worded as follows: "At Plume Creek station, Mormon family awaits you." Thereupon we cried out with joy. At last we were going to contemplate these seventeen-strong families with only one man!

We arrived at the station and caught sight of a Mormon who was waiting for us by his front door. He bade us welcome and showed us into a room in which a table was laid in grand style. A young woman was casting a last glance at her arrangements. She greeted us graciously and fled to the kitchen.

"Here is the first," I thought to myself, "she is quite pretty. I wonder what the others are like?"

I bravely entered the kitchen on the pretext of asking for water. The young woman was there, talking with an old woman who was busy cooking. "My mother-in-law," she said, introducing her to me. . . . While I chatted with these women, I looked about, from the corner of my eye to see where the others might be.

---

[24] Actually, non-Mormon contractors such as J. F. Nounnan did the grading between Green River and Echo Canyon. On 21 May 1868, Brigham Young signed a contract for $2,125,000 to perform "all grading, tunneling, and bridge masonry from the head of Echo Canyon to Ogden." Young subcontracted most of the work to his son Joseph A. Young and his partner, Bishop John Sharp, with smaller jobs parceled out to a number of other bishops, notably Lorin Farr and Chauncey West. However, in early June, Salt Lake newspaper notices called for anyone who wanted work to report to Joseph A. Young, Brigham Young Jr., or to John W. Young, and the prophet's three sons "stood out as important participants in the work." See Athearn, "Contracting for the Union Pacific," 16–23; and Bain, *Empire Express*, 495, 659. The Union Pacific did not meet its contract obligations, and ultimately settled the debt with building materials and rolling stock, which Young used to build the Utah Central Railroad. See Foster, "'That Canny Scotsman': John Sharp and the Negotiations with the Union Pacific Railroad," 197–214.

[25] "Mr. Durand" was "Mr. Union Pacific," Dr. Thomas Clark Durant, a ruthless manipulator who earned the title "First Dictator of the Railroad World" as the company's vice president. See Bain, *Empire Express*, 151–52.

"Mormonism in Paris." Albert Robida lampooning Audouard.
Paris-Caprice 13 March 1869.

"L'académie transformée." Albert Robida lampooning Audouard.
Paris-Caprice *13 March 1869.*

"They must be locked away somewhere," I said to myself. "No doubt this Mormon does not wish to shock us by the sight of his harem in full array."

The young woman asked me if I would like to wash in my room before dinner, and I accepted eagerly, hoping to catch sight of the others. She led me to a little room, quite clean and tidy, and simply-furnished. "If you would like," she said, "to invite the other ladies to come upstairs, there is my mother-in-law's room, which they are welcome to use."

This timber house gave the impression of being one of those boxes with everything in it: it is very much the fashion in the Far West, and so to speak the second step before a palace. A large room downstairs, a kitchen beside it; two rooms upstairs and an attic. Well, I could see the open attic, and it was filled with potatoes, preserved fruit and bottles of cider, but not the slightest trace of a woman could be seen there. In the two inhabited rooms, there were only two beds: the mother-in-law's and the married couple's bed.

I could not have been more intrigued, so, arming myself with all my courage, and at the risk of appearing indiscreet, I inquired of my hostess, "But where on earth are the other wives?" She burst out laughing and replied with a touch of raillery, "Ah! that's right, Madam, you suppose that a Mormon with only one wife is not a Mormon. But you see, our husbands have the right and not the obligation to take several wives. So it's four years now since I got married, and Charles finds one wife is enough. Besides, if you go to Salt Lake City, you will find enough to convince you that all the stories written about us are fables invented by the maliciousness of our enemies!" I was astonished, and, I have to admit, a little put out. If I was going to discover on my arrival at *Salt Lake* that Mormon was the synonym of a faithful husband, what would people say in France? I went down to the dining room, where I found everyone gathered together.

"Gentlemen and ladies," said I to my traveling companions, "we have been robbed, duped; our host has but one wife, and he has been married for four years!"

The stupefaction and disenchantment were general. The following day, we were going to stay with another Mormon. All our hopes lay in that direction: that host would probably introduce us to his seventeen wives.

We were disappointed once again, only a little less so, since on entering the dining room, we saw two young women setting the table. I discovered a third, not as young, doing the cooking. I quickly spoke to one of the young women, "Is it to the mistress of this house that I have the honor of speaking?"

She smiled as she gave me her reply.

"To one of the mistresses of the house, since there are three of us!"

Three ... I breathed a sigh of relief: I had before my eyes some real Mormons.

I felt obliged to take a suitably sad expression to say to her, "Ah! That other young lady is therefore your rival . . . ?"

"My rival?" she replied with an astonished expression, "why so? She is simply my sister, and doubly so, for she is my sister by consanguinity and by the will of God, being like me Mrs. Williams."

"What?" I cried, "how can your own sister consent to be your rival?"

"But," she said to me, now with a slight edginess, "she is not my rival at all: she is simply the wife of my husband, like me."

I understood that, without wishing to, I was shocking this lovely Mormon woman, who looked as though she found my astonishment out of place, and so I said to her, with as much gentleness as possible, "Excuse my curiosity, but I am French and I am very curious to know the customs of your country to get a clear idea as to what difference there may be between the Mormonism of *Salt Lake* and that of Europe."

My status as a Frenchwoman appeared to win me her good graces. She changed her tone and said to me very graciously, "Since you come from so far away to visit us, you are welcome. The Latter-day Saints will receive you with pleasure, and I am happy to be the first to prove it to you. I shall pray God to send you the gift of the Holy Spirit, so that he may open your heart to the restored Gospel."

The hope of seeing me converted to Mormonism frightened me horribly, and I could not restrain myself from saying "Oh! No thank you. I have had a French husband, enough to say that I already know about Mormonism by experience, and I have had enough of it."

She smiled at this riposte, without being discouraged, and continued with these words: "If one day, the spirit and the light come into your soul, then you will become our sister and I shall be happy indeed, for I already feel friendship for you." On this cordial declaration, she asked me if I wished to come into the kitchen to see her third sister.

While chatting with these three women, I noticed that a clear cordiality reigned among them; all three of them were gay and laughing. Four children played in a corner. Mary, the young woman to whom I had spoken first, was stroking a little girl in her arms.

"Do you see," she said, "how pretty she is? Well, she is even sweeter than that." The little girl was kissing her, playing with her hair and seemed to love her greatly.

"How old is your little girl?" I asked.

"She's four years old. But she isn't my daughter; she's the daughter of this lady," and she pointed to the cook. "I myself have only a little boy."

"Yes, she's my aunt," said the little girl.

"Whom do you love best, your mother or your aunt?"

"Why, both as much," she replied.

The young woman, who had guessed my thoughts, said to me, with a smile, "This will astonish even more, Madam, but, do you see, we love the children of our sisters in God almost as much as our own!"

I certainly was astonished . . . and that expression *"sister in God"* shocked me. Why not rather *"sister in love"*?

The greatest fault I find with the Mormons is for mingling God and religion with so unedifying a situation. They remind me of a Don Juan who swore that he was only paying court to ladies by divine order, and who pressed them to yield their favors in the name of morality and religion.

A devout or hypocritical Don Juan, that is a character to draw! I amused myself with making my hostesses talk and I learned from them a few details about how these polygamous households are organized.

All the work is classified and divided into weeks. Each of the wives has her week, during which she sees to the household chores: she cooks, does the laundry, and even has time for going out and for visits. I confined myself to these few details which removed from me any wish to know more.

The second day following this first encounter with the Mormons, we were at the camp of Mr. Reed, the chief engineer, when we were told that Brigham Young's two sons wished to see us: Young Younger and John W.[26] They came to welcome us to the state of Utah, the domain of the Latter-day Saints, on behalf of their father. They brought with them exquisite fruit and some champagne from *Salt Lake*.

They were introduced to me: I spoke with them, being very desirous of knowing who these sons of the Mormon pope were. I was very astonished, once again, when I found them very gentlemanly, with simple, natural yet elegant manners, not without distinction.

Young-Younger is the elder son of the great Mormon leader, the one who will succeed him one day.[27]

Younger had come to Paris two years previously. So he knows our country and he immediately began to speak with me. This Mormon was witty, and his wit was seasoned with a touch of raillery that was far from displeasing. Among others, he had a subtle way of mocking the curiosity of Parisians to see a Mormon:

"Frankly," he said to me, "I thought that in that country where the practice of having many women is so widespread, a poor Mormon from Salt Lake City would go unnoticed. But no!" And he thereupon recounted to me

---

[26] Vermonter Samuel B. Reed, who began his career working on the Erie Canal, helped build the first railroad into Chicago and, as Union Pacific superintendent of construction, laid out and built the line between Green River and the Great Salt Lake. For information on Brigham Young Jr. and John W. Young, see Athearn, "Contracting for the Union Pacific," 16–23; Bishop, "Building Railroads for the Kingdom: the Career of John W. Young," 66–80; Compton, "John Willard Young," 111–33.

[27] Audouard explains to her French readers that Young in English means "young" and that his son is therefore "Young-Younger."

the weird, unseemly questions he had been asked in Paris. In particular, he spoke very amusingly of the way he had been received by an important lady whose husband was in a very eminent position.

"I thought," he said to me, "that I could make so bold as to offer some books on our religious institutions of which so little is known in Paris. I was even assured that people in the upper echelons were somewhat curious to know about them.

"So I had several of our books bound, and I carried them to Mr. ***. The manservant told me, 'Mr. *** has gone out'.

"'Well then,' I replied, 'take my card into Mrs. ***'."

"I knew that the French did not lock their women away in harems, and allowed them to receive visits without any unseemly inference being drawn.

"I waited in an antechamber with several doors opening into it. Suddenly, I heard a woman's voice ring out, with horror-struck note.

"'A Mormon! Dear God! Why, no, I shall not see him. . . . Tell him I am unwell'.

"The manservant came back to me, and discharged his duty as his mistress had bidden him. So I told him, with a smile, 'Convey all my regrets to Mrs. *** at my being unable to pay my respects to her, and take these books into her, asking her to deliver them to her husband on my behalf'.

"I sent in a second visiting card with my richly-bound books. I waited for a moment, and the same voice cried out: 'Books? Let us see what they are!'

"A few minutes' silence ensued. Perhaps the books were being leafed through. The silence was followed by angry exclamations: 'Mormon books. . . . *Fi!* Horror! What, am I to give these awful things to my husband? Never! Quickly, take all this away, hand him back these books, and forbid him—do you hear?—forbid him to leave a single one in my house. I do not wish such horrors to besmirch my home!'

"I took my books away with me, very surprised at the horror I had inspired in this great lady. I told a Parisian friend of mine about the matter, and he laughed uninhibitedly.

"'I can well imagine she was afraid! She has very good reasons for wanting her husband to believe that plurality is permitted only for wives . . . never for husbands'."

"Aha!" I [Audouard] replied, "do Mormons also speak ill of women?"

"Why no, Madam, we would not even allow ourselves to think of such a thing: I am only repeating a witty but cruel Parisian remark."

I expressed to these gentlemen my eager wish to know the Mormon institutions and to study their religion.

"I absolutely wish," I said to them, "to see with my own eyes how your women put up with their humiliating condition, and I want to ask them what they think."

"That will be easily arranged for you, Madam, and we will introduce our wives to you, and they will gain you admittance to all the Mormon households you wish to visit."

John W. added, "One of my wives is of French extraction on her mother's side. She speaks French well and will be happy to help you."

The two sons of Brigham Young, especially John W., are very good young men, very lively, and well-educated and intelligent as well.

The following day, I made my entrance into Salt Lake City, in the president's carriage, driven by his third son, Josaphat.[28]

I was cordially and eagerly welcomed there, and I had the opportunity of seeing more than two hundred households, and of conversing with a multitude of Mormons. So many fables have been spun about these Latter-day Saints that I am afraid of making my readers mistrustful by keeping strictly to the truth. People have willfully misrepresented the men as Pashas, owning fifty or sixty wives, and thinking only of satisfying their evil passions. Most of the travelers, when they return from the Mormons, feel themselves obliged to enrich their accounts with extravagant anecdotes to stir the curiosity of a certain kind of public. I hope the gentlemen concerned will not feel animosity towards me if I shed light on their misrepresentations. How can they know the home life of families, since the men who arrive at *Salt Lake* cannot gain entry to them: they are received by the President, the consuls and other dignitaries, and that is all. Of what happens in the families, in the privacy of home life, they can know nothing. And when they speak, they embroider, or else they repeat a few hoary old chestnuts invented by American journalists to discredit a social custom which offends them. There is a story that has gone the rounds in the New World, an exaggerated American story, that is completely forgotten today. Well, believe it or not, a traveler returning from Salt Lake City thought it was a funny idea to give this fable a fresh airing, and to tell it straight-faced, giving it a thin veneer of authenticity. Here is the story:

One day, a lady comes into the office of a Mormon and makes a request of him. He looks at her in astonishment and says to her, "But I don't understand why you are making this request to me, why me?"

"But to whom should I make it, if not you?"

"Who are you, then?"

"Why, don't you recognize me?"

"No, not in the least.... Look here, though, it seems to me that I have already had the pleasure of seeing you somewhere ... but where? I don't know...."

---

[28] Josaphat probably refers to Joseph A. Young, who was involved with his two brothers in completing the railway line from Echo Canyon to Ogden.

"Well, I shall remind you. You saw me at your home, in your boudoir, since I am your wife!"

"You, my wife? But that's impossible. What is your name, then?"

"Juliette...."

"What is your number?"

"Thirty-seven."

The Mormon opens his register, looks up number 37 and does indeed see the name Juliette.

So he extends his hand to her and says in a friendly tone, "Do sit down; it's quite true, you are my wife; tell me what your request is and I shall do my best to satisfy it."

The story is funny, doubtless. It raised laughter for a whole summer season among the Yankees that read it in their little local newspapers. But it is inaccurate and improbable, since there is not a single Mormon who has such a large number of wives. Only the President has many (I am going to explain to you why), and even then, he only has seventeen. As he spends his evenings with them, dines with them and takes them out to shows, he knows them all, and obviously does not need to scan his registers to find their numbers. The current President introduced to me his seventeen wives, naming each of them by her name, and telling me when he had married them, how old they were, and the country of their birth! His memory was very faithful to the facts on that score. The truth has the sober privilege of being less amusing than lies and exaggeration.[29]

In spite of that, I shall simply tell the truth about these much-discussed Mormons, whom people delight in making the subjects of ridicule, and I shall add nothing of my own invention. If people want to find amusement in the subject, there is little point in trekking 2,801 miles to study the Mormons. It would be simpler and more convenient to stay in Paris and give free rein to the imagination. As I see it, an account of a journey must above all be faithful and accurate....

Let us return to our Mormons, whom one might term cosmopolitan Mormons, since there are Germans, Swiss, Swedes, Norwegians, English, and even Yankees. There is only one Frenchman; not one Italian, and not one Spaniard![30] *Salt Lake* has been, as can be seen, the meeting-place of all those people who, before leaving their home country, had already rid themselves of all prejudice, and who, having the courage of their opinions, had resolved beforehand to accept the responsibilities of polygamy.

---

[29] Brigham Young married fifty-six wives and fathered fifty-seven children. Jeffrey Ogden Johnson, "Determining and Defining 'Wife': The Brigham Young Households," 62, 69, lists fifty-five wives, but Johnson has since identified one more.

[30] As noted, a number of Italian converts had moved to Utah. See Homer, "The Italian Mission, 1850–1867"; Stokoe, "The Mormon Waldensians"; Homer, "Like a Rose in the Wilderness"; and Homer, "An Immigrant Story: Three Orphaned Italians in Early Utah Territory."

This cosmopolitan, freethinking element, indifferent to old forms, heedless of the future, but drawn towards an ideal by aspirations that I believe to be honest, grouped itself together under the name of Mormons to transform itself into a social order of doubtful legality, one may argue, but of which the purpose is the search for a new form. Onto all this, a new religion became grafted, as in the times of Fourier and the Saint-Simoniens!![31] It is curious, I grant, but it is too serious today to see only the ridiculous side of it. What seems to me incredible is that in this nineteenth century, which represents to our thinking the quintessence of past centuries of civilization, a new religion should have been capable of becoming established on a firm footing and of finding such a large number of supporters! This proves perhaps that there are neither absolute truths nor absolute lies when dealing with matters that are the province of faith. . . .

[*The history and doctrine of the Mormons are discussed.*]

After these six hard months of trekking, the Mormons found themselves on dry ground, without any vegetation, without water, in a corner of the earth where it almost never rains. . . . Their provisions had run out, and they were reduced to eating roots. . . . And yet, without losing heart, it was on this soil, seen in a dream by their prophet, that they bravely pitched their tents. Once established, they went into the mountains to seek the greening water, and brought it into the plain by digging canals. They established an irrigation system like that existing in Egypt, tilled and sowed the land, and some of them even fetched trees from Mexico, California, and the United States! They also understood that the nature of the soil there was well-suited to the vine, and planted vineyards that today produce an excellent champagne and an exquisite sweet wine.

In short, they arrived in this desert in 1847 numbering 2,700, and today they have reached 125,000 in the state of Utah alone.[32] Their capital, Salt Lake City, is a delightful little city of 18 to 20 thousand inhabitants. It is surrounded by well-tended orchards yielding superb fruit. As far as the eye can see, there are nothing but wheat fields and fertile pastures. Water flows throughout the city, the tents have given way to large and beautiful houses. All these people have a prosperous, contented air. One might have thought oneself to be in a city founded long ago, having passed gradually through all kinds of improvement. The streets are wide and lined with handsome trees. I found everywhere an air of cleanness and comfort that charmed me. One can even mention a building worthy of the ancient civilizations, and perhaps without parallel anywhere in the world: the colossal temple built to the glory of God and capable of holding 12,000 persons. It is covered by an immense

---

[31] Robert Owen, Charles Fourier, and Henri de Saint-Simon were prominent Utopian Socialists.
[32] These population figures were inflated. The 1870 census counted only 86,786 people in Utah.

dome which has an excellent aeration system. The interior is modeled on the ancient Roman circuses, that is, as an amphitheater.[33]

Salt Lake City boasts a very beautiful theater built on the model of the Italian theaters, with the difference that there are only two boxes next to the stage: one for Brigham Young and the other, facing it, for his sons and their wives; all the other seats are stalls. The décors, manufactured by Mormon workers, are in good taste, even luxurious. All the actors and actresses are Mormons. Many of them have never seen another theater and have only studied dramatic art at Salt Lake City and yet, they act well. There is even a young woman who is a genuine artist. The plays that are staged at this theater are just our French plays translated into English. Is there not enough pillaging of these poor authors? Even the Mormons are involved in this!

There are several free schools, and even a small conservatory to teach singing and music to the young Mormon women. There is no dearth of pianos, but I should say that they shine more by their number than by being any good.

There are two major newspapers at Salt Lake City: the New Descret [sic] [*Deseret News*] and the New Telegraph [*Salt Lake Daily Telegraph*]. Mr. Stenhausse [T. B. H. Stenhouse], the editor of the first named, is an eminently well-educated man. A German by origin, he speaks French with a very pure accent. His wife, born a Frenchwoman, is a sociable, kindly, charming woman, very well-educated, a good musician and the mother of thirteen beautiful children. She is a former sister of Charity [Daughter of Charity], and the only Catholic Frenchwoman among the Mormon women.[34]

Also to be found at *Salt Lake* are large stores filled with all the articles from Europe, in no way adversely competing with the two or three indigenous factories. The glove factory has a well-deserved reputation: the so-called Mormon gloves are excellent; they are made of fine, supple buckskin, and trimmed with fur gauntlets. Trade with the United States, especially San Francisco, is sizable. With the Indians, it is confined to buffalo-hides that they buy from them, and grisly [grizzly bear] skins (a small, vicious bear [sic]). I could mention a fair number of bankers, men of letters, teachers in every subject and distinguished farmers.

I go into these details, which might appear extraordinary if one were writing about any other country, because I have often been asked such incongruous questions about the Mormons, I have come to realize that people entertain the weirdest misconceptions about them. As an example, I was

---

[33] Audouard confused the temple with the tabernacle.

[34] Stenhouse was editor of *The Salt Lake Daily Telegraph*, foil for the *Union Vedette*, published at Camp Douglas. He and his wife were actually British, but both had lived in Geneva, Switzerland, while Thomas served as mission president from 1850 to 1854. Long one of Mormonism brightest defenders, Stenhouse became disenchanted with Brigham Young and left the LDS church shortly after Audouard's visit.

once asked whether, like the savages of Africa, they wore a primitive costume. I might as well have been asked whether they walked on all fours! Well, I shall give this answer once and for all: the Mormons would cut a credible figure, even in Paris. And as for their style of dress, it is so proper that they wear a white tie and tails on every occasion, not forgetting the famous, obligatory stovepipe hat.

As Salt Lake City is, or rather as the Mormons are formed into a kind of community termed religious, a few persons believe that everything is held in common among them, even wives. This is not so. Polygamy there is, but not wives held in common. Goods are not held in common, either: each Mormon has his own business, his own industrial concern, if he is not a farmer. His wealth is entirely personal.

If a new proselyte arrives in Utah, people come to his aid, lending him money to set up, and according to his abilities he chooses a way of life. The richest form a kind of emergency fund for those in need. The priests of the temple have no other occupation but to go and visit the sick and the poor, and to distribute alms to them. If a Mormon dies leaving no wealth, but leaving widows and orphans in hardship, as one of the fundamental rules of this religion is that man must always work for woman and never leave her in need, the rich Mormons diligently marry these women *spiritually* and adopt their children. This gives no right of possession to the man over the spiritual wife: his duties are confined to supplying her with her subsistence and taking care of her children. However, the spiritual wife retains the right to marry the man she chooses. Only in this case does the spiritual husband cease to provide for her expenses. There have been spiritual unions that became outright marriages, if the two spouses were suited to each other, but these cases are infrequent.

Young women and widows choose their husbands freely. They have the right to divorce if their husbands behave badly towards them. For the husband, divorce is allowed only if adultery is proven.

In America, I was told that the Mormons, plunged as they were in the sweetness and delights of the harem, forced their women to work in the fields, and made them perform the heaviest tasks. Well, throughout the entire state of Utah, I never saw a single woman laboring in the fields. I never saw any woman dragging heavy carts, as can often be seen in the streets of Paris. The wife of a humble farmer has nothing else to do but look after her children and her household, and as there are often three wives, each is only responsible for a third of the household chores!

Materially speaking, the Mormon woman is happy: her only concern, the only task required of her, is to bring lots of children into the world. She performs this so conscientiously that it is not infrequent to find women with sixteen or seventeen children.

After all that I had heard said, I had expected to find in the person of Brigham Young, the great apostle of Mormonism, the pope and king of the Latter-day saints, a kind of deluded madman, or even a basely self-seeking man, a grotesque character arraying himself majestically in his threefold grandeur. The love of the truth forces me to admit that I found him to be a gentlemen, impeccably turned out in correct European dress, with simple, affable manners, loving the world, and still, despite his sixty-eight years, an excellent dancer; he also had the good taste, once outside the tabernacle and away from his official functions, to make one forget, and himself forget, his all-powerfulness. In a word, he was a simple, unassuming man with no posing about him, living on terms of the closest intimacy with all his subjects, with no usher, gilded or ungilded, at his door, and graciously receiving all those who come to see him. And yet the high position occupied by this former glazier might well have gone to his head! He must therefore be admitted to have much tact and wit, since he has successfully resisted the temptation of becoming a kind of idol or fetish.

He is both pope and emperor. As pope, he is infallible ... an infallibility that none of his subjects would ever dream of denying. As a temporal sovereign, his power is as unlimited as that of Tsar Alexander of Russia. His rule is entirely personal, just like any other personal sovereign. But in one point, he has superiority over that government with which, sadly, we have become acquainted, in that he is joyfully accepted by all, he maintains his rule with neither needle guns nor a standing army. . . . This good Brigham Young does not even have a squad of town police at his orders. . . . His prestige alone, the esteem and friendship he inspires in his subjects are sufficient to maintain his threefold powers—threefold because his is also supreme judge: his judgements are without appeal and no one complains about them. Surely this is enough to inspire envy in more than one sovereign of Europe. If a sovereign who relished personal rule succeeded in maintaining his power in this way, then he really could call himself the elect of the nation, Majesty by the grace of God and of the people.

The absence of soldiers and policemen at Salt Lake City is only noticeable in the budget, which is proportionately less weighty: the most perfect order reigns just the same. I saw gatherings of twelve thousand persons. There was not a single instant of disorder.

Thefts and murder are unknown in Utah. . . .

Mormon polygamy is entirely opposite to Muslim polygamy. The latter is rather based on inconstancy than on sharing. A Turk marries a young and lovely woman, and he adores her. But his love survives neither youth nor beauty. The torrid climate of the Orient and life in the harem soon fade women's charm. The Turks often change wives, but usually, the first becomes a stranger, as soon as the second settles into the household.

Since the Mormons have mingled God with the devil, having put religion in the service of their passion, they have established their polygamy on a sharing basis. Each wife is entitled to an equal share of affection. They must divide their tenderness into three or five equal shares, depending upon the number of their wives. This appears very difficult, and yet they achieve the impossible. They are as tender, as loving towards the wife of forty who has little beauty allotted to her, as towards the one who is twenty and a great beauty. They find all this quite natural.

An Englishman, Mr. Dixon, has just published a book on the Mormons in which he says, "Only women of low breeding, common women without learning, docilely put up with polygamy, whereas the higher-bred women, women of the higher classes, are indignant at it and endure it only with a feeling of pained humiliation."[35] I question the accuracy of this appraisal, for how can it be reconciled with the very positive fact of being initiated to the practice beforehand? In any event, only women born of Mormon parents would have the right to say, "we endure polygamy, but it is hateful to us," and here again, they have the resort of refusing to marry, since marriage is not compulsory for young Mormon women. They contract it freely and in full foreknowledge of the situation.

As for the women who arrive every year at Salt Lake City, converted to Mormonism by the preachers that Brigham Young sends out all over the world, there is no casting doubt as to their full endorsement of polygamy, since before being admitted as members of the Mormon church, they must be subjected to long sermons, become steeped in that doctrine, and swear that they believe in it and hold fast to it. Still more is required. Mormon polygamy has wider duties and obligations. It is not enough for a wife not to oppose her husband's second marriage, but she must even have the delicate attention of offering a second or third wife to her husband, and what is more, she must love her rivals and treat them as sisters.

Does a woman who accepts this role, and who swears to resign herself to her lot, have the right to complain of it afterwards? I confess to you that my womanly feelings made me believe that Mormon women were nothing but poor victims, deceived and abused, held in bondage against their will and bearing only painfully this hateful sharing of married love. I had expected to find many an ill-concealed woe, dark jealousy and implacable hatred.

I duly sounded these women's hearts, I scanned their looks, observed their expressions. There are certain small details that cannot escape a woman's glance; we are more perspicacious than men, in reading the labyrinthine secrets of a woman's heart. Well, I can assure you that I was never able to discover the slightest sign of jealousy. These women, nearly all of them Protestant, have that coldness and rigidity specific to Anglicans: correct, devout

---

[35] See Dixon, *La nouvelle Amérique*, 178–89.

and prudish. If you talk to them of jealousy, they become offended and are ready to cry out, "Shocking!"

"*We* feel jealous," they say, "Why, fie! jealous of what? Of our husbands' affection? But they are so tender and so attentive to us. Why might not the heart have affection and tenderness for several persons at once? We could only then be jealous of their sensual love, and we reject such a suspicion, since our hearts are so purified by grace and by our holy baptism, that we cannot be sullied by a coarse, impure love! In a word, I discovered that these combined Don Juans and Tartuffes[36] are so thoroughly conversant with the devout, prudish character of Anglican women, that they have made jealousy synonymous with impurity. To display jealousy, according to these men, is to be too much attached to carnal love, a fault that deserves severe censure! That is very shrewd of them, and it succeeds perfectly, so much so that each Mormon woman loses no time, after a very short spell of married life, in asking her husband: "Dear, will you not soon take a second wife? Dear, would this lady be to your liking? Do you prefer my young sister?"

Note that, for the second marriage to be valid, the first woman must herself present the rival to her husband and say to the priest, "It is I myself, entirely voluntarily, who offer this second or third wife to my husband." If a wife does not consent to a second marriage, her husband cannot go through with it; only she is required to make her reasons known to pope Brigham Young. If these reasons appear insufficient, he exhorts her to make her change her mind. But if she holds firm, her husband cannot act against her will. He may never give his wife a rival she does not like. He is forced to choose a person who is to the liking of her and the other wives too, if he has several.

Marriages are celebrated in the houses that are called endowment houses. The marriage ceremonies are copied from the Bible, and have the features of both a civil wedding and a religious one.

The figure three is the number usually adopted by Mormon households. Few have less than three wives, except the young, and very few have more. I do not know the reason for their preferring this cabalistic number, but I found it to be very widespread among them. . . .

I was invited to small evenings, to great dinners, and I saw husbands surrounded by their wives. Well, I can affirm that they were attentive and equally amiable to all of them. The ladies too showed great affection for each other. When it came to introductions, I must confess to being seized by a hearty laughter that I had great difficulty in restraining.

Mr. Williams, for example, took a young lady by the hand and brought her to me, saying, "Mrs. Williams, my wife!" Then he went and fetched a second, repeating the same words to me. And then finally a third, and still,

---

[36] Tartuffe, a character in a Molière play, is a plausible hypocrite.

Mrs. Williams, my wife! To someone unused to this situation, it is comic to the point of being burlesque!

Obviously, all the wives have to bear their husband's surname.

As the lord of this country, Brigham Young has no rights over the wives of his subjects, but he has the most populous harem: as I said earlier, he has seventeen wives.

His first, who is aged seventy, was his helpmeet when he was but a humble glazier. He still displays great friendship towards her, and shows her much consideration. This lady, for her part, appears to have for her husband a tenderness that amounts to veneration. One day I was on my way to the theater with her, to sit in Brigham Young's box. He did us the honors there with perfect grace. This old lady looked radiant. During an interval, she leant toward me and whispered to me, "Ah, I am so happy this evening, since, did you see, Madam, when I can spend a few hours with my husband, it puts a ray of sunlight into my heart: he is so kind, so excellent to me."

This old lady too, really has an excellent character, since it was as her husband that he became a Mormon!

Since that time, she has seen sixteen other women enter the conjugal home, and in spite of that, she venerates her husband and congratulates herself on his kindness! Truly there are things that one would not believe if one did not see them with one's own eyes!

Brigham Young also has three other elderly wives whom he married in Illinois. The remaining ones, those whom he married in Salt Lake City, are younger. One of these wives is very beautiful, as well as being elegant and distinguished. She has the assumed air of a stately lady and appears to take her role as sovereign lady very seriously. She is called Amelia. Or rather, people call her the fair Amelia. She had been the wife of a rich Yankee from New York. Of a dreamy, romantic turn of mind, and unoccupied, she dreamed of something whimsically out-of-the-ordinary happening to heal her of the spleen that tormented her in the prosaic social environment in which she lived.

The newspapers were telling of the famous Brigham Young, both pope and sovereign. Strange stories were told concerning him. . . . Amelia read this, and one day, she said to herself, "I want to become the queen of Salt Lake City. With my beautiful eyes, I want to enslave that man and gain such a hold over him that he will renounce polygamy." She took a pen, some ink, a beautiful sheet of paper, and wrote him the following note: "I believe I have been overcome by grace. I wish to become a Mormon, if you will marry me."

The reply was not long in coming: "Come, you will be welcomed with open arms and you will become my wife."

Amelia petitioned for divorce, which she obtained, without speaking of her project. Once she was free, she left for Salt Lake City with a guard of honor sent to her by the sovereign of Utah. Her arrival caused a sensation. Never before had the Mormons seen a woman as beautiful and elegant as her. Brigham Young was enchanted, smitten. He gave her a queen's welcome and covered her with flowers, lace and diamonds. As she had foreseen, she gained a great hold over him, and he fell in love with her for good and all.

Amelia then bethought herself of achieving her goal, which was to destroy polygamy. But Brigham Young was inflexible on that matter. "God has imposed it upon us," he would invariably tell her, "ask me what you will, and I will do it. But despite all my love for you, I cannot go against the will of the Most High."

Amelia remained a Mormon as a matter of fancy, not of conviction. She was a stately lady who had sought distraction in an out-of-the-ordinary whimsy. I believe she even repented her impulse more than once, but she has ended up making the best of her lot. Since she is not a prisoner, she could have left Salt Lake City, but the society she had left would have been without mercy towards her. It was better for her, therefore, to endure the consequences of her folly, and that is what she has done, only the fair Amelia has a slight air of a dethroned queen, or a lady who has lost her ideal.

Concerning her, I shall not say that jealousy was unknown to her. It is stated that especially when she had a great influence over the President's mind, she ill-treated the other wives and took pleasure in giving them a hard time. That, besides, is what put an end to Brigham Young's vertiginous feelings of love for her, since he was very kind by nature and could not bear his other wives being victimized by her. To punish her, he married three others![37]

A man in Brigham Young's position is seldom forced to go and look for new spouses. It is rather they who come and offer themselves to him. In this connection, a short while ago, here is what a woman from Boston wrote to him: "Mr. President of Utah, my husband is a drunkard and a lazy man. He goes out to drink all the money he earns and when he returns home, instead of bread he gives me blows, me and my poor little children, too. I think a religion that allows such bad husbands to exist is a bad religion. I am therefore ready to embrace the Mormon religion, if you promise to marry me and provide for me and my children." Brigham Young replied, "Come!" and he sent money to that woman for her journey.... He even married her, but I do believe he confined himself to spiritual marriage only.

I had a great surprise when I found in Salt Lake City the daughter of General de La Harpe. This lady has been a Mormon for twenty years. Of an eager disposition, given to analysis, of a very high intelligence, she has

---

[37] Brigham Young married the twenty-three-year-old Harriet Amelia Folsom in 1863 as his fiftieth wife. For her own recollections of the marriage, see Schindler, "Brigham Young's Favorite Wife," in *In Another Time: Sketches of Utah History*, 158–61.

become a zealous follower of this religion. Here is how she told me of her conversion: "I was born into the reformed religion [Protestant], but as I grew older and my ideas matured, my mind became concerned with matters of the next world, with the soul of God the creator. I thought with anxiety of what we would find after the grave. . . . I studied all religions, their dogmas and beliefs. I felt that I was living a lie, and that the religion in which I had been brought up was a pure human invention.

"Since my mind was troubled, and my heart discontented, I set out to search for the truth, which had become my ideal, and I cast myself into the study of philosophy. . . . My spirit found in all these brilliant doctrines an irresistible charm, but my heart quietly told me, 'These are only sentences and paradoxes'.

"Finally I became the friend of Fourier and one of his most ardent followers. His doctrine pleased my mind, but my heart rejected it. I still had the feeling I was in falsehood: I saw in this system more a work of man than a divine inspiration. . . ."

"Now," said this lady to me, "I am happy. A gentle quietness has taken the place of that painful uncertainty that devoured me. I have been a Mormon now for twenty-two years, and I swear to you that it is only since I have been, that I have an exact idea of our mission on earth, of our future life, and I can begin to understand the grandeur and the eternal beauty of the one we call God."

This lady is a woman of the finest breeding. In Europe, she lived in the best society. In Russia, she even had a high position. Her intelligence genuinely is superior, her heart, kind and affectionate.[38]

Well then, was it out of fanaticism or conviction? The fact is, though, that she had sacrificed everything: her husband, her daughters and her position, to lead a modest, precarious existence at *Salt Lake*, and to devote herself to her new religion. To join the Mormons, she had trekked for two months under grueling conditions in the American desert. Her family even organized a search for her. The French Minister was instructed to arrest her and send her back to Russia. She has resisted everything, entreaties as well as threats, and for twenty-two years she has been living beside these great lakes, with but one dream, only one desire, to succeed by her letters in converting her daughters to Mormonism.

When she intimated this wish to me, I could not help saying to her, "Do you really think so? Bringing your daughters here, making them leave Russia, where they are married and enjoy a good position. But it's absurd!"

---

[38] Tsar Alexander I made his former tutor, Swiss statesman Frédéric César de la Harpe (1754–1838), a Russian general when allied forces entered Paris in 1814 and helped de la Harpe secure recognition of cantons Vaud and Ticino as members of the Swiss Confederation at the Congress of Vienna. His daughter, Joséphine de la Harpe Ursenbach, was closely associated with prominent Mormon women until her death in 1878.

"No," she replied to me; "it is not as mad as you think. On the contrary, it is very wise. I would far prefer them to be here, like me, the wives of a humble gardener (for Mademoiselle de La Harpe is married to a modest gardener), and to see them working out their salvation, than to know them rich and happy in Russia, while they are walking in the darkness and will not, like me, reach the heaven of the Mormons."

Ah, fanaticism! To what lengths does it not drive those who are smitten with it!

Besides that, this lady has remained a woman of the world: she talks well, the literature of every nation is known to her; she charmed me by her wit, and astonished me by her ardent adherence to this religion, as well as by the assurance she gave me with great seriousness that she, too, had revelations. If, in 1851, Mr. Bertrand wrote a long letter to Napoléon III to convert him to Mormonism, Mademoiselle de La Harpe for her part attempted to convert Victor Hugo.[39] I have held in my hands a copy of this long epistle. It was not without originality.

To conclude on this subject, I will say that, alas, not all Mormons are on the shores of the salt lake. Europe has a great many of them. To count those in Paris would be a long and thankless task. But between the Mormons of Europe and the followers of Brigham Young there is an immense difference, much indeed to the credit of the latter. First, the Mormons of *Salt Lake* have the courage of their convictions. Bravely, they lay themselves open to the jests and catcalls of their European colleagues. Next, one is bound to acknowledge that the American ones at least do not violate their oaths; they do not swear fidelity to their wives. On the contrary, they say to them, "You are clearly warned that you will have rivals. Reflect, and see whether you will have sufficient strength of character to put up with polygamy."

The Europeans, for their part, swear fidelity to their wives, and young women are not sufficiently aware that men only make such oaths to give themselves the pleasure of not keeping them. These women are naïve enough take their promises seriously. . . . The disillusionment is terrible.

The Mormons of *Salt Lake* must also be credited with the following: they have not invented a children's home to send their children to; they have not ever written into their code this immoral, inhuman sentence: 'The search for paternity is prohibited'.[40] The sad result of this sentence is that, out of three children born, in Sweden and Norway, one is a bastard; in Austria, the average is one in five. In France, the average is roughly the same. All these children are doomed by their fathers to misery and shame. Misery and shame

---

[39] Louis Alphonse Bertrand also tried to convert novelist Victor Hugo while residing on the Isle of Jersey.

[40] Title VII, Chapter III, Section II, Article 342 of the Code Napoléon specified, "A child shall in no case be admitted to search whether for paternity or maternity."

lead some to the penal colonies, and others to the hideous wretchedness of prostitution.

The Mormonism of Europeans, even if it is not legal, is nevertheless strongly safeguarded by the laws, and its results are ten times worse: it has caused the degradation of women, by creating the demi-monde, the third-of-the-world, the quarter-world and the world of the streets. These worlds show us women who are sad to look upon, very guilty no doubt, but even more unhappy. They were almost all born honest. They are nothing but the unfortunate victims of European Mormonism.

At *Salt Lake*, there are no degraded women. There are only women well-thought-of by all, bearing the name of the man they live with. Their position as quarter-spouse has nothing humiliating about it, since it is legal. The man who has married these wives can never abandon them. He is obliged to work to maintain them; they are never in the position of finding themselves in want. All the children they bring into the world have a proper status, and the name of their father who is forced to feed them and bring them up. There are innumerable families among the Mormons. It is not infrequent to see a man surrounded by his forty children. If he has married several wives by a guilty surrender to the force of his senses, at least he has borne in a gentlemanly fashion the consequences of his incontinence.

Brigham Young has thirty-six daughters, all of them tall, strong and robust, and in addition, seventeen sons.

A curious point to note is that all Mormons have one-and-a-half times as many daughters as sons. God, they say, indicates by this that every man must marry at least two wives. An interesting conclusion.

In short, my opinion is that polygamy well and truly is a hangable offence, a horrible thing that assimilates man to beast, destroying that pure, strong, divine love that is the inspirer of all great and beautiful things. However, to choose between one kind of polygamy and another, I prefer the legal polygamy of the Mormons to the illegal, tolerated and protected polygamy of the Mormons of Paris, for, I repeat, the latter has still more disastrous consequences.

Salt Lake House, Salt Lake City.
Used by permission, Utah State Historical Society, all rights reserved.

Chapter 5

"THE KING OF THE NEW JERUSALEM"
Riding the Rails through Utah, 1869–77

The completion of the transcontinental railroad by the Union Pacific and Central Pacific railroads in 1869, and the construction of a connecting line between Ogden and Salt Lake by the Utah Central Railroad in 1870, transformed travel to Utah. Brigham Young had enthusiastically supported construction of the railroad for decades, and in 1867 he called on Congress and the Union Pacific to "hurry up, hasten the work! We want to hear the iron horse puffing through this valley. What for? To bring our brethren and sisters here."[1] Young was disappointed that the railroad's mainline bypassed Salt Lake City, but during the season that followed the driving of the golden spike, more visitors passed through Salt Lake than at any time since its founding.[2]

Although Young and his followers celebrated the opening of the railroad—seven thousand Mormons assembled in the Tabernacle the day after the golden spike was driven—they also worried about the impact of "Gentiles" who settled in their previously isolated territory. They took precautionary measures, including the establishment of a protectionist economy that required faithful Latter-day Saints to shun non-Mormon merchants.[3] Gentiles and dissenting Mormons "thought that Young's attempts to maintain Deseret as a distinct and semi-isolated entity were unwisely placing the Saints in the path of an irrepressibly expanding American nation." They believed that such attempts were futile because God had "doomed the iso-

---
[1] Young, 26 May 1867, "The Union Pacific Railroad," *Journal of Discourses*, 12:54.
[2] *Deseret Evening News*, 6 January 1870, cited in Athearn, "Opening the Gates of Zion," 313.
[3] Arrington, *Great Basin Kingdom*, 248–50.

lation of Utah to pass away."[4] They also hoped that a flood of visitors and settlers would undermine the power of Brigham Young's theocracy and contribute to the end of polygamy.

With the arrival of the railroad, the federal government's assault on polygamy became much more aggressive. Brigham Young was arrested for cohabitation in 1871, George Reynolds was convicted of cohabitation, and the U.S. Congress passed the Poland Act, which broke the church's hold on jury selection and increased federal control over the territorial legislature. A new band of Mormon dissenters known as the Godbeites flexed their muscles, and the *Salt Lake Tribune* became an important independent voice in the territory. At the same time prominent Mormons such as T. B. H. Stenhouse, Fanny Stenhouse, Ann Eliza Webb Young, Bill Hickman, and John D. Lee all left the church and published books explaining their reasons for doing so. Politicians and preachers, meanwhile, continued to rail against the illegal practice of polygamy.

A good example of the fascination many Americans had with Mormonism's most provocative doctrine is a letter published in *L'Eco d'Italia*, an Italian-language newspaper published in New York. "What would your readers say if I were to boast an offspring of 62 children?" the letter's author, calling himself Gian Domenico Pellegrini, claimed. "And remember that I am only 50 years old so that I can expect a still greater number of children from my 22 wives, all of them healthy and able to procreate."[5] Had the readers known that there was no one named Gian Domenico Pellegrini living in Utah Territory, it would not have dampened their interest in the subject matter of the letter.

During the 1870s entrepreneurs—especially the railroad tycoons—began selling the West. More than twenty-five railroad guides were published during the decade following 1869, and the number of passengers increased from 30,000 in 1871 to 75,000 by 1875. Companies began organizing and selling package tours across the continent to California. In spring 1872, Thomas Cook, a Baptist missionary and teetotaler who owned a successful "package" travel company in England, advertised in *The Times* of London promoting an around-the-world tour. During the summer and fall periodic notices of Cook's journey appeared in *The Times* and were repub-

---

[4] Walker, *Wayward Saints*, 177.

[5] Correspondence, *L'Eco d'Italia*, 10 June 1874, 2, cited in Schiavo, *Four Centuries of Italian American History*, 171.

lished in the English periodical *Excursionist* in April 1873. Although a Sacramento newspaper had claimed—shortly after the completion of the railroad—that "a journey around the world can be made in eighty days," Cook's tour took 222 days to circumnavigate the globe.[6]

When Cook's entourage passed through Utah Territory, they detoured from Ogden to Salt Lake City and met the Mormon prophet. "All my party were astonished at the magnitude and business characteristics of Salt Lake City, which is rapidly filling with a smart Gentile population," Cook wrote. "My party visited Brigham Young, and most of them also visited the military camp which is located a short distance from the city. . . . I called to see one of my once near neighbors in Leicester, who left his home and friends 19 years since, as a journeyman carpenter. At my request he showed the produce of his farm, which was perfectly astonishing. . . . It is unquestionable that Brigham Young and his adherents have raised a city, cultivated the greater part of the territory of Utah, constructed railways, and executed other public works, and have pioneered the way to the formation of another State of the Union."[7]

High circulation periodicals—particularly *Harper's Weekly* and *Frank Leslie's Illustrated Newspaper*—increased their coverage of Utah after 1869. Frank Leslie, who began his career as an engraver for the *Illustrated London News*, dispatched Joseph Becker, one of his best illustrators, to the territory, and *Harper's Weekly* sent two French artists in 1873. Leslie organized a celebrated coast-to-coast trip and in August 1877, Leslie, his wife, and an entourage of reporters visited the City of the Saints, where Mrs. Leslie interviewed Brigham Young only a few weeks before his death. The newspaper's account of the excursion featured engravings frequently pirated by later visitors, and Mrs. Leslie published an account of the excursion after she returned to New York City.[8]

The completion of the railroad coincided with the end of the Franco-Prussian War and the beginning of the longest period of peace and economic growth in modern European history. Continental tourism to the American West boomed as European newspapers sent reporters to cover the Centennial Exposition in Philadelphia in 1876—which included exhibits by

---

[6] Withey, *Grand Tours and Cook's Tours*, 264, 270–71.

[7] Cook to *The Times*, San Francisco, 31 October 1872, published 27 November 1872, 4. Cook successfully introduced package travel and travelers' checks to the world, and his company has survived into the twenty-first century.   [8] Leslie, *California: A Pleasure Trip from Gotham to the Golden Gate*, 72–103.

Thomas Cook & Son and Frank Leslie—and many of them then headed west to report from the young nation's frontier. They included a French scientist, Sicilian and Belgian noblemen, diplomats from Austria and Prussia, and even an escaped political prisoner, and they were all drawn to Utah to speak with the modern prophet universally acknowledged as "the sovereign of the desert."

Joseph Alexander, Baron von Hübner: Sovereign of the Desert

Diplomat and writer Joseph Alexander, Baron von Hübner (1811–92) was born in Vienna, but the circumstances of his birth are obscure. He used the name of his mother until 1834. The Hapsburg chancellor, Prince Klemens von Metternich (who some sources claim was Hübner's father) provided for his education, and in 1833 he began his distinguished career as a secretary in Metternich's cabinet. He was appointed consul general in Leipzig in 1844, and four years later he was sent as Metternich's emissary to Lombardy-Veneto during uprisings in Milan. Hübner arrived shortly before the *cinque giornate*, and the provisional government arrested and incarcerated him for more than three months. The episode won him lifelong fame in Austria.

Upon his return to Austria, Hübner supported anti-democratic forces during uprisings in Vienna and eventually became secretary to the new president, Prince Felix zu Schwarzenberg. Schwarzenberg sent him to Paris in March 1849 as a special emissary to Louis Napoléon, where he eventually became the Austrian minister. In 1854 he was made a baron. He remained in France until he was recalled after the outbreak of war between Austria, France, and the kingdom of Sardinia—the Second War of Italian Independence—in 1859. When he returned to Austria he served as police minister in the Rechberg cabinet. He was subsequently posted for three years to the Papal States as the Austrian minister in 1865. During his tenure he negotiated the abolition of the 1855 concordat between the Papal States and Austria. Hübner retired from the diplomatic corps in 1871 and embarked on a two-year trip around the world, and he published an account of his trip on his return to Austria that appeared in France, Germany, Italy, England, and the United States. His literary work helped him become a popular lecturer. Hübner was made a permanent member of Austria's House of Lords in 1879, and ten years later Emperor Franz Joseph made him a hereditary count.

JOSEPH HÜBNER, *PROMENADE AUTOUR DU MONDE*
[TRAVEL AROUND THE WORLD], 73–110.
TRANSLATED BY LADY HERBERT.

At five o'clock we came to the Ogden station, situated at the northern extremity of the Salt-Lake, and forming the terminus of the line called the Union Pacific Railroad. From hence to Omaha, the distance is 1,032 miles; to St. Francisco, 882 miles; while a branch line, thirty-seven miles long, constructed by Brigham Young, leads to the Salt-Lake city. Ogden is in its Sunday best. The steps, the platform, and the waiting-rooms of the station are crowded to overflowing with smart folk. We are in the heart of Mormonism. The little town is today honored by the presence of no less a person than the great prophet Brigham Young, who has deigned to visit and preach in its tabernacle. At this moment, he is going to depart. Although the ordinary train starts for the Salt-Lake city in a quarter of an hour, Brigham Young, with some of his wives and a numerous suite, travels by special train. That is quite fair. Is he not sovereign of the desert? The king of the new Jerusalem? Standing on the platform, he salutes majestically with a wave of his hand to the crowd of Mormons, male and female, who take off their hats and curtsey low to the great man. It was a regular court scene, such as we often see in Europe on the arrival or departure of our crowned heads. There was, however, a shade of difference: here nothing was artificial, nothing conventional. And yet there was not a shadow of enthusiasm or pleasure on those gaping faces, or in those bent bodies that remained immovable even for a minute or two after the prophet had disappeared! Was it a simple demonstration of respect? Or an act of etiquette? I do not think so. It seemed to me rather a manifestation of a superstitious belief, tormented, though perhaps not troubled, by vague fears. It was the adoration of a Supreme Being who had your fate at his disposal, and to whom you are irrevocably bound; but whom you dread far more than you love. . . .

What strikes me, is the European look of this crowd which throngs the steps. The stationmaster gives me the key of the enigma. All these men dressed as workmen on Sundays, all these women wearing evidently their best gowns, are English, Norwegian, and Danes; but the British element predominates. Wales furnishes the largest contingent. After the departure of the great man, the crowd mounted sadly and quickly into the railway cars. Women and babies swarmed. The women looked melancholy and subdued; the men vulgar and insignificant. The most distinguished personage in the mob was an Indian warrior with a plumed head-dress and his face all begrimed with yellow ochre; he looked at the Mormons, who are defiling before him, from head to foot, with supreme disdain. In the carriage where I have installed myself, I have an opportunity of watching one of the effects of polygamy. The great part of the men are traveling with two wives; some even have brought three with them; but the youngest is evidently the favorite.

The husband does not trouble his head about any of the others, he only talks to her and buys her cakes and fruit at the station. The other neglected wives sit by, resigned to their fate, with sad and cross expressions. This scene is perpetually being repeated. In fact, it is in the nature of things.

We spend two whole hours in making the thirty-seven miles that separate Ogden from the Mormon capital. Every five minutes we stopped at some little hamlet or isolated farm. The railroad follows the line of the Salt-Lake, which is an immense sheet of water of a dull, metallic color. Steep rocks, empurpled by the setting sun, rise from its bed, like branches of coral thrown on an imperfectly enameled dish. The country is fine, and the effects of the light magical. If it were not for the golden and crimson tints of the sky, the extraordinary clearness and transparency of the atmosphere, and the complete absence of those vaporous clouds that hang toward evening over the southern countries of Europe, one could fancy oneself in Europe on the coasts of Sicily or of Andalusia. At nightfall we arrive at Salt-Lake city, and I alight at the Old Townsend's, that is, at one of the most abominable inns which I have ever had the misfortune to meet within the two hemispheres.[9]

From the 4th to the 7th of June

What a curious town! The houses are invisible. Entirely surrounded by fruit-trees, they are hidden from sight. Acacias and cotton-trees (unknown east of the Missouri, whose flower resembles balls of cotton), form a thick green curtain stretched all along what seem apparently interminable avenues. As in all American towns, these avenues cross one another at right angles, from north to south, and from east to west. On both sides, mountain torrents—the great treasures of the country—roll in abundant if not limpid streams. According to the tales of the first adventurers who visited this unknown land when it still formed part of Mexico, freshwater was not to be procured for love or money. If you are to believe their stories, outside the Salt-Lake there was nothing but pools of brackish water. But Brigham Young has changed all this. The "Elect of God," the Moses of the Mormons, has caused water to gush out from the stony rock, and so conferred an inestimable blessing on the town....

---

[9] Although prominent in Mormon affairs for fifty years, James Townsend has nearly vanished from history. Wilford Woodruff ordained him an Elder in February 1838 in his native Maine, and Townsend soon followed Woodruff westward. He told Artemus Ward and Richard Burton that he was forced to sell his property in Nauvoo for fifty dollars. He established the Salt Lake House in 1854 on East Temple Street (today's Main Street) between First and Second South, where it served as Salt Lake's Pony Express station. He sold it ten years later to go on a mission to England and on his return built the Townsend House on the corner of First South and West Temple, where the Marriott Hotel stands today. "How impressive he may be as an expounder of the Mormon gospel, I don't know," wrote Ward. "His beefsteaks and chicken-pies, however, were first-rate." See Ward, *Artemus Ward: His Travels*. Others, like Burton and Hübner, were less impressed with Townsend's innkeeping skills.

TOWNSEND HOUSE.
Used by permission, Utah State Historical Society, all rights reserved.

During the whole of my walk, I have only met one or two women and a little group of children with books and satchels on their backs, coming from school, and walking quickly without talking. On their little pale faces you already see the care and preoccupation of riper years. The sight of a stranger excites their curiosity; they scan me with a searching look. Not a smile or a shadow of fun is to be seen on any one of those countenances. Then they pass on. Everywhere there is solitude and silence. An Indian warrior from Utah, proudly careering on his thin jade, passes me at a gallop. His black, long, straight, shining hair, falls on his shoulders from under a diadem of feathers; his face is painted yellow and red; his features are fierce to the last degree; he is armed to the teeth, and his appearance is really terrible. Behind him, running on foot, are his two squaws, the very types of misery and female degradation.

I turn my steps toward Main-Street, the principal avenue of the town, and suddenly find myself in a regular city of the Far West. If it were not for the Indians, and for the extraordinary number of women and children who, even in this busy quarter, far outnumber the men, one would forget that one was in the centre of Mormonism. Here there are no trees. Houses line each side of the street. The greater portion are built of brick or rather of "adobes," which are made of mud dried in the sun; others of wood and beams covered with canvas, tell of the first immigrants. The more modern buildings have some pretension to architecture. In all of them, the first floor consists of open shops. The walls are, without exception, covered from top to bottom with gaudy advertisements.

The streets are thronged with bullock-wagons and carriages of every description. A stagecoach, drawn by ten horses, belonging to Wells, Fargo, and Co., a firm well known in the States, draws a crowd and increases the confusion. Formerly these coaches were the only resource of the impatient traveler; but since the railroad opened, they have nearly disappeared. Porters, miners on foot or on donkey-back—in a word, a whole body of strong, intelligent-looking men, with tanned, weather-beaten faces and brawny arms, whose life is one continual fight with savage nature, and who are justly termed the pioneers of civilization, jostle one another in the crowded thoroughfares, all intent on their respective business.

The ancient masters of the soil, the Utahs [Utes], of a finer and less degraded race than the greater portion of the Indians on the borders, mingle their warriors with the crowd. They are encamped just outside the town, and come into it now and then, each followed by his wives. They hold their heads high and examine carefully, without betraying the smallest surprise, all the wonders of modern civilization. I met several in one of the most elegant of the Main Street shops. They looked at everything exposed for sale very minutely, all the time maintaining their air of dignity and proud indifference. The looking-glasses only put them out, and then what bursts of laughter! They could not believe their eyes or cease admiring themselves. . . .

In the forenoon, "Old" Townsend took me to see the tabernacle. It is a long, low hall, entirely bare and destitute of religious emblems, with a raised daïs at one end, on which were placed the armchairs of the prophet and bishops, the whole being covered by a heavy oval cupola, which is rightly compared to a dish cover such as they use in England for covering hot joints. Alongside they are building a new temple, which is to be an immense edifice of cut stone, in the Roman style. But only the foundations are as yet laid: and no one hopes or seems to wish for the new tabernacle to be completed. There are scarcely any men at work on it, for both money and fervor are wanting.

The theatre is far more popular. This is one of the thousand schemes of Brigham Young and the great resource of the inhabitants of the Salt-Lake City. It is opened every night. The house is badly decorated and still worse lit. In the pit I saw groups of children, who had evidently come all alone. On benches and in the galleries sat a number of men in blouses with their wives (two or three apiece) dressed with a certain amount of care. The Prophet, who has reserved for himself the best box near the stage, had not, contrary to his usual custom, made his appearance that evening; but I saw through the curtains, one of the youngest of his wives, who was very graceful and pretty, and in toilet that might be called elegant. One of Brigham's own daughters,

Mrs. Alice Clawson, whose talent is justly appreciated, played the principal part. She married a man in easy circumstances, which, however, does not prevent her accepting a good salary.[10] The piece, a sensational drama that had a great run in England some years ago, and is full of English habits and institutions and contrasts singularly with the public of the New Jerusalem. Society of the Middle Ages, as painted by Shakespeare, is not farther afield than is highlife in England at this moment compared with the social state of the Mormons. Nevertheless, the play was listened to with great attention, although there was neither laughter nor clapping. I am told that Brigham Young, who is himself the censor, and excludes all indecent pieces, is very anxious to encourage people to go to his theatre. It is in his hands a kind of school of art, whereby he strives to refine the habits of a society that has been reduced by circumstances, as we shall see, to a condition of perpetual forced labor.

It is two o'clock—the heat is terrible; the sun is at a white heat. It is the dinner-hour of the place, and the guests at "Old" Townsend's are waiting with no small impatience. A large company is gathered in the veranda. . . . All this society is composed of gentiles, miners and their families, commercial travelers, clerks, and government agents. In consequence, the head of the establishment, the "gentleman" at the office, and even the waiters, look at us with an evil eye, and the service corresponds with their hostile feelings. This influx of unbelievers irritates and frightens them. Alas! the good old times of Mormonism are over. The masses, perhaps, do not realize it; but no intelligent man can doubt the fact. Certainly, Mr. Townsend, the dignitary of the tabernacle, is not a model innkeeper. He pays little or no attention to this house and still less to his guests. He leaves everything to his two wives, who bear the burden and heat of the day, if not civilly, at least with a patience and resignation worthy of a better cause. I was really sorry for them. . . .

At last the signal is given. The ladies enter first, gravely, in single file. Afterwards, every man runs, stumbles, treads on the other's toes, or fights with his elbows, one more vigorously than the other. Doctor C. has fortunately taken me under his protection. He is a man of mark, who, in consequence, has a place reserved for him, and manages to squeeze me in alongside. These meals have but one merit, and that is to be able to be dispatched in ten minutes. They give you nothing but one dish of hard, badly cooked meat and one or two biscuits. For dessert, you have very good wild strawberries—for drink, pure water. The bar or taproom does not exist: the law forbids it. Nevertheless, the Mormons manage to elude the commandment, and wine and spirits abound in their own houses. The only happy

---

[10] In 1856 Alice Young and in 1868 her half-sister, Emily Augusta Young, married Hiram B. Clawson, a protégé of their father who eventually had four wives with whom he fathered forty-two children. See Ellsworth, ed., *Dear Ellen: Two Mormon Women and Their Letters*, 32–34.

moment is when one can leave the dinner table with the proud satisfaction of feeling one has accomplished a painful duty....

Since the opening of the Pacific Railway, the number of visitors has increased daily, but Brigham Young has not tired of being stared at, examined, and commented upon as an object of curiosity. To see him requires letters of introduction.

My host, "Old" Townsend, offered to present one that had been given to me at New York, and to arrange an interview. One morning accordingly, at ten o'clock, we went together to the President's house. Some bishops and one or two elders whom we met on the road begged to accompany us. I had to run the gauntlet of the usual questions, but I did not spare them either, and they answered me with very tolerable grace. They were all Americans, for, as a general rule, the Americans alone aspire to the higher grades of elders or bishops, and are evidently better educated and better brought up than the greater portion of the Mormons, three parts of whom are Europeans. Simply though decently dressed, these men bore no sign of their ecclesiastical dignities. Their faces told one nothing whatever. There was no trace of fanaticism, affectation, or hypocrisy about them; still less of anything clerical. Nothing betrayed the habit of meditation or prayer, or even a wish to pretend anything of the kind. They looked just what they were—men of business, farmers, shopkeepers, or commercial travelers. It was impossible to be what the English call more commonplace. There was only one exception—the Bishop of —. I never saw a more slovenly dress, dirtier linen, or a more threadbare coat; but he was, on the other hand, the only one of the lot who had a jolly, open countenance, and a frank, hearty laugh. "I have got three wives," he exclaimed; "so I am very well off."—"Not the least in the world."—"Don't you ever feel any scruple about it?"—"On the contrary; I should be scrupulous if I didn't. In having several wives, I am simply obeying God's special commandment. I feed my children and send them to school—that's all that is necessary. But as for the rest, you can't understand it, for you are not one of the elect. Now, we are not only one of the elect, but of the privileged few. God has given us the privilege of inspiration, and all that we do is right and well done. That's the reason we have been made bishops. Inspiration is granted to a man or not, as God pleases. He alone can give or refuse it."

He then entered into a confused explanation that he said was a development of this theory; but in spite of all the trouble I gave myself to follow his line of thought, it was utterly and entirely unintelligible. It was simply nonsense, balderdash, and gibberish, delivered with a kind of careless, indifferent ease, like a schoolboy who is repeating a lesson by heart without understanding or thinking of a single word he is saying.

The most remarkable man of the company was Mr. George Smith, called the historian, who must not, however, be confounded with Joe Smith, the founder of the sect, who was murdered. George is more educated than the other dignitaries of the tabernacle, and so holds the first place in the church after the President, Brigham Young. He assisted the latter in guiding the Saints at the time of their terrible journey from the borders of the Mississippi to those of the Salt Lake, and took part likewise in the works consequent on the first establishment of the New Jerusalem. He gave me a great deal of curious information, and likewise a pamphlet which he wrote two years ago.[11]

Walking very slowly, for the heat was overpowering, and seeking the shade of the acacia and cotton trees, which bordered the long avenue, we at last arrived before the President's house surrounded by a high wall and composed of several distinct buildings and separate apartments for the use of his wives and children. A great room at one of the angles of the enclosure is a school for the exclusive use of the latter. We crossed the threshold and were shown into the parlor, a little room simply furnished and ornamented with twelve oil paintings representing the Mormon apostles. The first place was reserved, of course, for the portrait of Joe Smith. The secretary and son-in-law of the President, a little deformed youth, after having offered us chairs, began to cross examine me in a loud voice in the usual American way. Whilst I was answering, I thought I saw a shadow behind the half-open door. Twenty minutes passed in this way. The conversation went on; but the President still kept us waiting. At last I got up and said: "Mr. Young has doubtless his own occupations. I have mine. I have nothing to say to him, and do not care to wait any longer to see him. Besides, they are waiting for me at Fort Douglas." At that very moment, the door, which had attracted my attention, opened suddenly, and Brigham Young appeared on the threshold. He was dressed with great care, and looked as if he had just come out of the hairdresser's hands. For some minutes he looked at me in silence; then he walked toward me in a solemn manner, only acknowledging the low bow of his people by a slight wave of the hand. He had his hat on his head but took it off hastily when he saw me deliberately putting on mine, and then, sitting down, motioned me to an armchair alongside of him. The bishops and elders took their places at a respectful distance. On a sign to his secretary, the latter, standing before his master, read my letter of introduction out loud.

The conversation that followed lasted nearly an hour. I give the main

---

[11] George A. Smith (1817–75), a gregarious cousin of Joseph Smith Jr., became an apostle in 1839. He led the founding of the first settlements in southern Utah in 1851 and became LDS church historian in 1854, but he was not well educated. After watching him remove his false teeth, toupee, and spectacles, Indians called the portly, bald, and, at times, vain apostle *Non-choko-wicher*, "Man-Who-Takes-Himself-Apart." See Van Wagoner and Walker, *A Book of Mormons*, 270–74. Smith probably gave Hübner his *The Rise, Progress, and Travels of the Church of Jesus Christ of Latter Day Saints*.

points, which I noted down in my journal as soon as I got back to the inn, and was struck, while doing so, at the trouble I found in seizing a single intelligible thought amidst the grand phrases and the confused and illogical statements with which his conversation was interlarded. (Mr. Young said nothing very remarkable; nothing but what he said to everybody, everywhere, and especially in his very short sermons in the tabernacle. I do not, therefore, fear to commit an indiscretion by giving publicity to his words.)

"The world," he began, "is full of prejudices. A man must be of a privileged caste to rise above them. God gives this privilege only to His elect. What they teach is the truth, for they only speak or act by inspiration. Faith and work—this is the sum total of our task . . . the object of our religion is to make the bad good, and the good better. Read the Book of Mormon. It has been translated in all languages, and is sold in Main Street. You will find in it a correct account of our origin and history. The first Mormons emigrated in the time of King Solomon(!) The last immigration was 600 years before our Savior (!) Today they pour in from all sides. The hour will come when they shall be spread over the whole earth."

On my remarking that he, Brigham Young, seemed to me to unite both temporal and spiritual powers in Utah, he answered sharply: "You are quite mistaken. The Mormon is free. Everything is done by compromise between the contending parties, or by arbitration. I am not afraid of the railroads, as people fancy. We did not leave Nauvoo to fly away from the gentiles. We left it simply because we were turned out."

I then attacked him on the subject of polygamy. "In Europe," I said, "you are well known. Everyone appreciates the energy of a man who has made his will a law to his disciples and who has learned how to transform a desert into a garden. But on the other hand, I cannot conceal from you that there is but one cry of indignation against you for the polygamy you practice and you have introduced into your community. The general opinion is that it is a shame to women and a disgrace to the century in which we live." Here the audience gave an ominous growl of dissent. The President started but constrained himself. After a few moments of silence, he said, speaking in a low voice and with a slightly disdainful smile: "Prejudice, prejudice, prejudice! We have the greatest of all examples—the example of the patriarchs. What was pleasing to God in their day, why should it be proscribed now?" He then went into a long explanation of a theory which was new to me, regretting that men did not imitate the example of animals, and treating the subject of the relations of the sexes in so confused and at the same time so ambiguous a manner, that it was next to impossible to understand his meaning; but he arrived finally at the conclusion that polygamy was the only effective remedy for the great social evil of prostitution. Then he interrupted himself by exclaiming, "As for the rest, what I do, and what I teach, I do and teach by the special command of God." When I got up to take my leave, he took my hand, drew me toward him and murmured, closing his eyes, "Blessing, blessing, luck!"

Brigham Young, who was born in Vermont State, has just completed his seventieth year, but appears much younger than he really is. He is above the middle height, holds himself very upright, and seems to enjoy perfect health. His crisp, curly, light-brown hair, with a tinge of red in it, carefully brushed and combed, shades a broad head well placed on a pair of good square shoulders. His eyes, which never look you straight in the face, betray more cunning than intelligence; his mouth is thoroughly sensual; his square and almost disproportionately massive chin indicates an energy that I should fancy would border on cruelty. Taking it altogether, his face is one which can only belong to a remarkable man. It fascinates and repels you at the same time. One understands how this man exercises the charm of a serpent that immobilizes its victims by the terror it inspires and crushes them without scruple or pity the moment they strive to escape its clutches. I do not say that Brigham Young *is* like this, I only say that his appearance gave me that impression, which I share with all the other strangers who have described their visits to the Mormon chief. Certainly one ought not to judge a man by the external appearance only, or after one short interview; therefore I am only writing down the effect which his appearance produced upon me, and which was most unfavorable.

As to his manners, I find them just as unsympathetic. They are wanting in simplicity, or rather they bear the stamp of affectation,—one moment pompous, the next familiar, now unctuous, then joking, now severe, then oily. Brigham Young never for a moment forgets the part he chooses to play as prophet. Before intoning one of his sententious phrases, he bends his head, assumes an air of majesty, and fixes his eyes on the ground. When he speaks, it is slowly, with a tone of authority, and an interval between each word. Then suddenly he lifts his head, throws it back and shows his great white teeth, and his huge sensual mouth gleaming with a sinister smile. Then he shuts his eyes again and lowers his voice; that's when he wishes to be funny. These fits of forced and unnatural gaiety did not win me in the least. I know not what kind of grossly theatrical pretence in these sudden changes from the sublime to the ridiculous, from tragic effect to vulgar comic; but I suppose the ignorant public are carried away by this claptrap and are willing to let themselves be humbugged. I remarked, too, that at such times the bishops and elders all pretended to be electrified.

Judging by his exterior, his manners, and the bosh he has the impudence to tell to you, Brigham Young is the most audacious hypocrite under the sun. But look around you! Listen not to what his acolytes tell you, who adore him as a divinity, but impartial witnesses, or rather men who have no sympathy with him, but who know both him and his works: listen to what they will tell you of the obstacles he has overcome, the dangers he has surmounted, the wonders he has wrought,—and not the least of these miracles is having captivated, subdued, and broken the will of nearly 200,000 human beings;—let all this be told you on the spot by impartial men, well acquainted with the state of things, by the commandant of the federal troops at Fort Douglas, for instance, or by his officers; by the Chief Justice, by the Attorney-General, by the doctors, by those who have been resident here for years, by the miners who come and go; and your disgust will give place first to astonishment, and then to something bordering on admiration!—admiration, not certainly for the doctrines Brigham Young has inculcated, nor still less for his practices, nor even for the extraordinary success of his colonization, for others besides Mormons have done as much in other parts of the American Continent; nor for the motives that have actuated him, and which, being unknown to us, we have not a right to judge—but for the talents and ability which Providence has vouchsafed to this most extraordinary man; for the clear instincts of this uneducated mind, for his indomitable energy, his marvelous perseverance, and especially for the mysterious and absolute power he exercises over his sect. Many books, pamphlets, and innumerable articles have been written on Brigham Young, on Deseret, and on the faith and practices of the Mormons. The greater part of these accounts are exact enough in their descriptions. Nothing can be more attractive than the picture of New Jerusalem by Hepworth Dixon. The portrait is exact as far as it goes. But neither this author, nor any others who have written on this subject, have been able to find out the secret of the terrible power of this man, which has enabled him to establish in the center of America a state of things which politically, religiously, and socially is a direct negation of the manners, ideas, and belief of the century in which we live....

On Sunday Brigham preaches sometimes in his Tabernacle. I did not hear him; but according to the unanimous testimony of his hearers, these sermons are a mixture of incoherent quotations from the Bible, denunciations of persons or hateful insinuations, vulgar personalities, and unctuous or commonplace phrases. His language is coarse, sometimes injurious, and always stamped by the most profound ignorance. He has not a shadow of natural eloquence. For a long time the Prophet has chosen polygamy as the subject of his homilies, so as to answer thus indirectly the attacks of the American press, which, in this, is the faithful echo of public opinion in the United States.

As he pretends to tolerate every form of religion, he opens the Tabernacle occasionally to preachers of other sects. An Anglican clergyman, on one occasion, availed himself of this permission, and, putting on a surplice, addressed the congregation. After him, Brigham, wrapped in a bed sheet, got into the pulpit amidst shouts of laughter from the audience, and delivered a comic speech, which was a coarse parody of the sermon they had just heard.

(I found this fact mentioned in some book or paper. I forget where. But it was confirmed to me on the spot by credible witnesses.)

In one word, it is absolutism carried to its utmost limits and personified by the head of the religion. On the part of the sectarians, the most blind faith in the person of the Prophet. No divine worship, for the short Sunday sermons and a few occasional hymns sung in the Tabernacle do not deserve that name. In general, speaking of the masses, no religious feeling or sentiment whatever; or rather, the whole of their religious sentiments are concentrated in a fanatical worship of Brigham Young. Work and faith are proclaimed the governing principles of the sect: work, manual and forced, and pushed to an extreme; for besides earning their bread, they have to pay their debts to the President (this excessive labour explains the marvellous and rapid progress of the colony). A monopoly which embraces everything and extends to everything, exercised by the Prophet only. The intervention of the latter, either personally or through the medium of his bishops, in the most intimate family relations and in the most private affairs, whether of business or other matters: in all difficult and critical moments, recourse only to one man, the oracle, Brigham Young: and to sum up all, polygamy, declared a duty and a privilege, and practised for twenty years—such is the essence of Mormonism.

Rudolph Schleiden: He Disapproved When Any Mormon Drank Wine or Beer

Rudolph Schleiden, a native of Bremen, was a member of the German Reichstag and served as the Hanseatic League's minister in Washington. During his first visit to the United States in 1858, he saw the ruins of the Nauvoo temple and became infatuated with the history of Mormonism, and in 1872 he finally visited Utah. His recitation of Mormon history and its beliefs, using the Mormon catechism as a reference, and his account of why they settled in Utah are not always accurate. Schleiden concluded that despite what others had written about the people of Utah, their existence and activities had been nothing but a boon to the United States.

>Rudolph Schleiden, *Reise Erinnerungen aus den Vereinigten Staaten* [Memories of Travel in the United States of America], 28–72. Translated by tsc.
>
>The first president of the Mormons does not look as though he was born as far back as June 1, 1801, and is therefore in his 72nd year. His hair is light brown and only his beard has some gray in it. He is of average height and

powerfully built with a slight tendency toward corpulence. A black overcoat, pants of the same color, a white vest with a gold chain and small smoke topaz pendant give him, as does his whole being, more the appearance of a bank or railway president than a prophet. For he is also reputed to be well-to-do and a very able businessman. His facial expression is friendly and mild but lets evidence of a keen mind show through. His speech is clear, yet not very loud; he has a pleasant-sounding voice and an elegant manner of expressing himself. No one would ever be able to tell that he had, as President Smith told me, attended school for only eleven days, been a gardener (at Seward's father-in-law's) in his youth, and later been a carpenter and joiner.[12] He himself said to me, with his particular modesty, that Hebrew was the only foreign language that he had mastered later in life, along with some other knowledge, but that with improvisation he could make himself understood by all the various nationalities among his people. Yet, the next day, when he introduced me to a German-speaking American, it gave me an opportunity to notice that he understands even more German than one should assume, given this remark. President Young seems to not like to speak about the teachings and customs of his sect, at least not in front of strangers, but prefers to discuss national economic questions, and most particularly everything concerning the development of the territory that is prospering under his direction. At first he, himself, was somewhat cautious in this regard. Only after we had conversed for a time and he was certain that we had not come to speculate in mining or other enterprises, but were rather only seeking to be informed and entertained, did he become communicative. Since having studied the Mormons' exodus and having seen Brigham Young's accomplishments in Utah, I have no scruples about calling him an organizationally talented person and the founder of a state. As to the means he is supposed to have used in part to achieve them, I can judge them just as little as his religious faith. The Mormons trust him unconditionally and call him the "lion of the Lord." That he jealously upholds the reputation of his people and strives to improve them morally, intellectually, and materially, I also do not doubt.

Brigham Young began the conversation by commenting that, although being mindful of his childhood memories from New England (like Joseph Smith, he was born in Vermont) he strictly keeps the Sabbath and as a rule does not receive visitors on Sunday, he would gladly make an exception for us because we had been recommended to him by Seward. After expressing his admiration for the former Secretary of State with lively accolades, he changed the topic to Utah and its affairs. He expressed his hope that the ter-

---

[12] In 1817 the future Mormon prophet worked as an apprentice carpenter on a house in Auburn, New York, later owned by Lincoln's secretary of state, William C. Seward. See Palmer and Butler, *Brigham Young: The New York Years*, 11–16. In 1869 Seward visited Young in Salt Lake.

ritory would be admitted into the Union as a state should Greeley, whom he called a good man, be elected president. Already while taking a fleeting look around the spacious room whose furnishings were respectable and comfortable though simple, I had noticed a picture of Greeley, as well as a couple of good landscapes of the Wasatch Mountains and the portraits of the brothers, Joseph and Hyrum Smith and many other prominent Mormons. As I was able to have a closer look at it two days later, I discovered that it was a gift from Greeley and bore an inscription in his hand which read, "Yours, for universal amnesty and impartial suffrage, Horace Greeley."[13] Regarding relations with the present Union government, Brigham Young commented that he hoped they would turn out favorably; but that at any rate the Mormons were no worse off than the first Christians. In reply to my question about relations with the Indians, he answered that generally they were very good. He had, right from the start, sought to successfully win the Indians over with friendly, charitable treatment. The stealing and killing, which have recently been on the increase once again, are essentially the result of bad management by Indian agents, for they very often used the provisions earmarked for the impoverished Indians for themselves and let the Redskins suffer. Corruption has actually gone from bad to worse in recent years, and it is impossible to foresee how it will end.

He reported very favorably on the diligence, moral uprightness, and sobriety of the Mormons, decreeing that no spirits would be found in a Mormon home, and that he disapproved when any Mormon drank wine or beer. When I thereupon reminded him that, according to the scriptures, Noah planted grape vines, he had an appropriate answer close at hand, and said that Noah, himself, also had soon experienced the evil consequences thereof.

At our departure, the prophet conferred his blessing on us with simple, pleasant words.

The next day we got to know and better assess the second president, George A. Smith, as he most kindly acted as our driver during an excursion of several hours. A tall, very powerfully built man with a full face, he looks to be at least 50 years old. At our first meeting, he seemed a bit slow-witted and unrefined to me. But this impression disappeared completely as I got to know him better. He proved to be a very good-natured man with a very healthy intellect and a great, well-placed sense of humor. There was something touching about the unpretentious way in which he spoke of his difficult childhood. We found none of his fellow-believers to be as willing as he

---

[13] In what some regard as the first published newspaper interview, editor Horace Greeley of the *New York Tribune* questioned Brigham Young for two hours on 13 July 1859. Young, the editor noted, "assumed as undeniable that outside of the Mormon church, married men usually keep mistresses—that incontinence is the general rule, and continence the rare exception. This assumption was habitual with the Mormons." See Greeley, *An Overland Journey*, 219. Greeley won 40 percent of the popular vote in 1872 as the Liberal Republican Party candidate for president but died three weeks after the election.

was to enlighten us with apparent openness, about all circumstances and questions. His fellow-Mormons have given him the nickname "Pillar of Truth." He was elected to his present high office in 1868 after the death of Heber C. Kimball. His colleague, President Daniel H. Wells, did not give the same impression of confidence. The hard features of his constantly twitching face very likely had some influence on creating such an impression. Nevertheless, we also are only able to praise the great courtesy and obligingness of this obviously very clever man....

In 1871 Brigham Young was accused of having 16 wives. He resides with these and has forty-nine surviving children with them, ranging from two to forty years in age. In addition, a string of old spiritual wives are sealed to him, of whom not all are personally known to him. Most of his family lives with him in the same large, orderly house which is appropriately named "The Beehive." A few family members live nearby. For his first wife, who is still held in the highest esteem, he has a particularly pleasant country-house (White House); for his school-aged children he had his own school house built and Mr. Young, himself, is involved in their instruction. Although the much-heard complaints about there being domestic misfortune where several wives share one husband may be well-founded, to Brigham Young's credit, it is said that his family lives happily together in the greatest degree of harmony. This has also been confirmed to me by Seward, who is perhaps the only non-Mormon that the Prophet has included in his family circle as a friend....

One of our most interesting experiences in Utah was organized by Brigham Young. It was an excursion to Lehi in the Utah Valley on the South Railroad, which had been opened only a few days before our arrival. It gave us some insight into the social life of the Mormons and a more accurate understanding of the wonderfully rapid development of the region's natural resources. Aside from my two friends and myself, and much-loved ex-governor Fuller and his dear wife, who are now resident in Salt Lake City, the gathering consisted only of distinguished Mormons.[14] Several of them, including their top leader, were accompanied by their wife or one of their wives. Some mothers had their babies with them. Occasionally, the Mormons have been compared to the Moslems. Common to both is polygamy as the pronounced carnal element and a close association between church and state. But the Mormons have neither formally trained clergy, nor do

---

[14] Physician, lawyer, dentist, author, lecturer, railroad executive, reporter, and military recruiter Frank Fuller served as acting governor of Utah during the Civil War. Abraham Lincoln declined to send Brigham Young a message when he appointed Fuller territorial secretary, but "I will say to you that if Brigham will let me alone I'll let him alone." See "Frank Fuller, War Governor of Utah," *New York Times*, 1 October 1911. Fuller later became a Washington agent for the LDS church and appears to have been the federal official who betrayed Gov. John Dawson, leading to the assault in which Dawson was "half emasculated" on New Year's Eve 1862.

they exclude and socially diminish the female sex. On this excursion we were able to confirm the latter. However, I remained doubtful whether the oft repeated saying, "In America, more than anywhere else, women are the better half of Creation," can be applied to Mormon women. Some of the ladies we met were rather beautiful, and many were pleasant and well-mannered. Nevertheless, when it came to intellectual bearing and genuine culture, I found that most of them seemed second-rate to the men, who of course included the pillars of the Mormon community.

Louis Laurent Simonin:
Stenhouse Promised to Introduce His Two Wives

Louis Simonin (1830–86) attended the school of mines at Saint-Etienne and eventually visited mines in France, England, and the United States before becoming a professor of geology at the Ecole centrale d'architecture in 1865. He soon made his first trip to the Far West.[15] He did not visit Utah but he discussed the Mormon presence in the West and their role in the California gold rush. Simonin visited Salt Lake City in 1872 on his second trip to the U.S., and his more serious observations of the Mormons avoided sensationalism and proved quite complimentary.[16] Simonin was so interested in the natural history of the territory that he dug for Indian artifacts near the Great Salt Lake. He also donated skulls to the Paris Museum, which evidently considered them to have some scientific or anthropological importance. Simonin also conducted the requisite interview with Brigham Young. He was admitted to the waiting room, and eventually into the president's office ahead of others, because of the distance he had traveled.

> Louis Simonin, *A travers les Etats-Unis, de l'Atlantique au Pacifique* [Across the United States from the Atlantic to the Pacific], 66–67, 70, 79–80, 107–9, 112–21. Translated by Rick Grunder.
> One morning at the Townsend Hotel, I had a visit from the son of Brigham Young.[17] He was then acting on behalf of his father in the work

---

[15] See Simonin, "Le Far West américain," *Le tour du monde* 1 (1868): 225–388; and Simonin, *Le grand-ouest des Etats-Unis*. An Italian translation was published in installments in *L'Universo Illustrato*. See Simonin, "Viaggio in California," *L'Universo Illustrato*, and in book form as Simonin, *Il Far-West degli Stati Uniti*.

[16] Simonin, "De Washington à San Francisco à travers le continent américain," *Le tour du monde* 1 (1874), 161–240; Simonin, "Da Washington a San Francisco: Attraverso il continente Americano," *Il Giro del Mondo* 20 (1874): 24–41; and Simonin, *Attraverso gli Stati Uniti dall'Atlantico al Pacifico*.

[17] This probably refers to John W. Young.

T. B. H. Stenhouse (1825–1882).
Used by permission, Utah State Historical Society, all rights reserved.

related to the railroad. He explained to me what he was doing, his projects, his enterprise. "You see here all the capital we brought with us," he said, showing me his large hands. "If we have earned a little money, if we have even become rich, we owe it only to this." He expressed regret that his activities at the moment were too pressing to allow him to take me in his car and show me the area around the city and part of the work on the tracks. I have not seen him since, but I retain the highest regard for him, as I do for his father. . . .

Stenhouse, a highly able journalist in a country that already counts so many good journalists, came to Europe to preach Mormonism in Switzerland and speaks French very properly. He graciously offered me the columns of his journal to tell about the excavations I commissioned (as will be explained below) in the mound at the Great Salt Lake.[18]

Stenhouse promised to introduce his two wives to us, but he always forgot to do it. They lived separately, not out of jealousy, at least to hear him tell it, but to raise their children better. He was getting ready to take a third wife soon. "It is not I who will choose her," he told us, "but one of my wives. We generally take those whom they point out to us, and who have some particular talent that the first wives lack. The one makes jam better (and you know Salt Lake fruit preserves are renowned); another irons better

---

[18] Simonin's footnote reads, in part: "M. Stenhouse has since been expelled by the pope with one of his wives, after having been attacked and insulted by the Saints."

or darns the linen better; a third cooks better, and so on with the others. The household thus becomes complete. Beyond this, the pope would not allow us to marry a new wife if we did not have the means to support her. It is the same here as in Turkey: you have to be able to maintain the wives you take; that's why we don't have more."

We were everywhere given the same observations about polygamy. Savage, who needed a second wife for his photography studio, his bookstore, his stationery shop, went to get her from among the emigrants recently arrived from Wales. We saw her working in the artist's studio. She has a kindly appearance, so gracious, classical features, even pretty; she is one of the most pleasing people I met in Utah, and one would be well taken with her in any country. . . .[19]

George Smith, Church historian and one of the twelve apostles, gladly opened his archives to our view; he showed us journals, various curious documents, shorthand sermons. He is plump, forthright, likes to laugh, and his appearance reminds one of a jolly friar. . . .

One Sunday my comrade and I participated in afternoon services. At a certain point, they passed a large white metal cruet around the room, in the shape of those one sees in all the homes of the United States, in all the hotels, filled with ice water, winter as well as summer, from which all who are thirsty drink. They carried this vessel around, and everyone drank out of it. I thought this a considerate precaution by the presiding bishops to refresh the pious throng, for the weather was very hot. I drank like the others, and passed to my neighbor on the left the chalice I had received from my neighbor to the right. Meanwhile, noticing that everyone drank, I said to myself that it was not possible everyone would have equal thirst, and so, turning to the one who had passed me the vessel said, "What ceremony are they performing just now?"

— The sacrament; it is our communion.

— And to take a drink is to commune?

— Certainly; we partake of the emblem of water.

— So, I have taken the sacrament?

— You said it.

— And what does communion make of me?

— The beginnings of a Mormon; it only remains for you to accept baptism.

---

[19] Renowned frontier photographer Charles Roscoe Savage (1832–1909) was born in poverty in Southampton, England, and only learned to read and write after Stenhouse converted him to Mormonism in 1848. He served a mission to Switzerland and conducted Italian and Swiss converts to New York in February 1855. Savage journeyed to Salt Lake in 1860, opened a photographic studio, and later formed partnerships with Marsena Cannon and George M. Ottinger. His work won prizes at World Expositions in Chicago, St. Louis, and San Francisco. Savage married Annie Adkins in 1856, Mary Emma Fowler in 1871, Ellen Fenn in 1876, and Annie Clowes in 1895. See Richards, *The Savage View: Charles Savage, Pioneer Mormon Photographer*.

SALT LAKE THEATRE, SALT LAKE CITY.
Used by permission, Utah State Historical Society, all rights reserved.

— And then?
— To marry several wives to be a complete Saint.
— Fine; but in my country polygamy is a hanging matter; to each their laws. *Locus regit actum*, as goes the Roman judicial adage.
— In that case, remain here, that's the best thing to do.

And the Saint went back to reading the Bible of Nephi (which he had not closed for a moment except to answer me), while I took to consider that I could call myself a little bit Mormon, like the medical man of New York who had posted on his door: "Licensed Medical Practitioner of Sorts, Soon to be Doctor." . . .

At some distance from the Salt Lake, on the slopes of the mountain that borders the lake on the south, we encountered, not another mound, but a burial cave. . . . The cavern had already been rummaged. They had taken out two skulls, one with its jawbone, the other worn to the bony cavity; beside the skulls were the skeletons which had not taken long to fall to dust. One of these skulls served at the Salt Lake Theater for the productions of Hamlet: *Alas! poor Yorick!* They were both generously offered to me through the intervention of Mr. Savage and Mr. Ottinger, and I made a gift of them to the Paris Museum. One can study them in the fine anthropological collection of that establishment.

Max Joseph August Heinrich Markus Buchner: Brigham Young Sat on His Sofa Slumped Down

Max Buchner (1846–1921), born in Munich, Bavaria, was a diplomat and world traveler. He circumnavigated the globe via India, Hawaii, San Francisco, and New York, visiting Utah while traveling on the transcontinental railroad from the West to the East Coast. In his memoirs he described his visit to Utah, apparently in 1876, and his observation of Brigham Young. Buchner traveled extensively in Africa as a Prussian diplomat from 1878 to 1882, serving as Prussian consul in Cameroon. He signed the West African treaty that made Togoland a German protectorate.[20]

> Max Buchner, *Reise durch den Stillen Ozean*
> [Travel across the Pacific Ocean], 436–47. Translated by TSC.

At Ogden the scenery once again became somewhat tolerable and continued that way during the slow two-hour ride to Salt Lake City. Indeed, there were no trees aside from those artificially planted, and yet the numerous farmsteads were surrounded by a green that, after two days of privation was doubly pleasant to see. Even the mountains were adorned with particularly appealing colors. Large patches of soft pink heather covered the peaks, while the rest of the slopes were gray-green and yellow, and a cold white marked the steeply plunging cliffs. Stretched out to the right was the dark blue salty expanse of the lake inside its marshy shore. Salt deposits covered dried-up pools along its periphery.

The broad valley, gently rising up to the mountains, was populated with a multitude of friendly looking houses scattered among gardens. Where they clustered most densely, the unwieldy gray shingle roof of the Tabernacle rose up above them like an elephant standing among the crowded stalls of an Asian market or a whale rising out of a choppy sea—that was Salt Lake City.

Here I hoped to get a couple of days' rest. A streetcar with two lively mules took me away from the train station's slovenly wooden shacks into the city. Shady, tree-lined walks bordered unusually wide dusty streets that crossed at right angles. Next to the sidewalks ran fast-flowing streamlets. The houses were surrounded by gardens and pleasantly concealed by shrubbery and trees. Only on the first two or three business streets did the buildings stand side by side without a break.

Salt Lake City has a population of about 25,000 and is quickly traversed. Main or East Temple is the primary business street which looks quite generally American. A couple of hotels, shops of all kinds, a drugstore, several

---
[20] Beatrix Heintze, ed., *Max Buchners Reise nach Zentralafrica, 1878–1882*.

beer parlors and saloons are all assembled together with colorful signs bearing pompous-sounding names.

Most noticeable of all is a specific Mormon oddity, the so-called Bee Hive Store, a large three-story brick building with massive glass windows in front. Glittering above the entrance is a golden eye of God [the All-Seeing Eye] and around it in golden letters is the inscription "Holiness to the Lord. Zions Cooperative Mercantile Institution." If we step inside under this tasteless emblem of sanctimoniousness, we will enter into an enormous bazaar, in which one can find all the possible items that any person might ever require, from thrashing machines to sewing needles, from Indian bearskins to kitchen aprons, from color prints to office stationery. The ground floor and a triple row of galleries one on top of the other are cluttered with wares. Banking transactions are carried out in an area divided off by a metal grill. The lively hustle and bustle of buyers and sellers somewhat justifies the name "Beehive Warehouse." The best thing about this establishment is that it operates at the expense of, and for the benefit of the whole community, so that it constitutes a consumers' co-operative of the largest size. Only Mormons may partake of its advantages. . . .

The majority of the streets have a quiet, peaceful, rural character. You do not meet many people. Everywhere there are shade trees and orchards, long walls and fences and murmuring brooks that flow hurriedly toward the lower-lying Jordan River. Salt Lake City is very pleased at its good fortune of having an abundance of water without which no agriculture would be possible because of its dry climate. The constantly cloudless sky, the hot sun, the clouds of dust, and the mules with red tassels pulling streetcars are reminiscent of Mexico and other southern lands. On these streets one hardly notices a trace of Mormonism's quintessential polygamy. It is not as if husbands went for walks here with ten wives and fifty children in tow. At best, out in the country, you would see a farmer driving along with two or three younger women seated behind him. . . .

It fortunately just so happened that a larger gathering of the saints took place while I was in Salt Lake City. The entire imposing hall was full of men, women, and children. Crouching at one of the entrances were two Indian women, faces painted red, tattered and covered with dirt. They too belonged to the Mormon assembly.

The members of the throng paid little attention to the words of the apostle who was then speaking. I saw not a single resolute or focused face of the kind displayed by a typical American, and most of those present held their mouth open. The women were ugly and the modest, orthodox bonnets many wore did nothing to improve their looks. Crying children and the noise of constant coming and going drove me to the front so that I could hear some of the message.

Brainless faces seemed to predominate among the apostles, across from whom three or four scampish faces suggested a kind of intelligence. Several spoke one after the other, revealing much drivel and little intelligence. The perpetual refrain was that the Mormons were supposed to be better than all other people. "Where does the Kingdom of God begin? With Fathers and Mothers. Let the fathers be pure of heart and let the mothers be pure of heart. And then the children and the entire family will also be pure of heart. Abraham, Isaac, and Jacob were also pure of heart. Because they were the founders of the Kingdom of God and we are the latter-day saints; and because we are the latter-day saints, we are pure of heart. Here we stand before the nation, here we stand before the whole world. But we are pure of heart and belong to the Kingdom of God." This is word for word what an old fellow with a crafty gallows-bird face was saying with the greatest complacency. He looked more intelligent than his sermon suggested. It must have been good enough for the stupid mob in front of him, since he obviously did not think it worth the trouble of exerting himself.

After him a not-too-bright-looking apostle stood up and said approximately the same thing, as though he were trying to show that he had been carefully paying attention. Perhaps what a Gentile confided in me is true—that the apostles among them only have about a dozen sermons with which to edify their patient flock year in and year out. I was most intensely repulsed by all of the shopkeeper and butcher types who, far from possessing any ideal qualities, passed themselves off as having been anointed by the Lord and tossed memorized phrases about from the pulpit. What mass of human folly allowed such apostles to rise to power?

Brigham Young sat in his sofa slumped down so low that only the upper part of his old head was visible over the armrest. He was reading a newspaper and paid no attention to the nonsense the others were uttering below him.

Finally, he straightened up slightly as his son approached and sat down beside him. The earnest conversation that then ensued between the two gave me an opportunity to look more closely at the famous prophet. He wore dark glasses and already looked very broken and weak with age. His thick, shapeless neck seemed to hardly have the strength to carry his large bald head, half of which was framed by an American style of beard. I could not notice anything imposing or venerable about him. There was something venomous and malicious about the look on his face. My general impression of him was that of a completely ordinary profiteer, with one foot in the grave, tormented by remorse, and who had never been capable of thinking a lofty thought throughout his lifetime.

There was a pause in the preaching. None of the saints seemed to feel inspired. So, Brigham Young gave his son a nudge, whereupon the latter started to speak while lolling his elbow crudely on the armrest. The junior Young also already had a bald head and he might have been in his late forties. He wore an ordinary gray jacket, and his facial features were ordinary, too. Yet the short speech he gave was the only one among those I had heard that had some intelligence and fire.

When he finished, the organ started up a melody and the good, powerful voices of the mixed choir behind the prophet's sofa sang a hymn that sounded very pleasant to me, as I had not heard anything of that kind for a long time. After this, the entire assembly went through the simultaneously opened doors and departed to all points of the compass. . . .

Now, of course, Mormonism's might is finished and the giant temple with six towers that Brigham Young had planned will remain incomplete, save for the already finished walls and the stark, abandoned framework pointing up at the sky. The Pacific railway gave the Kingdom of the Saints its death blow. Ever more gentiles have been coming to Salt Lake City and the Chosen Flock have had to withdraw more and more before them. Internal disputes have been gnawing at their vitality. The Apostles are being exposed as common criminals, thieves, and murderers by disdainful secular righteousness. Converts are becoming ever rarer and only a large number of immoral women coming particularly from Denmark, Norway, and Sweden, and who have run away from their husbands, are still providing continued growth. The crudeness, contempt and ridicule that the gentile press is producing against the Mormons is unequaled in America. A person only needs to take a look at one single edition of the Salt Lake Daily Tribune to realize immediately that Mormonism has lost every bit of its power.

As for other noteworthy curiosities, Salt Lake City has a theater, a museum for everything, a small but terrible collection of paintings, the palace of the prophet, a Gothic Methodist church and hot springs with bathing facilities. The dwelling of Brigham Young and his many wives is just as tasteless as most of the products of his intellect: it is surrounded by a thick wall of quarried stone and mortar with a great number of little conical towers made of the same material. There is a dilapidated wooden eagle perched above the gate and below it, staring once again out of its triangular garland of rays, is one of those very popular all-seeing eyes of Jehovah. The best building of the whole town is still the theater, even though a pedantic art connoisseur might take offense at the overly slender Doric columns in the entrance hall. One comes across Scandinavian names remarkably often here, but there is no lack of Germans, Frenchmen, and Italians, and the slit-eyed "Yun Lee" or "Sun Wau" with his stereotypical "Washing and Ironing" has already arrived here as well.

The Mormons boasted proudly of being a microcosm unto themselves, of covering all their necessities themselves and not requiring any foreign products. Traces of this aspiration are noticeable everywhere, but its negative effects are predominant. Isolation and paranoid rejection of stimulating outside influences have never brought a communal system very far. A stagnation of talents and abilities is the only result of such a system.

I would perhaps not even have made the side trip to Salt Lake City if the salt lake with its twenty percent salt content had not tempted me to bathe in it. It used to be possible to obtain one ton of salt from four tons of its water by means of evaporation, but now five tons are needed to do this. The lake is becoming more dilute, its level is rising, possibly as a result of a constant uplift of the entire landmass whose ever higher-rising mountain tops are able to wring ever more moisture from the clouds.

The city is separated from the lake by a wide, yellow marshy area through which the Jordan snakes with its green border of willows and poplars. To bathe in the lake, you have to ride two hours on the Western Utah Railway to Lake Point where the mountains rise directly from its shore. The Western Utah Railway had only been operating for a short time and is not yet very frequent. It ran as far as Ophir City, a lead mine about twice as far away as Lake Point, and every day a train would run there and back. It moved so slowly it would have been possible to walk alongside it. The locomotive only had to pull three open cars occupied by miners....

Lake Point consists only of a two-story hotel, a pier jutting out into the lake where a steamboat used for pleasure cruises is docked, as well as several bathing huts. It is a charmingly quiet, lonely spot. Only rarely is the prevailing quiet interrupted by a twittering bird. Grasshoppers go whirring over the clumps of yellow grass. Among these I frequently saw a variety that I at first mistook for a mourning cloak butterfly. It had exactly the same black wings with yellow edges, and exactly the same fluttering but prolonged flight of that kind of butterfly.

I proceeded immediately into the dense salt brine of the lake and proved to myself the fact I had already read, that you cannot dive underwater in it. It was an extremely peculiar, foreign feeling to be held up in that way. Nevertheless, a non-swimmer would just as surely drown in this twenty percent liquid as in distilled water. This flexible medium seeks to keep your body continually horizontal, and at the slightest movement you find yourself turning about your own axis so that your face and thereby the openings for your indispensable airways face upwards, then quickly downwards, if you do not know how to fight against it with appropriate behavior. I did not find it difficult to keep my precarious balance for a prolonged period in an upright position with my arms crossed. You then find yourself resting in deep water sinking down only up to your nipples like a living aerometer. I found propelling myself forward less easy and extremely tiring. A Leander or a Captain Webb would hardly be thinkable in Utah's Great Salt Lake.[21]

I also made another discovery. If the usual four-percent salt water of the sea has a horrible taste, then the taste of this water is all the more intense. During my various experiments, some drops of water got into my throat through my nose and the interesting but unpleasant result was instant vomiting. As I was later informed, there has not yet been a person who has been able to experience such an irritation without having such a reaction. . . .

When the dawdling train from Ophir City picked me up again in the evening and we were chugging our way back to Salt Lake City, we took an even longer time to cover the short stretch than we had in the morning. One time we went off on a side track that ran into a nearby sand pit to attach a sand wagon. Twice we had to stop in the middle of the flatland, first because a farmer had left his empty cart behind on the tracks until the locomotive engineer pushed it off into the ditch, and later because three obstinate oxen insisted on trotting comically along in front of us with their tails held up high. And while we just happened to be going full throttle, I still had enough time to jump off quickly, capture a careless snake creeping along the embankment, catch up to the train again, and get back on it.

Before I left Salt Lake City for good, I took a walk to Camp Douglas. About thirty years ago, when Brigham Young felt sufficiently strong and far enough away to defy the government in Washington, it sent an army under General Douglas [*sic*] at great expense to defeat him. Camp Douglas, the expedition's once-fortified encampment, is on a height of land back toward the mountains from which it controlled the city.[22] Today, it still speaks of that story and lodges a small garrison, even though Mormon power has long since been broken.

Victor-Henri Rochefort, Marquis de Rochefort-Luçay: Mr. Stenhouse . . . Resolved to "Confine" Us

Political journalist Victor-Henri Rochefort, Marquis de Rochefort-Luçay (1830–1913) provoked a series of French governments but refused to be intimidated by frequent arrests and imprisonment. He wrote for *L'Evénement*

---

[21] Steamship Captain Matthew Webb became the first person to swim the English Channel on 25 August 1875, while Greek mythology describes how Leander swam the Hellespont to make love to Hero.

[22] Col. Patrick Edward Connor named Camp Douglas after Illinois senator Stephen Douglas, who turned against his old Mormon allies in 1857. The post was never fortified but continues to occupy a commanding site in Salt Lake City as Fort Douglas. For an excellent history, see Hibbard, *Fort Douglas, Utah, 1862–1991*.

and *Le Figaro* and was sacked in 1868 because of his hostility to Louis Napoléon's second empire. He founded *La Lanterne*, which Bonaparte quickly suppressed, and Rochefort was fined and sentenced to prison. Rochefort relocated to Belgium and continued to publish the journal and distribute it clandestinely in France. In 1869 he was elected to the Chamber of Deputies in France. He returned to Paris, where he started a new paper, *La Marseillaise*. Again condemned, the revolution of 1870 kept him in business, but Rochefort's hostility to the Thiers government led it to deport him to New Caledonia in 1871. Within three years he escaped and traveled on an American vessel to San Francisco. Rochefort visited Utah Territory on his return to Europe, and his *Retour de la Nouvelle-Calédonie de Nouméa en Europe* appeared in Paris, without attribution, in 1877. Rochefort probably preferred anonymity since he lived in Geneva until the amnesty of 1880 allowed him to return to Paris, where he became the director of *Intransigeant*. He was again condemned and sentenced to serve life in prison in 1889, but he escaped to England and continued to collaborate with his editors. He returned to Paris in 1895 and wrote for the journal *La Patrie* until his death.

Victor Rochefort-Luçay,
Retour de la Nouvelle-Calédonie de Nouméa en Europe
[Return from New Caledonia from Noumea to Europe], 246–75.
Translated by Hugh MacNaughton

To reach Ogden, we follow the desolate shores of a dismal, leaden lake, with water that looked like mercury and was five times more salty than seawater. Not a fish can live in it, not a bird ventures across it. The disgust of men had to run deep indeed for people to come and settle in the midst of such a wilderness. A branch line leaves Ogden leading, in less than two hours' railroad journey, to Salt Lake City, the metropolis of Mormonism. . . .

An omnibus took us to one of the main hotels of the great city. We followed a road lined with villas, most of them built of stone in European style. Our hotel is the last word in comfort. A lift to go up to the rooms, all of which have an alcove with twin doors opening themselves to reveal a bathtub in which the bath seemed to run itself.

Although Salt Lake City lies four thousand feet above sea-level, backing onto permanently snow-clad mountains, the heat was stifling. The hotel lobby, transformed into a bar, was thronged with inquisitive onlookers who were slaking their thirst while awaiting our arrival, which had been telegraphed from one of the previous stations.

Salt Lake City has a number of non-Mormon inhabitants, and we realized straightaway that a veiled hostility reigned between the Americans of the Union and the disciples of the prophet. The former, as soon as we arrived, sought to monopolize us, evidently fearing the influence the latter might gain over us.

While several leading Mormons offered to introduce us to Brigham Young, a number of the prophet's enemies sought to dissuade us from all visits. A former Mormon priest, Mr. Stenhouse, who had become the most active opponent of his former employer, accusing him of the blackest misdeeds, appeared resolved to "confine" us to prevent all dealings between us and the prophet, who, heavily calumniated by the American press, might have thought of calling on the French press in his defense. . . .

[It was Sunday and everything was closed.] But the Tabernacle was open, Brigham Young was to officiate in person, and we were sure to meet at this ceremony almost all the faithful, who had deserted their homes to be there. We resolved to offer ourselves this consolation. Mr. Stenhouse, who had made himself our guide, vainly strove to draw us away elsewhere, and when he saw that we had determined upon going to the Tabernacle, he made a virtue of necessity and went with us.

"You will see how ridiculous all this jugglery is," he told us. . . .

Our eyes blinked as we entered, upon seeing a congregation of some eighteen-hundred obviously sincere women seated entirely unselfconsciously beside each other. The men, perhaps three hundred or so, sat in the front seats. We chose the last places reserved for the sex to which we belonged, the better to scrutinize the faithful of the sex to which we did not belong. A few of the latter-day women saints were elderly, but the young made up the vast majority of the society. Many young girls dressed with an evangelical simplicity.

We had imagined, almost in spite of ourselves, that the Mormon women must have acquired from their bizarre condition a special demeanor and almost a special physiognomy. We were surprised and even a little put out to find nothing in their attitude to reveal malicious intentions or even attract attention. A good many of them were very pretty, but that could not be an aggravating circumstance. Preceded among the Mormons by the rumor of our coming, we had thought that we would make some impression upon entering the Tabernacle. We were disappointed. The women did not appear to forsake their meditations on our account, nor did their glances give us any preference.

Brigham Young, seated at the foot of the pulpit, had caused an announcement to be made at the start of the ceremony to the effect that, having fallen prey to a severe cold, he would not be able to speak. Despite his discomfiture of the moment, and the worries of every kind that his wife may have caused him, he appeared to us as a man aged not more than fifty-five. We learnt that he was seventy-two.... The habit of exercising absolute power had left in his eye a certain harshness, compensated by a likeable set of the mouth due to the prominence of his lower lip....

The Lord had appeared to [Brigham Young], saying to him: "You have two hundred and fifty million at the Bank of England and owe nothing to anyone. Use them to settle your people near the Salt Lake." And Brigham Young had spent his millions without stinting, to obey the Lord.

"You see," said Mr. Stenhouse, "he holds himself out as a Moses in direct communication with the Most High, and the first duty of the Neophytes is to regard Mormonism as a revealed religion."

"Our Moseses do absolutely the same," I replied, "only when times are hard, instead of giving us their millions, they take ours...."

"For some time," [Brigham] shouted in the very Tabernacle, "I notice below your waists some unusual bulges. What is the meaning of these ridiculous fashions? Leave, all you women and come back here when you have deposited this worldly attire in your homes. It is not behind you, do you understand, but on your bellies that you should have humps." And, angrily rolling his eyes, he added, "I find that, in the past six months, people have been making very few babies in this country...."

When the sermon ended, a choir of young ladies standing on either side of the organ sang powerfully effective hymns under that huge vault. Seeing that devout congregation praying in its own way, under persecution and even under the guns of the United States government, one could not help thinking of the undercover priests of the Protestant *camisards*, and this whiff of dragonnade [referring to French soldiers firing on Protestants] gave Brigham Young the color of a martyr....

On leaving the Tabernacle, we went to buy some photographs, from a Mormon French photographer, of views of the Salt Lake and of the various houses where the prophet quarters his wives. We questioned the photograph-seller, and realized that he had become a complete fanatic.[23] Although Brigham Young had received, it seems, only a limited education, this goodly collaborator of the sun revealed that his leader knew everything, and that even the most recondite sciences held no secrets from him. We readily agreed, having scarcely any more reason for disputing the divine essence of the Mormon prophet than for affirming that of Jesus Christ, who never said to his apostles a single word about America, Central Africa or Oceania....

As we went back down to the hotel, we passed a young lady wearing a nankeen dress, and sheltering beneath a white parasol her beautiful fair head.

---

[23] This was surely Louis Bertrand, who recalled that he had "traveled as a professor of that admirable invention" from "the time of the first productions of the daguerreotype." See *Mémoires d'un Mormon*, cited in McClellan, "Not Your Average French Communist," 3.

"That is one of the prophet's daughters," said Mr. Stenhouse to us.

[*Stenhouse invites the party home to meet his wife.*]

Mrs. Stenhouse had acquired fame of a kind, in America, through her very startling break with Mormonism and her lampooning of the leader of the sect. She received us sitting in the dreamy attitude and with the hair falling over the shoulders of almost all the portraits of the famous bluestockings. The moment we set eyes on the woman, her tawny eyes and resolute air told us what share should be attributed to her in her husband's apostasy. She took from a console a gleaming bound copy of her book on the Mormons and wrote in a firm hand a dedication and presented it to me. All this with the gestures of Corinne improvising on Cape Misena.[24]

Although it took some effort for the ice to break, Mrs. Stenhouse could no longer forbear from launching, in fairly correct French, on an indictment of the polygamy to which she owed so many sufferings. The summary of her complaints was actually this:

"So long as my husband had no other wife than me, I was a Mormon down to my little finger. We went to Switzerland to recruit followers and preach the conversion of gentiles, which suited me all the more since our journey was paid for and everything was found for us by our Church. It is only when my husband, to fulfill his duty as a faithful Mormon, took a second, then a third wife, that jealousy opened my eyes to the drawbacks of a religion so mortifying to my self-esteem."

She had obviously used all her charms to remove her weak husband from the ascendancy of Brigham Young and one day, the former priest had declared to his pope that he intended to return to the bosom of monogamy, and regarded himself as divorced from his wives, except one alone who would replace for him all the others. He had also warned the prophet that he was laying down his priesthood, and renouncing forever Mormonism, its pomps, its works and its women.

It was at this juncture that a tragic event had occurred which, told by anyone else, would have filled us with indignation but which, in the telling of it by the victim herself, took on such a burlesque incongruity as to force us to bite our lips down to the chin, failing which we would have burst out into unseemly and inextinguishable laughter.

Mrs. Stenhouse took on an appropriately tragic voice to relate to us, entirely unembarrassed as we observed, and with details that doubled the horror of the event, the dreadful vengeance that Brigham Young, at the height of exasperation, had not shrunk from premeditating against her, and that he had succeeded in bringing about with the most deplorable consequences.

---

[24] Fanny Stenhouse's *A Lady's Life Among the Mormons* and *"Tell It All": The Story of a Life's Experience in Mormonism* were wildly popular exposés. The reference is to the odes of the poetess-heroine of Madame de Staël's *Corinne; ou, L'Italie*.

One evening, returning unsuspecting to the matrimonial home, she was thanking the Lord for having delivered her from the clutches of the devil, when in a dark alley, she was suddenly seized by three masked men who first gagged her, then dragged her off into a small clump of trees. She at once realized that all resistance was useless and bravely underwent the ultimate dishonor.

Her vile aggressors had not spoken one word, and it was only when they left, leaving her as good as dead, that one of them spat these significant words at her: "You have sinned out of pride; the Latter-day Saints are punishing you in your pride."

"You can imagine that this attack caused some stir," continued Mrs. Stenhouse in a tone of deliberation, while Mr. Stenhouse nodded by way of confirmation. "The following day, the entire city was informed of the misfortune that had befallen me. All the ladies came to call and make their condolences."

"The drawing-room just never emptied," added the worthy Stenhouse, not without the merest trace of vanity.

Mr. B. laughed so much that he was weeping—that was what saved him. Olivier Pain had slid slowly down behind the back of his armchair, where he writhed with unrestrained mirth. As for myself, being overrun with hilarity, I no longer knew how to cope with this great grief. I essayed a few remarks so as to disguise my nervous quiverings. "Since the matter had thus been made public," I said, "why did you not take it to court?"

"I knew that those who were guilty were emissaries of Brigham Young," replied the interesting narrator; "but so long as he had bound them to secrecy, they would sooner have let themselves be killed than reveal the secret. In any case, it is not them I am after, it is him alone. They did nothing but obey blindly, according to Mormon law. I forgave them long ago."

For one moment, we thought she would regale us with a plea in their favor. In her rancor against the high priest of polygamy in America, she unhesitatingly made him responsible for a crime that probably had no political motive. To have sought to explain that it should probably be put down to three common malefactors would have needlessly bereft her of her most consoling illusion, that of having suffered for her faith. Such a construction is not consistent either with other authors' accounts of good public order, or with the testimony of the wronged woman herself, if she was speaking the truth.

It will be rightly conjectured that Mrs. Stenhouse's book reflects that state of feeling. All the good that was done in the State was in spite of Brigham Young. All the untoward events were imputed to Brigham Young. Her unfairness went as far as blaming him for the cholera which, in 1853, struck down the Swiss emigration during the journey from Geneva to the Salt

Lake.²⁵ Comparing Mormon polygamy to Turkish polygamy is no less unfair. The one is only a refinement to the satisfaction of the senses, a useless or ruinous luxury, a source of physical and moral abasement. The other is conducive to work and wealth, and a force added to the development of creation. Mrs. Stenhouse was not loath to repeat to us, "I escaped from Mormonism as you escaped from your fortress."

In this, she was much mistaken, since the Ducos peninsula was incurably barren, whereas Mormonism is above all a devotion to fertility.

We had some difficulty in deflecting from its course the tumultuous torrent of recriminations of the outraged Mrs. Stenhouse. By dint of cleverness and concessions, we nevertheless obtained information of some precision on the home life of a Mormon household, particularly the private life of Brigham Young, with whom she and her husband had long been on intimate terms. Despite the truly Corsican, tenacious hatred she felt for him, from her anathemas and malevolent insinuations, we gathered as much truth as to say that, apart from the mission with which he claims to be invested by God Himself, the prophet is an excellent father and an entirely good man. When he gets married once again, he gathers together all his wives and introduces his new conquest to them, and they all come forward in turn to greet and embrace her. As a rule, he dines with all his spouses, at an immense table where he sits at the head, and is always alone of his sex, since contrary to what people in Europe would imagine, moral standards are extremely rigid in Utah, and although a wife may sometimes have only one-seventieth of a husband, as is the case in Brigham Young's household, adultery is quite exceptional there.

There is no legal age for a young woman to get married. It is rare for her to tie the fateful knot before fifteen. It is also rare for her not to have found a husband by seventeen. The prophet does not like wasted time. At eighteen, a young woman is regarded as unmarried, and at twenty she becomes an old maid.

What appeared to arouse particular indignation in Mrs. Stenhouse were the whimsically equivocal situations arising in families from unions that radically upset the family ties. One of her neighbors had married a young woman, while his son had married her sister. Thus, the father was at the same time the brother-in-law of his son, one of the spouses was mother-in-law to her own sister, while the latter found that she had become the daughter-in-law of her brother-in-law. We pointed out to her that no French or American law prevented a son from marrying the sister of his father's wife, and that myth and legend, to say nothing of the Bible, offered us far odder examples of wedlock. . . .

---

²⁵ Seth Blair's party in 1855, many of them Waldensians, lost more than a third of its members (and probably more) near Mormon Grove in Kansas to "the terrible destroyer," cholera.

A marriage in Utah is annulled almost as easily as it is contracted. Except that, while it is the men who marry, women only are entitled to divorce. Mrs. Stenhouse conceded that she felt this stipulation to be irreproachable. . . .

The well-informed woman who supplied all these details to us made as if to refuse to lift the veil concealing Brigham Young's private life. "His wives and children are sacred to me," she told us. "In any case, however infamous his conduct toward me may have been, I have made it a rule never to attack anything except the public man, the false prophet who, if people are not careful, will soon drag America into a cataclysm."

Francesco Varvaro Pojero:
He Would Convert You Immediately

Francesco Varvaro Pojero was a minor Sicilian nobleman who read Tocqueville, Trollope, Dickens, Laboulaye, and even Appleton's guide. He was also familiar with the travel accounts of William Hepworth Dixon, Alexander von Hübner, Richard F. Burton, and Louis Simonin that had been published by the Milanese publisher Emilio Treves.[26] Even though he was only twenty when he first traveled to the U.S. in 1876 to visit the Centennial Exposition in Philadelphia, he had already written travel books about Europe. Several Italian newspapers sent representatives to the Centennial Exposition. Edoardo Sonzogno, the Milanese publisher of *L'Emporio Pittoresco*, dispatched a correspondent to Utah to do a series of five articles describing the territory along with articles about "Colburn Peak" in Utah, and "I Mormoni."[27] Other prominent Italian newspapers and magazines, such as *L'Universo Illustrato*, Fratelli Treves' *L'Illustrazione Popolare*, and *L'Emporio Pittoresco*, published stories about Utah.[28] They included illustrations from American periodicals such as *Harper's Weekly*, and *Frank Leslie's* as well as books by Rémy, Stansbury, and Piercy. Emilio Treves published Varvaro

---

[26] Burton's *City of the Saints* was serialized in *Le tour du monde* 2 (1862), 353–400, as "Voyages à la cité des Saints, capitale du pays des Mormons." A French edition, *Voyages du Capitaine Burton à la Mecque, aux grands lacs d'Afrique, et chez les Mormons*, appeared in 1870. Treves published an abridged edition as *I Mormoni e la città dei Santi* in 1875. Varvaro Pojero consulted Dixon's *The White Conquest*, which was abridged and serialized in Italian as "La Conquista Bianca," *Il Giro del Mondo* 4 (6 and 13 July 1876), 90–106; and Dixon's *New America*, which was published in France as *La nouvelle Amérique*.

[27] Sonzongo, ed., *L'Esposizione Universale di Filadelfia Illustrata*, 1:130–32; 2:418–19, 427, 442–43, 452–54, 460–62, 546–47.

[28] For example, see "I Mormoni," *L'Universo Illustrato* 4:25 (20 March 1870), 418–22; "L'arresto di Brigham-Joung," *L'Illustrazione Popolare* 3 December 1871), 75–77; and "Il gransacerdote Brigham-Young e le donne fra i Mormoni," *L'Emporio Pittoresco* 9:383 (31 December–6 January 1872).

Pojero's travel narrative, so it is possible that Treves dispatched him to the Centennial Exhibition as well. Varvaro Pojero certainly had connections, since he met President Ulysses S. Grant while in Washington.

Varvaro Pojero remained in the U.S. for only three months, but at the conclusion of the exposition he took a train to California. It is hard to argue with historian Andrew Torrielli's conclusion that he was "prejudiced against America."[29] American women were beautiful, he thought, but they lacked good taste and manners. The lack of culture and fine arts in the U.S. compared unfavorably with European culture. "They have a great aversion to the ancient, for the old; old is particularly a word of contempt. They call Europe *the old country*, almost to the point of derision."[30] Varvaro Pojero considered most public building in the United States to be monotonously ugly, but even though he criticized most American theater, he complimented the plays he saw in Salt Lake City.

On their visit to Utah, Varvaro Pojero and his Japanese traveling companion, Matsmoto, scheduled an appointment with Brigham Young. This excerpt begins with a preliminary discussion with a "pezzo grosso" (someone who considered himself important) while waiting in the Beehive House for the Mormon church president to arrive.

>   Francesco Varvaro Pojero, *Una Corsa nel Nuovo Mondo*
>   [A Race through the New World], 82–83, 89–91, 92–93.
>
> — These principles give honor to your religion; they should bring to you the esteem and respect of all; but that does not happen because everyone forgets the good part of your institution, and remembers the bad.
>
> — What is the bad?
>
> — Do I need to tell you?
>
> — Polygamy? Even you have this prejudice against the patriarchal life?
>
> — I don't believe it is prejudice. The world is populated by approximately the same number of man and women; don't you believe that nature or providence, call it what you want, with the two sexes in this proportion, wanted to assign one woman to a man? Even beyond these considerations, I will tell you frankly that I can't imagine any good coming from a family with plural wives.
>
> — And why?
>
> — For many reasons, and because of jealousy above all, which must necessarily destroy the domestic peace.

---

[29] Torrielli, *Italian Opinion on America*, 20.

[30] Varvaro Pojero, *Una corsa nel Nuovo Mondo* II:262, as quoted in Torrielli, *Italian Opinion on America*, 224.

— You are deceived, the Mormon said to me. I have had many relations with gentile families, and in my calling I know intimately the conditions of many Mormon families. There is no question that jealousy always causes small domestic troubles, but I can assure you that our families enjoy more peace then your families.

I could not help but smile.

— Oh the thing seems absurd, but let's think about this: A woman in Christianity, in Islam, in Paganism, and in Mormonism is always jealous by instinct. Doesn't it seem to you natural that she would be less jealous when she sees her husband with another woman, and she knows that he is with her only because he is following the precepts of his religion?

— Fine, but husbands do not necessarily neglect their wife; not all of our husbands betray them. . . .

[*Varvaro Pojero and his traveling companion have a short discussion with another Mormon*]:

— I see that you are not yet convinced of the great truth of our religion, but I can assure you that I will convince you, if you will give me your time.

— I leave in another hour.

— But that really disappoints me. I wish you could meet some of our missionaries, and that you could give them a chance to convert you.

— What country do you live in?

— In Italy

— Oh then no doubt you know our brethren Toronto and Lorenzo Snow, who were missionaries in your country.

— I have never heard of them.[31]

— That is shocking. Lorenzo is a great missionary, and he would convert you immediately. He would be able to demonstrate to you the evidence which supports the sweetness of polygamy, and you would not have any difficulty overcoming your aversion to it.

— Tell me how many wives do you have? I ask him. The Saint lowered his eye—I have but one, he said to me humiliated. . . .

[*Brigham Young has a very short conversation with Varvaro Pojero and Matsmoto*]:

Nothing in our conversation is really worth mentioning because it was not really very interesting . . . and Young demonstrated a firm desire not to engage in religious subjects and to do so he kept the discussion as far away from Mormonism as possible.

He began by asking Matsmoto if the Japanese people also suffer from rheumatism and then he asked me if it was known in Italy; from our responses he decided that rheumatism is common in both hemispheres.

---

[31] Several years later Paolo De Vecchi, an Italian doctor who had settled in California, wrote a letter to the *Gazzetta Piemontese* in Torino, in which he described some Italians who had settled in Utah after they were converted to Mormonism by Joseph Toronto. Paolo De Vecchi, "I Mormoni Italiani," *L'Eco d'Italia*, 8 January 1881.

Then he spoke of the Japanese language, praising the Japanese alphabet for its abundance of letters and criticizing ours for the scarcity of letters. He spoke of vowels, said that there were too many, and he denied that they were necessary for the pronunciation of words and spoke against them—poor vowels—which he hates profoundly. This grand reformer, in his mania to reform also wanted to apply his reforms to the alphabet.

Passing on to all other subjects, I spoke many words praising the city.

— It is the most beautiful city in the United States, said Brigham.

I also praised the cooperative he had constructed.

— It is the most beautiful warehouse in the world, said Brigham.[32]

The Prophet, before becoming prophet was an American.

I could not bring myself to applaud the architecture of the Tabernacle, but, having to say something, I said it was a new design, a real invention.

— It is my work, added the Prophet, I did the design, and I directed the work.

Following our discussion concerning the Tabernacle, Brigham's son said to my Japanese companion—You did not hear the organ, didn't you?

His father corrected him.

— What kind of talk is that, you give the question and the response, and the response prior to the question, this is a vice of the Yankees, I can see that we need to send you to school again.

Baron Arnold de Woelmont:
One of the Most Astonishing Figures of Our Time

Belgian Baron Arnold de Woelmont (1849–1903) wrote several books about his adventures in the American West. His description of Salt Lake City emphasized the progress made since its settlement, but Baron de Woelmont's view of the Mormon community was not as rosy as many other commentators. He noted the contentious relations between the Mormons, the gentiles, and apostates and the Mormon ban on mining. He felt Brigham Young maintained an economic hold over his subjects, not allowing his faithful to enrich themselves, while extending to them the all-embracing facilities of a welfare state.

De Woelmont emphasized the personal rule of Brigham Young and his state within a state, and observed that Washington was reluctant to subdue it. His tone varies from the sympathetic and dispassionate when describing

---

[32] For the story of ZCMI, Zions Cooperative Mercantile Institution, see Bradley, *ZCMI: America's First Department Store.*

something he admires, to a mild irony when confronting something strange or discomfiting about the Mormons. One of the last, if not the last, European aristocrats to have an audience with Brigham Young (by the time his recollections were published, Young was dead), Baron de Woelmont concluded "the former carpenter will remain one of the most astonishing figures of our time"—a conclusion borne out by time.

ARNOLD DE WOELMONT, *SOUVENIRS DU FAR-WEST*
[RECOLLECTIONS OF THE FAR WEST], 164–73.
TRANSLATED BY HUGH MACNAUGHTON.

At one o'clock, we arrived at the Presidential palace. He was there in his office, accessible to all. Two negresses were coming out as we went in. Might they be future devotees? Hitherto, the Mormons had not wished to have colored women. This old prejudice no longer has any reason to exist in a century such as our own....

The prophet's apartment was among the most modest: on the walls were the portraits of the prophet-martyr, Smith, the apostles and a few elders, all of them Mormons. We noticed a large frame with fifteen or twenty portraits of women whose Baptismal names were inscribed below. These were the Mrs. Brigham Youngs: almost all of them blonde, a few of them really pretty. The president had taken the lion's share.

Most Mormon women are far from being pretty, and in a country where beauty is so common, the contrast is all the more striking. One could not help but think that Utah was a refuge for those women who could not find a husband elsewhere. No child's portrait was displayed, but we knew that Brigham was the father of his people....

Brigham did not keep us waiting. He came up to us, shook hands with us, and most ceremoniously bade us sit down. I had expected to see something like Bluebeard: in front of me was a man of an austere exterior. Brigham, who had been born with the century, appeared twenty years younger. He was tall, well-built and still had all his teeth and hair.[33] His eyes were clear, the gaze piercing and resolute, the forehead high, the lips thin and pressed together, with no moustache, the chin square; everything in him portrayed the able diplomat, the intelligent meditative mind combining with an unshakeable firmness. He was dressed like a Protestant minister, and under his long, silky, grizzling beard, he wore a large white scarf to hide a goiter.

His speech was slow, in a low, yet clear voice. Each of the words he pro-

---

[33] Young had his teeth replaced in the early 1860s with excellent dentures. Shortly afterward, he directed George Q. Cannon "to purchase for me a liberal assortment of the best quality of artificial teeth, mostly upper gums, for gentlemen and ladies." See Young to Cannon, 7 January 1862, Brigham Young Collection, LDS Archives.

nounced fell from his lips like an oracle or a biblical word of wisdom. One felt he was accustomed to monologue.

"You have seen," he told us, "our city, its roads that intersect at right angles, its telegraph, its gas, and its trams. Not thirty years ago, in 1847, we opened our route hither. . . . You can see what we have put in place of the desert. . . ." After a pause in which he seemed to listen to the echoing of his own voice, Brigham, seeing us meditating his words while examining him from head to foot, spoke to us of the exhibition in Philadelphia, telling us that he wouldn't ever be seen there; then, suddenly, he added, "I hope you will go and see my shop; examine it carefully. It is lit from above: an innovation of which I am the author, and which will soon become widespread."

When we stood up to take our leave, he asked us to write our names in a register. The latter opened of its own accord at the 23rd of April of this year, on which date Dom P. d'Alcantara, the emperor of Brazil, had deposited his own signature. . . .

As far as I am concerned, and I have no shame in admitting it, I felt more sadness than horror at the fanaticism and sincerity of the numerous devotees of this detestable religion. From this visit I have retained great admiration for the achievements at the Salt Lake, and for the strong-mettled character and sagacity of the prophet Brigham Young.

I have simply sought to tell how he appeared to me among his own people, surrounded by his agricultural and apostolic works. I had no intention either of criticizing or of making a panegyric of his life. A temporal leader and a spiritual pontiff, who had created a State of his own in the United States, a Church amidst the Churches, the founder and pastor of his people, autocrat and lawmaker, pope and prophet, the former carpenter will remain one of the most astonishing figures of our time.

Chapter 6

"Excursions in My Own Mind"
European Fantasy Accounts of the Mormon West

No bright line separates fantasy accounts from travel narratives that often blur fact and fiction. Many fiction writers strain to assure their readers that the events described in their books really took place, but such claims are not always totally convincing. Jacob D'Ancona's account of his six-month visit to China—four years before Marco Polo—is suspected to be a forgery.[1] There are even some scholars who question whether Polo actually visited the Far East at all, or even any of the places described in the fabulous narrative of his adventures in the thirteenth century.[2] Closer to home in Utah, there will always be debate between believers and non-believers as to whether Lehi and his family actually traveled to the Americas in 600 B.C.

Armchair writers have much greater latitude than travelers. Samuel Taylor Coleridge wrote that "From whatever place I write you will expect that part of my 'Travels' will consist of excursions in my own mind."[3] Fictional accounts are often more widely read and therefore form the foundation for one's images of time and place more than the experiences of real travelers. Beginning with Homer's *Odyssey* and *Iliad*, some of the best literature consists of fantasy travel. Such tales were so enduring that seven hundred years later Publius Virgilius Maro (70–19 B.C.) was inspired to transfer Aeneas from Troy to Italy in *The Aeneid*. During the late Middle Ages Sir John Man-

---

[1] D'Ancona, *The City of Light*. For discussions about D'Ancona's authenticity, see Wasserstein, "Jacobo Spurioso," 15; and Letters to the Editor, *Times Literary Supplement*, 21 November 1997, 19.
[2] For example, see Wood, *Did Marco Polo Go to China?* Another contemporary of Polo whose work became popular was Odoric of Pordenone, *The Travels of Friar Odoric*.
[3] Coleridge, "Letter II: To a Lady," *Biographia Literaria*.

deville (ca. 1300–72) wrote a series of *Travels* that were "an eyewitness account of the wonders of the east by a man who never stirred from his study," and in England tall tales are still referred to as "Sir John Mandeville's."[4] Other examples of stay-at-home travelers who still stir the imaginations of stay-at-home readers are Daniel Defoe's *The Life and Strange Surprising Adventures of Robinson Crusoe of York, Mariner . . . Written by himself*; Jonathan Swift's *Gulliver's Travels*; and William Combe's *Dr. Syntax* trilogy.[5] Some of these writers insisted that their excursions were not limited to the "mind." Similarly, in 1836 the *New York Sun* reported that British astronomer Sir William Herschel had discovered life on the moon after a voyage on a ship supported by hydrogen balloons.[6]

The Mormon West was merely one element in the European fantasy of the American West that sprang from a variety of sources. James Fenimore Cooper was the first American novelist to achieve worldwide fame. His "Leatherstocking Tales" recounted the adventures of settlers and Indians on the American frontier, and beginning in 1823 they were translated into French, German, Italian, and other European languages. Even though Cooper also insisted that his stories were not "an imaginary and romantic picture of things" they were clearly based more on his reading than on his limited experience with Indians. Many Europeans, including Balduin Möllhausen, Karl May, and Emilio Salgari, imitated Cooper's formula in their tales and they added many details—including the presence of Mormons—to their Westerns, while American authors, such as Francis Parkman and Mark Twain, attempted to correct Cooper's image of the noble savage.

Mormonism became a favorite topic of many fantasy writers after moving its chief stake of Zion to the Far West. As Larry McMurtry observed, "Lies about the West are more important to them than truths," so it is not surprising that fictional accounts of life in Utah are more widely read than more sober and boring travel accounts, but it is ironic that the image of Utah crafted by authors who did not visit the territory become, more often

---

[4] Henisch, *Medieval Armchair Travels*, 5.

[5] Defoe, *The Life and Strange Surprising Adventures of Robinson Crusoe of York, Mariner . . . Written by himself* (Defoe claimed that this was not a novel but a real adventure); Swift, *Travels into Several Remote Nations of the World, in four parts, by Lemuel Gulliver* (Swift wrote Gulliver's travels in part, Leo Damrosch noted, "to show that truth and fiction are more closely intertwined than we normally acknowledge: 'facts' can never be established with certainty, and every story (certainly Robinson Crusoe) is suffused with imagination." See Damrosch, "New Introduction," *Gulliver's Travels*, v–vi); Combe, *The Tour of Doctor Syntax*; *The Second Tour of Doctor Syntax*; and *The Third Tour of Doctor Syntax*.   [6] See Galluzzo and Dura, *Delle scoperte*.

than not, the primary source for Europeans wanting to know more about life in Utah.[7] It thus tells us more about the European image of America than it does about the actual reality of what was occurring in Utah.

Terryl Givens identified fifty-six novels written between 1850 and 1900 that use Mormonism as a backdrop or plot device because it was "salacious, lucrative, pious, chivalrous, and patriotic all at once."[8] More simply stated, Mormon polygamy was illicit sex, and illicit sex has always sold books. Most authors poked fun at the "peculiar institution" and exploited horrifying details of life in the Far West. Such stories certainly reassured British readers about the superiority of their own society even as it warned of the consequences of the American democratic experiment. Some of the first "historical novels" involving Mormons were written by minor authors such as George Frederick Ruxton, whose *Life in the Far West* was published posthumously in 1849; Antonio Caccia, whose *Europa ed America: Scene della vita dal 1848–1850* was published in 1850; and Mayne Reid, who wrote *The Wild Huntress* in 1861.[9] Other minor authors who used the Mormon theme include Annie Argyle in *Cupid's Album*, in 1866; and Joaquín Miller in *The First Families of the Sierras*, first published in 1875 and subsequently republished as *The Danites of the Sierras* in 1881. Similar accounts continue to be written and perpetuate the familiar image of Mormons in Utah Territory.[10]

Eventually more prominent writers such as Artemus Ward, Mark Twain, Robert Louis Stevenson, Arthur Conan Doyle, and Zane Grey wrote about Mormons in the West. Similar accounts were written by European authors Karl May, Jules Verne, and Emilio Salgari in Germany, France, and Italy, where their popularity remains strong almost a century after their deaths.

---

[7] McMurtry, *Walter Benjamin at the Dairy Queen*, 55.

[8] Givens, *The Viper on the Hearth*, 143.

[9] Italian Gustavo Strafforello popularized both fiction and non-fiction books about the West. See his novel *Il nuovo Monte-Cristo. Memorie d'un emigrante*, as well as *Storia popolare del progresso materiale negli ultimi cento anni* (which mentions Mormon participation in the discovery of gold in California); and *Letteratura Americana* (in which Strafforello recommends reading J. H. Beadle, Artemus Ward, and Mark Twain). See also Strafforello and di Hellwald, *America Settentrionale secondo le notizie più recenti*, in which he gives a short history of the Mormons and opines that they were the most important American sect and had created "a state within a state." Ibid., 135.

[10] Gregory, *The Great Railroad Race*. Gregory's book is part of the "Dear America" series that includes fictional diaries of young girls during important periods in American history. Libby West's story is set in 1868–69 and culminates when the Union Pacific and Central Pacific railroads met in Utah Territory at Promontory Summit. Gregory's book includes references to the peculiar aspects of Utah, including polygamy, the counsel of Mormon authorities not to associate with "Gentiles," and Brigham Young's heavy-handed leadership style.

Their distorted snapshots of frontier Mormonism are now frozen in time, but they are key sources from which thousands of Europeans have formed their opinions of Utah and the Latter-day Saints, not only in the nineteenth century but also in the twenty-first.

Paul Duplessis: Abandon All Hope of Leaving

Paul Duplessis (1815–65) was born in Rennes, France, and as a young boy visited Mexico and northern Africa with his family. In 1848 Duplessis published his first book of poetry, *Chansons*. He began writing plays in 1850, including "Les Chercheurs d'or du Sacramento et Donna," "Une Fortune à faire," and "Les Boucaniers," along with many adventure stories. He was part of a new school of "realists" that included Mayne Reid, Gabriel Ferry, Gustave Aimard, Balduin Möllhausen, and Emilio Salgari.[11] He published *Les Boucaniers* and *Les Grands Jours d'Auvergne* in 1853; *Les Etapes d'un volontaire*, *La Sonora* and *Le capitaine Bravaduria* in 1854; *Le Batteur d'estrade* in 1856; *Juanito le harpiste* and *Le Tigre de Tanger* in 1857; *Le Coeur de marbre* in 1858; *Les Mormons* in 1859; *Aventures mexicaines* in 1860; and *Les Peaux-Rouges* in 1864. Several stories that were published serially before his death in 1860 were published posthumously in book form.

In *Les Mormons* the president of the Mormon church seduces two Parisian sisters to travel to Salt Lake City. A non-Mormon adventurer, Joaquín Dick, agrees to help their brother, Georges d'Hédouville, to follow their wagon train to Utah and rescue them. On his way to Deseret, Joaquín meets Captain Kennedy, a government spy going by the name of "Williams." As a baptized Latter-day Saint, Williams manages to compile evidence against the Mormons and pass it along to Joaquín before the Danites discover his deception and arrest him. In a surreal scene in the wilds, the two rebellious women are tortured by torchlight while Captain Kennedy bravely endures his own interrogation and awaits his execution.

Paul Duplessis, *Les Mormons* [The Mormons], 1:337, 2:229–33.
Translated by Rick Grunder.
Great Salt Lake City is open to all the world, but it is like Dante's hell: when one has entered, one must abandon all hope of leaving! Once the Mor-

---
[11] Billington, *Land of Savagery, Land of Promise*, 37.

mons take hold of their prey, they do not let it escape again. How will we throw down the invisible, invincible barrier that shuts away the unfortunate detainees of this human hell? I do not know! Heaven has given me courage and presence of mind; my checkered life of adventure has made me used to danger, has given me calm in moments of crisis. . . . As for you, you are insanely, righteously in love . . . these are precious ingredients of success. Courage, young man, the situation is not yet hopeless. . . .

The Martyr

Whether Williams' executioners wanted to prolong his agony, or—as is more probable—hoped to extract his confession, the fact is that instead of a clerk to read the sentence, it was a judge who stepped from the crowd of Mormons.

This judge was one of the group of six Elders who Caton had consulted before giving Alice her freedom.

— Williams, he said in a solemn voice, if your crime is great, the mercy of the Lord—of Whom we are the direct representatives on earth—is beyond compare, without limits. There is no sin that a sincere and complete repentance cannot redeem! . . . By complete candor, you can yet obtain pardon for your error. Are you ready to answer my questions?

— What is the point of this ridiculous sham of justice?, said Williams with a disdain he did not bother to hide. You are neither judges nor even executioners. . . . You are plain and simple assassins! I am your enemy, you have me in your power: kill me!

— I will point out to you, prisoner, resumed the Mormon without showing offense at this response, that you have nothing to gain by your silence, and much to hope from your confessions. . . . What is your name?

— Williams! replied the unfortunate young man after a short hesitation, submitting to this interrogation.

— You lie! that is not your real name at all.

— What does it matter?

— Your name is Kennedy.

The spurious Williams betrayed no sign of surprise, but did not answer.

— What is your position in society?

— I am a merchant.

— No, you are a captain in the Union army!

— Well, then, yes! That is true, and I hold it as an honor, exclaimed the young man with pride.

— What motive brought you to Deseret?

— The desire to purge the United States of bandits who form a league today, but tomorrow may become a nation and threaten the prosperity and independence of my beloved country!

— You speak of the Latter Day Saints?

— I said "bandits!" Isn't that the same thing?

— Who assigned you this criminal mission?

— Those who had the right.... But I must add that I requested it, and requested it earnestly.

— What did they pay you for your espionage?

— An inestimable prize! exclaimed the captain.

— But what, then?

— Glory!

The pretended judge paused to cover his discomfort with these answers from the secret agent of the government in Washington. He had counted on the fear that approaching death would produce in the spurious Williams, but instead, here was a man making himself a pedestal for his scaffold.

— Captain Kennedy, he resumed after reflecting, what will you do, if we let you off?

— My duty!... I will pursue the course of my investigation; I will assemble as much proof as I can to show the nation clearly that the annihilation of your sect is indispensable to the security of the United States!

— During the time you have lived with us and among us, you must have gathered many of these pretended proofs, which I would call calumnies?

— Yes, many! declared Captain Kennedy with the most emphatic satisfaction.

— And yet, nothing was found at your place the night you were arrested. ... Have you hidden, destroyed or entrusted these documents to someone?

— Those documents are safe.... They will arrive at their destination, you may be certain.

— You lie! exclaimed the Mormon with a fire he had not shown from the beginning of the interrogation.

— Oh! you know full well that I do not! replied Captain Kennedy; otherwise I would not be so calm! It isn't the certainty that I will later be avenged that gives me this tranquility at the edge of my grave, he continued with fervor; what saves me from grief in my final moments is the consoling thought that my life will not be given for my country in vain. I have the conviction, the certainty, that my efforts are not wasted. Another hand will plant the ground I have broken, but nothing can now prevent the seed from coming to light.

The Mormon judge, probably discouraged, went to find his colleagues. The conference of Elders, among whom was Caton, lasted scarcely five minutes: the sham judge returned immediately to the condemned man.

— Captain Kennedy, he said, my words will be grave, the last I will speak to you. Consider carefully, then, before you answer. You can yet avoid the just punishment that awaits you. Deliver the name of your accomplice, the man to whom you have entrusted your notes and your documents; swear to renounce your errors, to enter sincerely into the bosom of our Church. And, at that very instant, you will be set at liberty. . . . Do you accept?

— No! replied the martyr-patriot in a vibrant voice that awakened the echoes of the forest.

— Misérable! cried the Mormon who, forgetting his role of judge, struck the captain's face with his fist.

The noble young man grew more pale, his eyes burned more brightly, but he remained unmoved.

— This deed will reverberate through history, and my country will hold me in thanks, he said to himself, with elation.

The Mormon's violence broke, as it were, the sort of solemnity which, up until then, had presided over this horrible scene. From all sides arose the call for death.

— Let justice take its course! . . . said the judge, addressing the Danite subordinates; and he rejoined the group of Elders.

— Pride of my fondness, murmured Caton, leaning to Alice's ear, the Latter Day Saints, as you have just seen, are patient and indulgent so long as they hope to meet with true repentance! But, once convinced of the sinner's incurable perversity, they show their implacable severity! I am not threatening you here, angel of my life! . . . No, this is simple advice that I give you. . . . Take care that your future conduct does not force me—much to my regret—to apply to you the rigorous means I possess as an influential member of our holy Church! May the example of Kennedy's just punishment impress and teach you a lesson, my sweet Alice! . . .

The young woman only replied by nodding her head, full of humility and submission; she was too terrified by the spectacle before her eyes to be able to pronounce a single word.

Heinrich Balduin Möllhausen: Polygamy is Common amongst Them

Heinrich Balduin Möllhausen (1825–1905) enjoyed a reputation as a novelist throughout Germany from the 1860s until the end of the century and was known as "der alte Trapper" and the "Cooper of Germany."[12] After serving in the military during the revolutions of 1848, Möllhausen traveled to the United States in 1849, where he spent a year hunting in Illinois near the Missouri and Kaskaskia rivers before joining the widely traveled

---

[12] Barba, *Balduin Möllhausen, the German Cooper*.

explorer Duke Frederick Paul Wilhelm of Württemberg as an artist on an expedition over the Oregon Trail that terminated at Fort Laramie.[13] When he returned to Germany in 1852 he became acquainted with the famous naturalist Alexander von Humboldt, and through Humboldt's encouragement and introductions Möllhausen returned to the U.S. in 1853, where he joined the railroad survey expedition led by Lt. Amiel Wecks Whipple as an artist and topographer. The Whipple Expedition, which was commissioned to plot the route of a Pacific railroad line along the thirty-fifth parallel, traveled from Arkansas to Los Angeles. He returned to the States in 1857 for a third time to participate in the expedition led by Joseph Christmas Ives that explored the Colorado River to the Grand Canyon. Möllhausen's illustrations were included in the official reports of the Whipple and Ives expeditions.

When Möllhausen returned to Germany in 1858, he wrote and published two books recounting his adventures during the Whipple and Ives expeditions. His first book, which included an introduction by Humboldt, was about the Whipple Expedition. It was published in German, English, and Dutch in 1858, and republished in German in 1860.[14] The volume on the Ives Expedition, which William H. Goetzmann called "one of the best travel books of [the] age," appeared in 1861.[15] In it Möllhausen mentioned several encounters with Mormons; he described them as "stout energetic looking fellows, who, trusting to their good fortune and their good weapons, were making their way toward a distant goal—the great Mormon city on the Salt Lake." He reported the murder of Captain Gunnison and, relying on the descriptions of Gunnison and Stansbury, he published an account of Mormon history and culture, observing that the Mormons "endeavor to render themselves independent of intercourse with all other nations, although they call themselves Americans, and acknowledge the government of Washington." Möllhausen believed that "the government of the United States has treated this peculiar sect with great liberality and

---

[13] For Möllhausen's life, see David Henry Miller's 1970 dissertation, "Balduin Möllhausen, A Prussian's Image of the American West"; Lamar, ed., *The New Encyclopedia of the American West*, 727–28; and Garland, eds., *Oxford Companion to German Literature*, 590–91.

[14] Hermann Mendelsohn published Möllhausen's *Tagebuch einer Reise vom Mississippi nach den Küsten der Südsee* in 1858. The English translation appeared the same year in London as *Diary of a Journey from the Mississippi to the Coasts of the Pacific with a United States Expedition*. The two-volume Dutch edition, *Reis van den Mississippi naar de kusten van den grooten oceaan*, appeared in 1858 and 1859.

[15] Möllhausen, *Reisen in die Felsengebirge Nord-Amerikas*; and Goetzmann, *Army Exploration in the American West*, 310.

indulgence." Mormon behavior, he wrote, even included conspiracy with the Indians to cause bloodshed among "Gentiles." Möllhausen described Thales Haskel, a Mormon scout, as a "spy, who with pernicious intentions toward us planned to go to the Mohaves. Although he demonstrated much cunning and carefully avoided giving himself away owing to an unheeded word, nevertheless the glances of a deeply rooted hatred with which he regarded us when he believed himself unobserved, did not escape us.... Yet on our part he wasn't exactly greeted with best wishes, for repeatedly I perceived remarks which intimated that our men would rather have seen him hanging from a tree, as in our skiff."[16] "We camped in woods on the bank of the Colorado and were surrounded by 2000–3000 Mohaves," Möllhausen reported to his wife in August 1858, during the Ives Expedition, "who were incited by the Mormons, and who owing to their fearful painting and by their weapons of war, and the absence of their women and children and owing to the shooting of one of our mules, only too clearly gave evidence of their hostile intentions."[17]

His American experience, Möllhausen claimed, provided the factual basis for his fiction. Following publication of his travel diaries, he began writing the first of several hundred novels that he claimed were accurate down to the precise details. Even in his fantasy tales Möllhausen insisted, "I relate what I have seen and observed ... and even if I have not personally experienced that which I narrate, I have heard it ... from old hunting companions around a secret campfire in an inhospitable wilderness."[18]

Das Mormonenmädchen, published in 1864, is considered one of Möllhausen's best works.[19] The book's subtitle is "A Story during the time of the United States military action against the 'Latter-day Saints' during the years 1857 and 1858." Not surprisingly, the novelist focuses his story on polygamy. The story begins with the failed escape of a polygamous wife and her one-year-old child from "Mormon City." He then transfers the story to New York City, where a new group of Mormon converts has just arrived from Europe. Herta Jansen is a Swedish convert who is immigrating to Utah,

---

[16] Möllhausen, *Reisen in die Felsengebirge Nord-Amerikas*, 2:309, 325, 319, 398–99, quoted and translated in Miller, "Balduin Möllhausen," 188.

[17] Möllhausen to Carolina Möllhausen, Colorado River, 20 August 1858, in Barba, *Balduin Möllhausen, the German Cooper*, Appendix II, 173–74; translation from Miller, "Balduin Möllhausen," 190.

[18] Quoted in Ashliman, "The Novel of Western Adventure in Nineteenth Century," 142–43.

[19] Ashliman, "The Image of Utah and the Mormons in Nineteenth-Century Germany," 218, citing Spiero, *Geschichte des deutschen Romans*, 11. I have relied on Ashliman for the short summary of the book's plot.

where she will become the second wife of a Mormon leader, and two Mormon agents are making arrangements to smuggle weapons to Utah to prepare for the Utah War. The Mormons successfully leave New York with both women and weapons while the hero of the book, Lieutenant Weatherton of the United States Navy, follows them to Utah, where he saves Herta and the United States. Of course, Weatherton also marries Herta at the end of the story. The excerpt from *Das Mormonenmädchen* appeared in Möllhausen's introduction, which contains a "short description of Mormonism" based on Howard Stansbury's report, Captain Gunnison's book, as well as what he called "personal experiences I gathered when meeting with Mormons."

HEINRICH MÖLLHAUSEN, *DAS MORMONENMÄDCHEN*
[THE MORMON GIRL], 7–17. TRANSLATED BY ROSE EDWARDS.

To give a better understanding of the following tale, and especially to not be forced to interrupt the flow of the story through explanations—and especially when they might be inappropriate in some parts—(and then I might be forced to give a hint) it seems appropriate to precede the story with a short explanation of Mormonism and its history.[20]

The Mormons, who lately attracted so much attention of the entire civilized world, form a religious sect whose unique institutions certainly merit a special mention and description.

Their capital and main settlements are found in the valley of the Salt Lake. This lake lies between the Mississippi and California; in other words, west of those States where people, through good business sense and hard work obtain, what people in the West greedily take out of the gold-bearing terrain.

The valleys in and around the large Salt Lake are totally severed from habitable parts of the country. Toward the north and south are vast desert regions, toward the east rise—as a dividing wall—the columns of Rocky Mountains, while toward the west sand steppes and stiff mountain ranges form a difficult-to-cross barrier. . . .

The faith of this sect, which works with such incredible efforts and sacrifices to spread its message over the whole world, is founded on the unshakable conviction that all Christian sects or Gentiles (as they call them) act in

---

[20] Möllhausen included a footnote: "This short description of Mormonism is put together from notes taken from the official 'report' of United States Captain Howard Stansbury in the year 1852, as well as from the discourse on Mormonism, which was also written in 1852 by Captain Gunnison (who was murdered later by Indians who lived in Utah). I also included my personal experiences I gathered when meeting with Mormons."

ways that will not lead them to heaven, and that the eternal bliss can only be imparted to disciples of the "Melchisedec priesthood.". . . .

The Mormons' homes' furnishings are completely and totally different from any other Christian sect due to the system of the "spiritual wife."

When the Mormons were driven out of Illinois, polygamy was brought up as one of the main accusations against them, though they firmly denied it at that time. However, this is now proven for the longest time, and for years they haven't kept it a secret that polygamy is common amongst them.[21] Even the preachers declare openly from the pulpit that they are at liberty to take thousands of wives, if they would like to, and they challenge everybody to prove to them the opposite from the Bible.

Joseph Smith's opinions about polygamy were probably never published, however he made known to his adherents, that he had the privilege—the same as those who he deems worthy, similar to the ancient patriarchs Jacob, David, and Solomon—to take as many wives as he is able to sustain, to establish a holy house for the service of the Lord. They admit that the Book of Mormon says that each man should have a wife and each woman should have only one husband. Because the word "only" is only used with women, this means that polygamy is permitted for the man. And they declare that the principles of this institution are absolutely moral and holy. They even indicate that Jesus had three women, Mary, Martha, and the other Mary, whom he loved, and that he married all of them at the marriage feast in Canaan.

If a husband wishes to take on a second helpmeet, he has to first receive the agreement of the parents of the girl and then also the permission of the elder or the president. Then the new wife will be "sealed," and from that point on she is in every regard on equal footing with the first wife. Such marriages are deemed totally moral and honorable, and all subsequent wives claim the same position in their society as if they were the only wife or the first one chosen. The Mormons declare that such marriages are stronger and more binding than all other religions and sects. The more so, since according to their opinion the future life of the man as well as the woman is directly dependent on the marital relations on this earth. The church teaches that a woman who has no husband is not able to obtain heavenly joys in the future and neither is a man without at least one wife. The degree of bliss of the man depends partly on the number of women he had while on earth.

Each thought of sensuality, as a reason for wrong relations, is denied

---

[21] "When traveling in the region of the upper Missouri a few years ago, I experienced that amongst the Mormons that had gathered there it was common that not only the women, but also the men denied practicing polygamy," Möllhausen noted. "Obviously this happened to deceive the married women, as some of them might have taken exception to following their husbands to Salt Lake, from where their return was impossible; and there the men took other wives."

strongly, as the main goal of all is to establish a holy generation as fast as possible that is supposed to build the Kingdom of the Lord on earth.

Because the elder or the president of the church alone has the power to permit such marriages or to dissolve them, it is understandable what great influence such power must give to the person who holds it in his hands and what care and wisdom is expected of the person who presides as the trusted counselor of families and stands as both church and political head.

On top of it, each unmarried woman has the right, if she is neglected or forgotten, to demand a husband for the salvation of her soul. One way or another the president then has to provide for her and he even has the authority to force any man, whom he deems best for her to join her into marriage, just as each man is obliged to rescue the soul of the girl who is offered to him.

There are other strange customs of Mormonism, but I'm just trying to bring up those which will be touched on in the story below so there won't be a need for an explanation.

Concerning the worldly position of the Mormons, one could expect that in a household in which there are up to thirty wives, there would be incessant bickering and fighting; however, totally to the contrary, in most homes there is peace, unity and sisterly affection amongst the companions. It might be difficult for some young girls to become the thirty-second wife of a husband, just as it would bring sadness to a young woman who for a long time has been the only companion of a husband, when she is informed from time to time of a new engagement and marriage of her husband. . . .

It is known that the Mormons, through the building of schools, universities, factories of all kinds, and through the continual betterment and expansion of agriculture and cattle raising are seeking independence from interaction with other people as soon as possible; though they call themselves citizens of the United States and recognize the government in Washington. The future will show how far they will succeed in this undertaking, because their form of government and their resistance to submit to the orders given by Washington already brought on one break in the relations with the United States. Now that the civil war in America has ended, I suppose that once again the question of polygamy will be in the limelight— sooner or later.

I am sure that theologians of all sects—each in their own way—decided a long time ago what aspects of the Mormon sect can be praised or reproved. The lay person though, who is a reverent worshipper of nature and its wise laws, must disapprove of all that contravenes those laws and should form special opinions, slowly but surely, about any religion which doesn't acknowledge that any other faith, besides its own, is capable of saving souls.

Let this suffice for an introduction. Concerning this novel, I can only repeat that I kept the same purposes in mind when I wrote it, as in similar writings that I published earlier.

A possible question that someone could ask me is whether *The Mormon Girl* is a novel, a description of a journey, or if it was written from descriptions of nature. I answer in the following manner: I tried to combine the one with the other to a rounded whole. A work guided by such purposes is a task that is often quite difficult to achieve and so demands even more friendly leniency.

Just as historical fiction simultaneously combines entertaining as well as instructional elements, so am I guided in my tales by the desire to combine in similar manner the useful with the entertaining. If characters in which all despicable characteristics are displayed are allowed to appear in novels as main characters, shouldn't nature, with all the qualities that are inherent to it, be allowed to own the same right: to be treated with preference? That which demands reverence or abhorrence in nature we regard with worshipful reverence or deep fright, because we fear that which we see has crushed our human fate as a weak reed; however, if nature treats us kindly, we love it the more as is builds a lofty promise opposite to the raging vices of mankind.

After the outbreak of animosities, the Mormons thought to exterminate the expedition (of which I was part) in the Colorado River valley;[22] and even though it isn't their fault that I am still alive, I was in no way guided by hatred against them in the subsequent descriptions. Free from prejudices against sects and positions in society, I took my characters nearly exclusively from real ones. That was greatly facilitated because I either knew them myself, though I was not always very close to them, or I had seen them, or was often—without my intervention—filled in with necessary information about them. But it would be futile to try to seek out this one or that one, because except those natives, who are unforgettable because of their faithful service to me, not a single one is introduced by their real name.

And so, full of faith, I deliver this work to the public.

---

[22] Möllhausen's footnote at his point in the text cites his own *Reisen in die Felsengebirge Nord-Amerikas*, 1:409. In that book Möllhausen noted that "a small group of natives, led by the traitorous Captain Jack" were in the area where the Ives Expedition was grazing its animals, and that "one could not leave the grazing animals unattended because apparently the Mormons had asked Captain Jack to cause us trouble in order to instigate hostilities, which did not come about because of the calm reasoning of the brave train leader." According to Möllhausen, "it had become apparent that the Mormons had spread false rumors about the purpose of our journey, which the natives believed only too willingly"; and that "the Mormons were nearby and they knew very well how to use harmless warriors for their pernicious purposes" (ibid., 410). When Ives was finally informed that "the natives had started to shoot their arrows at the herds," he had difficulty "holding back the young, eager officer from opening fire on the natives." They assumed "that the wild men were still influenced by the Mormons who lived nearby" (ibid., 407, 409, 414). During this period Mormon leader Jacob Hamblin was still operating under Brigham Young's August 1858 instructions that the Indians "must learn that they have either got to help us or the United States will kill us both." See Brooks, *Mountain Meadows Massacre*, 34–35.

The person who has no caring heart for nature, who wants to stubbornly have the foreign—yes—the unknown measured with conditions here at home, and who can't divorce the pictures taken from reality from those which were completed by imagination, that person should lay aside those books unread and disregard them, because their contents will not satisfy him. But the person who loves to gaze across the close boundaries, who—guided by a safe hand—enjoys letting his spirit wander through the endless wilderness of the "Far West," who enjoys taking in, even if just second hand, the overpowering impressions of the one who visited the places himself and who is able to feel and sympathize with the same forces that inspired the author, that person may discover in this book something that may reconcile him with the way the story is told, and may move him to overlook some obvious deficiencies.

Der Fanatiker was Möllhausen's second story with a Mormon subplot. The book was published in 1883, and like *Das Mormonenmädchen* it "begins with the description of a heinous Mormon crime" and the plot revolves around "a naïve Scandinavian beauty who has been tricked or forced into joining the Mormons and who is to be married into polygamy by an unscrupulous guardian." The story begins on a secluded stretch of the overland trail "in the northern part of Salt Lake Valley." Dowlas, a Mormon apostle, and Billot, chief of the Danites, view the remains of a party of eighteen Missourians, who have been recently killed in a massacre similar to that which took place at Mountain Meadows. But a survivor of the massacre observes Dowlas and Billot and even hears them mention a third accomplice named Brandvold. He immediately vows vengeance.[23] Meanwhile the Mormons return to the scene of the crime and quickly discover that their deception, to blame the atrocity on the Indians, has been discovered. Needless to say the Mormon scheme to cover up the massacre is eventually revealed, the survivor takes his vengeance, and the young Scandinavian beauty is rescued from the Mormons.

MÖLLHAUSEN, *DER FANATIKER* [THE FANATIC],
5: 7–18. TRANSLATED BY ROSE EDWARDS.

The morning sun of a clear late summer day shone on Emigrant Street, a road leading north of Salt Lake and to cutoffs leading to other territories. Frightening desolation stared from the bare mountain slopes and the ravines and gorges that run between them.

---

[23] Ashliman, "The Image of Utah and the Mormons," 220. The quotations in the plot summary are from Ashliman.

The desolation wove like a curse through the deep solitude—uninterrupted by any living thing—like a curse from which even the angel of mercy shied away. Even the sun rose coldly over the jagged eastern summits and the haze in the atmosphere veiled its countenance. A breath of hell hung over this deep rocky ravine.

As they laid there so quietly—the eighteen dead men, who just an hour ago had trusted in their own strength, and the strength of their tough fast mules, had looked hopefully into their future, as if the drive through the deserts that stretched before them would have just been child's play.

As they laid there so quietly, a few of them in front of still-smoking campfires, others between opened crates, bales and harnesses close to the six heavy wagons, others next to the feebly flowing brook and in the middle of the sharply limited pasture, where they were murdered by the bullets of treacherous enemies safely hidden to ambush. They didn't even have time to reach for their weapons. And all this happened an hour ago, just as they were preparing for the continued journey to the golden land.

Now again there was dead silence in this green corner of the valley. The contrast between light and darkness equalized more and more, and the rocky desert became more and more illuminated until it was finally a stiff picture of death.

The sounds of the trotting herd of mules was muted in the narrow pass that served as an exit, when two men leaving the valley in the rough clothing of the western settlers, with their rifles over their shoulders, used a pass in the valley to climb toward the highest jagged crag they could reach. By and by a sharp mountain ridge hindered their view into the valley as they slowly moved upward. They were seeking an unobstructed view of the landscape. As they were in deep conversation and were looking down on the sharply rising ground before them, they didn't notice a short distance away a stoutly built man who was pressed against a rock on the only accessible part of the crag when he slid over the mountaintop and then disappeared on the other side. There he rolled down a ways, and stopped barely a few inches from a hundred-feet deep abyss. After laying a few minutes in his doubtful hiding spot, he heard the noise of feet searching for safe ground, and soon he discerned voices and words that he could clearly understand.

"I tell you, Dowlas, this was an excellent strike, we could never have thought to succeed better against those heathen," stated the younger one, a medium-built man with a seemingly weakly built body and with an eastern-looking countenance, as they reached the summit of the crag.

"May they be cursed," replied Dowlas, a man of impressive appearance, "may they be extinguished with fire and sword in the whole world just as they were extinguished here on a small scale." He sent a fleeting glance into the valley and added with hypocritical enthusiasm: "The Lord slew them in his wrath. They suffered no other fate than the bitter enemies of our purified dogma would like to offer to every single one of our people."

"True enough," Billot, chief of the Danites—a union of secret Mormon police—agreed with the apostle. Then he put his rifle down in front of him, brushed his thin blue-black bristly beard, while his small piercing brown eyes blinked mockingly. "A sensitive strike, even if only on a small scale, we taught them once more; and their mules and other valuables are also not to be despised."

"Well, alright," Dowlas agreed hesitantly, "we just can't have any mishaps with the distribution so that the matter will not be known amongst the people. Even Mormon tongues can gossip."

"All participants have sworn secrecy," replied Billot calmly. He pointed casually down to the valley, "I would like to see that person who would declare that this is the work of anyone but the red man (Indian), and unless we commit any stupidities, the Mormons will be the last to fall under suspicion."

"Where was Brandvold?"

"I informed him of everything," came the reply. The man in his hiding place could not hear any more, as the two Mormons continued down the rocky path.

For a while longer the fugitive remained motionless. Then he crept cautiously up the rim. He peered down the valley that his enemies used as a path with their eyes sharpened because of his fear of death. But it lay quiet and desolate. He slid quickly over the rim again to the other side, and kneeling hard on the top cliff, he spied again into the valley.

Finally the two Mormons entered the pass and disappeared immediately behind a cliff.

The fugitive slid back from his lookout and sat down. The terrible predicament he found himself in for over an hour, as well as the sight of the horrifying scene, had exhausted him completely. For a long, long time he sat with his arms on his knees and his face buried in his hands.

"Brandvold, Dowlas and Billot" he murmured with clenched teeth, as if to familiarize his ears with the sound of their names; "Oh, I won't forget you or the faces of your twelve accomplices. I'd recognize every single one of you even amongst hundreds of people."

With a forceful movement he stood up, and with his arms crossed over his broad chest, he stood in his well-worn travel suit like a young giant who felt in himself the strength to meet his enemies even without weapons in life-or-death combat. His deportment, however, sloughed off shortly. In his mind he pictured his travel companions who had crossed the Missouri with him and who he watched bleed to death by the hands of murderers. It was just by chance that he didn't share their fate, just by chance that through him somebody still lived who could ensure through his testimony that those criminals would not escape without punishment since he could testify about the murder of his companions.

After he climbed down the pass he turned to the site of the murder. Seeing the horrible destruction, the color faded from his countenance and his movements became halting.

He walked from one dead comrade to the next. Clear tears flowed out of his honest eyes, as he became convinced that not a single heart beat anymore. Every eye was broken. He counted the wounds inflicted by gunshots, counted the arrows, which were shot at the end into the lifeless corpses to produce a deception. After he bid farewell in this manner to his companions, he walked over again to the wagon. He searched for weapons, but in vain. Axes and knives were taken. However all kinds of food and pieces of clothing lay around in abundance, because no crate was left unopened, no bale uncut. He took as much food as he could carry comfortably, as well as two woolen blankets to serve as protection against the cool of the autumn nights. As he was heavy with sleep he staggered toward the mountain pass. Only after several rock walls were between him and the valley did his movements become more relaxed. When he reached Emigrant Street, with the sun shining on the hazy air, the tracks divided. Five riders took the fork to the Salt Lake, but the tracks of the stolen herd and its keepers lead southeast toward the Wahsatsch Mountains.

The lonely traveler didn't reflect for a long time. If he went toward the Mormon settlements he would hardly get far, so he decided to follow the herd. He hoped to take possession of one or two of the mules that might have fallen back without being noticed.

And so he wandered until the tracks became invisible with the fading of the last glimmer of daylight. He bedded down for safety's sake on a hill when he noticed several small fires in a long gorge about whose significance he had no doubt.

About thirty-six hours had passed since Dowlas and Billot had left the scene of their criminal activities, but now they drew closer to that dreadful place again. Between them rode a tall, well-built, yet lean man whom they treated with respectful politeness. The reason for this was his attitude and dark personality, because he had not yet attained any clerical honors above those of his fellow travelers. At the most he was only a little more than fifty years of age. His short-cropped hair and well-trimmed beard were so mixed with white hair that it was difficult to guess its original color. His countenance, his high forehead, and large brown eyes, might have been more striking in his youth, but he was less handsome now because of his serious expression and a severity that bordered on cruelty. Brooding gloomily, he was usually looking down. But when he lifted his eyes they shone with that unbridled religious fanaticism that shows itself impatient with anything that is not in agreement with it.

A short distance away a troop of eighteen to twenty followed on horseback. All carried weapons, hoes and spades in their saddles. They watched several crows and vultures that were circling above the bare rocks of the mountains in front of them. The birds shot down swift as an arrow only to rise again and reappear just as swiftly in a different place, as if they wanted to express their displeasure about this or that disturbance of the day.

"I wonder what's with those birds," remarked Brandvold, who rode between the apostle and the Danite chief. "I've been watching them for a quarter of an hour. It seems that something is making them anxious."

"It's the wolves that fight with them over the spoil," countered Dowlas, as he observed the movements of a vulture.

"Not the wolves," declared Billot confidently, "To the contrary, the wolves are anxious themselves, or they'd hardly roam around out here—there—look there is another one. They don't seem to really know where to go. I'd hardly be surprised if we met a band of Shoshones down in the bottom of the valley. Those dogs aren't too shy to pull a shirt off the bones of a skeleton, and to put it on their own warty bodies."

"Then they can only belong to those who caused that blood bath." said Dowlas.

"Without fail," admitted Billot. "After they secured the first booty, they have returned to get the rest. The real culprits might even send some other ones."

"So, they count as murderers too, and we need to make sure none will escape alive," decided the apostle. "None," Brandvold confirmed darkly. "It is our duty, a duty ordered by God, to meet the culprits with the edge of the sword." "That would be the surest way to nip in the bud any suspicions about who did this; as surely suspicions will arise in the East against our parish," replied Dowlas calmly.

"In spite of that, the band of korah will not hesitate to at least accuse us of knowing about this crime," replied Brandvold, who then fell silent.[24] He and his companions halted their horses and looked sharply toward the ravine, which was the continuation of the narrow path leading out of the valley.

About three hundred meters away several horsemen came into their view. They recognized two as white men while the third seemed to be a native. They had hardly left the gorge when seven or eight heavily loaded horses and mules appeared behind them, followed by three Indian riders. "I said so,"

---

[24] In Numbers 26:9, Dathan and Abiram "strove against Moses and against Aaron in the company of Korah, when they strove against the LORD."

mentioned Dowlas after a short pause and a devilish malignant delight illuminated his countenance. "From the first moment when I saw the dead I knew that white men had their hand in this." "If they took part in this assault, may God be merciful to them," spoke Brandvold with deep conviction, "he who has shed blood, will also shed his, says the Lord and the name of the Lord shall be praised for ever and ever."

Silently they looked toward the arrival of the strangers, but the little hunting party obviously didn't think anything of it. On the contrary, their leader, a gray-bearded, weather-beaten trapper spurred his horse, and as a sign of his joy to meet civilized people he swung his hat, calling: "Gentlemen, I see by your hoes and shovels what brings you here. By God, it is high time; because behind me," and he swung his hat in the direction of the valley, "there it's horrible. Eighteen of them are lying there, and whoever committed this horrible deed—to deceive me and my companions' eyes—those villains should have been smarter. Natives could have done it, but you would have to be blind as a rattlesnake who is skinning if a single native had any hand in this deed. Awkward hands from the closest distance shot the arrows into the already dead bodies, and the tracks of the moccasins show the style of half a dozen different tribes, the type of moccasins you could get at a barter shop. By God, this surpasses everything I have ever experienced; and if I will get from you Mormons—and I suppose, I am not wrong if I call you such—just a little bit of help, I could find the criminals in eight days."

The Mormons took in this long speech silently, which was carried with deep indignation. In the meantime, Dowlas exchanged a worried look with Billot. Then he observed carefully a second hunter who rode closer, accompanied by a slim half Indian, then turned again to the old trapper: "Yes, we are Mormons," he started, "and we are on our way to give a Christian burial to a number of people of a different faith who were shamelessly murdered in the neighborhood of one of our colonies."

"Well spoken, man," interrupted the old hunter appreciatively, "and we shall be the ones to give you a hand. We would have done it ourselves if we had the right tools."

"Don't worry about that, but for now, I'd like to ask for some information—where are you coming from and where are you going?"

"A justified question in this part of the country," came the willing reply. "I, my comrade and the young half-Indian—my son, by the way—are coming from the other side of the mountain range. There, the three Indian Dakotas, reliable fellows, joined us and so we were on our way southward to the tributaries of the Colorado, when we noticed from Emigrant Street the birds, which are still circling there over the valley of murder. We rode over there, sensing nothing good, and what we found—well, if you haven't been there yet, you will see it soon enough and be horrified."

During the lively communications of the old man, neither he nor his companions watched how the Mormons had successfully surrounded them. They noticed even less that some, through unambiguous signs, had demanded that the Dakota Indians discontinue moving with their loaded animals. As soon as he finished, the apostle continued his interrogation: "For trappers who are on their way to hunting grounds, your animals are loaded down nearly too much, and it appears to be marvelous that you not only carry three guns over your shoulder but you also have the fur of a fox hanging on your saddle, as may be the fashion in New York on Broadway, but not here in the wilderness. As I can see, your three comrades are also equipped with all kinds of curiosities."

"If you check the load of our pack animals, you will find a lot more," replied the hunter unsuspectingly, "whatever we could carry, we tried to save and bring—together with the terrible news—to Salt Lake City. Because if others came after us, we calculated—and the vultures show the most poor and dumb person the location more than half a day's journey away—they may not deal with it honestly. And the guns, you say? Well, one is my own, and the other two I took, because there are names engraved on them, which I deemed important to identify the persons."

"Deliberately done," countered Dowlas with a mocking smile, "but another question: Would you have chosen Salt Lake City as your goal, if you would not have met us?"

The old hunter looked sharply into Dowlas' eyes, then into the dark closed countenance of Branvold, and then danger seemed to dawn on him.

"Hallo," he exclaimed, and his weather-beaten face became a shade darker because of his feelings of deep indignation, "the gentlemen seem to consider me and my companions scoundrels?"

"I'm not saying that," replied Dowlas, "but I would like to know how many loads you have carried away since yesterday morning?"

"Quiet," the old man turned to his companion, who wanted to give a sharp reply, "wild speeches don't lead to a meeting of minds, and after all, in this case you may excuse some mistrust," then turning to Dowlas: "Why don't you ask us straightforward if we were those who, together with others, laid waiting for the caravan?"

"Would you confess being guilty, if the crime rested on you?" replied Dowlas, looking first to the dark Brandvold and then turning to his people he smiled spitefully.

"That hardly," answered the old hunter, "and I certainly would not have been so simpleminded as to run into your arms."

"Hum," pondered Dowlas, "chance often leads wonderfully. But that is beside the point. Just answer this one question: Did you take any of the property of the murdered persons?"

"Did I deny this?" he shouted vehemently. "Or didn't I already talk about this? And didn't I add, that it would be easy for me and my companions to find the murderers? Damn it! I repeat, whoever committed this crime, in their effort to deceive experienced eyes, committed as many stupidities, as the footprints printed with their moccasins, which were worn by those who are used to wearing leather shoes."

Dowlas looked away, so as not to reveal that he grew slightly pale.

"What do you think?" he asked the Danite chief. "I don't want to take the responsibility only on my shoulders; what would you do in my place?"

"I'd check into this affair right here and would deal immediately with the convicted murderers," came the calm reply.

"And you?" Dowlas turned to Brandvold.

He observed the hunters, looking at them somberly. For him, the blind fanatic, even the tiniest suspicion was sufficient to recognize in any person of different faith a criminal.

"I wouldn't be too hasty," he spoke with a conviction that announced nothing good, "but we should take the culprits with us to Salt Lake City and put them in front of a lawful jury."

Jules Verne: At a Speed of Twenty Miles an Hour, A Course of Mormon History

Jules Verne (1828–1905) was born in Nantes and began studying law in Paris in 1847 and witnessed some of the violent demonstrations the following year when revolution broke out in the city. His father introduced him to Paris' literary salons, where he met a handful of luminaries, including Alexandre Dumas. After passing his law exams in 1849, Verne spent the next eight years writing plays, comedies, and short stories. Before his marriage in 1857 he supplemented his meager writing income by working at the Théâtre Lyrique, where he maintained contact with the Parisian literary community, and thereafter he worked as a stockbroker.

Between 1859 and 1862 Verne traveled widely and published accounts of his experiences.[25] When he wasn't traveling, he spent many hours in the libraries of Paris studying geology, engineering, and astronomy. He became famous in 1863 after publishing *Cinq semaines en ballon* in *Magazin d'éducation et de récréation*, which inaugurated the genre of science fiction. The periodical was published by Pierre-Jules Hetzel, who was also the publisher of Alexandre

---

[25] He traveled to England and Scotland [*Voyage en Angleterre et en Ecosse*] and Norway and Denmark.

JULES VERNE (1828–1905).
Courtesy of L'Association des Amis d'Albert Robida.

Dumas, Victor Hugo, George Sand, and other prominent authors. Hetzel quickly agreed to publish Verne's successful story in book form. A recent discovery reveals that Verne also wrote the futuristic *Paris au XXe siècle* in 1863, but Hetzel rejected it, and the story was not published until 1994.[26] Nevertheless, Verne published more than sixty books with Hetzel in a series of *Voyages extraordinaires à travers les mondes connus et inconnus* between 1863 and 1911.

Verne abandoned his unsuccessful brokerage business by 1864 and devoted the rest of his life to writing adventure stories and futuristic tales. He traveled with his brother to the United States—he did not visit Utah—in 1867. When he returned to Europe, he visited London, where he was beginning to attract an English audience. His first book translated into English and published in England and the United States was *From the Earth to the Moon Direct in Ninety-seven Hours and Twenty Minutes* in 1869.[27] At the outbreak of the Franco-Prussian War in 1870, Verne enlisted in the coast guard at Le Crotoy (Somme).

In 1872 Verne completed *Le tour du monde en quatre-vingts jours*, which introduced the unforgettable rational English gentleman, Phileas Fogg, and his wise and loyal French servant, Passepartout. Traveling west on Central Pacific Train No. 148 from Elko, Nevada, to Ogden, Utah, Passepartout encountered Elder William Hitch, who lectured on the mysteries of Mormonism. Passepartout and thirty other passengers attended (although Fogg did not), but the French servant was the last remaining listener when he left the car prior to the end of the lecture. As one author noted, Elder Hitch created "no delay, but a bit of aggravation." Just as Phileas Fogg conceived the idea of his trip after reading an article in the *Daily Telegraph* at the Reform Club in London, Verne may have conceived the idea of placing his characters on the transcontinental after reading about Thomas Cook & Son's package tour across the continent in the *Times* of London.[28]

Before his death in 1905 Verne became increasingly reclusive, but he continued to sail; travel to England, Scandinavia, and America; and attend

---

[26] Verne, *Paris au XXe siècle*. Random House published an English translation as *Paris in the Twentieth Century* in 1996.

[27] Verne, *From the Earth to the Moon Direct in Ninety-seven Hours and Twenty Minutes*. Another futuristic tale was *To the Sun? A Journey through Planetary Space*.

[28] Withey, *Grand Tours and Cook's Tours*, 264, 267, 270–71. Verne had many sources to consult for his episode concerning Mormonism, including Rémy, Bertrand, Burton, and Audouard.

meetings of the Geographical Society in Paris. In addition to his science fiction, he also wrote travel adventures and a series of books recounting the experiences of real travelers.[29] His books appear in 148 languages, and he is among the most-translated novelists in the world.

> JULES VERNE, LE TOUR DU MONDE EN QUATRE-VINGTS JOURS
> [THE TOUR OF THE WORLD IN 80 DAYS], 203, 210–17.[30]

"From ocean to ocean,"—so say the Americans; and these four words compose the general designation of the "Great trunk line" which crosses the entire width of the United States. The Pacific Railroad is, however, really divided into two distinct lines: the Central Pacific, between San Francisco and Ogden, and the Union Pacific, between Ogden and Omaha. Five main lines connect Omaha with New York.

New York and San Francisco are thus united by an uninterrupted metal ribbon, which measures no less than three thousand seven hundred and eighty-six miles. Between Omaha and the Pacific the railway crosses a territory which is still infested by Indians and wild beasts, and a large tract which the Mormons, after they were driven from Illinois in 1845, began to colonize.

The journey from New York to San Francisco consumed, in former times, under the most favorable conditions, at least six months. It is now accomplished in seven days.

During the night of the 5th of December, the train ran southeasterly for about fifty miles; then rose an equal distance in a northeasterly direction, towards the Great Salt Lake.

Passepartout, about nine o'clock, went out upon the platform to take the air. The weather was cold, the heavens gray, but it was not snowing. The sun's disk, enlarged by the mist, seemed an enormous ring of gold, and Passepartout was amusing himself by calculating its value in pounds sterling, when he was diverted from this interesting study by a strange-looking personage who made his appearance on the platform.

This personage, who had taken the train at Elko, was tall and dark, with black mustaches, black stockings, a black silk hat, a black waistcoat, black trousers, a white cravat, and dog-skin gloves. He might have been taken for a clergyman. He went from one end of the train to the other, and affixed to the door of each car a notice written in manuscript.

Passepartout approached and read one of these notices, which stated that Elder William Hitch, Mormon missionary, taking advantage of his presence

---

[29] Charles Scribner's Sons published *Verne's Famous Travels and Travelers* (1879); *The Great Navigators of the Eighteenth Century* (1880); and *The Exploration of the World* (1881).

[30] This translation is taken from the first English edition of Verne's book, published in 1878.

"And you, my faithful..."
Elder Hitch preaches on the train.
Verne, Le tour du monde en 80 jours, *153*.

on train No. 48, would deliver a lecture on Mormonism in car No. 117, from 11 to 12 o'clock; and that he invited all who were desirous of being instructed concerning the mysteries of the religion of the "Latter Day Saints" to attend.

"I'll go," said Passepartout to himself. He knew nothing of Mormonism except the custom of polygamy, which is its foundation.

The news quickly spread through the train, which contained about one hundred passengers, thirty of whom, at most, attracted by the notice, ensconced themselves in car No. 117. Passepartout took one of the front seats. Neither Mr. Fogg nor Fix cared to attend.

At the appointed hour Elder William Hitch rose, and, in an irritated voice, as if he had already been contradicted, said:—"I tell you that Joe Smith is a martyr, that his brother Hiram is a martyr, and that the persecutions of the United States government against the prophets will also make a martyr of Brigham Young. Who dares to say the contrary?"

No one ventured to gainsay the missionary, whose excited tone contrasted curiously with his naturally calm visage. No doubt his anger arose from the hardships to which the Mormons were actually subjected. The government had just succeeded, with some difficulty, in reducing these independent fanatics to its rule. It had made itself master of Utah, and subjected that Territory to the laws of the Union, after imprisoning Brigham Young on a charge of rebellion and polygamy.[31] The disciples of the prophet had since redoubled their efforts, and resisted, by words at least, the authority of Congress. Elder Hitch, as is seen, was trying to make proselytes on the very railway trains.

Then, emphasizing his words with his loud voice and frequent gestures, he related the history of the Mormons from Biblical times: how in Israel, a Mormon prophet of the tribe of Joseph published the annals of the new religion, and bequeathed them to his son Mormon; how, many centuries later, a translation of this precious book, which was written in Egyptian, was made by Joseph Smith, Junior, a Vermont farmer, who revealed himself as a mystical prophet in 1825; and how, in short, the celestial messenger appeared to him in an illuminated forest and gave him the annals of the Lord.

Several of the audience, not being much interested in the missionary's narrative, here left the car; but Elder Hitch, continuing his lecture, related how Smith, Junior, with his father, two brothers, and a few disciples, founded the church of the "Latter Day Saints," which, adopted not only in America, but in England, Norway and Sweden, and Germany, counts many artisans, as well as men engaged in the liberal professions, among its members; how a colony was established in Ohio, a temple erected there at a cost of two hundred thousand dollars, and a town built at Kirkland; how Smith became an enterprising banker, and received from a simple mummy showman a papyrus scroll written by Abraham and several famous Egyptians.[32]

The Elder's story became somewhat wearisome, and his audience grew gradually less, until it was reduced to twenty passengers. But this did not disconcert the enthusiast, who proceeded with the story of Joseph Smith's bankruptcy in 1837, and how his ruined creditors gave him a coat of tar and feathers; his reappearance some years afterwards, more honorable and honored than ever, at Independence, Missouri, the chief of a flourishing colony of three thousand disciples, and his pursuit thence by outraged Gentiles, and retirement into the far West.

Ten hearers only were now left, among them honest Passepartout, who was listening with all his ears. Thus he learned that, after long persecutions, Smith reappeared in Illinois, and in 1839 founded a community at Nauvoo, on the Mississippi, numbering twenty-five thousand souls, of which he became mayor, chief justice, and general-in-chief; that he announced himself, in 1843, as a candidate for the Presidency of the United States; and that finally, being drawn into ambuscade at Carthage, he was thrown into prison, and assassinated by a band of men disguised in masks.

---

[31] Although Brigham Young was arrested in October 1871 for "lewd and lascivious cohabitation," he was never tried on the charge. Young was, however, sent to prison for twenty-four hours in March 1875 for failing to pay alimony to a young wife who was suing him for divorce.

[32] Verne's probable source for this discussion was Jules Rémy, who commented at length on these papyri. Bertrand also discussed the papyri.

Passepartout was now the only person left in the car, and the Elder, looking him full in the face, reminded him that, two years after the assassination of Joseph Smith, the inspired prophet, Brigham Young, his successor, left Nauvoo for the banks of the Great Salt Lake, where, in the midst of that fertile region, directly on the route of the emigrants who crossed Utah on their way to California, the new colony, thanks to the polygamy practiced by the Mormons, had flourished beyond expectation.

"And this," added Elder William Hitch,—"this is why the jealousy of Congress has been aroused against us! Why have the soldiers of the Union invaded the soil of Utah? Why has Brigham Young, our chief, been imprisoned, in contempt of all justice? Shall we yield to force? Never! Driven from Vermont, driven from Illinois, driven from Ohio, driven from Missouri, driven from Utah, we shall yet find some independent territory on which to plant our tents. And you, my brother," continued the Elder, fixing his angry eye upon his single auditor, "will you not plant yours there, too, under the shadow of our flag?"

"No!" replied Passepartout, courageously, in his turn retiring from the car, and leaving the Elder to preach to vacancy.

During the lecture the train had been making good progress, and toward half past twelve it reached the northwest border of the Great Salt Lake. Thence the passengers could observe the vast extent of this interior sea, which is also called the Dead Sea, and into which flows an American Jordan. It is a picturesque expanse, framed in lofty crags in large strata, encrusted with white salt,—a superb sheet of water, which was formerly of larger extent than now, its shores having encroached with the lapse of time, and thus at once reduced its breadth and increased its depth.

The Salt Lake, seventy miles long and thirty-five wide, is situated three miles eight hundred feet above the sea.[33] Quite different from Lake Asphaltite, whose depression is twelve hundred feet below the sea, it contains considerable salt, and one quarter of the weight of its water is solid matter, its specific weight being 1170, and, after being distilled, 1000.[34] Fishes are of course unable to live in it, and those which descend through the Jordan, the Weber, and other streams, soon perish.

The country around the lake was well cultivated, for the Mormons are mostly farmers; while ranches and pens for domesticated animals, fields of wheat, corn, and other cereals, luxuriant prairies, hedges of wild rose, clumps of acacias and milk-wort, would have been six months later. Now the ground was covered with a thin powdering of snow.

The train reached Ogden at two o'clock, where it rested for six hours. Mr. Fogg and his party had time to pay a visit to Salt Lake City, connected with

---

[33] The Great Salt Lake is actually only slightly more than four thousand feet above sea level.
[34] Lake Asphaltite is the Dead Sea.

Ogden by a branch road; and they spent two hours in this strikingly American town, built on the pattern of other cities of the Union, like a checkerboard, "with the sombre sadness of right angles," as Victor Hugo expresses it. The founder of the City of the Saints could not escape from the taste for symmetry which distinguishes the Anglo-Saxons. In this strange country, where the people are certainly not up to the level of their institutions, everything is done "squarely,"—cities, houses, and follies.

The travellers, then, were promenading, at three o'clock, about the streets of the town built between the banks of the Jordan and the spurs of the Wahsatch Range. They saw few or no churches, but the prophet's mansion, the courthouse, and the arsenal, blue-brick houses with verandas and porches, surrounded by gardens bordered with acacias, palms, and locusts. A clay and pebble wall, built in 1853, surrounded the town; and in the principal street were the market and several hotels adorned with pavilions. The place did not seem thickly populated. The streets were almost deserted, except in the vicinity of the Temple, which they only reached after having traversed several quarters surrounded by palisades. There were many women, which was easily accounted for by the "peculiar institution" of the Mormons; but it must not be supposed that all the Mormons are polygamists. They are free to marry or not, as they please; but it is worth noting that it is mainly the female citizens of Utah who are anxious to marry, as, according to the Mormon religion, maiden ladies are not admitted to the possession of its highest joys. These poor creatures seemed to be neither well off nor happy. Some—the more well-to-do, no doubt—wore short, open black silk dresses, under a hood or modest shawl; others were dressed in Indian fashion.

Passepartout could not behold without a certain fright these women, charged, in groups, with conferring happiness on a single Mormon. His common-sense pitied, above all, the husband. It seemed to him a terrible thing to have to guide so many wives at once across the vicissitudes of life, and to conduct them, as it were, in a body to the Mormon paradise, with the prospect of seeing them in the company of the glorious Smith, who doubtless was the chief ornament of that delightful place, to all eternity. He felt decidedly repelled from such a vocation, and he imagined—perhaps he was mistaken—that the fair ones of Salt Lake City cast rather alarming glances on his person. Happily, his stay there was but brief. At four the party found themselves again at the station, took their places in the train, and the whistle sounded for starting. Just at the moment, however, that the locomotive wheels began to move, cries of "Stop! Stop!" were heard.

They do not stop trains in motion. The gentleman who uttered the cries was evidently a belated Mormon. He was breathless with running. Happily for him, the station had neither gates nor barriers. He rushed along the track, jumped on the rear platform of the train, and fell exhausted into one of the seats.

Passepartout, who had been anxiously watching this amateur gymnast, approached him with lively interest, and learned that he had taken flight after an unpleasant domestic scene.

When the Mormon had recovered his breath, Passepartout ventured to ask him politely how many wives he had; for, from the manner in which he had decamped, it might be thought that he had twenty at least.

"One, sir," replied the Mormon, raising his arms heavenward,—"one, and that was enough!"

Albert Robida:
They Too Were Tired of the Solitary Life

Albert Robida (1848–1926) was not only a prolific writer of adventure and travel stories but was also a gifted illustrator. Nevertheless, his fantastic novels were never as successful as Jules Verne's. While Verne's around-the-world adventures blurred fact and fiction, causing some readers to suspend disbelief, many of Robida's tales were parodies whose exaggerations lampooned "true" adventure stories.

Robida was born in Compiègne, France, and, like Verne, began his professional life as solicitor. He abandoned law to become an illustrator for *Journal Amusant* and other magazines before founding *La Caricature* with Georges Decaux. In 1869, at age 19, he drew a series of cartoons entitled "Le Mormonisme à Paris" that was published in *Paris-Caprice*. Robida satirized Mormonism and the prominent feminist Olympe Audouard, who was surprisingly sympathetic in her treatment of Mormon polygamy after she visited Utah earlier that year.

Robida toured Europe from 1875 to 1879 and demonstrated his outstanding artistic and writing talent in two travel narratives, *Les vieilles villes d'Italie*, published in 1878, and the following year in *Les vieilles villes de Suisse*. His first book of fiction, *Voyages très extraordinaires de Saturnin Farandoul dans les 5 ou 6 parties du monde et dans les pays connus et même inconnus de M. Jules Verne* [The Quite Extraordinary Travels of Saturnin Farandoul in 5 or 6 parts of the World and in all countries known and unknown by Jules Verne], appeared in 1879.[35] Robida had obviously read Verne's *Le Tour du monde en quatre-vingts jours*, including his chapter on Mormonism, but his satire of Verne's

---

[35] The title used on the book's cover in 1882 for the second part in a five-volume set was *Le tour du monde en plus de 80 jours* [Around the World in More than 80 Days].

ALBERT ROBIDA (1848–1926).
Courtesy of L'Association des Amis d'Albert Robi

romance had detail about Mormon history, doctrine, and truth claims that was not included in Verne's book.[36]

Robida was one of few graphic artists of his generation to both write and illustrate. Whereas Verne's book had only one illustration accompanying the text relating to the preaching of Elder Hitch there are more than twenty illustrations in Robida's two books relating to Utah and the Mormons. During his career he drew more than 60,000 illustrations and wrote and illustrated more than two hundred books, including such classics as the *Arabian Nights*, Rabelais' works, and Jonathan Swift's *Gulliver's Travels*. And Robida's Farandoul has been used by subsequent graphic artists. He has been the subject of the Italian cinema (in 1913), Italian television (in 1957), and in comics beginning with Topolino (Mickey Mouse) in 1938–39, Paperino Girandola (Donald Duck) in 1959, and in a less well known parody (Marzolino Tarantula) in 1979. Today the Robida Society publishes *Le Téléphonoscope* to celebrate his literary works.

---

[36] This may be the reason that the editors of *Le Téléphonoscope* were somewhat incredulous when I asked why Robida included Mormons in his book: "Un universitaire de Salt Lake City ne nous demandait-il pas récemment, via Internet, les raisons qui avaient conduit Albert Robida à s'intéresser aux Mormons!" See Editorial, *Le Téléphonoscope* (May 1999), 2.

The departure of the sailors for the city of the Mormons. *Robida, Voyages très extraordinaires, 171.*

ALBERT ROBIDA, *VOYAGES TRÈS EXTRAORDINAIRES DE SATURNIN FARANDOUL* [THE QUITE EXTRAORDINARY TRAVELS OF SATURNIN FARANDOUL], 168–216. TRANSLATED BY HUGH MACNAUGHTON.

Tired out with the great enterprises in which that scarred heart remained solitary and sad, convinced that in life it is from time to time necessary to do something for that organ, Farandoul resolved that he would betake himself to the land of the Mormons. Mandibul and the fifteen men of the good ship *Belle Léocadie* were summoned that very evening, and Farandoul acquainted them with his plan. Strange to say—it proves to what extent these men were of one mind—they too were tired of the solitary life and their thoughts had also turned toward the great city by the Salt Lake.

There was but one shout of acclamation: "Hurrah for Mormonism! All Mormons together!" Mandibul even declared that he had always dreamed, as far back as he could remember, of spending a happy life as the head of a Mormon line, surrounded by a family identified by serial numbers instead of commonplace forenames.

The preparations did not take long. The idea had been received by one and all with such enthusiasm that in two hours every man was ready, and they all set out at once.

Six days by railroad did nothing to dampen the ardor of the neophytes. At the first station, Farandoul had sent a telegram to Brigham Young, the high priest of the Mormons, to let him know of their arrival. Brigham had replied, and throughout the journey a conversation had become established between the high priest and the new convert.

Brigham Young, delighted and flattered to have won for his religion such an important recruit, said he was placing himself at the entire disposal of Saturnin.

During the last few hours of the journey, the telegrams flew to and fro:

"Found a splendid opportunity. Senator just divorced from spouses. Sixteen well-assorted women. Would throw in seventeenth into the bargain. Do you wish to avail yourself? Many applicants, but you would have preference. —BRIGHAM YOUNG

"Accepted. Thank you. Lieut. Mandibul wonders whether similar opportunity for him." —FARANDOUL

"Six negresses and a Chinese for the asking. Don't speak French. Do we negotiate?" —BRIGHAM YOUNG

"Mandibul additionally asks for half-dozen white women for the sweet chit-chat in the home." —FARANDOUL

"I've found them. Asked before closing whether Lieut. Mandibul is fair-haired." —BRIGHAM YOUNG

"Blazing fair hair. Another request. Tournesol [Sunflower], thirty-three, volcanic temperament. Would like Mexican women?" —FARANDOUL

"Mandibul match made. A big lot of Mexican ladies for Tournesol. I shall be at the station." —BRIGHAM YOUNG

Brigham Young had organized everything beautifully. Before his friends had even disembarked, he had them married, and had found them the seventeen apartments that were needed, that is to say, two large houses for Farandoul and Mandibul, and fifteen cottages for the sailors.

The announcement that the famous Farandoul and his men were arriving had caused a great stir in the city of the Saints. The high council, the bishops and the elders had met, and it was decided that they would be given a grand reception.

The station was decorated with bunting everywhere and long before the train arrived, a huge crowd had flocked there in festive garb. The high coun-

The formal reception at Salt Lake City. *Robida,* Voyages très extraordinaires, *173.*

cil was there with Brigham Young at its head. In front of the Elders, a white-clad cohort of women drew the tenderly admiring gaze of the onlookers.

Dressed in white, with garlands of flowers, the newlywed brides stood waiting, repressing the beatings of their hearts, for their husbands to arrive.

They were in all shades of complexion and of every nationality. To present a pleasing sight for the arrivals, Brigham Young had sought to gather together as complete an assortment as possible of Mormon beauties, and you can be sure that he had entirely succeeded.

Finally, the train appeared and all hearts were beating; the repeated whistles and increasingly loud siren-calls from the steam-engine were drowned all of a sudden by the explosion of a salvo of applause fit to make the great temple collapse.

The travelers leapt to the ground, replying to the popular acclamations by sweeping their hats off, and they made their way toward the group of ladies.

Brigham Young came forward, shook both Farandoul's hands and pronounced a welcoming speech steeped in the most heartfelt cordiality, to which Farandoul replied with a few deeply felt words.

Next the introductions were made. Farandoul was consumed with eagerness to get to know his spouses; Mandibul and the sailors were trying to make out theirs from among the numerous collection gathered together by Brigham Young.

Perhaps it should be said straightaway that all were entirely satisfied of the choice, and Brigham did not have to deal with any complaints.

Mandibul alone negotiated a small exchange with the Breton, Trabadec, a simple, gentle-natured man. Trabadec had been fairly well done by the choice of wives allotted to him; Brigham Young had bound him together with four charming young Parisian women, among them a little dramatic artiste who had come over with an operetta troupe to San Francisco; but Trabadec instantly realized that none of his brides understood his dialect of Breton, and went to explain his plight and his despair to his superior.

Mandibul, ever the kindly soul, took the four Parisian women for himself, and allotted four of his negresses to the enchanted Trabadec.

Since all had turned out to the general satisfaction, nothing else remained but to get on with the ceremony.

At the station exit, the cortège went straight to the temple, where the registry documents had been prepared. All that was needed was a few rapid signatures and everyone repaired to the Great Polygamy Hotel, in the gala room of which, a magnificent banquet for three thousand had been provided by the municipality of Salt Lake City the new converts.

Brigham Young, the bishops, and the elders honored this gigantic dinner with their presence, and seas of Champagne were poured in honor of Farandoul. We have no intention of reporting all the incidents, or of enumerating the toasts which were proposed to Mormonism, to the old and new faithful, and to their amiable fractions, as Mandibul said, referring to his wives, who were too numerous to be called his *moitiés* or better halves.

We should like to transcribe here just the opening words of the speech made by our hero to tumultuous applause and acclaim, culminating in such a rending explosion of hurrahs that several gas lamps were blown out in the street. These were the words with which Farandoul began:

"Ladies and Gentlemen: It is not, believe you me, without mature reflection, not without having meditated long and deeply that I decided to come

The toast to the amiable divisions of Mandibul.
Robida, Voyages très extraordinaires, 175.

to the City of Saints to ask you to make room for one more member of the faithful!

"It is a man beaten by the stormy seas, shaken by wind and weather, who comes hither seeking the happy, peaceful haven in which, in the calm waters of virtue well understood, to rest from the fatigue and agitation of an existence hitherto dedicated to the defense of great, renovating and humanitarian ideas.

"The Mormon ideal is great, too! To return to the true role of women in Biblical tradition; to raise the family to its rightful dignity; following the example of the Patriarchs, to widen the conjugal home and make room for an indeterminate number of wives! Your prophet, Brigham Young has said it: 'The heart of man is vast, vast too must be his home!'

"Another very imperious reason militates in favor of polygamy: How many examples have we seen of those sad monogamists, whiling away their colorless, almost useless existence in a continual state of coldness and hostility to their sole spouse! Since the sharp edges of their characters jarred together at every instant, the result was stony silences, quarrels, every kind of unhappy episode for both, whereas if they had bravely adopted the principles of polygamy, the household made wide open would have regained its allure, through some degree of balance produced by the variety of characters, failings and qualities which succeeded in offsetting themselves against each other, forming a sum of conjugal bliss that can never be attained with the restricted household.

"Yes, polygamy alone can cushion existence!

"Accordingly, we renew the home life, we elevate man and we raise up womankind, too. But our action does not stop there. Gradually, we shall change the face of the world; in my view, monogamous nations are doomed to swift decadence and degeneration, and the time has come when, if they are to forestall the onset of this decadence, they must fling themselves into our arms! The role of polygamous nations will begin. We must and shall be the initiating nation!

"Just one example, Gentlemen, of the power of the polygamous idea; I give it not for yourselves, the strong and convinced, but for the world which has its eyes upon us.

"When was the period of the highest prosperity for Turkey, the period of expansion and grandeur for the Ottoman empire? Precisely that period when polygamy was considered by all as an absolute religious duty. Turkey only began to decline when morals had become loose, when polygamy was observed only by the great statesmen, the pashas, and the sultans!

"That is why I say that the renewal of the old world will come from the Mormon nation, and why I am ready to contribute as far as my feeble means will allow to the triumph of our great, pacific and humanitarian idea!!!"

FARANDOUL'S SEVENTEEN WIVES
THE HOUR OF TRANQUILITY HAS NOT COME
BOUND TO AN INDIAN WAR STAKE!

We spoke earlier of the emotion aroused by Farandoul's speech in the Mormon gathering; an attentive observer would have noticed that Brigham Young alone had not contributed his share of congratulations to the orator and that his face, which had been smiling and cordial at the start of the feast, had gradually changed through all the fine shades of discontent. With pressed lips and frowning brow, he saw the Mormons milling around the one whom he began to view as a possible rival, and who he repented having welcomed in such style.

However, one of the most venerable onlookers asked to be allowed to speak.

"I have only two things to say," he shouted in a burst of enthusiasm, "a bishop's see is vacant on the high council; I propose that we elect our eloquent friend Farandoul to it without delay! Believe me, my candidate will honor the Mormon church!"

This motion was greeted with thunderous applause. The lips of Brigham Young became even more firmly pressed-together, his fists clenched, he made as if to stand, but a thought restrained his impulse; he fell back onto his seat with an evil smile.

"The entire council of elders is gathered together at this table;" resumed the orator, "we can vote by acclamation!"

All hands were raised. A great shout arose: "Farandoul for a Mormon bishop!"

Saturnin Farandoul had just been unanimously elected.

"The honor you do me is immense; I shall endeavor to show myself worthy!" cried our hero who, in the twinkling of an eye became overwhelmed with the handshakes and hugs of his friends and his wives.

This incident reminded him that he was the head of a family.

"Honor to the ladies!" said he, "overwhelmed with the weight of all the favors with which you so generously ply me, I have not yet been able to make the acquaintance of my spouses! It would be unpardonable of me if I were to neglect any further these fair ones who have consented to adorn my household."

"Bravo! Bravo!" cried all those who were present, "we shall lead you in triumph to your abode. The town band awaits you in the street."

Brigham Young had disappeared, and with him a few gloomy figures who had not joined in the general rejoicing.

The elders took up their place at the head of the procession. Farandoul and his wives, Mandibul and his, and the sailors' families came next. The procession moved forward to the strains of the Mormon national anthem, sung in chorus by the entire assembled multitude:

Great King Solomon had a good three hundred wives! etc.

Farandoul's villa was charming, and the purest good taste had presided over the furnishing of all the rooms.

After a few last acclamations beneath its windows, the procession had moved on to see Mandibul and the sailors to their homes. A personage who seemed to be the grand master of ceremonies had left a paper in the hands of Farandoul: it was the copy of his marriage certificate.

"Very good!" said Farandoul, "I shall at last get to know the forenames of my amiable better fractions! Let us first call the roll to see that there is no mistake and no stray wife of Mandibul's has got mixed up with mine. Let us begin:

Sidonie Brulovif, 26 years old, born in Bordeaux;[37]
Lodoïska Ratakowska, 30 years old, born in Cracow;
Balthazarde Marcassoul, 18 years old, born in Marseille;
Chloé Vanderboeuf, 30 years old, born in San Francisco;
Athenaïs Plumet, 32 years old, born in Paris;

---

[37] *Brûle au vif* or *brûlot vif*, in French, means "burn alive" or "a lively firebrand."

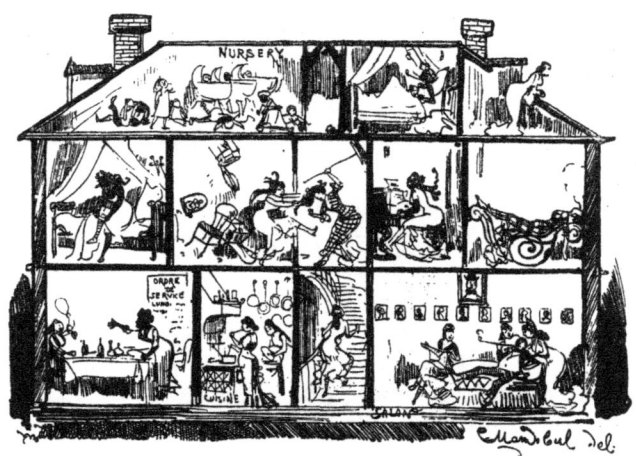

Sectional view of a Mormon home, according to a sketch by Lieutenant Mandibul. *Robida*, Voyages très extraordinaires, *177*.

Calypso Zanguebar, negress, age and place of birth unknown;
Theodosia Niggins, 18 years old, born in New York;
Cora Millington, 16 years old, born in Chicago;
Dolorès Castañetta, 22 years old, born in Mexico;
Diana Pickington, 17 years old, born in Philadelphia;
Pulchérie O'Cobbler, 26 years old, born in Baltimore;
Angelina Farthing, 26 years old, born in Dublin;
Olga Biscornoff, 22 years old, born in Saint Petersburg;[38]
Juanita Pachéco, 18 years old, born in Lima;
Clarisse Dickinson, 25 years old, born in Liverpool;
Kaoula Ka-ou-lin, 28 years old, born in Litchou Fou, near Pekin;[39]
Marguerite Schumaker, 20 years old, born in Berlin.

No error was discovered, each lady answered the roll call and Farandoul discovered with satisfaction that they truly were charming; Brigham Young had good taste. Saturnin promised to himself that he would show his gratitude.

The luggage arrived. Farandoul, his mind occupied, saw to his settling in.

In his life, events were hurrying forward with such rapidity that they scarcely left him any time for thought.

---

[38] In French, *biscornu* means "misshapen" or "oddly-shaped."
[39] In French, a pun on *kaolin*, China clay.

Twenty-two days earlier, he had still been in Brazil. Without letting up, he had spent fifteen days at sea on a steamer and six days journeying by railway, with scarcely any time taken to settle accounts at New York. And finally, he had only been a Mormon for six hours, and already seventeen wives were the ornament of his home, and he was already a bishop! . . .

The ringing of the bell roused him from his ponderings; the seventeen ladies discreetly withdrew, leaving him alone with his visitor.

The latter had simply come to tell him that a meeting of the council of elders would be taking place that very evening, and Brigham Young asked the new bishop to honor the occasion with his presence, if the rigors of the journey allowed him to.

"Lead on!" said Farandoul.

And the indefatigable Saturnin, pausing only to offer a few words of explanation to the ladies, followed in the departing footsteps of Brigham Young's messenger.

Alas! The hour of tranquillity, after so many hard fortunes and adventures, had not yet rung for our hero. New perils were hanging over his head; the infamous Brigham Young, in his jealousy and anxiety, had thought it prudent to make away with the man who could become a dangerous rival to him.

Night had fallen. Our hero was walking down the dark avenue that led to the Great Mormon Temple. Unsuspecting, he had not noticed some shadowy figures following him noiselessly, while other shadows hid behind each tree. His thoughts returned to his seventeen wives, and the smiling future which beckoned to him. Not a single dark shadow on the horizon, not a cloud in his sky. . . .

Suddenly, an owl-hoot sounded behind him, and a cascade of human beings bore down upon his shoulders before he realized what had happened, and despite a desperate struggle, his assailants had thrown him to the ground, then bound and gagged him.

These men were masked! Even so, Farandoul thought he could make out among them two of Brigham Young's followers whom he had glimpsed at the banquet. It was all plain to him!

Horses were brought, and the bandits tied Farandoul tightly onto the liveliest of the steeds and leapt into their saddles.

Without a word, the cavalcade made off at a fast gallop toward the country; after two hours' ride, the gang halted at the borders of a wood. A few owl-hoots were uttered; others replied, and a new group of horsemen came into sight.

These riders were redskins. By the light of the moon, Farandoul glimpsed strange tattooings, further accentuating the fierceness of the faces, the animal-skin hats, the warlike hairstyles adorned with eagle and vulture feathers, saddles hung with terrible scalps.

"Here is the man!" said the chief of Brigham Young's henchmen.

"Good," said a tall Indian, "our father the paleface with a hundred wives is a great chief; his enemy shall die! The Apache warriors and the palefaces of the Great Salt Lake are friends; the redskin warriors will be able to go and fetch firewater in their city. The war-ax is buried for ever. How!" . . .

After much nonsense, Farandoul wins over the Apache warriors but soon fell from grace by being too partial to their wives. He runs off with one and two warriors pursue them. To save their lives, Farandoul kills two grizzlies and they disguise themselves in the skins. They meet two trappers who first shoot at them, mistaking them for real grizzlies, and then offer to take them to Santa Fe, two days' journey away. Farandoul's first thought was to telegraph Mandibul at Salt Lake City. The reply was not long in coming: upon learning of the disappearance of their chief, the pirates had gone, abandoning their wives.

BATTLE OF GIANTS IN A LOCOMOTIVE

Farandoul returned to the telegraph office; a message in the following terms was dispatched to Brigham Young:

You rascal, what have you done with my seventeen wives?

FARANDOUL REPLY PAID.

Brigham Young replied with a telegram which betrayed his astuteness and hypocrisy.

Sir, After your incomprehensible flight, which showed us that you were not a sincere Mormon, your spouses, blushing for shame at having ever, for one instant, been united to a man so bereft of convictions, are petitioning for divorce. An honorable Mormon, Matheus Bikelow, appointed Bishop in your stead, has afforded the shelter of his home to them. He has married them and will not abandon them!

Once again, Sir, your conduct has been unworthy, and I would suggest that you never show yourself again in the city of the Saints.

BRIGHAM YOUNG

Since the reply had been paid, Brigham, as we can see, had not been over-spare with his words. Farandoul turned next to Bikelow, and asked for his seventeen wives back.

Notes were exchanged between the rivals, bittersweet at first, but soon turning threatening. Bikelow accepted the challenge, but could not make up his mind on any weapon; Farandoul suggested first the tomahawk, then the rifle, the cannon, the balista, the catapult, the ironclad ship, the ball, etc. etc.

The press had got hold of the matter, so that in every city in the United States the talk was all about this duel. As people were beginning to tease Bikelow, who had such difficulty in coming to a choice of weaponry, he ended up proposing a classic American duel, asking that the two adversaries, each armed with a rifle, should both leave at the same time, one from New York and the other from San Francisco, searching for each other throughout the whole Yankee territory.

Here is Farandoul's reply:

Idea accepted in principle, with just one little modification. Each adversary shall be mounted on a locomotive. Both trains shall leave at the same time from New York and San Francisco, to collide in the middle of the Central Pacific Railroad line.

Bikelow had to accept Farandoul's challenge. In Nevada, where they had searched in vain for their captain, the pirate crew learned of Farandoul's duel with Bikelow. They join Farandoul as he prepares to leave New York, riding the special train with which he is to confront Bikelow. The opponents are to do battle at the Devil's Bridge, spanning the Nebraska River. The duel had attracted considerable public attention, and people were in Nebraska waiting for the two trains, armed with swivel-mounted cannon, to come together. As they meet, a murderous exchange of fire damages Farandoul's train, but Bikelow's train causes the bridge to collapse and plunges over a hundred feet into the river. The speed of Farandoul's train causes it to reach the abutment in time. Farandoul's popularity notwithstanding, he does not wish to stand for political office. The expenses connected with the duel make inroads into Farandoul's accumulated wealth, but with his honor satisfied, Farandoul declares, "I renounce all seventeen ungrateful women; please telegraph the fact to Brigham Young."

After a digression into the earlier adventures of Horatius Bixby, Farandoul and his crew embark on further picturesque and improbable adventures in South America and elsewhere, involving at one point Phileas Fogg and Passepartout of *Around the World in Eighty Days*.

In contrast to his Mormon pirate fantasy, Robida's *Le vingtième siècle* (published in 1882) is futuristic humor. The setting is France and England in 1953. Since 1910, the United States had become three nations: a Chinese republic in the West, with its capital at New Nanking (San Francisco), a German empire in the East with its capital at New-Berlin (formerly New York City), and a Mormon republic (formerly "the old states of Utah, Colorado, Arizona, etc."), headquartered at Salt Lake City. The Mormons, sensing that their country would become the inevitable battlefield and plunder of the two larger American nations, turned to their mother country of England, particularly when the British government fled to India. "Perhaps through the transatlantic tunnel the great Mormon republic of Great Salt Lake City, which comprises the ancient states of Utah, Colorado, Arizona, etc.," one character speculates, "sent its legions of missionaries to proselyte and indoctrinate England and convert it to Mormonism."[40] In ten years, the Mormonization of England was complete: the land of the expression "shocking!" has become the most *shocking* country on the planet. The House of Lords is now the House of Bishops, and to be eligible for election to the House of Commons, one must have at least eight wives. New landmarks include the Great Temple, modeled after the Salt Lake Temple, and, in Hyde Park, the palace of the head of state (who is both pope and president of the Mormon republics of Europe and America). Windsor Castle is now a retirement estate "for widows of bishops and archbishops." Monsieur Ponto, a Parisian financier, has sent his son Philippe to England, now the most dangerous country in Europe, on a crucial banking matter. Philippe has dropped out of sight, and his father's concern is only heightened when he finally receives a letter—which is rare in this modern day of telephone calls.

ROBIDA, *LE VINGTIÈME SIÈCLE* [THE TWENTIETH CENTURY],
312–18. TRANSLATED BY RICK GRUNDER.

Bachelor's-Prison, August 7, 1953
My dear father,
Such a funny country Mormonism has made of this New-England—how I would laugh if I were not in prison at the moment! Rest assured that I have murdered no one, nor committed the slightest misdemeanor. I am simply locked up in *Bachelor's-Prison* as a *matrimonial insubordinate*. Don't laugh, this is very serious! ...
After coming out of the Calais tunnel, I found the aerocab of our London correspondent, Mr. Percival Douglas, as planned, and this gentleman looked after me himself. Just as we were leaving for the bank, I noticed a crowd on the docks in front of two enormous transatlantic dirigibles swarming with people. People were running, jostling to get close to these.

---

[40] Robida described an American continent that included three nation states controlled by China, Germany, and the Mormons. For a more recent fantasy map, which included "Utah Theocracy" as a nation-state in 2092, see "Canada and the United States in the year 2092," *The New York Times* (21 October 1992).

"So what is that?" I asked Percival Douglas.

"It is an arrival of wives," he replied coolly.

I began to laugh, naturally, and asked to see the arrival a little more closely. Our aerocab parked ten meters above the docks. On the decks of the dirigibles I saw hundreds of young ladies and women of all colors and conditions, some well dressed and covered with jewels, draped in superb clothing—others poorly clothed.

"What is this?" I said: "yellow women, white or swarthy, even Negresses. . . ."

"It is the overflow of the Indies, of America, and Australia," replied Percival; "there, they only marry one wife. Many young women therefore remain unprovided for; the agencies which we have in the five parts of the world enroll them for the promised land of the New-England. . . ."

"Then all the ladies of this arrival will find spouses?"

"They will be conducted to the *Marriage Docks*, where they will remain until they receive a proposal."

I broke into laughter. Since the institutions of the New-England are not widely known, I was ignorant of such useful docks! . . . they look like a massive Eastern inn. Four groups of buildings, eight stories of rooms, kitchens, and work rooms where the young women demonstrate their abilities to visitors, drawing rooms, a garden where all are admitted. Superb! The structure is surmounted by a lighthouse . . . the *Marriage Beacon*. Its emblematic fires shine over the entire city of London, reminding those who are interested that they can come to the docks to light other flames. A civil officer of the state, established in the lighthouse itself, keeps his registers open all hours of the day and night. . . .

The first person I saw the next day was a preacher who came to talk to me about the beauties of Mormonism. As he left, he gave me an assortment of Bibles and pamphlets: *Mormon Virtue*, by Rev. J. F. Hobson; *Shame on the Bachelor, Pity the Monogamous*, sermon preached at the great temple by Mr. Clakwell, vendor of imitation Champagne wines, and archbishop; *The Art of Managing Women*, treatise by Mr. Fred. Twic, Mormon archbishop, etc., etc. . . .

This strange country! The men drink, smoke, or sing hymns in the taverns while the women stay at home and work. Only the poor devils who have but one or two wives need labor. For the others—the lucky gallants fortunate enough to bring seven or eight "misses" before the civil officer—life is tranquil and happy. I made it into several patriarchs' homes and saw that the motto was *order and discipline!* The husband is head; he is venerated and pampered. Besides, in each district and ward there is a sort of guardroom or house of correction for wives who might be contrary or rebellious. One word from a husband to the superintendent of police and the policewomen come to find the guilty wife and take her to the Correctional House, where solitude and the sermons of preachers assigned to the institution induce salutary reflection. . . .

Last Sunday morning, as I was descending from the aerocab to the pavement of Regent Street (with the idea of taking a walk before lunch), I noticed that passers-by looked at me strangely. Fathers threw me irritated looks, and when ladies saw me, their gestures showed I was an object of horror to them. I racked my brains in vain to figure out the reason for these repulsive manifestations when suddenly, two policewomen, sent by an old woman, came and seized me by the arms.

"*Are you married?*" they asked me.

"*No!*" I replied, surprised.

"*No spouse?*"

"None at all!"

"Oh!!!"

And they grabbed me resolutely by the collar. I offered no resistance. We thus arrived at the coroner's. This magistrate began by putting the same question to me: "Are you married?—No, Sir, not yet!—Then, you are a bachelor?—Apparently!—This is serious! very serious!"

The coroner murmured, regarding me with a disapproving air. "I shall be obliged to send you to bachelors' prison."

— "But I am a foreigner!"

— "Everyone we arrest says that!"

— "But listen to me, you can tell very well from my accent that I am French!"

— "Everyone speaks French, more or less—that doesn't prove anything. Do you have papers?"

— "You know very well there haven't been passports since the Middle Ages."

— "Then too bad for you, I'm sending you to Bachelor's Prison. Enter your protests as you are able."

The episode seemed so funny that I let them take me to Bachelor's Prison, curious to experience this Bastille of unfortunate celibates.

But, oh! the walls, ten meters high, the barred windows, the massive doors: this is a serious prison. The turnkey-esse (for at Bachelor's Prison the turnkeys are turnkey-esses) listed me coldly on the register and had me taken to a cell furnished with a bed, a table, and a chair. Another jailor-esse brought me a bundle of old ropes and uttered a single word: "Work!" I asked for an explanation. I am condemned to eight days of forced labor: if I want to eat lunch and dinner, I must unwind the hemp of these old ropes, without cease, from six o'clock in the morning until six o'clock in the evening. At six o'clock I eat, and at seven o'clock I go to chapel where I hear Mormon sermons until midnight.

This sort of existence hardly seems entertaining, and I dream of getting out.

In the end, it turns out that Percival Douglas is letting poor Philippe rot in Bachelor's Prison until he might agree to marry the Douglas daughters. Philippe is saved in the nick of time by his father's secretary, sent to London and appearing at the prison, pretending to be Philippe's wife.

Karl Friedrich May: We Will Not Give Up

Karl May (1842–1912) was born in Ernstthal, Saxony, on 25 February 1842.[41] May's father encouraged him to read at an early age, and he became especially fond of adventure stories. He completed his studies to become a teacher in 1861, but was sacked a year later when he was accused of stealing a watch from a colleague. Subsequently May had repeated problems with the law, including impersonating a medical doctor, a policeman, and a notary's assistant, and he was incarcerated for eight of the next twelve years. His prison reading reawakened his interest in adventure writing, and following his release in 1874, he began writing stories that eventually made him one of Germany's most popular writers.

May wrote and published more than one hundred novels. At least twenty of these volumes, written between 1886 and 1909, were centered in the American West. After the publication of his initial adventures in *Collected Travel Novels* in 1892, May amassed a substantial personal fortune. His most popular stories, however, were *Treasure of Silver Lake* (1890), *Winnetou I, II, III* (1893), and *Old Shatterhand* (1894). Old Shatterhand and Winnetou were the heroes in at least twelve of May's western epics whose foils were Yankees, mixed bloods, Chinese, malevolent Indians, and Mormons. Richard Cracroft has noted that Old Shatterhand, when asked if he belonged to the Latter-day Saints replied, "I am not a Mormon by a long shot."[42]

May remains obscure in the U.S., but his stories have been translated into at least twenty-eight languages and sold over eighty million copies. Like Möllhausen, he has been called "Germany's James Fenimore Cooper."[43] Scholars recognize that his stories "had a remarkable impact on generations of Young Germans," and that he was "a major influence in shaping Ger-

---

[41] For May's biography, see Cracroft, "The American West of Karl May"; Phillips and Axelrod, eds., *Encyclopedia of the American West*, 3:947–48; and Lamar, ed., *The New Encyclopedia of the American West*, 686–87. See also Garland, eds., *The Oxford Companion to German Literature*, 590–91.

[42] Cracroft, "The American West of Karl May," 116.

[43] Read, "Karl May, Germany's James Fenimore Cooper," 4; and Barba, *Balduin Möllhausen, the German Cooper*.

many's idealized image of a mythic American West."[44] Readers in Germany, Austria, and Switzerland as diverse as Berta von Suttner, Heinrich Mann, Thomas Mann, Karl Liebknecht, Hermann Hesse, Albert Einstein, Albert Schweitzer, Karl Zuckmayer, and Adolph Hitler admired May's work.[45] Unlike Möllhausen, most of May's books are still in print and Karl May festivals continue to be held in Germany.

Most of May's adventures were written as first-person narratives, and he claimed his American stories were based on personal experiences in the West, but he did not visit the U.S. until after he had written most of his tales. His visit to North America in 1908 was limited to New York City, Buffalo, and Toronto, Canada. Cracroft has noted that May's books were "grounded in 'authentic' detail gleaned from reference books," which undoubtedly included "atlases, encyclopedias, dictionaries, geographical and ethnological studies, and an inexhaustible imagination."

The myth of the American West fascinated the Germans—and still does—and May could rely on a wealth of German material about the Mormon West.[46] Like many Europeans, May's most personal encounter with the West might well have been viewing Buffalo Bill's immensely popular Wild West Show, which visited Munich in 1898 and 1913. May was also familiar with Möllhausen's novels. His books with the greatest Mormon content are *Unter Geiern* [Amongst Vultures] (1888) and *Die Felsenburg* [The Cliff Stronghold] (1893). In the *Unter Geiern* a Mormon missionary named Tobias Preisegott (Praise God) Burton persuades John Helmers, an inn keeper who is a hospitable German immigrant, to let him stay at his inn. Old Shatterhand is also lodging there, and he suspects that the Mormon missionary is guilty of murder and robbery.

KARL MAY, *UNTER GEIERN* [AMONGST VULTURES], 319–23, 339–41.
TRANSLATED BY ROSE EDWARDS.

Just as Helmers was about to answer, his attention was diverted toward a man who ever so slowly slid around the corner of his house. He was completely covered in a black cloth and carried a small bundle in his hand. His figure was tall, slim, his chest narrow, and his face haggard and sharp. The

---

[44] Lamar, ed., *The New Encyclopedia of the American West*, 686; and Phillips and Axelrod, eds., *Encyclopedia of the American West*, 948.

[45] Ashliman, "The Image of Utah and the Mormons," 221. For Einstein's fondness for May, see Cracroft, "The American West of Karl May," 4–6.

[46] See Ashliman, "Mormonism and the Germans: An Annotated Bibliography, 1848–1966," 73–94.

high hat, sitting deep in his neck, and his bespectacled face gave him the look of a clergyman.

He approached with strangely slinking footsteps, and touching slightly the edge of his hat, greeted: "Good day, mesch'schurs. Is this correct—am I arriving at John Helmers, Esquire?"

Helmers checked out the man with a look on his face that made you realize that he was not pleased with what he saw, and answered him. "Yes, my name is Helmers, but you may just as well leave out esquire. I am not a judge, and I don't like any such remarks. They are only rotten apples and a gentleman doesn't like to have those thrown at him. As you know my name, may I ask for yours?"

"Why not, sir. My name is Tobias Preisegott Burton and I am a missionary for the Latter-day Saints."

The stranger said this in a self-confident and unctuous tone. However, this failed to make the impression he had hoped for with the farmer, because Helmers answered, shrugging his shoulders: "Ah, so you are a Mormon? This is by no means a recommendation for you. You call yourselves the Saints of the Latter Days. This is pretentious and presumptuous. As I am a humble man I have no use for your self-righteousness. I'd suggest you might as well be on your way in your pious missionary boots. I don't tolerate any purchasing of souls here in this settlement."

This was said very bluntly, even offensively, but Burton kept his obligatory air about him, touched his hat again very politely and responded: "You are mistaken, sir, if you think I would want to convert the people of this blessed farm. I only ask to rest for a while and to quench my hunger and thirst."

"I see. Well, if that's all you want you should have it, provided you can pay for it. I hope you have got some money on you."

Helmers again looked over the stature of the stranger with a sharp and discerning look and twisted his face as if he had seen something not very pleasing. The Mormon lifted his face toward the sky, cleared his throat and declared: "Though I am by no means blessed with the treasures of this sinful world, but for food, drink and a place for the night, I am prepared to pay. Although certainly I had not counted on this expense, as I had heard this household is most hospitable."

"Ah, and who told you that?"

"I heard it in Taylorsville, where I just came from."

"You were told the truth. But they seem to have forgotten there to add that I only show my hospitality to people I welcome."

"And that's not the case with me?"

"No, absolutely not."

"But I didn't do anything."

"Maybe that is so. But when I look at you, it seems to me that only unpleasant things could come from you. Don't take this amiss, sir. I am an honest fellow, and am used to tell everybody openly what I think about him or her. I don't like your face."

Even now, the Mormon pretended not to be offended. He touched his hat for the third time and said in a mild voice: "In this life it is the fate of the just to be misjudged. I can't help my face. If you don't like it, it's not my fault."

"But you don't have to let anybody tell you this. It takes a great lack of self respect to take something like that calmly. By the way, I confess that I don't have anything against your face. I just don't feel good about the way you carry it. On top of it, it seems to me, this is not your true face. I suppose you make a totally different face when you are by yourself. And then there are other things I don't particularly like about you."

"May I ask you to tell me what you mean?"

"I'll tell you even without you asking me. I have a lot against you saying you came from Taylorsville."

"Why? Do you have any enemies there?"

"Not a single one. But tell me, where are you heading to?"

"Up to Fort Elliott."

"Hum. And the closest way passes by here?"

"No, but I heard so many lovely and good things about you that I had a longing in my heart to get to know you."

"Don't wish for that, Mr. Burton, that might not be the best for you.— But go on! Where is your horse?"

"My horse? I don't have one. I came on foot."

"Oh! Don't try to pull the wool over my eyes. You hid the animal some place and I suppose very strongly that it's not an honorable reason that prompted you to do so. Here, every man, every woman, every child rides a horse. Without a horse you can't get around in this area. A stranger who hides his horse and then denies he owns one certainly doesn't seem to have any good intentions."

The Mormon wrung his hands and pleaded: "But, Mr. Helmers, I swear, I truly don't own a horse. I walk humbly on foot throughout the land and I have never even sat in a saddle."

Hearing that, Helmers got up from the bench, stepped toward the stranger, put his hand heavily onto his shoulder and rebuked him: "Man, you are telling this to me who has lived so long at the frontier? Do you think I am blind? I certainly see the wool on the inner side of your pants threadbare from riding. I see holes for spurs on the side of your boots, and . . ."

"That's no proof, sir," the Mormon cut in. "I bought those boots second hand. The holes were already in the boots."

"I see. Since when are you wearing them?"

"Since two months."

"In that case, the holes would be filled with dust or dirt. Or are you by any chance taking the pleasure to bore new holes into them daily? It rained last night. Your boots would be completely dirty from such a long hike. Seeing them that clean is sure proof that you rode. On top of it you smell like a horse, and look, look at that! If again you'll put spurs into your coat pocket, make sure they don't hang out. He pointed to the brass spurs, which hung out from his pocket.

"I just found them yesterday.". . .

The setting is still on Helmer's ranch, where several of his friends are talking about people who ride through the wilderness carrying valuables. In the meantime, they have been keeping an eye on the Mormon, who has been accused of stealing from a gentleman by his former black servant, Bob. The black man, accompanied by his Indian friend Bloody-Fox, has vowed to avenge his former master and to kill the Mormon as soon as he leaves the farm.

The day was coming to an end, and dusk, which is extraordinarily short in these regions, set in. It was already so dark that you couldn't see very far any more. In spite of their lively conversation, Bob and Bloody-Fox kept an eye on the Mormon at all times. Burton tried hard to pretend he wasn't paying any attention to their conversation. Most likely the others thought that a Mormon, who had the complete appearance of a Yankee, would not understand any German. Therefore, they spoke so loudly that he could hear every word.

When Jungle-Fred talked about the six men he was supposed to lead through the Llano Estacado, Burton's features tensed up. When he heard that the six seemed to have a lot of money on them, a contented smile played around his thin lips, though it wasn't noticed because of the fading light.

At times he lifted his head impatiently toward the direction he had come from. He knew he had to consider himself nearly a prisoner, because the eyes of the black man focused on him incessantly. From minute to minute he felt more alarmed. He had to think about the threats of the Negro, and he didn't trust the black man.

Now that it was nearly totally dark, it seemed possible for Burton to get up and leave, something that might be more difficult later on. He reached for the bundle he had brought and pulled it slowly toward him. He intended to suddenly jump up and quickly run around the corner of the house. Once behind some bushes, he would hardly have to fear any pursuers anymore.

But he didn't count on Bob. Like most Negroes, once he decided something, he pursued it with great persistence. The black man had observed the Mormon closely, endeavoring to secure his bundle, and he got up so fast from his seat, at the very moment the other one wanted to jump up, that he nearly pushed down Helmers. Therefore Jungle-Fred's question, what could be the matter. Bob replied: "Masser Bob has seen that thief want away. Already pull bundle. Want fast escape. Masser Bob want to beat him up away from here, therefore go with him and watch him always." He moved to the farthest part of the bench, so that he was very close to the Mormon, who sat at the other table.

"Let the fellow go," remarked the host. "He's probably not worth watching so closely."

"Massa Helmers is right. He not worth it, but money worth it that he stole. He not get away without Bob accompany him."

"Who is this man anyway?" asked Jungle-Fred in a low voice. "I didn't like him from the moment I set eyes on him. He looks like a wolf that runs around in sheep's clothing. When I caught sight of him, it seemed as if I had already seen this sharp, haggard grimace once before, and under circumstances that don't speak well for him."

In *Die Felsenburg* a villainous group, consisting mostly of Mormons, is attempting to transport a number of European immigrants to a mercury mine in the Sierra Madre in northwestern Mexico, where they will be forced into slave labor. Old Shatterhand and his friend Winnetou foil the scheme. The passage begins in the city of Guaymas, Sonora, Mexico, where Old Shatterhand encounters another Mormon missionary named Harry Melton. Shatterhand is suspicious of Melton especially when he discovers that Melton is pretending to be a Roman Catholic, and that he drinks, smokes, and swears. Eventually Melton confesses that he is working undercover for his church and that he is investigating the possibility of moving the main Mormon settlement from Utah to Mexico where he claims polygamy is not forbidden.[47]

> KARL MAY, *DIE FELSENBURG* [THE CLIFF STRONGHOLD], 18–27.
> TRANSLATED BY ROSE EDWARDS.

All of a sudden, in the middle [of the domino game], the innkeeper stopped and hit his forehead with his hand.

"How could I have forgotten? You [Shatterhand] wanted to travel by way of Hermosillo, Señor, and I totally forgot that you have a splendid opportunity. Señor Enrique is expecting a ship, that will put down anchor here, and then keep on going toward Lobos."

---

[47] I have relied on Richard Cracroft's excellent summary. Cracroft, "The American West of Karl May," 116–18. The earliest federal judges sent to Utah attempted to prosecute polygamists under the Mexican common law. See Homer, *The Judiciary and the Common Law in Utah Territory*, 105.

"This place would indeed be very convenient. But who is the man you call Señor Enrique?"

"He is a guest of mine, whose name is written in the register right before yours. You didn't read his name yet?"

I hadn't done that. So I reached for the book [*Book of Mormon*] and read: "Harry Melton, Latter Day Saint."

These words were written in English. So, a Mormon! How did he get here? What affair could have brought him so far south to Guaymas from Great Salt Lake City?

"Why do you look so pensively at the book?" asked the innkeeper. "Does anything strike you about the entry of this guest?"

"Actually, no. Did you read the words?"

"Yes, but I didn't understand them. The señor is so serious, so proud and so pious, that I didn't want to bother him with questions. I probably mispronounced his name, and so he explained to me, that Harry is the equivalent of the Spanish Enrique. That's why I call him that."

"So, he lives with you?"

"He sleeps here, leaves in the morning and returns at night."

"What's he up to during the day?"

"I don't know. I don't have time to worry about each of my guests."

Yes, the little man played and slept and slept and played and couldn't possibly have time to pay that much attention to each guest.

"I only know his name and that he is waiting for a boat to Lobos," he continued. "The señor talks very little. His piety is worthy to be praised. Just a pity, that he can't play dominoes."

"How do you know, that he is so pious?"

"Because he continually lets the rosary glide through his fingers, and he never comes or goes without bowing in front of the picture of the saint in the corner and taking some holy water from the vessel at the door."

I wanted to reply but decided it would be wiser to say nothing. A Mormon with a rosary! Polygamy and holy water! The Book of Mormon and bowing before a Saint. This man was definitely a hypocrite, and his hypocrisy had to have a reason.

I wasn't able to continue this train of thought, because Señorita Felisa now brought me a cup, which contained some brown thick stuff, and wanted me to eat. . . .

Just as I finished my last bite, wiped my knife on my sleeve, and stuck it back into my belt, in came the man whose appearance I had looked forward to with great curiosity: The Mormon.

The light of the lamp reached the door, and as I sat across from the lamp, I saw him enter. He bowed toward the corner, where the picture hung, dabbed the top of his fingers into the small vessel of holy water, and only after that he turned to greet us briefly. When he saw me, a stranger, he stopped for a few moments to look me over. Then he came over quickly, opened the guest registry that still laid on the table, and quickly read my notice. Then wishing us a good night, he retired into the semidarkness where the hammocks for the guests were fastened.

All that happened so fast, that I could not check out his face. But now I noticed what respect he had instilled in the innkeeper, because he said in a hushed tone to his family:

"Senor Enrique wants to sleep. Lay down and don't make any noise...."

[*Our traveler wakes up after a night in the yard, and enters the inn. Old Shatterhand describes Harry Melton, the Mormon gang leader.*]

The Mormon sat at a table, apparently having waited for my arrival, for I saw that he was observing me sharply. I didn't let him notice that I did the same with him, but it became difficult to turn my eyes from him. He had a peculiar personality.

His muscular body was well and carefully dressed, and his face was smoothly shaven. But what a face he had! Seeing his face reminded me immediately of the strange expressions that the master pen of Gustave Dore had lent the devil. The similarity was so great that you could have thought the Mormon had modeled for Dore's painting. He couldn't have been much older than forty. Around his high, broad forehead rolled deep dark curls, cascading down his neck to nearly his shoulders; it was truly gorgeous hair. His large, night-dark eyes had the almond-shaped cut that nature seems to have reserved exclusively for oriental beauties. His nose was slightly bent and not too sharp, the trembling movement of the lightly pink nostrils let you conclude that he was very present minded. The mouth nearly resembled that of a woman, but yet was not effeminate or weakly formed. Its corners were slightly bent downwards, revealing a rather strong will. His chin was delicate and yet at the same time strongly built, the type that is found on people whose spirit is superior to their animalistic instincts. Every single part of his head and his face was beautiful in itself, but only if you looked at that part alone, because in their totality there was a lack of harmony. But where there is a lack of harmony, there is absolutely no beauty. I can't say if others felt the same, but I felt repulsed. The putting together of singular beautiful forms to a whole that lacks harmony, gave me the impression of something disagreeable, something ugly. There was one other thing on top of that. I immediately was struck with the similarity to the picture of Dore. But the more often I looked at the man, the clearer I felt that his face resembled another one I had seen someplace and at some other time, and that in circumstances that couldn't possibly serve to recommend him. I thought and thought, but could remember neither place nor time, nor did it become clear to me who the person was that had this face. Even in the course of the next few days, during which I met the Mormon regularly in the morning and in the evening, I was not able to remember, though I became more and more convinced that I had met a very similar person, who had acted in animosity either against myself or against one of my friends.

As often as I saw Henry Melton, he measured me with sharp eyes. . . .

[*The Mormon offended the innkeeper, and so the innkeeper retired, which was apparently the intention of the Mormon, as he wanted to be alone with the traveler.*]

"You have been here for 15 days. Are you intending to stay here in Guaymas?"

He didn't speak in the tone of polite inquiry. I sensed that he tried to be friendly, but he couldn't manage it. And so his question sounded like an overseer speaking to a person very below his rank.

"No," I replied. "I don't have any business here."

"Where are you heading to?"

"Maybe to La Libertad."

I named this town, because it was near Lobos, and, as I had heard, the boat, for which he was waiting.

"Where do you come from?"

"I came down from the Sierra Madre."

"What were you doing there? Looking for Gold? Did you find any?"

"No," I answered truthfully, without giving any further replies to his inquiries.

"I thought so. I can see that you are a poor devil. At any rate you chose a very unhappy trade."

"Why?"

"Well, I found in the guest registry, that you are a writer, and know that in this trade most of the people go hungry. How could you dare to venture into this region? You are a German. If you had stayed in your fatherland, you could write letters or keep accounts for people there who don't know how to write. Through such work, you could earn at least enough money to not suffer hunger."

"Hmm!" I muttered, as I didn't want him to notice that I felt amused. . . .

Emilio Salgari: Strange Rituals and Polygamy

Emilio Salgari (1862–1911) was one of the most prolific and widely read Italian adventure writers during the late nineteenth and early twentieth centuries, even though he did not travel to the many exotic settings of his books. Salgari was born in Verona in 1862. As a youth he briefly visited Venice, which spawned a lifelong interest in the sea, and in 1880 he was a passenger on a mercantile ship that traveled from Venice to Brindisi along the Dalmatian coast. Despite his limited travel experience, Salgari was a voracious reader. During the 1880s he began writing stories for newspapers in Verona (*Nuova Arena*), Livorno (*Telefono*), and Milan (*La Vaglia*).

The Milanese publisher Guigoni accepted Salgari's first book, *La Favorita del Madhi*, in 1887.[48] He transferred his family to Torino, where he contracted with the publisher Fratelli Speirani to write adventure novels. For the next eighteen years he wrote books that were published in Genoa, Florence, Milan, Livorno, Rome, Palermo, and Turin. He also wrote about the future in *Le Meraviglie del Duemila* (1907) [The Marvels of 2000]. Despite this impressive output, Salgari was never financially secure. He attempted suicide for the first time in 1909, and after his financial and personal condition deteriorated over the next two years, he finally succeeded.

Although Salgari never traveled to the U.S., he was extremely interested in the American West. The Buffalo Bill Wild West Show performed to sold-out audiences throughout Europe in 1898, and Salgari and his family attended a performance in Verona. Prominent Italian publishers had distributed books about Utah and the Mormons for at least four decades before Salgari's death. One of Salgari's publishers, Fratelli Treves, published the travel accounts of Richard Burton, Louis Simonin, Alexander von Hübner, and Francesco Varvaro Pojero. Each author included rich descriptions of Utah and the Mormons. In addition, popular Italian travel periodicals and newspapers, including *Il Giro del Mondo*, *Giornale popolare di viaggi*, *L'Esploratore*, and *L'Universo Illustrato*, published travel accounts and general histories about the Mormons. Finally, Arthur Conan Doyle's *A Study in Scarlet*, perhaps the most famous Mormon melodrama of all time, was published in Italian in 1901 and republished in 1907, 1908, and 1911.[49]

Salgari began to take an interest in Mormonism during the last decade of his life. His Western adventures—*Avventure tra i Pellerossa* (1900); *La Sovrana del Campo d'Oro* (1905); and *Sulle Frontiere del Far-West* (1908)—included conflict with "Red Skins" as well as Mormons.[50] In *Sulle Frontiere del Far-West* the author assured his readers that the events described take place before the Mormon emigration and before the territory had "been invaded by the Mormons, and there were no cities, no villages, no railroads, and no

---

[48] One Italian observer noted that "there is not a corner of the planet that has not be Saglarized by his pen." See Leonardi, "Introduzione," *Jolanda la figlia del Corsaro Nero*, xii.

[49] See *Un dramma misterioso* (1901); *Uno strano delitto* (1907); *Sherlock Holmes il poliziotto dilettante: lo scritto rosso* (1908); and *Il segreto di Hope* (1911).

[50] Stories attributed to Salgari continued to be published under his name (and a coauthor named Luigi Motta) after his death. These included books about the Far West, such as *I cacciatori del Far West* (1925).

steamships." He also described the Great Salt Lake country and the Mormons in *Avventure tra i Pellerossa* and in an unpublished manuscript, apparently written in 1911 that was tentatively entitled *Un massacro di Mormoni nell'Utah*. Interestingly, both stories describe mythical Indian battles with at least passing similarities to the Mountain Meadows massacre. The first involves the slaughter on the Rio Pecos of a Salt Lake–bound Mormon wagon train from Texas. While there was a substantial overland emigration between Texas and Utah, any Mormon train that wound up on the Pecos would have been hopelessly lost—and Salgari's ruthless Indian attack resembles nothing that ever happened on Western wagon trails.

To set the scene, a "poor Mormon emigrant" has helped Ralph, Randolfo, Mary, and the Alligator of the Salt Lake fend off a night Indian attack in the middle of a forest. As they await their fate, the Mormon tells his story.

> EMILIO SALGARI, *AVVENTURE TRA I PELLEROSSA*
> [ADVENTURES AMONG THE RED SKINS], 82, 85–91.
>
> That poor man had received a blow from an ax on his left thigh. The wound was so bad that it continued to bleed.
>
> Randolfo tore off a bandage and placed it tightly around the wound he had cleaned with brandy for quick healing.
>
> We have been around. It will take you a couple of weeks to recover from your wounds, he said. Rest assured that we will not abandon you.
>
> You are too kind, Sir, the emigrant said.
>
> Are all of your companions dead?
>
> All of them, Sir, he responded with emotion.
>
> What a massacre! What a horrible disaster!
>
> Were there a lot of you?
>
> There were 150 men, women and children.
>
> And where were you going?
>
> To Salt Lake City, responded the emigrant. We were all Mormons and as you know that city is the settlement of all of our brothers.
>
> While the Indians leave us in peace tell me your sad story. We can forget our sad state.
>
> Listen to me, the Mormon said. You will see how cruel the Indians are.
>
> Oh! We know them, said Randolfo. Tell us your story friend....
>
> Harry Burklay—that is what the wounded man called himself—had left the Mexican frontier twenty days earlier. He led a caravan that consisted of 150 men, women and children, with a great procession of wagons driven for the most part by horses.

His intention was to cross Texas and arrive in Utah, where the Great Salt Lake is located, which is the place where the Mormon sect has found refuge.

They crossed the Rio del Norte so as not to arouse suspicion among that part of the population that did not have a high regard for this emigration that depopulated a good part of the district which was previously thriving. Throughout the day the caravan traveled through the prairie by following the banks of the Rio Pecos.

The journey across the rich plains, which were overflowing with deer, bucks, antelope, bison and wild turkeys, provided the emigrants with an abundant fresh supply of meat, could not have been more tranquil.

Until one evening, the emigrants got scared when they saw several riders near the Rio Pecos. The sight of waving hair, war bonnets and long spears was enough to convince them they had seen Indians.

Burklay was aware that tribes of Comanche warriors were in the vicinity and became concerned about his own hair and the safety of the caravan too. So he gathered the most seasoned explorers together to consult and decided to immediately travel toward the edge of the Rio Pecos.

They reached the river in a short time, crossed it at a ford, and then set up their outlying camp on the other shore.

The wagons were drawn up in a Saint Andrew cross shape to insure their safety. Afterwards as they were short on food several hunters were sent out for new game.

For three days they had been busy hunting and tying ropes to stakes driven into the ground to dry meat when in the evening of the fourth day one of the hunters came back with a wounded arm caused by an Indian hatchet. The Mormon leader asked him what happened and he began to tell how he had been followed and wounded by the numerous Comanches. Soon there was great fear of an attack. It was about midnight when one of the men standing guard on the Rio bank saw something moving.

He was about to ask another guard 100 feet away if he could distinguish anything when an Indian hatchet hit him hard and crashed his head. He was able to give the alarm when an Indian jumped and scalped him. As soon as the men heard the signal they grabbed their guns and used the wagons as a barricade. . . .

The Indians had crossed the river in the cover of darkness and now little by little the emigrants could see them riding two by two and coming toward the camp brandishing their long spears.

They were outnumbered by 200 warriors whose proud and war-like attitude showed their thirst for scalps. They knew they would receive no pity from their long-enduring mortal enemies and they did not hesitate to open fire when the first ones came near.

The Indians responded with war-cries furiously urging their horses toward the wagons, attacking them with spears and throwing clouds of arrows. Scared by the gunfire they retreated leaving 6 or 7 dead behind.

But this was just a false maneuver. Burklay who knew better ordered his men to remain in their positions and get ready for a second attack soon to come. . . .

When Burklay saw his men were giving up he gathered all those remaining and rushed the enemy. Instead of being successful this move proved to be fatal for the Mormons.

They had just started the fight when the rest of the Indians came running out from the woods behind them. . . . Then a terrible massacre began between the Red-skins and the Pale-faces. Spears and guns became useless. They were now fighting with hatchets, knives, crushing their heads, tearing open, fighting, biting, strangling, trampling on, escaping and pursuing each other. In every corner one could hear swearing, curses, the cries of the wounded, the moans of the dying echoed by women's screams and children's cries and the blood-thirsty Indians' yells and shouts.

The outnumbered Whites gathered around their women who were demonstrating great courage with hatchets and hot brands, but they could not overcome the powerful Comanche assault. The men were scattered or killed in the wagons and the women and children were carried away by the Indians.

In that terrible situation, Burklay did not lose self control. He gathered the last survivors and tried to save about 20 women from the victorious enemy but failed. His companions fell dead one by one by the hatchet and he, too, was wounded in his thigh and rolled under a wagon and played dead.

The poor one spent the night in tremendous suffering and anxiety as he had to watch the savages' uncontrolled violence.

In the morning when the Indians had gone, he cleaned his wound and left that place to fall again into the hands of these ruthless enemies.

Unfortunately he could not go far because of his serious wound. He lost his senses, fell and his horse ran away.

He certainly would have lost all his blood if he had not met the God-sent Ralph, the Salt Lake Alligator, and Randolph.

This was the dramatic story of the poor emigrant we found in the woods in such a bad state.

When Salgari died, he left an unfinished manuscript entitled "A Massacre of Mormons in Utah." The only surviving portion of the manuscript suggests that Salgari was expanding the story of the Mormon massacre previously told in *Avventura tra i Pellerossa*.[51]

---

[51] The missing manuscript was not reported until 1980. See *E Salgari spezzò la penna*, Gazzetta del Popolo, 16 March 1980, 5.

Emilio Salgari, *Un massacro di Mormoni nell'Utah*
[A Massacre of Mormons in Utah], from an unpublished manuscript.

Since the Mormons are frequently mentioned, especially during the last few years, everyone knows that they have been gathered for a long time on the shores of the Great Salt Lake where they established [Salt] Lake City, better known as the Holy City. They have gone there to escape the attention of the great American republic, to avoid further interference with their strange rituals and to maintain polygamy, which is a prescribed dogma of their religion. They are separated by thousands of miles from the President of the Republic, in a territory that was almost forgotten and was inhabited only by those horrible red skins that ran around the desert. The Mormons, one could say, have established an independent kingdom which rules, much more so than the legislative assembly of Utah, and which is made up exclusively of men who are members of the faith.

Since it was the aim of the church to become strong and numerous, with the hope that they might establish a separate republic almost in the middle of the United States, they have searched for all possible means—persuasion, illusions, cunning, gold, and also force—to find proselytes.[52] Many Mormons are located throughout the various cities of North America who actively spread propaganda and scrape together a certain number of persons. One fine day, they deceived the local authorities and took these converts to the Great Salt Lake. They often traveled great distances over the prairies and the Rocky Mountains. It is not uncommon for them to be massacred by the Indians, who are the sworn enemies of any white men.

But note that one of these caravans of converts, just ten years ago, which left San Giovanni on the North River, was headed toward the Holy City of the Lake. The caravan had over one hundred fifty persons, gathered from ten different countries, the major part "squatter" and "peons" with their wives and children and heavy wagons pulled by prairie mustangs which are used to store food.

Guillaume Apollinaire: So Much Fertility after the Sterility of the Salt Desert

Guillaume Apollinaire (1880–1918) was a successful French poet and novelist who was known for his exoticism, irony, and buffoonery. *La femme assise* (which was published two years after the author's death) is a meandering,

---

[52] This is an obvious reference to Albert Robida's *Le vingtième siècle* and its portrait of Mormonism as a successful world theocracy that enforced the practice of polygamy.

mediocre novel set in early twentieth-century Paris, but the central portion of the novel is a reminiscence of Mormonism in the mid-nineteenth century. The author is fascinated by polygamy, polygyny, populating, and promiscuity. Philosophy is kept simple here, piqued by occasional gratuitous sexual allusions. Although unabashed, Apollinaire was never explicit. Elvire Goulot, the protagonist, flits through a half-dozen lovers, but the liaisons are scarcely interesting. The bulk of the novel—the Mormon portion—seems to be inserted into the middle of an otherwise short and rambling book. The excuse to inject Mormon content is Elvire's visit to an old acquaintance of her grandmother, who converted to Mormonism in the 1850s and lived for a time in Salt Lake City, before she disappeared in Europe. The novel is neither artfully constructed nor homogenous. There are few if any passages of arresting literary interest. The Mormon portion, which covers 115 out of the book's 268 pages, reveals occasional examples of specific knowledge of Mormon characters and doctrine, but the book is as bad as similar works because of its careless and gratuitous errors.

The book's title, *The Seated Woman*, is taken from a brief episode in which Mormons in a parade in Salt Lake City carry a large seated female mannequin, representing democracy in America, a land where great (or substantial) women give birth to giants. In a last-moment attempt to tie the final unrelated chapters of the book to this theme, Apollinaire (or his posthumous editors) reflects in the final two paragraphs of the book how the sight of Elvire, seated at an easel in her studio, reminded the novel's narrator of a worthless Swiss coin, "which, in my youth, one had to be careful not to accept." Elvire becomes, in large part, "what all women are: like the Swiss ecu, false and unacceptable."[53]

For all its drawing-room shallowness, *La femme assise* paints a colorful and amusing portrait of theocratic Utah. The first excerpt is part of an extremely long, spurious letter (apparently based on a close reading of Louis Bertrand's *Mémoires d'un Mormon*), written by John Taylor in Paris in December 1851 to Brigham Young. Taylor relates his personal adventures on the streets of Paris when he tried to negotiate his way to his lodgings during the *coup d'état* that left Paris occupied by government troops who won a sanguinary victory over dissidents on 3 and 4 December 1851. As government soldiers approach, John Taylor saves himself by crying, "Vive la

---

[53] Apollinaire, *La femme assise*, 268. For a discussion of Appollinaire, see Decoo, 2: 266–70.

République!" and lives to convert Pamela—the future grandmother of the central protagonist in the novel—and send her to Utah. Many years later, in 1916, an aged former acquaintance of Pamela (Otto Mahner) tells Elvire about her grandmother's adventures in Salt Lake City. It is a long story, and Pamela's experiences are narrated by the old man she once knew, as Elvire listens to a description of the arrival of exhausted new converts (mostly women, including Pamela, the only French one in the lot) in Salt Lake. They are met by rude, immodest children, shopkeepers, and hoards of women in a state of advanced pregnancy.

There follows the majestic arrival of the Council of the Twelve, including such luminaries as "Weber" C. Kimball, the Herald of Grace; "Perley" P. Pratt, the Archer of Paradise, and, incongruously, William Smith, "the Patriarchal Staff of Jacob."[54] Brigham Young, the Lion of the Lord, is introduced to the new converts by Lorenzo Snow. Brigham picks out a Norwegian, an English woman, and a Hungarian who has not learned a word of English. Pamela refuses all offers, including Brigham's, and begins to miss the comforts left behind in France. Brigham then begins to preach until the people are on all fours, barking and howling like dogs, rolling on the ground, or hopping like toads and contorting themselves like "unknown reptiles." The pregnant women seem as if they will give birth, while other Mormons grovel in the dust until sunset as Brigham continues his preaching and begins to sing.

There is a description of a parade in Salt Lake City. The stores are closed. This is 19 September 1852, a day of great celebration "when Brigham the Prophet proclaimed the revelation on polygamy to the Mormon people." The ritual procession begins at the tabernacle. One sees various Mormon dignitaries, Indians, even a "Missouri Negro" who interrupts the procession briefly to proclaim: "I have seen Christ-Adam descend from a golden sky with his wives and countless gods, traversing space to announce the redemption of the Blacks." Heber C. Kimball laughs riotously at this, but Brigham is outraged. Four members of the Seventy leave their ranks in the parade to borrow Pamela's scarf with which they hang the black man. The Mormons watch, laughing and celebrating, until his agony ends, upon which the parade continues.

---

[54] Mormon journalist W. W. Phelps invented these enduring sobriquets in a toast of the Mormon apostles on New Year's Day 1845. See Van Wagoner and Walker, *A Book of Mormons*, 208.

GUILLAUME APOLLINAIRE, *LA FEMME ASSISE* [THE SEATED WOMAN], 68–70, 84–86, 113–15, 152–54. TRANSLATED BY RICK GRUNDER.

I [John Taylor] arrived at Paris in April from Copenhagen where I was fortunate to make a large number of Danish converts that you have probably had the joy of welcoming to our holy city.

Having visited Paris a number of times, I knew what a hard life brother Curtis Bolton was living, charged with the difficult undertaking of converting Parisians. Despite a thousand obstacles, he had made at least four hundred conversions, and I must say that he was hardly favored by his circumstances.

For seven years, he lived in a garret in the town of Tournon, and despite his efforts, he surely earned no more than six francs per month, which forced him to live on dry bread and plain water. I felt it was time he rested, and since my arrival I have undertaken—knowing enough French—to proof his translation of the Book of Mormon. This work will most likely appear during the course of next year.[55]

I sent brother Curtis Bolton to some of his relatives in England, who received him well, and the enthusiastic letters he sends me indicate that his ministry is feted with balls (you know how agreeable these are to the gods), concerts, excursions, garden parties, and the most pleasing games.

And wasn't he in Jersey with some of the Saints and a bunch of young ladies who are ready to become our sisters! Throughout this vacation, all was preaching, hymns and the fulfilling of the desires of the flesh according to laws human and divine which require polygyny according to the example of the patriarchs, and that of Christ who had three spouses, as one can see in the Gospels. . . .

[COUNTER-REVOLUTION IN PARIS]

Suddenly, it began to rain, and the rapidly forming mud was, in places, red with blood. Some passing rioters hurried to regain their barricade, at times ducking to avoid projectiles, or proudly defying the armed forces with insolent calls. They never stopped for a moment, however, hoping to avoid the soldiers who were coming from both directions. But I, certain that I could not escape them, prepared to die. At this moment, a band of stylishly dressed young men and women passed nearby, laughing. I decided to follow them, for they seemed little concerned by the disturbance, indeed immune to danger; but even while laughing and sporting, these debauchees—and there is no other word for them—turned around and knocked me aside with their canes, saying:

"Mind your own business, man, we're not on your side."

---

[55] When John Taylor left Paris in February 1852, the mission office was transferred from Rue du Paradis–Poissonnière, 37, to Rue de Tournon, 7.

And one of the young women who had also turned around, picked up an empty bottle that she found at her feet near a shako and dead soldier, and threw it at me violently, yelling:

"Hurry now, Pamela, and be careful of this socialist."

At the same moment, the bottle hit my forehead, stunning and wounding me above the right eyebrow. Forthwith, I heard a kind voice saying:

"Poor man, you're bleeding."

And then, a close rustling of silk as well as a delicate hand stopping the blood from my wound with a perfumed handkerchief.

At first, I thought it was the angel Moroni appearing on the field of battle, come to save one of Joseph's faithful. . . .

[WELCOME TO SALT LAKE]

Other troops of women pressed close behind. Like surging rivers, they flowed through all the streets until wherever the emigrant women turned, all they could see were women, and almost all were pregnant. There were so many of them that one could not see beyond them, nor could one see the assembly of Mormon men or the gentiles. And bit by bit, there were so many of these pregnant women that Union Square seemed to contain nothing but their enormous bellies, shuffling like ripples on a lake upon which they floated like corks, with little heads with faces disfigured by pregnancy.

And the emigrant women were surprised to see so much fertility after the sterility of the salt desert. The religion they had embraced in Europe a few months ago was that of fertility. Then, mingling among the group of foreign women, the fertile matrons boasted of their happiness, described their happy homes, praised the strength and intelligence of their spouses:

— Come with me, young woman, we are already four wives and we live together with our husband. Come share our communal tenderness. Our children are still young, they will never know who among us is their mother, and their filial piety will encompass all five of us.

— O come with me, young woman, five wives live at our house, and our husband has three more wives, two of whom have already lived and one who will be born three centuries from now.

— O come with me, young woman, you will be fertile in the nation of fertility. Our nation will cover the world, and then will come the time of bliss.

— O come with me, young woman, my husband has fifteen wives and you will be the most pampered, being the most beautiful.

— O come with me, young woman. There are twenty of us wives and each has her own home in an orchard full of fruit and our husband visits us each in turn.

— O come with me, young woman, I once also came from Europe. I had lost my only true love. Now here is the city without love. And what happiness compares to that of the flesh satisfied, once the mind can no longer know jealousy?

And these pregnant wives wanted to seduce the European women to lead new wives to their husbands. They talked with enthusiasm about their happiness without love, without jealousy. And all had forgotten old wishes for tenderness between two beings....

[AFTER THE LYNCHING]

Then, after the Missouri Negro's final spasm, the procession resumed its march before the fixed stare of the dead man, rigid as an opium eater.

In front of all passed a large mannequin representing a seated woman crowned with stars, the wheels invisibly hidden in the base, pushed by two men who could not be seen, while a third made the head turn as if on a living woman. And from time to time, the stupendous image spoke, and it was these men who shouted inside the machine:

"I am the Democracy of America, land of great women and turbulent men who will beget giants greater than the huge sequoias!"

Then there was the council of bishops and quorums of lesser priests, followed by shamans of the Ute race, in turn followed by the Documents of the Press wagon, where they had assembled the papyrus of Abraham, the manuscripts of Joseph Smith's Book of Mormon translation, the first books and journals printed by the Mormons, while, leading the oxen that pulled the wagon, and surrounding it, marched the remaining members of the family of Joseph Smith. On the wagon, the patriarch, a young man who kept his eyes closed, carried in a little silver chest the Urim and Thummim, divine instrument of clairvoyance

PIERRE BENOIT: LET ME REMIND YOU ... I AM INFALLIBLE

Pierre Benoit, a "manufacturer of adventure novels," was a prolific writer of fiction who, like many authors, chose topics that had popular appeal.[56] His choice of nineteenth-century Mormonism in *Le lac salé*, demonstrates that this was still a subject that could titillate the French imagination even during the early twentieth century. Some Mormon missionaries, who served in France during the second half of the twentieth century, were not surprised when people they contacted said they first became aware of Mormonism in *Le lac salé*.

Wilfried Decoo notes that Benoit learned much about Mormonism from Jules Rémy, and Benoit does quote Rémy on the title page: *"Les truites*

---

[56] Marcel Girard as quoted by Decoo, "The Image of Mormonism in French Literature," 2:271.

qui y descendent quelquefois par les ruisseaux meurent immédiatement" ("The trout that sometimes descend from the streams into [the Great Salt Lake] die immediately"). This quotation prepares readers for what is an evil-of-polygamy novel with better-than-typical character development for stories of this genre. It is set in 1858 during the presence of the United States Army in Utah. Annabel Lee, a young Catholic widow, lives in deserted Salt Lake City, in one of the city's finest homes along with her houseguest, friend, and protector, Father Philippe of Exiles, a Jesuit priest. The first half of the book plods along, with interminable conversations and occasional brief philosophical or literary asides. Rev. Jemini Gwinett, a Protestant chaplain from the federal camp just west of the Jordan River, visits for dinner and suddenly falls desperately ill. Annabel, who had been ready to leave for the East momentarily, has the entire household unpacked and keeps the invalid in her villa for weeks while the servants nurse him back to health.

The action picks up when, almost without warning, Annabel decides to marry Gwinett. She agrees to give up her cherished Catholic faith and is naïvely cooperative in helping her future spouse calculate her vast assets at home and abroad. The nighttime wedding ceremony "for time and eternity" seems bizarre, but she is not familiar with what she takes to be Protestant liturgy. She submits without protest. Not until the morning after does she discover that she is wife No. 2. "Reverend" Gwinett has in fact converted to Mormonism and is at that very moment being groomed as Brigham Young's eventual successor. Father Philippe of Exiles has already been reassigned to Idaho, so Annabel writes a desperate letter to a friend still stationed in Utah Territory, Lieutenant Rutledge, who would probably have been only too glad to marry Annabel a few months earlier.

Rutledge gets permission from Gen. Albert Sidney Johnston to go into Great Salt Lake City to rescue Annabel. Unfortunately, Annabel's Mormon husband has intercepted her letter to Rutledge, who arrives in the city only to receive a summons to have lunch with Governor Cumming. Cumming warns Rutledge of the impracticality of rescuing Annabel and obliges him to return directly to camp.

It is only through a chance meeting with travelers in Idaho that Father Philippe learns of Annabel's unfortunate marriage, her undoubted misery, and her manipulative husband's immediate sale of her former villa. The priest hurries to Salt Lake, presents himself at the Lion House, and through masterful conversation and insider knowledge of Utah and Brigham Young's secret banking schemes, convinces the Mormon prophet to have a revelation forthwith to release Annabel and let her leave the city. When Annabel is brought into the prophet's office, she is emaciated, poorly clothed, and virtually uncommunicative. Father Philippe takes her away immediately under cover of darkness with Young's promise to call off the Destroying Angels. Brigham returns to a meeting with the General Authorities, whom he directs to chant psalms all night to give Father Philippe and Annabel time to get out of town. Sadly, the next morning, when Father Philippe awakens at the mountain postal station where he and Annabel have taken refuge, he arises to discover the woman outdoors, staring blankly at the city far below. She has lost her mind and her former free spirit, and distractedly insists on returning to the house to prepare lunch for her husband and the other wives. No words can convince her to continue East.

Father Philippe, utterly disheartened, travels south to Lake Sevier and presents himself to the Indians, who had pronounced a sentence of death on him *in absentia* a few years earlier for having revealed their massacre of Gunnison to federal authorities. The Indians treat him civilly and offer him every opportunity to defend himself legally in their council, but he defers, waiting patiently for a humane execution the next morning: this is his means of ending his life without committing the sin of suicide.

Years later, now-General Rutledge has been appointed the new governor of Utah Territory. During his first official tour of Salt Lake City, his party takes refuge from a sudden rainstorm by touring the East Temple Hospice for aged destitutes. At the end of the brief tour, the enthusiastic director insists that the distinguished visitors see the kitchen. In the corner sit three miserable old derelicts peeling vegetables. At the sight of one of the women, Governor Rutledge pales suddenly. The woman, with a sudden outcry, grabs a handful of scraps from the floor and throws them in the governor's face, ending the hopeless story.

PIERRE BENOIT, *LE LAC SALÉ* [THE SALT LAKE], 315–33.
TRANSLATED BY FLORENCE AND VICTOR LLONA.

Six days later, shortly before dark, Père d'Exiles entered Salt Lake City. After stopping just long enough to entrust Mina to a small store-keeper of his acquaintance, he presented himself at the President's mansion.

After some discussion, he was received by Young's general secretary and confidential man, Herbert Kimball. See President Brigham! he exclaimed.

Impossible! He is at the Assembly of the Elders.

Until when?

Until seven o'clock, at least. And there are people waiting for an audience with him.

I am not worried about them, said Père d'Exiles. He will see me before any one else. But seven o'clock is too late for me.

Well, you don't think I am going to get the President, do you? Kimball asked insolently.

That's exactly what I expect you to do, answered the Jesuit.

What! You want . . . spluttered Kimball, dumfounded. And do you suppose for a minute that he will leave the Assembly of the Elders, the Assembly constituted according to the rite of Esdras by the twenty-sixth revelation!

He will, said Père d'Exiles.

I'd like to see it, said Kimball.

You will, all right. All you have to do is to whisper in his ear that there is some one in his private office with bad news from the Crosby Bank of New York. He'll come.

But . . .

Let me add, Brother Kimball, that knowing as I do that President Brigham is not in a good humor every day, it is to your own interest not to defer my message any longer.

So saying, Père d'Exiles settled himself in one of the big leather armchairs in the President's private office.

A quarter of an hour later, Kimball entered the hall where the Congregation was assembled. The light of forty clay lamps, hung near the ceiling, flickered upon the eighty persons present.

The room became silent. Kimball mounted the presidential dais and whispered to Brigham, who arose with dignity. His enormous shaven face was unmoved.

You must excuse me, Brethren. Brother Herbert informs me that the Almighty requires my presence elsewhere. Brother Orson Pratt will please preside over the ceremonies until I return.

Once outside, he interrogated Kimball with the same composure.

Did he tell you anything else?

Nothing else.

Good! said Brigham.

And the obese giant accelerated his pace with an alacrity of which he hardly seemed capable.

He found Père d'Exiles examining a sepia sketch of Salt Lake's future tabernacle, which hung on the President's study wall.[57]

---

[57] Benoit is referring, of course, to the Salt Lake Temple. Rick Grunder prepared the plot summary and reviewed this translation.

The two men exchanged a few courteous phrases.

A splendid structure, said Père d'Exiles.

The architect, said Brigham, is Brother Truman Angell. We expect that his work will soon leave the rest of the world far behind. Thus the two towers of the Amiens cathedral are 201 feet high, if I remember correctly.

The south tower is 201 feet high, the north 198 feet.

Ah, you see! The six polyhedral spires that are to embellish our tabernacle will each be 226 feet high! Besides, take a look at this. This block of grey granite is a specimen of the stone we will use to build the House of the Lord. We quarry it in the mountains nearby at great expense.

Nothing is too good for the Lord, said the Jesuit.

Nothing, said Brigham.

For a few moments they exchanged sundry remarks on the construction of religious edifices. Père d'Exiles cited Robert de Luzarches and Viollet-le-Duc. Brigham stood his ground. He was playing with the tiny compass adorning his watch-chain. Altogether, he was content to have met with an adversary worthy of him.

At last he asked in a tone of extreme indifference: So there is bad news from the Crossby Bank?

I have come out of the desert, said Père d'Exiles continuing his examination of the projected tabernacle, and so I really couldn't tell you anything absolutely certain about the bank's affairs; however, I believe they have never been better.

Ah! said Brigham, manifesting no surprise whatever.

They looked at each other smilingly.

Might I ask then, said the President, what interest there is in coming here to discuss the Crossby Bank with me?

It must be your own, if any, said Père d'Exiles, judging by the rapidity with which you left the Assembly of the Elders, the Assembly constituted according to the rite of Esdras by the twenty-sixth revelation.

Brigham braced himself in his arm-chair.

You want something of me?

Yes, said the Jesuit.

What?

The dissolution of the marriage that united Mrs. Lee to Mr. Jemini Gwinett.

Impossible, said Brigham.

Impossible, did you say?

I have no reason and no power to pronounce such a dissolution.

Of course you know to whom I refer, said the Jesuit.

The shepherd knoweth his flock, said Brigham ironically. Mrs. Gwinett Number Two, formerly Mrs. Lee.

Widow of Colonel Lee, specified Père d'Exiles.

As to Brother Jemini, there you have a remarkably intelligent man, so intelligent that . . .

That he aspires to succeeding you some day, finished the Jesuit.

That's just what I was going to say, said Brigham biting his lip imperceptibly.

Now we know just where we stand, said Père Philippe. So I repeat my question—will you or will you not pronounce the dissolution of this marriage?

I cannot, and I will not.

It is irony to say that you cannot, Brother Brigham. You can do anything, being infallible yourself and having revelations from on High at your disposal.

Don't jest, said Brigham. Infallibility is not to be laughed at. There are problems that can only be solved by resorting to absolutism. Sooner or later, I tell you, your pope shall be obliged to come to the same conclusion.

Far be it from me to sneer at infallibility, said the Jesuit. Quite the contrary, for I said that you could if you would, pronounce the divorce I spoke of, since you may resort to principle when you see fit.

That's where you make your mistake, said the President. To be wholly effective, the principle must be applied with moderation. You can't play it on every occasion, because if you do, it's certain. . .

What's certain, my dear President, is that we are wasting our time.

Brigham protested amiably. Perhaps you are, my friend. I'm not. On the contrary, there is nothing more profitable for me than an occasional chat with an able representative of another sect.

I ask you for the last time, said the Jesuit, will you or will you not pronounce the dissolution of this marriage?

I have already answered—I cannot and I will not.

Is that all you have to say?

Momentarily, yes.

Momentarily! Ah, what an admirable reservation! Come, my dear President, confess—for the past hour you have been dying to have me tell you a story, the story of the Crossby Bank.

Admitted, said Brigham.

He arose, went to the door, opened it. The corridor was empty. Brigham returned to the table, sat down.

You may begin.

Don't you smoke here? Our religion forbids it, said Brigham, and he continued with the tolerant smile. But you know, as the great pontiff Aurelius Cotta used to say in Rome, between intelligent people, religion is one thing, and . . .

So saying, he opened a little ebony cabinet and took out a box of cigars.
Take your choice, he said.
Then he helped himself.
I am listening.
They settled down in their respective armchairs, leaning their heads back, gazing at the ceiling, where crept the smoke of their cigars.
There was in New York, around 1848, began Père d'Exiles, a bank that was exceptionally well patronized, the William Crossby Bank.
Correct.
It was then that the first Mormons who had discovered gold in California, were coming back to Salt Lake City. By a full-fledged revelation, the Mormon Church forbade gold digging. Gold therein was it made known unto us. . . .[58]
Spare me the text of that revelation, said Brigham with a show of impatience. As its promulgator, I ought to know it.
I should think so. But there is something that you perhaps don't know.
What?
What I am about to tell you. The Mormon pioneers brought back about eighty sacks of gold dust from California.
Exactly eighty.
Well, out of those eighty sacks, sixty-two were used to coin five and ten dollar gold-pieces by order of President Brigham Young—an operation that permitted the notes issued by Kirtland's Mormon bank to climb back to par.
Well?
Well, doesn't something strike your attention?
I don't quite see what.
The simple difference between the figure 80 and the figure 62, said the Jesuit. How much does that make?
Why . . . 18.
Eighteen, just so.
Sixty-two sacks were used by the Bank of Utah, while it had received eighty. That makes a leftover, an excess or a difference of eighteen sacks whose fate it would be interesting to know, above all, when you take into account that the market value today would be the sum of $800,000.
Perhaps you have some private information on the subject.
I have.
Would it be indiscreet?
Not all. About that time, Colonel Lee, one of Brigham's friends, left Salt Lake City, where the first walls were being erected. He had been given a con-

---

[58] Brigham Young opposed gold mining but never issued a revelation on the subject.

voy of five wagons. Well, two of the wagons where loaded with the very eighteen sacks we were taking about.

Dear me, everything comes out in the end, said Brigham.

Colonel Lee, continued the Jesuit, arrived in New York. The eighteen sacks in question were deposited in the Crossby Bank. Stop me if I am making mistakes.

Go on, said Brigham.

In exchange, they game him a receipt for fifteen sacks!

Fifteen instead of eighteen?

The difference of three sacks was his commission. The receipt for the fifteen sacks was made out in the name of a certain . . .

Nathaniel Sharpe, said the President with a smile.

And do you know who was this Nathaniel Sharpe?

Myself, said Brigham with great simplicity.

He took a huge portfolio from the pocket of his frockcoat, opened it, drew out the paper folded twice.

And here is the receipt in question.

The two men looked at each other.

What do you think of my story? asked the Jesuit.

I think, said the President, that Colonel Lee was a less reliable friend than I thought. It seems to me that he gave me his word. . . .

He kept it, Brother Brigham. I happen to be acquainted with these details because I was the Colonel's confessor.

You are bound to secrecy, said Brigham.

I am. Theologically, however, one thing might release me—that you should not keep the promise you made Colonel Lee, a promise to watch over his wife.

Just so, agreed Brigham.

The situation is now quite clear, it seems to me, said the priest.

How does it strike you?

Like this. When after the great exodus from Nauvoo, Brigham Young arrived with his followers upon the site of the town that was destined to be built under the name of Salt Lake City, he had little confidence in the future of the Mormons. He took advantage of the first gold from California to assure, come what may, his own material welfare. What would his people say today, if they learned that he, the Prophet of God, had doubted the Holy Cause? What would they say, these faithful people, if they knew that the Head of the Church had kept part of the gold whose use he forbade publicly? What kind of an effect do you thing such a disclosure would produce?

A very bad one, said Brigham. He beamed. You would have to furnish the proof of your statement. Well, I have the receipt.

Yes, said Père d'Exiles, but there exists a duplicate.

A duplicate! said the President, whose heavy eyelids fluttered slightly.

A duplicate, or about the same things, the Jesuit said with aplomb, a copy, signed by Colonel Lee as depositor, and by the agent who received the deposit.

And, as Brigham gazed at him covertly:

Oh, rest assured that the copy would not be on my person when I came to visit you! concluded Père d'Exiles.

There was a moment's silence.

Another cigar? said Brigham.

With pleasure.

The conclusion, said the President with a pained expression, is that Colonel Lee distrusted me. It wasn't quite the thing. I never would have thought it of him.

The scanty protection you afforded his widow recently proves at any rate that his distrust was not unfounded, returned the priest.

The President was playing with his watch-charm.

Well, what about this, duplicate?

It is in the hands of trustworthy friends at present.

Trustworthy friends are a token of the Almighty, stated Brigham.

They have the duplicate of this receipt in their possession, pursued Père d'Exiles. And in addition, they are commissioned to publish it in the most influential newspapers of the United States if—today is January fifteenth—if I am not in St. Louis on the first of March to stop them.

Suppose, said Brigham Young, reflecting, that for some reason or other I could not prevent its publication, in your opinion, what do you think the result would be?

You said it a while ago—a very bad one.

To specify?

Your followers would be highly edified. Perhaps, but not necessarily. It wouldn't be the first time I have been calumniated. I would contest the authenticity of the document. I would transform the affair into a religious quarrel. If need be, I would use a revelation. Let me remind you in my turn that I am infallible.

As far as the Mormons are concerned, perhaps, said the Jesuit. But as far as the rest of the country is concerned, no! It would make a fine scandal, I assure you. And I know that you have no desire to cause one in any way whatsoever.

Quite so, said Brigham, meditatively. Then . . .

Then take steps immediately for me to be in St. Louis on March the first.

I will help you to the best of my ability so that the first of March will find you safe in that charming town.

I don't doubt it. But you know that is must be in the company of Mrs. Lee.

Mrs. Gwinett.

Mrs. Lee, if you please.

I repeat, Mrs. Gwinett, said Brigham dryly. Oh! You know me well enough to realize that I am not a man to be stubborn about a name. I regret that you do not seem to understand immediately what I mean by Mrs. Gwinett.

Père d'Exiles looked at the President, who smiled.

Let it not be forgotten, he said in an indefinable tone, that as High Priest and Supreme Head of my flock, the custody of the laws devolves upon me. Thus I could not dissolve a lawful union. But Mrs. Gwinett might escape, leave her husband's bed and board, with my knowledge and, in that case, very likely you would both take the same road.

And your Danites will not pursue us? asked Père d'Exiles distrustfully.

My poor Angels of Destruction! guffawed Brigham. Their exploits have been highly exaggerated. A man of your intelligence, to be taken in by such a clumsy humbug! I am astonished, my dear friend. Such mean suspicions when you succeeded so well in interesting me in the happy outcome of your journey!

It's my turn to say quite so, said the Jesuit laughingly.

Brigham rang. Kimball appeared.

Brother Herbert, commanded the President briefly. Go to Brother Jemini Gwinett's right away. He is at the Tabernacle, so you won't run into him, but, understand, you have to arrange things so that you locate Mrs. Gwinett Number Two and bring her back here, without being seen by a soul, do you hear? Go and make haste.

Kimball bowed.

Mrs. Gwinett Number Two, Anna, is it clear? Repeated Brigham. I am waiting.

The messenger went out.

You have to be precise, said the President coming back and sitting across from Père d'Exiles. What in the world would we say if that good old fellow brought us back Sarah or that simpleton of a Bessie, instead of Sister Anna?

It's true, said the Jesuit. Brother Jemini has three wives already.

Three, said Brigham. Three. And they're not beyond his resources.

And they continued to chat like the best of friends in the world.

Chapter 7

"The Country of Apotheoses"
The First European Visitors to Southern Utah

Spanish missionary-explorers Francisco Domínguez and Silvestre Vélez de Escalante became the first known Europeans to visit southern Utah after they gave up their attempt to find a route from New Mexico to Monterey in late 1776, but they would hardly be the last. American fur hunters such as Jedediah Smith and Thomas L. "Pegleg" Smith became familiar with the country during the 1820s, and John C. Frémont followed the Spanish Trail, a pack-train route between Santa Fe and Las Angeles opened in 1830, on his return from California in early 1844.

Latter-day Saints first laid eyes on the region's wonders when Mormon Battalion veterans headed south from Salt Lake in October 1847 to bring back desperately needed supplies. As part of his expansive plans to colonize every arable spot in the Great Basin and open a seaport on the Pacific, late in 1849 Brigham Young sent Apostle Parley P. Pratt to make the first formal Mormon survey of the country.[1] Within a year, Young dispatched some 118 men under the leadership of George A. Smith on the Iron Mission, whose purpose was to settle the Little Salt Lake Valley and exploit the rich iron ore deposits Pratt's explorers had discovered.[2]

Despite the valiant efforts of its colonists, southern Utah would remain one of the most remote spots on the globe for decades, but the first European tourists arrived during the mid-1850s. Jules Rémy and Julius Brenchley crossed the region in the fall of 1855 and subsequently described their visit, but they were preceded by a band of Germans whose experiences the

---

[1] Smart and Smart, eds., *Over the Rim*, 9.   [2] Larson, ed., "Journal of the Iron County Mission," 11–14.

anonymous "Th. Gr." recounted.³ No European descriptions of southern Utah in the 1860s are known, and it remained for John Wesley Powell to open the country to European visitors. Powell's exploration of the Green and Colorado rivers between 1869 and 1872 literally put the region on the map. Thereafter, an increasing number of visitors toured the rural colonies of Utah, including John Codman, Ernest Ingersol, Phil Robinson, and even Albert Tissandier and Carlo Gardini. Camp Floyd, Provo, Spanish Fork, Payson, Nephi, San Pete Valley, Cove Fort, Fillmore, and Scipio became part of the grand tour of Utah. The travelers would be, as any summertime visitor to Utah's national parks can see, the first of thousands of their countrymen to visit the singular wonders of canyon country.

TH. GR. [ANONYMOUS]: MORMONS ARE COMMUNISTS

The best experts believe that this anonymous account by Th. Gr. is "a genuine narrative of a journey of 2,000 miles on horseback. Six Germans and five Americans left Westport 15 May 1854 or 1855. They went through Ft. Atkinson on the Arkansas, near which they met immigrants bound for California by way of New Mexico and the Gila, carrying rocking chairs in their wagons." The sojourners passed Big Timbers, the ruins of Bent's Fort, the Huerfano River, and reached Ft. Massachusetts on 5 June. They crossed "Coochatope Pass" (translated here as "Buffalo Gate"), the flooded Laguna River, the Rio Grande, and the Colorado, arriving at Green River on 24 July, where they met a party of Mexican traders returning from Mormon country. This account is one of the earliest descriptions by an outsider of the new settlements at Paragonah, Parowan, Cedar City, and Santa Clara, who reported that the settlers bartered whisky and beads to purchase Indian children to use as house servants. The Germans followed the Spanish Trail, now largely a Mormon wagon road, into California, crossing Cajon Pass on 19 August after traveling 1,852 miles in one hundred days.⁴ Chad Flake included this account in *A Mormon Bibliography* in 1978, but Becker's fourth edition of Wagner-Camp eliminated the entry, probably because it appeared in a periodical rather than in a book, which put it outside the scope of the bibliography. The author's descriptions of southern Utah's early settlements, however, make it an important, if little-recognized, narrative.

---

³ Rémy described the trip from Fillmore to Los Angeles in *A Journey to Great Salt Lake City*, 2:347–456.
⁴ Wagner, *The Plains and the Rockies*, 421–22. Internal references, such as to Ute leader Wakara, who died in January 1855, and that Parowan had been settled for less than two years, suggest this trip took place in 1853 or 1854.

"Ein Ritt nach Californien," in *Das Buch der Welt*
["Riding to California," in The Book of the World],
34–40, 44–48, 52–57, 61–64. Translated by TSC.

[We met a pack train of] Mexicans returning from a trading expedition to the Mormon colonies at the Vegas de Santa Clara. . . .[5] On July 24, we reached the Green River, the second "fork" of the Rio Colorado. . . . The Vegas de Santa Clara, with their small Mormon colonies in the great Utah Territory, was our next destination. It is estimated that it is 242 miles to the Little Salt Lake, not to be confused with the Great Salt Lake which lies several hundred miles farther north and near which the Mormons have built their capital city. The first 90 miles took us through an infertile flatland, frequently crossed by dry river beds. Nothing grew there aside from wild sage and cactus, but then again, we were no longer bothered by mosquitoes and horseflies, as these scourges of America are only found along waterways. Above this, within just 20 miles we found 20 good camping sites with grass and fresh water. We had to cross a great number of tributaries of the Green River. These rivers were not large in size and caused us few difficulties. The largest were the San Rafael and the Rio Del Moro (The Castle Stream), thus named because the wild, rocky cliffs of the mountains where it has its source looks exactly like the old, gray fortresses and mountain castles that can be seen in Europe on the hill tops along the Rhine and the Neckar Rivers.

From the Rio Del Moro onward, we once again entered a mountainous area consisting of the foothills of the great Wahsatch Range. We crossed over a long row of hills that were separated from one another by wide valleys. This region is particularly fertile, the valleys all being moistened by life-giving water, and possessing an overabundance of grass, wood and game. The boundary of these rows of hills is formed by the Vegas (mountain meadows) of Santa Clara, at the foot of which the first of the Mormon colonies are located. We reached these after riding for eight days, and on the 2nd of August arrived at Paragonah in the valley of the Little Salt Lake. It is located at the foot of the Vegas de Santa Clara, just four miles away from the lake. This colony was very small consisting of barely thirty houses. Still the settlement had a friendly look and the entire region was characterized in particular by its extraordinary fertility. Here we found much wild rye with such heavy heads that the best cultivated field in Europe could not produce any better. The houses were built of adobes—sun-dried bricks—and covered with a flesh-colored paint which gave them a very friendly appearance. Together they formed a large square and the gaps between the individual buildings were equipped with palisades so that the entire little village was like a fortress that could, for a time at least, hold out in case of an attack from without. Surrounded by a picket fence, the "Field" is located outside

---

[5] On his second expedition, John C. Frémont broadly applied this name to the entire region between the headwaters of the Santa Clara River and today's Parowan.

of the small village. It is the land that is commonly held by all, jointly cultivated by all and from which the entire community obtains its food. For the Mormons are "Communists" in the full sense of the word, and for this reason every one of their colonies has such a "communal field." The one at Paragonah might have been 60 Morgen[6] in size. The whole field could be irrigated with the water of a small river that flowed across it. But we were not able to stay here because all the inhabitants had just received an order from their "apostle, pope and governor," Brigham Young, to give up the colony and move to the neighboring town, Parowan, located a good hour's journey away. And the people obeyed the order as though it were the Will of God! All this beautiful land that they had barely converted to the present state of cultivation with two years' worth of work, all their possessions, their houses and dwellings—all of this they left happily, without complaint, because He, the one who at the same time was both their spiritual and their worldly shepherd, had ordered it. Doors, windows, furniture and provisions of all sorts were loaded onto wagons and taken to Parowan, as were horses, cows, mules and other livestock. They left everything else behind or destroyed it so that it might not fall into the hands of the "enemy."[7]

The reason for this move, or much rather for this order from Brigham Young, was the threatening manner in which the Utah Indians had recently been acting and threatened to continue to act. A daring chief of the Utes had brought a large portion of his scattered Indian tribe together under his leadership. This chieftain was called Wahkah, in honor of an old American hunter by the name of Joe Walker, the man who had discovered the Walker Pass through the Sierra Nevada in California. However, he was not a Utah Indian by birth. Rather, as a small child he was kidnapped and raised as a "Ute" by his Indian foster parents. (His parents were probably Americans who were traveling through this desert region.)[8] He had developed an extraordinary degree of both mental and physical skill already as a youth, and was soon able to bring the bravest of the young warriors around him together under his command. Now he is recognized as the chief of the entire tribe. He has developed such a reputation, that his name creates fear and alarm in the colonies of the white men whenever it is mentioned. His people enthusiastically support him and he is expanding his raiding expeditions not just in Utah Territory and the Mormon colonies, but even to Sonora and New Mexico. Everywhere he steals whatever he can find, horses, mules and other livestock most particularly. Up to now all his undertakings have been so shrewdly planned and so daringly carried out that not one has

---

[6] German for "acre," a land measurement equaling 4,048 square meters or 4,040 square yards.

[7] The author saw the results of Brigham Young's policy of "forting up," gathering scattered settlements into consolidated walled settlements, which was implemented as a result of the conflict with the Utes known as the Walker War.

[8] Wakara was probably a Ute Indian by birth.

yet failed. The Mormons have been particularly afflicted by him, and therefore they also have placed a price of $15,000 dollars on his head. But who would earn this reward? Wahkah does not harass the "North Americans" much. His scouts, for example, soon ferreted out our small party, but after he was informed that we were "Swabs" (North Americans in the Utah language), he let us continue on undisturbed. This would soon change, however, if the North Americans try to erect "permanent dwellings" in these areas, for Wahkah claims the entire Utah Territory along with the smaller Sonora and the northern part of Mexico as his heritage, and this is a land on which he is determined not to tolerate any white men.[9]

Of course the few Mormons in Paragonah could not defend themselves against such an enemy, and that is why they were instructed to resettle in the much larger Parowan. So, we likewise rode to the latter town. However, it did seem somewhat miraculous to us when, here in this lonesome place cut off from all civilization, we came upon a beautiful country road, a real, genuine country road with bridges over even the smallest of streams! Yes, we even found "signposts" at "crossroads" and "mileage indicators"! This contrasted greatly with what our journey through the wilderness had hitherto been and seemed almost like a fairy tale to us.

Parowan was a town with about a hundred houses, which (as in Paragonah) are laid out to form the perimeter of a large square. The front of each house faced the open area in the middle of the square and every dwelling had a small, easily watered garden next to it. This was because the small brook that flows through the middle of Parowan was so ingeniously divided up into canals that it flowed past every house, thereby supplying the inhabitants with wonderful drinking water. The large square in the middle of the town was planted with trees, which allowed one to take lovely, shady walks. The "communal field" outside of the town was surrounded by a high, palisade-like fence and planted with wonderful maize and wheat. It might have been about 400 Morgen in size and was likewise irrigated in an appropriate manner. We could only be amazed at how much these men had been able to accomplish in such a short time, for the entire settlement was barely two years old. We were even more amazed as we toured the nearby ironworks. For the world's most lovely iron ore is found in the mountains nearby and the Mormons did not hesitate to make use of it. It was also an extraordinary bit of luck that on the way to the iron pits, they also discovered coal pits many of which are found just 18 miles away along the so-called "Coal Creek." The coal is of high quality, as high as any English coal could be and the deposits appear to be inexhaustible. Of course, many immigrants are settling near these coal mines, particularly Englishmen who were already familiar with coal mining back in

---

[9] Th. Gr. provides a typical and fairly accurate report on Wakara, although the Ute war leader and his many "brothers" were part of one of the tribe's most powerful kinship groups. For the most recent perspective on the legendary "Napoléon of the Desert," see Stephen Van Hoak's "Waccara's Utes," 309–30.

their old homeland. So it was no accident that Cedar City, the third Mormon colony to which we came, was enjoying a booming development. This was because the coal mines lay closest to this city of cedars and already back when we were there, it was much larger than Parowan.

Cedar City lies directly at the foot of the Vegas de Santa Clara, and numbers about 300 houses. The building style is exactly the same as that in Parowan and Paragonah, but the inhabitants mostly work at coal mining. For this reason the "communal field" is relatively smaller than it would have to be if all of the people were dependent on agriculture. Raising cattle, on the other hand, is a much more extensive activity, but it does not require much manpower. This is because the Vegas or mountain meadows of Santa Clara are world famous, so to speak, for the lush grass that they provide, and for their mild climate, which allows livestock to find enough nourishment in the open throughout the winter. They extend for about 150 miles in length and are so plentifully supplied with water that every day a person travels across them, he must cross dozens of streams. The water is cool and fresh, even during the hottest summer. Their highest peaks are covered with dense woodland consisting mainly of cedar trees (thus the name Cedar City), but they do not rise to any considerable elevation for they are essentially only foothills of the Wahsatch Mountains. It is within these Vegas that the coal mines I have just spoken about are located, as well as a few salt mines, which are indispensable despite the close proximity of the "Little Salt Lake." This is because the salty water of this lake is saturated to such an extent with lye and gypsum that it is hardly suitable for cooking and the salt obtained from it by evaporation is practically unusable. Therefore, the Mormons obtain all their salt from the rock salt mines on the Vegas de Santa Clara.

Before we leave the Mormons I cannot help but mention a peculiarity that is one of their customs and that may not yet have become widely known. I naturally do not mean the custom of polygamy, even though we also could not avoid being lectured on this topic (about the history and the wisdom of the custom, about the examples given by the patriarchs, and about the benefit it has provided to all the Orient), but rather the Mormons' habit of buying small children from the Indians and raising them to be "valets," stableboys, and handmaidens. The Mormons do not keep black slaves, but rather "red ones"! They do, by the way, treat them well and raise them in their religion. That is why such a "domestic slave," who addresses his owners as "Father and Mother," returns to the Indians when he becomes an adult. The New Mexicans also practice this custom of "buying children" and unloving parents who sell their progeny for poor-quality firearms, "whiskey or beads" or other paltry things, are only too easily found. They, however, all belong to the Pahutah tribe, the lowest, most fiendish rabble to be found on the prairie, but with which we were not able to become acquainted until now.

Albert Tissandier: Wild, Forsaken Places

Albert Tissandier (1839–1906), was born in Anglure, Champagne, France, attended the Ecole des Beaux Arts in Paris, and became an architect and municipal official. But his real passion, and that of his brother Gaston (1843–99), was aeronautics. They began experimenting with Montgolfier hot-air balloons—pear-shaped balloons with baskets and no guidance or propulsion systems—in the 1860s, and they designed, constructed, and tested dirigible (navigable) airships, making at least forty-four ascents in balloons.[10] During the Franco-Prussian War of 1870 to 1871 they made numerous ascents over the city as part of the army of Loire.[11] After the war, they organized two ascents in 1875 aboard a Montgolfier named the "Zenith" to study the atmosphere. Their first voyage was to test duration (they spent twenty-four hours in the air from Paris to Bordeaux) and the second was to test elevation (they ascended to 8,000 meters). During the second ascent Gaston lost his hearing, while his two fellow passengers died from asphyxiation. Following this tragedy, the Tissandier brothers became well-known throughout France, and although they made no further experiments in hot-air balloons, they did design and construct a screw-propelled dirigible airship and in 1883 they successfully traveled at eight miles per hour.

Albert Tissandier traveled in the U.S. during 1885 and 1886, arriving in New York City in April and making a westward journey by train, coach, horseback, and foot. He made more than 225 sketches documenting American urban and rural scenes.[12] When he arrived in Utah in May 1885 he seemed particularly interested in the Great Salt Lake,[13] but he was also very anxious

---

[10] The first manned balloons (hot air, hydrogen, and hybrid) were successfully tested in France in 1783. The first manned dirigible airships (which had cigar-shaped frames with gas bags on the side) were successfully tested for the first time in France in 1852.

[11] During the Franco-Prussian War the French government sponsored at least sixty-five balloon missions. They were deployed to evacuate 167 people from Paris, deliver military dispatches to troops at Tours, and drop propaganda pamphlets to Prussian troops.

[12] The Utah Museum of Fine Arts at the University of Utah owns 225 of Tissandier's sketches. The museum lent twenty of Tissandier's drawings to the Utah Arts Council in 1984 for an exhibition in the Governor's Board Room of the Utah State Historical Society. See McCoy, *Albert Tissandier, Six Months in the United States*. In 2001 the Utah Museum of Fine Arts, University of Utah, exhibited a larger selection of 225 Tissandier sketches from the museum's collection. See Francy, *Albert Tissandier: Drawings of Nature and Industry in the United States, 1885*.

[13] P. A. Van Tassell, one of the first itinerant balloonists in Utah, made several ascents in Salt Lake City during the summer of 1883. Subsequent balloonists made ascents at resorts on the Great Salt Lake and Utah Lake, including Lake Park and Garfield Beach. See Carter, "Daredevils of the Sky—Early Aeronauts in Utah."

to visit rural Utah and headed south, anticipating future European travelers who today visit Utah's national parks. Tissandier became one of the first Europeans to make a detailed description of the wonders of southern Utah and on the Arizona strip. Tissandier's book on his trip to America appeared in 1886, with excerpts appearing in the French travel journal *Le tour du monde* and in the periodical *La Nature*.[14] While most travelers used existing, and often hackneyed, illustrations, each of Tissandier's publications included a few of his original sketches. The article in *Le tour du monde*, which focused on his experiences in rural Utah and the Arizona strip, included sketches of Pipe Springs, Kanab, Kaibab, Mount Trumbull, and Toroweap.

After returning to France, Tissandier was a member of several French delegations sent between 1887 and 1890 to the Far East on diplomatic and scientific missions, and in 1892 he returned to North America and visited Canada, Alaska Territory, and the state of Washington.

ALBERT TISSANDIER, *SIX MOIS AUX ETATS-UNIS*
[SIX MONTHS IN THE UNITED STATES].
TRANSLATED BY HUGH MACNAUGHTON.

The regions of southern Utah, the province of the Mormons, and of the Kaibab plateau, in northern Arizona, are virtually unknown to the Americans. How can Europeans be expected to know them? For fifteen years, Mr. Powell, the director of the Washington Geological Survey, has been conducting numerous explorations into this curious country.[15] Aided by Mr. Thompson and other geologists, he has drawn remarkable maps of these quite extraordinary countries.[16] Thanks to Mr. Powell and his good advice, I was able to explore them myself. I wish to express my indebtedness to his kindness and charming welcome.

From Salt Lake City, the railway takes thirteen hours to reach Milford, which is where the great excursion begins.[17] This short journey by railway in the country of the Mormons is scarcely like any other. As far as the view extends after leaving the valley and the shores of Lake Utah there is only the

---

[14] See Tissandier, "Voyage d'exploration dans l'Utah et l'Arizona, Kanab et le plateau de Kaibab," *Le tour du monde* 51 (1886), 353–68; *La Nature* (1888). Gaston Tissandier was the editor of *La Nature*.

[15] For excellent biographies, see Worster, *A River Running West: The Life of John Wesley Powell*; and Stegner, *Beyond the Hundredth Meridian: John Wesley Powell and the Second Opening of the West*.

[16] Alma Harris Thompson, known as Harry, was Powell's brother-in-law and partner.

[17] Spanish explorers Domínguez and Escalante visited Milford Valley in October 1776. Ranchers and miners arrived in western Beaver County in the 1870s, but Milford was born when the Utah Southern Railroad extension, built to serve the nearby Horn Silver Mine, arrived on 15 May 1880. (The line became part of the Utah Central Railway.) Early visitors described the settlement as a "perfect mudhole." See "Milford," in Powell, ed., *Utah History Encyclopedia*; and Bradley, *A History of Beaver County*, 39, 160.

"View of the Great Salt Lake, Utah."
Drawing of Albert Tissandier. *Used by permission of the Utah Museum of Fine Arts, University of Utah.*

prospect of arid, sandy deserts. The stations where we stopped were very primitive. One of them, named Juab, perhaps the most remarkable, consists of only five or six wooden houses. It is the railway that brought it into being, and it barely survives except by the railway. At the end of the day, we dined with the driver and his assistants beside the luggage wagon.

Only one traveler, Mr. Lund, kept me company in the train.[18] Cooking is performed in a frying pan. While the provisions of the employees are modest, they are at any rate offered with a ready grace: the payment for them is insignificant.

The severe prospect of the mountains and plains unfolded rather sadly to our gaze.

At nine o'clock at night, we arrived at Milford. A small house made of planks acts as the hotel there.

At seven o'clock in the morning, I climbed with Mr. Lund, my amiable traveling companion, into the postal coach that was to take us to Silver Reef. It had no suspension, and its seats were stuffed with the stones of some American fruit whose species I could not discover. A rented tarpaulin formed the ceiling of this primitive conveyance and, as it was impossible to lean back onto any kind of a seatback, to take a few moments' rest during the great heat of the day, traveling in this way was really quite tiring. Only the barest outline of roads contrived to stir up an intolerable cloud of dust. I must therefore renounce attempting to describe the number of jolts and the disagreeable state of our persons owing to the fine clouds of dust stirred up by the wheels of our carriage.

Numerous flocks and herds, left to themselves year-round, graze in these solitary wastes. We saw them from far away. If a cow or a sheep had died of hunger and fallen by the barely discernible roadside, no notice was taken of it. The carriage turned slightly out of the way to avoid the carcass, which would lie there until completely decomposed.

A number of jackrabbits ran before us, frightened by the noise of our horses' hooves. They ran for cover under the meager, blue-leafed bushes that are the only shrubs in these desert wastes, and from there they watched us go by. We also saw chipmunks running away from us: these are tiny, charming sand squirrels; several times we saw wolves [coyotes], anxious and wild, wandering far away.

A shroud of dust almost continually robbed us of the sight of the beautiful flowers that grow in these forsaken lands and of the skyline of blue mountains. Twelve hours went by in this rather charmless way, until finally we arrived at Cedar City, a Mormon village that seemed like an oasis after the long, monotonous journey since that morning.

---

[18] This man's name was probably not Lund but Lunt. He may have been Henry Lunt (1824–1902), who led the party that established Cedar City in 1851, or one of Lunt's descendants.

Cedar had beautiful avenues lined with handsome trees, beautiful brick-built houses and hedged enclosures filled with fruit and vegetables. Freshwater streams flowed down the mountainside, crisscrossing the place with their currents, finally mingling their waters with those of a small river whose joyous babble is to be heard.

Cedar lay huddled in the shelter of a tall mountain of red sandstone. Around the town were fields and pastures. Mr. Lund was a Mormon. He knew all the inhabitants, and his first concern was to lead me to the bishop of Cedar, who gave us supper and a bed for the night.

The bishop was a farmer. He had two wives, it seems, but I saw only one of these ladies, undoubtedly the older of them.[19] She appeared to me intelligent and educated; it was she who served us at table.

The house, which was spotlessly clean, was used to shelter the infrequent travelers on their way through Cedar; it was also the telegraph office. In the sitting room, a warm fire comforted us; there were carpets everywhere. Newspapers lay open on the table. The fireplace was adorned with a large frame containing the pious rules that the family must follow every day.

To conclude the evening, the bishop's young daughters played the organ. One of the farm hands (or so I had taken him to be when I arrived) came in, clean and decently dressed. He sang romances with the daughters.

Mr. Lund then took me to see several other Mormon farmers in Cedar. In every house, I could see the same order, the same fastidious neatness, the same comforts. One would never have thought oneself to be in a country so far from any civilization.

At three o'clock in the morning, we had to be on our way: Mr. Lund was coming with me. We said good-bye to the kind bishop and his family. The entire household arose to wish us a safe journey in the traditional way.

Toward one o'clock, we arrived at Silver Reef, which lay at the entrance to the grandiose rocky landscapes of Utah. This country's scenery, and that of Kaibab in Arizona is surely unlike anything to be seen in Europe.

The grass of the prairies grew on sandy soils with the brightest colors of green, white, pink, golden-yellow and other sandstones. The mountains, most of them sandstone, are vividly striped with similar colors. All these widely varied tints, so close to one another, and often without any transition, have an uncanny effect that is hard to describe. Under the light and the fierce heat of the sun, the appearance of the soil and the mountains made weird, improbable impressions on me, the more so since the vegetation was hardly less strange in appearance. Bright June flowers, Cedars with dark green needles, bluish sagebrush added still starker contrast to this mixture and extravagant gush of colors. I rested for one day at Silver Reef, a small

---

[19] Christopher J. Arthur (1832–1918) succeeded Henry Lunt as bishop at Cedar City in 1877 and served until Lunt replaced him in 1884. Arthur was actually married to four women.

"The Salt Lake, Utah: Bathhouse and Open Air Cafe."
Drawing of Albert Tissandier. *Used by permission of the Utah Museum of Fine Arts, University of Utah.*

town of some 400 inhabitants drawn from multifarious origins. Chinese, some nomadic Indians, Irish, Canadians, and Americans, and finally a few Sisters of Charity who had courageously organized a mission to help the sick. Silver Reef was prospering, because of the silver mines discovered there a few years before, most of them fairly sizeable.[20]

At the recommendation of my traveling companion, Mr. Allen, the manager of one of these mines, was kind enough to show me around. It was some 270 feet deep, and its workface was 1300 feet in length. In the six years it had been operating, it had already earned 18 million dollars or 90 million French Francs. A ton of rock could yield an average of 25 dollars or 125 French Francs. The ore lay chiefly in the fossil layers of aquatic plants. Silver was extracted from those layers as the chloride, and sometimes also as the sulfide. In the clay shale layers, native silver was encountered in small, thin sheets.

This mine was dug into thick banks of green and white sandstone. The silver was removed from the ore by amalgamating it. This operation was performed at a factory in Silver Reef, located close to the mines.

Before bidding me farewell, Mr. Lund introduced me to the driver who would take me to Kanab. So here I was with a new companion. He was a Canadian who spoke French well. He had been brought up in Canada in a relatively well-to-do family, and his father had wanted above all to make him familiar with our language. This man was a curious fellow. By the time he had come of age, he had squandered all his fortune. He enlisted as a seaman and went whaling. Then he turned miner. At San Francisco he became rich, but ruined himself three times in a few years in mining speculations and became a menial worker. Finally, he had come to live at Silver Reef. He hired carriages there, and was convinced he would remake his fortune a fourth time.

We settled into a carriage as uncomfortable as the one we had taken to Silver Reef and the roads were no less bumpy. Fortunately, the landscape was as splendid as before. The Virgin River rocks were pink and silver-gray, and I looked in amazement at their outline, carved and filigreed into thousands of fantastic shapes.

We passed through the middle of the village of Toquerville, whose houses are all hidden under trees and behind flowers.[21]

---

[20] William Tecumseh Barbee heard rumors of silver deposits in a sandstone formation some eighteen miles northeast of St. George and by October 1876 had netted over $40,000. Miners drawn from the closed mines at Pioche, Nevada, established a tent camp at "Rockpile" to compete with Barbee's Bonanza City, and renamed it Silver Reef. The town boomed, boasting fifteen hundred residents and producing over a million dollars in silver annually. The boom ended and by 1884 the town was dead. For more legends, see Brooks, "Silver Reef," 281–87.

[21] Veterans of the Mountain Meadows massacre established Toquerville in 1859, named for a local Paiute leader, about thirty miles south of Cedar City.

The lonely wastes resumed; nothing but desert all day. Then we ran alongside the Vermilion Cliffs, a long mountain chain of red sandstone standing tall above the wide prairies where numerous flocks grazed.

The moonlight shone a fairy light on all this grandiose scenery. It was midnight. Our horses, tired with their fifteen hours' journeying, halted before Pipe Spring, a farm completely isolated in the sands and scrublands.[22] Despite the late-night hour, we were graciously received. When we called, a hangar door opened and we spent the rest of the night there wrapped in our blankets.

The following day, at noon, we were at Kanab. It lies beside a river that is almost always close to dried-up, but with the snowmelt, it swells and overspills extensively in floods, washing away sand and putting the entire country roundabout under water. Huge red-sandstone rocks (the Triassic escarpment) sheltered the village on one side; on the other, the scrublands stretch away out of sight. It housed perhaps 500 inhabitants.

Their isolation would have been complete, but their own industriousness has succeeded in forging links with the most prosperous and civilized in their country. The telegraph was installed there! I could not help thinking that many French villages were less remote than little Kanab, at the confines of the province of Utah, and yet our farmers would hardly have dreamed of setting up at their own expense a telegraphic network to receive interesting news of their locality, even if they had permission to do so.

Each house is bounded by an enclosure of yellow-rose hedges. The avenues are lined with acacias. The water of the Kanab river was brought into the center of town by an open wooden aqueduct a few miles long. By paying a water subscription charge, the townsfolk can cultivate a few vegetables and fruit. The Mormons love gardens and take great care of them. In each enclosure, they even have a few vines, which give them a very small yield, but they appreciate it as the reward of their work and of their constant struggle against drought.

My entry into Kanab, it seemed, had caused great emotion. The Mormons at the time were watchful. The government of the United States, tired of their eccentric ways, wished to bring them under the general rule of law and prohibit their bigamy. Since the decree of 1882 against polygamy and "cohabitation," they were prosecuted, sentenced to jail and to pay fines. In the small village of Panguitch, two men were abducted and borne off to jail. They were being required to repudiate their non-legitimate spouses and only keep the one they had married first, along with her children. Under

---

[22] James Whitmore received a land certificate for a 160-acre tract at Pipe Spring in 1863. Four years after Whitmore's murder in 1866, Brigham Young hired Anson P. Winsor to use the site for the church's tithing herd. Winsor built a classic Mormon ranch fort that John Wesley Powell allegedly dubbed "Winsor Castle," which is preserved today as Pipe Spring National Monument.

"The House of Nathan Adams, my Mormon Guide at Kanab, Utah."
Drawing of Albert Tissandier. *Used by permission of the Utah Museum of Fine Arts, University of Utah.*

"Main Street in the Village of Kanab (Kane County, Utah)."
Drawing of Albert Tissandier. *Used by permission of the Utah Museum of Fine Arts, University of Utah.*

these threats, the Mormons were in constant fear of police patrols and of being taken by surprise. Instead of making a boast of having several wives as in the old days, they deny the fact, especially in front of strangers, whom they always mistrust.

In any case, the Mormon religion remains very mysterious for a person who does not stay for long in the country. He can glean a few facts only from the newspapers that relate from time to time the scandals caused by the battles amongst women who are jealous of each other. But these rumors themselves would need to be verified in their exact detail. My arrival having been reported, a few inhabitants had crept out of the village and hidden among the rocks. Less timidly, the wife of my future guide received me at the front door of her house. Mr. Powell had given me a very special letter of recommendation, which I handed to her.

"My husband is out," she said to me before having read it. "You will not see anyone here."

These last words clearly expressed a mistrust that instantly evaporated after she had read the letter. Nathan Adams thereupon showed himself without fear, and I was made thoroughly welcome by all these poor people as soon as they were convinced that I was coming to them simply as a tourist and not as a government *detective*. They gave me hospitality, since there is no hotel in Kanab; one has either to lodge with the inhabitants, or camp out in the scrublands.

Kanab is the focal point from which one can branch out and embark upon the main excursions to the grand cañons. The goals of my first journey, agreed with Nathan, my future guide, were Mount Trumbull and the Toroweap gorges. The tour takes seven whole days; the difficulty in finding water in the deserts that must be crossed means that during this exploration hardship sometimes has to be endured.

At Kanab, from the only store in the village, we purchased tin cans, tea, coffee, and a few other necessaries; there was scarcely any variety or choice available.

Nathan brought his son with him, who was to be a valuable help. We had one horse each and a fourth for our baggage.

The ordinary life of a tourist once he leaves Kanab is organized roughly as follows: get up at four A.M., breakfast at five: Nathan laid our places on the grass. We had bacon, tinned salmon, water, and bread he made himself three times a day for each meal. This bread consisted of patties cooked in a frying-pan over a fire of dry branches that are nearly always easy to find in these deserts.

The horses, left to roam free each evening, foraged where they could for their food. As a precaution, however, to prevent them from going too far away during the night, their forelegs were hobbled with a kind of leather bracelets connected with a strong, thick strap. These poor beasts, who were very tired, often had nothing to eat save meager grass and sometimes had no water. They were used to this diet. Even so, they must have been brave, since on some days, they walked for twelve or fifteen hours: a grueling schedule.

Each morning, the main subject of conversation between Nathan and his son, when they had run after the horses to bring them back, was where we could make the next resting stop so that it would be close to a spring to fill our water flasks and water our horses.

Sometimes we spent the entire day without any drinking water. The burning heat of the sand made the stored water barely drinkable; the only recourse was to content ourselves with a little coffee. The horses, on the other hand, were lucky if they could find in some hole in the rock a remnant of water from the snow-melt or from a recent thunderstorm.

We rested in the afternoon. In the evening, towards seven, we stretched out our blankets on the desert sand, or in the forest, and went to sleep under the stars.

That is the way Mormons journey in Arizona. A Parisian tourist may quite legitimately wonder about it during the first day of the journey, but the originality and splendor of the scenery greatly compensate for the utter lack of comfort. One soon gets used to such small discomforts.

On leaving Kanab, we had to return to Pipe Spring, one of the few places with a freshwater spring. Its amiable inhabitants had already extended to me their hospitality; this time, I was received with a cordial eagerness by the mistress of the house and her daughters. If I was astonished in Cedar City by the welcome and the style of the bishop's dwelling, I was still more so at Pipe Spring. I want to be perfectly sincere. These Mormon ladies are distinguished and well-educated, even though in reality they are nothing but farming women living in wild, forsaken places. Deep in our French countryside, in the most forgotten corners of our provinces, our rural lady fellow-citizens are certainly in less deserted environments than those of Utah or Arizona, and yet, I have to admit that they are usually less civilized.

All around Pipe Spring, large herds graze, watched over by cowboys, hardy young men who are used to privation. Alone, living always in these vast scrublands, completely remote from all society, these Mormon shepherds nevertheless lead an active existence, and not devoid of interest. For entertainment they have hunting and the contemplation of the grandiose natural scenery of these desert regions. Then, still on horseback, chasing their cattle or bringing it back, often from very far away in various parts of the scrubland, the work is toilsome and arduous.

They have to see to the reproduction of their animals. The totally wild state of the latter often makes this occupation difficult and even dangerous at times. Among other duties, they must brand the newborn calves. Each owner has his own brand, which is marked on the flanks of the young animal. Without this precaution, it would be impossible to recognize his own property. In the United States, livestock farmers have books in which it is easy to look up the names and brands of the various herd owners.[23]

I was told that fifteen years before, the cattle had been more numerous than was the case today in the neighborhood of Pipe Spring; the reason is that the animals, when they eat grass, pull up the roots, which can scarcely hold in the sandy soil. Consequently, the seeds dry up before they can shoot, the prairie is not re-seeded, and the desert makes further inroads. The numerous skeletons of animals on the wayside attest to this degradation of the scrubland.[24] Another development is that antelopes and wild horses, which were formerly abundant, are drawn farther and farther away, or die in the sand.

I said goodbye to my gracious hosts at Pipe Spring. A few cowboys wished me good health and "fresh water to drink" during my excursion, as they helped me to saddle my horse.

We left the high escarpments of the Vermilion Cliffs and soon entered the true desert with its desolate prospects.

The horses walked with difficulty in the dusty, yielding sand. The smallest breath of air raises small swirls of sand that are visible from far away. And yet, under our feet grew numerous flowers in widely spaced clumps forming bouquets. But we were in June. A little later, all would be burned by the sun, and on the earth nothing would be left save an arid, mournful drought.

Still riding onward, we came across a few antelopes; further on, we startled a herd of wild horses, about fifty of them who, followed by their young foals, galloped off ahead of us.

At the end of the day, we left the sandy regions at the approach to Mount Trumbull. Numerous traces of volcanic slag covering the earth attested to the disorders and disasters of former centuries. The volcano has long been extinct. Nearly all its craters are covered with centuries-old pine forests. Formerly it had flooded the plateaus of Uinkaret with its immense lava flows, over which we were traveling today. The forest attests to these revolutions of bygone ages. Beneath roots and plants can be discovered whole banks of basalt rock shattered by wind and weather.

Farther on, the scenery changes, and a sort of lava sea can be seen uncovered, a relatively more recent flow, not yet overrun by vegetation. Only a few stunted oaks eked out an arduous existence there.

A mountain covered with a thin verdure concealing volcanic slag as black

---

[23] For local examples, see Cracroft, "The Heraldry of the Range: Utah Cattle Brands," 217–31.

[24] Tissandier's comments on rangeland degradation are perceptive. For a study of the affect of livestock grazing in southern Utah, see Beckstead, *Cowboying: A Tough Job in a Hard Land.*

as the Styx adjoins this magnificent flow. Far off, the gorges or cañons of Kanab, lit by the rays of the declining sun, form on these high plateaus immense clefts resplendent with light. They make an astonishing contrast with the black of the lava and make the bizarre silhouette of Mount Trumbull's volcanic cones stand out more prominently.

We threaded a precarious path down all these rocks, holding our mounts by the bridle. Most of the horses in this country are not shod, so that the volcanic slag hurts their feet and they can only walk with difficulty. In any case, there was no other road we could follow to reach the sandy Toroweap valley near the canyons. Long and relatively narrow, this valley was surrounded by colossal rocks with colors that constantly surprised.

In the evening, we had no complaint to make about our encampment at the foot of a fortress-like rock wall. Under the shadow of an old cedar, we were on an immense sandstone plateau of rounded rocks, worn by the snows of winter. Numerous flowers and stunted trees or *agaves*, some of them growing more than twelve feet in height, and reddish or golden cactuses charmed us as though they were decorations on these colorful stones. Beyond that prospect, our gazes rested on the saw-toothed rock walls that stretched on and on and barred the skyline.

After a little rest, we walked over enormous stones, often scrambling up them using hand- and footholds, or leaped over wide clefts. Spellbound by the grandeur of these strange desert lands, I moved forward with an indefinable feeling of astonishment.

The scene changes, but was not less dizzying: here at my feet lay the grandiose precipices of Toroweap, at the foot of which runs the Colorado. What an uncanny spectacle are these eroded gulfs, some 2,000 to 2,600 feet deep, with steep-sided walls or gigantic tiers descending to the torrent itself.

From the edges of the upper plateau, my eye followed in amazement the outline of these rocks, which thrust forward into promontories describing the most fantastic of curves above the precipices.

We were constantly having to make detours, and at each instant, new and ever more admirable prospects came into view. In immense clefts, a geologist can read with ease the entire series of different layers that form the sidewalls of the gorge, and one's imagination entirely fails to grasp the incalculable ages that must have elapsed since the successive formation of all these marvels....

We could not camp for long on Toroweap plateau, for we were getting short on water. Nathan and his son had discovered a little snowmelt in a cleft of the rock, but only our horses were able to drink it.

We returned to Kanab by the same route to organize an excursion to the Kaibab plateau. When we came into the village, we learned that the Indians who often camped in the area, among whom I had hoped to find a guide, had left shortly before to hunt buck in the Kaibab forests: I was told that they would not be seen again for a month. I could not wait that long, and I began to fear that I might not be able to continue my journey. Nathan knew the country, but he did not want to take responsibility for guiding me alone in those solitary parts. He said to me, "I need an Indian with me; only they know how to find their way in the virgin forests."

The Mormons advised me to go straight to the Indians' camp. They were supposed to be settled by a spring a long day's journey away from Kanab. Once there, Nathan, who knew a few words of the Ute language, would certainly succeed in finding the guide he felt was necessary.

I followed his advice eagerly, and we set off at once.

That very evening, at sunset, threading our way along the winding desert ways, and through picturesque woods of cypress, we arrived at Mangum Spring, where we duly found the camp that the Mormons of Kanab had indicated. It was a temporary encampment of eight or nine tents in a clearing. Some twenty Indians lived there with their wives and a few children. They had chosen the spot with most exposure to the sun. Their tents were made of a few branches cut from nearby trees and tied together in pyramidal bundle. A wretched piece of cloth or an animal skin covered these simple shelters.

Mr. Powell dwelt at length in his book on these wretched barbaric tribes, whose customs were primitive, but whose ways were gentle.[25] American explorers, it seems, have never had cause to complain of the relations they contracted with them. We decided to camp near the Indians so that we too could take advantage of the spring.

Our horses, for their part, lost no time in fraternizing with those of the savages, and disappeared into the thicket.

Alongside us, under the pines, are two cabins of Americans. They had some cattle there and, like the Indians, lived in the forest with their wives and children. However, their living arrangements were less primitive.

After our evening meal, the Indians came to visit me and to keep warm beside my fire. I gave them a little bread made by Nathan and a few drops of coffee. Two almost-naked children drew close to me. Their hair was all tousled and they looked at me with the expression of little wild beasts. I put a few grains of caster sugar into the palm of my hand and gently offered this to them, taming them instantly in doing so: they came and kept warm by my side. Several of these Indians were young and well-knit. Two or three had painted faces. All their skin is colored with yellow ochre, except for a little vermilion under the brows and on the eyelids, and two roundels of the same

---

[25] For Powell on the Paiutes, see Powell and Ingalls, House Exec. Doc. 157 (43-1), 1874; and Knack, *Boundaries Between: The Southern Paiutes, 1775–1995*, 116–17, 126, 317–18.

color, as big as a 5-Franc piece (a silver dollar), painted on their cheeks. They reminded me of our country circus clowns at home.

Ethnically, these savages are of fairly characteristic type. Their face is slightly flat, with very prominent cheekbones. Their eyes are large. They have dark skin of a golden-yellow tint resembling that of old Florentine bronzes. Magnificent jet-black hair grows down to their shoulders, plaited in front, forming long tresses interwoven with red cotton, like the ancient Gauls. Around their necks shine a few rows of glass beads. Their clothes are in poor condition, most of them even in rags and tatters, being of European cut and consisting only of trousers and a sort of calico print shirt adorned with floral designs. On their heads they wear a small cap of oriental form.

As best he could, Nathan explained to the Indians the reason for my presence in their forest and the purpose of my journey.

Our American neighbors in their turn came up to us. They asked me the latest news of Kanab. We chatted, and so, in the heart of the forest, we entertained each other with spring water and coffee to refresh us. When our fire went out, we withdrew, each to his preferred plot of grass, and tucked ourselves up into our blankets.

The following morning, I returned the call the Indians had paid us the evening before, and I saw their women, who unfortunately cannot be called pretty. Even so, they have magnificent hair, and their eyes have a sparkle that astonishes. But their faces are faded and wizened, and it would be difficult to guess exactly how old they were. Burdened with the most arduous tasks, especial those of the encampment, these poor women are worn-out and old before they even reach the age of twenty. One of them carried her baby on her back, in a sort of wickerwork creel. Its face, too, was dyed with yellow ochre. Poor little creature! What a ridiculous figure it gave him! His body was wound in baby-clothes, and thrust standing into the creel. His head, which was all that was visible, was held at the forehead by a band of wickerwork, no doubt to attenuate the jolts of his mother's walk.

Nathan told me that an Indian woman normally sits with her baby behind her back, or hangs it in the branches of a tree. It was carried by a long tape threaded through the creel and held by her forehead. I wanted to draw the child, but its mother forbade it, saying that I would have cast an evil spell on it, but the Indians did let me sketch their encampment, and I finally did sketch the creel and the child in secret.

These savages were very busy during my visit. Helped by their wives, they were cutting up a bullock and carefully laying out the pieces on a rock to dry them in the sun. A few of them wove baskets for their use. The women, dressed in long, ample coats made of sewn-together jack-rabbit skins, lit fires near their tents. They called anxiously to those of their children who came close to me to see what I was doing with my paper and pencil.

Meanwhile, Nathan had gathered information about a guide. At his request, a young Indian, who was busy grooming himself in his tent, decided to accompany us. He was called John Panichkos (I cannot be sure of the spelling of his surname). His face was painted. I could not have dreamed of a handsomer guide. He asked for 6.25 French Francs for himself and his horse. This was agreed on the spot and so we set forth.

The following morning, my Mormon guide said that John was put out. His face paint had almost worn off, and he did not have the necessary ointments to renew his adornments of the day before. I laughed heartily at this minor mishap as I saw my Indian, rendered much handsomer in my opinion, with his natural skin, white teeth and magnificent eyes.

My second excursion lasted thirteen days. We lived in the virgin forest of Kaibab.[26] Nothing could be greater or more interesting. Naturally, there were no roads cut through these woods and, and as has frequently been observed, the Indians must have one sense more than we have to recognize where they are, some faculty such as racing pigeons. I had to make my way up never-ending hills and down dales through centuries-old pine forests and dense thickets, then scramble over fallen tree trunks lying on the moss. Sometimes it was so dark under the vegetation that I wondered whether night had suddenly fallen. In some parts, the thickets were so dense that I could not see my companions a few paces away. From time to time, we came across the skeletons of deer or does.

Some parts of forests had been burned by the Indians. To heat themselves during the night and to cook their meager meals, they choose the biggest pine tree in the forest and set fire to it. The resin-filled tree burns easily and often sets fire to nearby branches until there occurs, if there is wind, thoroughgoing disasters in these vast forests. The Indians give such things little thought and go and camp elsewhere, burning more trees without ever thinking of taking a few precautions.[27]

Fallen trees were obstacles in every case for our poor horses. At any moment they were compelled to leap over the pine trunks lying on the ground or to make detours when they are too big. Since we were compelled to strike a path through the branches to see, we were unable to avoid scratches to our hands, and rents in our clothes.

At the top of a rise, which was covered with the most magnificent trees, John suddenly cried out and pointed to the marvelous panorama. There lay the Grand Canyon, the *Scotingat*. That is the name my Indian guide gave me. I was obviously unable to verify its exact spelling, but he gave me to understand that he called those huge gorges by that name on account of the plants growing in the rocks that covered many places.

---

[26] The area Tissandier visited is now part of the Kaibab National Forest.

[27] For a modern perspective on Indians' use of fire, see Stewart, *Forgotten Fires: Native Americans and the Transient Wilderness.*

I stopped, astounded and fascinated at such an unparalleled heap of walls built one on top of another, giant amphitheaters, fairytale palaces, towers and fortresses the like of which the Titans might have built. When contemplating such perspectives, one cannot believe oneself to be on earth any more. It is the country of apotheoses. The forces of the imagination are powerless before the immensity of these prodigious proscenia, these towering walls, these fantastic plateaus that overlook them and succeed each other with ever-differing colors, fading only at an infinite distance into the distant blue of the sky. I was dreaming, I could not think any more. For several days, I felt the same sentiment of awe.

At the spot known as Thompson Springs, sizeable flocks of sheep grazed on grass of little substance in that season. It was curious to see them walking in bands toward the large salt licks that the Mormons are careful to place here and there in the scrubland. They come each in turn and lick the salt, and seem very fond of this delicacy that the stock-farmers of Utah and Arizona regard as very beneficial.

We arrived at the Sublime Point. This is one of the highest points on the Kaibab plateau at 8,500 feet above sea level. At this height, the rocks form a sort of cape and from that unfolds the entire cañon country of Arizona, with walls named the Hindu Amphitheater, and the heights of Kwagunt Valley, the Temple of Shiva, etc.

The Kaibab plateau is the most interesting of all the plateaus of Arizona, since it is covered with forest up to its highest peaks, unlike the other plateaus discovered from Sublime Point, which are bare, giving an endless prospect of arid, fearsome desert. It is truly both a sublime and moving sight.

Between colossal fissures, I caught glimpses of the Colorado from time to time, its waters boiling at the foot of the precipices and becoming lost to sight as its course wound its way about in fantastic detours some 6,000 feet below.

One of the most striking features of the Kaibab is the total lack of water courses. Even so, the climate there is very humid. Rain falls frequently in the summer and the snow lies deep in winter. The water stands in hollows of land forming numerous lagoons, surrounded by vegetation of such luxuriance that in such places one has the illusion of a delightful park.

Wishing to visit all these marvels at leisure, I camped for three days beside a beautiful marsh, the Forest Lagoon, surrounded by white poplar and old pines. From there I could easily strike outwards and enjoy all the main sights of interest. Numerous birds with brilliant plumage, the *Pyranga ludoviciana*, which has a yellow body, a red head, and black wings, and also many humming birds that announced their presence by the slight rustle of their wings, flew among the flowers, the cedars, and the arbutus, and were among the greatest attractions of this charming spot.

I was overjoyed to observe a humming bird at very close quarters, near a small cedar. Its wings beat so fast that it was almost impossible to see them, but it rested at last, to go and sit on its tiny, beautifully constructed nest. There were two eggs in it, of the size of a small bean. The bird flittered about all the time and seemed in no way disturbed at my presence. It lay on its nest, which it then arranged coquettishly with its long beak and then flew off again. I could see nothing more charming than this tiny dance of the bird with the glittering colors. It had a pearly-gray breast and the top of the wings and the head were colored green with emerald glints.

Our Indian, during the times when I was drawing, went off to hunt buck, armed with flintlock rifle from goodness-knows-what period. He killed a few, and skinned them in the twinkling of an eye, keeping only the hide, which he would go and sell in the Mormon villages. Thanks to him, we had a few meals that were not as bad as usual.

After our moonlight walks among the fairy rocks, we would go to sleep by the fire. John sang Indian songs while he unraveled his long plaits of black hair.

When we left the Forest Lagoon, we had to go down, through tracts of impenetrable forest, to Pagump Valley. Two young Americans living there in a small cabin, had been raising horses and cattle for two years. They lived alone in these desert wastes, with one cowboy. Our arrival was a welcome change for them. An Indian, a Mormon, a Frenchman and four horses, appearing suddenly from the silence of their valley, could not fail to arouse their interest. They ran up to see us, very glad to have conversation with mortals who had as if by enchantment descended from the forests of Kaibab lying 1,600 to 2,000 feet above their cabins.

Nathan introduced me, telling them I was a Parisian who had come among them to draw the cañons of Arizona. I showed my sketches, and at the sight of them, Messrs. Gibson and Gillett became enthusiastic.

"Stay with us," they said, "we have a treasure to show you. Your horses are worn out. We will lend you others, while yours rest up." This lively pleasantness charmed me. The treasure of these two gentlemen consisted of the view of immense cañons that Nathan did not know about: the Marble Cañons. I accepted their proposal.

John, seeing that we could get back to Kanab without his assistance, disappeared into the forest with his horse and without saying goodbye or concerning himself with the money he was owed. Nathan had told him he would be paid at Kanab the next time he went by there. That was enough for him: he was trusting.

It needs a long day's journey to get from Pagump Valley to the Marble cañons and visit them. It was one of the most wonderful excursions of my journey. These cañons do not have the same aspect as the other gorges of

Kaibab. The aridity is greater than elsewhere among these vast amphitheaters: before one's eyes is a spectacle of desolateness of the utmost grandeur.

In the evening, partly thanks to our provisions, we had the recreation of a big dinner in the log cabin of our two gentlemen hosts. The following day, our hosts wished to show us their herds of 1,800 cattle and 80 horses in their rangelands.

"This season we were in luck," said Mr. Gibson, "five hundred calves were born; if it continues this way, another few years of our solitary, savage life, and we'll have enough dollars to go and return your visit in Paris, then finish up our existence in one of the big American cities."

Our farewells were full of affection.

On the return leg, about a third of our way towards Kanab, we camped at Kane Spring.

One morning, it was four o'clock, and I was washing close to a spring framed by beautiful pink and golden rocks. All of a sudden, I heard shouts and neighing. A hundred free-roaming horses, led by a cowboy, were galloping hard toward the solitary spot where I had just spent the night, attracted by the spring. After slaking their thirst, they returned at the same breakneck pace to graze the grass in the far-off deserts. The effect had been enthralling. This eager, hurrying troop, in such a picturesque site, lit by the morning sun, struck me as an original sight, peculiar to America.

The cowboy, a young man of scarcely twenty-five, very trusting of his animals, had stayed behind. He asked to be allowed to accompany us when we left. This favor I found no difficulty in granting him. Meanwhile, Nathan was busying himself with making our daily supply of bread.

The cowboy pointed out to me a small troop of mounted Indians with large pots hanging from each side of their saddle. They were coming to fill them with fresh water to take back to their encampment, newly set up in the desert, under the full light of the sun. Among them I recognized my John, newly-painted this time with two red roundels on his cheeks. He was at the head of his friends, and would have been glad to have a little flour and coffee. Fortunately, I still had some left. The other Indians then wanted to know what I had marked in my album: John had spoken to them of my studies in the forests. When they recognized from my sketches the Forest Lagoon and a few details of the cañons, they started laughing among themselves, then began speaking together endlessly in the Ute language. I should have liked to understand them; besides, they seemed to be saying nothing but honorable things about me. They enjoyed a further gift of coffee for their goodwill, and afterwards, they disappeared with their mounts behind the rocks but without in the least bidding us farewell: it was not their custom.

We left Kane Spring with Nathan and my cowboy. We had a fairly hard stage of the journey to make, crossing the desert for five hours in the blazing sun before we reached House Rock, a spring almost as solitary as the one we were leaving behind us, except that beside it stood a cabin tenanted by an old man and a youngster who stayed there to tend the herds and give hospitality to the infrequent cowboys who passed that way.[28]

The young Mormon was a merry soul, and we chatted together. I wondered how this honest lad's mind could have thought up all the questions he asked me about Europe, Paris, etc. Was I really so far away in the deserts with a herder?

I spent my last night in Arizona at Navajo Well, a solitary place if ever there was one. In this spot, between two rocks barely emerging from the ground, a water hole is to be found. It is a sort of natural cistern, a holding tank for rainwater or snowmelt from the winter. People came from a long way off, across sands and forest to drink. It was curious to see the birds flocking to this detestable, almost brackish water. That was of little consequence to them: it was their only resource. On our arrival at sunset, we were already aware that this water reserve was not far off, from the number of wild turtle-doves and crows that flocked there to slake their thirst. They approached the cistern almost singly, queuing as though outside a theatre, and patiently waiting their turn as they flew about or walked on the sand.

I began by filling our vessels with this turbid water. We had to water our horses first, then I waited a little to have clearer water for ourselves. During our taking possession of the spring, about a hundred turtle doves, disturbed by my presence, landed scarcely ten yards from me and were joined by other birds. I stood as still as possible so as not to frighten these graceful little creatures; accordingly, I was soon surrounded by a prodigious gathering of birds. They had a pressing reason for not being frightened away: it was at the last hour of daylight, six o'clock, and they needed to drink before sleeping. I was glad to yield the ground to them.

Navajo Well is a wide open place; red walls colored the horizon; the failing light of day slowly faded. The crescent moon was beginning to shed its light for us. Among the sagebrush and the flowers, the crickets gave us a final concert, mingled with the plaintive calls of the turtle doves hidden in the stunted cedars and the tinkling of our horses' bells—a delightful interlude in the absolute calm of these immense plains. I shall never forget the magic natural scenery at Navajo Well and that evening spent under the stars.

On my return to Kanab, I thought that it was time to return to Salt Lake City and to American civilization, and I began my return.

This last part of the journey was not without interest. From Kanab to Panguitch, the countryside was as improbable-looking as in Arizona. It was

---

[28] Located in the Kaibab National Forest, House Rock gives its name to a spring and valley. The nearest settlement is Jacob Lake, Arizona.

even more curious, more bizarre, perhaps, although it was not as grandiose. The colors of the sandstone rocks of Utah are absolutely extraordinary.

Our horses followed for a long time the bed of the Kanab river, almost dried out in June, walking in wet sand between two banks of cream-colored sandstone. Above the banks, rose orange-colored hillocks, partly covered by dark-needled cedars and bluish sage. Farther away stood rock walls of white-veined pink sandstone. Lastly, at the horizon the enormous rounded rocks of the White Cliffs contrasted to the colorful foreground by their dazzling whiteness. Along a certain stretch of its banks, the Kanab river is lined by a long bank of volcanic stone overlooked by the White Cliffs. On these sandstone rocks. polished over the centuries, one can see the long swathes cut by the former glaciers.

At Panguitch, I made an excursion into the mountains surrounding the fertile valley where this small city is built. For a long time, we crossed great prairies dotted with villages of a particular kind: the cities of the prairie dogs. There were many of these. When I had crossed the Nebraska plains by railroad, I hardly had any opportunity to see these graceful animals, but in these sandy regions around Panguitch, I could observe them at leisure.

They were not shy creatures, and as they saw us quietly going our way on horseback, they continued exercising and happily romping together. They utter a sort of short, jerky bark, or rather more a yap, which is the only point of resemblance with the canine race. Their bark was probably the reason this little rodent was given the name of prairie dog. At first sight, one has the impression of seeing a large marmot. Its back is a tawny red; the fur on the flanks and belly is much lighter in color, almost white. Its tail is carried upright, like a squirrel's, being three to four inches long and ending in a tuft of dark hair. My guide told me that an owl is almost always to be found in the burrows of prairie dogs, which is its roommate; they live together as friends. Its food consists of a few roots and stalks of a plant fairly common in these parts of Utah or the Upper Missouri, *Seleria dactyloides*. During the winter, it huddles down inside the burrows it has tunneled and goes to sleep, and like marmots, awakes only in the spring.[29]

Nothing is more amusing that to see the lively bustle that reigns in a prairie-dog city: constant comings and goings, leaps and joyous cries. They seem to be egging each other on to play and run better and better. They play hide-and-seek, and suddenly disappear down their burrow to reappear in another place, then jostle each other just like schoolchildren after school has ended for the day. The Mormons try to destroy these animals whenever they can, since their numerous burrows are so harmful to their crops. The flesh is quite tender, it seems, but the animal is too small to be worth hunting

---

[29] Now a threatened species that is protected year-round, the Utah prairie dog (*C. parvidens*) is the smallest of all prairie dogs.

them. People simply lay down a sort of rat-bait in the burrows. The unfortunate prairie dog is driven by greed, and dies quite quickly, being buried naturally in the home it built for himself.

We soon traveled into mountain territory. In the middle of green sandstone lands, almost apple green, stand a group of rocks of the same matter. They form tall bare hills of loose ground. The thunderstorms and the melting winter snows crisscross these high banks with innumerable streams, cutting them into strange shapes in every direction. A number of kidney-shaped stones often remain on the top of small, gradually crumbling sandstone bluffs. More singular places cannot be imagined, and I never ceased to marvel at the green-colored rock in the foreground contrasting with the forest-crowned pink ramparts that barred the horizon.

As I write, in Paris, I wonder if I really haven't dreamed what I drew and have just attempted to describe.

In the curious gorges around Panguitch, I saw many rattlesnakes. They are not very developed in these areas of Utah, but they sound the rattles on their tails admirably: they can be heard for a long time before they can actually be seen. I killed a few, 35 to 39 inches or so in length. One of them lay motionless on the path, with a menacing look, as if to lunge at my horse, which came to a sharp halt when he saw it. Horses are very afraid of these creatures. Mine was getting ready to bolt. A well-aimed stone thrown by my guide put an end to our slight upset: the reptile was crushed.

Mormons are hardly at all afraid of these snakes. If someone is bitten, the remedy is to make them drink spirits until absolutely inebriated. The effects of the venom are assured to be totally cancelled out in this way and a few days' rest suffice for the victim to be entirely healed.[30]

In the province of Utah, the country is far less arid than in the area near cañons in Arizona. The Mormon villages have succeeded in creating fertile lands thanks to arduous and extensive irrigation. Numerous herds of cattle and troops of horses can be seen on the high plateaus that lie along the Sevier River. Near Marysvale, there are magnificent places in the mountains. Among others, the Bullion cañons are interesting to visit. Apart from the small rattlesnakes that are frequently to be encountered there, reminding one where one is, one might think oneself to be in one of the rocky defiles of the Pyrénées: the vegetation is the same, and the waterfalls are similar. One could be forgiven for being mistaken.

Returning from my excursion, I was dying of hunger. For dinner, my hostess served me pancakes, canned pear purée, tea with milk and as much water as I wanted. What a strange, uncomforting meal! That morning, I had been given eggs, bacon that could not conceivably be eaten, and honey. The

---

[30] Like many folk remedies, this one may have allayed the pain, but it actually encouraged the distribution of the poison.

Mormons undoubtedly do all they can to accommodate you, but one can scarcely get any nourishment staying with them. . . .

The Mormon families live in these remote regions in the manner of ancient pastoral peoples. They are often isolated. All that can be seen in their houses are a few books and maps pinned to the wall of the family living room. Seldom do these solitary folk receive news from outside: there are not many letters to look forward to in the prairies. Even so, a postman makes his rounds fairly regularly in a primitive cart, with room for one passenger, but he does not often call at the door to deliver mail. In a spot known to all, on the barest outline of a road in through the grass, a small white-wood box is fastened to a post to receive letters or parcels. The Mormon who is expecting news of a friend or relative often comes from a long way off on horseback to see if this box has something addressed to him, and he returns happily to his log cabin if he has found what he was hoping to receive.

The Mormons appear to have a lively faith in their bizarre religion. They receive baptism and say that their will is to follow Biblical customs as closely as possible. Thus they defend their polygamy: "Abraham and Jacob had several wives: we believe that we have the right to do as they did." But I scarcely saw any bigamous household. The truth is, I feel, that these poor people usually have a single wife with many children. Once however, at the house of a Mormon who was the husband of two young wives, I asked one of them if she was the mother of a pretty little girl who was running about, playing among the wild flowers.

"She's our daughter," they both said together.

I did not seek to inquire any further. That reply on its own appeared to prove to me that they were not jealous of each other. Their husband assured me that they both lived like sisters who loved each other. The household appeared to be a happy one.

The driver I had when I left Panguitch, an intelligent young man but one of the strongest believers in his religion, complained bitterly of the persecutions the Mormons suffered. Although he was only twenty-eight, he had already married two wives with whom he had four children, and he was still thinking of marrying again. Along our way he pointed out to me the high mountains that hemmed the valley in.

"It was in these rocks," he said, with an air of conviction, "that God ordered Joseph Smith our prophet to go and find the gold plates on which our laws are inscribed. Joseph Smith talked many times with the Lord, and if we are to come into the Kingdom of God, we must follow his commandments." The gold plates were found by the prophet and seen, it appears, by three Mormon apostles who had copied the laws from it. Those are the laws which are currently obeyed by them. My driver did not seem to doubt the truth of this strange legend. As for the gold plates, they have disappeared long since, if ever they existed, and the Mormons still receive from their faithful one-tenth of their yearly earnings. This tribute is paid either in cash or in kind.

After my curious stay in the province of Utah and in Arizona, I can affirm that the Mormons are hospitable, kind to strangers, gentle, and fairly well-educated. Most of them take an interest in all matters of civilization. I shall always remember with pleasure their cordial, touching welcome. They received me like a brother: what more could I ask of them?

Carlo Gardini: A Little Worried the Indians Would Scalp Me

Italian physician, journalist, and impresario Carlo Gardini became interested in the United States as a youth after reading *Storia della guerra dell' Indipendenza d'America* by Carlo Botta (1766–1837), the first European history of the American Revolution. A lover of opera and ballet, he married the prima ballerina at La Scala, American dancer August Maywood (1825–76), in Milan in 1848. Following her retirement, they moved to Vienna and started a ballet school but soon divorced. Gardini returned to Italy where he met the Hungarian soprano Etelka Gerster (1855–1920), who debuted at La Fenice in Venice in 1876. They were married in 1877, the same year that Gerster appeared at Covent Garden in London. James H. Mapleson asked Gerster to perform for his Academy of Music in 1878, and she debuted that year in New York. Gardini's wife became one of the world's most heralded sopranos, and between 1878 to 1886 he spent considerable time in the U.S. She joined Mapleson's opera company's coast-to-coast tour of the U.S. in 1883, and during March and again in April the Gardinis visited Salt Lake City. In March 1883 Gerster "gave Salt Lake the greatest production of Grand Opera witnessed up to that date."[31]

Sometime during this period Gardini traveled south on his own and saw more of Utah Territory than any other nineteenth-century Italian traveler. Gardini's lifelong curiosity about Indians took him beyond Ogden and Salt Lake, the usual haunts of most visitors, aboard the Central Utah Railroad and rickety stagecoaches to the southern settlements of Provo, Milford, Cedar City, Silver Reef, Toquerville, Pipe Spring, and Kanab. Although Gardini was extremely critical of Mormonism, he was well-received by the

---
[31] Pyper, *The Romance of an Old Playhouse*, 356.

Mormons and wrote that "hospitality among the Latter Day Saints is a cordial thing." Yet he called the church a "bizarre sect" and its followers "fanatics." (His story of his encounter with a young missionary is so similar to Haussonville's account that it appears to be appropriated.)[32] Like other observers of the 1880s, he predicted the eventual demise of the religion.

Following his wife's retirement, Gardini moved to Sasso-Marconi, near Bologna. The famous Bolognese publisher Nicola Zanichelli printed Gardini's memoirs of his four visits to America, *Gli Stati Uniti—Ricordi*, in 1887. Gardini intended his two-volume account to "serve as a guide for Italian travelers and to provide scholars . . . with enticements for more exhaustive studies on particular aspects of American life" and to "dispel the silly notions" that Italians still had about it.

CARLO GARDINI, *GLI STATI UNITI—RICORDI*
[THE UNITED STATES—MEMORIES], 1:130–38, 166–71, 177–200, 204–5.

I traveled on the same car again on the railway line to Salt Lake with that sad looking and silent young man who was my companion on the sleeping car from Cheyenne to Ogden. Being curious to know more about him, I forced myself to ask him some questions.

— Excuse my curiosity. Are you perhaps also going to Salt Lake?
— Yes, sir, I live there.

Assuming that my companion was a Mormon, I asked him:
— Is it true that the Mormons call Salt Lake City the New Zion?
— Yes, because it is located where God, through a vision, ordered our prophet Brigham Young to build the New Zion.

Another traveler sitting near us, after he heard that the young man was a Mormon, very rudely interrupted our conversation and asked him how many wives he had:
— I am not yet married—he replied.
— In that case you are not a good Mormon the traveler added harshly.
— Certainly I am not yet at the point where I should be; but I am trying my best.

Hearing these humble words, I felt better disposed toward my companion because he was a true believer who was in good faith.

We then commenced an interesting conversation during which the young Mormon told me that his father had four wives and about twenty children. After my companion became an adult, he was called by the Supreme Council of the Church, to join a group of missionaries that was sent each year to Europe to make converts, especially among women.

---

[32] An English extract of Haussonville's one-day visit to Utah had appeared by 1883.

He had been sent to Norway, which seems to be one of the most favorable places to proselyte. He also traveled to England, where some people made fun of him and insulted him while he was preaching in public meetings; but he hoped that his preaching of the holy doctrines would some day bear good fruit and that many English blondes would take the road of Supreme Grace and become good Mormons.

He became sick after overextending himself in study of the doctrines and mysteries of his religion in order to demolish the objections of the protestant ministers. He therefore decided to return to his country and recover with the help of the healthy environment afforded in his native mountains. Although this decision pained his sense of religious fervor, at least he had the consolation to see again, after three years, his real mother and stepmothers, his brothers and sisters, both full and half-blooded.

When I told him that I was Italian, he said that some of his missionary companions were also sent to Italy and France; but there they had to spread the holy work with maximum secrecy, because the governments do not allow public meetings (what problems there would be if the poor Mormons risked to preach in public places in Italy!) and that he considered this restrictive prohibition to be the only reason that conversions are so rare in those countries.[33]

When the missionary perceived from my facial expression that I had little faith in his assertions, he felt a little offended and continued at a higher pitch:

The Almighty chooses his elect children from all over the world to add them to the fortunate people who enjoy his special favors that were anciently reserved to the people of Israel. We too are a bible people, and the name of our church and of its members is The Church of Jesus Christ of Latter-day Saints, which refers to the Saints of the Primitive Church that we try to imitate faithfully. As much as possible, we have kept the same organization so our church is the most similar to the Primitive Church of all other churches. We are convinced that we have been chosen by God to preach and spread to the entire world the revelation received by our first prophet, Joseph Smith, which is the fulfillment of the revelation of Christ.

Who knows whether my companion, in his Mormon fanaticism, was dreaming of converting all the people who were on the coach because apparently, as best as I could ascertain, none were latter day saints. To calm him down, I asked him another question:

— Dear sir, could you explain to me why you Mormons, who accept and believe the fundamental doctrines of Christianity, do not follow its moral doctrine, in which polygamy is condemned as a grave sin?

---

[33] In 1848 King Carlo Alberto granted the Constitution of the Kingdom of Italy, known as "Lo Statuto," but it did not grant freedom of religion and it was technically illegal to proselytize in public.

— Polygamy (he started) which was added to our doctrines by Brigham Young is absolutely not the foundation of our religion. However, polygamy was formerly authorized by the Bible; Abraham and Jacob, as you know, had many wives, and the Gospel, according to our correct interpretation, does not forbid polygamy. By taking various wives, we follow the commandment God gave to man at the beginning of the Creation: to multiply and replenish. Polygamy favors the most rapid growth of the human family. In your countries very many women waste their lives in harmful sterility, which is contrary to that precept. On the other hand, among us all the young women find a husband, and we have great faith that polygamy is very effective in protecting social morality. Also, you should know that not all Mormons are destined to have more that one wife. Plural marriage is a particular grace that God grants only to those who, by living a sinless life, are deserving of his divine favor, and therefore, to be able to marry many wives, one must obtain the permission from the presidency of our church. We all know that the *gentiles*[34] think that we conduct our lives like oriental sultans seeking erotic pleasures in a kind of harem full of favorites and slaves. But this is a big misconception: the marriage between a man and woman, sanctified by our church and that spiritually binds the man and the woman for all eternity, lasts longer in our families and it is considered more sacred than in yours. Each of our wives is lawfully wedded, lives in her own house, or at least in a separate apartment and each of them is entitled to equal affection and consideration and to the same attention and treatment. If a husband pays more attention to one of his wives, forgetting the other, this would be the greatest of mortal sins, and if such a situation is made known to our civil authorities, which according to our laws is aligned to the ecclesiastical, they would certainly condemn the culprit to a very severe punishment. Every good Mormon husband must live at equal intervals with each one of his wives, and if possible, he visits those with whom he is not living at least once a day. This is how my father behaves with his four wives, whom he dearly loves and equally respects like a husband would do with his only wife.

Since the young missionary was becoming more and more enthusiastic about praising and defending polygamy, to avoid any further escalation of his zeal, I did not tell him that I absolutely did not believe in his celebration of polygamy, especially his claim that a husband gave the same amount of affection for each of his wives. I made the observation that it seemed impossible that the various wives of a single husband could get along without frequent jealousy and quarrels and that the domestic peace would always be undermined.

— Oh no!—replied the blond missionary—our wives live in separate houses and they only think of helping their husband in his work. With

---

[34] Author footnote: "Under this name the Mormons denote all persons that are not members of their sect."

industry, and they use all their savings to furnish the house with furniture and everything else that will make their homes comfortable and attractive, so that their husband is enticed to visit them as often as possible. If competition exists, it is a kind of noble rivalry that exists among them for a good cause. I have to add, that our church teaches that the wife is not the only and exclusive principal of her husband. She has a peaceful God-given role and if she is ever tormented by jealousy, with the help of her faith she will find the way to tame this feeling. You, monogamists, boast that you have and you love only one woman; but, please, why do so many husbands have mistresses and so many wives have lovers? In our communities there is no adultery, and if it happened, the adulteress would be stoned, as written in the Law of Moses. In a few minutes you will arrive in our New Zion; you will personally witness the high level of morality and the material prosperity among our people. Unlike in the big cities, you will not find abandoned children in the streets. The Mormons take great care of their children, of their schooling and education, and I am sure that the day will come when we will be given full justice, and the world will be renewed by us Mormons.

While the fanatic apostle was preaching, with tears almost coming to his eyes, and doing all he could convert the world to Mormonism, our train arrived at the station in Salt Lake City. I saluted the missionary and thanked him for his kind invitation to be a guest at his home, which I thought was best for me to decline. I went directly to the Continental Hotel where, being very tired, I went immediately to bed because I wanted to get up early the next morning and visit the New Jerusalem at my leisure. . . .[35]

I went to visit the Tabernacle. From outside it looks like an enormous barracks, rather low and elliptical, covered by a kind of flattened cupola with no ornaments, unless one considers a series of rough brick pillars around the building as such. The Mormons are as proud as if it were the eighth wonder of the world because, according to the revelations of Brigham Young, it is similar to the temple of Solomon.[36] It is completely built with wood and inside it looks like a covered piazza in an oval shape, which corresponds to its external appearance. The walls have no decorations at all. Only an organ of gigantic proportions, with golden pipes, breaks the sad monotony of the building and records its religious character. To give the reader an idea of its vastness, I will add that 13,000 people can be accommodated comfortably when one includes the seats in the gallery.

The only praiseworthy feature in the Tabernacle is its truly surprising acoustics. Whether it is empty or full of people, and at whatever distance one sits, one can clearly hear every word of the preacher, even if he speaks with a feeble voice. This excellent resonance, which perhaps is best in the

---

[35] The Continental Hotel was located on the southwest corner of West Temple and First South.

[36] Gardini confused the temple and the tabernacle. The temple, which was under construction and not completed until 1893, was compared with Solomon's Temple, not the tabernacle.

world, is probably due to the elliptical shape of the Tabernacle, to the particular ceiling, to the specific properties of wood and especially, because the position of the preacher at the focus of the ellipsis. But a *saint* near me whispered in my ear, full of religious fervor, that this happened because God granted a miracle to Brigham Young.

On the day of my visit, the ceiling of the Tabernacle was decorated with garlands of evergreens and many kinds of artificial flowers, especially sunflowers. All the dignitaries were in front of the congregation that filled the seats of the Tabernacle and which, on special occasions, is illuminated with electrical lights.[37]

Below the stand there was a table, which represented the holy supper, with many baskets of bread and several trays with huge silver cups were filled with water. Several bishops were seated around that table and they broke the bread into small pieces for the Communion.

At two sharp, the organist started to play. The biggest pipes of the colossal instrument resounded with such a deep and unique intensity that ideally seemed to imitate the combined buzzing of all the swarms of the enormous Beehive of *Deseret*.[38]

After the musical introduction and prayers of the high ecclesiastical authorities, the choir, consisting of many men and women, started to sing a few hymns with a fascinating effect, but more theatrical and profane than ascetic.[39] This music made me think of what now happens in Italy where it is fashionable in the Catholic churches to perform the most popular and beautiful pieces of the operas. An English writer, commenting on this trend, said that the Italians did not want Satan to have a monopoly on the most seductive melodies. . . .

At the end of the meeting, after all the people left, I walked throughout the inside of the Tabernacle, but I did not find anything particularly interesting. . . . After the religious meetings, the other activity, other than farming and business affairs, to which the *saints* dedicate a large part of their leisure time, is the theatre. In the New Zion, I saw three relatively large theaters decorated with uncommon luxury.[40] The Great Prophet often attends the performances, sitting with his wives in a special box overlooking the stage. The performances are mostly plays in which, contrary to what happens in European theatres, the most scrupulous morality must be maintained from begin-

---

[37] Gardini visited the Tabernacle during LDS General Conference in April 1884.

[38] Author footnote: "Name given by the Mormons to the country of Utah."

[39] Author footnote: "The words of these religious hymns are very famous and were as they were written by the poet Eliza Snow, one of the spiritual wives of the deceased prophet."

[40] Two Salt Lake venues booked traveling companies in 1884: the Salt Lake Theatre, located on the northeast corner of State Street and First South, which was built in 1862 and razed in 1928; and the Walker Opera House, located on the south side of Second South between Main Street and West Temple, which was built in 1882 and destroyed by fire in 1891. The third theater that Gardini mentioned was the 1852 Social Hall. As he noted, performances were held in the Mormon Tabernacle.

WALKER OPERA HOUSE, SALT LAKE CITY.
Used by permission, Utah State Historical Society, all rights reserved.

ning to end. The actors are typically faithful believers, and it is not unusual to find the daughters of the Great Prophet among the actresses.[41]

When I arrived in Salt Lake City, the people were still full of enthusiasm for *Lucia* and *Sonnambula*—which had been performed a few days earlier by the Italian Opera Company of New York in the Walker Opera House—and also for the grand concert performed by the same company in the Tabernacle.[42] The two most celebrated living opera singers performed in that concert—a luxury that never happened even at *State Concerts* at Buckingham Palace in London—and it collected $15,000, or 75,000 Lire; and the Pontiff had even allowed the impresario to use the Tabernacle *gratis*.

As an example of the enthusiasm that was generated, as I was strolling

---

[41] The "great prophet" was Brigham Young's successor, John Taylor (1808–1887). Oscar Wilde met Taylor in 1882 and was taken by the beauty of one of his daughters. See Hart-Davis, *The Letters of Oscar Wilde*, 111.

[42] As manager of the "Italian Opera Company" from "Her Majesty's Theatre, London," Col. James Henry Mapleson organized three American tours that included performances in Salt Lake City. Gardini's "two most celebrated opera singers" were prima donnas Andelina Patti (1843–1919) and Gardini's wife, Etelka Gerster, who appeared as Lucia in Donizetti's *Lucia di Lammermoor* on 6 March 1884. Patti gave a concert on 2 April in the Tabernacle that included selections from Bellini's *La Sonnambula*, *I Lombardi*, and *Semiramide*. The company performed again in Salt Lake City on 26 February 1885 (*Il Trovatore*) and on 18 March 1886 (*Carmen*). See Mapleson, *The Mapleson Memoirs*. During their Salt Lake tour in March 1884, Mapleson enlisted Patti to obtain permission from John Taylor to book a concert in the Tabernacle. One writer claims she entertained the Mormon prophet on her private railway car: during dinner Patti apparently told Taylor that she was interested in joining the LDS Church. See Cone, *First Rival*, 64.

down *Main Street*, my attention was attracted by surprisingly beautiful peaches in the window of a fruit store. Since I wanted to buy one or two of them I entered the store. I was not yet inside when the owner, a thoroughbred Mormon, greeted me with a big smile and shook my hand and asked what country I was from. When I told him that I was Italian, he told me with rough but frank manners:

— Take as much fruit as you want and accept it as a gift, in exchange for the great pleasure that your fellow countrymen have given to me both in the opera and at concerts.

For a moment I remained a little undecided; but it was impossible for me to resist such a spontaneous and sincere proposition. I accepted his offer and left with a handful of fruit.

The theatre is not, however, the only recreational activity of the Mormons. I was told that, especially in *Social Hall*, they organize great dances, always preceded by a prayer given by the Prophet himself, who, like a second David, begins the dance with the Mormon *Cotillion* in which the knight always holds the hands of two women, perhaps as a symbol of polygamy....[43]

The first encounter I had in the New Jerusalem, after returning from the Great Salt Lake, was the young missionary. He asked me again, in the most kindly manner, to be his guest at his home, adding that he would be pleased if, on the same evening, I would have dinner with his family especially since he had to depart the following day for his missionary assignment in Toquerville in Southern Utah, in the *Grand Canyon District*,[44] where a few Indian bands were camping.

Since I was rather tired, perhaps because of swimming in the Great Salt Lake, I did not accept his invitation for dinner—but I proposed that I accompany him on his travels, because I was very curious to see the Redskins in their camps, and to visit the marvelous natural habitat of that area, which is still practically wild, and which is so accurately described by Mr. Clarence E. Dutton in his monographs published in Washington.[45]

At dawn the next day, the missionary—who had graciously accepted my

---

[43] Built of adobe with a shingle roof at 39 South State Street, the Social Hall was the first public building in Utah and was used for celebrations, dances, lectures, and theatrical and musical performances. Torn down in 1922, its foundations were inadvertently excavated in 1991 and are now preserved as the Social Hall Heritage Museum.

[44] Author footnote: "The Grand Canyon District, that country where the waters collect in the Grand and Marble canyons, of the Colorado River, two-thirds of which is located in northern Arizona and the rest is located in southern Utah. From the northwest to the southeast the length is approximately 300 kilometers and from the northeast to the southwest the width is approximately 200 kilometers."

[45] Soldier-scientist Clarence Edward Dutton (1841–1912) saw "pretty rough service" in the U.S. Army's Ordnance Corps during the Civil War and joined the U.S. Geographical Survey in 1875. His *Tertiary History of the Grand Cañon District* and its accompanying atlas was an artistic and geologic masterpiece. For Dutton's career, see Wallace Stegner's "Clarence Edward Dutton: Geologist and Man of Letters"; and Donald Worster's *A River Running West: The Life of John Wesley Powell*, 321–28.

proposal—and I were already sitting on a car of Central Utah Railroad, which, after twelve hours of travel (226 miles), would reach Milford.

After 48 miles on the railroad, which is constructed close to the shore of Utah Lake, we passed through Provo, a town of 5,000 people situated on a river of the same name, in which are located woolen mills that are the most important in the region between Omaha and San Francisco.

Beyond this city, the countryside begins to look dryer and more and more desert-like. Around noon we stopped at Juab,[46] a village of two or three shacks, and in the evening, after crossing the Sevier River valley, we arrived at Milford where we bedded down in a rustic cottage that the local people called a *hotel.*

My traveling companion told me about the civil laws the Mormons had vigorously adopted in Utah Territory and explained that they were taken directly from their religion, which integrated spiritual and temporal power. Being governed by divinely inspired laws, he said, the Mormon people could be nothing less than morally and materially the happiest in the world. Excessive freedom is, he added, for any people and the nation in which they reside, a much heavier burden to bear than slavery. We have universal suffrage like all the other American states, but it is subordinate to the influence of a brand of theocracy, and our Prophet leads it for the benefit of the believers.

At dusk the missionary took me to board a vehicle that was as primitive as a rustic cart. This "stagecoach" had no suspension and was shaded by two canvass covers on a wood frame that formed a kind of tent. Inside, the seats were made of wood boards with no backrests.... Because of my reaction to that primitive cart, my companion tried to comfort me with repeated assurances that in a year or two the railroad would come through, and no one wanted to invest money to purchase more modern carriages for such a short-term enterprise. I will leave my readers' imagination the shaking and tremors I suffered during that pilgrimage, in which the dust and stifling heat increased the tedium and the annoyance.

The countryside was dry with only sparse vegetation: a few willows and cottonwoods. Among the light-gray leaves of the absinthe, which was the predominant tree, were several strangely contrasting flowers of different vivid colors, many of whose names I did not know and which probably would not grow in Europe. During the whole day, we did not encounter a single human being. We traveled in the midst of a solemn calm that gave me the impression of living many, many centuries in the past, at the beginning of history. As for animals, not counting a few herds of poor-looking cows, I only noticed some rabbits rapidly fleeing from us as soon as they heard our horses and chipmunks that were scampering along the road trying to show some sign of life

---

[46] Located six miles southwest of today's Levan, Juab was terminus of the Utah Southern until 1880. Banking mogul Jay Cooke persuaded the railroad to push on to Milford and Frisco, near his Horn Silver mine.

in that deep solitude. My companion told me more than a few wolves lived in the area, but the noise of our cart scared them into hiding.

It was almost night when we arrived in Cedar City, a flourishing village of about eight-hundred people, all of them Mormons, and thanks to the connections of our missionary, we were able to lodge at the residence of the highest ecclesiastical leader [bishop], who was also the leader of the community. Hospitality is sacred among the Mormons, so you will easily understand that the whole family was occupied in preparing an excellent dinner as well as comfortable beds, which, after twelve hours on that pre-Adamic cart, was a true relief for us. The countryside surrounding Cedar City is liberally watered by abundant springs and has a totally different aspect from the one through which we had traveled. There are ample pastures, wheat fields, vegetable gardens, and fruit trees. When I was able to see all that fertile land the next morning, I thought I was in a different world, even more so because I had not forgotten that the night before, we were surrounded by beautiful and cheerful girls, all of whom were about the same age, and who were the daughters of the various wives of that bishop. In my heart I forgave polygamy since it had provided me such a sincere and cheerful welcome.

With the whole family wishing us a safe journey from the door of their home, and with the family patriarch waving his handkerchief, we again resumed our travel toward Silver Reef which would take about seven hours on that same carriage.

My companion informed me that Silver Reef had been settled about five years earlier and that it was already a respectable village of about thousand people of all races who came from everywhere because they were attracted by silver ore discovered in the area.

The landscape was changing little by little and soon the beautiful fields of Cedar City disappeared and we arrived in a sandy terrain streaked with a thousand colors which was enhanced by the intense light of the sun and that had a unique appearance. Some spots were completely barren while others were covered by curious vegetation with a strange mixture of colors. I noticed the same phenomenon on the mountainsides. As we traveled, I admired the landscape painted with a rich palette of various colors alternating in such a strange way.

At Silver Reef we changed stagecoaches, but not the situation. We resumed our travels on the same type of vehicle with the resulting shaking, dust, and heat which were not just the same but actually became worse. The only benefit we got from the shaking was the easier digestion of the indigestible food we were served at Silver Reef.

The region south of Silver Reef forms the entrance to the high rocky mountains of Utah. Their majestic peaks arise along the banks of the Virgin river with alternating stripes of a beautiful light red and a shining metal gray that looks like chain mail. One is treated to a spectacle of nature quite different from what one commonly see in the Alps of Europe.

The missionary, my only companion on the stage, knew the road very well because as a missionary of his faith *in partibus infidelium* (!) he had already been there several times, where one encounters a few *Pelli-rosse* [Redskins], among whom he had made several conversions.

He told me that the savages, who actually reside on the border of southern Utah, are of a very quiet and peaceful nature. Not only had he never personally experienced any trouble with them, he had also never heard of any other traveler who had been disturbed by them.

These Indians, like those of many other tribes, accepted a peace agreement several years ago with the *Gran Padre di Washington* ("Great Father in Washington," the name which the Indians give to the President of the United States), in which they promised that they would never harm any *faccie pallide* [pale faces], that they would live peacefully on their Reservations, and that they would receive, in exchange for these promises, their land, a certain amount of money and supplies from the government, including clothes, tobacco, tools for hunting, fishing and cooking. . . .[47]

We arrived at Toquerville, which was the end of my travels with my companion. Here we were also the guests of an excellent family that treated us very cordially, a trait that distinguishes every Mormon. Almost all the houses in Toquerville, with a population of no more than five hundred people, are surrounded by beautiful flowers and vegetable gardens, and the lots are surrounded by rows of fruit trees. The village seemed to me like a corner of the Promised Land in the middle of the desert. The missionary could not find an expert guide to accompany me to Kanab and to the Indian camp, and, since I could not get there on my own, with rare and delicate kindness he offered to accompany me and said he was happy to do so because he could easily postpone his duties for a few days.

The following morning, on a stage which was a twin to the other ones, we began our trip to Pipe Spring, which would take about 12 hours. Along the way we only encountered a few herds of cattle that were being driven by those famous cowboys that the reader learned about previously. My mentor told me that, unfortunately, the number of cows, antelope, and wild horses was diminishing every year because the soil was sandy and soft, and the animals were tearing up the grass and the roots that prevented seeds from maturing and therefore germinating. I was able to see, not very far from the road in the direction we were traveling, a range of high precipices that naturalists had named, because of their color, the Vermillion Cliffs. . . .

At 8 P.M., we arrived at Pipe Spring, a cluster of poor shacks at the bottom of the southernmost end of the Vermillion Cliffs. Travelers to southern Utah consider this place very important because of its good, fresh spring water, which is very rare in the middle of this wilderness. We slept

---

[47] Utah Indian Superintendent O. H. Irish signed a treaty with the Mormon-appointed leaders of the Southern Paiutes in 1865.

under a shaky shed, lying on a bench, wrapped in our travel blankets. Even with a bed so uncomfortable, and not be entirely confident because of the danger of wild animals, I was so tired that I slept very well until the moment it was time to recommence our trip at the first dawn.

The distance from Pipe Spring to Kanab is approximately 25 miles. The road, which is sufficiently good, first took us directly east, then passed by the spectacular and gigantic *Low-Permian Terrace*, and traveled in a northerly direction. We arrived in Kanab, which is built on the banks of a river and is protected on the other side by a large red rock formation. The inhabitants numbered approximately four hundred in the latest census and are all Mormons, like my companion. You can easily imagine how we were treated with much hospitality at the home of the leader of the community. Although Kanab is not as pretty as Cedar City and Toquerville, nonetheless all its homes have yards that are full of flowers and trees, similar to the style of all of the Mormon villages.

The first thing that my companion did was to inquire about Indian encampments. He was told that the Indians had been camped two or three hours walk from Kanab, but they had left a few days earlier for other locations along the Colorado River. But we were directed to another camp located within one day's walk in a southerly direction and next to a spring, the name of which I do not remember.

After we retained a young Indian boy as a guide, the missionary immediately began to decide what items we needed for our excursion. It was not prudent to wait even another day as the season was so late and the temperature was still exceptionally favorable. The most important items we needed were two good horses, and finding them was not an easy task. It was not the local custom to shoe horses and the animals tend suffer to injuries to their hooves. However, with the help of our lodger, we were able to obtain two excellent horses and sufficient provisions for at least three days, since there were no eating establishments or water in those mountains or any other sign of civilization. We were also able to obtain various boxes of preserved meat—in America they are better prepared than in either France or England—and coffee, tea, cognac, and some canteens full of water. We could not take any utensils to prepare food except for a small kettle in which to boil water for our coffee and tea. These were the only hot items that we were able to procure without losing time. I brought along some moccasins, a special type of shoe which are used by American explorers, that I had bought to climb Pike's Peak. But the thing that gave us the most pleasure, and proved the most useful at the same time, were two magnificent buffalo skins that the good head of household loaned to us. They are almost indispensable when one has to spend a night in the desert.

At 4:00 A.M. the next morning, we had already begun our journey and our Indian boy was setting the pace with admirable cleverness, choosing the least difficult path. We traveled past giant rocks almost stripped of any vegetation and similar to the vermilion cliffs we saw on our journey from Pipe Springs. We walked until almost midday when our guide advised us to stop near a little lake that terminated in a ravine. Pools of relatively clear water deposited from the hurricanes that commonly rage in this region were located at the end of the ravine. Nearby few parcels of ground were covered with grass where our horses could graze and drink at their leisure. During our stops in the desert, the horses were allowed to roam freely to search for their own food. We took the precaution of attaching hobbles to their front legs so they would not wander too far.

After about three hours of rest, we recommenced our journey and traveled until evening to a spring we had been told about in Kanab. Not far away we noticed a group of attentive Indians in a very narrow south-facing canyon. The camp consisted of about a dozen tents spread among a few shrubs. The tents were made from tree branches stuck into the ground and tied together at the top and draped with pieces of greasy canvas or animal skins. Fewer than two-dozen Indians lived in them. The missionary and our guide said a few good words to them, but only the men responded with a few signs denoting courtesy. The women and children looked at us firmly without uttering a word. In an effort to befriend them, we gave them a little tobacco, a few pieces of multicolored cotton, and various glass beads we had brought from Kanab for this specific purpose, but they failed to change the attitude of the savages. My gifts were accepted with such coldness that I was almost mortified. But the missionary made me realize that this way of acting is innate to the Indians who maintain their haughtiness and impassiveness as a way to deal with their extreme misery.

In the center of their camp, or rather den of animals, a fire crackled, and a kettle hung over the fire attached to a rough wooden frame made into a pyramid. We could see that at that moment the redskins—which from the darkness of the night and the light of the fire resembled fantastic shadows—were cooking their food. I reflected on memories from my boyhood travels, and they called to my mind the nomadic people, or gypsies, that one encounters in Hungary, Croatia, and Russia. But I also realized that the gypsies were very different from the savages who were now before me, and I was convinced that the Indians were original and unique among human species.

The color of their skin has an intermediate tint between the color of chocolate and red iron, which explains why they were baptized by Columbus with the name "Indians," since they are so similar to the inhabitants of India. They are of medium stature with a straight spine. Comparing them with our own race, one will recognize that the skeletal structure of the Indians is smaller and that their skulls are smaller and that their body parts and muscles are less well rounded, less solid and less robust. Their hair is very black, long, thick, and some of them wear it twisted into braids, with strips of red cotton, whereas others let their hair fall onto their shoulders. Their eyes seem to be shallow and less expressive, but of course that may depend on whether they have been continually exposed to the sun, the wind, or the smoke of their wigwams, things that without doubt influence negatively the eyelids and obscure the vibrancy of the eye. Their faces are oblong, their foreheads are low and oblique, their cheekbones jut out, their noses are large. They have large lips that lets one see their very healthy teeth even in their elderly persons, but their teeth even if they are white like black persons have, are covered with an enamel that is yellowish in color. Generally, the Indians are not blessed with beards, and those very few who do have them, destroy them by continually pulling out the hairs when they begin to grow because, among the Indians, to shave is considered something that is not acceptable but contrary to the dignity of man.

The women carry their children on their backs inside a type of basket attached to their shoulders. They appeared to be very ugly in the face and body, perhaps in consequence of being morally brutalized by the way they live and because they are condemned by their own religion, which teaches that the men must hunt while the women must toil—the two occupations that are the most difficult and undesirable. Their clothing, consisting of a small shirt of printed material, is dirty and half torn, and made me feel sorry for them. The men were also wearing poor clothing. If I remember well, they wore a pair of pants and a short shirt of a designed material, and a little hat similar to the "fez" of the Turks. They painted their cheeks, and around their eyes, with red dots and stripes. Although I did not understand a word they were saying to the missionary, I believed they were talking about religion and that some of them were Mormons because I heard them pronouncing with reverence the names of Enoch and of Smith.

The campsite that the guide and the missionary selected was nice and grassy, had a gently slanted slope with a few old trees, and was not too far from the Indian camp. The guide gathered a pile of dead branches and started a fire, which he kept illuminated through the night. After we merrily ate dinner and had a cup of excellent homemade coffee, we spread our wonderful buffalo skins on the grass and lay down to take some rest. It was the first time in my life that the walls of my bedroom were strange looking mountains and the ceiling was a sky with stars that seemed to shine more brightly than anywhere else. The view was sublime and the desert was silent, but I could not sleep, even though the missionary had reassured me several times, but I was a little worried the Indians would scalp me.

At dawn we got up and, while the guide was preparing the horses, we had a little breakfast and coffee. I decided to return right away to Kanab because I regretted having taken advantage of the courtesy of my companion. But I regretted the fact that I could not continue my trip up to the Grand Canyon district that is Totoweep, in the Uinkaret-Plateau, the Kaibab Plateau, as well as Marble Canyon. I postponed that adventure until the next year.

Chapter 8

"THE MANY SCANDINAVIANS WHO LIVE IN UTAH"
Northern Literary Lights in the Mormon West

The first Scandinavians who settled in Utah were Norwegians who joined the LDS church in Illinois beginning in 1842. When Brigham Young sent missionaries for the first time to continental Europe in October 1849, he chose apostle Erastus Snow to go to Denmark. William Mulder has noted that from 1850 to 1905 some thirty thousand Scandinavians emigrated to Utah as Mormon converts.[1] Scandinavians soon rivaled the number of British converts in Utah, and this exodus from Denmark, Sweden, and Norway produced future church leaders Anthon H. Lund (1844–1921), John Widtsoe (1872–1952), historian Andreas Jensen (1850–1941), artist C. C. A. Christensen (1832–1912), and many farmers and artisans.

Scandinavian converts aroused the curiosity, distrust, and anxiety of novelists and travelers; some even suggested that Mormon missionaries targeted Danish women "as fresh recruits" for polygamy. The Danes and Swedes obtained much of their information about Utah and the Mormons from translations of W. G. Marshall, John W. Gunnison, Maria Ward, William Chandler, and William Hepworth Dixon.[2] One bookseller in Stockholm assured this editor that W. G. Marshall's *Genom Amerika* is still the "classic" Swedish travel account on Utah and the Mormons, even though it was written by an Englishman. Another bookseller claimed that

---

[1] Mulder, *Homeward to Zion*, vii. Mulder's is the best account of the Scandinavian mission and the immigration to Utah. Concerning Scandinavian immigration to Utah, see Schmidt, *Oh, Du Zion I Vest*. It is available only in Danish. Concerning Scandinavian immigration to the United States, see Dorothy B. Skårdal, *The Divided Heart*. [2] Mulder, *Homeward to Zion*, 68–69.

the best Swedish accounts were written by Arthur Conan Doyle, and he then produced Swedish translations of *A Study in Scarlet* and *Our Second American Adventure*. Although Scandinavians were surely influenced by American and British writers, they were also able to read the accounts of northern literary lights who had visited Utah. Representative of these writings are the observations of Danish writer Vilhelm Kristian Sigurd Topsöe; Swedish newspaperman and writer Jonas Jonsson Stadling; Swedish author, legislator, and religious instructor Paul Peter Waldenström; and Danish editor, journalist, and author Paulus Henrik Cavling.

Vilhelm Kristian Sigurd Topsöe: The Era of Mormonism is Irrecoverably Over

Danish author Vilhelm Kristian Sigurd Topsöe (1840–1881) received a Bachelor of Laws degree in 1865 and began his literary career composing satirical sketches for the newspaper *Dagbladet*. He went on to write political pamphlets and entertaining travel accounts of Switzerland, France, and America. Topsöe became editor of *Dagbladet* in 1872 and formed a journalists' union. He was in his early thirties when he first traveled to North America. After arriving in New York and spending time in the city, he visited Philadelphia, Washington (where he had an audience with President Ulysses S. Grant), Chicago, Louisville, and Omaha, where he took the Union Pacific Railroad to Ogden. From Ogden he made a short trip to Salt Lake City. After arriving at the Utah Central Railroad station, Topsöe was taken to the Townsend House. While in Salt Lake he met the editor of *The Salt Lake Tribune* ("the heathen newspaper"), probably Fred T. Perris (1837–1916), who was then the newspaper's business manager. The account of his visit to the United States, which includes more than thirty pages about Utah and the Mormons with six illustrations, was published in Stockholm in 1874. Topsöe spent his last years writing novels concerning the spiritual aspects of modern times.

Vilhelm Topsöe, *Från Amerika* [From America],
320–21, 323–25, 327–30, 335–36, 340, 344–45, 349, 352.
Translated from Danish into Swedish by O. Strandberg.
English translation by Teodor Södergren Berg.

How strange it feels to step onto a train belonging to Brigham Young and find it looking much too ordinary to take a person to that city which seems to lie beyond the inhabited world. As a matter of fact, this train, with its locomotive and cars, baggage agents and conductors, looks just like trains and people in all the other places of America, and this business of buying a ticket in the little wooden building that serves as station isn't at all biblical. ... Curious, we try to catch sight of the city ... this friendly, alluring place called Salt Lake City. ...

The train stops and we step out onto a sandy place in front of the station. Even here, quite as though we were in heathendom, omnibusses from the hotels stand waiting. One of these, "Townsend House," belongs, we discover, to a Mormon. Naturally, we choose it. We rattle off down some streets—that is, broad sandy ways between leafy gardens in which dwellings are hidden— and catch a glimpse of the tabernacle in the distance, another glimpse of a wall which surrounds the houses of Mormon dignitaries, then halt in front of a friendly verandah which looks exactly as though it belongs to a large private house; this is the Townsend House, and we are among Mormons. ...

The countryside around is abundantly fruitful and in all respects well cultivated, and the city itself presents an extraordinarily friendly appearance. There are busy business streets with fair-sized stone houses and large shops, but most of the city consists of small isolated houses half hidden in green yards. Streets are very wide, 130 feet, and, so far as I remember, planted with beautiful trees, and—giving the city a remarkable impression—they are margined with small, flowing, clear creeks; a little river has been diverted into a web of rivulets which ripple and murmur along under avenues of shady acacias, spreading freshness and coolness on all sides and providing for the whole city the necessary water for sluicing and rinsing streets and paths. The streets are unpaved, and, on the whole, the city has a certain rural stamp. You may have whatever slight sympathy with Mormons as you please; still you'd have to say there's something friendly, you could almost say cozy, permeating everything.

The basic notion behind this city, if one may use such an expression, is to let the streets divide land into four-cornered blocks of ten acres, each block with eight lots of 1¼ acres, each lot assigned to a household. In the business district and in the poorer quarters, however, these lots are again divided into smaller parcels.

Houses that in the beginning were built of simple materials are now almost all built of stone. For the most part, they are small, one- or two-story. Larger ones are usually spread out in length and have separate entrances. However, one can also come across quite spacious private residences. Not to talk of Brigham Young's house, which occupies an entire block, there's also the house of Daniel Wells, Salt Lake City's mayor and Lieutenant General of the Mormon Legion, a lovely home among those of the upper priesthood. The house from which Apostle George Q. Cannon prints and publishes his newspaper *Deseret News* is also a good-sized establishment.

The yards are lovely, carefully maintained, closely planted, and generally the house stands in the middle, concealed by trees and shrubbery. So it happens that you can see less of Mormon domestic life than you would like. In evenings, when house lamps are lit and doors and windows stand open, you can catch a glimpse of figures inside as you wander about the calm, quiet, and dark streets. Evenings are apparently leisure time. The men sit surrounded by wives and children. Now and then you see people talking together, sometimes making music, but, whether pure chance or not, nowhere do you see anyone sitting and reading.

The most important business street, "Main Street," is long and wide. It is rather lively on the streets, and the public that busy themselves there have an odd character. You can see many "city-clad" people, but you also meet many country folk who fully look the simple life they lead. You don't know exactly why—maybe you just know—but business seems to a large degree to still have the character of a trading post: everything looks as though business is carried on in an entirely different manner than in any other town you've visited. Many of those familiar wagons covered with linen tents standing in the street in front of a shop have brought produce to trade for clothing and tools.

The large Mormon stores are set up with the same system as in the provincial towns of Scandinavia: one can buy everything from *eau de Cologne* to iron bars. Those genuinely Mormon shops have an odd sign which, for the above-mentioned cooperative, looks like this:

This eye with its inscription recurs on other signs, and this eye—"bull's eye," as the heathens call it—watches everywhere in the city. The fact is, in 1868 a conference issued the decision that all good Mormons who were merchants, manufacturers, or handicraftsmen of any sort whatsoever would put up this sign on their buildings in a prominent place to show that they were pure of faith. Furthermore, Mormons were instructed not to do business with anyone not having this sign.

This actually reached the point where many "gentiles" were compelled to leave the Territory because they couldn't carry on a trade. A few stayed, and among them was a bold man named Trumbo, who ordered up a sign to counter the Mormon one. After referring to a place in the Bible that talks about monogamy, it had this caption: "I AM THE LORD THY GOD: TRUMBO'S CREED."

This sign, however, didn't last long. After a day's lapse, during which people stared at it in dumb astonishment, it was torn down the next morning by a crowd of the young faithful and dragged through the streets with scorn and derision. Since that time there hasn't appeared any rebellious signs. . . .[3]

Now there is being built a new, magnificent temple that will supersede the tabernacle. This central building will be 100 feet high; above this will rise towers, three at each end of which the middle one will be 200 feet high. They haven't gotten any further than the foundation, and you don't get the impression that they are working along with any particular zeal, although there was quite a bit of zeal to collect the money for the project. The building will be constructed of granite, is reckoned to cost 3 million dollars, and it will certainly, if it is ever finished, become one of America's most beautiful buildings. On the other hand, there is certainly no building whose future prospects are as uncertain as this one's. . . .

To attain that freedom between the sexes, which so many souls in this century secretly sigh for and have sighed for, there come Romanesque, materialistic, God-renouncing people of the south to establish a new religion among the Gothic-Germanic people.

A glance at the multiple sects in America shows how many there are whose secret pulse and driving force is to freely exercise fleshly lusts. Mormonism, even though it's unclear whether it had this tendency at the beginning, is one of these sects. The teaching of polygamy is an odd adjunct to modern socialism's open marriage. Significant also is the sympathy with which socialist newspapers watch Mormonism in far-off America and report letters and anecdotes from Salt Lake City. People feel a peculiar sympathy for these folks with their hard, strict, everything-regulated economic system and their new sensual morality.

Mormonism arose in America among a slew of attempts to put into practice ideas of the older socialism. Here were two such attempts: the one by thieves who carried out Owen's plans, to which he himself gave the impulse,

---

[3] Topsöe lifted this tale directly from a guidebook. Auctioneer and merchant John K. Trumbo reportedly put up the sign on 26 February 1869. "All day wandering crowds of people of all classes, little and big, hovered about the premises, and many opinions were expressed as to the propriety of the sign, and whether it would be allowed to remain by the Mormons; but at about 7 o'clock in the evening the problem was solved, by a charge made by several young Mormons, who, with ladders climbed upon the building and secured ropes upon the sign, while the crowd below tore it down, and dragged it through the streets, dashing it to pieces." See Dadd, *Great Trans-Continental Railroad Guide*, 101. Trumbo, a friend of Mark Twain, had married a Mormon woman in Carson Valley, and his son Isaac was instrumental in securing statehood for Utah.

and the other by bandits who pushed through Fourier's beautiful theories.[4] Mormonism, whose earlier history, by the way, is shrouded in deep darkness, is contemporary with the first attempt. Joseph Smith could, thanks to angel Moroni's revelations, busy himself with not only a new temporal order but also with a new religion, whose prophet was himself. Quite rapidly he acquired followers, and, while Owen's "harmony" dissolved into utter disharmony, Smith's young society gained strength. The many persecutions to which Mormons were subjected from the beginning also contributed quite a bit. . . .

It was a motley, patched-together society that took upon themselves the building of Utah. Diligence was needed, and diligent they were. No loafer to be found here! It is quite surprising to talk with people here and to hear them tell of the incomparably harder work they must undertake here than in the land they left. The highest men in the church don't have enough with performing the duties of office as prophet and apostle but they must engage in work at the mill—an especially holy deed—farm work, management of a book press, publication of a newspaper, etc. It's also part of higher church duties to see to it that people can work and that they carry out their work in a satisfactory manner. . . .

Most Mormons, both men and women, believe without doubt that in polygamy they fulfill their religious duty, but the practice of this doubtlessly falls more lightly upon men than upon women. . . . Naturally enough, men find it easy in such a situation to regard their wives as merely objects for their lust and as servants. Sermons constantly preach submissiveness and obedience as women's first duty. Their husband is only their master.

That wives truly feel dejected and unhappy, even though they don't right out say so to strangers nor run away in droves to mountain camps of Union troops, is easy to discern through the Mormons' own testimony. It speaks worlds about these poor women's plight that it is so necessary to constantly inculcate upon them their duty to obey, and in Young's own sermons there is to be found many such remarks: "It is often the case that women say they are unhappy, and one can hear men declare, 'My wife, though she's the most splendid woman, has not had a happy day since I took my second wife.'". . .

The first generation of Mormon young people has now grown up, but it is almost unanimously said that they don't seem very eager for polygamy. However, it's quite hard to escape this net. George Cannon, one of the most prominent men in Utah, assured the author during a discussion of these matters that he had raised all his children to see that they would be able to live even among heathens as faithful Mormons; but one can report a great many examples among less prominent families, at any rate, where daughters

---

[4] Robert Owen (1771–1837) was founder of a socialist community in New Harmony, Indiana. Charles Fourier (1772–1837) was a French socialist who advocated small cooperative communities.

are lectured about being a sole wife to a "gentile" before becoming a fractional wife to a Saint. . . .

Since the opening of the Pacific railroad one doesn't hear anymore of those acts of outrageous violence that used to occur frequently. Slowly but surely the heathens stream in. Now with its authority so close to Utah's gates, even if the Union had decided not to intervene, Mormonism undoubtedly would have gradually split from within. Since Summer 1871 the heathens have lived secure and worry free and become more numerous day by day. . . . The era of Mormonism is irrecoverably over. It has a perhaps gradual but for sure relentless enemy in the Pacific railroad.

Jonas Jonsson Stadling:
Mormons Pay for Theatre Tickets with Watermelons

Swedish newspaperman and writer Jonas Jonsson Stadling (1847–1935) studied at Uppsala University and in Switzerland and England. From 1880 to 1883 he made an extended journey through North America that included a short sojourn in Utah. Like most Scandinavian travelers he arrived in New York and traveled to New England. But Stadling visited Iowa, Missouri, Kansas, Colorado, New Mexico, California, Oregon, and Washington before visiting Utah. He also toured up the Mississippi and visited Minneapolis and St. Paul in Minnesota, as well as the states of Wisconsin, Michigan, and Ohio and the cities of Baltimore and Washington, before returning to Sweden. In Utah he visited not only Salt Lake but also the Mormon settlement that had grown up around the abandoned army camp at Camp Floyd as well as Tooele. On his return to Sweden, Stadling lectured and wrote for a newspaper in the Swedish Free Church movement, an evangelical revival movement to free churches from state control and the established Lutheran church. During the famine of 1892 he traveled to Russia and represented an American philanthropist in supporting Leo Tolstoy's relief activities, which he chronicled in *In Hungry Russia*. Tolstoy's son claimed that his father often expressed surprise that such an excellent writer as Stadling was not better appreciated in his own country. As a newspaper correspondent he accompanied Salomon August Andrée's 1897 arctic expedition to Spitzbergen. The following spring Stadling crossed northern Siberia by reindeer sled and dog team and went up the coast in an open boat in a fruitless attempt to find Andrée's ill-fated balloon. Stadling's long life was filled with writing and philanthropic activities.

J. Stadling, *Genom den Stora Vestern* [Through the Great West], 228, 232–33, 242–43, 251, 254, 256, 257.
Translated by Teodor Södergren Berg.

It was already dark when we reached our destination. The first sight to meet my eyes upon arrival to Zion's city was a group of half-naked Indians sitting around a campfire near the train station with long black hair hanging down over their faces. Some of them had tattooed their bodies, which presented an appearance as artistic as those found on the cover of certain illustrated journals. . . .

A Bierstadt should depict these lantern slides.[5] He should sit at the window of my hotel room on the top floor while the sun goes down behind the Oquirrh Mountains: turning his gaze toward the Wasatch Mountains in the east, at the foot of which lies Salt Lake City with its yards of fruit trees and parks, he would see the changing colors and with his artistic eye follow those long shadows as they quietly slip up the slopes to the foot of the mountains, then he would behold the dark hues climb higher and higher among the picturesque cliffs until they reach the snow-covered tops and suddenly change into sunlight, which lingers a moment then disappears. . . .

One day a Swedish elder introduced me to the twelve apostles and "the prophet, seer, and revelator" John Taylor at an appointed time in his office, the same once used by Brigham Young. . . . This room with its low ceiling was humble but quite tastefully furnished. Conversation with the prophet and apostles lasted about twenty minutes and was very cordial. After we talked about the weather and wind and his questions on how I liked Utah and Salt Lake City, the prophet spoke highly of the many Scandinavians who live in Utah—between thirty and forty thousand—and hastened to add as an explanation of their splendid qualities: "But this isn't strange either, for the Lord is at work now to make a selection among the heathen folk and to lead his people to Zion. What's more, it lies in the nature of things that only the best characters feel deepest the yoke of European tyranny and have the courage to shake it off and respond to the gospel." I asked him whether polygamy is much practiced by the Scandinavians, to which after a few moments of silence he answered: "Not everyone strives equally after the glory of heaven." I got a more favorable impression than I expected of this 70-year-old prophet, whose hair was sprinkled with plenty of snow. He has gone through most of the persecutions to which Mormons have been exposed right from the beginning of their history. He was one of the twelve whom "the Lord" called to be "apostles" in 1841 [1838]; he was in

---

[5] German-born artist Albert Bierstadt (1830–1902) immigrated to America as a child but returned to Düsseldorf to study painting. He accompanied the Pacific Wagon Road survey and painted a number of classic western landscapes. For Bierstadt's western experience, see Houston and Houston, "The 1859 Lander Expedition Revisited," 50–71.

jail with Joseph Smith in Carthage when Smith was shot, and on this and other occasions he received various bullets—one struck his pocket watch, which miraculously saved his life—and he has always been an outstanding man among the Saints, even at times showing an uncommon degree of independence toward the demands of Brigham Young. He has great willpower and is often fierce in his attacks on "the heathens," for which one can almost excuse him when one stops to think that his body still carries three bullets received from "heathens" that plague him off and on. One would scarcely believe that this grave old man would, of all things, keep a half dozen young wives, but so he does; nonetheless, while on a mission to France some years ago, he publicly swore that polygamy was not practiced in Utah—although he himself at the time had five wives![6]

One of the leading Mormons with whom I had a long conversation said that society in our day tends toward polygamy, but only the Mormon church has regulated this tendency on the grounds of divine authority. Outside the Mormon church, said he, people hypocritically embrace monogamy while actually practicing polygamy—that's the only difference. I suggested that, nevertheless, there is a difference between a committed offence recognized as such and an offence turned into a virtue.

I visited the Tithing House and saw how the Saints come with heavy loads of seed, vegetables, fruit, meat, cheese and butter, etc., to "sacrifice a tenth to the Lord's altar." I visited the Mormon shops belonging to Zion's Cooperative Mercantile Institution and there saw Mormons exchange their produce for merchants' wares; yes, I even saw Mormons pay for theatre tickets with watermelons and butter. Mormon shops belonging to a cooperative whose establishment is through a special vision from "the Lord" have over their entrance this motto: "Holiness to the Lord." Every Mormon is strictly forbidden to do business with "the heathens." Still, a couple of "fallen off" Mormon merchants, Walker and Brothers, have kept afloat and even grown rich, though mostly through mining operations....

Mormons are already split into two classes: the bigots and the liberals. The former hold vigorously to polygamy and would drive "the heathens" out of the Territory if they could. Their influence is diminishing, while the liberals' are increasing. Superstition and animal lust are allies of the former; railroad, newspaper, and education are on the side of the latter....

Likewise, "the heathens" can be divided into two classes: troublemakers who spread all sorts of preposterous rumors about Mormons and would make themselves important in order to achieve position, and those who mind their own business and exercise a peaceful influence on their neighbors.

---

[6] See Taylor, *Three Nights' Public Discussion*, 8–9.

But now it is time to leave Mormon theology to continue the journey. The train rushes past the foothills of the Oquirrh Mountains and soon we find ourselves in sight of the pretty little town Tooele. Tooele doesn't resemble those monotonous American towns with their stereotypical straight streets and blocks but consists of unregulated and picturesque clusters of houses with gardens and parks. I dare not think of these fruit trees and vines, loaded with apples, pears, peaches, and grapes, for then I am overcome with a longing for Zion! I don't wonder that many become Mormon just to "sit under their own grape arbor and fig tree" and enjoy such delicious peaches and grapes as grow there. I was invited to as much fruit and many meals as I could eat, and I would be ungrateful and unfair if I said anything but good about the hospitable, peaceful, and happy Mormons in charming little Tooele. . . .

The Mormon bishop Carter is everything in the Mormon village of Camp Floyd. He watches over people's bodily and spiritual interests, gives advice, judges disputes, and heals the sick through prayer and the laying on of hands, which generally seems to cure as well as the doctor's concoctions of poisons. But they say the good bishop has learned that "laying on of hands" doesn't work so well with himself. He has always had only one wife; but, not long ago, it was revealed to him that he should take yet another. However, Mrs. Carter didn't see the angel who brought her husband this message, the angel having carefully avoided her. One lovely day the bishop went off to Salt Lake City "on business" and returned at evening with a second wife. It was then that the bishop experienced a mighty laying on of hands, and Mrs. Carter number 2 felt a mighty laying on of broom. The feminine muscle-and-broom Christianity triumphed over divine revelation and "spiritual sanction," but the difficulties were resolved so that the bishop finally married Mrs. Carter number 2—to another man.

I was introduced to a man of 93 who was father to sixty children, of whom the oldest was 75 and the youngest 67. The frail old man now waited for the bountiful rewards of his having contributed so much to the "increase of the earthly realm" and to the number of blessed souls in Mormon heaven. Still, I hadn't the satisfaction of seeing this venerable patriarch play with his little lads or let them "ride horsey" on papa's knee. The old fellow told me to not let myself be fooled by the current notion that God is a spirit, for if that were the case how could man be created in his image? No, God goes on two legs, sees through two eyes, smells through his nose, and otherwise behaves himself like a man with a natural body. . . . God the Father stands in the same relationship to other persons in the Godhead as an old man does to his sons.

Paul Peter Waldenström: Here Comes Satan!

Swedish author, legislator, and religious instructor Paul Peter Waldenström (1838–1917) received his doctorate of philosophy from Uppsala University in 1863 and was ordained a minister of the Lutheran Church in 1864. He played a leading role in the growing split between the state church and its pietistic faction, the Mission Friends. Waldenström edited the weekly *Pietisten* for nearly fifty years, and he is still considered one of Sweden's greatest evangelical preachers. Waldenström made three trips to North America. In 1889 he arrived in New York and made a cross-country journey that included Philadelphia, Boston, Chicago, Des Moines, Omaha, Topeka, Denver, Salt Lake City, and San Francisco. He also journeyed to visit Scandinavian immigrants in Minnesota.

In Utah he made some surprising observations concerning persecution and the impossibility of affording anyone "absolute religious freedom," in the context of the United States government's treatment of Mormons because of their belief in and practice of polygamy. According the Waldenström, "full-blown religious freedom will exist only when there are no laws to hinder people in the practice of their beliefs." As early as 1910, he argued for the separation of church and state in Sweden. As an influential member of parliament, he introduced the first bill calling for universal suffrage.

P. Waldenström, *Genom Norra Amerikas Förenta Stater* [Through North America's United States], 508–9, 513–15, 517–18.
Translated by Teodor Södergren Berg.

[In the tabernacle] . . . after the water was blessed it was passed around in large silver pitchers in the same way the breadbasket went from pew to pew, from person to person. As the sharing began, the bishop again strode up to his pulpit and continued his sermon. . . . About the same time the water pitchers finished their rounds, the bishop finished his sermon. A song followed from the choir, accompanied by organ, violin, and cornet. After this came a prayer and benediction and a song from the congregation. The whole service took about 1¾ hours. I can hardly describe the impression all this made upon me. If it could have made a difference, I would have stood up and shouted out loud. But how would that have helped? May God through his mercy open those blind eyes!

During the service I took three photographs of the congregation and preacher. Those Mormons sitting nearest gave me grim looks. Out on the street we stood awhile and watched the people.

"Look, here comes Satan!" said one of my friends. He pointed to a lanky, thin gentleman who looked to me to be about 60 years old. I'll get a shot of that rascal, I thought; I've never seen his likes before. I raised my camera and took a picture.

But who was this Satan? He was a Mormon belonging to the priesthood. At a marriage betrothal in Utah, the story of Creation and The Fall is theatrically performed. So, naturally, there also has to be the temptation through which Satan brought about The Fall of Man, and the man who usually represents Satan on these occasions was the gray-clad gentleman....

Mormons naturally consider themselves persecuted. And persecuted they really are. That can't be denied. I pointed out for my friends how impossible it is for a country to have absolute religious freedom. As a matter of fact, it's not to be found anywhere.

"That America doesn't at all have it," I said, "can be seen in the way Mormons are treated."

"Yes," they answered, "that's clear, but Mormons are persecuted not for their beliefs but for the way they behave toward the law."

"Yes, you're right," I answered in turn. "But that's just it. People everywhere are not persecuted for what they believe but for *acting* in accordance with beliefs conflicting with the law. But a full-blown religious freedom will exist only when *there are no laws* to hinder people in the practice of their beliefs."

"No," they replied, "here it's not merely a question of *practicing a belief* but of an *immoral lifestyle*. And no law can allow that."

"Well, sure," I rejoined, "but what is immoral or moral the Mormons, as do we, wish to determine from their Holy Scripture. When they see the Old Testament considering it a natural thing to have many wives, they wish to follow the example of those old holy patriarchs, and they don't for a moment admit there's anything immoral about it. However one turns the matter over, the Mormons are subject to persecution from the State. What do you think? If the State took upon itself to forbid child baptism under pain of punishment but Lutherans nevertheless continued to baptize their small children, they would naturally be persecuted by the authorities. But think if someone then said: 'Complete religious freedom *prevails* here. You see, these baptizers of children are not persecuted for their religious belief but for acting in accordance with beliefs conflicting with the law.' What should one make of such talk?"

Such reasoning might seem absurd to many, but if one looks at it seriously it becomes an important matter, for if one accepts the premise that the State is entitled to establish laws which hinder certain citizens in the exercise of their religious beliefs and also, because of acting upon those beliefs, exclude them from their civil rights and lay upon them civil punishment,[7] then one has surrendered the principle of complete religious freedom. Then the question becomes only this: *How long* can the State have the right to restrict religious freedom? Meanwhile, one can no longer talk about countries that lack religious freedom and countries that have religious freedom but only of countries where religious freedom is more or less restricted.

Paulus Henrik Cavling: You Have Seen God's Face

Danish editor, journalist, and author Paulus Henrik Cavling (1858–1933) traveled to the United States in 1895. He divided his itinerary into the East, the West, the South, and Scandinavian settlements. In the East he visited New York City, Washington, and Niagara Falls. In the West he visited Chicago, Omaha, Salt Lake City, and San Francisco. In the South he went to Atlanta and Key West. He also visited Scandinavians in Wisconsin, Illinois, Iowa, Minnesota, South Dakota, and North Dakota. When he arrived at the Utah Central railway depot (300 West between North Temple and South Temple) in Salt Lake he met O. P. Thomasson, the clerk of the Utah Central Railroad, who showed him around the city and invited the Danish novelist to stay with his family during his first evening in Salt Lake. When he returned to Denmark he published *Fra Amerika*. In it he included a short history of Mormons in Denmark, including the account of John Ahmanson. Although he visited after the Manifesto of 1890, Cavling confirmed that the practice of polygamy continued, was very critical, in a sectarian way, of its practice, and seemed curious that some of his fellow Scandinavians were attracted to it. After the turn of the century Cavling was a leader in press reforms that resulted in the modernization of newspaper reporting in Denmark.

> Henrik Cavling, *Fra Amerika* [From America], 468–71, 477–78.
> Translated from Danish into Swedish by Petrus Hedberg.
> English Translation by Teodor Södergren Berg.

The train rushed down the Utah valley through rich pastures and yellow acres. Farmers, who quickly looked up from their work in the fields and gazed after us, reminded me by their looks of the country folk back home. They were fair-haired and most certainly had blue eyes. The land was unusually well cultivated, and nowhere could be seen the weedy patches and aban-

---

[7] Author footnote: It is the Mormons' polygamy that prevents Utah from gaining statehood in the Union, although it has a population that has long since exceeded the number required to elevate a Territory into statehood.

doned strips of ground that characterize so much of the American landscape. If the valley had not been bordered on both sides by mountain ranges, one could believe that he was somewhere in Skåne.[8] One can find here in this Utah valley all the green, brilliant luxuriance that is so characteristic of the region around Öresund. . . .[9]

A golden shower of evening sunrays fanned out over the valley as I wandered up to Zion's city. Church bells ushered in peace and rest for the Saints, and I began to think about how many thousands of Scandinavia's sons and daughters had wandered this way under other circumstances. Back home we have been quite harsh toward these countrymen of ours, who after all are hardly to be reckoned among the worst. Indeed, what else drove them out here but a longing that, sometime or other, probably grips every single person, a longing to find peace on earth?

I met a little boy, greeted him, and asked the name of the river that ran along here. "It's called the River Jordan," said the boy. "And that mountain there?" "Mount Sinai." I heard a hymn being sung from a house. A cloud scattered above the peaks and for some minutes the whole landscape lay bathed in a heavenly light. The biblical names stood in full harmony with the surroundings.

Then I headed for the city, which didn't seem to have any other distinction to offer than that it is cleaner and more rustic than other American cities. Streets are beautiful and well cared for, and the sidewalks are broad and separated from the carriage roadways by a row of blooming acacias and broad stone gutters where rivulets of water from the mountains purl. On all of Salt Lake City's streets there are these watercourses, and one continually hears the lively purling sound. In the stillness of the night it's like a whispered conversation.

The houses I walked past were small villas surrounded by well-tended yards. Lamplight cast its glow over the flowerbeds and shrubbery and laid a quiet mood of peace and comfort over the scene. But soon these rural environs gave way to the actual city. I took off down Main Street, Salt Lake City's pulsing artery, where electric streetcars rushed and elegant boutiques, newspaper offices, and hotels stood entirely like other cities of the West.

My first evening in Salt Lake City I spent with one of the elders, a man named O. Thomasson, who, remarkably enough, had three wives who were sisters. Thomasson lived together with his oldest wife in a house of ten or twelve rooms; the two other wives lived in a couple smaller houses near the main house. The Edmunds Act, which passed in 1882, forbade polygamy, and the law of 1887 made wives legal witnesses in cases concerning polygamy.

---

[8] Skåne is Sweden's most southwest province, comprised of plains and rolling farm land.
[9] Öresund is the name of the sound located between Skåne and Denmark.

Here was aimed a deathblow against divine marriage. Mormons who had wedded several wives, and they did so as well as those among them who were the wealthiest, were now forced to choose between separating from their concubines or receiving a stiff prison sentence. For this reason they had to make personal arrangements such as those my host now had.

It was a circumvention of the law but a circumvention hard to get at. The fact is, to get a Mormon convicted of polygamy required witnesses to testify that he had violated the marriage contract with his first wife. The sheriff of Salt Lake City, who badly wished to acquire such witnesses, had now set up a corps of police spies who by night sneaked around the city, creeping over courtyards and hiding in backyards where they could watch entrances, especially to small buildings, and catch these lighthearted Mormons red-handed. In vain these hard-pressed, sincere men tried to defend themselves with the help of bloodhounds and high palings—the spies found their ways anyway, and during the years 1887 to 1890 there hardly passed a single night without a Mormon being led to jail, usually in the depths of undress. Tumultuous scenes sometimes turned into comic surprises, as when the spies one night surprised the sheriff himself in a Mormon bed.

But the Edmunds Act with its later addendum caused polygamy almost immediately to cease. Polygamy had never been popular with the generation following Brigham Young, and even without the Edmunds Act it would not have lasted very far into our time. Those Mormons who still have plural wives are all older men. If one expects to see in Salt Lake City a picture of life's pleasure through sex, it's time to abandon that illusion. Polygamy is already less practiced in its homeland than in San Francisco and New York....

If you would like to enjoy Salt Lake's peculiar beauty undisturbed, you may sit in a boat and sail out to one of the nine islands that stick above the water surface in various directions. Each offers an enchanting view away to the snow white peaks that stand around the lake and to the blue skies vaulted above these snowy mountains. Remarkably, you can notice at the same time the scent of trees from the forests and the salt-tasting breeze from the lake. It is as though one were making a trip through the Alps while out on the ocean.

Unforgettable is the impression you get when early in the morning standing on a mountain peak you let your glance glide away over the sky that lies before the eyes like a billowing ocean. The atmosphere is so pure and blue, so high and clear, that you breathe freely and feel yourself boundlessly elevated above all of life's petty problems. For a long time your thoughts roam about through this measureless space. You still stand there on high even while climbing down, and wake only at the first sight of smoking chimneys, people, and locomotives. Still, all that day, and for many days thereafter, your eyes have a special light. You have seen God's face.

Chapter 9

"BITTER, SALT, AND HOPELESS"
The Last Struggle for Statehood,
1878–96

When Brigham Young died in 1877, there was widespread belief in many quarters of the world that without his iron fist Mormonism could not survive.[1] Thereafter the United States government became more aggressive in its efforts to eradicate polygamy, especially after 1879 when the Supreme Court ruled in *United States v. Reynolds* that the Morrill Act, which made bigamy illegal, was constitutional. Following *Reynolds* the United States passed the Edmunds Act in 1882, which strengthened the ability of federal officials to prosecute polygamists, and prevented them, or those who believed in polygamy, from voting, serving on juries, and holding public office.

But Young's successors were still in a fighting mood. On the Fourth of July 1885 Mormon leaders denounced the federal government and flew the American flag at half-staff.[2] Two years later Congress passed the Edmunds-Tucker Act, which disenfranchised female voters, abolished spousal immunity, eliminated the Perpetual Emigrating Fund, disincorporated the LDS church, and authorized the escheatment of most church property.[3] Eventu-

---

[1] Glazier, *Peculiarities of American Cities*, 447. "The people who founded [Utah], together with the faith to which they cling, should disappear from the face of the earth and be forgotten, like the lost tribes of Israel, which they believe themselves to represent." Even in Italy the *Nuova Enciclopedia Italiana* predicted that "the day is not far off that it will be forced to dissolve itself or transform itself." See *Nuova Enciclopedia Italiana* (Torino: Unione Tipografico-Editrice Torinese, 1882), 14: 811. *L'Illustrazione Popolare* noted Young's passing by publishing a drawing of a "caravan of new Mormons traveling toward Salt Lake." See "Le nostre incisioni," *L'Illustrazione Popolare* 14: 46 (16 September 1877), 720, 723.

[2] For a description of the "half mast" incident, see Bigler, *Forgotten Kingdom*, 327.

[3] Some sectarian observers, such as Father Lawrence Scanlan, were careful to encourage the goodwill of Mormon leaders, while others, such as James Cardinal Gibbon, blasted Mormonism. LDS leaders in St. George invited Scanlan to hold a Mass in the St. George Tabernacle in 1879, and the local choir (*continued*)

ally social, economic, and political pressures caused the pragmatic Mormons to capitulate and abandon the practice of polygamy. This change in policy opened the way for Utah to be admitted as a state in 1896 after a nearly fifty-year wait.[4]

In the midst of these dynamic events, Utah Territory continued to be a stopping place for many travelers. The Union Pacific Railroad published a guide in 1881 that recommended "sights for tourists" in Utah Territory, predicted that the future of Salt Lake City depended on mining and the railroads, and criticized the continuing power and influence of the LDS church.[5] During the same year the Boston firm of Raymond & Whitcomb began organizing cross-country tours that stopped in Chicago, Omaha, Cheyenne, Denver, Ogden, Salt Lake City, San Francisco, and Monterey. In fact, Salt Lake City was chosen as one of the Sunday stopovers to allow Sabbath worship "in appropriately inspiring settings."[6] And in 1891 Morris Phillips included an account of a stopover in Salt Lake in a book that focused on England, Paris, and California.[7]

Throughout this period the practice of polygamy continued to attract the most attention. When Oscar Wilde lectured in Salt Lake City in 1882, he visited the Salt Lake Tabernacle—which he described as "an enormous affair about the size Covent Garden, and holds with ease fourteen families"—and later wrote, with a hint of sarcasm, his personal satisfaction that John Taylor, "a nice old man," had not only granted him a private audience but also "sat with five wives in the stage box" during his lecture.[8] The Reverend Henry Ward Beecher made similar observations in 1883 after his visit to Utah.[9] But in 1888 Rudyard Kipling was convinced that Phil Robinson had taken too much sun when he visited Utah and concluded that "the

---

even sang the Mass in Latin. See Harris, *The Catholic Church in Utah*, 331. James Cardinal Gibbons's famous statement in 1889 that Mormonism was a "plague-spot on our civilization" was a throwback to similar statements made about slavery. See Gasparin, *America Before Europe: Principles and Interests*, 316. Gibbon wrote that divorce "is an evil scarcely less deplorable than Mormonism" since divorce "leads to successive polygamy." See Gibbons, *Our Christian Heritage*, 485–86; and his *The Faith of our Fathers*, 88.

[4] Firmage, "Religion and the Law: The Mormon Experience in the Nineteenth Century," 765–803.

[5] Williams, ed., *The Pacific Tourist*, 129–58. Other guides, including *Appleton's General Guide to the United States and Canada*, made similar recommendations for railroad travelers.

[6] Withey, *Grand Tours and Cook's Tours*, 307.

[7] Phillips, *Abroad and at Home: Practical Hints for Tourists*, 239–42.

[8] Holland and Hart-Davis, eds., *The Complete Letters of Oscar Wilde*, 161. See also Hart-Davis, *The Letters of Oscar Wilde*, 110–11; and South, "Oscar Wilde in Salt Lake City," 8–11.

[9] Beecher, *A Circuit of the Continent*, 12–17.

Mormon was almost altogether an estimable person." For his part, Kipling expressed his gratitude that he was not "a brick in the up-building of the Mormon church, that has so aptly established herself by the borders of a lake bitter, salt, and hopeless."[10]

While these visitors expressed their distaste for polygamy, others were more kind in their assessment of other characteristics they observed in Utah. Willard Glazier, who was critical of the Mormon marriage system, wrote that the Mormons of Utah had "challenged the admiration of the world, and have set patterns in industry, and in a system of government, which seems to consider the well-being of all." He was also impressed that of "all the cities which have sprung into being and grown and prospered, since the discovery of the American continent, there is not one with which is associated so much interest, and which attracts such universal curiosity as Salt Lake City," and he was also confident that "Salt Lake City is destined to become an important point in the western section of our country. Her future is assured."[11] Czech traveler Josef Korensky observed in 1893 that "Main Street seems very orderly and full of life" and that Salt Lake City "used to be a desert until the Mormons created their biblical paradise from it," and further that "the [Tabernacle] choir's music was incredible. The Mormon singers were very talented and could win many competitions."[12] Even the Utah Commission—whose mission was to confirm compliance with anti-polygamy laws—found that the citizens of Utah "possess many traits of character which are well worthy of emulation by others."[13]

Some visitors also praised the Mormons for their agricultural success in the desert. John Wesley Powell lauded Mormon irrigation in his *Report on the Lands of the Arid Region* in 1878. William Smyth included the "Mormon Commonwealth" in an 1895 selected list of "real utopias of the arid west," noting the similarity in the geography of Utah and the Holy Land. "Brigham Young and the State he founded furnish stronger and clearer light for the future of domestic colonization than any other experience than can possibly be discovered," he concluded.[14]

---

[10] Kipling, *From Sea to Sea and Other Sketches*, 2:117–29.
[11] Glazier, *Peculiarities of American Cities*, 438–39.
[12] Korensky, *Cesty Po Svete*, 171, 178.
[13] Carlton, *The Wonderlands of the Wild West, with sketches of the Mormons*, 10.
[14] Smythe, *The Conquest of Arid America*, 75–76. Smythe's observations about Utah were originally published in 1895 in *The Century Magazine*.

Charles-Louis-François André: An Undulating Plain Garnished with Sauges en Brousailles

French scientist Charles-Louis-François André (1842–1912) began teaching at the Lycée de Nevers in 1865. That same year he started working at the Observatoire de Paris, where he became an expert in astronomy. André journeyed to New Caledonia in 1874 (when Victor Rochefort-Luçay was probably still incarcerated there) to observe and photograph the transit of Venus. Four years later he obtained financial support from the French National Academy and the Ministry of Public Instruction to travel to Utah Territory to make a scientific observation of the passage of Mercury over the sun. When André and his colleagues landed in Washington, they learned that the U.S. Army Corps of Geographical Engineers had installed a small observatory in Ogden, and the Corps made the facility available to them.

André's scientific expeditions to New Caledonia and Utah established his reputation in France and helped him secure an appointment as a professor of astronomy at the University of Lyon, where he successfully established a national observatory. For the next thirty years he made observations, trained astronomers, held conferences, wrote reports concerning his observations, and won many prizes for his accomplishments.

> Charles-Louis-François André, *Rapport sur le passage de Mercure sur le soleil, observé à Ogden (Utah) le 6 mai 1878*
> [Report on the Transit of Mercury over the Sun Observed at Ogden, Utah, on May 6, 1878].
> Translated by Hugh MacNaughton.

André described the country surrounding the plateau on which the observatory was located as

> an undulating plain garnished with sage brush and planted here and there with little farms. The placement was thus very well chosen for establishing an observatory; its only inconvenience, inherent in the nature of the soil, is an intense dust that is lifted by the slightest wind and which occasionally makes the operation of the instruments impossible. As far as the building itself, it is constructed of brick, and is composed . . . of a little central edifice supporting a hemispheric cupola of five meters in diameter, flanked by two lateral wings. . . .
>
> The following day, April 3rd, we went to Camp Douglas, the center for

the Utah garrison, to make contact with the military authorities of the Territory.

Camp Douglas is situated some 8 kilometers from Salt Lake City, at the summit of a plateau that overlooks the capital city of Utah. It should not in any way be compared to one of our French military camps; four hundred infantrymen and a few old cannons form the entire garrison. On the other hand, the quartering of the men is infinitely more comfortable; each officer has his own little house, standing in a garden, and the common bedrooms of the soldiers are of a neatness bordering on elegance.

The purpose of our visit was soon accomplished, and we spent the afternoon visiting the holy city of the Mormons, which they call the *modern-day Zion*. After crossing the Great American Desert lying between Ogden and Omaha, this city of 40 000 inhabitants had the effect of a veritable oasis of civilization. Besides, the character of the Mormon people has imprinted a special stamp on it with its *Tabernacle*, the Mormon temple. Its roof is ellipsoidal and its organ was built entirely at Salt Lake City itself under the leadership of the venerable Brigham Young. The streets of the city are all lined with trees, and bordered with small streams constantly fed by water coming down from the mountains, giving the whole city the appearance of a vast garden, in the middle of which the banking and commercial establishments seem at first sight to be of minor importance.

That evening, the Utah Central railroad brought us back to Ogden.

The scientists were surprised to find their work hindered by bad weather, which included a dust storm, and then snow, and a twenty-four-hour downpour stopped their work entirely. Brighter weather resumed, however, in time to host weekend visits.

The following day, Sunday 28th, the visitors flocked to the observatory. Sunday rest is more sacred still to the Mormons than to the English and American Protestants. We had just about finished setting things up, and it would do nothing but good for us to satisfy public curiosity.

A bizarrely sorrowful incident marred the visit of the Frenchmen when the sergeant whose quarters they were using as an office entered and shot himself in the head in front of the party. This event deeply affected the scientists.

On May 1st, we were visited by the Mayor and Deputy Mayor of Ogden; on May 2nd, it was the Governor of Utah, the administrator delegated by the central government to manage the civil affairs of the territory occupied by the Mormons; on May 3rd, we received the visit of the Mormon bishop Sharp and his family, and the central administrative staff of the Utah Central Rail Road.[15] For the Mormon ecclesiastical dignitaries are not confined to their religious duties; rather, they are fully involved in public life and, apart from the seat they occupy in the Tabernacle during services, and the larger number of wives that their dignity allows them to marry, nothing distinguishes them in everyday life from the rest of their fellow-citizens. Thus Bishop Sharp was at the time Superintendent of the Utah Central Railroad.[16]

The bishop asked to visit the observatory and view the heavenly bodies through the scientists' instruments. That evening, a special train halted at the foot of the hill where the observatory stood. The scientists did all they could to welcome the local dignitaries. André was struck by the intelligent curiosity of the visitors, some fifty in all. The following day, three or four hundred inhabitants of Ogden joined the city band (André translated its name as "Philosophical Harmony"), which played to wish the observers luck. André was touched by these spontaneous acts of welcome. Despite all the planning, a combination of sand and snowstorm arose during the evening of 5 May 1878 and ruined the observation of Mercury's transit. Eventually, a slight break in cloud cover allowed André and his team to record the final passage of Mercury over the sun's surface, but it only lasted about one minute.

Rudolph Meyer:
A Lot Can Be Learned from the Mormons

German journalist Rudolph Meyer (1839–99) began his university studies in Berlin in chemistry and physics but eventually concentrated on history, philosophy, literature, and economics and developed a deep interest in political and social issues. He worked as a private tutor in Hungary in 1864, but three years later he returned to Berlin and began his career as a journalist and writer. He received his doctoral degree in Vienna in 1874. The following year he was an unsuccessful candidate of the Conservative party for the Prussian parliament. Beginning in 1877 Meyer became the economics editor for the conservative periodical *Vaterland*. He developed contacts with many influential people in society and politics and eventually allied himself

---

[15] Lester J. Herrick was mayor of Ogden in 1874. The territorial governor was George W. Emery, who implemented the secret ballot in Utah and later had a county named after him.

[16] As noted, Bishop John Sharp was a Young family business partner.

with the conservative critics of Bismarck. The political views expressed in his writing led to his conviction for libeling Bismarck and two of his ministers, for which he was given an eighteen-month sentence. Rather than go to jail, Meyer fled the country and began residing in Vienna.

During his exile Meyer published a book about corruption in Germany and helped create an exile organization in Switzerland, but he eventually lost contact with his conservative colleagues in Germany. He began accompanying rich Hungarians on study trips to England, France, Italy, Canada, and the United States. In 1881 he visited Utah Territory and recorded his observations in *Ursachen der amerikanischen Konkurrenz* (1883). In the book he confirms his clear anti-capitalist leanings. He traveled to Canada in 1884, where he purchased a farm and became a British citizen. He obtained amnesty from the German government in 1888, but he did not return to Germany until 1897.

Rudolph Meyer, *Ursachen der amerikanischen Konkurrenz* [Causes of American Competition], 512–48. Translated by TSC.

It is not my assignment or intention to write about "Mormonism" as a peculiar Protestant sect or confession. Yet, once tradition is set aside, I do not see why Mormonism should be less legitimate than the other Protestant confessions to which of course I myself belong. It is not likely because of polygamy, although Count Philipp of Hess and King Friedrich Wilhelm II of Prussia practiced polygamy with the approval of the religious officials of their respective Lutheran Confessions, for it was by such officials that their marriage to their several wives had been consecrated.[17] I believe that nothing valid can be brought against Mormonism from a Protestant viewpoint, and neither from the Catholic standpoint can anything more valid be brought forward than against any other Protestant confession. But I do not regard such an observation of any value, since it concerns an area in which those who feel they have a vocation move as they wish, and I would not presume to pass judgment in such a matter. Mormonism interests me because it provides proof "that religion can be productive" even if it may be based on an erroneous belief. This, of course, is known by anyone who knows history.

It was not only in the Middle Ages that monks were cultural pioneers and teachers of agriculture, the trades, and the arts. Rather, they also achieved the same advances in the Americas during recent centuries, examples being the Jesuits in Paraguay and the Franciscans in California. I visited San

---

[17] For polygamy in the early Reformation, see Cairncross, *After Polygamy Was Made a Sin: The Social History of Christian Polygamy*; and Smith, "Strange Bedfellows: Mormon Polygamy and Baptist History," 41–45.

Gabriel, one of the Franciscan missions that was founded only 110 years ago and still today owns the most beautiful olive, fruit and palm orchards in southern California. All these establishments of the Catholic Church, whose remnants, ruins, and leftovers are still worthy of admiration, had been destroyed purely by economic forces through the emancipation of the Spanish colonies brought about by revolution, and a historically uninformed journalism takes pleasure in characterizing faith in God and economic progress as being antagonistic.

The Mormon Colonies in the Great American Desert deliver the most telling evidence that religion and faith are achieving miracles and moving mountains in the field of economics even today—that "religion is productive" and that a church, which intelligently organizes the care of its members' social and material conditions, will thereby also maintain a decisive influence on the State....

It is certainly worth the effort to become thoroughly acquainted with such a community, one which developed before our eyes and continues to develop further every year, which originated in a desert without capital and now has developed America's greatest farming system, which has used with masterly skill the modern power of steam and capital, railways and banks, and has achieved the greatest degree of excellence in agriculture and animal husbandry, but which, at the same time, is first and foremost a religious community....

[The Great Salt Lake] has often been compared to the Dead Sea in Palestine. I am not acquainted with the latter, but if this comparison is intended to denote something desolate and forbidding, then it is incorrect, for the Great Salt Lake is an exceptional beauty.[18]

I visited many farms, the best of which belongs to a Mr. Winder, who came here fifteen years ago with very small means, but who had a thorough knowledge of English farming. He chose to settle not far from town and bought eighty-five acres of land with water rights about three miles from Zion that had already passed into private ownership. He paid twenty-five dollars per acre. The land was still unplowed, bare and very rich in alkali and therefore needed to be frequently flushed with water. Now he has built a handsome house on it and enough stalls for his livestock.[19]

---

[18] The Great Salt Lake impressed many travelers, including John C. Frémont, Howard Stansbury, Jules Rémy, Richard F. Burton, Fitz Hugh Ludlow, and William Elkanah Waters.

[19] John Rex Winder (1821–1910) converted to Mormonism in Liverpool in 1848 and emigrated to Utah with his wife and three children in 1853. Following the Utah War, Winder purchased a farm south of Salt Lake. He began delivering milk products in 1880 and bottling milk for distribution in 1907. Winder was active in church and civic affairs as Salt Lake City assessor and collector (1870–84); as a member of the Salt Lake City Council (1872–78); and as city water master (1884–87). He was called in 1887 as counselor in the LDS Presiding Bishopric and was a member of the First Presidency from 1901 until his death in 1910. Descendants moved the Winder Dairy to Granger in 1931, where it continues to operate under family ownership. See Winder, *John R. Winder.*

This makes it impossible to calculate the cost of production of a cubic meter of grain in such a colony, for who can put a dollar value on those services that a well-organized ecclesiastical congregation provides to its "Brethren"? They are inestimable. And for an individual new settler who comes here from Europe, it is much more difficult to set himself up on his own. It is already completely impossible in Utah, for he is unable to install an irrigation system by himself, and the Mormons of course will not include him in their water co-operative.

And in fact, the Mormons control not only Utah, but the entire American desert as I have described it and the mountains along its boundaries. This is because they are the only farmers worthy of note and the only party in this area which has more than 100,000 well-off, independent men along with a number of very rich people who blindly follow the orders of their church government in Zion. Even if not appearing as such, the Great American Desert is a Mormon kingdom. Mr. Taylor, the president of the Church's Board of Governors, who, along with Joseph Smith, had been wounded in 1846 [1844] but escaped with his life, controls the American desert even though he in no way holds any political position within it! In all political and community elections, Mormons naturally vote with one voice and therefore are the decisive factor in all these elections.

Utah was thus a true Mormon state in which the Church was both the State and a religious institution. We have here the noteworthy appearance of a purely hierarchical political system, albeit only in the last ten years.

I visited a 64-year-old man who, two years ago at the age of 62, after more than twenty-five years as a gardener in Zion, took possession of a homestead in the desert and started a new life as a farmer. I found him hard at work with some of his sons building a massive barn. He had four wives, three of whom were still alive, and had forty-six living children, of whom many were already married and in turn had a great many children. Two of his wives lived in town. A third one who lived with him had borne him fourteen children, the youngest of whom was three years old. This is truly an amazing reproductive capacity.

A lot can be learned from the Mormons!

They have demonstrated, first of all, that the Great American Desert can be cultivated in many locations and that, as agriculture is practiced, the rainfall will also increase, thereby increasing in its turn the cultivable land area. This also significantly affects Europe, because the fewer foodstuffs miners and railway people of the desert require from California and the eastern States, the more of it is shipped over to Europe, consequently depressing agricultural commodity prices, which in turn will force down land rents and all the sooner destroy the way of life of the landowners.[20]

---

[20] Fortunately for European farmers, the "rain follows the plow" myth that Meyer accepted did not reflect reality.

They have further proven what poor people with a strong religious faith are capable of doing, and that Faith is a powerful factor in productivity. And finally, they have proven that a church is powerful among its membership and within the State, and will remain so if, in addition to its religious duties, it cares for the material interests of its people in an ordered, methodical way.

GIOVANNI VIGNA DAL FERRO:
DO NOT BELIEVE THAT THE MORMONS ARE SAVAGES

Giovanni Vigna dal Ferro, a journalist from Bologna, visited Utah in 1881 after serving as secretary of the Italian commission to the Centennial Exposition in Philadelphia. While in the U.S. he acted as Sarah Bernhardt's interpreter before traveling with Jehan Soudan, a correspondent for *Voltaire* of Paris, across the U.S. During the journey Vigna dal Ferro wrote a series of letters to *La Patria*, a newspaper in his home city. Some of his observations were also published in *L'Eco d'Italia*, an Italian-language newspaper published in New York City.[21] When he returned to Italy Vigna dal Ferro collected some of his articles and published them in a small pamphlet, *Un viaggio nel Far West Americano*. Ferro was "[d]efinitely not a close student of American life—he was so disappointed to discover that Indians no longer whooped and attacked trains," Joseph Torrielli noted. He wrote "nothing new or penetrating."[22]

VIGNA DAL FERRO, *UN VIAGGIO NEL FAR WEST AMERICANO*
[A TRIP IN THE AMERICAN FAR WEST], 30–31, 33–34.

We spent the day among the Latter Day Saints, or, as they are more commonly called, the Mormons. We arrived while they were in a great celebration, holding their annual meeting of the church, attended by all Mormons, both from within the city and outside its borders.... We met the president, old John Taylor, George Smith and some apostles....

The first impression that a traveler has upon arriving in Salt Lake City is the marvelous beauty of the place and all that has been accomplished in little more than thirty years, for the Mormons have been able to transform it from a desert into a real garden place. The valley of the Great Salt Lake is

---

[21] See Vigna Dal Ferro, "Carteggio dell'Eco d'Italia," *L'Eco d'Italia* 19 April 1881. Paolo De Vecchi, a correspondent for the Torino *Gazzetta Piemontese*, was another Italian writer who visited Utah in the 1880s. In Salt Lake he interviewed relatives of Joseph Toronto, who said they were anxious to return to Sicily. See "I Mormoni Italiani," *L'Eco d'Italia*, 8 January 1881. De Vecchi "condemned as a body those travelers who swept through the land in a few months and emitted pompous brays of disapproval." See Torrielli, *Italian Opinions on America*, 34. See also Bohme, "Vigna dal Ferro," 149–51.   [22] Torrielli, *Italian Opinion on America*, 21.

situated at the base of the high and snowy Wasatch Mountains and is irrigated by a river, which the Mormons have named Jordan, from which, a few miles before running into the [Great Salt] lake, water is diverted to irrigate the city and other portions of the territory....

The city of the Great Salt Lake or the New Jerusalem, which is what the Saints call their capital, is a beautiful little city which has, like other American cities, square blocks, which are bordered by trees and canals, which contain water to irrigate their gardens, and for use in the homes of the Saints....

Among the numerous discourses that were given in the Tabernacle while we were in attendance, those which surpassed all others in their eloquence were explanations concerning the mysteries of the *Book of Mormon*, and the injustices which the Mormons have endured because of the Gentiles and American government, given by President Taylor, his counselor George Smith, the Apostle Cannon and others. They also urged church members to continue to make contributions to the church to help defray the many expenses it had to satisfy to guarantee the community's continuing prosperity.

To my great surprise, the fiery George Smith, during one of these discourses, reproached the holy fathers—the heads of households—about sending their children to the Gentile's schools.[23] During his speech I heard the name of Father Gavazzi mentioned and I later learned that our celebrated citizen spoke on the same subject in a room in this city some time ago when he addressed the Protestants against the Catholics.[24]

Do not believe that the Mormons are savages. Seeing that their society will eventually, sooner or later, come to an end, they are content to shed tears inside the walls of their temple, while outside the walls they are men of affairs who have accumulated capital in the mines, on the railroads, in agriculture, and in commercial enterprises of every type. In their affairs these men do not find it difficult to transact business with gentiles. They have done business with them for a number of years, and especially after the discovery of rich minerals in Utah Territory. These gentiles have started to invade the city of the Saints and polluted it by introducing Yankee institutions that were previously unknown among the Mormons, such as saloons that have a relatively plentiful supply of drinks including whiskey-grog, sherry-cobbler, gin-cock-tail, and many other creations that American bartenders have invented to tempt the taste buds of their numerous customers.

---

[23] Vigna dal Ferro apparently heard Second Counselor Joseph F. Smith since George A. Smith died in 1875.

[24] Alessandro Gavazzi (1809–89), a monk in the Barnabite Order, was Garibaldi's confessor during the Roman Republic in 1848. When Pope Pius IX reasserted political control over Rome, Gavazzi went into exile in England, where he became a Protestant and wrote tracts against the Jesuits. He traveled to the U.S. and lectured in 1853 and 1854. See Gavazzi, *Father Gavazzi's Lectures in New York* (1861). When King Victor Emmanuel II annexed Rome in 1870, Gavazzi helped found the Evangelical Free Church, returning to the U.S. to raise funds for the new church. During this second visit he spoke in Utah. He remained the leader of the Evangelical Free Church until his death in 1889. See Spini, *L'Evangelo e il Berretto Frigio*, 14–17, 33–63.

Friederick Martin von Bodenstedt: A Variety of Things Are Missing Here

Born into a poor German family, Friederick Martin von Bodenstedt (1819–92) apprenticed as a merchant before attending the University of Göttingen to study history and foreign languages. From 1840 to 1843 he was the private tutor for the children of Princess Galitzin in Moscow and then briefly taught school in Tiflis in today's Georgia. After returning to Germany in 1845 he continued to travel, especially to Italy and Switzerland. For the next ten years he worked as an editor in Trieste, Berlin, Bremen, and Vienna. He began writing poetry and in 1851 published his first book of verse, which established his literary reputation. His later collections were not as well received.

King Maximilian II of Bavaria employed Bodenstedt in 1854 to teach Slavic languages in Munich. During this time he became a respected translator of many Russian authors, including Pushkin, and brought many of these authors to attention of the German reading public for the first time. He also translated eight works of Shakespeare and other English writers into German. He began managing a theatre in Meiningen in 1867, where he remained until he retired to Wiesbaden in 1874.

Following Bodenstedt's stay in Russia, he wrote an account of his experiences, and he subsequently described travel to the Far East, Denmark, and England. After his retirement he visited the U.S. in 1880 and published an account of his experiences in 1882. During his visit he boarded the transcontinental railroad in California and stopped briefly in Salt Lake City.

FRIEDERICK BODENSTEDT, *Vom Atlantischen zum Stillen Ocean* [From the Atlantic to the Pacific], 387–426. Translated by TSC.

On June 10th, 1880 at 7 o'clock in the morning, we reached the first town in Utah. Its name, Corinne, was prettier than its appearance. I found the bare, mournful, dreary sight that it offered all the more surprising because I had repeatedly read about it as though it were a pleasant, thriving town. No Mormons live here, and they therefore call it the City of Gentiles.[25] What a completely different impression one gets of Ogden, the next city the train

---

[25] Founded in March 1869 where the Union Pacific crossed Bear River, Corinne was named after U.P. agent Gen. J. H. Williamson's daughter, who the *New York Herald* reported was named after "the heroine in Madame de Staël's novel." The town's dream of replacing Salt Lake as Utah's commercial capital never materialized. For the history of "the burg on the Bear," see Brigham D. Madsen's *Corinne: The Gentile Capital of Utah*.

takes you to in not much more than half an hour from Corinne. It really does look like a thriving town! Here, in Ogden, it hardly sounds strange when the Mormons boast, while making reference to Corinne, that everything flourishes in the land of the Saints much better in their communities than in those of the unbelievers. . . .

After a two-hour train ride that passed quickly for me, I arrived in Salt Lake City in the best of spirits. . . . After shaking the dust from my feet, having a bath and a bite to eat, I made my way to Professor Park's dwelling.[26] At the hotel no one knew where it might be found, but I was told that I could inquire at the nearest school and that a driver was available for me.

I had barely left through the hotel's main entrance, when two ladies met me a few steps to the left of it where a sign with golden letters indicated a special entrance for ladies. They gave me a most friendly greeting and on discovering where I was headed, asked me to take them along, which I gladly did, for in America it is always best to travel in the company of women.

We first visited a school where about fifty boys and girls (the latter being in the majority) sat on segregated benches. A male teacher was busy with the boys, a female teacher with the girls. The latter appeared to be the person in charge, because I was directed to her when I asked for Professor Park upon entering. I was informed that he had gone for a ride to the country to attend a school celebration and that he would not return to town until four o'clock. I wrote a couple of lines on my card and requested that it be given to him.

I asked to observe the class instruction for a while with my two lady companions, and permission was gladly given. The lady teacher was teaching English grammar while the gentleman teacher was giving religious instruction. The method was exactly the same as I had found in other American schools. There was a small text book for each subject with questions and answers that the children had to memorize at home so as to be able to give an account of it in school and, at intervals, hand in written reports about it.

I discovered that none of the children were of German extraction. They were all very quiet and were generally clean but plainly dressed. Only two or three girls, the oldest of whom most likely was fifteen years old, were exceptions and seemed to belong to more well-to-do parents. One even wore an elegant watch on a golden chain.

We stayed only as long as was necessary to assess everything, and then toured all the main sights of the city: the Temple, the Tabernacle, the Theatre, the Lion House and the Beehive Store. . . .

In all the travel accounts about Salt Lake City with which I have become familiar, two different kinds of comments are repeated. First there is admiration for the city's beautiful location and thriving appearance, and secondly

---

[26] John R. Park (1833–1900) was the president of the University of Utah from 1869 to 1892.

amazement at the serious, sober aspect of its inhabitants. I have also found this to be the case, but basically not more than in any other American city with the exception of San Francisco. It is just more visible in Salt Lake City because a variety of things are missing here, things that do not exactly make the hustle and bustle of streets in other cities more inviting but which give them a livelier character. Most lacking are unruly young people who make themselves very noticeable everywhere else. Also lacking are yelling hustlers and newspaper vendors, as well as bums, beggars, and rowdies, and all other questionable characters whether in male or in female attire. In short, there is a lack of all the romantic accessories that go with street life in a big city.

Gabriel Paul Othenin de Cléron, Comte d'Haussonville: Polygamy— That's What Always Troubles the Gentiles

Comte Haussonville (1843–1924), a native of Gurcy-le-Châtel, France, earned his law degree in 1865 and practiced the profession for the next thirteen years. During the Franco-Prussian War he served as a lieutenant in the *garde nationale* of Seine-et-Marne and was awarded the *Légion d'honneur* for his good conduct. After the war he was elected to the National Assembly. During his tenure (1871–76) he became a close confidant of the duke of Paris of the Orléans family and lobbied for the restoration of the monarchy. Haussonville collaborated with a number of French periodicals including *Le Figaro, Le Gaulois, L'Echo de Paris*, and *Revue des deux mondes*. When he failed to be reelected in 1877 he became an adviser to the Orleans family.

The U.S. government invited Haussonville to attend the 1881 centennial celebration of the Battle of Yorktown. Following the ceremonies, he boarded the transcontinental railroad, and though he did not plan to visit Salt Lake, he accepted an invitation from a Mormon to stop in Ogden and make the short trip to the Mormon capital the next day. His memoir, which was published in Paris in 1883, was a very favorable account of his one-day visit to the city. The material on Utah was translated by Leo Haefeli and published by Deseret News Company the same year. In his preface the translator called the count "an unbiased thinker." Upon his return to France, Haussonville remained a convinced monarchist. He dedicated himself to French literature, and in 1888 he was elected to the Académie française and in 1904 to the Académie des sciences morales et politiques.

Gabriel Paul Othenin de Cléron, Comte d'Haussonville,
 A travers les Etats-Unis [Across the United States], 305–7,
 Translated by Rick Grunder; 307–335, Translated by Leo Haefeli.

Among my traveling companions, I had noticed (owing to his gentle demeanor and good manners) a young man who appeared to be about twenty years old. His hair and beard were light blond, his eyes a clear grey, his comportment rather timid and his manner of dress agreeable if rather groomed—he seemed enough like a young Englishman doing the grand tour. I had certainly not had occasion to converse with him directly, and I scarcely knew the sound of his discreet voice, when, on the second day out of Omaha, my attention was sparked by a rather lively discussion which arose at the far end of the car, and of which he appeared to be the focus. I leaned forward, listened, and realized that he was discussing with a federal army chaplain (my bunk-mate, incidentally) whether or not polygamy was forbidden by the gospel. The chaplain held the affirmative, naturally; but his young contradictor stood firm, and I was struck by the passion he brought to the argument—all the while noticing that he interjected neither sarcasm nor the slightest hint of disrespect.

I asked myself with what sort of person the chaplain had engaged himself in conversation. Then, certain words and points exchanged between the speakers cleared up my mystery: this young man with the polite manner, so carefully groomed and with the soft voice—was a Mormon, and that was why he held the subject of polygamy so close to heart. Little by little, the word that a Mormon was present echoed throughout the train. A circle formed about him and the discussion became more general, everyone wanting to put in a word—right down to the sleeping car conductor, who, just like the chaplain, presumed to argue against the Mormon with every reference he could cite. Perhaps I am mistaken, but I cannot envision a train conductor in France quoting Bible verses.

But soon the discussion degenerated into personalities.

— How many wives do you have? (asked one traveler, quite brusquely).

— I am not yet married (he replied).

— Then you are not a good Mormon.

— I am probably not as good a Mormon as I ought to be (he replied mildly—I had to strain to hear him).

I remembered the answer of Saint-Preux to Wolmar: "Are you a Christian?—I strive to be;" and it was this kind of humility that made me favor the Mormon. A few minutes later, he was to give an even more striking proof: a young woman muttered some remark, and he asked her with all politeness to repeat it:

— I wasn't talking to you, sir (she said, with insulting haughtiness).

The Mormon flushed under the insult, but contained himself and replied very politely:

— I beg your pardon, madam; I thought that you had spoken to me.

I was shocked at such unchristian rudeness, so when I conversed with him on my own turn, I took care to show every respect. But this painful incident had rather chilled the discussion, and it came to a standstill.

My politeness, however, was not lost. Toward the end of the journey the young Mormon came and took a seat by me and renewed the conversation. His name was Lorenzo Farr and he related to me his history.[27] His father had five wives and thirty-five children. He himself was the fourth or fifth (I cannot now remember his number more exactly), and at the age of twenty years he had been appointed by the supreme authorities of the Mormon Church to form one of those bands of young missionaries which the Council sends annually to Europe to make recruits to their faith. He had passed some time at Paris, but without much success; and although there were in France, he assured me, some agents of Mormonism, he complained bitterly of our restrictive legislation which did not permit him to hold public meetings. It was principally in England that he had labored on his mission, but not without seeing meetings held by him disturbed by hostile manifestations of the populace. But at the same time he was not without hopes that the seed sown by him had taken root in some hearts. Unfortunately he had overexerted his brain by studying day and night the Scriptures and theology, in order to be able to hold his own with the Reverends who would come to argue with him in the meetings; and he had arrived at such a condition of mental exhaustion that he had to abandon, at least for the time being, his vocation as a missionary and to take repose at the paternal hearth—a hearth, by the way, which he had not left deserted; for with the exception of one of his sisters who is married, and two of his brothers, the other children of his father have remained with him.

By degrees my new acquaintance returns to the conversation of the morning and becomes somewhat warm in telling me:

"You have seen how that lady has answered me; and yet I have spoken to her quite politely. This is the way they treat us in America, us Mormons. They think they are acting righteously by insulting us. They calumniate us without knowing us; and yet we ask only to be known, for there is nothing in our lives we need conceal. I am glad to have prevailed upon the chaplain, with whom I discussed before, and who is a correspondent of the Evening Star at Washington, that he would stay a day in Salt Lake City, and would give an impartial account in his journal of all he would see."

The idea strikes me at once that I might take advantage of this occasion to gather information to use in one of the French monthly magazines. I

---

[27] Lorenzo Erickson Farr (1858–1915) was the son of Lorin F. Farr (1820–1915), founder of Farr West, Utah, who was first president of Weber Stake of Zion and first mayor of Ogden City. Lorenzo was actually the first son of Lorin Farr's fifth wife, Nicholine Ericksen.

inform my newly made friend that without being correspondent of a journal I have some literary connections in France and I would be disposed to give an account—with an impartiality at least equal to that of the chaplain—of all I would see if I were permitted to join him. He jumps with joy at the idea.

"You will stay with my father," says he. "He lives at Ogden where we will arrive, this evening. You will pass the night under his roof and, to-morrow, I will take you to Salt Lake City myself, where I will make you acquainted with some people. We will return in the evening to Ogden and you then can take the train of the Central Pacific to San Francisco."

At first I hesitate a little to accept this invitation, thinking there might be some indiscretion on my part to witness this family reunion. But then I reconsider. "After all," I say to myself, "this father of thirty-five children cannot have too great a tenderness for each one, and the return of one of them to the fold, even after an absence of three years, cannot probably evoke a great emotion." I finish by accepting the offer, loathe to lose this unique occasion to sleep under the roof of a Mormon, and I communicate with the Chaplain, whose curiosity is as excited as my own. By and by the rumor spreads in the car that a correspondent of the Evening Post and a "French Count" are going to stay over night with a Mormon: and we become the objects of a certain curiosity, the more, they say, because what has been offered is very rare, and because the Mormons, generally, very jealous like all polygamous people, do not like to admit strangers in the presence of their wives.

Shortly before our arrival at Ogden the conductor of the sleeping-car takes me to one side and asks me if it is true that I intend to publish an account of my visit among the Mormons in a French work, or whether I have only used it as a pretext for accompanying the Chaplain. I answer him that, without binding myself to anything, it is quite possible that I will publish some notes on what I have seen. He thereupon requests me not to fail to send him my account....

We arrive at Ogden at nightfall, and the Chaplain, the Mormon, and myself step down, in a complete darkness on the plank sidewalk of the depot. "I think somebody has come to meet me," says our friend. Scarcely has he uttered these words when he falls in the arms of four large young gentlemen who surround him and shake his hands with outbursts of joy. A little back stands an aged gentleman, with whom, in his turn, our young friend goes to shake hands with a certain deference. The Chaplain and I surmise it is his father and stand aside. But in a few minutes he comes to us. "My father is not in town," says he; "the day before the dispatch announcing my return arrived he left to accompany some relatives to Arizona. But this is no reason why you should not come and stay with us. My mother will be very much pleased to receive you, and my uncle here will also come and spend the evening with us." . . .

[*After arriving at the young Mormon's home, the count and the chaplain meet the young man's uncle.*]

Our new interlocutor was a man of tolerably advanced age, but straight, dry, with the features, almost, of an ascetic.[28] He had entered the room with a big cane and a lantern in his hand, a broad-brimmed black felt hat on his head, and wrapped to his feet in a heavy cloth cloak held together at his neck by a little brass chain. Thus, my imagination would easily have pictured the old Silas Deans in the "Prison of Edinburg."[29] We were at first a little embarrassed; for, even when one is invited, it is always a delicate matter to interrogate a man on his faith and above all on his manners. The chaplain, to whom I naturally left the key of the conversation, at last asked him: "Have you been in the country a long time?" This trivial question sufficed to break the ice.

"On, yes," answered the old gentleman; "I am one of the few survivors who have come here with Brigham Young. You know that after the infamous massacre of our leader, Joseph Smith, at Carthage jail, Brigham Young gathered all the faithful for whom there was no more security in the State of Illinois, where that horrible crime had been committed; and that he undertook, in accordance to orders he had received from God, to guide them through the desert to a new land."

This whole long account had been delivered with a gravity and a concentrated emotion which could not fail making upon me a certain impression. I do not know if it was the same with the Chaplain; but, at any rate, he asked with much seriousness: "You believe, then, that your people is the object of a particular protection of God as was formerly the people of Israel, and that it is His hand which has conducted you here?"

"This is our conviction," replied our interlocutor; "we are a Bible people; hence, though you call us Mormons—undoubtedly on account of the Book of Mormon, which is indeed one of our sacred works—the name we give ourselves is that of Church of Jesus Christ of Latter-day Saints, in remembrance of the Church of the Former-day Saints, whom we are trying to resemble; and as they did we call Gentiles all those who do not belong to our Faith. We have, indeed, preserved, as much as possible, the organization of the primitive Church, which we believe to approach nearer than any Christian community, and we have the firm belief that we are called to preach and

---

[28] Aaron Freeman Farr (1818–1903) joined the LDS church at Kirtland and settled at Nauvoo. A veteran of Brigham Young's 1847 pioneer company, he later served a mission to the West Indies, as president of the St. Louis Branch, and as U.S. deputy marshal.

[29] Silas Deane was the first agent the Continental Congress sent to France, and Edinburg Castle was a notorious prison for American sailors during the American Revolution, but Haussonville's reference is obscure.

to spread throughout the universe the revelation of Joseph Smith, which is only the complement of the Christian revelation."

At these words our miens (mine and the Chaplain's) probably expressed some surprise, for he continued eagerly: "I astonish you, don't I? Well, that is just how you are, you Gentiles. You judge us without knowing us and you slander us. You only know one thing of the Mormons, that is that they practice polygamy, and you conclude from that that we are a debauched, pagan people, possibly even idolaters. You do not know that we believe all that is true in your faith, and that there is not an article of faith in the true Christian religion which we have not adopted. Only we believe something else, too, and we have made complete the Christian revelation by the revelations of Joseph Smith whom we consider the greatest benefactor of mankind after Christ."

"Then you believe everything that we Christians believe?" said the chaplain, no less astonished than myself.

"Certainly."

"Will you allow me to make sure of that? I will repeat the Creed of the Apostles, and you will be as kind as to interrupt me when there is any article you don't at all accept."

Said was done.

"But then," said the chaplain, collecting his courage, "if you accept the dogmas of Christianity, you must also accept its morals. How is it, then, that you practice polygamy?"

"That's where I expected you," retorted the old Mormon with fire. "Polygamy—that's what always troubles the Gentiles when they speak of us. They believe this is the very corner stone of our faith, and they don't know that it is only one of the features of our faith. But I will answer you on that point. You will not dispute that polygamy is positively authorized in the Old Testament, and we see no part in the New Testament where it is forbidden. By each of us having several wives, we believe we put in practice the commandment God has given to man in the beginning of the world—'Increase and multiply.' Polygamy favors the rapid growth of the race. As there always are a certain number of men who are either unable or unwilling to marry, one sees among the Gentiles a great number of old maids who spend their lives uselessly in sterility and bitterness. There is nothing like this among us."

"Do there not sometimes arise between your wives quarrels, aroused by jealousy and which disturb the peace of your households?"

"Certainly," replied the Mormon, "this may sometimes occur. Susie may complain that you show too much affection to Bessie, or Bessie that you are too attentive to Susie; but these are the light clouds that a good husband knows quickly how to disperse. Are there no quarrels in your monogamous households? Well, will you allow me to speak frankly? (And here the old gentlemen grew animated and began to express himself with some degree of eloquence.) You people who practice monogamy, you lay claims to virtues which you are incapable to practice. You say you have and love only one woman. All good and well. But how many husbands are there amongst you who take mistresses, and how many women are there who have lovers? In our midst, as far as our people are concerned, adultery is unknown; and an adulterous woman is a great an offender in our eyes as in the eyes of the ancient Israelites whose laws condemned an adulteress to be stoned to death. Tomorrow, when you take a walk through the streets of Salt Lake City, you will not see a single Mormon child abandoned or begging. How many children are there on the pavements of your great cities who do not know their father? In our midst illegitimate births are unknown. We take care of our children, and we have them taught. If you find an habitual drunkard, it is a Gentile and not a Mormon. This does not mean that the using of wine is positively forbidden to us, but it suffices us to have read in the Scriptures of the sins which the children of Israel committed through drunkenness, in order that we be on our guard against the vice. The principal difference between you and us is that we obey our law while you do not observe yours. Hence we are convinced that some day or other the world will do us justice, and that the world will be regenerated by and through us."

It was time to retire for the night. They gave me the choice of sharing the large bed of the Chaplain in the finest room of the house (that of the head of the family, undoubtedly) or of enjoying all to myself a narrow couch in a small room. I chose the latter, and it was with difficulty that I at last fell into a sleep somewhat agitated. I dreamed I had become a Mormon and the husband of several wives, and that, undoubtedly, for the lack of knowing how to arrange matters as well as the old gentleman, I could not succeed in bringing Susie, Bessie, and several others to live in peace.

[*The next morning, Haussonville, the chaplain, and their host take the train to Salt Lake.*]

The trip from Ogden to Salt Lake City lasted about two hours. During this trip we became acquainted with a Judge of the country, appointed by the Federal Government, consequently a stranger to the Mormons and presumably in a condition to speak of them with independence.[30] I asked how it came that, although polygamy had been prohibited by a bill of Congress (as I had just learned), the Mormons yet could continue the practice. He explained that the application of that law had hitherto only been held in check by the impossibility of finding in the Territory of Utah women who would prosecute, witnesses who would testify, and Juries who would condemn. Our new acquaintance, by the way, was very severe on the Mormons.

---

[30] Federal judges serving in Utah in 1881 included Philip H. Emerson and Stephen P. Twiss, but Haussonville probably spoke with Jacob S. Boreman.

"They are," he told us, "a licentious and debauched people who live in lewdness. Polygamy only serves to conceal their disorderly habits and the promiscuity of women existing among them."

This is a little contrary to what the old Mormon told us the evening before. Therefore I retort:

"Are the habits of the Mormons, then, so very bad, aside of polygamy, which, certainly, is a great evil? Yesterday, we were told that adultery and illegitimate children were unknown among them."

"To be just," yielded the Judge, "I cannot say that they have exactly bad habits. Men and women marry very early, and the Mormons have cleverly understood to persuade their women that their happiness in the other world depended on the happiness they had made for their husbands in this life. Thus the husbands are the instruments of their future salvation without whose help they could not obtain their blessings. On that account the women prove scrupulously faithful to their husbands, and as a Judge I have never learned of a single case of adultery among them."

"Well, that is something," I could not help telling him, "the more as a faithfulness so little repaid is the more meritorious. But is it equally true, as they pretend, that they are so much superior to the Gentiles in all other respects and that crimes are very scarce among them?"

"The Gentile population in Utah," said the Judge with some embarrassment, "leaves something to be desired in respect to morality. They are very often adventurers who come here, as they formerly did in California, attracted by the mineral riches of the soil. This race of miners is always a turbulent and greedy race. Drunkenness, brawls, followed by murder, are frequent among them; and I am compelled to confess that of every ten crimes nine are by Gentiles. But I must repeat that it is altogether an exceptional population and and that it would not be equitable to take it for a basis of comparison."

I did not want to tell the Judge that the harshness of his judgment on the Mormons did not appear to me quite justified after all he had himself conceded, and our arrival at Salt Lake City put an end to the conversation.

Stéphane Jousselin: I Demand to See the Women

Like other travelers who visited Utah after the Mormons abandoned plural marriage, Stéphane Jousselin expressed surprise and even regret that he did not meet polygamists with large numbers of wives trailing behind them. Another French writer, Léon Paul Blouët (1848–1903), who wrote under the pseudonym Max O'Rell, complained in *La Maison John Bull & Cie*: "Polygamy is not tolerated anymore by the new American laws. If Artemus Ward were still alive, and he wanted to use Mormons as the subject of one of his hilariously humorous talks, and be kind enough to extend an invitation to one of them, he would no longer have to write on the invitation 'Please admit the bearer and *one* wife.' Salt Lake City is striking for its cleanliness, its quietness, and its air of prosperity, and you have to admire the tabernacle and the new temple; but it is only interesting by the memories it evokes. Mormons continue to believe they are saints and to call themselves so—a harmless conceit." Writers like Jousselin agreed with O'Rell that, among the many regrettable changes which occurred at the *fin de siècle*, was the change that made Utah a much less interesting place to visit.

> STÉPHANE JOUSSELIN, *YANKEES À LA FIN DE SIÈCLE*
> [YANKEES AT THE TURN OF THE CENTURY], 275–78.
> TRANSLATED BY HUGH MACNAUGHTON.

We arrive at the valley of Utah, and, at a distance, the dome of he tabernacle emerges next to the unfinished towers of the temple of the "Latter-day Saints" as they modestly call themselves.

Poor Mormons! They really have it hard! Wherever they go, they work strenuously to fertilize the ground, cultivate abandoned land, and build cities, but when they reach the point where they could finally enjoy their work, the gentiles start flooding in, infiltrating their businesses, and they end up becoming the masters. And my poor Mormons are forced to look for other settlements where, sure enough, they will also be hunted down, particularly if they succeed.

In the meantime, what they did in Salt Lake City is really imposing: the city is very beautiful, with big avenues, a theater, superb buildings, in brief, everything needed to make an important metropolis.

Where are the women? I demand to see the women.

Another legend! Too bad, they are only legends! Mormons now only have one woman: the disciples of Brigham Young are reduced to stare everyday at the same wife, and to be happy with her; otherwise, the most severe punishments will fall upon them. Rigid legislators have thus decided, which made one Mormon say: "All of this is pitiful; we are hunted down because of our honesty, to practice publicly what others do with hypocrisy!" Nothing is left from the blessed time when the Mormon could, as he wished, go from the brunette to the blonde, and from the redhead to the brunette. One can hardly even see the bed of the Prophet, of Brigham Young himself. Oh! That bed! What a bed! A bed big enough to house a whole battalion from Cythère. Today, the venerable piece of furniture lay abandoned and full of dust. The current head of the sect cannot look at it anymore, afraid to be disturbed by its sight and to be reminded of his loneliness. The bed brings back memories which are too painful, and spiders silently build their webs between the columns where the fires of polygamy used to burn!

Today I saw the river that the Mormons, to follow biblical tradition, named Jordan, and which ends up at the great Salt Lake; new converts were being baptized: a very simple operation, a plunge under the water, and the mystery is accomplished. I am told on this subject, that the offspring of the Prophet are many; the gigantic bed and multiple spouses had living consequences. What a man this Brigham Young! If the young Brigham follows his sample, in fifty years we will have a whole Brigham population, another curse our children are not prepared for!

By the way, I just found proof that the French are the most spiritually minded people of the universe. I researched the Mormon records: not a single French person! This is spirituality, or I am really ignorant! It is futile of course to search so far for something so obvious. . . . On the other hand, I found many virtuous English and Saxons; not as many however since the unfortunate edict to only have one legitimate wife.

Some say that the Mormons will go to Mexico, a more liberal country, to see about the possibility of having another little harem; the noble sons of John Bull will no doubt rush in with enthusiasm. It is said that one of them, who compared Salt Lake City to Mohammed's paradise, incurred the fury of his numerous mothers in law. To solve the problem, he found nothing better than to marry them all: it was the best way to silence them. They all became his wives! This is a solution I heartily recommend to European sons-in-law.

Chapter 10

"AMERICANS LIKE ALL THE OTHERS"
Accommodation after Statehood, 1896–1930

Although travelers continued to flock to Utah even after the Mormon church abandoned the practice of plural marriage and Utah achieved statehood, some visitors complained that without polygamy Utah was simply "ordinary." Many of them highlighted the historical practice to add a little spice to their travel accounts. When Arthur Conan Doyle visited Utah in 1923 on a missionary tour promoting Spiritualism, he criticized polygamy and claimed that it "had nothing whatsoever to do with the original teaching of Smith's revelation, but was entirely a later growth, and is now heartily repudiated. But the memory of it remains to show the danger of so-called inspirational teaching in worldly matters."[1] Three years later Jerome K. Jerome lampooned polygamy after his visit: "A leading Elder put us up in Salt Lake City. He introduced us to his wife. He noticed I was looking expectant. 'There are no more,' he explained. He put his arm round her. 'The modern American woman,' he continued, 'has convinced us that one wife is sufficient for any man.'"[2]

Even after the first manifesto in 1890 and the second in 1904, polygamy remained an ingredient of many tales about the Mormons. Zane Grey published *The Heritage of the Desert* in 1910 and *Riders of the Purple Sage* in 1912; Charles Pidgin wrote *House of Shame* in 1912. Insiders such as Frank J. Cannon and outsiders such as Gertrude King Majors continued to criticize the church for vacillating on the issue. The movie industry began to take advantage of the image of Utah and Mormon beginnings with the absolutely horrible movie *Trapped by the Mormons*, which is still "in print" in the twenty-first century. The

---

[1] Doyle, *Our Second American Adventure*, 97–98. Doyle commented on Mormonism in his first book and in his last. See Homer, "Arthur Conan Doyle and his Views on Mormonism," 66–81.

[2] Jerome, *My Life and Times*, 257.

issue of plural marriage was also alive and well in Washington. Brigham H. Roberts' election to Congress in 1898 and his eventual rejection by the House of Representatives; Reed Smoot's election to the Senate in 1903 and his eventual acceptance by that body in 1907; the LDS hierarchy's authorization of post-manifesto polygamous unions and its subsequent attempt to distance itself from them; and the election victories of the anti-Mormon American Party in 1908 all kept polygamy in the limelight.

While travelers and the media continued to write about polygamy when describing Utah, the new state began its long march into mainstream America. The Rio Grande Western Railroad published a map emphasizing parallels between the Promised Land in Palestine and "Deseret."[3] The Mormons established their patriotic zeal and proved their commitment to the American dream in the Spanish-American War, and the LDS church built a resort at Saltair that it hoped would be the next "Coney Island," where alcohol was served and the gates remained open on Sunday. During World War I, Mormon youth volunteered for military service and experienced combat, while German prisoners of war were interred at Fort Douglas, where at least twenty-one of them died and were buried.

Jules Huret: Christians with Mohammedan Instincts

Born and raised in Boulogne, French journalist Jules Huret (1864–1915) moved to Paris in 1885 and found work on the Left Bank with a textbook publisher. Within a year he began writing for *L'Evénement*, but he soon became a freelance writer for a variety of newspapers including *Le Gaulois*, *La Presse*, and *La Lanterne*. He became a correspondent for *L'Echo de Paris* in 1890, where he was quite well known for his interviews. Five years later, *Le Figaro* commissioned Huret to travel to the United States and write investigative articles that he subsequently collected and published. His first travel book, *En Amérique de New-York à la Nouvelle-Orléans*, recounted his first visit to the U.S. He traced his travels in 1903 from New York to Boston, Philadelphia, Pittsburgh, Cincinnati, and finally New Orleans. He returned to the U.S. the next year and published *En Amérique de San Francisco au Canada* (1905), which contained his observations about Utah and the Mormons and showcased his well-developed interview technique. His observations

---

[3] See Smyth, *The Conquest of Arid America*, 54.

influenced subsequent writers and foreshadowed a more modern approach that promised a guided tour of each itinerary.[4] Huret received the Grande Médaille by the Société de géographie commerciale in 1905. He continued to travel and write for *Le Figaro* from 1907 to 1912 and subsequently published six books about Germany and South America.

> JULES HURET, *EN AMÉRIQUE DE SAN FRANCISCO AU CANADA*
> [IN AMERICA FROM SAN FRANCISCO TO CANADA], 106–12, 115, 141–60.
> TRANSLATED BY HUGH MACNAUGHTON.

The city of the Salt Lake, where I was headed to visit the Mormons, is thirty-six hours' rail journey from San Francisco. I could not repress the excitement I felt at what I have to acknowledge was one of the most curious goals of my journey: to see Mormons! Men and women who have made laws and a moral teaching for themselves alone, and who bowed only to persecution and exile. Whoever could these headstrong polygamists be? What is the doctrine followed by these Christians with Mohammedan instincts? For a long time, I had thought they were savages, the remnants of Indian tribes slowly dying out in the lonely wastes of the Far West. It was not so. It seemed that they were Americans like all the others, and that some are still to be found around the Salt Lake, worshipping and living according to their customs, in secret like the early Christians.

But I realized how little reliance could be placed in this country on information gathered at any distance. Each man is so intent on his own business, he invests so much rectitude and precision in his own affairs, that he is frighteningly vague about the rest of humankind. Utterly indifferent to the affairs of others, he even ignores them altogether. So I was all agog to see these Mormons with my own eyes, these fabled polygamists whose ideas on love had already haunted my dreams as an adolescent. And I was finding—inquisitive people will understand me in this—that the train was not traveling fast enough....

The nearer we drew to Utah, the more dismal the landscape became. At dawn and dusk, vast solitary blue and pink, gorse-clad scrublands stretched away to infinity. For hour upon endless hour, the plain stretched between snow-clad mountain ranges which drew away, then came up close on each side; and this alternation was the only distraction to the eye for the greater part of the day. Soon, the ground became covered with a sort of shining rime that might have been taken for traces of half-melted snow. At one halt, I got down from the train, and rubbed my finger along the white ground and tasted it: it was alkali. We were at the approaches to the Salt Desert. Noth-

---

[4] Arnoux, *Les étapes de la démocratie nord-américaine*, 125–26.

ing grows there except wormwood. Not a single tree. Once, on looking out from the train, we were surprised to see galloping cowboys in their shirtsleeves driving a mixed herd of cattle and horses. What could those poor beasts possibly find to eat, as they leaned their heads over the bare, gray earth, above the old, dust-covered reeds like a powdered wig?

Not one major city stood on the way. The stations boasted nothing save a few plank sheds covered with earthen roofs. Laundry and blankets drying on a rough fir-wood balustrade. Nothing more. And on for another two or three hours more. The solitude closed in once again, with only the rails and the telegraph poles bearing witness to man's passage through these wastes. The sky was empty of birds, the earth was bare. Twice I saw the sun set on this uniform desolateness.

The effect on one was curious. One was constantly telling oneself that it was going to end, that a different landscape, other vegetation, new colors, something else, at last, would appear. Nothing did. Only the pattern of the mountains slightly varied the skyline. The last day, the sun setting behind the purple mountains shot molten pearls into the waters of the Salt Lake. We were arriving! . . .

I was in the State of the Mormons.

My first surprise was the city. Walking around it the day after my arrival, I was struck straightaway by the order that prevailed and the generally well-turned-out impression. I had thought I was arriving in the midst of a tribe of dreamers, shamefaced recusants, encamped in a corner of the Salt Lake. To my great surprise, I found myself in a large American city, cleaner and prettier than most of the ones I had visited. The streets of Salt Lake City are straight, and laid out in a checkerboard plan, as in the rest of America; they are all a hundred and thirty feet wide! Trees are planted along the sidewalks—something I had seen nowhere else. Electric streetcars move along them from north to south and from east to west. The guide who was my informant pointed out to me that the terrain has two slight slopes in these directions, facilitating the drainage of water and sewage into the lake by the Jordan, a little river 65 feet wide that flows into it.

In the commercial part of the city, the buildings adjoin each other, and many are seven or eight stories high, whereas the residential quarters have cottages with one or two story, with verandahs and surrounded by gardens. To the north and east, the city is encircled by a belt of hills and tall mountains; to the South, the valley stretches out to a width of some 20 miles, while some 15 miles to the West, it is bounded by the Salt Lake, which is ten times the size of Lake Geneva, being 89 miles long and 40 miles wide. It is close to 1,200 meters above sea level and the city itself lies at an altitude of some 1,600 meters.[5]

---

[5] Salt Lake's official altitude is 4,330 feet or 1,320 meters.

"But look," I finally blurted out to my guide, "I should like to see some Mormons!"

He looked at me in astonishment: "Most of these men and women that you cross in the street are Mormons," he told me. "I myself am one. You can look at me." And he beamed from behind his spectacles. He was a short, bearded man, with a tranquil, dreamy air, very plainly dressed. He explained to me that he was Swiss and that, having been converted in his home canton by a Mormon missionary, he had felt it preferable for his salvation to draw closer to the mother Church.

"That is why I came to America. I don't regret having done so. I am married; I have several children; I am employed at the Zions Cooperative Mercantile Institution founded by the apostle Brigham Young (it is a sort of big department store where just about everything can be found, from a ton of iron to a grand piano), and I live happily. Besides, I have a rank in the priesthood of the Latter-day Saints. . . ."

"Naturally, I suppose you are polygamous?" I asked.

"Not at all."

I was disappointed.

"Not all Mormons are polygamous," he explained. "To be so, you need to have wealth, since twenty or so children cost a good deal to raise . . . Besides," he added, "polygamy is now forbidden by the laws, and officially there are no more polygamists." . . .

"You will know all," the man replied placidly. "And you will even be able to talk about them with the Chief of the Apostles, should you wish to. He is very busy with running his bank, and speaking with him is a favor. But the fact that you are a stranger from so far away will make it easier for you to meet him. . . ." It seemed to me, I know not why, that the priests of this strange religion ought to be clothed in white or purple flannel with strange hats; I conceived them to be something between a pagan Roman votary and a Buddhist priest. So when I was shown into the office of Mr. Cutler, one of the most important bishops of Salt Lake City, I was momentarily surprised. It was a small business office, with a table, a few chairs, some file-boxes and a telephone. And I found myself facing one of the largest sugar-producers in Utah.

The man in front of me was an American differing little from any other, with his pointed, grizzling beard, his keen eye and his amiable, reserved smile. In his physiognomy could be read something other than the ordinary preoccupations of a man of business. Furthermore, he was elegant in his well-fitting morning coat, with a politeness uncommon in these far-flung regions. Naturally, he only spoke English.[6]

---

[6] Huret met John Christopher Cutler (1846–1928), who served as the second governor of the state of Utah (1905–09). Cutler apparently served as a ward LDS bishop but never served as a general authority.

My bishop, in-between his sugar concerns, engaged in all sorts of other speculations, to do with banking, industry, and commerce. This was even, one should suppose, his main function. His title of bishop, which was purely honorary, gave him authority in the hierarchy; but as there is no worship in Mormonism, no confession, nor communion, nor even any ceremony other than the Sunday lectures, baptisms and marriages, which fall within the province of the secondary priests, his priesthood amounted to little. I told him the purpose of my journey, and he promptly gave me his entire attention, answering my questions unhesitatingly. So I soon found out that he had or had had five wives and nineteen children, of whom fifteen were living and engaged in business in the four corners of the world, in Australia, China, the Indies and Europe. "All of them good Mormons," he told me.

He went on to recount to me all the old persecutions suffered by the Mormons. And by this route, we came to discuss his religion itself. According to him, Adam was a holy man who had done his duty on another planet, and whom God had brought to earth to become the prince of the human lineage as the reward of his virtue.

To become a good Mormon, it is necessary to believe in the doctrine of the revelation, that is, what God told to Joseph Smith, and that the Book of Mormon, or Western Bible, is as authentic as the Eastern Bible.

"Is it true," I asked him, "that all Mormons pay a tenth of their income to the church?"

"That's quite right," he replied, adding, "And isn't that very fair? The believing people must nourish the ones who preach the word of God. So in the future of mankind, the human community will work, not to pay interest to idle capital, but to support its intellectual élite, which will think and sing for it and make life beautiful." He informed me that of the early Mormons, the most zealous, the most fervent were Danes and Swedes. Since then, the Church had continued to take in Scandinavian converts. There were even, it seems, French people drawn—I said to him—by polygamy, but the majority of believers were of Germanic origin.

I asked him if I could see the chief of the Apostles, the President of the Mormon Church. He volunteered to take me to him himself.

"President [Joseph] F. Smith is also President of the Zions Cooperative Mercantile Institution and of several other banks," he told me; "he is a very busy man, but I hope we shall see him, if only for an instant. You probably know that he is a blood relative of Joseph Smith?"

We went out. I was very cold. Thick snow covered the ground. As we passed in front of the blue granite temple, with its six spires reaching skyward, the bishop said to me, "When he arrived here, Brigham Young, the successor of the prophet, declared, 'here is where we shall build the Temple.' And so it was done."

The street running the length of the temple is peopled with banks and trust companies. Nearly all these banks are Mormon. The greater part of commerce and industry in the area is in the hands of the Mormons. I was beginning to understand that I was dealing with wonderful businessmen. . . .

When we reached the bank of the head of the Apostles, he was just leaving. He stopped when he saw Bishop Cutler walking beside me. Bishop Cutler murmured a few words in a low voice, and President Smith walked towards me.

Very tall, with a grizzling beard, and long hair flowing backward, he cut a benevolent figure, lively and open. He was dressed in a long black frock coat, under which one could see a white tie (the twelve apostles wear a white tie). But behind his gold spectacles, one observed his eye, which, like that of the bishop, tried to read one's eyes, and this visible preoccupation, which one sensed to be habitual, put between him and the person with whom he spoke some indefinable barrier of mistrust, arousing the sensation one has when in the presence of people whose profession is to deceive, or who wish to appear clever, like diplomats, for example.[7]

I told him of the curiosity which had led me to the Salt Lake and I touched upon the wealth of the Mormons. His lips smiled. "It is true we are rich," he replied to me. "But it is our economy, our sobriety and especially our work that have given us wealth. Smith said 'Build your house.' A good truth, Sir!"

"And, above all, we have the faith! When the Mormons arrived here in July 1847, they found themselves in the middle of an immense desert, alone, far from the help of man, with no provisions other than wild roots, and no spare clothes. Another people with another faith would have given way to despair and become the prey of Indians and wild beasts, or fallen into degradation and anarchy. One of their number, Samuel Brennan [sic], just returned from California, endeavored to persuade Brigham Young to leave this inhospitable region, describing in the most glowing terms the beauty and abundance of the Pacific coast. In vain. Brigham Young and his companions were of the stuff of heroes of whom persecution and adversity could do nothing but strengthen the character. 'Here,' said Brigham Young, thrusting his stick in the earth, 'we shall build the temple of our God!' And he built this temple that you saw.[8]

"Another story: a trapper, James Bridger, who had visited the Salt Lake and knew Utah, advised the Mormons, when he met them in 1847, to abandon their project. And as he saw he could not sway them from their purpose, he offered them one thousand dollars for the first bushel of wheat harvested

---

[7] Joseph F. Smith (1838–1918) was church president from 1901 to 1918. He testified before the United States Senate at the Smoot hearings in 1904 and shortly thereafter issued his famous second manifesto confirming that polygamy was no longer sanctioned by the Mormon church.

[8] For the life and adventures of Samuel Brannan and this story, which was told in a discourse by Wilford Woodruff, see Bagley, ed., *Scoundrel's Tale*, 214.

in the region! And sure enough, Utah would have remained a desert still, had the Mormons not used irrigation and drainage—according to the methods of the Spanish and the Egyptians—which, in their hands, became the salvation and wealth of all the arid region of the Rocky Mountains. Today, all the streams that come down from the mountains are harnessed for this purpose, along with many artesian wells we have dug.

"And did you know that, today, few lands are as productive as the soil of Utah? Do you wish to have proof of this? In 1889, one of the leading agricultural journals of the United States, the *American Agronomist*, offered a prize for the highest yield of wheat per acre anywhere in the U.S. The prize, as it happens, was awarded to a farmer of Salt Lake City, who harvested 80 bushels of wheat per acre (a bushel weighs 60 pounds, 2.8 bushels = 1 hectoliter, and there are 2.47 acres to the hectare). That is not all, Sir. At the same time we were making Utah an agricultural country, we were building roads, bridges, and factories of all kinds, mining for asphalt, coal, and iron, and quarrying for marble, onyx, and sandstone, and we were producing 150,000 tons of salt per year. In a few years, we shall have blast-furnaces and foundries; and the Eastern railways are made with rails from Utah, for we have near Cedar City—not counting the others—the Iron Mountain which, itself alone, contains 50 million tons of iron ore. And again, that is not all, Sir. We are richly endowed with gold, silver, copper and lead mines. In 1900, the total income from our mines—still not exploited to the full at the time—came to 234,703,580 dollars, equivalent to 1,174 million francs. Our dividends paid in 1901 came to 22 million francs."

"I was told," I interrupted him, "that your religion prevented you from working the mines?"

The two elderly divines look at each other and smiled, as is becoming for divines: "No," said the chief of the Apostles, continuing to smile, "nothing forbids us from working mines, or even owning them. I myself own shares in several mines. Besides," continued the Mormon pope, "in Utah we have 40 oil companies. I spoke to you of sugar and wheat, but I have told you nothing of the woolen mills, the electricity generating plant, and the foundries that already exist. Sugar, now, the bishop could tell you about it. We produced 16 million kilograms of it in 1901–1902...."

"By the way," I asked, "how is your Church organized?"

"The whole territory that is occupied by the Mormons," the Mormon pope replied, "that is, not only Utah but also part of Idaho, Wyoming, and Arizona, is divided into ecclesiastical districts, with a bishop presiding each district; the bishop, with his two counselors, is responsible for the temporal and spiritual prosperity of his flock; he gives judgment in the difficulties and disorders that arise among members of his brotherhood; he receives and administers the tithe and the offerings, sees to the needs of the poor without receiving any fixed wage, being remunerated only according to his own needs and the time he devotes to the Church. I would mention in passing that the Church sends out a number of missionaries each year to all parts of the world (there are currently some fifteen hundred of them) to preach the Gospel, without wages; this mission lasts two to three years, after which others go out and replace them."

"How do you recruit them?"

"Most of these missionaries are young men aged between eighteen and twenty, with no experience of the world, no university education, but like Christ's disciples of old, filled with the Holy Spirit, preaching the primitive Gospel in all its purity. Most of our schools are full: try looking for a little truant in the whole of Utah; you won't find *one*. Our schoolteachers, some 270 men and women, earn an average wage of $515 (2,600 Francs of the day) for 40 weeks' teaching. The Mormons have a Sunday-school system probably unsurpassed elsewhere; there are more than 500 such schools throughout the Church, with nearly 100,000 pupils and men and women teachers, and 23,541 volumes in their libraries; $15,000 are spent annually on the purchase and publication of religious books and tracts. Besides this, there are young people's associations for improving mental and bodily fitness; ladies' societies for the relief of the poor. Old people are not forgotten; each year, a big excursion is organized for all persons aged over seventy. Last year, 1,700 old people of both sexes, all religions and all races were transported to Ogden, the second-largest city in Utah, and entertained there free of charge.

"I don't need to tell you that not only does universal suffrage exist in Utah as in the remainder of the United States, but in addition, women vote and have the same civil rights as men."

"If you have rendered so many services to your country, and made so much progress, then how do you explain the persecutions waged against you?"

"Envy. When in 1849, the earliest gold mines were discovered in the West, we were the owners by law of the entire Salt Desert. And when gold was discovered in the desert, an unreasoning wave of hatred rose against us."

"So it is not your religion that was being persecuted?"

"No. Our religion is very moral, even severe. The old Mormons and the good Mormons of today take neither alcohol nor any kind of stimulant, which is wonderful in such a harsh region. That does not prevent us liking pleasurable pursuits, the theater and dancing, but provided nothing ever offends decency."

"I know," I said, "that Mormons married before 1890 have kept their wives. But now that the law forbids plural marriage, is there no trace of polygamy?"

The Head of the Apostles, his gaze fixed firmly earthwards said to me,

"The Latterday Saints may have several spiritual sisters who chose them for husbands..." He stopped speaking. And I saw that I ought not to insist....

I had expressed the wish to meet a few Mormon women, of those who were part of a polygamous family. I was extremely curious to see them first of all, to speak with them, to ask them questions, to gain my own impression of their state of mind. A five o'clock tea was arranged for me, and one evening, at six, I found myself in a little, old-fashioned drawing-room at Mrs. [Emmeline B] Wells', a respectable, white-haired lady, of a fine and distinguished expression, still pretty in spite of her being over sixty. A firm gentleness was delineated in her noble, regular features.[9]

She explained to me that she had invited several of her lady friends to come, chosen from among the most remarkable women of the sect. One was even a daughter of the famous Brigham Young, the extraordinary man who had succeeded Joseph Smith in the Presidency of the Church and who had led the exodus of the Mormons from the Mississippi to the Salt Lake, through the Rocky Mountains, in the depth of winter, under continual threat from the Indians. She told me of the impression left by Brigham Young in the minds of all those who knew him: "He was tall, he was strong, he was handsome, he was powerful; everyone obeyed him as they would have obeyed a king, a god. He had twenty-one wives."

The Mormon ladies arrived soon after, excusing themselves for being a few minutes late. They had just come from their club, or from some charitable work. There were seven of them. I scrutinized them as discreetly as I could, but with intense inner curiosity.

At first blush, there was nothing to mark them out from the other women of every country, apart from a certain simplicity of dress and adornment, yet not without a feather in a hat, and a ribbon: the attire of the lesser gentry in the English-speaking Protestant world. But on closer examination, especially when they spoke, it was easy to note an intense exaltation of thought, a sort of ardent mysticism, an energetic faith that no objection could cause to waver.

When I began to explain the reason for my curiosity, I clearly saw that it was I, in my turn, who had become the phenomenon. They regarded me curiously, smiling benevolently, like people astonished at the astonishment of others, as we would regard the surprise of Papuans viewing our civilization.

I avowed my ignorance of the Mormon religion and their customs, and apologized in advance for the indiscretion, naïveté and perhaps the bluntness of my questions. These ladies smiled with the condescending air that I just spoke of, and Mrs. Wells assured me that I should not feel myself to be under any restraint. I was delighted to hear this.

---

[9] Pioneering feminist Emmeline Blanche Woodward Wells (1828–1921) was the widow of Apostle Daniel H. Wells. She was the fifth president of the Relief Society from 1910 to 1921.

I then went on to explain the difficulty Europeans have in understanding, and especially allowing, that women who were not Orientals would agree to share a man that they loved with an indefinite number of rivals.

"But first of all," Mrs. Wells replied to me, "they are not rivals. All the wives of a Mormon must love each other. Nothing is more natural for the human race than to feel drawn towards those who have the same tastes as ourselves. Unlike your way of thinking, therefore, two women who love the same man should, as a rule, get on together."

"I grant you that," I conceded, "but you say, *as a rule*. Does not this fellow-feeling actually cease the moment one of the women takes from the other the love of the man to which she felt entitled?"

"No, if the man knows how to distribute his love fairly. It is a question of power and tact. And that is why not all men are worthy of plural marriage."

"Surely," I went on, "you claim that man and woman are, if not equal, at least equivalent. Now, say there is a woman who makes a man the complete gift of herself, wholly and unreservedly: is she not naturally inclined to require the equivalent of what she gave? And is there equivalence if the man goes around distributing in pieces, all the smaller for the shares being many in number, the totality of the love she believes she deserves?"

This object appeared to cause Mrs. Wells to hesitate for a moment. But one of my other lady companions spoke up: "As for myself, I would rather be the tenth wife of a superior man than the single wife of an inferior man."

"I can understand you, Madam," I said, surprised at the passionate energy she had put into her rejoinder; "but would you not prefer to be the single wife of a superior man? That is what I should like to know."

She replied, "Certainly. But it is a fact that, in a family of twenty children—for example, ten boys and ten girls—the girls are generally superior to the boys. Now, since there are more superior women than superior men, the women must be content to share the superior men."

I had not expected such a thrust, and the argument, which I could not verify, left me tongue-tied.

I nevertheless managed to reply, "It would need to be proved that your calculation is accurate."

They all cried out at once, "It's a fact, it's a fact!"

"No matter," I replied, "that fact would not dispense you from suffering, if you were very loving and very sensitive, from seeing the object of your love squandering his own . . . In France, a woman who could bear that with indifference wouldn't love her husband . . ."

Mrs. Wells, who had been thinking, repeated, "The man would need to share his love equally . . ."

"Would you not therefore need," I insisted, "to be entirely ignorant of the sentiment of jealousy? . . ."

One of the ladies who had not yet spoken, timidly essayed a reply: "If one suffers, one does not show it. *One must not show it.*"

"But what if the suffering is violent . . . It is a question of sensitivity . . ."

She responded: "It's a question of discipline."

I shook my head. These women could say what they liked. If they loved otherwise than with their heads exalted above their hearts and their mystical imaginings, they would have in their eyes something other than that icy gleam which is the sign of their virtue and also the secret of their facile resignation. I felt like telling them so, but I felt that I would be unable to make myself understood by these creatures who had been naïve enough to let themselves be taken in by this childish fable that is the Mormon religion, so disciplined and so cold that the very notion of jealousy appeared foreign to most of them.

And I went on to address a different line of enquiry.

I knew that they accepted plural marriage. How had they managed, with their monogamous upbringing, to understand and allow it? One can conceive of such a thing in Oriental women, oppressed for centuries by the customs of the harem. But these women, of English, Scandinavian, or Germanic origin, brought up in the austerity of Protestantism, what way had their prejudices taken so as to accept this incredible reversal of their original customs?

I asked them this. And very seriously, so seriously that I inwardly thought she was mocking me, Mrs. Wells gave me this reply: "Polygamy is useful to Mormons, men and women, for their glory to be greater in heaven. But the more numerous their offspring, the more wondrous and overwhelming will their glory be. They shall reign over their innumerable families forever and ever. Think of the sadness of a virtuous man with no descendants. The first wife of the current head of the apostles, President Smith, was barren. What would he have suffered, if polygamy had not been part of our faith?"

I could not believe my ears. "And it is this idea that has led you to accept this sharing?"

"Is it not sufficient?" she replied in a tone of simple sweetness. "Is not glory in eternal life worth this small service, even admitting that it is one? What does earthly life amount to, compared with the glorious happiness that obedience to the law of God promises us?"

"So it is God who ordained polygamy for Mormons?"

"Why, yes!" said she in surprise. "Did you not know that Joseph Smith received from God himself the revelation of the fitness of plural marriage? Besides, did you not also know that the patriarchs of old . . ."

"Yes, yes, I know," I interrupted, amazed at such credulity, and also at the astonishing power gained over these simple souls by the businessmen—prophets of Mormonism. I continued my inquiries: "What was the life of

Mormon households during the time when polygamy was allowed? How did the five or six wives of the same man get on in practice, and what became of the children in all this babble of confusion?"

A young, pretty, woman spoke up. She had dark hair and dark eyes, and was aged about thirty or thirty-five: "I can tell you quite well. I am one of the forty-six daughters of Brigham Young. I lost my mother when I was three, and all my other mothers loved me very much, I should say almost as much as my natural mother. In the days when I was at home—I was born at the Lion House, which you can see near here—we were eighteen sisters, and my father's twelve wives lived with us. There was never quarreling of any kind, nor even any misunderstanding. My father came to the house every evening at six. He said prayers, kissed all his children, took dinner with my mothers, and I saw no more of him until the following evening at six. My mothers lived together as friends. They were of one accord in admiring my father's genius, his strength, intelligence and kindness. Their conversations turned on our upbringing and the Mormon religion. My father had twenty-one wives in all."[10]

I listened to these matters, which were new to me, with growing curiosity.

"Note also," said Mrs. Wells to me, "that there are virtually no invalids or badly developed children among the polygamists. This is very important."

"Finally," I concluded, "you do not envy the lot of women in Europe?"

She gave me the following reply, which I found ironically appropriate:

"They are not to be envied. Their husbands are unfaithful to them; if they are not aware of this, then the lie they live is very unhealthy. Or else they do know, and they suffer on that account. Why not agree that man is polygamous? If it were agreed, as with us, they would not suffer from it, or at least, not as much."

Another of the ladies added, "The wives of polygamists are much happier than the others. They even become rapidly superior to them. They don't have to take care of their husband all the time, so they have more leisure to cultivate their mind. Since the man's ill humor is scattered over several women, none of them suffers much from it. And lastly, as of necessity we see each other less often, we are not constantly together, so love does not become commonplace, and the joy of loving remains more intense and at the same time, more pure . . ."

My curiosity had spent itself. The interview came to an end.

---

[10] The daughter of Brigham Young that Huret met was most likely Phoebe Louisa Young Beatie (1854–1931), who was three years old when her mother, Clarissa Ross Young, died on 20 March 1858. However, Phoebe would have been fifty years old in 1904. Another possibility is Evelyn Louisa Young Davis, who was two years old when her mother, Margaret Maria Alley, died 5 November 1852 (two years before the Beehive House and four years before the Lion House were built), which would have made Evelyn fifty-four in 1904. According to the best expert, Jeffery Ogden Johnson, Brigham Young had fifty-six wives and fifty-seven children, including thirty-one daughters.

Before I left, Mrs. Wells handed me a copy of the newspaper she heads, a journal of women's causes, and a copy of an anthology of poems she wrote in English, *Rêveries et souvenirs*.[11] Her engraved portrait was the frontispiece of her work. Her finely chiseled, angelic face with its serious expression sheds a sympathetic light on those candid pages: I have read them since. It is all of a mysticism at once exalted and puerile. Canticles of thanksgiving; slow, gentle requiems; psalms and melodies in which recur unceasingly the names of Eternal and Most High. The most worn-out metaphors crowd together in these verses with a kindly ingenuousness: the voice of the nightingale and the kingfisher, the rays of the silvery moon, the breath of the westerly breeze, the brightness of daisies shining on the lawn like the stars in the sky are, for her, divine messengers that sing a hosanna to the glory of the Creator. God is everywhere, and she unceasingly sings of him, in pastures, dales, roses and lilies, the scents of spring, the sun's golden rays, and whatever else?

. . .

What a strange mixture of vague religiosity, juvenile outpourings, banality and credulity, to the extent that one is hesitant whether to feel sorry for her, to admire, or to smile.

In the end, though, one has to smile.

G. A. Zimmer: Such Blind Fanatical Zeal

The German Evangelical Christusgemeinde (Christ Church) sent G. A. Zimmer of Albersdorf, Germany, to Utah in July 1902 as a missionary-pastor to the German Evangelical Synod of North America. The synod, founded in 1840 in a country parsonage near St. Louis, Missouri, was a legitimate daughter of the Prussian State Church that by 1902 had more than one thousand clergy and thirteen hundred congregations in nineteen districts extending across the U.S. and Canada. Zimmer was sent after Rev. G. A. Schmidt, the president of the mission district in Denver, traveled to Salt Lake City in the winter of 1901–02 on the Denver and Rio Grande Railway's express train, to determine if there were evangelical Germans in the city. He located a few married couples who had not been in a church since their confirmation but who told him that they would attend a church if "a liberal-minded fellow" came to be its German pastor. He encouraged the Synod's Central Office for Home Missions, located in St. Louis, to

---

[11] Wells was the editor of the *Women's Exponent*, a semi-monthly newspaper for Mormon women, from 1877 to 1914. George Q. Cannon & Sons published her book of poetry, *Musings and Memories*, in 1896.

send G. Niebuhr from Saint Charles, Missouri, to Utah to explore the matter further. Niebuhr had been a pastor to German immigrants in California and was familiar with life in the West. Niebuhr arrived in Salt Lake City on 10 July 1902 and visited Ogden and other settlements but had to return to the East after three months due to other responsibilities. Zimmer came to Utah shortly thereafter. He wrote about his experiences in Utah while serving as "a modest country pastor in Soto, Missouri, right in the middle of the blessed uplands of the Ozark Mountains."

G. A. Zimmer, *Unter den Mormonen in Utah*
[Among the Mormons in Utah], 73–89. Translated by tsc.

I arrived in Salt Lake City on a bright, sunny day with the words of the following verse on my lips: "Jesus go before me and lead me along life's way." Brother Niebuhr recommended the Hotel St. James for lodging. It was a plain, modest guest house on Main Street in the center of the city, which I arrived at after asking for directions here and there. Mr. Jones, the manager, told me right away without beating around the bush that he was a Mormon, but he was quite accommodating when it came to business. He had good reason for that. Service was nil, the food miserable, the room, particularly my bed, full of bedbugs. With time I ceased to get upset about the last-mentioned matter, since they appear to be a standard feature of all guest houses west of the Rocky Mountains. For only a single, narrow room I paid three dollars per week. For three meals a day, I paid five dollars per week. It is with great pleasure that I think back to my first lodging in Salt Lake City. It was from there that I undertook my first exploratory walks. That same evening I made a pilgrimage up Main Street to Moroni's Temple. On its eastern central tower, the angel Moroni gazed eastward with a golden trumpet in his right hand, inviting the people of the world to enter into Mormon's Zion. There was something fascinating about that sight. It was there, in front of the gigantic Mormon Temple made of monstrous granite blocks, that the embodiment of this demonic teaching's imposing power first confronted me.

Since the gates of the approximately five-meter high wall surrounding the large, quadrant-shaped Temple Block were closed, I walked along Brigham Street past the statue of Young to his roomy Lion and Beehive house. In his old harem, where Young, the "Leader of Israel," had lived like a Turkish Pasha with his twenty-six wives, there now are the offices of the high priesthood, the world mission, and also the residence of the current president, Joseph F. Smith. Since this prophet, seer and revelator of God had five wives sharing his love, each of whom lived in her own handsomely furnished house, he still had to have had an official residence where the members of his church could contact him during several hours of every day.

In the Beehive House, where none of his wives lived, I saw some small, rather cheeky little boys running about, and later some girls as well. This made me conclude that a portion of his *forty-three* children lived and slept there.

The Eagle Gate, the former entrance to Young's private property, is located right beside the Beehive House. His grave is a few steps to the northeast of it in the corner of an austere square surrounded by a high iron fence.[12] Neither a wreath nor flowers decorated his resting place nor those of several of his wives who are also buried there. On the horizon the snowy peaks of the Wasatch Mountains glowed in the last rays of the sun. Far to the west, the wide silver ribbon of the Salt Lake glistened.

The next morning I began my assigned missionary work among the many dead and completely faithless Christians and the several thousands of former Evangelicals who had converted to the Mormon sect. It was not a very encouraging beginning. I had received a few addresses from Pastor Niebuhr. Using these, I first went to see the English Baptist minister, Reverend Frank Barnett. He had already allowed Brother Niebuhr to hold worship services in his church and he offered the same privilege to me in exchange for $1.00 per service. I then made my initial pastoral visits, the first one at the home of a certain Mr. Meier. This man came originally from the area of Lippe and moved here after having lived in two other communities in the Union. Once a man of deep religious understanding, his pursuit of money had turned him into a Demas (the rich man in the story of Lazarus and the beggar) who had won the world. On hearing my invitation to take part in worship services, he replied, "Go to church? No Pastor, I go to my [Masonic] lodge." And this continued to be his answer, even though I invited him weekly for two years. His wife received my invitation with gratitude but never attended either. She was also from the area of Lippe and had been raised by devout parents, but had sunk down so low in Utah's immoral atmosphere that it killed off all moral judgement. She defended polygamy with the following words: "But it is something beautiful! I'd have no objection if my husband became a Mormon and took another one or two young wives. Then I'd also have it a bit easier doing housework." This blatantly honest confession left me speechless. So, women themselves see nothing offensive about polygamy! I briefly refuted Mormon teachings and practices using God's Word and took my leave but was preaching to deaf ears, for in parting this woman said to me, "Well Pastor, you wouldn't be hoping to convert any Mormons here, now would you? That would be quite ridiculous!"

---

[12] Brigham Young's grave, a stone box sealed with a heavy granite block and surrounded by an elaborate wrought-iron fence, is in what is now called the Mormon Pioneer Memorial Cemetery on a hilltop on the south side of First Avenue between State and A streets. His son, Joseph A. Young, daughter Alice Young Clawson, and wives Mary Ann Angel, Eliza R. Snow Smith, Lucy Ann Decker Seeley, and Mary Elizabeth Rollins Lightner Smith are buried nearby.

That same evening, I unintentionally ended up in an authentic, large Mormon house. While passing by, I heard German speech coming from within and in good faith believed that German evangelical Christians might be living there. So I stepped inside and asked for the man of the house who soon appeared and invited me to dinner. As I was very hungry, I gratefully accepted the invitation. Before I could put forward my invitation to an evangelical worship service, the man introduced me to his three wives and seventeen children and giving his six grown-up daughters an inviting glance asked me, "Are you already married?"

"No," I answered.

He continued with, "Yes, you did say that you are a preacher of the Gospel. If you were to die today already, do you believe you would die in peace and that Jesus would mercifully receive you?"

Myself. "Most certainly I shall be received."

He: "That is precisely where you are mistaken, Pastor! One day the Lord will say to us, 'Where are those I gave you?' And yet you would then come before Him with empty hands."

Myself. "Well, well, what you say is quite remarkable."

He: "It is not at all remarkable. The Savior will not receive you into Eternity above. He will tell you, 'Return to earth and do your duty.'"

"What then will I have to do on earth?"

"Have children, nothing but have children." Thereupon, the simple-minded man quoted scriptural passages that he vehemently spewed forth whether they were appropriate or not. He was so convinced of his salvation through the begetting of children that I would have started a heated argument had I made a just reply. But I did not want to do this after such short acquaintance and after I had been so graciously invited to dinner. Therefore I thankfully took my leave. The threefold husband gave me another searching look and said, "Preacher, you aren't far from the Gospel. Tomorrow, buy yourself *The Book of Mormon* and read it prayerfully. Then you will find the truth sooner than you think. For it is not in vain that God has sent you into the land where the Children of God are gathered together."

Despite myself, I had to think of the words that Jesus spoke as he looked upon the Centurion from Capernaum: "Not even in Israel have I found such faith." Where are the Christians who immediately recommend their religion with a true ring of conviction to someone of another faith like this old German man? Such blind, fanatical zeal is proof of the great demonic power that the Mormon hierarchy holds over its followers. The man came from the area around Tuttlingen in Württemberg and was so convinced of Prophet Smith's God-given mission that he thought providence had lead me to Utah so that I might receive his teachings!

So the first Sunday came. Three people, a man and two women, came to the first worship service. Attendance improved extremely slowly. After half a year there were already seven! And yet during this time I was making about thirty-two visits every week in the city, which was saying a lot because of the great distances I had to travel to find the German Evangelicals. The church service was also announced every Friday and Sunday morning in three to five daily newspapers.

Most of the Germans living there persistently put up a passive yet ironclad resistance. When I visited them, most received me in such a cold and heartless way that I still inwardly shiver when I think about it. I soon found out that many of these compatriots had stormy and adventurous pasts. Some had to get out of Germany with haste. Others had abandoned a wife and child in the eastern part of the Union and were living here in common-law relationships with other women. Others had fraudulently declared bankruptcy somewhere and were happily living in ease under assumed names on the funds they had illegally obtained. There were counterfeiters, known swindlers, and anarchists among them. They were the dregs of German society who, after many vagaries, had taken refuge here where they found a comfortable place of rest for their sins among the immoral Mormons with whom they have been residing in a friendly, neighborly fashion. Such people hate a German pastor with the depths of their souls. They find a visit from one distressing, for they do not like to be reminded of the time when, as youthful communicants, they stood in front of the altar of their home church. . . .

To keep the few worshipers together, I appointed three men to a provisional executive [committee] to actively recruit members. They signed agreements which committed them to contributing fifty cents to one dollar per month. After a few months, the president died of pneumonia. Of the two remaining members of the executive, one was the treasurer. He hailed from Genthin near Magdeburg. His wife came from Fehrbellin in Brandenburg and was born Catholic. When she was only fourteen years old, Mormon missionaries converted her whole family to their sect. When she was sixteen, those missionaries induced them to emigrate to Utah. There she soon got married. As her husband was not a Mormon and earned good money as a cutter in a men's clothing store, she was partly successful in getting away from the Mormon Church. Both attended the worship service every Sunday and I liked the young couple a lot and appointed the husband as treasurer. But I had to collect the contributions when they were due. Otherwise no money would have come in, for the treasurer found such work beneath his dignity and left it to the Pastor, who in no way found it pleasant. Then the couple had their first child, a daughter. Despite admonitions on my part, her baptism was constantly put off. When the child was already several months old, it suddenly became sick. What did these people, who wished to be Christians, do? They had the child "blessed" by a Mormon bishop who lived nearby. (Mormons are not baptized until they have completed their eighth year of life.) When I entered their home barely ten minutes afterwards and found out what had been done, the child's father said, "Pastor, if the child gets worse, would you be so kind as to also baptize it. Maybe that would be better after all!"

That such people cannot be made members of the executive of an evangelical congregation is clear. Another example of the muddled views about baptism among the Germans in Salt Lake City would be timely here.

On a quiet Sunday afternoon, in October 1903, I went to the home of a grain and seed wholesaler to baptize his fifth child with all the family present. As the mother and godmother did not understand any German, I had to conduct the baptism in English. Afterward the godmother admitted she was a Mormon when I asked which church she belonged to. In reply to my interjection that she therefore had no right to take over the role of godmother in this case, the father of the baptized child said, "See here Pastor, you do know that I am a strict Lutheran from Hanover, do you not? My wife is the second daughter of the seventeenth wife of the apostle John Taylor. My oldest boy, now eleven years old, was baptized a Mormon in the Jordan River two years ago. My second boy was baptized by the English-Lutheran Church, the third by the German Missouri Lutheran Church, the fourth by a Presbyterian pastor and the fifth, a girl, is the one you have just baptized. I have had my children baptized into such a variety of religions because I do business with all of these people. It's all one and the same since the only purpose of baptism is for children to receive a name. When they grow up, they'll all become Mormons anyway. My father-in-law will see to that and you just can't do things any other way here!"

And then how did things go with my treasurer? His Mormon-blessed child died a few days later. His wife, who was once again ensnared by the Mormon faith, insisted that her husband have the child buried in the Mormon cemetery. This was because Mormons strictly believe that only those buried in their cemeteries will be resurrected on the judgement day, whereas all those laid to rest elsewhere will have to sleep for eternity. The funeral sermon was given by the nearby Mormon bishop and a few words were said by some spice merchants. From then on both spouses turned their backs entirely on my evangelical church. On both Sunday and workday evenings, they attended the Mormon meetings where they were soon completely won over by this religion.

Just to what extent this conversion succeeded became evident a year later. The young woman longingly wished to have another child, but this wish was not being fulfilled. But every faithful Mormon woman has no greater wish than to bear children, since "woman will be saved through bearing children" (I Tim. 2:15). Now she had an older sister who had also married a Mormon soon after her arrival in Utah. He, however, ran off to California with another who pleased him more, whereupon Prophet [Joseph] F. Smith divorced her from him. She had no children and her sister, the cutter's wife, induced her husband, who had meanwhile converted to Mormonism, to also marry her sister so that at least one of them would have children by him. And so it came to be that my former congregational treasurer was married to his sister-in-law by a bishop behind the closed doors of the Temple on January 16, 1904. This was after he had already had sexual relations with her, for she gave birth to a child as early as June.

So this man, whom I had at first regarded as a quiet Christian, had given up his faith and his self respect and surrendered himself body and soul to the demon of Mormonism. In the time following this, I got to know many other men and youths who saw sexual enjoyment, which the Mormons make as accessible as possible for everyone, as the greatest joy in their lives. Thousands in the land of the Mormons still founder every year on the rock of sexual pleasure. . . .

While I was in Utah, I published a monthly Evangelical paper for the congregation entitled "Das Licht von Utah" (The Light of Utah). I sent several hundred copies free of charge to the German Mormons I was unable to visit because they lived too far away. For most of these people, this was the first Christian paper they had seen in Utah. I learned from their letters that this paper brought great joy to the many living in Utah's heartland who had been thinking for a long time about casting off the spell of Mormonism, but could not leave due to unfavorable circumstances. The idea that the German Evangelical Church they had left still cared about them was quite new. Bitter anger was aroused in others, however, especially when I revealed in detail the sad fate of many newly arrived proselytes. . . .

Yet once again during my pastoral visits the very next day, I was struck to see how the power of Mormonism extended into all facets of life. The wife of one of the best members of my congregation related to me how the Mormon bishop of her municipal district had told her husband he had to pay a temple tax of 125 dollars instead of seventy-five to support the tabernacle choir in Salt Lake City. It was voluntary, of course, but since he owed the success of his business to the Mormon customers, he would lose these if he did not agree to this suggestion. And the bishop's request was granted without a second thought. The wealthy high priests of the "saints" received 125 dollars, while the German Evangelical congregation, which can barely make ends meet, only got thirty dollars from this member. The money of the "heathens" they curse every Sunday is accepted with pleasure. After all, "No one knows where it came from!" . . .

The Mormons do not shy away from issuing threats, either. On 8 November 1903, the leadership of the German Mormons in Salt Lake City sent me a message by way of Frau L———, a so-called ward teacher, or religion teacher, which said, "If you write another article against the Mormons like the one that was published recently in the Konigsberg (East Prussia) 'Evangelischen Brüderboten,' you will vanish in the dead of night."

However, there are also encouraging experiences, such as the one I had at our Christmas celebration of 1903. More than 160 German Mormons attended our worship service where they sang German Christmas carols with us under the brightly lit Christmas tree, carols that Mormonism had taken from them. We listened together to the tidings of the angels, "Unto you today a savior is born!" After this truly beautiful celebration had ended, an old German with a white beard stepped up to me, shook both my hands heartily, and said, "Herr Pastor, I have lived as a Mormon for thirty-seven years in Utah, but this evening for the first time I once again took part whole-heartedly in the celebration of Christmas. It was exactly like this at home. Ach, now I know again, after travelling so long on the wrong path, that the dear Christ child was born for an old sinner like me, too." Wiping the tears from his eyes, he continued, "It's true, isn't it? That the beloved savior you preached about will even have mercy on a Mormon who grew old in sin?" I spoke to him a long time about Jesus' love for sinners. Fourteen days later, he died of a heart defect in a miserable hut, and I was able to be with him once again before his death. Since he had been a "High Priest" for decades, he was buried with Mormon ceremonies. But after a repentant confession of his sins, he passed away peacefully and gently as a child of God whom Jesus had forgiven.

A sign of success for our missionary work in Utah is the fact that the Mormon leaders are now much more reluctant to undertake or provoke vile acts that offend Christian feelings. . . .

These poor people are withering away spiritually because they never see a Christian book or paper. The only suitable reading material for them is the German Salt Lake City Beobachter [Observer].[13] This paper was founded and edited for a time by the Mormon elder J. H. Ward. A former Methodist preacher, he wanted to offer something of worth to the community. Therefore, he reprinted Christian poems from Knapp, Gerok, Spitta, the Swiss Hugendubel, etc., as well as commentaries from Gerolt's Psalmenerklarung (Psalm Commentary), as well as from the sermons of Hofacker, Goßner, Frommel, Kogel, and other Evangelical men. In his later years his heart had simply turned away from Mormonism. During one of his visits to me, I broached the subject of his behavior, telling him at the same time that no one could take him to task for it. He replied, "I have to do it because our German saints are used to better things from their homeland. We have

---

[13] See Broadbent, "The Salt Lake City Beobachter," 329–52.

almost no religious literature, and the people will go to the dogs entirely if they hear nothing of God's word. If, as has already happened, someone takes me to task because of these ideas, then I always say that these articles were written by a high apostle of our church who wishes to remain anonymous. This calms our readers down." Since Ward passed away, however, the Beobachter brings so much stale nonsense from the revelations of the prophet and founder Smith, among others, that what little good content the paper had before is now ruined.

Due to the spying sanctioned by the Mormon bishops that extends even to the most remote settlements, it is very difficult for German Mormons to read the better quality German newspapers sent from the eastern part of America. The postmasters, usually Mormons themselves, not only rifle through the mailboxes, but often simply hold back the mail. And the response to this, as to all other violations, is silence. For there are spies everywhere who report the least word of discontent to the leaders of the church. And woe to him, if the local bishop learns that anything has been said against the Church of Latter-day Saints! In collaboration with his colleagues, he will certainly know how to get hold of the source of such sin and cut him off as much as possible from the basis of his livelihood.

David Bosio: I Was Lucky Enough to be Able to Gather Many Waldensians

David Bosio (1885–1950), a Waldensian pastor from San Germano Chisone, studied in Florence and Edinburgh before being consecrated in 1911. The Waldensians were Protestants in northwest Italy from which several hundred had immigrated to Utah between 1854 and 1913. From 1911 to 1913 Bosio served as a pastor in Palermo. In September 1913 he traveled to Utah where he visited Protestant congregations as well as Mormon converts who had emigrated from the Waldensian valleys. He wrote two letters that were published in October 1913 in the Waldensian newspaper *L'Echo des Vallées*.[14] Bosio claimed that the LDS church still permitted polygamy and that the British government was concerned about Mormonism because "their missionaries go to England principally to marry women and take them away with them." He also expressed concern for "our Waldensians" regardless of whether they had joined Mormonism or remained Reformed Protestants.

---

[14] *L'Eco delle Valli Valdesi* is currently part of *Riforma*, the official Italian newspaper of the Waldensians, Methodists, and Baptists.

DAVID BOSIO (1885–1950).
*Used by permission, courtesy of
Emanuele Bosio, San Germano Chisone.*

Bosio also recognized that some of the initial Mormon converts from the valleys were from San Germano and that some of the converts had returned to Italy as Mormon missionaries. Jacob Rivoire and his wife, Catherine Jouve, proselytized in Piedmont from 1879 to 1880; James Beus returned to San Germano in 1882–83; James Bertoch was a missionary in the valleys in 1892 and 1893; and Paul Cardon spent some time among the Waldensians in 1900. During the same decade that Bertoch lived with his cousins in San Germano, another wave of Waldensians left the valleys and some of them settled Utah.[15] Most of them went to Utah for work and not as Mormon converts.

When he returned to Italy, Bosio served as a chaplain during World War I. After the war he resumed his duties as a pastor in Torre Pellice, Torino, San Germano Chisone, and Genoa. He served for five years as a member of the church's governing "Tavola" and for two years as the vice moderator of the church. From 1930 until his death twenty years later, Bosio was a professor of theology at the Waldensian College in Rome.

Following Bosio's visit, no other Waldensian pastor visited Utah until

---

[15] Watts, *The Waldenses in the New World*, 227–32.

February 1965, when Ermanno Rostan, the Waldensian church moderator, participated in a service in Salt Lake City that included LDS general authority Marion D. Hanks and some descendants of nineteenth-century LDS converts from the Waldensian valleys. Rostan noted during the meeting that he wanted "to make some friends for the Waldensian Church." The following year he criticized the tenants of Mormonism in a Waldensian church publication.[16] When a group of Waldensians representing the Centro Culturale Valdese and the Società di Studi Valdesi visited Utah in September 1997, they met primarily with Presbyterians in Ogden.[17] But in September 2002, the church moderator, Gianni Genre, hosted a Salt Lake County delegation and recounted the arrival of the first Mormon missionaries in the Waldensian valleys in 1850.

> DAVID BOSIO, *NOS VAUDOIS DANS L'UTAH* [OUR WALDENSIANS IN UTAH].
> TRANSLATED BY ROBERTO MONGIA.
>
> The Waldensians who came to Utah sixty years ago [1854–55] were converted to the Mormon sect by missionaries who were sent to Italy. After they arrived in America, they crossed the Plains by foot or on horses and today their children occupy very good positions, generally speaking. Among the pioneers two families were from Saint-Jean [San Giovanni], one from Prarustin, who were followed later by a young man from Angrogne, a family from Pramol and another from Saint-Germain [San Germano]. These Waldensians probably did not find the saints that the missionaries had described, and some of them have conceded that they felt very disappointed, but after living here, they were confronted with the terrible punishments that the Mormons inflict on those who abandon their faith and therefore they gradually adjusted to their new faith. Anyway, apart from two or three exceptions, none of them have ever practiced polygamy and most of them still have deeply religious feelings.
>
> The Waldensians who came here later [1890–1900] were not attracted by the Mormon religion (about which they were probably uninformed), but rather by the agricultural opportunities Utah offered. Some of them were not so strong, as we would like to expect, concerning the religion of the Mormons, but also in general, they have kept faithful to the faith of their fathers.
>
> Most of the Waldensians live in Provo and Ogden. They are located about four hours from each other by train. Most of our Waldensians came from

---

[16] Rostan, *Chi sono I Mormoni*.
[17] Renzo Turinetto, "Sulle tracce dei valdesi del Nord-Ovest degli Stati Uniti d'America," *L'Eco delle Valli Valdesi*, 17 October 1997, 8.

Saint-Germain and from Pramol and we can really consider Utah Valley as a branch of Val Perouse. With few exceptions, they all own beautiful farms, with good irrigation, even though the elevation of this valley is about 1,500 meters. The climate is so favorable that they can cultivate both corn and grapes.

The most profitable product is fruit: berries, strawberries, peaches, and apples, which they send to the cities in the East in refrigerated boxcars. But lately, the price of fruit has plummeted because of oversupply, and last year most of the farmers did not even bother to harvest the fruit because the margin of profit was so low.

I was fortunate to be able to gather many Waldensians for a religious service held in French during the morning of Sunday September 7, [1913] in Provo, at the house of our sister Clémentine Richard, who has been disabled for many years, and, during the evening of the same day, in Ogden, at the chapel of a local congregation that was kindly offered us for that occasion. Most of our Waldensians participated in these meetings: it was the first time they had been visited by a Waldensian minister; other Protestants from France and Waldensians who had converted to Mormonism also joined us at the meetings and all of them gave generous contributions for our church in Italy, and we collected 200 francs. . . .

We can calculate that there are about fifteen families who came either directly from the Valleys or from the colony of North Carolina; but if we also include the families of our brothers, their sons and grandsons, the number becomes much larger.[18] There are also Waldensian families that I could not meet because they live far from the cities that I visited.[19] . . . But they are so scattered that it would take many weeks for me to visit them. Therefore I only visited the families living in Ogden and Provo and I leave it to one of my successors the charge of visiting the other ones. Almost all our brothers in Utah belong to an American church. Many of them, especially the older people, have great difficulty participating in religious meetings because they do not understand English, and they therefore rarely go to church. They can still find spiritual consolation for their souls in their old family Bibles but only if, naturally, they do not allow them to be covered by dust.

---

[18] Besides Utah, Waldensians settled in North Carolina, Texas, and Missouri. During the 1890s, a number of Waldensians settled around Valdese, North Carolina, whose three thousand residents are still largely Waldensian today. Bosio used "sons" and not "children" because in the Waldensian culture the female line was usually ignored in church records, making it difficult for genealogists to trace the maternal line.

[19] Bosio mentioned that a family from San Germano named Rochon lived in Lund, Utah. A year before Bosio's visit, Louis Rochon wrote to Etienne Vinçon of San Germano asking for money. Although he had been in America for awhile, "I have not yet made my fortune," he explained. Rochon had moved to Utah from California to homestead 320 acres, which he wrote was like a "journée," the amount of land one can work in a day, in the old country. The climate was not as good as California, where he had left his family, and he would return if he was unsuccessful. See *Cartella Vinçon di borgata Savoia fascicolo Etienne Vinçon*, 14 April 1912.

All the youngsters understand English and many of them go to meetings. The difficulties they encounter in their religious lives are caused by the social environment in which they live. Some of them have married Mormon women and this has caused painful religious divisions, which often creates indifference.

The most evident evil that we find among the Mormons is materialism; this is the most widespread attitude that our youngsters encounter in dealing with their neighbors and companions: this is the single thing we are most worried about. We pray that God will protect them and keep them in his love.

There is some hope for the future. Mormonism is diminishing and a greater and greater number of Christians are coming to dwell in these cities. This situation will make it easier for a Christian to marry another Christian, and little by little the religious atmosphere will become more spiritual and pure. We can look to the future with hope and wait for better times; we invite the Church of the Valleys to remember these faraway children, who still look to her with loving memories, in their prayers.

Comtesse Madeleine and Mlle. Jacqueline de Bryas: Mormons Looked Just Like All Other Human Beings

The Countess Madeleine de Bryas, a French lawyer, and her sister Jacqueline were patricians from Bordeaux. The de Bryas family had a long history of public service and philanthropy. The Marquis Charles de Bryas possessed an immense fortune and was a deputy in the French Parliament and mayor of Bordeaux.[20] The De Bryas sisters visited the United States during World War I.[21] They arrived in Salt Lake City at the Denver and Rio Grande Railway Station where they were greeted by a "committee of reception." Thereafter they visited Saltair, where they "dipped our tired persons into the lake or, more truthfully, sat on it." They also attended an organ rehearsal at the Tabernacle, where "a good looking Mormon . . . spoke about the war and the Liberty Loan Drive." But according to the sisters, "what excited our feminine curiosity most was to find out how all the Mormon wives got on together." The most interesting part of the reminisces of Salt Lake concern their encounter with Emmeline B. Wells (1828–1920)

---

[20] Henry Dunant, founder of the International Committee of the Red Cross, noted that de Bryas went to Italy in 1859 "on his own initiative for no other purpose than to help the wounded soldiers."

[21] See Tinling, *With Women's Eyes*.

who at 90 years old was still the president of the Female Relief Society. Their reaction to this encounter demonstrates that many visitors continued to be fascinated by the practice of polygamy almost thirty years after the Woodruff manifesto.

> COMTESSE MADELEINE AND MLLE. JACQUELINE DE BRYAS,
> *A FRENCH WOMAN'S IMPRESSIONS OF AMERICA*, 205–14.

Distances are tremendous in this country, and we generally had to travel many hours to get from one town to another. From Pueblo to Salt Lake City was a twenty-four-hour journey amid the most wonderful and gorgeous scenery imaginable, and we would willingly have traveled many miles more to be certain of reaching the famous Mormon city of which we had always heard such extraordinary tales!

To begin, I must say that to all appearances the Mormons looked just like all other human beings. No particular exterior sign distinguished them from the rest of the population, although we had expected to find them dressed in what we thought would be the Mormon fashion. We expected to see men with long hair and sandals and long white robes, staves in hand; we expected the women to be dressed in a similar style, with their hair braided and low over their ears. Nothing of the sort was there to be found, for the Mormon men and women were dressed in twentieth-century fashion. They live in extremely comfortable houses, just as do the citizens of Salt Lake City, for their town is not solely inhabited by those of their own faith, but also by people of all other religions.

Our train arrived three hours late, and immediately on arriving we had to attend a reception given in our honor. Then some of the ladies on the committee of reception suggested that we should go to Saltair, the big salt lake renowned all over the country for its invigorating power. We had literally to rush out of the reception room and into the train, by which, in three quarters of an hour, we reached Saltair, where we dipped our tired persons into the lake or, more truthfully, sat on it. For the water is so charged with salt that it requires a special effort to really sink down into it, otherwise one remains floating on its surface like a cork.

Now had we both gone there alone without having been prepared for what would happen to us, we could have believed that a miracle had taken place, and could have thought the blessings of the Almighty had come upon us in giving us the power of sitting comfortably on the surface of the waters! But when several hundred people are all "doing it," you easily understand that you are not specially privileged, but that it is simply and only a curiosity of nature!

An organ rehearsal was given for us in the Tabernacle, which is one of the largest auditoriums in the world, seating from six to eight thousand people.

EMMELINE B. WELLS (1828–1921).
Used by permission, Utah State Historical Society, all rights reserved.

It is arched over by an immense vaulted ceiling of wood, being dovetailed and so constructed without a single nail, and this self-supporting wooden roof is considered a remarkable work of engineering.

In questioning some members of our party we learned that the reason for this entirely wooden construction lay in the fact that the building was erected before the railroads reached the state, and so wood, on account of its lightness, was chosen as material. Therefore heavy nails were replaced by wooden pins.

The acoustic properties of the building are perfectly astounding and unique. We were told that a pin dropped on the ground could be heard at a distance of two hundred feet. As the Tabernacle was crowded that day we did not try the pin experience, but listened to the wonderful organ that rises majestically at one end of the building and enjoyed the concert. This great organ is believed to be the most perfect one of its kind, and the notes resound wonderfully through the huge church.

We were told that at the religious meetings held in the Tabernacle, a member of the congregation, man or woman, is frequently called upon to preach to the faithful ones, and this generally without having been given notice beforehand. "For, once in the pulpit, they are always inspired," explained a Mormon lady.

This sounded so remarkable that we decided the next afternoon to attend one of these meetings. We did so, and took seats near the entrance door at the opposite end from the pulpit. A good-looking Mormon was called upon to address the assembly, and in a monotonous voice he spoke about the war and the Liberty Loan Drive. It was a discourse just like the ones we heard every day, and were beginning to know pretty well-human imagination being limited! But when an inspired Mormon speaks like the non-privileged ones of any other faith, the only thing to do is to look for the door, (which fortunately was quite near) and get a little air on the lovely grounds around the Tabernacle....

But what excited our feminine curiosity most was to find out how all the Mormon wives got on together, so with a most amiable smile we asked a member of this faith the following question:

"Do all your wives live together in the same house?" For which we were rewarded with a most horrified look and the words:

"I have only one wife, the law forbids us now to have more than one."

I was later drawn aside by a non-Mormon who had heard this conversation and who said: "They all protest that they have only one wife, but we others are sure they still have several."

"The other day," another non-Mormon whispered in our ear, "a teacher received two new pupils in one of our schools.

"'Tell me your name and your age?' he asked the first boy.

"'I'm called Peter Jones, and I'm seven!'

"'And yours?' asked the teacher.

"'I'm Josephus Jones,' answered the second boy, 'and I'm seven.'

"'Then you're twins, I suppose?' inquired the teacher.

"'Perhaps,' answered one, 'anyhow, we're twin brothers by our father!'"

What was I to think of all this? My mind was in a whirl, when a charming old lady entered the room, looking as if she had just stepped out of an old picture. She was sweet and smiling and draped in a cashmere shawl and wore a fascinating little bonnet.

"This is Aunt Emmeline," my neighbor said.

"Come and meet Aunt Emmeline!" said another lady.

"How are you to-day, Aunt Emmeline?" I heard a third voice ask.

"But who is Aunt Emmeline?" we asked with astonishment and curiosity.

And then we learned that Emmeline B. Wells was a celebrated Mormon woman, ninety years of age, who enjoyed great popularity in Salt Lake and was called Aunt Emmeline by all its citizens. Her late husband was a pioneer who had seven wives, and she was the last survivor of this happy—as it cannot be called couple, let us call it "octuple."[22] Emmeline Wells had journeyed with the pioneers from the State of Illinois to find the Promised

---

[22] Despite her age Emmeline B. Wells was still the Relief Society president at the time of the de Bryas visit.

Land. After selling all their belongings, they traveled some on horseback, others in wagons drawn by horses and oxen, until they reached about where Omaha stands to-day, and there they established their winter quarters. Aunt Emmeline gave birth to a child during this long and fatiguing journey—a journey made up of hardships and privations, and during which they encountered the Pawnee Indians.

We were told that after the cold weather was over, Brigham Young left these winter quarters to search for the Promised Land, taking with him one hundred and forty-three men, three women, and two children. This statement brought the thought to my mind that the problem was just the reverse at that time, for instead of seven wives for one man each of the three women had from forty-seven to forty-eight men—a unique case truly sufficient to break up a religion! But to avoid such a complication, I imagine that nine hundred and ninety-eight additional women soon followed to allow the one hundred and forty-three men their normal number of seven wives each! Finally the pioneers reached the valley of the great lake, settled there, and divided the land into lots of equal size.

The temple is a beautiful piece of architecture, and rises majestically, its six lofty pinnacles towering to the skies, seeming to call the attention of Heaven to itself. We could not enter this building, as visitors are not allowed to cross its threshold. So our feminine curiosity naturally induced us to ask why the temple doors were closed to the public, and we heard that inside that impressive building were performed marriage and baptismal ceremonies and other sacred rites.

"Why are outsiders not admitted to all these ceremonies?" we asked a follower of that faith, and he replied as follows:

"Our Prophet Joseph Smith revealed to his followers that in celestial spheres the marriage relation exists eternally, and it is only in our temple that this sacred ceremony can be performed in its eternal significance. Those of our people who are married outside our temple are married for this life only."

"Ah! those are the lucky ones," thought I!

ZOPITO VALENTINI:
I DID RAISE THE SUBJECT OF POLYGAMY

Zopito Valentini visited the United States in 1925 and published his travel narrative, *Un anno senza rondini*, five years later. "Rondini" are swallows that usher in springtime, and his title represents his pessimism of having experienced "a year without springtime." His account included a very sensational—and suspect—description of his experiences to Utah. The same year Valentini also published a book in Salt Lake City, *Attività Italiane nella Intermountain Region*, in which he described Italian Americans who lived in the Intermountain West, including those in Utah. The two books were quite different in tone and outlook. While the first was critical of Mormon polygamy, which had been abandoned officially, if not in reality, forty years earlier, the second book is positive, even glowing, in its description of Utah and the Mormons. The stark contrast, as well as the historical fantasies contained in his travel account, demonstrates that travel narratives are often written to sell and usually contain both fact and fiction.

Although Valentini's travel narrative was never intended to be read by a Utah audience and its fictional elements are easily detectable it is more difficult to determine what portions of the account are accurate. Valentini was obviously disappointed that polygamy had been abandoned by the Mormons before he could visit the state. But unlike other writers, he improvised, claiming that polygamy was still practiced among the Mormons. According to Valentini, LDS Church President Heber J. Grant told him modestly that he had six wives and twenty-four children at a time when many had forgotten Grant's two dead polygamous wives. Simply put, Valentini's recollections are unbelievable. One may wonder whether John Taylor told Leonetto Cipriani—the first Italian to visit Utah—in 1853 that polygamy would not survive, but no one would believe that one of Taylor's successors told a later Italian visitor that polygamy had survived.

<blockquote>

ZOPITO VALENTINI, *UN ANNO SENZA RONDINI*
[A YEAR WITHOUT SWALLOWS], 267–307.
TRANSLATED BY ROBERTO MONGIA.

I began making friends with the priests with long flowing beards, with the exquisitely hospitable apostles and with the patriarchs who had an air of serenity. Among these I found a very nice person, a certain Mr. Harris, who acted as my very helpful guide. He was frank and simple with blue eyes, but who was also without doubt very powerful. All doors, even difficult ones, were opened to us during our travels. . . .

My guide took me into the waiting room of the Pope, who had courteously granted my request for an audience. I was expecting a very interesting "spectacle" but instead he was simply introduced, he was a very kind old gentleman who was like anyone in a very ordinary office. The Pope, the head of the apostles, as we would call him in Italy, received me with much affability. I told him about my journey and he asked me specifically about
</blockquote>

Rome, including the Vatican palaces and even Italian politics. For my part I asked him about the practices that one must follow in order to become a Mormon and he briefly enumerated them:

Faith in Jesus Christ.

Repentance.

Baptism by immersion.

The laying on of hands in order to receive the gift of the Holy Ghost.

Out of fear that he would give me a long lecture I did not ask him specific questions but I did raise the subject of polygamy. The Pope told me that many early Christians spoke benevolently about it, and he reminded me of the words of St. Augustine: "Jacob had four wives; this was not a crime when one considers the times." I then asked the leader of the Mormons how many wives and children he had. Six wives and twenty-six children he responded modestly. I gave neither condolences nor congratulations but rather sat like an idiot, looking tranquilly at the small, good-natured man. As I was about to leave, Mr. Harris proposed that I visit some of his wives, some of whom were old and some of whom were young, two were over sixty and a few were not yet in their twenties. As we went from house to house, my friend explained to me that every woman raised her own children, and that—a funny thing—no feeling of jealousy or rivalry exists among the wives. They visit one another and since they are often together they are always in agreement. I found one of the wives of Mr. Harris to be much more interesting than the others. She was not beautiful, she had a strange olive colored and irregular face, but her fleshy mouth and her very restless eyes made her quite interesting. She was also small and slender, very nervous and could not keep still even a moment. In her skinny hands she held a fan which she used nervously. She was an Italian American but she spoke Italian with a bizarre accent and she also spoke French. She was very enthusiastic about her religion and exalts in it with ardor. She explained to me that polygamy is the best remedy of all that is bad because when a husband equally distributes his love, the women, who are tied together in a common spirit, love each other as sisters. The man—she said—has his black periods; his work and preoccupations make him nervous. If one can overcome these times of frazzled nerves and bad times with ten persons then life is possible, if, on the other hand, a man only has one woman to support him in his fits of anger and in his reprimands, then home can be a real hell. I listened with great interest but I detected in her cunning eyes an ice-cold reflection and I could not refrain from asking her in Italian—so that the man would not understand—"You are not convinced of what you are saying. I take it that you are repeating, with great ability, an interesting part." The woman, with a natural air, responded in an indifferent tone: "Come and see me tonight at 8:00 and I will explain everything better." It did not even occur to the man to inquire what we had just said to one another. At 8:00 that evening I arrived punctually at the woman's home. (Mormon women do not take their husband's names but instead keep their unmarried name.) She greeted me with these words:

— You have exceptional intuition, Sir.

— Me, why do you say that?

— I spoke with such zeal today so that I would not arouse suspicion.

— In Mr. Harris, but not with me.

— Well, then that means that you read my soul.

— But no Signora. The thing is quite simple. It was enough to look at your eyes to convince me that you were making it all up. As long as you were talking from the perspective of men I would have found the whole discourse natural. All men are practically a little "Mormon." But women—no way. If it was the other way around, that is every woman had ten men at her disposal, maybe I would have been convinced, but for a girl, as young and beautiful as you, to accept their love one drop at a time and for you to content yourself with a tenth or one fifteenth of Mr. Harris is something that is impossible to believe.

The signora set the table.

She seemed more nervous than earlier in the day. Her hands were really trembling.

— I released the maid so that I could be alone with you.

— And is Mr. Harris coming?

— No he is not. But if he does come we will tell him that I telephoned to invite you. It is natural that I would entertain a fellow countryman.

I had the curious desire to close the mouth of this striking woman, who was like a bitter fruit, with my bite so that she could say no more. When she had finished setting the table she invited me to sit next to her.

— Do you have children, Signora?

— I don't have any. I am alone in the home with my maid.

— But in this Mormon country only men make them?

— As you can see, she responded freely, we are doing it ourselves tonight.

She burst out with a loud and strange laugh, which amounted to a tremor.

— But it does not happen very often, is that right?

— Oh no, it only rarely occurs. While the city has many women, there are very few men. Being well supplied (some men have twenty-five wives) they never take care of other men's women.

— The Mormon system reduces women to a form of slavery.

— You have (can we use the familiar form with each other?)

— Of course.

— You have understood immediately. I do not believe any of the stories told today. They are all gossip. Such enthusiasms are required around men like my husband. But in reality everything is much different my dear—oh yes, much different.

— I would imagine.

— Mormonism gives a man a way to satisfy his libido and vices as he wishes; but it places a woman on a pedestal, like an object of art, like a piece of china. The man comes home once a week or every ten days, he spends an hour with his wife and then he disappears again. A Mormon woman's youth vanishes, and then her smile disappears, in her solitude and silence. In every home in Salt Lake City one can find unsatisfied desires and deep sorrow. As long as we can speak to each other with an open heart, woman to woman, I find that among women in their souls the same anxiety, the same grieving pain as mine.

— But why are you, an Italian woman—here in Utah?

— When my parents settled in America, they had to become Mormons to obtain land. I was born here. I grew up here. It was impossible not to marry one of theirs. I have at heart assured my own well being

— And every husband provides for every single wife?

— How could it be otherwise?

— The Mormons are all very rich then?

— Those with less money have fewer wives, and those with more riches have more wives. But, I repeat, in every case where there is an appearance of tranquility, there is really agitation and throbbing, within the closed walls, many saints have unsatisfied aspirations which are painful. Woman who are close to me have talked.

I could feel the woman's passionate breath on my cheeks as she spoke to me. The light in her eyes was twinkling as fast as lightning. I kissed her fleshy lips and her kiss had the strength of a twisting reptile, the thrill of a storm, and the shivering of hidden torment.

Afterword

"Lovers and Hunters of the Picturesque"
Utah in the Twenty-first Century

Several years ago in Cody, Wyoming, I met a couple from Portsmouth, England, who were on their way to Salt Lake City. "Will we be safe?" they asked, explaining that they had read Arthur Conan Doyle's *A Study in Scarlet*. I assured them that they would be fine.[1] It is now more than 150 years since Brigham Young founded Salt Lake City, but many Utah tourists continue to focus on its religious origins and the fanciful stories told about its rough-and-rowdy early days as a "New Jerusalem." The legacy of early storytellers such as Jules Rémy, Richard Burton, Karl May, and Arthur Conan Doyle runs deep.

The nineteenth-century sojourners who passed through Deseret "on the way to somewhere else" left us complex, colorful, contradictory, entertaining, and instructive records of their visits, and many of them draw incomparable word portraits of Utah's plainspoken prophets, such as Rudolph Schleiden's observation that Brigham Young had "more the appearance of a bank or railway president than a prophet." They include insightful comments on the nature of frontier Mormonism's relations with their "Lamanite" neighbors and the religion's experiments with marriage, theocracy, communalism, and even irrigation. These travelers' tales provide invaluable insights into how seriously early Latter-day Saints took their faith and its millennial prophecies, and how different Utah Territory was from its modern counterpart.

---

[1] I told this story when I delivered the Utah History Address at the annual meeting of the Utah State Historical Society in 1998. See Janelle Biddinger Hyatt, "Sherlock Holmes on the Mormon Trail," *The Ogden Standard Examiner* (27 September 1998), 1E–4E.

But many modern visitors fail to recognize the differences. "I must confess," French author Bernard-Henri Lévy wrote in 2005 after visiting Utah, the LDS church "looks like nothing I've ever seen before." Traveling in the "footsteps" of Tocqueville, Lévy found Salt Lake City "a surreal and artificial place, orthogonal and rigid, built in the nineteenth century in the middle of the desert." Like many of his predecessors, he toured the tabernacle and found an "uneasy mixture of the prophetic and the mundane, the intensity of fervor and the triviality of rites." Lévy also visited Brigham Young's successor: "Instead of the holy man I was expecting, instead of a dignified heir to Joseph Smith, the church's founder, whom I had imagined as an apostolic figure come to re-establish the plenitude of the Gospel on earth, I discovered a little ninety-four-year-old man, cautious and dapper, dressed in a double-breasted navy-blue suit with gold buttons, closer to a Cinzano drinker than to a WASP Dalai Lama."[2] As the Preacher said, "What has been will be again, what has been done will be done again; there is nothing new under the sun."[3]

The failure of prophecies that Mormonism would not survive Brigham Young's death (and subsequent predictions that it would disappear after the abandonment of polygamy) only revitalized the perception that church and state remain interconnected and interdependent in Utah. Despite the unambiguous rejection of polygamy by the modern LDS church, the press in Europe is often fast and loose in its descriptions of polygamists as "fundamentalist Mormons." Mormons are also lampooned because they are, by Hollywood standards at least, excessively conservative, while Utah is criticized for lacking religious, ethnic, and political diversity and faces charges that non-Mormons are marginalized.

Both the LDS church and the state of Utah have worked hard to modernize and improve their images in the world. Early in the twentieth century when church leaders recognized that polygamy had tainted the image of Mormonism throughout the world, they embarked on a new course to change that image. Plural marriage was vigorously uprooted from the church, and those who resisted and insisted on its continued vitality were excommunicated. Thereafter the church encouraged broader participation in national politics and eventually achieved greater political influence. A major watershed occurred in 1907 when the United States Senate voted to retain apostle

---

[2] Lévy, "In the Footsteps of Tocqueville (Part 3)," *The Atlantic Monthly* (July/August 2005). Lévy felt that the "real story" in Salt Lake was the Family History Library. [3] Eccles., 1:9.

Reed Smoot, who had been elected to that body in 1903 by the Utah State Legislature. "The Senate's vote to retain Smoot marked the beginning of the nation's acceptance of the Latter-day Saints on the same denominational terms as other American religions," argues Kathleen Flake.[4] Almost a half century later President Dwight D. Eisenhower selected another apostle, Ezra Taft Benson, to be in his cabinet as secretary of agriculture. The Benson family's appearance on Edward R. Murrow's "People to People" confirmed to the nation how mainstream Mormons had become.

These apostles and other church members in government successfully convinced the powerful elite that the LDS church had committed itself to working within the American system of government and that it was part of mainstream religious life. But there have also been bumps on the road to respectability. Prior to 1978 the LDS church banned blacks from holding priesthood office. This became a major source of embarrassment to the church and its membership after the blossoming of the Civil Rights movement in the 1960s. Even though the church initially resisted calls for change, it failed to articulate either a historical basis for the policy or a theological justification. Most church members, who were much less prejudiced than their nineteenth-century grandparents, were relieved and even applauded when church leadership finally discontinued the practice in 1978. Less than thirty years later many non-Mormons are completely unaware that the LDS church ever denied priesthood offices to blacks.

The hierarchy's willingness to discontinue polygamy and priesthood denial demonstrates that neither it, nor rank and file church members, cling to anachronistic nineteenth-century doctrines that are no longer considered fundamental. On the other hand, the church hierarchy has been vigilant in upholding moral standards that it considers to be core doctrines and practices. Church teachings concerning the family, marriage, premarital sex, homosexuality, the role of women, drugs, and even the use of coffee, tea, alcohol, and tobacco have been strengthened and reemphasized. As a result, twentieth-century Mormonism developed an image as a conservative religion that upholds moral values, while also experiencing dramatic growth.[5] Some have claimed that it is on the verge of becoming a world religion that

---

[4] Flake, *The Politics of American Religious Identity*, 157.

[5] Shipps, "Surveying the Mormon Image since 1960," 58–72. "LDS critics who have declared victory over nineteenth century anti-Mormon stereotypes in literature have seriously miscalculated the persistence of these stereotypes," Michael Austin has warned. "Mormons remain relatively unknown to a large segment of the American public." See Austin, "Troped by the Mormons," 54, 70.

is as different from Christianity as Judaism is from Christianity, but the more important development is that by the end of the twentieth century Mormons had become clean-cut monogamists who were fiercely patriotic and conservative.[6]

In contrast, public perception of Utah and its relationship with Mormonism has been more difficult to modify. *The New York Times* published a cartoon in 1992 that depicted the United States in the year 2092, which included "Utah Theocracy" as a nation state.[7] Ironically, this map was similar to Robida's description of a Mormon republic in *Le Vingtième Siècle*, which included the old states of Utah, Colorado, and Arizona. Utah (and Mormonism) is also satirized in movies, television, and in popular literature.[8] Because of these simplistic perceptions Utah has not always kept pace with its western neighbors in attracting business investment and tourism dollars. At the turn of the last century Salt Lake City was one of the largest cities west of the Missouri River. But during the next one hundred years it was often eclipsed by Denver, Phoenix, and Seattle and sometimes by even smaller markets in Portland, Boise, Reno, and Las Vegas. Salt Lake business executives have lamented that the city lacks the cachet of other Western urban centers and that it is often difficult to convince business professionals from other parts of the country to transfer to the state.

The media and other purveyors of popular culture continue to link Utah and the Mormons. The LDS church accounts for more than 60 percent of the state's population, and church headquarters are located in Salt Lake City. Temple Square is the most visited location in the state and the Family History Library is a hit not only on the internet but also among tourists. Many Mormons agree with church leaders on moral issues—the church has run successful lobbying campaigns on the Equal Rights Amendment, liquor laws, and the rights of women and homosexuals—even if some of

---

[6] Shipps, *Mormonism: The Story of a New Religious Tradition*, 148. Ironically, Mormon writers struggle to convince the Christian world that Mormons are as Christian as Catholics and Protestants. See Blomberg and Robinson, *How Wide the Divide?* They also fail to provide a rationale to support their thesis that Mormonism will become the newest world religion. Sociological studies focus on past growth and projections rather than historical analysis. See Stark, "So Far, So Good: A Brief Assessment of Mormon Membership Projections," 175–78; and "Extracting Social Scientific Models from Mormon History," 174–94. The rate of LDS growth has been slower than other fast-growing churches such as Pentecostals, Jehovah's Witnesses, and Adventists. Retention rates are also controversial. See Peggy Fletcher Stack, "Keeping members a challenge for LDS church," *The Salt Lake Tribune*, 26 July 2005, B1.

[7] "Canada and the United States in the year 2092," *The New York Times*, 21 October 1992.

[8] Vince Horiuchi, "TV Writers take digs at Utah, Mormons," *The Salt Lake Tribune* 15 August 2005, A1, A5.

those positions rub the religion's liberal minority the wrong way. Travelers, who wish a place to remain static, are sometimes surprised when their imaginings of Utah are not confirmed by their real observations. Stéphane Jousselin and Jules Huret were disappointed when they discovered that polygamy was no longer sanctioned and was only practiced underground.

Perhaps Utah's most dramatic attempt to moderate the "Mormon" label occurred when it made repeated bids to host the Winter Olympic Games. "One of the reasons we embrace the Olympics is we hope it will clarify what Utah is and that we're not all strange out here," said Spence Kinard, director of the Utah Travel Council.[9] Some thought the international press had fallen in love with Utah's charms after foreign newspapers showed new interest in the state after it was finally chosen to host the 2002 Winter Olympics.[10] But when Salt Lake became embroiled in a bidding scandal, the international press began acting like a jilted lover, and the city "never quite shook the sense that it had some inadequacy or provincialism to overcome" and felt "a need to make a name for itself . . . and to shed a bit of its insular history as the central city in the Mormon religion."[11] One of the nation's most prominent Mormon businessmen expressed concern that because of the scandal the state had become "the laughing stock of the world" and that post-scandal public relations efforts were misguided because they reinforced the notion that some of the games sponsors were attempting to use them to bolster the image of the LDS church: "Diversity in the Olympic Games is what it's all about," said Jon Huntsman Sr. "These are not the Mormon Games."[12]

Fortunately, the Salt Lake City Olympic Games were a huge success, the Mormon church agreed not to proselyte visitors, and the individuals caught up in the scandal were exonerated. While Salt Lake may usually lack, in the words of Friederich Bodenstedt, "all the romantic accessories that go with street life in a big city," including "yelling hustlers and newspaper vendors,

---

[9] Michael Vigh and Kevin Cantera, "Polygamy Trial Gives World Titillating Look at Utah," *The Salt Lake Tribune*, 21 May 2001.

[10] Christopher Smith, "International Press Has Fallen in Love With Utah's Charms," *The Salt Lake Tribune*, 28 August 1996, A1.

[11] "From an Innocent Bid to Olympic Scandal," *The New York Times*, 11 March 1999, A14.

[12] "Huntsman Complains About Oly Fundraising," *Salt Lake Tribune*, 11 July 1999, A15. The fear that the Salt Lake Olympics would be perceived as the "Mormon Games" caused both the Salt Lake Organizing Committee and the LDS church to reconsider, and eventually modify, the church's role in the games. See Mike Gorrell, "LDS Role in Games under Review," *Salt Lake Tribune*, 22 June 2001, E1.

as well as bums, beggars, and rowdies, and all other questionable characters whether in male or female attire," it did become such a city during the Winter Games.[13] And while Salt Lake City demonstrated that it could host an international event, travelers from around the world also learned firsthand about other parts of Utah that have nothing to do with religion and everything to do with sacred place. These places are representative of the vision that early inhabitants of Utah had concerning place, which included not only the natural geography of Salt Lake Valley, with its salt sea connected to a freshwater lake by the "River Jordan," but also the surrounding mountains, which many believed were a fulfillment of Isaiah's prophecy that in the last days "the mountain of the Lord's house shall be established in the top of the mountains, and shall be exalted above the hills; and all nations shall flow unto it." The Mormons actually adapted a hymn written by Felicia Hemans (1793–1835), written to celebrate the mountains surrounding villages located in Piedmont, Italy (the homeland of Stephen Malan and Daniel Bertoch before they immigrated to Utah in the 1850s), which they retitled "For the Strength of the Hills We Bless Thee."[14]

Richard V. Francaviglia has described these places as among America's "most unique and underappreciated." They include not only Olympic venues and other world-class ski resorts, which were highlighted in the 2002 games, but also the state's five national parks—Zion, Bryce, Capitol Reef, Canyonlands, and Arches—seven national monuments—Cedar Breaks, Hovenweep, Natural Bridges, Rainbow Bridge, Timpanogos Cave, Dinosaur, and Grand Staircase—and many other outdoor wonders, such as the Colorado River and the Great Salt Lake.[15] International travelers who walk in the footsteps of Rémy, Gardini, and Tissandier and visit these outdoor wonders are often astonished as they hear foreign languages ricocheting off canyon walls.[16]

The Olympics were also a catalyst for boosting Utah's economy and for increasing its immigrant workforce. "Utah ranks among those states with the very highest rates of increase in diversity and is prominent among the

---

[13] Bodenstedt, *Vom Atlantischen zum Stillen Ocean*, 398.

[14] Homer, "The Waldensian Valleys: Seeking 'Primitive Christianity,'" 136.

[15] See, Francaviglia, *Believing in Place*, xiv. See also Williams, *Refuge*, 237; and Chisholm, *Following the Wrong God Home*, 321–84.

[16] For an example of an Italian writer who has used southern Utah as a backdrop for a love story, see Soria, *Kodachrome*.

newly emerging gateways of immigrants," the David Eccles School of Business at the University of Utah reported in 2004. This will result not only as an economic boon for the state, but it will also aid in "transforming the formerly monolithic culture and homogeneous population of the state, creating a new era of cultural, racial and ethnic diversity for Utah."[17] According to Governor Jon Huntsman Jr. this will create greater diversity as well as greater balance between Republican and Democrat party affiliation in the state.[18] At the same time Salt Lake City's geographical location at the "crossroads of the West" has helped the state to develop a more successful convention industry and attract airlines that use the city as a hub for national travelers.

Despite these developments and transformations, some travelers will continue to sweep into the state and, in the words of Paolo DeVecchi, discharge "pompous brays of disapproval."[19] The combatants in culture wars and religious disputes are more familiar with the frozen nineteenth-century image of Utah as a land of polygamy and patriarchy. But as Utah continues to reorient itself (as many states and cities have done) to appreciate not only its religious origins but also its sacred places, increasing diversity, and growing economy, then its nineteenth-century image will become a more distant ancestor.[20] As that happens the "lovers and hunters of the picturesque" will increasingly appreciate that Utah's sacred soul transcends the enduring stereotype.[21]

---

[17] University of Utah News and Public Relations, 16 July 2004 Press Release relating to a study completed by the Bureau of Economic and Business Research, David Eccles School of Business, University of Utah, entitled "Immigrants Transform Utah: Entering a new era of diversity," published in the *Utah Economic and Business Review*, May/June 2004.

[18] Matt Canham, "Mormon portion of Utah population steadily shrinking," *The Salt Lake Tribune*, 17 October 2005, B1.

[19] Torrielli, *Italian Opinion on America*, 34.

[20] Majanlahti notes that "modern Rome is only the great great great grandchild, at best, of its ancient predecessor." Majanlahti, *The Families who made Rome*, 1.

[21] Charles Dickens called upon "lovers and hunters of the picturesque" to observe not only the "gay Neapolitan life" but also "the miserable depravity, degradation, and wretchedness, with which this gay Neapolitan life is inseparably associated." The British author believed that one can only appreciate the world if one associates a "new picturesque with some faint recognition of man's destiny and capabilities." See Dickens, *Pictures from Italy*, 240.

Selected Bibliography

This bibliography has separate sections for books, periodicals and articles in books, theses and dissertations, and manuscripts.

Books

Abdy, E. S. *Journal of a Residence and Tour in the United States of North America from April, 1833, to October, 1834,* 3 vols. London: John Murray, 1835.

Ahmanson, John. *Vor Tids Muhamed.* Omaha: Press of the Danish Pioneer, 1876. Republished as *Secret History: A Translation of Vor Tids Muhamed.* Trans. by Gleason L. Archer. Chicago: Moody Press, 1984.

Aitken, W. *Journey up the Mississippi River from its Mouth to Nauvoo, the City of the Latter Day Saints.* Ashton-Under-Lyne: John Williamson, n.d. [1845].

Alderson, Jo Bartels, and J. Michael Alderson. *The Man Mazzuchelli, Pioneer Priest.* Madison: Wisconsin House, Ltd., 1974.

Allen, James, and Glen Leonard. *The Story of the Latter-day Saints.* Salt Lake City: Deseret Book Co., 1976.

———, Ronald W. Walker, and David Whittaker. *Studies in Mormon History, 1830–1997: An Indexed Bibliography.* Urbana: Univ. of Ill. Press, 2000.

André, Charles. *Rapport sur le passage de Mercure sur le soleil, observé à Ogden (Utah) le 6 mai 1878, par M. Charles André. Extrait des Archives des Missions Scientifiques et Littéraires.* Troisième Série. Tome Septième. Paris: Imprimerie Nationale, 1881.

Anquetil, Georges, ed. *La maîtresse légitime: essai sur le mariage polygame de demain.* Paris: Georges-Anquetil, 1923.

Anquetil, Georges, and Jane De Magny. *L'amant légitime ou la bourgeoise libertine.* Paris: Georges-Anquetil, 1923.

Appleman's hand-book of American travel. N.Y: D. Appleton and Co., 1871.

Apollinaire, Guillaume. *La femme assise.* Paris: Editions de la Nouvelle Revue Française, 1920.

Argyle, Archie. *Cupid's Album.* N.Y: M. Doolady, 1866.

Arnoux, Jules. *Les étapes de la démocratie nord-américaine (1707–1907).* Paris: Librairie Gedalge et Cie, ca. 1907.

Arrington, Leonard. *Brigham Young: American Moses.* Urbana: University of Illinois Press, 1986.

———. *Great Basin Kingdom: An Economic History of the Latter-day Saints, 1830–1900.* Cambridge: Harvard Univ. Press, 1958.

———. *From Quaker to Latter-Day Saint: Bishop Edwin D. Woolley.* S.L.C: Deseret Book Co., 1976.

Audouard, Olympe de Joaral. *Les mystères du sérail.* Paris, 1863.

———. *Le canal de Suez.* Paris, 1864.

———. *Les mystères de l'Egypte dévoilés.* Paris, 1865.

———. *L'Orient et ses peuples.* Paris, 1867.

———. *A travers l'Amérique: Le Far-West.* Paris: E. Dentu, 1869.

———. *A travers l'Amérique: North-America.* Paris: E. Dentu, 1871.

———. *Les nuits russes.* Paris, 1876.

———. *Au pays des boyards.* Paris, 1881.

Bagley, Will, ed. *Scoundrel's Tale: The Samuel Brannan Papers.* Spokane, Wash: The Arthur H. Clark Co., 1999.

Bain, David Haward. *Empire Express: Building the First Transcontinental Railroad.* N.Y: Viking, 1999.

Baird, Robert. *De la religion aux Etats-Unis d'Amérique.* Paris: L. R. Delay, 1844.

Barba, Preston. A. *Balduin Möllhausen, the German Cooper.* Publications of the Univ. of Pa. American Germanica, XVII. Philadelphia: Univ. of Pa., 1914.

Beadle, John Hanson. *Life in Utah; or, the Mysteries and Crimes of Mormonism, being an Exposé of the Secret Rites and Ceremonies of the Latter-day Saints, with a Full and Authentic History of Polygamy and the Mormon Sect from Its Origin to the Present Time.* Philadelphia: National Publishing Co., 1870.

Beckstead, James H. *Cowboying: A Tough Job in a Hard Land.* S.L.C: Univ. of Utah Press, 1991.

Beecher, Henry Ward. *A Circuit of the Continent: Account of a Tour through the West and the South.* N.Y: Fords, Howard & Hulbert, 1884.

Belisle, Orvilla S. *The Prophets; or, Mormonism Unveiled.* Philadelphia: Wm. White Smith, 1855.

Beltrami, Luca. *Padre Samuele Mazzuchelli.* Milan: n.p., 1928.

Benjamin, Israel Joseph. *Drei Jahre in Amerika: 1859–1862.* Hannover: Selbstverlag des verfassers, Druck von Wilh. Riemschneider, 1862. Republished as *Three Years in America, 1859–1862.* Trans. by Charles Reznikoff with an intro. by Oscar Handlin. Philadelphia: Jewish Publication Soc. of America, 1956.

———. *Le voyage d'Israël.* 1854.

———. *Cinq années de voyage en Orient, 1846–51.* 1856.

Benoit, Pierre. *Le lac salé.* Paris: Albin Michel, Editeur, 1921. *Salt Lake.* Trans. by Florence and Victor Llona. N.Y: Alfred A. Knopf, 1922.

Bertoch, James. *Missionary Journal and Letters to His Family.* Ed. by Michael W. Homer S.L.C: Prairie Dog Press, 2004.

Bertrand, Louis A. *Mémoires d'un Mormon.* Paris: E. Jung-Treuttel, 1862. *Mémoires d'un Mormon.* Paris: E. Dentu, 1862. Typescript trans. by Gaston Chappuis in the Donald R. Moorman Collection, Special Collections, Stewart Library, Weber State Univ., Ogden, Utah.

Beverley, James A. *Counterfeit Code: Answering the DaVinci Code Heresies.* Brooklyn: Bay Ridge Books, 2005.

Bigler, David L. *Forgotten Kingdom: The Mormon Theocracy in the American West, 1847–1896.* Spokane, Wash: The Arthur H. Clark Co., 1998.

———, and Will Bagley, eds. *Army of Israel: Mormon Battalion Narratives.* Spokane, Wash: The Arthur H. Clark Co., 2000.

Billington, Ray Allen. *Land of Savagery Land of Promise, The European Image of the American Frontier in the Nineteenth Century.* N.Y: W. W. Norton & Co., 1981.

Bird, Isabella. *A Lady's Life in the Rocky Mountains.* Introduction by Daniel J. Boorstin. Norman: Univ. of Okla. Press, 1960

Blomberg, Craig, and Stephen E. Robinson. *How Wide the Divide? A Mormon and an Evangelical in Conversation.* Downers Grove, Ill: InterVarsity Press, 1997.

Bodenstedt, Frederich Martin von. *Vom Atlantischen zum Stillen Ocean.* Leipzig: F. A. Brockhaus, 1882.

Botta, Carlo. *Storia della guerra dell' indipendenza degli Stati Uniti d'America.* Parigi: D. Colas, 1809.

Bowersock, G. W. *Fiction as History.* Berkeley: Univ. of California Press, 1994.

Bowles, Samuel. *Across the Continent: A Summer's Journey to the Rocky Mountains, the Mormons, and the Pacific States.* Springfield, Mass: Samuel Bowles & Co., 1866.

———. *Our New West.* Hartford: Hartford Publishing Co., 1869.

Bradley, Martha Sonntag. *ZCMI: America's First Department Store.* S.L.C: Zions Cooperative Mercantile Institution, 1991.

———. *A History of Beaver County.* Salt Lake City: Utah State Hist. Soc., 1999.

Brooks, Juanita. *The Mountain Meadows Massacre.* Stanford, Calif: Stanford Univ. Press, 1950. Reprinted Norman: Univ. of Okla. Press, 1962.

Brown, Dan. *The Da Vinci Code.* New York: Doubleday, 2003.

Brown, J. Newton, ed. *Encyclopedia of Religious Knowledge.* Brattleboro, Vt: Brattleboro Typographic Co., 1838.

Bryant, Edwin. *What I Saw in California.* N.Y: D. Appleton & Co., 1848. Reprinted Palo Alto, Calif: Lewis Osborne, 1967.

Bryson, Bill. *The Lost Continent.* N.Y: HarperCollins, 1990.

Buchner, Max. *Reise durch den Stillen Ozean.* Breslau: J. U. Kern's Verlag, 1878.

Burnstein, Dan. *Secrets of the Code: The Unauthorized Guide to the mysteries behind the DaVinci Code.* New York: CDS Books, 2004.

Burton, Richard F. *The City of the Saints and across the Rocky Mountains to California.* London: Longman, Green, Longman, and Roberts, 1861. N.Y: Harper & Brothers, 1862. *Voyages du Capitaine Burton à la Mecque aux grands lacs d'Afrique, et chez les Mormons.* Paris: Librairie Hachette, 1870. *I Mormoni e la città dei santi.* Milan: Fratelli Treves, 1875.

Busch, Moritz. *Die Mormonen: Ihr Prophet, ihr Staat und ihr Glaube.* Leipzig: Verlag von Carl B. Lorck, Druck von Breitsopf und Härtel, 1855.

Caccia, Antonio. *Europa ed America: Scene della vita dal 1848–1850.* Monaco: Giorgio Franz, 1850.

Cairncross, John. *After Polygamy Was Made a Sin: The Social History of Christian Polygamy.* London: Routledge & Kegan Paul, 1974.

Canning, Ray R., and Beverley Beeton, eds. *The Genteel Gentile: Letters of Elizabeth Cumming.* Salt Lake City: Tanner Trust, 1977.

Cannon, George Quayle. *Writings from the "Western Standard."* Liverpool: By George Q. Cannon, 1864.
Carlier, Auguste. *Le mariage aux Etats-Unis.* Paris: Hachette et Cie., 1860.
Carlton, Ambrose B. *The Wonderlands of the Wild West, with sketches of the Mormons.* N.p., 1891.
Carriker, Robert C. *Father Peter John De Smet, Jesuit in the West.* Norman: Univ. of Okla. Press, 1998.
Carvalho, Solomon N. *Incidents of Travel and Adventure in the Far West.* N.Y: Derby & Jackson, 1857. *Incidents of Travel and Adventure in the Far West.* N.Y: Derby & Jackson, 1860.
Cavling, Henrick. *Amerika.* Stockholm: Wilh. Siléns Forlag, 1898.
———. *Fra Amerika,* 2 vols. Glydendal, 1897.
Chandless, William. *A Visit to Salt Lake; Being a Journey Across the Plains, and a residence in the Mormon settlements at Utah.* London: Smith, Elder, and Co., 1857. Reprinted N.Y: AMS Press, 1971.
Chaney, Edward. *The Evolution of the Grand Tour.* London: Frank Cass, 1998.
Chard, Chloe. *Pleasure and Guilt on the Grand Tour: Travel Writing and Imaginative Geography, 1600–1830.* Manchester: Manchester Univ. Press, 1999.
Chasles, Philarète. *Etudes sur la littérature et les moeurs des Anglo-Américains au XIXème siècle.* Paris: Amyot, 1851.
Chisholm, Clive Scott. *Following the Wrong God Home.* Normam: Univ. of Okla. Press, 2003.
Cipriani, Leonetto. *Avventure della mia vita,* 2 vols. Bologna: Nicola Zanichelli, 1934. *California and Overland Diaries of Count Leonetto Cipriani from 1853 through 1871, Containing the Account of His Cattle Drive from Missouri to California in 1853; A Visit with Brigham Young in the Mormon Settlement of Salt Lake City; The Assembling of His Elegant Prefabricated Home in Belmont . . . Later to Become the Ralston Mansion.* Ed. and trans. by Ernest Falbo. Portland, Ore: Designed and Printed by Lawton Kennedy, San Francisco, for Champoeg Press, 1962.
Codazzi, Angela. *L'opera del missionario milanese Padre Samuele Mazzuchelli O. P. nel Nord America.* Milan: Atti del X Congresso Geografico Italiano, 1927.
Coleridge, Samuel Taylor. *Biografia Literaria: or, Biographical Sketches of My Literary Life and Opinions,* 2 vols. London: Rest Fenner, 1817. New York: Kirk and Mercein, 1817. James Engell and W. Jackson Bate, eds. Princeton: Princeton Univ. Press, 1984.
Comettant, Jean Pierre Oscar. *Les civilisations inconnues.* Paris: Paguerre, 1863.
Commager, Henry Steele. *America in Perspective: The United States through Foreign Eyes.* N.Y: Random House, 1947.
Cone, John Frederick. *First Rival of the Metropolitan Opera.* N.Y: Columbia Univ. Press, 1983.
Conybeare, William John. *Essays, Ecclesiastical and Social.* London: Longman, Brown, Green, and Longmans, 1855.
Cooley, Everett L., ed. *Diary of Brigham Young 1857.* S.L.C: Tanner Trust Fund, 1980.
Combe, William. *The Tour of Doctor Syntax, in search of the picturesque: A Poem.* London: R. Ackermann, n.d. [1802].
———. *The Second Tour of Doctor Syntax, in search of consolation: A Poem.* London: R. Ackermann, 1820.
———. *The Third Tour of Doctor Syntax, in search of a wife: A Poem.* London: R. Ackermann, n.d. [1821].

Crépeau, Rosemary. *Un apôtre dominicain aux Etats-Unis, le Père Samuel-Charles Gaetan Mazzuchelli*. Paris: J. DeGigord, 1932.

Dababie, F. *Récits et types américaines*. Paris: F. Sartorius, Librairie-Editeur, 1860.

Dadd, Bill [The Scribe]. *Great Trans-Continental Railroad Guide*. Chicago: Geo. A. Crofutt & Co., 1869.

D'Ancona, Jacob. *The City of Light*. Ed. and trans. by David Selbourne. London: Little, Brown & Co., 1997.

Davidson, Levette Joy, and Prudence Bostwick, eds. *The Literature of the Rocky Mountain West, 1803–1903*. Caldwell, Idaho: The Caxton Printers, 1939.

De Charencey, Hyacinthe. *Le mythe de Votan*. Alencon: Imprimerie de E. De Broise, 1871.

De Bryas, Comtesse Madeleine, and Jacqueline de Bryas. *A Frenchwoman's Impressions of America*. N.Y: The Century Co., 1920.

De Smet, Pierre-Jean. *Cinquante nouvelles lettres du R. P. de Smet, de la Compagnie de Jésus et missionnaire en Amérique*. Paris: Rue de Tournon, 1858

———. *Oregon Missions and Travels over the Rocky Mountains in 1845–1846*. N.Y: E. Dunigan, 1847. *Missions de l'Orégon et voyages aux Montagnes Rocheuses aux sources de la Columbie de l'Athabasca et du Sascatschawin en 1845–1846*. Gand: Vander Schelden, 1848.

———. *Life, Letters and Travels of Father Pierre-Jean De Smet, S.J., 1801–1873*, 4 vols. Ed. by Hiram Martin Chittenden and Alfred Talbot Richardson. N.Y: Francis P. Harper, 1905.

Defoe, Daniel. *The Life and Strange Surprising Adventures of Robinson Crusoe of York, Mariner . . . Written by Himself*. London: 1719.

Desmons, Frederic. *Essai historique et critique du Mormonisme*. Strasbourg: Berger-Levrault, 1856.

Dickens, Charles. *Pictures from Italy*. London: Bradbury & Evans, 1846. Ed. by Andrew Lang as *American Notes and Pictures from Italy*. London: Chapman & Hall, 1898.

Dixon, William Hepworth Dixon. *New America*, 2 vols. London: Hurst and Blackett, 1867. *La nouvelle Amérique*. Paris: Librairie Internationale, 1869.

———. *White Conquest*. London: Chatto and Windus, 1876. *La conquête blanche*. Paris: Librairie Hachette et Cie., 1877. *La conquista bianca*. Milan: Fratelli Treves, 1877.

———. *Les Etats-Unis d'Amérique. Impressions de voyage*. Paris: Librairie Hachette et Cie., 1879.

———. *Spiritual Wives*, 2 vols. Philadelphia: J. B. Lippincott & Co., 1868. German ed. Leipzig: Tauchnitz, 1868.

Dolan, Brian. *Ladies on the Grand Tour*. N.Y: HarperCollins, 2001.

Domenech, Emmanuel Henri Dieudonne. *Journal d'un missionnaire au Texas et au Mexique*. Paris: 1856. Trans. as *Missionary Adventures in Texas and Mexico*. London: Longman, Brown, Green, Longmans, and Roberts, 1858.

———. *Seven Years' Residence in the Great Deserts of North America*. London: Longman, Green, Longman and Roberts, 1860. *Voyage pittoresque dans les grands déserts du Nouveau Monde*. Paris: Morizot, 1862.

Doyle, Arthur Conan. "A Study in Scarlet" in Beeton's Christmas Annual. London: Ward, Lock & Co., 1887, 1-95. Italian ed. Un dramma misterioso. 1901. Uno strano delitto. 1907. Sherlock Holmes il poliziotto dilettante: lo scritto rosso. 1908. Il segreto di Hope. 1911.

———. *Angels of Darkness, A Drama in Three Acts*. N.Y: The Baker Street Irregulars, 2001.

―――. *Our Second American Adventure*. London: Hodder & Stoughton, 1924.
―――. *Through the Magic Door*. London: Smith, Elder & Company, 1907.
Dunant, Henry. *A Memory of Solferino*. Geneva: International Committee of the Red Cross, 1986.
Duplessis, Paul. *Les Mormons*. Paris: A. Cadot, 1859.
Dutton, Clarence E. *Tertiary History of the Grand Cañon District*. Wash: Government Printing Office, 1882. Republished Santa Barbara: Peregrine Smith, 1977; and with an introduction by Wallace Stegner and a new foreword by Stephen J. Pyne. Tucson: Univ. of Arizona Press, 2001. *Atlas to Accompany the Monograph on the Tertiary History of the Grand Cañon District*. Wash: United States Geological Survey, 1882.
Ekins, Roger Robin, ed. *Defending Zion: George Q. Cannon and the California Mormon Newspaper Wars of 1856–1857*. Spokane, Wash: The Arthur H. Clark Co., 2002.
Eliason, Eric A., ed. *Mormons and Mormonism: An Introduction to an American World Religion*. Urbana and Chicago: Univ. of Ill. Press, 2001.
Ellsworth, S. George, ed. *Dear Ellen: Two Mormon Women and Their Letters*. S.L.C: Univ. of Utah Library, [1982].
Erdan, Alexandre. *La France mystique*. Amsterdam: R. C. Meijen, 1858.
Eyma, Louis Xavier. *Excentricities américaines*. Leipzig: Durr, n.d. [1860].
Faithful, Emily. *Three Visits to America*. N.Y: Fowler & Wells Co., 1884.
Ferris, Benjamin G. *Utah and the Mormons: The History, Government, Doctrines, Customs, and Prospects of the Latter-Day Saints, from personal observation during a six months' residence at Great Salt Lake City*. N.Y: Harper & Brothers, Publishers, 1854.
Ferris, Mrs. B. G. *The Mormons at Home; With some incidents of travel from Missouri to California*. N.Y: Dix & Edwards, 1856.
Flagg, Edmund T. *The Far West: or, A Tour beyond the Mountains*, 2 vols. N.Y: Harper & Brothers, 1838.
Flake, Chad J., and Larry W. Draper. *A Mormon Bibliography, 1830–1930*, 2 vols. Rev. edition. Provo: Religious Studies Center, Brigham Young Univ., 2004.
Flake, Kathleen. *The Politics of American Religious Identity: The Seating of Senator Reed Smoot, Mormon Apostle*. Chapel Hill: Univ. of North Carolina Press, 2004.
Francaviglia, Richard V. *Believing in Place: A Spiritual Geography of the Great Basin*. Reno and Las Vegas: Univ. of Nevada Press, 2003.
Francy, Mary F. *Albert Tissandier: Drawings of Nature and Industry in the United States, 1885*. S.L.C: Utah Museum of Fine Arts, 2001.
Franklin, John B. *A Cheap Trip to the Great Salt Lake City*. Ipswich, England: J. Scoggins, 1864.
Furniss, Norman F. *The Mormon Conflict, 1850–1859*. New Haven: Yale Univ. Press, 1960.
Galluzzo, Leopoldo and Gaetano Dura. *Delle scoperte fatte sulla luna dal Sigr. Herschel*. Naples: L. Gatti e Dura, 1836.
Garland, Henry and Mary, eds. *The Oxford Companion to German Literature*, 3d ed. Oxford: Oxford Univ. Press, 1997.
Gardini, Carlo. *Gli Stati Uniti―Ricordi*, 2 vols. Bologna: Nicola Zanichelli, 1887.

Gasparin, Count Agénor de. *L'Amérique devant l'Europe. Principes et intérêts.* Paris: Michel Lévy Frères, 1862. *America Before Europe: Principles and Interests.* N.Y: Charles Scribner, 1862.

Gates, Susa Young. *History of the Young Ladies' Mutual Improvement Association of the Church of Jesus Christ of Latter-day Saints, from November 1869 to June 1910.* S.L.C: Deseret News, 1911.

Gavazzi, Alessandro. *Father Gavazzi's Lectures in New York.* N.Y: De Witt and Davenport, 1853.

———. *Sermons du Père Gavazzi.* Paris: Poulet-Malassis et de Broise, 1861.

Gee, John. *A Guide to the Joseph Smith Papyri.* Provo, Utah: FARMS, 2000.

Gibbons, James Cardinal. *The Faith of our Fathers.* Baltimore: John Murphy Co., 1876.

———. *Our Christian Heritage.* Baltimore: John Murphy Co., 1889.

Givens, Terryl L. *The Viper on the Hearth: Mormons, Myth, and the Construction of Heresy.* N.Y: Oxford Univ. Press, 1997.

Glazier, Willard. *Peculiarities of American Cities.* Philadelphia: Hubbard Brothers, Publishers, 1884.

Goetzmann, William H. *Army Exploration in the American West, 1803–1863.* New Haven: Yale Univ. Press, 1959.

Goodrich, Samuel Griswold. *Les Etats-Unis d'Amérique.* Paris: Guillaumin et Cie, 1852.

Greeley, Horace. *An Overland Journey, from New York to San Francisco in the Summer of 1859.* N.Y: C. M. Saxton, Barker & Co.; San Francisco: H. H. Bancroft & Co., 1860.

———. *Recollections of a Busy Life.* N.Y: J. B. Ford & Co., 1868.

Green, Nelson Winch. *Fifteen Years among the Mormons: Being the Narrative of Mrs. Mary Ettie V. Smith.* 2nd ed. N.Y: H. Dayton, 1859.

Gregg, Josiah. *Commerce of the Prairies: or the journal of a Santa Fe trader, during eight expeditions across the great western prairies, and a residence of nearly nine years in northern Mexico*, 2 vols. N.Y: Henry G. Langley, 1844.

Gregory, Kristiana. *The Great Railroad Race: The Diary of Libby West.* N.Y: Scholastic Press, 1999.

Griffiths, D., Jr. *Two Years' Residence in the New Settlements of Ohio, North America: with Directions to Emigrants.* London: Westley and Davis, 1835.

Gunnison, John W. *The Mormons, or, Latter-day Saints, in the Valley of the Great Salt Lake.* Philadelphia: Lippincott, Grambo & Co., 1852.

Hafen, LeRoy R., ed. *The Utah Expedition, 1857–1858: A Documentary Account of the United States Military Movement under Colonel Albert Sidney Johnston, and the Resistance by Brigham Young and the Mormon Nauvoo Legion.* Glendale: The Arthur H. Clark Co., 1958.

Hamilton, Thomas. *Men and Manners in America*, 2 vols. Edinburgh: William Blackwood; and London: T. Cadell, 1834.

Handlin, Oscar. *This Was America: True Accounts of People and Places, Manners and Customs, as Recorded by European Travelers to the Western Shore in the Eighteenth, Nineteenth, and Twentieth Centuries.* Cambridge: Harvard Univ. Press, 1949.

Hansen, Klaus J. *Quest for Empire: The Political Kingdom of God and the Council of Fifty in Mormon History.* East Lansing: Mich. State Univ. Press, 1967.

Hardy, Carmon. *Solemn Covenant: The Mormon Polygamous Passage.* Urbana and Chicago: Univ. of Ill. Press, 1992.

Hardy, Lady Duffus. *Through Cities and Prairie Towns: Sketches of an American Tour.* London: Chapman and Hall, 1881.

Harris, Dean. *The Catholic Church in Utah, 1776–1909.* S.L.C: Intermountain Catholic Press, 1909.

Hart-Davis, Rupert, ed. *The Letters of Oscar Wilde.* London, 1962.

Harazthy, Agostin. *Grape Culture, Wines, and Winemaking: with notes upon agriculture and horti-culture.* N.Y: Harpers, 1862.

Haussonville, Gabriel Paul Othenin de Cléron, Comte de. *A travers les Etats-Unis. Notes et Impressions.* Paris: Calmann Lévy, 1883. *One day in Utah. A Literary French nobleman's views on the Mormon question, from "A travers les Etats Unis."* S.L.C: Deseret News Co., 1883.

Hayden, A. S. *Early History of the Disciples in the Western Reserve, Ohio.* Cincinnati: Chase & Hall, 1875.

Hayward, John. *The Religious Creeds and Statistics of every Christian Denomination in the United States and British Provinces.* Boston: Published by John Hayward, 1836.

Heckman, Marlin L. *Overland on California Trail, 1846–1859: A Bibliography of Manuscript and Printed Travel Narratives.* Glendale: The Arthur H. Clark Co., 1984.

Heintze, Beatrix, ed. *Max Buchners Reise nach zentafrica, 1878-1882.* Köln: Köppe Verlag, 1999.

Hellwald, Frederich Anton Heller von. *Die Erde und ihre Völker. Ein geographisches Hausbuch von Friedrich von Hellwald. Funfte Auflage Neu bearbeitet von Ernst Waechter.* Stuttgart: W. Spemann, 1876.

────── and Gustavo Strafforello. *America Settentrionale secondo le notizie più recenti.* Torino: Ermanno Loescher, 1886.

Henisch, Bridget Ann. *Medieval Armchair Travels.* State College, Pa: The Carnation Press, 1967.

Hibbard, Charles G. *Fort Douglas, Utah, 1862–1991.* Fort Collins, Colo: Vestige Press, 1999.

Hibbert, Christopher. *The Grand Tour.* London: Thames Methuen, 1987.

Hickman, William A. *Brigham's Destroying Angel: Being the Life, Confession, and Startling Disclosures of the Notorious Bill Hickman, the Danite Chief of Utah.* Ed. by J. H. Beadle. N.Y: Geo. A. Crofutt, 1872.

Hingston, Edward P. *The Genial Showman, Being the Reminiscences of the Life of Artemus Ward.* Barre, Mass: Imprint Soc., 1971.

Holland, Merlin, and Rupert Hart-Davis, eds. *The Complete Letters of Oscar Wilde.* N.Y: Henry Holt and Co., 2000.

Hopkins, Sarah Winnemucca. *Life Among the Piutes: Their Wrongs and Claims.* 1883.

Hoskins, Nathan Jr. *Notes Upon the Western Country.* Greenfield, Mass: Printed by J. P. Fogg, 1833.

Hübner, Joseph Alexander, Graf von. *Ein Spaziergang um die Welt.* Leipzig: 1874. *Promenade autour du monde,* 2 vols. Paris : Librairie Hachette et Cie, 1873. *A Ramble Round the World, 1871,* 2 vols. Trans. by Lady Herbert. London: Macmillan and Co., 1874. *Passeggiata intorno al mondo 1871.* Torino: Unione Tipografico-Editrice Torinese, 1873; Second Italian ed., Milan: Fratelli Treves, 1879.

———. *Neun Jahre der Erinnerungen eines österreichischen Botschafters in Paris unter dem zweiten Kaiserreich 1851–1859*. Berlin: Gebrüder Paetel, 1904.

———. *Ein Jahr meines Lebens*. Leipzig: Brockhaus, 1891.

Huret, Jules. *En Amérique: De New-York à la Nouvelle-Orléans*. Paris: Bibliothèque-Charpentier, 1905.

———. *En Amérique: De San Francisco au Canada (avec un index analytique de l'ouvrage)*. Paris: Bibliothèque-Charpentier, 1905.

Hyde, John Jr. *Mormonism: Its Leaders and Designs*. N.Y: Fetridge, 1857.

Ingalls, Rufus. "Report of Rufus Ingalls to Major General Thomas S. Jesup, Giving an Account of a Trip with Colonel Edward J. Steptoe from Fort Leavenworth to Salt Lake City between June 1 and August 31, 1854." Senate Exec. Doc. 1 (34:1), 1850, Serial 811, 2:152–68.

Jerome, Jerome K. *My Life and Times*. N.Y: Harper & Brothers Publishers, 1926.

Jousselin, Stéphane. *Yankees à la fin de siècle*. Paris: Paul Ollendorff, 1892.

Kane, Elizabeth. *A Gentile Account of Life in Utah's Dixie: Elizabeth Kane's St. George Journal, 1872–73*. Ed. by Norman R. Bowen and Mary Karen Bowen Solomon. S.L.C: Tanner Trust Fund, 1995.

———. *Twelve Mormon Homes Visited in Succession on a Journey through Utah to Arizona*. 1874; S.L.C: Tanner Trust Fund, 1974.

Kelly, William. *Across the Rocky Mountains, from New York to California: with a visit to the celebrated Mormon colony, at the Great Salt Lake*. London: Simms and M'Intyre, 1852.

King, Ross. *Michelangelo and the Pope's Ceiling*. N.Y: Walker and Co., 2003.

Kipling, Rudyard. *From Sea to Sea and Other Sketches. Letters of Travel*, 2 vols. London: Macmillan and Co., Limited, 1900.

Knack, Martha C. *Boundaries Between: The Southern Paiutes, 1775–1995*. Lincoln: Univ. of Nebr. Press, 2001.

Koch, Albrecht Karl. *Reise durch einen Teil der Vereinigten Staaten von Nordamerika in den Jahren 1844 bis 1846*. Dresden and Leipzig: Arnold, 1847. *Journey Through a Part of the United States of North America in the Years 1844 to 1846*. Trans. and ed. by Ernst A. Stadler. Carbondale: Southern Ill. Univ., 1972.

Korensky, Josef. *Cesty Po Svete*. Prague: Nakladatelstvi J. Otty, ca. 1894.

Kurutz, Gary F. *The California Gold Rush: A Descriptive Bibliography of Books and Pamphlets Covering the Years 1848–1853*. San Francisco: The Book Club of California, 1997.

Laboulaye, Edouard. *Paris en Amérique*. Paris: Charpentier, 1863.

Lamar, Howard, ed. *The New Encyclopedia of the American West*. New Haven: Yale Univ. Press, 1998.

Langworthy, Franklin. *Scenery of the Plains, Mountains and Mines: A Diary Kept Upon the Overland Route to California, By Way of the Great Salt Lake*. Ogdensburg: J. C. Sprague, Book-Seller, 1855.

Larson, Charles. *By His Own Hand upon Papyrus: A New Look at the Joseph Smith Papyrus*. Grand Rapids, Mich: Institute for Religious Study, 1992.

Leonard, Glen. *Nauvoo: A Place of Peace, a People of Promise*. Salt Lake City: Deseret Book, 2002.

Leslie, Mrs. Frank. *California: A Pleasure Trip from Gotham to the Golden Gate.* N.Y: G. W. Carelton & Co., 1877.
Lester, John Erastus. *The Atlantic to the Pacific. What to see, and how to see it.* Boston: Shepard and Gill, 1873.
Lienhard, Heinrich. *Californien unmittelbar vor und nach der Entdeckung des Goldes.* Zurich: Fasi & Beer, 1898.
Lippincott, Sarah Jane [writing as Grace Greenwood]. *New Life in New Lands: Notes of Travel.* N.Y: J. B. Ford and Co., 1873.
Ludlow, Fitz Hugh. *The Heart of the Continent: A Record of Travel Across the Plains and in Oregon.* N.Y: Hurd and Houghton, 1870.
MacFadden, Harry Alexander. *Rambles in the Far West.* Hollidaysburg, Pa: Standard Printing House, 1906.
Madsen, Brigham D. *Corinne: The Gentile Capital of Utah.* S.L.C: Utah State Hist. Soc., 1980.
———, ed. *Exploring the Great Salt Lake: The Stansbury Expedition of 1849–50.* S.L.C: Univ. of Utah Press, 1989.
Mackay, Charles. *The Mormons: or Latter-Day Saints.* London: Office of the National Illustrated Library, 1851.
Majanlaht, Anthony. *The Families who made Rome: A History and a Guide.* London: Chatto & Windus, 2005.
Mapleson, James Henry. *The Mapleson Memoirs: The Career of an Operatic Impresario, 1858–1888.* Ed. by Harold Rosenthal. N.Y: Appleton-Century, 1966.
Margaret, Helene. *Father De Smet, Pioneer Priest of the Rockies.* Milwaukee: Bruce, 1940.
Marks, David. *The Life of David Marks.* Limerick, Maine: Printed at the Office of the Morning Star, 1831; *Memoirs of the Life of David Marks, Minister of the Gospel,* ed. by Mrs. Marilla Marks. Dover, New Hampshire: Free-Will Baptist Printing Establishment, 1846.
Marolla, Ed. *Mazzuchelli of Wisconsin.* Horicon, Wisc: Marolla Press, 1981.
Marquardt, H. Michael, and Wesley P. Walters. *Inventing Mormonism: Tradition and the Historical Record.* S.L.C: Smith Research Associates, 1994.
Marshall, W. G. *Genom Amerika.* Stockholm: Albert Bonniers Forlag, 1882.
Massara, Giuseppe. *Viaggiatori Italiani in America (1860–1970).* Roma: Edizioni di Storia e Letteratura, 1976.
Mattes, Merrill J. *Platte River Road Narratives.* Urbana: Univ. of Ill. Press, 1988
Maximilian, Alexander Philipp, Prinz von Wied-Neuwied. *Reise in das innere Nord-America in den Jahren 1832 bis 1834,* 2 vols. Coblenz: J. Hoelscher, 1839–41. *Travels in the Interior of North America.* London: Ackermann and Co., 1843. In Reuben Gold Thwaites, ed. *Travels in the Interior of North America,* Vol. III. Cleveland: The Arthur H. Clark Co., 1906.
———. *Reise nach Brasilien in den Jahren 1815 bis 1817.* Frankfurt: H. L. Brönner, 1820–21. Republished with maps as *Beitrage zur Naturgeschichte von Brasilien.* Weimar, 1825–33; and *Abbildungen zur Naturgeschichte Brasiliens.* Weimar, 1822–31.
May, Dean. "Mormons," in Eric A. Eliason. *Mormons and Mormonism: An Introduction to an American Religion.* Urbana: University of Illinois Press, 2001.
May, Karl Friedrich. *Unter Geiern.* Bamberg: Karl-May-Verlag, 1953. [First published 1886].

———. *Die Felsenburg*. Bamberg: Karl-May-Verlag, 1950. [First published 1893]

Mayernik, David. *Timeless Cities: An Architect's Reflections on Renaissance Italy*. Boulder: Westview Press, 2003.

Mazzuchelli, Samuele. *Casa di missioni e collegio fondati sul Sinsinawa Mound*. Milan: Boniardi-Pogliani, 1846.

———. *Memorie istoriche ed edificanti d'un missionario apostolico dell'Ordine dei Predicatori fra varie tribù di selvaggi e fra i Cattolici e Protestanti negli Stati Uniti d'America*. Milan: Boniardi-Pogliani, 1844. *Memoirs Historical and Edifying of a Missionary Apostolic of the order of Saint Dominic among various Indian tribes and among the Catholics and Protestants of the United States of America*. Chicago: W. F. Hall Printing Co., 1915. *The Memoirs of Father Samuel Mazzuchelli, O.P.* Chicago: The Priory Press, 1967.

———. *Positio Super Vita, Virtutibus et Fama Sanctitatis. Canonizationis servi dei Caroli Samuelis Mazzuchelli, O.P.* Romae: Congregatio Pro Causis Sanctorum, 1989.

McClure, A. K. *Three Thousand Miles Through the Rocky Mountains*. Philadelphia: J. B. Lippincott & Co., 1869.

McDermott, John Francis, ed. *Travelers on the Western Frontier*. Urbana: Univ. of Ill. Press, 1970.

McGreal, Sister Nona. *Samuele Mazzuchelli, O.P., A Kaleidoscope of Scenes from his Life*. Sinsinawa, Wisc: Mazzuchelli Guild, 1973.

McMurtry, Larry. *Walter Benjamin at the Dairy Queen: Reflections at Sixty and Beyond*. N.Y: Simon & Schuster, 1999.

Mérimée, Prosper. *Mélanges historiques littéraires*. Paris: Michel Levy, 1855.

Merriman, Frances. *My Summer in a Mormon Village*. Boston and N.Y: Houghton, Mifflin and Co., 1894.

Meyer, Rudolph. *Ursachen der Amerikanischen Concurrenz*. Berlin, 1881.

Miller, Joaquin. *The Danites of the Sierras*. Chicago: Jansen, McClure & Co., 1881.

Mintz, Lannon W. *The Trail: A Bibliography of the Travelers on the Overland Trail to California, Oregon, Salt Lake City, and Montana during the Years 1841–1864*. Albuquerque: Univ. of New Mexico Pres, 1987.

[Mitchell, A. W.] *The Waldenses: Sketches of the Evangelical Christians of the valleys of Piedmont*. Philadelphia: Presbyterian Board of Publication, 1853.

Möllhausen, Heinrich Balduin. *Tagebuch einer Reise vom Mississippi nach den Küsten der Sudsee*. Leipzig: Hermann Mendelssohn, 1858. Dutch ed: *Reis van den Mississippi naar de kusten van den grooten oceaan*, 2 vols. Te Zutphen, Bij A. E. C. Van Someren, 1858–59. Trans. as *Diary of a Journey from the Mississippi to the Coasts of the Pacific with a United States Government Expedition*, 2 vols. London: Longman, Brown, Green, Longmans, Roberts, 1858.

———. *Reisen in die Felsengebirge Nord-Amerikas bis zum Hoch-Plateau von New Mexico*. Leipzig: Hermann Costenoble, 1861.

———. *Das Mormonenmädchen; eine Erzählung aus der Zeit des Kriegszuges der Vereinigten Staaten gegen die "Heiligen der letzten Tage" im Jahre 1857–1858*. 6 vols. Jena and Leipzig: Hermann Costenoble, 1864.

———. *Der Fanatiker*, roman. 3 vols. Leipzig: P. List, 1883.

Monastier, Antoine. *Histoire de l'Eglise Vaudoise*. Geneva: Kessmann, 1847. Trans. as *A History of the Vaudois church: from its origin, and of the Vaudois of Piedmont to the present day*. London: Religious Tract Society, 1848.

Monk, Maria. *Awful Disclosures of Maria Monk*. N.Y: Howe & Bates, 1836.

Morton, H. V. *A Traveler in Italy*. N.Y: Dodd, Mead & Co., 1964.

Mulder, William. *Homeward to Zion: The Mormon Migration from Scandinavia*. Minneapolis: Univ. of Minnesota Press, 1957.

——— and A. R. Mortensen, eds. *Among the Mormons: Historic Accounts by Contemporary Observers*. N.Y: Alfred A. Knopf, 1958.

Nevins, Allan. *America Through British Eyes*. N.Y: Oxford Univ. Press, 1948.

Nibley, Hugh. *The Message of the Joseph Smith Papyri: An Egyptian Endowment*. S.L.C: Deseret Book, 1975.

Ollivant, Joseph Earle. *A Breeze from the Great Salt Lake; or, New Zealand to New York by the New Mail Route*. London: William Hunt and Co., 1871.

Olson, Carl E., and Sandra Miesel. *The DaVinci Hoax: Exposing the Errors in the DaVinci Code*. San Francisco: Ignatius Press, 2004.

Olshausen, Theodor. *Geschichte der Mormonen oder Jüngsten-Tages-Heiligen in Nordamerika*. Göttingen: 1856.

Ordoric of Pordenone. *The Travels of Friar Odoric, Trans. By Sir Henry Yule*. Grand Rapids, Mich: William B. Eerdmans, 2002.

Ortolani, Sergio. *S. Croce in Gerusalemme*. Roma, 1924.

Palmer, Richard F., and Karl D. Butler. *Brigham Young: The New York Years*. Provo: Charles Redd Center for Western Studies, 1982.

Parker, Samuel. *Journal of an Exploring Tour beyond the Rocky Mountains*. Ithaca, N.Y: By the Author, 1838.

Parkman, Francis. *The California and Oregon Trail: being sketches of prairie and Rocky Mountain life*. London: Putnam's American Agency, 1849.

Peck, John M. *A Gazetteer of Illinois*. Jacksonville, Ill: R. Goudy, 1834.

Peterson, H. Donl. *The Story of the Book of Abraham: Mummies, Manuscripts, and Mormonism*. S.L.C: Deseret Book, 1995.

Pfeiffer, Ida Reyer. *A Lady's Second Journey Round the World*. N.Y: Harper & Brothers, 1856. *Mein zweite Weltreise*. Vienna: C. Gerold's Sohn, 1856. *Mon second voyage autour du monde*, 2d ed. Paris: Librairie de L. Hachette et cie., 1859.

Phillips, Charles and Alan Axelrod, eds. *Encyclopedia of the American West*, 4 vols. N.Y: Macmillian Reference USA, 1996.

Phillips, Morris. *Abroad and at Home: Practical Hints for Tourists*. N.Y: Bretanos, 1891.

Pichot, Amédée. *Les Mormons*. Paris: Hachette et Cie, 1854.

Powell, Allan Kent, ed. *Utah History Encyclopedia*. S.L.C: Univ. of Utah Press, 1994.

Powell, John Wesley, and George W. Ingalls. *Report on the Condition and Wants of the Ute Indians of Utah; the Pai-Utes of Utah, Northern Arizona, Southern Nevada, and Southeastern California; the Go-si Utes of Utah and Nevada; the Northwestern Shoshones of Idaho and Utah, and the Western Shoshones of Nevada*. House Exec. Doc. 157 (43-1), 1874.

Powell, Lyman Pierson. *Historic Towns of the Western States.* N.Y. and London: G. P. Putnam's Sons, 1901.

Pyper, George D. *The Romance of the Old Playhouse.* S.L.C: Deseret Book Co., 1937.

Reed, Rebecca Theresa. *Six Months in a Convent, or the Narrative of Rebecca Theresa Reed.* Boston: Russell, Odiorne & Metcalf, 1835.

Reid, Mayne. *Les deux filles du Squatter.* Paris: J. Hetzel et. C., n.d.

———. *The Wild Huntress, or love in the Wilderness.* N.Y: R.M. DeWitt, 1861.

———. *The Man-eaters and Other Odd People.* N.Y: J. Miller, 1880.

Reininger, Anton. "Karl May—Il sogno dell'esistenza eroica." In *Salgari: L'ombra lunga dei Paletuvieri.* Udine: Associazione Friuliani, 1997.

Religious Tract Society. *Mormonism.* London: Religious Tract Society, 1851.

———. *The Doctrines of Mormonism.* London: Religious Tract Society, 1853.

———. *Is Mormonism True or Not?* London: Religious Tract Society, 1853.

———. *Reasons I Cannot Become a Mormonite.* London: Religious Tract Society, 1851.

———. *Remarkable Delusions, or Illustrations of Popular Errors.* London: Religious Tract Society, 1851.

Rémy, Jules. *Voyage au pays des Mormons.* Paris: E. Dentu, 1860.

———, and Julius Benchley. *A Journey to Great-Salt-Lake City, by Jules Rémy, and Julius Brenchley, M. A.; with a sketch of the history, religion, and customs of the Mormons, and an introduction on the religious movement in the United States,* 2 vols. London: W. Jeffs, 1861. *An Excerpt from A Journey to Great-Salt-Lake City, in 1855.* S.L.C: Red Butte Press, 1984.

Reybaud, Louis. *Etudes sur les réformateurs, ou socialistes modernes.* 7th ed. Paris: Guillaumin et Cie., 1864.

Reynolds, George. *The Book of Abraham.* S.L.C: Deseret News Printing and Publishing Establishment, 1879.

Rice, Edward. *Captain Sir Richard Francis Burton: The Secret Agent Who Made the Pilgrimage to Mecca, Discovered the Kama Sutra, and Brought the Arabian Nights to the West.* N.Y: Scribner's, 1990.

Richards, Bradley W. *The Savage View: Charles Savage, Pioneer Mormon Photographer.* Nevada City, Calif: Carl Mautz Publishing, 1995.

Ridley, Ronald T. *Napoléon's Proconsul in Egypt: The Life and Times of Bernardino Drovetti.* London: The Rubicon Press, n.d.

Roberts, Brigham H. *Comprehensive History of the Church of Jesus Christ of Latter-day Saints,* 6 vols. Salt Lake City: 1930.

Robida, Albert. *Le vingtième siècle.* Paris: Georges Decaux, 1883. *The Twentieth Century.* Ed. by Arthur Evans, trans. by Philippe Willems. Middletown: Wesleyan Univ. Press, 2004.

———. *Voyages très extraordinaires de Saturnin Farandoul dans les 5 ou 6 parties du monde et dans tous les pays connus et même inconnus de M. Jules Verne.* Paris: Librairie Illustrée, 1885. *Viaggi straordinarissimi di Saturnino Farandola nelle 5 o 6 parti del mondo ed in tutti i paesi visitati e non visitati da Giulio Verne.* Milan: Casa Editrice Sonzogno, 1919.

Robinson, Phil. *Saints and Sinners: A Tour Across the States, and Round them; with Three months among the Mormons.* London: Sampson Low, Marston, Searle, & Rivington, 1883. Boston: Roberts Brothers, 1883.

Rochefort-Luçay, Victor Henri, Marquis de. *Retour de la Nouvelle-Calédonie.* Paris: Ancienne Librairie Marinon, F. Jeanmain, Successeur, 1877.

Rolle, Andrew F. *The Immigrant Upraised.* Norman: Univ. of Okla. Press, 1968.

―――. *Westward the Immigrants: Italian Adventurers and Colonists in an Expanding America.* Golden: Univ. Press of Colo., 1999.

―――. *The Road to Virginia City: The Diary of James Knox Polk Miller.* Norman: Univ. of Okla. Press, 1960.

Rostan, Ermanno. *Chi sono I Mormoni.* Torino: Claudiana, 1966.

Ruxton, George Frederick Augustus. *Adventures in Mexico and the Rocky Mountains.* London: J. Murray, 1847. N.Y: Harper & Brothers, 1848.

―――. *Life in the Far West.* London: John Murray, 1849.

Salgari, Emilio. *Avventure fra le Pellerossa.* Torino: Ditta G. B. Paravia e Comp., 1900.

――― and Luigi Motta. *I cacciatori del Far West.* Milan: Bottega di Poesia, 1925.

―――. *Jolanda la figlia del Corsaro Nero.* Introduzione di Ruggerio Leonardi. Milan: Oscar Mondadori, 1999.

Schiavo, Giovanni. *Four Centuries of Italian American History.* N.Y: 1952.

Schiel, Jacob Heinrich Wilhelm. *Reise durch die Felsengebirge und die Humboldtgebirge nach dem Stillen Ocean.* Schaffhausen: Druck und Verlag der Brodtmann'schen Buchhandlung, 1859. *The Land Between: Dr. James Schiel's Account of the Gunnison-Beckwith Expedition into the West, 1853–1854.* Ed. and trans. by Frederick W. Bachmann and William Swilling Wallace. Los Angeles: Westernlore Press, 1957. *Journey Through the Rocky Mountains and the Humboldt Mountains to the Pacific Ocean.* Ed. and trans. by Thomas N. Bonner. Norman: Univ. of Okla. Press, 1959.

Schindler, Harold. *In Another Time: Sketches of Utah History.* Logan: Utah State Univ. Press, 1998.

Schlagintweit, Robert von. *Die Pacific-Eisenbahn in Nord-America.* Köln and Leipzig: E. H. Mayer; N.Y: L. W. Schmidt, 1870.

―――. *Die Mormonen; oder, Die Heiligen vom jungsten Tage von ihrer Entstehung bis auf die Gegenwart.* Köln and Leipzig: E. H. Mayer, 1874.

Schleiden, Rudolpf. *Reise-Erinnerungen aus den Vereinigten Staaten von Amerika.* N.Y: E. Steiger, 1873.

Schmidt, Jørgen W. *Oh, Du Zion I Vest: Den Danske Mormon-Emigration.* Copenhagen: Rosenkilde og Bagger, 1965.

―――. *Mormon Bibliografi 1837–1984: En dansk* [A Danish Mormon Bibliography, 1837–1984]. Lynge, Denmark: Forlaget Moroni, 1984.

Shipps, Jan. *Mormonism: The Story of a New Religious Tradition.* Urbana: Univ. of Ill. Press, 1985.

Sillitoe. Alan. *Leading the Blind. A Century of Guide Book Travel, 1815-1914.* London: Macmillan, 1995.

Simonin, Louis L. *Le grand-ouest des États-Unis. Les pionniers et les Peaux-Rouges. Les colons du Pacifique.* Paris: Charpentier, 1869. *Il Far-West degli Stati Uniti: i pionieri e i Pellirosse.* Milan: Fratelli Treves, 1876. *The Rocky Mountain West in 1867.* Lincoln: Univ. of Nebr. Press, 1966.

―――. *A travers les États-Unis, de l'Atlantique au Pacifique.* Paris: Charpentier et cie., 1875. *Attraverso gli Stati Uniti dall'Atlantico al Pacifico.* Milan: Fratelli Treves, 1876.

Skårdal, Dorothy B. *The Divided Heart: Scandinavian Immigrant Experience through Literary Sources.* Lincoln: Univ. of Nebr. Press, 1974.
Smart, William B., and Donna T. Smart, eds. *Over the Rim: The Parley P. Pratt Exploring Expedition to Southern Utah, 1849–1850.* Logan: Utah State Univ. Press, 1999.
Smith, George A. *The Rise, Progress, and Travels of the Church of Jesus Christ of Latter Day Saints.* Salt Lake City: Deseret News Office, 1869. Second revised ed., 1872.
Smith, Joseph. *An American Prophet's Record: The Diaries and Journal of Joseph Smith.* Ed. By Scott H. Faulring. Salt Lake City: Signature Books, 1987.
Smythe, William E. *The Conquest of Arid America.* N.Y. and London: Harper & Brothers Publishers, 1900.
Snow, Eliza R. *Biography and Family Record of Lorenzo Snow: One of the Twelve Apostles of the Church of Jesus Christ of Latter-Day Saints.* S.L.C: Deseret News Co., Printers, 1884.
Snow, Lorenzo. *The Italian Mission.* London: Printed by W. Aubrey, 1851.
Sonzogno, Edoardo, ed. *L'esposizione universale di Filadelfia illustrata,* 2 vols. Milan: Edoardo Sonzogno, 1877.
Soria, Piero. *Kodachrome.* Milan: Mondadori, 1997.
Spalding, Franklin Spencer. *Joseph Smith, Jr., As a Translator.* S.L.C: The Arrow Press, 1912.
Spiero, Heinrich. *Geschichte des deutschen Romans.* Berlin: W. de Gruyter, 1950.
Spini, Giorgio. *L'Evangelo e il Berretto Frigio.* Torino: Claudiana, 1971.
Stadling, Jonas Jonsson. *Genom Den Stora Vestern.* Stockholm: Författarens Forlag, 1883.
———. *Hvad jag hörde och seg i mormonernas Zion.* Stockholm, 1884.
Stansbury, Howard. *Exploration and Survey of the Valley of the Great Salt Lake of Utah.* Philadelphia: Lippincott, Grambo & Co., 1852.
Stegner, Wallace E. *Beyond the Hundredth Meridian: John Wesley Powell and the Second Opening of the West.* Intro. by Bernard De Voto. Boston: Houghton, Mifflin, 1954.
Stenhouse, Mrs. Thomas B. H. *A Lady's Life Among the Mormons.* N.Y: Russell Brothers, Publishers, 1872. *"Tell it All": The Story of a life's experience in Mormonism.* Hartford, Conn: A.D. Worthington & Co., 1874.
Stenhouse, T. B. H. *The Rocky Mountain Saints: A Full and Complete History of the Mormons, from the First Vision of Joseph Smith to the Last Courtship of Brigham Young.* N.Y: D. Appleton and Co., 1873.
Stevenson, Robert Louis. *Across the Plains.* London: Chatto & Windus, 1892.
———. *Essays of Travel.* London: Chatto & Windus, 1908.
———, and Fanny Van De Grift Stevenson. *The Dynamiter (More New Arabian Nights).* London: Longmans, Green, and Co., 1885.
Stewart, Omer. *Forgotten Fires: Native Americans and the Transient Wilderness.* Norman: Univ. of Oklahoma Press, 2002.
Stone, Eileen Hallet. *A Homeland in the West: Utah Jews Remember.* S.L.C: Univ. of Utah Press, 2001.
Strafforello, Gustavo. *Il nuovo Monte-Cristo. Memorie d'un emigrante.* Florence: Felice Le Monnier, 1856.
———. *Storia Popolare del Progresso Materiale negli ultimi cento anni.* Torino: Unione Tipografico-Editrice, 1871.

———. *Letteratura Americana*. Milan: Ulrico Hoepli, 1884.

———, and Federico di Hellwald, *America Settentrionale secondo le notizie più recenti*. Torino: Ermanno Loescher, 1886.

Swift, Jonathan. *Travels into Several Remote Nations of the World, in four parts, by Lemuel Gulliver, first a surgeon and then a Captain of several ships*. London: 1726.

Taine, Hippolyte Adolphe. "Les Mormons." In *Nouveaux essais de critique et histoire*. Paris: L. Hachette, 1865, 271–79. English translation appeared in Fife, "Taine's Essay on the Mormons."

Taylor, John. *Three Nights' Public Discussion between the Revds. C. W. Cleeve, James Robertson, and Philip Cater, and Elder John Taylor, of the Church of Jesus Christ of Latter-day Saints at Boulogne-sur-mer, France*. Liverpool: John Taylor, 1850.

Thomsen, Mads. *I Cowboyland*. Copenhagen: V. Pios Boghandel-Povl Branner, 1918.

Tinling, Marion, ed. *With Women's Eyes: Visitors to the New World, 1775–1918*. New Haven: Archon Books, 1993.

Tissandier, Albert. *Six mois aux Etats-Unis, voyage d'un touriste dans l'Amérique du Nord suivi d'une excursion à Panama*. Paris: G. Masson, 1886.

Tocqueville, Alexis de. *Democracy in America*. Ed. and abridged by Richard D. Heffner. N.Y: Signet Classics. 2001.

Topsöe, Vilhelm Kristian Sigurd. *Från Amerika, af V.C.S. Topsöe. Svensk med förf. samtycke utgifven uppl. Öfversättning af O. Strandberg. Med 50 illustrationer och 1 karta*. Stockholm: A. Bonnier, 1874.

Torrielli, Andrew Joseph. *Italian Opinion on America as Recorded by Italian Travelers, 1858–1900*. Cambridge: Harvard Univ. Press, 1941.

Toutain, Paul. *Un Français en Amérique. Yankees, Indiens, Mormons*. Paris: E. Plon et Cie, 1876.

Towle, Nancy. *Vicissitudes Illustrated*. Second ed., Portsmouth, New Hampshire: Printed for the Author by John Caldwell, 1833.

Townsend, John Kirk. *Narrative of a Journey across the Rocky Mountains to the Columbia River*. Philadelphia: Henry Perkins, 1839.

Trollope, Frances. *Domestic Manners of the Americans*, 2 vols. London: Whittaker, Treacher, 1832.

Turner, Jonathan B. *Mormonism in all ages: or the rise, progress, and causes of Mormonism*. N.Y: Platt & Peters, 1842.

Twain, Mark. *The Innocents Abroad, or The New Pilgrims' Progress*. Hartford: American Publishing Co., 1869.

———. *Roughing It*. Hartford: American Publishing Co., 1872.

Valentini, Zopito. *Attività Italiane nella Intermountain Region*. S.L.C: Intermountain Publishing Co., 1930.

———. *Un anno senza rondini*. Florence: Vallecchi Editore, 1930.

Van Orden, Bruce A., D. Brent Smith, and Everett Smith, Jr., eds. *Pioneers in Every Land*. S.L.C: Bookcraft, 1997.

Van Tramp, John C. *Prairie and Rocky Mountain Adventures; or, Life in the West. To which will be added a view of the states and territorial regions of our western empire embracing history, statistics, and geography, and descriptions of the chief cities of the West*. Columbus, Ohio: Gilmore & Segner, 1866.

Van Wagoner, Richard, and Steven Walker. *A Book of Mormons*. S.L.C: Signature Books, 1982.
Vasoli, Nidia Danelon. *Un Uomo del Risorgimento nella California del "Gold Rush." Avventure e disavventure Americane di Leonetto Cipriani*. Florence: Leo S. Olschki Editore, 1986.
———. *L'Archivio privato di Leonetto Cipriani*. Florence: Leo S. Olschki Editore, 1987.
Vavaro Pojero, Francesco. *Una corsa nel nuovo mondo*, 2 vols. Milan: Fratelli Treves, 1878.
Verne, Jules. *From the Earth to the Moon Direct in Ninety-seven Hours and Twenty Minutes*. N.Y: American News Co., 1869.

———. *Le tour du monde en quatre-vingts jours*. Paris: J. Hetzel, 1873. *The Tour of the World in Eighty Days*. Boston: James R. Osgood and Co., 1873. *Il giro del mondo in ottanta giorni*. Milan: Serafino Muggiani e comp., 1876. *Il giro del mondo in 80 giorni*. Casale Monferrato: Piemme, 1996.

———. *To the Sun? A Journey through Planetary Space*. Philadelphia: Claxton, Remsen & Haffelfinger, 1878.

———. *Paris au XX siècle*. Paris: Hachette, 1994.
Vigna dal Ferro, Giovanni. *Un viaggio nel Far West Americano*. Bologna: Tipografico Successori Monti, 1881.
Vogel, Dan ed. *Early Mormon Documents*, 5 vols. S.L.C: Signature Books, 1996–2003.
Vollmer, Carl G. W. *Kalifornien och guldfebern, Guldgrafvarnes, Mormonernas och Indianernas seder och bruk*. Stockholm: J. E. Fahlstedt, 1862. German ed., *Californien und das Goldfieber: Reisen in dem wilden Wester Nord-Amerika's: Leben und Sitten der Goldgraber, Mormonen und Indianer*. Berlin: 1863.
Von Rodt, Cäcilie. *Reise einer Schweizerin um die welt*. Neurenberg: F. Zahn, 1903. *Voyage d'une Suissesse autour du monde*. Neuchatel, 1903.
Wachtmeister, Hans. *Turistskizzer Från Andra Sidan Atlanten*. Stockholm: P. A. Norstedt & Soners Förlag, 1901.
Wagner, Henry R., and Charles L. Camp. *The Plains and the Rockies: A Bibliography of Original Narratives of Travel and Adventure, 1800–1865*. Third ed., Columbus, Ohio: Long's College Book Co., 1953. Fourth ed. by Robert H. Becker. San Francisco: John Howell Books, 1982.
Waldenström, P. *Genom Norra Amerikas Förenta Stater*. Stockholm: Pietistens Expedition, 1890.
Walker, Ronald W. *Wayward Saints: The Godbeites and Brigham Young*. Urbana: Univ. of Ill. Press, 1998.

———, David J. Whittaker, and James B. Allen. *Mormon History*. Urbana: Univ. of Ill. Press, 2001.
Wallace, Dillon. *Saddle and Camp in the Rockies*. N.Y: Outing Publishing Co., 1911.
Ward, Artemus. *Artemus Ward: His Travels*. N.Y: Carleton, 1865.
———. *Artemus Ward's Lecture*. London: John Camden Hotten, 1869.
Ward, Austin and Maria. *The Husband in Utah; or, Sights and Scenes among the Mormons: with Remarks on their moral and social economy*. London: James Blackwood, 1857. *Mannen Bland Mormonerna eller Tilldragelser i Utah*. Stockholm: Schuck & Josephson, 1857.
Ward, Maria. *Female Life Among the Mormons: A Narrative of Many Years' Personal Experience*. N.Y: J. C. Derby, 1855. London: G. Routledge & Co., 1855. Trans. by B. H. Révoil. *Les harems du Nouveau Monde—vie des femmes chez les Mormons*. Paris: Michel Levy Frères, 1856. Hungarian ed.: *Nöélet. A Mormonoknál*. Pest: Geibel Armin bizománya, 1858.

Watters, Leon L. *The Pioneer Jews of Utah*. N.Y: American Jewish Hist. Soc., 1952.

Watts, George B. *The Waldenses in the New World*. Durham: Duke Univ. Press, 1941.

Wells, Emmeline B. *Musings and Memories*. S.L.C: George Q. Cannon & Sons, Publishers, 1896.

Wetmore, Alphonso. *Gazetteer of the State of Missouri*. St. Louis: C. Keemle, 1837.

Wilberforce, Bertrand. *The Life of St. Louis Bertrand*. London: 1882.

Williams, Henry T., ed. *The Pacific Tourist*. N.Y: Adams & Bishop, 1881.

Williams, Terry Tempest. *Refuge: An Unnatural History of Family and Place*. N.Y: Pantheon Books, 1991.

Winder, Michael K. *John R. Winder: Member of the First Presidency, Pioneer, Temple Builder, Dairyman*. Salt Lake City: Horizon Publishers, 1999.

Winthrop, Robert C. *Life and Letters of John Winthrop*, 2 vols. Boston: Little, Brown, 1869. Reprinted N.Y: DaCapo Press, 1971.

Wischmann, Lesley. *Frontier Diplomats: The Life and Times of Alexander Culbertson and Natoyistsiksina'*. Spokane, Wash: The Arthur H. Clark Co., 2000.

Withey, Lynne. *Grand Tours and Cook's Tours. A History of Leisure Travel, 1750–1915*. N.Y: William Morrow and Co., Inc., 1997.

Woelmont, Arnold de, Baron. *Souvenirs du Far-West*. Paris: E. Plon et. cie. Imprimeurs-éditeurs, 1883.

Wood, Frances. *Did Marco Polo Go to China?* London: Secker & Warburg, 1995.

Woodruff, Wilford. *Wilford Woodruff's Journal*, 9 vols. Ed. by Scott G. Kenney. Midvale, Utah: Signature Books, 1983–85.

Woods, Kate Tannatt. *Out and About or, The Hudson's Trip to the Pacific*. Boston: D. Lothrop Co., 1882.

Worster, Donald. *A River Running West: The Life of John Wesley Powell*. N.Y: Oxford Univ. Press, 2001.

Young, Ann-Eliza. *Wife No. 19, or a Story of a Life in Bondage, being a complete expose of Mormonism*. Hartford: Dustin, Gilman & Co., 1876.

Ziegler, Alexander. *Der Geleitsmann: Katechismus für Auswanderer nach den Vereinigten Staaten von Nord Amerika, nach Mittel- und Süd-Amerika und Australien: mit besonderer Rücksicht auf die Ansiedelungen in Ungarn, den unteren Donaufürstenthümern, Algerien und dem Cap der guten Hoffnung*. Leipzig: Verlagsbuchhandlung von J. J. Weber, 1856.

———. *Meine Reisen im Norden, in Norwegen, auf den Orkney-und Shetland-Inseln, in Lappland und Schweden*, 2 vols. Leipzig: J. J. Weber, 1860.

———. *Meine Reise im Orient*, 2 vols. Leipzig: J. J. Weber, 1857.

———. *Reise in Spanien*, 2 vols. Leipzig: J. J. Weber, 1852.

———. *Republikanische Licht und Schattenseiten*. Dresden and Leipzig: 1848.

———. *Skizzen einer Reise durch Nordamerika und Westindien*. Dresden and Leipzig, 1848.

Zimmer von Ulbersdorf, G. A. *Unter den Mormonen in Utah: Mit Besonderer Berücksichtigung der Deutschen Evangelischen Missionsarbeit; Ein Beitrag zur Neueren Missionsgeschichte*. Gütersloh: Druck und Verlag von C. Bertelsmann, 1908.

Periodicals and Essays

Arrington, Chris Rigby. "The Finest of Fabrics: Mormon Women and the Silk Industry in Early Utah." *Utah Hist. Qtly.* (Fall 1978), 376–96.

Arrington, Leonard J., and Thomas G. Alexander. "The U.S. Army Overlooks Salt Lake Valley, Fort Douglas 1862–1965." *Utah Hist. Qtly.* 33:4 (Fall 1965), 326–50.

Ashliman, D. L. "The Image of Utah and the Mormons in Nineteenth-century Germany." *Utah Hist. Qtly.* 35:3 (Summer 1967), 209–27.

———. "Mormonism and the Germans: An Annotated Bibliography, 1848–1966." *Brigham Young Univ. Studies* 8:1 (Autumn 1967), 73–94.

———. "The Novel of Western Adventure in Nineteenth Century." *Western American Literature* 3 (Summer 1968).

Athearn, Robert G. "Opening the Gates of Zion: Utah and the Coming of the Union Pacific Railroad." *Utah Hist. Qtly.* 36:4 (Fall 1968), 291–314.

———. "Contracting for the Union Pacific." *Utah Hist. Qtly.* 37:1 (Winter 1969), 16–40.

Austin, Michael. "Troped by the Mormons: The Persistence of 19th-Century Mormon Stereotypes in Contemporary Detective Fiction." *Sunstone* (August 1998), 51–71.

Baer, Klaus. "The Breathing Permit of Hor." *Dialogue: A Journal of Mormon Thought* 3 (Autumn 1968), 116–17.

Barnes, Joseph W., and J. Hayward Madden, eds. "The Gold Rush Journal of Thomas Evershed: Engineer, Artist, and Rochesterian." *Rochester History* 39:1–2 (1977): 1–44.

Beltrami, Luca. "I Mormoni nelle memorie di un missionario Milanese." *Il Marzocco.* 1 January 1928.

Besana, Enrico. "I Mormoni nel 1869." *La Perseveranza,* 11–13 February 1869.

———. "Note di viaggio di un Italiano: Le grande praterie Americane e i Mormoni." *Giornale Popolare di Viaggio,* 2 (1871): 60–64.

Bishop, M. Guy. "Building Railroads for the Kingdom: The Career of John W. Young, 1867–91." *Utah Hist. Qtly.* 48:1 (Winter 1980), 66–80.

Bohme, Frederick G., ed. "Vigna Dal Ferro's *Un Viaggio Nel Far West Americano.*" *California Historical Society Quarterly* 41:2 (June 1962): 149–61.

Bosio, David. "Nos Vaudois dans l'Utah." *L'Echo des Vallées* 41 (10 October 1913) and 42 (17 October 1913).

Brimhall, Sandra Dawn, and Mark D. Curtis. "The Gardo House: A History of the Mansion and Its Occupants." *Utah Hist. Qtly.* 68:1 (Winter 2000), 4–37.

Broadbent, Thomas L. "The Salt Lake City *Beobachter*: Mirror of an Immigration." *Utah Hist. Qtly.* 26:4 (October 1958), 329–52.

Brodie, Fawn M. "Sir Richard F. Burton: Exceptional Observer of the Mormon Scene." *Utah Hist. Qtly.* 38:4 (Fall 1970), 295–311.

Brooks, Juanita. "Silver Reef." *Utah Hist. Qtly.* 29:3 (July 1961), 281–87.

Burton, Greg. "Leavitt's Lineage: Descended from Proud Polygamists." *The Salt Lake Tribune,* 18 June 2000, A1.

Carter, D. Robert. "Daredevils of the Sky—Early Aeronauts in Utah." *History Blazer* (May 1996).

Cavling, Henrik. "Mellem Mormonerne." In *Politiken* (13, 14, 15, 20, 22, 23 January 1889). "Hos Profeten" ["At the Home of the Prophet"]; "Polygami" ["Polygamy"]; "Bikuben" [The Beehive"]; "Edmund Bills"; "Gudstjeneste i Tabernaklet" [Religious Service in the Tabernacle"]; "Salt staden" ["Salt Lake City"].

Compton, Todd M. "John Willard Young, Brigham Young, and the Development of Presidential Succession in the LDS Church." *Dialogue: A Journal of Mormon Thought* 35:4 (Winter 2002), 111–33.

Conybeare, William John. "Mormonism." *Edinburgh Review* (April 1854).

Cracroft, Richard H. "The Heraldry of the Range: Utah Cattle Brands." *Utah Hist. Qtly.* 32 (1964), 217–31.

Damrosch, Leo. "New Introduction" in Jonathan Swift. *Gullliver's Travels*. N.Y: Signet Classics, 1999.

Decoo, Wilfred. "The Image of Mormonism in French Literature: Part I." *Brigham Young Univ. Studies* 14:2 (Winter 1974), 157–75. Part II. *Brigham Young Univ. Studies* 16:2 (Winter 1976), 265–276.

Devecchi, Paolo. "Letter to the Editor." *L'Eco d'Italia*, 8 Jan. 1881.

Ferrero, Flora. "Dalle Valli Valdesi al Grande Lago Salato: Un percorso di conversione." In *La Bibbia, la Coccarda e il Tricolore: I Valdesi fra due Emancipazioni (1798–1848)*. Torino: Claudiana, 2001, 531–38.

Fife, A. E. "Taine's Essay on the Mormons." *Pacific Hist. Review* (February 1962), 49–65.

Firmage, Edwin B. "Religion and the Law: The Mormon Experience in the Nineteenth Century." *Cardozo Law Review* 12:3/4 (February/March 1991), 765–803.

Foster, Craig L. "'That Canny Scotsman': John Sharp and the Negotiations with the Union Pacific Railroad, 1869–1872." *Journal of Mormon History* 27:2 (Fall 2001), 197–214.

Gr., Th. "Ein Ritt nach Californien." In *Das Buch der Welt*. Stuttgart: Hoffman'sche Verlags-Buchhandlung, 1859.

Homer, Michael W. "The Italian Mission, 1850–1867." *Sunstone* 7 (May–June 1982), 16–21.

———. "The Federal Bench and Priesthood Authority: The Rise and Fall of John Fitch Kinney's Early Relationship with the Mormons." *Journal of Mormon History* 13 (1986–87), 8–110.

———. "The Judiciary and the Common Law in Utah Territory, 1850–61." *Dialogue: A Journal of Mormon Thought* 21:1 (Spring 1988), 97–108.

———. "Gli Italiani e i Mormoni." *Renovatio* 26:1 (January–March 1991), 79–106.

———. "The Church's Image in Italy from the 1840s to 1946: A Bibliographic Essay." *Brigham Young Univ. Studies* 31:2 (Spring 1991), 83–114.

———. "Arthur Conan Doyle and his Views on Mormonism: From *A Study in Scarlet* to *The Edge of the Unknown*," ACD: *Journal of the Arthur Conan Doyle Society* 2:1 (Spring 1991), 66–81.

———. "'Similarity of Priesthood in Masonry': The Relationship between Freemasonry and Mormonism." *Dialogue: A Journal of Mormon Thought* 27:3 (Fall 1994), 1–113.

———. "LDS Prospects in Italy for the Twenty-first Century." *Dialogue, A Journal of Mormon Thought* 29:1 (Spring 1996), 139–58.

———. "'Like a Rose in the Wilderness': The Mormon Mission in the Kingdom of Sardinia." *Mormon Hist. Studies* 1:2 (Fall 2000), 25–62.

———. "L'azione missionaria in Italia e nelle valli Valdesi dei gruppi Americani non tradizionali." (Avventisiti, Mormoni, Testimoni di Geova). In *La Bibbia, la Coccarda e il Tricolore: I Valdesi fra due Emancipazioni (1798–1848)* (Torino: Claudiana, 2001), 505–530.

———. "An Immigrant Story: Three Orphaned Italians in Early Utah Territory." *Utah Hist. Qtly.* 70:3 (Summer 2002), 196–214. "Les premiers immigrants italiens en Amérique: des mormons. Histoire de trois orphelins piémontais au milieu du Grand Lac Salé (1854–1905)." In *Sectes, églises, mystiques: Echanges, conquêtes, métamorphoses*. Bordeaux: Pleine Page éditeur, 2004, 338–50.

———. "The Waldensian Valleys: Seeking Primitive Christianity in Italy." *Journal of Mormon History* 31:2 (Summer 2005), 134–87.

Honour, Hugh. "Italianizzatti." *London Review of Books* (13 November 1997), 9–11.

Houston, Alan Fraser, and Jourdon Moore Houston, "The 1859 Lander Expedition Revisited: Worthy relics tell new tales of a Wind River wagon road." *Montana: The Magazine of Western History* 49:2 (Summer 1999), 50–71.

Johnson, Jeffery Ogden. "Determining and Defining 'Wife': The Brigham Young Households." *Dialogue: A Journal of Mormon Thought* 20:3 (Fall 1987), 57–70.

Judt, Tony. "Anti-Americans Abroad." *The New York Review* (1 May 2003), 24–27.

Larson, Gustive O., ed. "Journal of the Iron County Mission, John D. Lee, Clerk." *Utah Hist. Qtly.* 20:2–3 (April, July, October 1952), 108–34; 253–84; 352–83.

Leonardi, Ruggero. "Introduzione." In Emilio Salgari. *Jolanda la figlia del Corsaro Nero*. Milan: Arnoldo Mondadori Editori, 1999.

Lévy, Bernard-Henri. "In the Footsteps of Tocqueville (Part Three)." *The Atlantic Monthly* (July/August 2005). Digital copy at http://www.theatlantic.com/doc/200507/levy.

Martin, Charles W. "John Ahmanson vs. Brigham Young: A Nebraska Legal Controversy, 1859–1861." *Nebr. History* 64 (Spring 1983), 1–20.

Mazzuchelli, Samuele. "Memoirs of Rev. Samuele Mazzuchelli, O.P." *The Young Eagle* (February 1898–December 1901).

McClellan, Richard D. "Not Your Average French Communist Mormon: A Short History of Louis A. Bertrand." *Mormon Hist. Studies* 2:1 (Fall 2000), 3–24.

McDermott, John Francis. "Dr. Koch's Wonderful Fossils." *Missouri Hist. Soc. Bulletin* (July 1948), 233–56.

Marks, David. *The Morning Star*, 28 April 1830, 1.

Maury, Alfred. "Sectes religieuses au XIXème siècle: Les Irvingiens et les Saints-du-dernier-jour." *Revue des Deux Mondes* 23 (1 September 1853), 965–68.

Mérimée, Prosper. "Les Mormones." *Le Moniteur Universel* (25, 26, 31 March and 1 April 1853)

Mitchell, Martin. "Gentile Impressions of Salt Lake City, Utah, 1849–1870." *The Geographical Review* 87:3 (July 1997), 334–52.

Mulder, Willam. "Through Immigrant Eyes: Utah History at the Grass Roots." *Utah Hist. Qtly.* 22 (1954), 41–55.

———. "Mormon Angles of Historical Vision: Some Maverick Reflections." *Journal of Mormon History* 3 (1976), 13–22.

Murphy, W. W. "Biography of Father Samuele Mazzuchelli." *The Republican Journal*, 9 December 1909 to 6 January 1910.

Nibley, Hugh. "A New Look at the Pearl of Great Price." *Improvement Era* 71:1 through 73:5 (Jan. 1968–May 1970)

Papanikolas, Helen Z. "Ethnicity in Mormonism: A Comparison of Immigrant and Mormon Cultures." In *"Soul Butter and Hog Wash."* Ed. by Thomas G. Alexander. Charles Redd Monographs in Western History, no. 8. Provo: Brigham Young Univ. Press, 1978, 102

Peterson, H. Donl. "Antonio Lebolo: Excavator of the Book of Abraham." *BYU Studies* 31:3 (Summer 1991), 5–24.

Ramseyer, A. A. "The Memoirs of a 'Mormon.'" *Improvement Era* (1907).

Read, Helen Appleton. "Karl May, Germany's James Fenimore Cooper." *The American-German Review* 2 (June 1937).

Reclus, Elisée. "Le Mormonisme et les Etats-Unis." *Revue des deux mondes* 32 (15 April 1861), 881–914.

Rémy, Jules, "Visite aux Mormons du Lac Salé." In *L'Echo du Pacifique* (January to February 1855). English translation published as "A Trip to Salt Lake." In *California Chronicle* (December 1855 to March 1856).

Révoil, B. H. "Souvenirs des Etats-Unis.—Religions bizarres prôfessées dans l'Union américaine.—Les Mormons." *L'Illustration, Journal Universel*, 15:373 (20 April 1850), 251–52.

Ritner, Robert K. "'The Breathing Permit of Hor' Thirty-four Years Later." *Dialogue: A Journal of Mormon Thought* 33 (Winter 2000), 97–119.

Schama, Simon, "The Unloved American." *The New Yorker* (10 March 2003), 34–39.

Schleiden, Rudolpf. "Utah und die Mormonen." *Allgemeine Zeitung* (Augsburg) (16–19 February 1873).

"The Sesquicentennial of Four European Translations of the Book of Mormon." *Journal of Book of Mormon Studies* 11 (2002), 28–49. The articles in this feature include Richard D. McClellan, "Traduit de l'Anglais: The First French Book of Mormon"; Gilbert W. Scharffs, "Das Buch Mormon: The German Translation of the Book of Mormon"; Michael W. Homer, "Il Libro di Mormon: Anticipating Growth beyond Italy's Waldensian Valleys"; and Ronald D. Dennis, "Llyfr Mormon: The Translation of the Book of Mormon into Welsh."

Shipps, Jan. "Surveying the Mormon Image Since 1960." *Sunstone* 118 (April 2001), 58–72.

Simonin, Louis. "Le Far West américain." *Le Tour du Monde* 1 (1868), 225–388.

———. "Viaggio in California." *L'Universo Illustrato* 3:7 (15 November 1868), 407–9.

Simonton, James W. "Letter from the Army of Utah: Matters in Mormondom." *San Francisco Evening Bulletin*, 21 July 1858, 3/2–4.

Slaughter, William. "In the City of the Saints: Sir Richard Francis Burton's Utah Exploration." *Salt Lake Magazine* (March/April 2000), 55–58.

Smith, George D. "Strange Bedfellows: Mormon Polygamy and Baptist History." *Free Inquiry* 16:2 (Spring 1996), 41–45.

Snow, Edwina Jo. "William Chandless: British Overlander, Mormon Observer, Amazon Explorer." *Utah Hist. Qtly.* 54:2 (Spring 1986), 116–36.

———. "British Travelers View the Saints." *Brigham Young Univ. Studies* 31:2 (Spring 1991), 63–81.

South, Will. "Oscar Wilde in Salt Lake City." *The Arts Magazine* 1:3 (December 1992), 8–11.

Stark, Rodney. "Extracting Social Scientific Models from Mormon History." *Journal of Mormon History* 25 (Spring 1999), 174–94.

———. "So Far, So Good: A Brief Assessment of Mormon Membership Projections." *Review of Religious Research* 38 (December 1996), 175–78.

Stone, Alvan. "Extracts from the Memoir of Alvan Stone." *Journal of the Ill. Hist. Soc.* 3:4 (January 1911), 85–97.

Thompson, Stephen E. "Egyptology and the Book of Mormon." *Dialogue: A Journal of Mormon Thought* 28 (Spring 1995), 143–60.

Van Hoak, Stephen. "Waccara's Utes: Native American Equestrian Adaptations in the Eastern Great Basin, 1776–1876." *Utah Hist. Qtly.* 67:4 (Fall 1999), 309–30.

Wasserstein, Bernard, and David Wasserstein. "Jacobo Spurioso." *Times Literary Supplement*, 14 November 1997, 15; Letters to the Editor, *Times Literary Supplement*, 21 November 1997, 19.

West, Joseph A. "Sir Arthur Conan Doyle's 'New Revelation' and 'Vital Message.'" *Improvement Era* 24 (1920), 6–13.

Theses and Dissertations

Cracroft, Richard H. "The American West of Karl May." Masters Thesis, Univ. of Utah, 1963.

Ferrero, Flora. "L'emigrazione valdese nello Utah nella seconda metà dell'800." Tesi di Laurea, Università degli Studi di Torino. June 1999.

McClellan, Richard D. "Louis Alphonse Bertrand: One of the Most Singular and Romantic Figures of the Age." Honor's Thesis, Brigham Young Univ., August 2000.

Miller, David Henry. "Balduin Mollhausen, A Prussian's Image of the American West." Ph.D. Dissertation, The Univ. of New Mexico, 1970.

Searle, Howard Clair. "Early Mormon Historiography: Writing the History of the Mormons." Ph.D. Dissertation, Univ. of Calif., Los Angeles, 1979.

Snow, Edwina Jo. "Singular Saints: The Image of the Mormons in Book-Length Travel Accounts, 1847–1857." Master's Thesis, George Wash. Univ., 1972.

Stegner, Wallace E. "Clarence Edward Dutton: Geologist and Man of Letters." Masters Thesis, State Univ. of Iowa, 1935.

Stokoe, Diane. "The Mormon Waldensians." Masters Thesis, Brigham Young Univ., December 1985.

Whittaker, David J. "Early Mormon Pampleteering." Ph.D. diss., Brigham Young Univ., 1982.

Manuscripts

Archivio di Stato di Torino, Registro delle Insinuazioni, Torino, Italy.
Bertoch, Daniel. Autobiography. Utah State Hist. Soc.
Bertoch, James. Missionary Journal and Personal Correspondence. Utah State Hist. Soc.
Bolton, Curtis. Journal. LDS Archives.
Cipriani, Leonetto. Cipriani Mss. Cipriani Archives, Bastia, Corsica.
Le carte di conte Leonetto Cipriani. Cipriani Mss. Biblioteca di Storia e Cultura del Piemonte della Provincia di Torino. Torino, Italy.
Corrispondenza della Tavola, Archivio della Tavola Valdese. Torre Pellice, Italy.
Emigration Records and Ship Roster, LDS Archives.
Jorgensen, Dan C. New Facts on the Life and History of Giovanni Pietro Antonio Lebolo. Unpublished paper. Univ. of Utah, October 1976.
Journal History, LDS Archives.
Lettres du Modérateur, 1850–59, Archivio della Tavola Valdese. Torre Pellice, Italy.
McCoy, Sue. Albert Tissandier, Six Months in the United States. Utah State Hist. Soc.
Malan, Stephen. Autobiography and Family Record, (1893). LDS Archives.
Mazzuchelli, Samuele. Mazzuchelli Archives. Mazzuchelli Guild, Sinsinawa, Wisc.
Nauvoo Legion Papers. Beinecke Library. Yale Univ.
Primrose, Archibald Philip. America, 1873. William Clements Library, The Univ. of Mich.
Record of Membership of the Italian Mission. LDS Archives.
Watt, George D. *A Series of Instructions and Remarks by President Brigham Young at a Special Council, Tabernacle, March 21, 1858.* Copy at Special Collections, Marriott Library, Univ. of Utah.
Young, Brigham. Collection. MS 1234, LDS Archives.

Index

Abdy, E. S: 31
Adams, David: 76
Adams, Nathan: 275, 276, 279, 280, 283, 284–285
Ahmanson, John A: 86, 315; account by, 96–99; bio. of, 94–96
Aimard, Gustave: 190
Alleman, Father J: 35, 37
Alexander, Edmund: 106
Alley, Margaret Maria: 355
"Among the Mormons" (play): 117
André, Charles-Louis-François: bio. of, 322; report of, 322–324
Anglicans: 140, 160
Antelope Island: 92–93, 94
Apache Indians: 226
Apollinaire, Guillaume: bio. of, 244–246; fantasy account by, 247–249
Argyle, Annie: 189
Arthur, Christopher J: 269
Audouard, Olympe de Joaral: 23, 26, 117, 209; account by, 126–145; bio. of, 123–124; drawing of, 125
Avventure tra i Pellerossa (novel): 240

Baird, Robert: 67
Baker Street Irregulars. *See* Holmes, Sherlock
Ballantyne, Richard: 82
Domenico Ballo: 52. *See also* Capone, Gennaro

Baptists: 29, 148, 358, 364
Barbee, William Tecumseh: 271
Barnett, Frank: 358
Baron von Hübner. *See* Alexander, Joseph
Beadle, J. H: 189
Beatie, Phoebe Louisa Young: 355
Beaver, Utah: 70
Becker, Joseph: 149
Beckwith, Edward Griffin: 61–62
Bee Hive Store. *See* Zions Cooperative Mercantile Institution
Beecher, Henry Ward: 320
Beehive House: 182, 357, 358
Beehive Warehouse. *See* Zions Cooperative Mercantile Institution
Bell, William A: 116
Benjamin, Israel Joseph: accounts by, 118–121; bio. of, 118; photo of, 119
Benoit, Pierre: bio. of, 249–251; fantasy account by, 251–258
Benson, Ezra Taft: 379
Bertoch, Antoinette: 90, 91, 93, 94
Bertoch, Daniel: 86; accounts of, 92–94; bio. of, 90–92; illus. of, 92
Bertoch, James [Jacques]: 90, 91, 93, 94, 365
Bertoch, Jean: 90–92, 102
Bertoch, Jean Jr: 90, 91
Bertoch, Marguerite: 90, 91
Bertrand, Daniel: 144
Bertrand, Louis (Dominican friar). *See* St. Louis Bertrand

Bertrand, Louis Alphonse: 86, 144, 177, 209; bio. of, 100–101, 102–105; conversation with Alexandre Erdan, 101–102; illus. of, 100. *See also Mémoires d'un Mormon* (book)
Besana, Enrico: accounts by, 122–123; bio. of, 121–122
Beus, James: 365
Bird, Isabella: 124
Blanc, Jean-Joseph-Charles-Louis: 111
Blouët, Léon Paul: 339
Bodenstedt, Friederick Martin von: 381–382; account by, 330–332; bio. of, 330
Bodmer, Karl: 32–33
Bolton, Curtis: 100, 101
The Book of Abraham: 69, 104
The Book of Mormon: 29, 30, 31, 36, 67, 85–86, 158, 197, 249, 348, 359; French translation of, 100, 247; German translation of, 67
Boorstin, Daniel J: 26
Boreman, Jacob S: 338
Bosio, David: account by, 366–368; bio. of, 364–366; photo of, 365
Bowles, Samuel: 116, 117
Bowring's Theater: 121
Brannan, Samuel: 48, 349
Brenchley, Julius: 49, 68, 259
Bridger, James: 349–350
British: 26, 48–49, 54, 78, 134, 151
Brooklyn (ship): 48
Brooks, Fanny: 118
Brooks, Julius Gerson: 118
Browne, Charles Farrar. *See* Ward, Artemus
Bryant, Edwin: 48
Buchanan, James: 48, 107, 110, 111, 112, 115
Buchez, Philippe: 100
Buchner, Max Joseph August Heinrich Markus: account by, 169–174; bio. of, 169
Buffalo Bill Wild West Show: 232, 240
Burt, Samuel: 89
Burton, Richard Francis: 26, 116, 152, 181, 209, 240, 326, 377

Cabet, Etienne: 43, 100, 101
Caccia, Antonio: 49, 189
Cajon Pass: 260
California: 42, 47, 48, 49, 51, 54
Camp Douglas, Utah: 174, 322–323
Camp Floyd, Utah: 260, 309, 312
Camp Scott: 106
Campbell, Alexander: 29
Canadians: 271
Cannon, Frank J: 343–344
Cannon, George Q: 185, 305, 308, 329
Cannon, Marsena: 167
Capone, Gennaro: 52–54, 55, 60
Cardon, Paul: 365
Carn, Daniel: 85
Carter (Mormon bishop): 312
Carthage, Ill: 212, 336
Carvalho, Solomon N: 118
Cass, Lewis: 111
Caswall, Henry: 32
Catholics: 34–35, 38, 86, 87, 236, 237, 250, 329
Cavling, Paulus Henrik: 304; bio. of, 315; memoir of, 315–317
Cedar City, Utah: 70, 260, 264, 268–269, 276, 289, 298, 300, 350
Central Pacific Railroad: 147, 209, 210, 335
Central Utah Railroad: 289, 297
Chandler, Michael: 69
Chandler, William: 303
Chandless, William: 48–49, 96
Chapuis, Louis: 94
Chasles, Philarète: 68
Chimborazo (ship): 102, 108
Chinese: 172
Christensen, C. C. A: 303
Christians: 368
Church of Jesus Christ of Latter-day Saints. *See* Mormons
Cipriani, Beppe: 51
Cipriani, Leonetto: 26, 49, 373; account by, 52–60; bio. of, 50–52; illus. of, 50

The City of the Saints (book): 116
Civil Rights movement: 379
Civil War: 115
Clark, John A: 32
Clawson, Alice (Young): 155, 358
Clawson, Emily Augusta (Young): 155
Clawson, Hiram B: 155
Clemens, Orion: 116
Clemens, Samuel. *See* Twain, Mark
Clements, Gilbert: 110
Codman, John: 260
Colfax, Schuyler: 117
Comanches: 242
Communism: 74, 100
Connor, Patrick Edward: 174
Continental Hotel: 293
Cook, Thomas: 148–149, 150
Cooke, Jay: 297
Cooke, Philip St. George: 107
Cooper, James Fenimore: 188
Corinne, Utah: 330
Council Bluffs, Iowa: 32, 43, 44, 45, 47
Cove Fort, Utah: 260
Culbertson, Alexander: 33
Cumming, Alfred: 102, 107, 109, 110, 115
Cumming, Elizabeth: 124
Cupid's Album (book): 189
Cutler, John Christopher: 347–348

Danish: 98
Danites: 28, 98, 193, 200, 202, 207, 251, 258
The Danites of the Sierras (book). *See The First Families of the Sierras* (book)
Das Mormonenmädchen (novel): 195–196
Davis, Evelyn Louisa Young: 355
Dawson, John: 164
de Bryas, Comtesse Madeleine: account by, 369–372; bio. of, 368–369
de Bryas, Jacqueline: account by, 369–372; bio. of, 368–369
de Gasparin, Agénor: 103

de la Harpe, Frédéric César: 142–144
De Smet, Pierre-Jean: 26, 32, 43; accounts of, 44–45; bio. of, 43–44
Dean, Silas: 336
Der Fanatiker (novel): 200
Deseret: 82, 88, 89, 109, 118, 147–148, 160, 191, 294, 344
Deseret News (newspaper): 136
DeVecchi, Paolo: 383
Devéria, Théodule: 69, 104
Devil's Gate: 97, 108
Dickens, Charles: 25, 26
Die Felsenburg (novel): 232, 236
Dilke, Sir Charles Wentworth: 116
Dixon, William Hepworth: 96, 116, 122, 139, 160, 181, 303
Doctrine and Covenants: 101
Domenech, Emmanuel Henri: 117
Dominican Order: 34, 35, 36
Douglas, Stephen: 174
Doyle, Arthur Conan: 27–28, 70, 189, 240, 304, 343, 377
Drovetti, Bernardino: 69
Drummond, William: 75
Ducloux, Marc: 101–102
Duke Frederick Paul Wilhelm of Württemberg: 193–194
Duplessis, Paul: bio. of, 190; fantasy account by, 190–193
Durand, Mr. *See* Durant, Thomas Clark
Durant, Thomas Clark: 126
Dutton, clarence Edward: 296
Dykes, George P: 67, 85

Echo Canyon: 112, 126
Edmunds Act: 316–317, 319
Edmunds-Tucker Act: 319–320
Eisenhower, Dwight D: 379
Ellerbeck, Thomas: 106
Emerson, Philip H: 338
Emery, George W: 324

Emigration Canyon: 44, 89, 96
En Amérique de New-York à la Nouvelle-Orléans (book): 344
En Amérique de San Francisco au Canada (book): 344
Episcopalians: 32
Erdan, Alexander: 101–102
Europa ed America: Scene della vita dal 1848–1850 (book): 189
Evangelical Free Church: 329
Excursionist (periodical): 149

Faithful, Emily: 124
Farr, Aaron Freeman: 336–337
Farr, Lorenzo Erickson: 334–336, 338–339
Farr, Lorin: 126, 334, 335
Farr, Nicoline Erickson: 334
feminism: 123, 124
Fenwick, Edward Dominic: 34
Ferris, Cornelia: 124
Ferry, Gabriel: 190
Fillmore, Utah: 70, 260
The First Families of the Sierras (book): 189
Flagg, Edmund: 31
Flandin, Jean-François Elie. *See* Bertrand, Louis
Fort Benton, Mont: 36, 43
Fort Bridger: 97, 106
Fort Laramie: 194
Fourier, Charles: 135, 308
Fourier, Jean Baptiste Joseph: 143
Francaviglia, Richard V: 382
Franco-Prussian War: 149, 265
Frank Leslie's Illustrated Newspaper: 149
Freemasons: 102, 118, 358
Frémont Expedition: 118
Frémont, John C: 259, 326
French: 26, 172, 283, 341, 348
From the Earth to the Moon Direct in Ninety-Seven Hours and Twenty Minutes (novel): 209
Fuller, Frank: 164

Gardini, Carlo: 26, 260, 382; bio. of, 289–290; account by, 290–302
Garn, Daniel. *See* Carn, Daniel
Gavazzi, Alessandro: 329
Gentiles: 73, 74, 76, 78, 83, 116, 147, 149, 155, 158, 171, 172, 175–176, 178, 184, 195, 196, 212, 248, 292, 306, 308, 311, 329, 330, 337, 338, 339, 340
German Evangelical Christusgemeinde (Christ Church): 356
Germans: 26, 32, 40–41, 67, 78, 134, 172, 232, 259–260, 348, 359, 360, 361, 363, 364
Gibbon, James Cardinal: 319, 320
Giovane Italia (Young Italy): 121
Glazier, Willard: 321
Godbeites: 148
gold rush: 47
Goodrich, Samuel Griswold: 117
Grand Canyon: 281, 302
Grant, George D: 94
Grant, Heber J: 373–374
Grant, Jedediah: 94, 108
Grant, Ulysses S: 182
Great Salt Lake: 56, 62, 92, 121, 151, 152, 173–174, 175, 177, 213, 265, 296, 326, 382
Great Salt Lake City. *See* Salt Lake City
Greeley, Horace: 116, 163
Greenwood, Grace. *See* Lippincott, Sarah Jane
Gregg, Josiah: 31
Grey, Zane: 27, 189, 343
Griffiths, D. Jr: 31
Gunnison, John W: 61, 96, 194, 196, 303

Hamblin, Jacob: 199
Hamilton, Thomas: 31
handcart companies: 94–96, 97
Haraszthy, Agoston: 102
Hardy, Lady Duffus: 124
Harney, William: 106
Harper's Weekly (magazine): 68, 116, 149, 181
Harris, Martin: 30

Harris, Sarah Hollister: 96, 103, 124, 303
Haskel, Thales: 195
Haussonville, Gabriel-Paul-Othenin-Barnard de Cléron, Comte de: 26, 290; account by, 333–339; bio. of, 332
Hemans, Felicia: 382Indian slavery: 264
Hemenway, Luther: 104
Herrick, Lester J: 324
Hickman, Bill: 98, 148
Hill, Isaac: 98
Holmes, Sherlock: 27, 70
Homestead Act: 115
Hoskins, Nathan: 30–31
Hotel St. James: 357
House Rock: 285
Howe, Eber D: 29–30
Howell, William: 85
Hübner, Joseph Alexander von: 51, 181, 240; account by, 151–161; bio. of, 150
Hugo, Victor: 101, 144, 209, 214
Humboldt, Alexander von: 194
Hungarians: 246
Huntsman, Jon Jr: 383
Huret, Jules: 26; account by, 345–356; bio. of, 344–345
Hyde, John: 44, 69

Icarian communities: 100
Idaho: 250
Illinois: 110, 193, 197, 210, 303
Indians: 32–33, 83, 151, 153, 157, 163, 170, 188, 195, 199, 200, 202, 204, 205, 206, 210, 240, 241, 242–243, 251, 260, 264, 271, 278–281, 284, 296, 299, 300–302, 310, 345
Ingersol, Ernest: 260
Intransigeant (newspaper): 175
Iowa (steamboat): 39
Irish: 271
Iron Mission: 259
Islam: 138, 164, 341, 345
Italians: 26, 78, 122, 172, 373, 374, 376. See also Waldensians

Ives Expedition: 194, 195, 199
Ives, Joseph Christmas: 194

Jacob, Alexandre-André. *See* Erdan, Alexander
Japanese: 183
Jensen, Andreas: 303
Jensen, Pottemager [Potter]: 98
Jerome, Jerome K: 343
Jesuits: 41, 43, 44, 253, 254, 329
Jews: 118, 119, 120
John M. Wood (ship): 88, 91
Johnston, Albert Sidney: 102, 106–107
Jousselin, Stéphane: account by, 340–341; bio. of, 339–340
Juab, Utah: 268, 297
Juliette (Mormon wife): 134
Juventa (ship): 88

Kaibab, Utah: 266, 269, 278, 279, 281, 282, 283, 284, 302
Kanab, Utah: 266, 272–275, 278, 280, 285, 289, 300
Kane, Elisha Kent: 110–111
Kane, John: 110
Kane, Margaret Fox: 111
Kane, Thomas L: 102, 108, 110–111
Kearny, Stephen W: 48
Keits, Mr: 93
Kelly, William: 48–49
Kidder, Daniel: 31–32
Kimball, Heber C: 54, 82, 164, 246, 251–252, 258
Kinard, Spence: 381
Kinney, John Fitch: 71, 74–75
Kipling, Rudyard: 320–321
Kirtland: 25, 29, 30, 212
Koch, Albert Karl: 32; account by, 39–40; bio. of, 38–39
Korensky, Josef: 321

La femme assise (novel): 244–249

La Liberté (newspaper): 104
La revue cosmopolite (journal): 123
La voix de Joseph (The Voice of Joseph) (pamphlet): 87
Labyrinthodon: 40
Lake Point, Utah: 173
Lamanites: 377
Las Vegas: 70–71
Latter-day Saints. *See* Mormons
Le lac salé (novel): 249–251
Le National (newspaper): 111
Le Papillon (journal): 123
Le Populaire (magazine): 100–101
Le tour du monde en quatre-vingts jours (novel): 209, 210–215; illus. from, 211
Le vingtième siècle (novel): 227–231, 244, 380
Lebolo, Giovanni Pietro Antonio: 69
Lee, John D: 148
Lehi (Mormon prophet): 187
Lehi, Utah: 70, 164
Leslie, Frank: 149, 150
Leslie, Mrs. Frank: 124, 149
Lévy, Bernard-Henri: 378
Life in the Far West (book): 189
Lincoln, Abraham: 164
Lion House: 73, 250, 331, 355, 357
Lippincott, Sarah Jane: 124
Little Salt Lake: 261, 264
Little Salt Lake Valley: 259
Livingston, Kincaid & Co.: 73
Livre de Mormon. See The Book of Mormon
Ludlow, Fitz Hugh: 116, 326
Lund, Anthon H: 303
Lunt, Henry [Lund]: 268, 269, 271
Lutherans: 314, 361

Mackay, Charles: 49
Majors, Gertrude King: 343
Malan, Barthélemy: 88
Malan, Jean Daniel: 87–88
Malan, Jean Etienne. *See* Malan, Stephen
Malan, Jeanne Dina: 88
Malan, Joseph: 91
Malan, Madeleine: 88
Malan, Marie Catherine: 88
Malan, Pauline: 88
Malan, Pauline Amelia (daughter of Pauline): 88
Malan, Stephen: 86, 91, 102; account by, 88–90; bio. of, 86–88
Manifesto of 1890: 315, 344, 369
Mapleson, James Henry: 295
Marcy, R. B: 107, 108
Margetts, Philip: 121
Marks, David: 30
Marquis de Rochefort-Luçay. *See* Rochefort, Victor-Henri
Marshall, W. G: 96, 303
mastodon: 38–39
Matsmoto (traveling companion): 182, 183–184
Maury, Alfred: 68
Maximilian, Alexander Philipp: account by, 33–35; bio. of, 32–33
May, Dean: 86
May, Karl Friedrich: 188, 189–190, 377; bio. of, 231–232; fantasy accounts of, 232–236, 236–239
Mazzuchelli, Samuele Carlo: 26, 32; account by, 36–38; bio. of, 34–36; illus. of, 35
McClure, Alexander Kelly: 116
McCulloch, Benjamin: 111–112
Mémoires d'un Mormon (book): 103
Mérimée, Prosper: 68
Merriman, Frances: 124
Methodists: 363, 364
Meyer, Rudolph: account by, 325–328; bio. of, 324–325
Meynier, Jean Pierre: 90
Milford, Utah: 289, 297
Miller, James Know Polk: 116
Miller, Joaquín: 189
Mills, William G: 109

mining: 115, 154, 155, 160, 162, 165, 173, 180, 236, 255, 259, 263, 264, 271, 311, 320, 327, 329, 339, 350, 351
Missouri: 24, 29, 30, 31, 45, 110
Mohave Indians: 195
Möllhausen, Heinrich Balduin: 188, 190, 232; bio. of, 193–196; fantasy accounts of, 196–200, 200–206
Mormon Battalion: 48, 259
Mormon Grove, Kansas: 91, 102
Mormonism in All Ages (book): 35
Mormonism Unvailed [sic] (book): 29–30
Mormonism: Its Leaders and Designs (book): 44, 69
Mormons: 29, 30, 31, 32, 33, 37, 40, 41, 42, 43, 44, 45, 66, 67, 117, 121, 194–195, 263, 264, 287, 296, 304, 328–329, 333, 334, 340, 345, 347, 365, 369, 378; beliefs of, 26, 30–31, 34, 37–38, 62–64, 69, 70, 76, 79–80, 82–83, 84, 95, 97–99, 102, 120, 158, 161, 167–168, 170–171, 176, 185, 288, 291, 313–314, 325, 336–337, 348, 351, 361, 372, 374; culture of, 47–48, 59, 73–74, 76–78, 83–84, 99, 136, 137, 138, 172–173, 276, 287–288, 289, 290–291, 299, 308, 311, 321, 327–328, 329, 332, 351, 362–363, 368, 379–380; fantasy accounts on, 188–189, 190–193, 195–196, 196–200, 200–207, 210–215, 217–227, 227–231, 232–236, 236–239, 241–243, 244, 245–249, 249–258; missions of, 85, 86–87, 87–88, 90, 94, 100–101, 183, 303; theocratic government of: 48, 49, 71–72, 83, 115, 117, 138, 148, 189, 228, 262, 297, 327, 350–351, 380. *See also* Indian slavery, polygamy
The Mormons (book): 49, 68
Moroni: 248
Morrill Act: 115, 319
Mount Trumbull: 266, 275, 277
Mountain Meadows massacre: 48, 241, 271
Mulder, William: 86

Nauvoo Legion: 105–106
Nauvoo, Illinois: 25, 31–32, 35–36, 37, 39–40, 41, 47, 100, 152, 158, 212, 213; temple of, 39–40, 41, 42, 48, 161
Navajo Well: 285
Nebraska: 94
Neki, Utah: 56
Nephi, Utah: 70, 260
Neumann, John N: 36
New America (book): 122
Niebuhr, G: 357, 358
Nounnan, J. F: 126

Oblasser, Albano: 69
Odd Fellows: 118
Ogden, Utah: 88, 147, 149, 151, 169, 175, 213, 214, 323–324, 330, 332, 335–336, 357, 366, 367
Olympic Games: 381
Omaha Indians: 45
Omaha, Nebr: 94, 96
Ophir City, Utah: 173
Oregon Trail: 194
O'Rell, Max: 339
Osborne, Dr. *See* Kane, Thomas L.
Ottinger, George M: 167, 168
Our Second American Adventure (novel): 304
Owen, Robert: 31, 32–33, 135, 307–308

Pacific Railroad Report: 61
Pacific Railway: 156, 210
Pahvant Indians: 61
Paiute Indians: 264
Palmyra, Utah: 56
Panguitch, Utah: 272, 286–287
Panichkos, John: 281, 283
Paragonah, Utah: 260, 261–262, 263
Paris au XXè siècle (novel): 209
Park, John R: 331
Parker, Samuel L: 30
Parkman, Francis: 48, 188
Parowan, Utah: 70, 260, 263–264

Pawnee Indians: 372
Payson, Utah: 260
The Pearl of Great Price (book): 69
Pellegrini, Gian Domenico: 148
"People to People" (TV show): 379
Perpetual Emigrating Fund: 85, 86, 87, 102, 319–320
Perris, Fred T: 304
Pfeiffer, Ida: 124
Phelps, William Wines: 30, 246
Pidgin, Charles: 343
Pipe Spring National Monument: 272
Pipe Spring, Utah: 266, 276–277, 289, 299–300
plural marriage. *See* polygamy
Poland Act: 148
polygamy: 23, 24, 47, 48, 52, 53, 56–58, 59–60, 63–64, 75, 78, 80–81, 83, 101–102, 116, 117, 120, 122, 124, 129–131, 133–134, 137, 138–141, 145, 148, 151–152, 156, 158, 160, 161, 164, 166–167, 168, 170, 178, 179, 182–183, 189, 212, 213, 214, 245, 247, 269, 272–275, 288, 291–293, 308–309, 311, 312, 313, 315, 316–317, 319–320, 321, 327, 333, 334, 335, 337–338, 338–339, 340–341, 343–344, 347, 351–355, 358, 369, 371, 373, 374–376, 378–379; in fantasy accounts, 197–198, 211, 218–222, 223–224, 226, 229–230, 236, 237, 244, 248–249, 250–258. *See also* Young, Brigham, family of
Polysophical Society: 109
Pottawatomie Indians: 43
Powell, John Wesley: 260, 266, 272, 275, 279, 321
Powell, Lazarus W: 111–112
Prairie and Rocky Mountain Adventures (guidebook): 117
Pratt, Orson: 48, 75, 82, 252
Pratt, Parley P: 36, 37, 39, 40, 82, 246, 259
Protestants: 31–32, 37–38, 86, 101, 139, 143, 177, 250, 325, 329, 364

Provo, Utah: 67, 70, 108, 112, 260, 289, 297, 366, 367
Pueblo, Colorado: 48, 369

Quorum of the Seventy: 246

Railroad Act: 115
railroads: 61, 115, 117, 126, 147, 148, 149, 152, 172, 173, 175, 210, 266–268, 290, 304–305, 309, 330, 334
Ransohoff, Nicholas S: 118
Raymond & Whitcomb: 320
Reclus, Elisée: 68
Reed, Samuel B: 131
Reid, Mayne: 189, 190
The Religions of America (book): 67
Rémy, Jules: 26, 49, 52, 103–104, 181, 209, 212, 249–250, 259, 326, 377, 382; bio of, 67–71; writings of, 71–84
Republican Party: 48
Rese, Frederic: 34
Revel, Jean-Pierre: 91
Révoil, B. H: 68, 103
Reynolds, George: 148
Richards, S. W: 99
Richardson, Albert: 117
Riders of the Purple Sage: 27
Rigdon, Sidney: 29, 30, 37
Rio Grande Western Railroad: 344
Rivoire, Catherine Jouve: 365
Rivoire, Jacob: 365
Roberts, Brigham H: 343–344
Robida Society: 216
Robida, Albert: 124; bio. of, 215–216; drawings by, 127, 128, 217, 219, 221, 224; fantasy accounts of, 217–227, 228–231, 244; photo of, 216
Robinson, Phil: 260, 320–321
Rochefort, Victor-Henri: account by, 175–181; bio. of, 174–175
Rochon, Louis: 367
Rockwell, Orrin Porter: 98, 116

Ruxton, George Frederick: 47–48, 189

St. Louis: 32, 35, 38, 39, 42, 43, 51
St. Louis Bertrand: 100
Saint-Simon, Henri de: 135
Salgari, Emilio: 188, 189–190; bio. of, 239–241, 243; fantasy accounts of, 241–243, 244
Salt Lake City: 23, 26, 44, 47, 49, 51, 52, 61, 62–63, 68, 70, 71, 76, 87, 89, 91, 92, 96, 97, 98, 99, 102, 104, 105, 116, 117, 118, 120–121, 122, 129, 131, 133, 134, 135, 136, 137, 138, 139, 141, 142, 143, 144, 145, 147, 149, 152, 153–154, 165, 169–170, 172, 173, 175–176, 184, 186, 190–191, 196, 228, 246, 248, 251, 290, 305–306, 310, 316, 317, 321, 328–329, 330, 331–332, 338, 345, 346, 349, 357, 368, 369, 377, 378, 380, 382; illus. of, 46
Salt Lake Daily Telegraph (newspaper): 136
Salt Lake House: 152; photo of, 146
Salt Lake Social Hall: 112, 121, 294, 296; illus. of, 79
Salt Lake Tabernacle: 62, 96, 99, 108, 110, 122, 135, 147, 154, 158, 160, 169, 176, 177, 184, 293–294, 313, 320, 323, 329, 331, 368, 369–370, 378
Salt Lake Temple: 55, 69, 172, 225, 252, 307, 331, 348, 357, 372
Salt Lake Theater: 60, 121, 136, 154–155, 168, 172, 294, 331; photo of, 168
Salt Lake Tribune (newspaper): 148, 172
Salt Lake Valley: 44, 45, 48, 88, 96
Saltair Resort: 93, 344, 368, 369; illus. of, 95
San Francisco: 51, 122
San Pete Valley, Utah: 260
Santa Clara, Utah: 260, 261–262
Sardinia: 86–87, 90–91, 150
Savage, Annie Adkins: 167
Savage, Annie Clowes: 167
Savage, Charles Roscoe: 167, 168
Savage, Mary Emma Fowler: 167

Savage, Ellen Fenn: 167
Scandinavians: 54, 78, 94, 134, 151, 172, 246, 303, 310, 316, 348
Scanlan, Lawrence: 319
Schiel, Jacob Heinrich Wilhelm: 49, 61–67; bio. of, 61; report of, 62–67
Schleiden, Rudolph: 378; account by, 161–165; bio. of, 161
Schmidt, G. A: 356
Scipio, Utah: 260
The Seer (book): 101
Seward, William C: 162, 164
Sharp, John: 92, 93, 126, 323, 324
Shelley, Mary: 123
silk industry: 105
Silver Reef, Utah: 268, 269–271, 289, 298
Simonin, Louis Laurent: 181; account by, 165–168, 240; bio. of, 165
Simonton, James W: 100
Sisters of Charity: 271
Smith, George A: 156–157, 163–164, 167, 259, 328, 329
Smith, Hyrum: 72, 163, 211
Smith, Jedediah: 259
Smith, John: 94
Smith, Joseph: 24, 29–30, 31, 35, 36, 37, 47, 48, 69, 72, 76–77, 79, 104, 110, 113, 162, 163, 185, 211, 212, 288–289, 308, 311, 327, 336, 343, 348, 359, 372, 378; in fantasy accounts, 197
Smith, Joseph F. (6th president of lds church): 329, 348, 349, 354, 357, 362
Smith, Thomas L. "Pegleg": 259
Smith, William: 246
Smoot, Reed: 344, 379
Smyth, William: 321
Snow, Eliza: 109
Snow, Erastus: 85, 101, 303
Snow, Lorenzo: 85, 86–87, 183, 246
Snyder, J. A: 65
Sonzogno, Edoardo: 181
South Pass: 103

Spalding, Franklin Spencer: 69
Spanish Fork, Utah: 260
Spanish Trail: 259, 260
Spencer, Orson: 85
Spiritualism: 343
Stadling, Jonas Jonsson: 304; bio. of, 309; memoir of, 310–312
Standing Army of Israel: 107
Stansbury, Howard: 181, 196, 326
Stenhouse, Fanny: 124, 135, 148, 178–180, 181
Stenhouse, T. B. H: 69, 85, 86–87, 117, 136, 148, 166–167, 176, 177, 178; photo of: 166
Steptoe, Edward: 74
Stevenson, Robert Louis: 189
Stiles, George P: 75
Stone, Alvan: 30
Strafforello, Gustavo: 117, 189
A Study in Scarlet (novel): 27, 70, 240, 304, 377
Sutter's Mill: 47
Swedish Free Church movement: 309

Taine, Hippolyte: 68
Taylor, John: 37, 51, 54, 55–56, 56–57, 60, 67, 85, 100–101, 110, 245–246, 247, 294, 295, 296, 297, 310–311, 320, 327, 328, 329, 361, 373
The Ten Tribes: Discovered and Identified (book): 88
Th. Gr. (anonymous): 260; account by, 261–264; background on, 260
Thomas Cook & Son. *See* Cook, Thomas
Thomasson, O. P: 315, 316
Thompson, Alma Harris "Harry": 266
Thwaites, Reuben Gold: 33
The Times of London (newspaper): 148–149
Tissandier, Albert: 260, 382; bio. of, 265; drawings of, 267, 270, 273, 274
Todd, John: 116
Tooele Valley: 104
Tooele, Utah: 312

Topsöe, Vilhelm Kristian Sigurd: 304; account by, 304–309; bio. of, 304
de Tocqueville, Alexis: 25, 26
Toquerville, Utah: 271, 289, 296, 299, 300
Toronto, Joseph: 86–87, 88, 92–94, 183, 328
Toroweap, Utah: 266, 278
Towle, Nancy: 30
Townsend House: 152, 155, 165, 305; illus. of, 153
Townsend, James: 152, 154, 155, 156
Townsend, John: 31
Townshend, Frederick Trench: 116
Tramp, John C. Van: 117
Trapped by the Mormons (movie): 343
Treves, Emilio: 122, 181–182
Treves, Fratelli: 240
Trollope, Frances: 25, 26, 123
Trumbo, Isaac: 307
Trumbo, John K: 307
Turner, Jonathan B: 31–32, 35–36
Twain, Mark: 116, 188, 189
Twiss, Stephen P: 338

Un anno senza rondini (narrative): 372–373, 373–376
Union Pacific Railroad: 92, 126, 147, 151, 210, 320
United States v. Reynolds: 319
universal suffrage: 351
Unter Geiern (novel): 232–236
Ursenbach, Joséphine de la Harpe: 142–144
Ursenbach, Octave: 105
Utah: 23, 25, 26, 27, 28, 43, 44, 49, 56, 63, 64, 65, 66–67, 69, 70, 71, 73, 74, 75, 76, 86, 88, 90, 91, 94, 96, 97, 98, 99, 101, 102, 104, 105, 109, 110, 111, 131, 135, 138, 142, 188, 189, 190, 211, 240, 303, 304, 345–346, 350, 362, 373, 380, 382–383; southern, 157, 259–260, 261–262, 266–268, 296, 297–298, 299–300, 312
Utah Central Railroad: 92, 147, 304, 315, 323–324

Utah Commission: 321
Utah Expedition: 44, 107
Utah War: 36, 48, 102, 103, 105–112, 115, 116, 121
Ute Indians: 154, 262–263

Valentini, Zopito: account by, 373–376; bio. of, 372–373
Van Vliet, Stewart: 107
Varvaro Pojero, Francesco: 26, 240; account by, 182–184; bio. of, 181–182
Vegas de Santa Clara: 261, 264
Vermilion Cliffs: 272, 277, 299
Verne, Jules: 189–190, 215–216; bio. of, 207–210; drawing of, 208; fantasy account by, 210–215
Viett, George: 67
Vigna dal Ferro, Giovanni: account by, 328–329; bio. of: 328
Vinçon, Daniel: 90
Vinçon, Etienne: 367
Voice of Warning (book): 36, 101
Voyages extraordinaires à travers les mondes connus et inconnus (book series): 209
Voyages très extraordinaires de Saturnin Farandoul . . . (novel): 215

Wakara (Ute chief): 262–263
Waldensians: 86–87, 91, 364, 366–368
Waldenström, Paul Peter: 304; bio. of, 313; memoir of, 313–315
Walker Opera House: 294, 295; photo of: 295
Walker war: 262
Ward, Artemus: 116–117, 152, 189, 340
Ward, J. H.: 363–364
Ward, Mrs. Maria. *See* Harris, Sarah Hollister
Wars of Italian Independence: 50–51, 52, 121, 150
Washington Geological Survey: 266
Waters, William Elkanah: 326

Wells, Daniel H: 106, 164, 305, 352
Wells, Emmeline Blanche Woodward: 352–356, 368, 371–372; photo of, 370
West, Chauncey: 126
Western Utah Railway: 173
Westport, Mo: 61, 260
Whipple, Amiel Wecks: 194
Whipple Expedition: 194
White Cliffs: 286
Whitmer, David: 30
Whitmore, James: 272
Whymper, Frederick: 116
Widtsoe, John: 303
The Wild Huntress (book): 189
Wilde, Oscar: 295, 320
Williams Ferry: 33
Williamson, J. H., daughter of: 330
Winder, John Rex: 326
wine industry: 102, 104, 105
Winter Quarters: 43, 47
Winsor, Anson P: 272
Winsor Castle: 272
Woelmont, Baron Arnold de: account by, 185–186; bio. of, 184
Wollstonecraft, Mary: 123
Woodard, Jabez: 87–88, 90, 91
"Word of Wisdom": 102
Woodruff, Wilford: 103, 152
Wooley, Edwin D: 97
Wronski, Hoëné: 100

Young, Amelia: 141–142
Young, Ann-Eliza Webb: 124, 148
Young, Brigham: 23, 25, 26, 43, 45, 47, 51, 54, 60, 62, 63, 71–72, 73, 74–75, 76, 77, 82–83, 85, 87, 92, 94, 95, 96, 98, 99, 103, 105, 107, 108, 109, 110, 111–113, 115, 116, 117, 118, 119–120, 126, 136, 138, 139, 147, 148, 149, 152, 154–155, 156, 157–158, 160–161, 162–163, 165–166, 171–172, 174, 176, 177, 178, 179, 180, 181, 182, 183–184, 184–185, 185–186, 212, 213, 259, 262, 272, 292, 293,

303, 304, 305, 310, 311, 319, 321, 323, 336, 340, 347, 348, 349, 352, 355, 357, 372, 377, 378; appearance of, 55–56, 72, 112, 118–119, 138, 157, 159, 161–162, 171, 176–177, 185, 310; family of, 57, 120, 122, 131, 133, 134, 141–142, 145, 151, 154–155, 164, 171, 177–178, 185, 358; in fantasy accounts, 211, 218, 219, 220, 222–223, 226, 227, 245–246, 251, 252–258; illus. of, 45

Young, Brigham Jr: 126, 131
Young, Clarissa Ross: 355
Young, Eliza R. Snow Smith: 294, 358
Young, Harriet Amelia Folson: 142
Young, John W: 126, 131, 133, 165
Young, Joseph A: 126, 133, 358
Young, Lucy Ann Decker Seeley: 358
Young, Mary Ann Angel: 358
Young, Mary Elizabeth Rollins Lightner Smith: 358

zeuglodon: 39, 40
Ziegler, Alexander: 32; account by, 41–42; bio. of, 40–41
Zimmer, G. A: account by, 357–364; bio. of, 356–357
Zion Cooperative Mercantile Institution: 170, 184, 306, 311, 331, 347, 348

The Editor

Michael W. Homer is a trial lawyer in Salt Lake City. He has published four books, thirteen chapters in books, and over sixty articles. He is the recipient of the David Kirby Best Article Award from the Arthur Conan Doyle Society for his article "The Absence of Holmes: The Continuation of the Mormon Subplot in 'Angels of Darkness'," *ACD: Journal of the Arthur Conan Doyle Society* 4 (1993), 57–74. He received the Lowell L. Bennion Editor's Award from *Dialogue, A Journal of Mormon Thought*; the T. Edgar Lyon Award of Excellence from the Mormon History Association; and the Best Article Award from The John Whitmer Historical Association for his article "'Similarity of Priesthood in Masonry': The Relationship Between Freemasonry and Mormonism," *Dialogue, A Journal of Mormon Thought* 27:3 (Fall 1994), 1–113. His community service includes Member, Board of Visitors, University of Utah, 2005–Present; Member, President's Club Committee, University of Utah, 1998–Present; Utah State Historical Society, Board of State History, 1997–present, Chair, 2003–present; and Member, Board of Trustees, Utah Opera Company, 1989–1998.

www.ingramcontent.com/pod-product-compliance
Lightning Source LLC
Chambersburg PA
CBHW031425160426
43195CB00010BB/618